Cognitive Behavior Therapy
in Clinical Social Work Practice

Tammie Ronen, PhD, is a social worker and an educational counselor. She is a professor and the head of the Bob Shapell School of Social Work at Tel Aviv University, and the head of the research center for treating aggressive children and their parents. She is the past president of the Israeli Association for Behavior and Cognitive Therapies. She publishes widely in the area of CBT with children and lectures and trains groups internationally.

Arthur Freeman, EdD, ABPP, is visiting professor in the Department of Psychology at Governors State University, University Park, IL, is clinical professor in the Department of Psychology at Philadelphia College of Osteopathic Medicine, and Director of Training at Sheridan Shores Care and Rehabilitation Center, Chicago, IL. He is a Distinguished Founding Fellow of the Academy of Cognitive Therapy. Freeman has published widely in CBT and has lectured internationally. His work has been translated into twelve languages. He holds diplomas in clinical, family, and behavioral psychology from the American Board of Professional Psychology and is a Fellow of APA.

Cognitive Behavior Therapy in Clinical Social Work Practice

Edited by

Tammie Ronen, PhD

Arthur Freeman, EdD, ABPP

SPRINGER PUBLISHING COMPANY

New York

Dedication

This volume is dedicated to the memory
of our friend and colleague
Michael J. Mahoney, PhD

Springer Publishing Company, LLC
11 West 42nd Street
New York, NY 10036

Acquisitions Editor: Sheri W. Sussman
Managing Editor: Mary Ann McLaughlin
Production Editor: Gail F. Farrar
Cover design: Joanne E. Honigman
Composition: Publishers' Design and Production Services, Inc.

09 10 11 / 7 6 5

Library of Congress Cataloging-in-Publication Data

Cognitive behavior therapy in clinical social work practice / [edited by] Tammie Ronen,
Arthur Freeman.
    p.   cm.
   Includes bibliographical references and index.
   ISBN 0-8261-0215-8
   1. Behavior therapy.   2. Cognitive therapy.   3. Social case work.   I. Ronen, Tammie.
II. Freeman, Arthur, 1942–

RC489.B4C64 2006
616.89'142—dc22

          2006044365

Printed in the United States of America by Yurchak Printing, Inc.

Contents

Contributors

G. Bert Allain, MSW, is the director of a multicounty substance abuse treatment and prevention program. He has authored four books on children's cognitive coping skills and was selected as the 2005 recipient of the Service Recognition Award by the Louisiana State University School of Social Work for his work in children's prevention services.

L. Stewart Barbera Jr., PsyD, MSW, is the Chair of the Counseling Department at St. Joseph's Preparatory School in Philadelphia, Pennsylvania. He is the cofounder of the Center for Family Enrichment, Aston, Pennsylvania, and a member of counseling staff at Life Counseling Services in Chadds Ford, Pennsylvania.

Steven K. Bordelon, LCSW, received his MSW from Tulane University, and an MA in Religious Studies from Loyola University, New Orleans. He has a private practice in Baton Rouge, Louisiana.

Amy Carrigan, MSSA, is on the faculty of the Department of Psychology and Counseling at the University of Saint Francis, Fort Wayne, IN where she teaches both undergraduate and graduate courses. Her area of expertise is lifespan development. She is also an adjunct professor of psychology at Indiana Institute of Technology. Amy is currently pursuing her Ph.D. at Walden University.

Lili Daoud, LCSW, is a graduate of the University of the Connecticut School of Social Work and is currently pursuing a Ph.D. in Christian Psychology. Lili received training in REBT at the Albert Ellis Institute in New York and completed the Behavior Therapy Institute's advanced training for OCD spectrum disorders. She is the clinical director of the

Connecticut Center for Cognitive Therapy, where she offers clinical service as well as supervises therapists in CBT technique.

Sharon Morgillo Freeman, PhD, holds a doctoral degree in sociology and master's degrees in both nursing and psychology. She is board-certified as an advanced practice Clinical Nurse specialist and certified as a Cognitive Therapist by the Academy of Cognitive Therapy. She is Director of the Center for Brief Therapy, PC in Fort Wayne, Indiana. Sharon is the senior editor of *Cognitive Behavior Therapy in Nursing Practice* (Springer, 2005) in addition to 20 chapters in edited volumes. She is President-elect of NAADAC, The Association for Addiction Professionals, and is on the board of the International Association for Cognitive Psychotherapy

Eileen Gambrill, PhD, is Hutto Patterson Professor of Child and Family Studies at the School of Social Welfare, University of California, Berkeley where she teaches both social work research and practice. She had been a visiting scholar at the Universities of Oxford and Tel Aviv University, and has been a Benjamin Meeker Fellow, School for Social Policy, University of Bristol, England. She served as Editor-in-Chief of *Social Work Research and Abstracts* from 1984 to 1988 and as Editor-in-Chief of *Journal of Social Work Education* from 2000 to 2003. Her most recent publications include *Social Work Practice: A Critical Thinkers Guide* (2nd ed., 2006), and *Critical Thinking in Clinical Practice* (2nd ed., 2006).

Susan Gingerich, MSW, is a full-time trainer and consultant based in Philadelphia, Pennsylvania, with over 20 years of research and clinical experience with consumers and families in a variety of settings, including inpatient units, outpatient clinics, residential treatment centers, state hospitals, and home visits. She is the co-author of *Social Skills Training for Schizophrenia: A Step-by-Step Guide, Coping With Schizophrenia: A Guide for Families, Behavioral Family Therapy: A Workbook, Coping Skills Group: A Session-by-Session Guide,* and several book chapters and articles related to working with consumers and their families.

Donald K. Granvold, PhD, LCSW, LMFT, is Professor of Social Work at the University of Texas at Arlington School of Social Work where he has been on the faculty since 1974. He has been a leader in the advancement of cognitive treatment and constructivist psychotherapy methods particularly as they are applied to couples treatment and divorce. He has authored over 45 book chapters and articles in social work and allied helping profession journals, and is editor of the volume, *Cognitive and Behavioral Treatment: Methods and Applications.* He is on the editorial boards of *Social Work* and *Brief Treatment and Crisis.* He is a Founding Fellow in the Academy of Cognitive Therapy.

Joseph A. Himle, PhD, is an Assistant Professor at the University of Michigan, School of Social Work and the Department of Psychiatry. He is also the Associate Director of the University of Michigan, Anxiety Disorders Program. He completed his doctorate in social work and psychology at the University of Michigan in August of 1995. Dr. Himle is an active clinician, teacher, and researcher in the area of mental health disorders and interventions.

Cedar R. Koons received her MSW from the University of North Carolina. She was on staff at the Women Veterans Comprehensive Health Center at the Durham VA Medical Center and was an adjunct clinical faculty at Duke University Medical Center. At Duke she founded the dialectical behavior therapy (DBT) program, taught and supervised psychiatry residents, and conducted research on the efficacy of DBT as compared to treatment as usual for women veterans with borderline personality disorder. She founded Santa Fe DBT Consultation, a group of practitioners providing comprehensive DBT treatment to adults and adolescents and was the first president of Marie Institute, a nonprofit organization formed to increase access to evidence-based clinical services for severe, multidisordered, difficult-to-treat clients.

Craig Winston LeCroy, PhD, earned his BSW from San Jose State University, his MSW from Western Michigan University, and his PhD from the University of Wisconsin. He is professor of social work at Arizona State University.

Catherine M. Lemieux, MSW, PhD, received her MSW from Barry University and her PhD from Florida International University. She currently serves as the Margaret Champagne Womack Associate Professor in Addictive Disorders in the School of Social Work at Louisiana State University, Baton Rouge, Louisiana. She has extensive practice experience with individuals and families affected by substance abuse. Her publications are in the area of substance abuse education, prevention, and treatment.

Catherine MacLaren, MSW, is a certified Fellow and Supervisor in Rational Emotive Behavior Therapy, Licensed Clinical Social Worker (LCSW) and Certified Employee Assistance Professional (CEAP). Formerly a staff therapist and training faculty member at the Albert Ellis Institute in New York, she coauthored *Rational Emotive Behavior Therapy: A Therapist's Guide* with Albert Ellis in 1998. Catherine is currently working with Community Counseling Center in Portland, Maine.

Ruth Malkinson, PhD, teaches at the Bob Shapell School of Social Work, Tel Aviv University. She is a past-president of the Israeli Association for

Couple and Family Therapy. Her field of expertise is CBT (the REBT model) and its application in therapy with a broad range of clinical problems. An author of numerous articles on loss, bereavement, and trauma, and cognitive grief therapy, she has coedited two books on the subject of loss and bereavement.

Donna M. Martin, PsyD, is a clinical psychologist who works for Penn Foundation Sellersville, PA. She was previously an assistant professor and the director of the academic support program at the Philadelphia College of Osteopathic Medicine (PCOM) where she received her doctorate in clinical psychology. Dr. Martin was the manager of the Center for Brief Therapy, PCOM's training clinic, and was involved in the supervision and training of psychology practicum students. Her interests include the use of CBT for anger disorders and working with adolescents who self-mutilate. Most recently she co-edited *Comparative Treatments for Borderline Personality Disorder* with Arthur Freeman, EdD and Mark Stone, PsyD, as well as co-authoring several chapters.

Rene Mason, LCSW, received her Master of Social Work degree from New York University. She is a Senior Social Worker and School Coordinator at the NYU Child Study Center School Based Intervention Program. She provides evaluations and cognitive behavior treatment for primary and secondary schoolchildren and parents experiencing symptoms of PTSD, anxiety, and depression. She also provides training for educators, administrators, and social workers in behavior management, functional behavioral assessment, anxiety disorders in children, and cultural diversity. Mason also assists in the implementation of research protocols in schools to test treatment efficacy.

Kim T. Mueser, PhD, is a licensed clinical psychologist and Professor in the Departments of Psychiatry and Community and Family Medicine at Dartmouth Medical School in Hanover, New Hampshire. Dr. Mueser has published over 200 journal articles, 8 books, and 50 book chapters on the treatment of schizophrenia and other mental illnesses, and has given numerous workshops and scientific and public presentations on the topic throughout the world. Dr. Mueser's research has been supported by a variety of different public organizations, including the National Institute of Mental Health, the National Institute on Drug Abuse, and the Substance Abuse and Mental Health Services Administration, as well as by private foundations.

Jordana Muroff, MSW, PhD, is a postdoctoral fellow at the VA Ann Arbor Healthcare System Center for Practice Management and Outcomes Research and the University of Michigan Center for Behavioral and

Decision Sciences in Medicine. She completed her doctorate in social work and psychology at the University of Michigan in 2004. Dr. Muroff's practice experience, teaching, and research are in the areas of mental health assessment and cognitive behavior interventions with a particular focus on anxiety disorders, and the influence of culture on clinical decision making.

Laura L. Myers, PhD, is an assistant professor in the Department of Social Work at Thomas University in Thomasville, Georgia. Laura L. Myers received her MSW and Ph.D. in social work from the University of Georgia. Her research interests include eating disorders, cultural diversity, and the various forms of child foster care. She lives in Tallahassee, Florida, with her husband and four children.

Donald Osborn, MA, MS, LCSW, LMFT, MAC, is licensed in Marital and Family Therapy, Clinical Social Work, and Mental Health. He earned an M.S. in Counseling Psychology from Indiana State University (ISU). He did postgraduate work in Marital/Family Therapy, and Psychological Appraisal and received an M.A. in Theology with a specialization in Psychiatry and Religion from Saint Mary of the Woods College. After graduation he completed the Addiction Studies certificate from Vincennes University and is completing his doctorate in Clinical Psychology. He is employed by the Department of Corrections at the Wabash Valley Correctional Facility as Program Supervisor in Substance Abuse and is also involved in the Cognitive Behavior Program.

Vaughn Roche, LCSW, ACT, is a social worker with the University of Utah's Huntsman Cancer Hospital where he is most closely associated with the Pain Medicine and Palliative Care Service. He also maintains a private practice in Salt Lake City. He has used cognitive behavior therapy in the treatment of patients with a broad range of medical illnesses. He is certified by the Academy of Cognitive Therapy. He has trained at the Beck Institute for Cognitive Therapy and Research as well as the Albert Ellis Institute.

Susan Dowd Stone, MSW, LCSW, received her clinical training from New York University and is currently the Managing Director of Blue Skye Consulting, LLC, a mental health resource serving the northern NJ/NYC area. While at Hackensack University Medical Center, she was a member of an intensively trained DBT consultation team. She writes, presents, and consults on a variety of affective and behavioral disorders/treatments including trauma, EMDR, bereavement, and the human-animal bond. She is the current President of Post Partum Support International, a member of NASW, AABT, The American Academy of Bereavement, The Green Cross, and The Delta Society.

Raymond Chip Tafrate, PhD, earned his doctoral degree in Combined Clinical and School Psychology in 1995 from Hofstra University. He is a licensed Psychologist in Connecticut and New York, and is a Fellow and Supervisor at the Albert Ellis Institute. An associate professor in the Criminology and Criminal Justice Department at Central Connecticut State University, he is the Director of the Graduate Program in Criminal Justice and teaches courses on anger and aggression management, correctional counseling, and research methods. He is the Director of the Connecticut Center for Cognitive Therapy in Avon, Connecticut.

Bruce A. Thyer, PhD, MSW, received his MSW from the University of Georgia and his doctorate in social work and psychology from the University of Michigan. He is currently a Professor with the College of Social Work at Florida State University and has published widely.

Beverly White, PsyD, LCSW is Founder and Director of Phillips-White Associates in greater Philadelphia. She teaches at Arcadia University and Philadelphia College of Osteopathic Medicine and is on staff at Brooke Glen Behavior Hospital. Dr. White received her master's in social work from Hunter College, and her doctorate at Philadelphia College of Osteopathic Medicine. Dr. White utilizes a cognitive-behavioral approach in her private clinical practice with traumatized children, adults, and families, and as a consultant with the Philadelphia Department of Human Services.

Marjorie R. Zahn MSS, LCSW, received her graduate degree in social work from Bryn Mawr College, Graduate School of Social Services and Social Research in Pennsylvania in 1986. She has worked with older adults in a variety of settings, including inpatient and outpatient mental health centers, assisted living facilities and long-term care facilities. Marjorie has also completed a graduate program in school counseling and works with children and adolescents.

Bruce S. Zahn, EdD, ABPP, is Associate Professor and Director of Clinical Training in the Psychology Department at Philadelphia College of Osteopathic Medicine. He is board-certified in Clinical Psychology and is a fellow of the Academy of Clinical Psychology. Prior to coming to PCOM, he was the Director of Psychological Services and Cognitive Therapy Program at the Presbyterian Medical Center of the University of Pennsylvania Health System, and was clinical manager for the Geropsychiatric Partial Hospitalization Program.

Foreword

Over the last 30 years, cognitive therapy (CT) has grown in many exciting directions. Had you asked me in 1977 how to best apply CT and to what particular patient populations, I would have said that we had excellent data on the treatment of depression, and that was where we needed to focus. Regarding the best techniques to treat depression—we were still growing and experimenting with a broad range of cognitive and behavioral interventions. I did not see with certainty the incredible impact that CT would have on the theory, research, and practice of psychotherapy. Once the basic ideas that underlie the cognitive therapy model were known, growth was exponential. Through the efforts of clinicians around the world, CT became widely disseminated.

From my early work in treating depression with cognitive therapy, I have seen CT applied to the broad range of clinical syndromes from the most common clinical disorders (depression and anxiety) to our more recent work in the treatment of patients with bipolar disorder and schizophrenia. Many talented clinicians were either trained at the Center for Cognitive Therapy, studied there for various periods of time, or consulted and collaborated with us. CT developed and grew rather quickly. It has now been applied to the treatment of all aspects of the anxiety spectrum disorders, personality disorders, and, more recently, bipolar disorders and schizophrenia. My answer to the same question regarding the focus of CT today is that CT has developed as a broad and empirically supported treatment for the range of psychiatric disorders. A recent review by Dr. Judith Beck identified the following ranges of application of CT: agoraphobia and panic disorder with agoraphobia, generalized anxiety disorder (GAD), geriatric anxiety, panic disorder, social anxiety/phobia, obsessive-compulsive disorder (OCD), posttraumatic stress disorder (PTSD) (CBT is effective in combination with stress management training and exposure), cocaine abuse, opiate dependence, schizophrenia (CBT is effective for treating delusions), geriatric depression, major depression, anger, binge-eating disorder, bulimia, anorexia, cancer pain, chronic pain (CBT, in combination with physical therapy, is effective for chronic pain in many medical conditions), chronic back pain, sickle cell disease pain (CBT that has multiple treatment components is effective), idiopathic pain, somatoform disorders, hypochondriasis, irritable-bowel syndrome, obesity (CBT is effective in combination with hypnosis), rheumatic disease pain (CBT that has multiple treatment components), smoking cessation (group CBT is effective, as well as CBT that has multiple treatment components, in combination with relapse prevention), marital discord, erectile dysfunction (CBT is effective for reducing sexual anxiety and improving communication), disorders concerning extreme dissatisfaction with body image, atypical sexual practices, sex offenders, geriatric sleep disorders, withdrawal from antianxiety medications, and bipolar disorder (CBT is effective for medication adherence).

CBT has been clinically demonstrated to be an effective treatment for children and adolescents for the following disorders and problems: anxiety disorders (separation anxiety, avoidant disorder, overanxious disorder), chronic pain, conduct disorder and oppositional defiant disorder, depression, adolescent unipolar depression, distress due to medical procedures (mainly for cancer), phobias, and recurrent abdominal pain. This is an enormous list of treatment applications, and one that I could not have envisioned in the early days.

Similarly, the therapeutic techniques of CT have become far more sophisticated as we have studied what has worked and what has been less successful in our treatments. I have seen CT grow from our early outpatient work at the Center for Cognitive Therapy, which was an outpatient facility that was part of the Department of Psychiatry at the University of Pennsylvania. The contemporary CT model, adapted from this early work, has been effectively applied to inpatient work in hospitals, applications for use in schools and other institutions, and residential, inpatient, and outpatient settings.

From our early work in treating adults and adult disorders, CT has been extended to the treatment of children, adolescents, elders, couples, families, and groups. Finally, I have seen CT extended from our early work in Philadelphia to be a truly international movement, with cognitive therapists now to be found around the globe. The International Association for Cognitive Psychotherapy (IACP) coordinates and sponsors international conferences on a triennial basis. In June of 2005, as part of the IACP congress in Gothenburg, Sweden, I had the honor and privilege of having a public discussion with His Holiness, the Dalai Lama. All of these markers of the development, growth, and maturation of CT have been very gratifying for me and my coworkers over the last four decades.

The Association for Advancement of Behavior Therapy has changed its name to the Association for Behavioral and Cognitive Therapies. Likewise, the European Association for Behavior Therapy has added "cognitive" to its name. The *Journal of Cognitive Psychotherapy, Cognitive and Behavioral Practice*, and other journals publish articles on the CT approach. The Academy of Cognitive Therapy has become a premier organization that certifies cognitive therapists internationally. The individuals that earn certification must meet the stringent criteria set by the Academy.

CT has made its greatest inroads in the fields of psychology and psychiatry. Other professional groups that deal with patients experiencing the broad range of mental disorders have been much more in the minority. Two of these groups, psychiatric nurses and clinical social workers, have not had the same training and materials available for teaching them the basics and advanced practices of CT. The former group, nurses, were addressed in the excellent text on *CBT in Nursing Practice*, edited by Sharon Morgillo Freeman and Arthur Freeman (Springer, 2005).

Following fast on the heels of that volume is the present volume designed and edited by Tammie Ronen and Art Freeman. Tammie is the Head of the Bob Shapell School of Social Work at Tel Aviv University. Art has been a colleague, coworker, and collaborator with me for many years. In this volume, the chapters have all been either authored or coauthored by a social worker, clearly stating that the social work perspective would be of paramount consideration in each and every conceptual and clinical discussion. Tammie and Art have put together a unique and talented group of contributors. They represent both academic social work and clinical social work. Several contributors are faculty members from some of the finest social work programs in the country. Other contributors are clinicians who are in the front lines of treating patients. The range of topics is equally impressive. They start with a basic overview of the confluence of interest between CT and social work practice and include chapters on evidence-based social work practice, and the importance of critical thinking in evidence-based practice. Of special interest is the chapter on developmental considerations. Too often, clinicians are not clear about the role of normal development in the manifestations that are diagnosed as psychopathological.

Newer additions to basic CT include mindfulness meditation and the use of dialectical behavior therapy (DBT). Perhaps the greatest strength of the book can be found in the clinical discussions. The richness and breadth of the clinical applications are impressive. All of the many applications are discussed: CT with children, couples, families, groups, school settings, elders, eating disorders, medical settings, and so many others.

Few volumes on CT are as comprehensive as the volume that Tammie and Art have edited. It is the first volume of its kind for this important professional discipline and group. With this publication, CT has moved yet another step forward.

Aaron T. Beck, MD
University Professor
University of Pennsylvania
Philadelphia, PA

Introduction

The present volume emerged from what must be viewed as a series of fortuitous circumstances that contributed to the eventual product. It might even be viewed as a series of karmic events. The first contributing factor was a long professional relationship between the editors, Tammie Ronen and Art Freeman, that dates back almost 20 years. Consistent with this was our customary meeting at the annual meeting of the Association for Advancement of Behavior Therapy (now the Association for Behavioral and Cognitive Therapies). As was our pattern, when we met we both caught each other up on the news of our lives some 6,000 miles apart. Where we had we traveled, what were our new and continuing life circumstances, and what projects we had in motion.

When we had the chance to meet and compare notes at the AABT meeting in 2004, Tammie announced that she had been elevated to the position of Head of the Bob Shapell School of Social Work at Tel Aviv University. This was wonderful news, and a well-deserved honor (though those of us who have held administrative positions in academe might question if this was a promotion or sentence). Given Tammie's position as an expert and well-published clinician and now a highly placed academic in a school of social work, the idea emerged of our putting our mutual interests in teaching cognitive behavior therapy (CBT) to diverse groups and advancing the field of clinical practice. We talked of applying CBT to the education of clinical social workers. We were both aware of the dearth of information and material on CBT in social work practice, and, more broadly, the limited impact of CBT on the field of social work. We both had the experience of workshops and courses in CBT being tenanted by many social workers, but few resources that could be identified as primarily social work oriented.

We were both excited by the prospect. We would design and produce a volume that merged our theoretical focus—CBT—with our belief that there was a need for a focused, comprehensive, and clinically relevant volume designed from the outset to be for social workers in clinical practice. We also thought (and hoped) that such a volume could be used in undergraduate and graduate social work training programs. Finally, our idea was to provide a volume that could be the nexus for other texts designed and focused on the work of clinical social workers.

We sought a quiet space at the conference exhibit area and spent the next two hours outlining this volume. What topics should we include? What clinical entities, settings, and modalities should we include? What authors could best make the CBT points that we wanted to make in this volume? What would be the length and coverage of each of the chapters and ultimately of the volume? For whom would the volume be designed? Who would be the best publisher to produce a high quality text and then to distribute it? We put some of our immediate thoughts to paper.

We then took the handwritten pages to Lauren Dockett, then the Social Work editor at Springer Publishing Company, New York. Springer seemed the natural choice for this volume. We had both published with Springer, they had a superb social work list, and the senior editors at Springer could help us to craft this volume into an excellent social work resource. The text that you will read through is a monument to our faith in Springer and their faith in us. The volume is more of a handbook in terms of its coverage, size, and comprehensiveness. If there are areas that the reader believes should have been included, authors that should have been invited, or particular clinical populations, clinical settings, or clinical syndromes that needed greater coverage, and weren't, we must apologize. Some authors were invited and were unable to participate because of other commitments. To present a broad range of topics while keeping the volume to an affordable price, some topics were merged. Otherwise, this volume would have required two volumes (an idea that we discussed briefly), and would have a cost that would make it prohibitive to own. Given our goal of making CBT accessible to clinical social workers, this would have been unacceptable.

We wanted to be sure that this would be a volume relevant to social workers and consistent with clinical social work practice. What we agreed to from the beginning was that every chapter would be authored or co-authored by a social worker. We wanted to showcase the many social workers that have been trained in, practice, or teach cognitive behavior therapy.

In this introductory chapter we would like to preview the superb contributions and offer a view of the prospects for a clinical partnership between social work and CBT. We will not be trying to offer a synopsis of each chapter; the author's or authors' chapter summary does that. We will be comparing and contrasting the points made by the contributors in each section, and then offering an integrative view of the three sections.

Part I contains those chapters that focus on the basic foundations of social work, the elements of CBT, broad clinical issues that relate to both CBT and social work (e.g., evidence-based practice), developmental considerations, technical and strategic interventions (e.g., the use of mindfulness in clinical practice) or specific models of treatment (e.g., dialectical behavior therapy).

The contributions in Part II focus on the applications of CBT to the treatment of children, adolescents, families, elders, and couples. To do this, treatment is described both in the consulting room, the group room, and the school. Alfred Adler described the school setting as of major importance for treatment in that it is the setting where we have the greatest access to children and adolescents, and also the best chance to observe them in their natural setting. The treatment of elders is one of those areas where we see the need for major development and growth over the next few years as we experience the "graying" phenomenon, worldwide.

The third part of the book focuses on the typical problems seen by clinical social workers. As the frontline troops in most clinical settings, social workers, social work interns, and social work supervisors are confronted daily with clients who present with the more common problems of anxiety and depression, substance misuse, grief and bereavement, eating disorders, personality disorders, and medical problems. It was in this final part that we had originally listed far more disorders, but decided to have several contributors write chapters that were inclusive of these disorders (e.g., PTSD, trauma).

HISTORICAL PERSPECTIVE

Historically, social work has grown from an almost "religious" calling to a key mental health profession. The clinical social worker is recognized as an independent and equal partner along with other health care and mental health care providers. All states have set up licensing guidelines for social work practice, and the establishment of a strong national organization has helped to give social work an identity.

Social work has its early roots in community-level practice. In social work terms, this would be called *macropractice*. The early settlement house movement was precisely about this macro level of practice. It was designed to offer social services, education, and to facilitate integration into the community. It was born out of a combination of two factors: the industrial revolution and ongoing waves of immigration to the United

States in the late 19th and early 20th centuries. With the postsettlement house movement, the Mary Richmond style "casework" approach (i.e., social diagnosis), social work as a profession began to flounder in terms of its identity. As it grasped at ideas about the goals, foci, and its potential client groups, social work moved more toward the fields of psychology and psychiatry, and social work practice began to mimic a medical model. This was especially true of clinical social work. Social workers saw clients as "patients" and their problems came to be defined through "diagnosis." Clinical social workers developed credentialing systems to certify that a "clinical" social worker was not the same as a "degreed" social worker. Clinical social workers were trained in individual, family, and group therapy, and could be found working in private practice, institutions, schools, and mental health settings.

Contemporary social work has moved away from the medical model in part because of the perceived negative effects of labeling attendant to diagnoses and in recognition of social/contextual issues that impact human capacities. Within social work today, there is greater emphasis placed on social policy development, reduction of oppressive systems and forces, and addressing environmental constructs that impair individual and community health. Social work has always been a profession that was interested in helping people change, trying to bridge gaps in society and addressing the needs of the weak, the voiceless, and the disenfranchised.

SOCIAL WORK AND CBT

Whether working in clinical practice, private practice, or institutional settings, public agency, policy, or administration social workers have become the backbone of mental health practice in most settings. Clinicians recognize the need for a model of treatment that is active, short-term, directive, problem-oriented, solution-focused, collaborative, structured, dynamic, and psychoeducational interventions. CBT meets that need. Contemporary mental health circumstances require the provision of high-quality services to as many individuals as possible. Dwindling resources and limitations of financial supports have had the consequences of decreased space, staff, and ability to provide services. As both a clinical issue and one of social policy, the use of a cognitive behavior model seems ideally constructed and consistent with the needs of social workers. As Ronen points out, there has been a shift in the position of the clients from the passive recipients of service to being active partners in their treatment.

One of the most significant characteristics of CBT is its dynamic nature. It is dynamic in many ways. First is the manner in which CBT is continually subjecting itself to an evaluation process. What works?

What works for whom? When does it work best? What is the evidence that supports what we do? The answers to these questions invariably fuel the process of change. Part of this change can be seen by looking at the way CBT has changed from its basic behavior therapy underpinnings in the early to mid 1960s with the work of Wolpe, Krasner, and Ullman, Lazarus, Brady, and many others, to a more cognitive base in the late 1960s and through the 1970s with the work of Beck, Ellis, Meichenbaum, Lazarus, Mahoney, and many others. In the 1980s and 1990s many of these basic models were expanded and new disorders were subjected to treatment with CBT. There was during this time an integrative movement to bring behavior therapy and cognitive therapy together as a combined model. There was also significant effort expended during this time to rethinking and reconceptualizing many of the clinical phenomena that have previously been the focus of psychodynamic therapy (e.g., dreams) into the CBT treatment. Terms such as *resistance*, *transference*, and *countertransference* entered the lexicon of CBT. Into the new century, CBT continues to grow and change, adding new components to its basic nature—*constructivism* over the 1990's and mindfullness in 2000.

CBT is dynamic because it is influenced by our developing society and because it guides therapists to modify their thinking and adapt their methods to the changing needs of individual clients. We can see the greater emphasis over the last few years on medical treatment, and on developing prevention and postvention programs.

As Ronen points out, there is the need for the keen recognition of issues of diversity (i.e., gender, culture, age, ethnicity, sexual identity) across myriad lines that are described in greater depth by Murdoff later in the volume. Over the last 30 years, CBT has developed, adapted, revised, and created a range of interventions in the areas of cognition, emotion, and behavior.

In their description of the basic CBT model, MacLaren and Freeman describe a treatment model that is active, directive, dynamic, psychoeducational problem-oriented, solution-focused, collaborative, and directive. By virtue of its structure, CBT seems almost specifically crafted for social work practice. Rather than focusing on the client's problems, CBT emphasizes the clients' strengths to help clients become their own therapist. Based on the works of Albert Ellis and Aaron T. Beck, Seligman's Positive Psychology has grown out of this basic CBT model. Over the last 25 years, the "cognitive revolution" proposed by Mahoney has come and gone. As with most revolutions, it has moved from the early revolutionaries banging on the gates of the establishment to the structure that they have built then becoming the establishment. CBT has become a model and buzzword for practice, and a meeting ground for behavioral and dynamic therapists. Through an extensive literature emerging over the last two decades, CBT has been applied to virtually every patient population, treatment context, and diagnostic category as Beck points out in his foreword. This revolution (and its literature) has circled the globe. There are associations for cognitive behavior therapy (CBT) in Europe, North America, South America, Asia, Australia, and Africa.

Emerging first within the discipline of psychology, CBT has been nurtured and has grown over the years to become one of the primary models of treatment. Interestingly, even though some of the earliest and most important contributors were physicians (Wolpe and Beck), CBT has only recently taken hold in psychiatry. Goisman attributed the problems of CBT moving into psychiatry being due to the power and influence of the more senior and psychoanalytically oriented professors. Social work, one of the most important areas of health and mental health practice, has not been part of the CBT revolution. None of the founders and only a few of their students have come from social work.

Contemporary psychotherapy treatment has moved away from clinical decision making based on "clinical experience" to a model that requires critical thinking and empirical support. While it is romantic and even a bit magical to present therapeutic successes in anecdotal form, it lacks the science that is being required by 21st century practice. The need for empirical support is driven not by the vicissitudes of managed care, but by informed clinical practice.

In some ways, social work practice has moved away from its basic roots in practical and objective changes in individuals, families, groups, and systems. The need for evidence-based practice in social work is a clarion call. Thyer, Myers, Gambrill, and Ronen (this volume) all describe the need for social work to embrace an evidence-based stance. Clinical reports, personal observation, and client statements of satisfaction are not enough to support practice. The use of a particular intervention for many years gives it longevity and can even be designated as clinical experience, but does not necessarily make that intervention the best or most efficacious. The necessity of outcome assessment now being required by many agencies and institutions requires that clinical social workers must work to not only help clients *feel better*, but to *get better* in measurable ways.

The goals of clinical social work must include helping individuals, families and groups to be happier, more personally fulfilled, and more productive. It is essential, however, that the strategies (goals) and interventions (techniques) used to reach these collaboratively set goals are measurable, reasonable, proximal, and realistic. It is far more important in the short term to *get* better than to feel better. It is, in fact, the quest for short-term gain that often will lead individuals into the avoidance seen in the anxiety spectrum disorders, substance misuse, or eating disorders.

The idea that I must respond to the immediacy of one's internal demands is a pattern that needs to be altered.

This is a theme that will emerge in greater detail in Parts II and III as the treatments of specific populations and disorders are considered. Similarly, the need to consider and craft treatment interventions in the light of culture, social conditions, family realities, and personal characteristics is essential. Being all things for all peoples is an unrealistic and unachievable goal. Most therapists would have trouble knowing all of the cultural expectations/demands of their own gender, social, ethnic, racial, or socioeconomic group. Muroff (Chapter 6) makes the point that being a culturally competent CBT social worker does not necessitate experience and expertise with persons of every culture and subculture. Instead it may entail an integrated approach that integrates general principles and broad techniques combined with skills that are likely to be encountered in work with a specific individual. What has made CBT a cross-cultural therapy is the focus and emphasis on identifying and exploring the client's schema. Rather than focus on content (e.g., the unresolved Oedipal conflict) the CBT clinician focuses on the beliefs and explanations that the individual holds that were acquired from early experience in the family of origin. It is these schema that then becomes the template for understanding one's world, choosing a particular strategy for coping, or for avoidance. The schema serves as a filter for expressive and receptive data for everyone, helping clients identify those particular schema that are both helping them cope and become successful (e.g., "If I ignore all social involvement and focus on work, I will achieve success, financial gain, and notoriety"). Obviously, the same schema will also serve to keep the individual isolated and alone. The choice of modifying the schema is the client's. The clinician's job is to make the schema manifest. We are familiar with the terms *genotype* (signifying the biological makeup of the individual) and *phenotype* (the physical expression of these characteristics. We would suggest the addition of a third construct, that of *sociotype* (the social context in which the genotype and phenotype are expressed). By using this third construct, we can include the social and cultural setting in which the individual exists.

A final set of issues raised in the initial section of the book relates to developmental considerations. Often, developmental factors are either not viewed, not raised, or not recognized. P. F. Kernberg (1983) in discussing the phenomenon of borderline personality disorder (BPD) in adolescents warns of the difficulty of making the diagnosis inasmuch as many of the normal developmental factors that define adolescence may be mistaken for BPD (manipulation, identity uncertainty, impulsivity, potentially self-damaging behavior, or relationship problems).

Our goal in Part I of the book was to group information in a manner to set the stage and base for all that follows.

TREATING CHILDREN, ADOLESCENTS, FAMILIES, COUPLES, AND GROUPS

In Part II, we address treatment across the lifespan. Nowhere is the social part of the term *social worker* more essential and vital than when dealing with clients' problems with coping deficits. Given that we live within social contexts, the problems of groups and families seem obvious areas for the social work practice. The bidirectional interactions of couples and the tri-, quad- or pentadirectional interactions that occur within groups and families make this area of treatment far more complex than it might appear on the surface. Children and adolescents must be treated within their family, school, cultural, and religious systems. The systems are the agencies that have helped create and maintain schemas and need to be addressed if any schematic modification is to occur (or if the modification will be maintained). One therapist speaks of how not paying necessary homage to the powerful and controlling mother of a 16-year-old client led to the eventual sabotage of the therapy, the withdrawal of the client from therapy, and the return of the presenting symptoms. It is unusual for child or adolescent clients to seek therapy. School social workers, by virtue of their work venue, are more likely to have "walk-ins" who have had a personal or social crisis, are experiencing overwhelming emotions, or have recognized the need to speak with a nonjudgmental adult. Few clinical social workers in institutional or private practice settings get these same referrals. The work with children and adolescents is further complicated by the need in many settings for parental approval of the treatment beyond an initial referral screening. A key ingredient stressed throughout this area of treatment is how one builds the client's active collaboration and participation in the treatment. The issue is not only how to develop motivation for change but to maintain that motivation through the demanding times of treatment. Ronen (Chapter 9) makes the point that the clinician needs to identify areas and issues that the client is willing and able to work toward changing. Further, she states, "CBT looks for and increases clients' support systems, strengths, and resources and helps them to help themselves." As DiGiuseppe states, "Children are not so much disturbed, but are more often disturbing to others" (1992, personal communication). Children and adolescents find themselves in conflict with their families and in their school settings. Their difficulties may be based on their frequent aggressiveness with peers, academic underachievement (or failure), misuse of drugs, or impulsive or apparently reckless behavior. We have all seen or experienced a child who is *acting out* in the classroom through some externalizing behavior. A particular teacher or educational system is motivated and trained to cope with this child. The same behavior in another classroom or setting creates a situation with which the system cannot cope. Similarly, the *acting in* or internalizing child may not even be noticed inasmuch as they may not cause the same level of disturbance as their externalizing classmate.

Therapy across the lifespan must be developmentally informed. For example, expectations of generalization of learning, the use of abstractions, or interpretations may fall flat with children, adolescents, and individuals with cognitive loss. Treatments for children and adolescents must take into account the need for rather concrete and focused approaches. One such approach is the use of metaphor and metaphorical fables to teach children and adolescents the connection between their thoughts and their feelings and actions. Useful in teaching problem solving, social skills, and the modification of negative thoughts, this approach stands as an exemplar of the structured, focused, and relevant treatment described by MacLaren and Freeman (Chapter 2). What is encouraging is the coping skills program (CSP) developed by Allain and Lemieux (Chapter 10). The goal of this treatment program is prevention through a CBT-based program. If youth can develop the skills to avoid problems, they can be more successful. A prime example of this is a CBT-based program that demonstrated that a group of freshman college students could be "inoculated" against the problems typically found in working with undergraduates. At the end of four years, the treated group had fewer referrals for mental health problems, higher graduation rates, fewer dropouts from school, and lower levels of depression.

Empowerment and *advocacy* have been two of the watchwords of social work practice. Abuse, whether directed toward children, elders, spouses, or partners appears to be a problem of increasing legal and mental health concern. The abuse may be verbal, sexual, physical, or psychological. It may come about as a result of acts of omission or commission. It may be overt, leaving visible marks and scars, or more covert and subtle, where the scars are not visible and the sequelae of the abuse only becoming visible years later. All states have laws that mandate the clinician to report suspected abuse. Both Mason and White (Chapters 11 and 21) address the issue of abuse. Mason addresses abuse from the perspective of treating children, and White focuses on adult survivors of sexual and physical abuse. The chapters offer quite parallel points, that is, the need to move the abused individual from victim to survivor, learning to cope with the fear and arousal that are frequently evoked by seemingly neutral stimuli, and the need for having and using a support network to get through the hard times. The issue for both populations is not an emphasis on cure, but on developing effective coping strategies. Here again, the importance of developmental, cultural, and systemic factors must be addressed. For children, spouses, and elders, protection and safety are the first concerns. Treatment cannot proceed effectively in the midst of abuse. Working with an abusing family or spouse is rendered ineffective as long as the abuse continues. Unless a safety plan is in place and the abuse has stopped, the therapy will be compromised.

The schematic work described earlier is compounded in couples work as there are several potentially conflicting sources of schema. There are the schematic patterns for each of the partners that represent the sum total of each individual's development within their family, the schematic pressures that are brought to bear by families and friends of the couple, and the cultural and subcultural schema regarding being (and staying) in a relationship. The multidirectional schema must also include the schema that derive and are reciprocated regarding "it," the relationship per se. We see this in such schemas and myths as, "when you are in a committed relationship, sex does not need to be discussed," or "my partner should know what I want without my having to discuss it," or "the best way to get what I want is to show anger." As Granvold (Chapter 14) points out, these schematic patterns are often displayed by one partner and reinforced by the other partner. The use of anger is a prime example of emotional reinforcement. Anger may be met with compliance, thereby inadvertently reinforcing anger as a useful and even desirable way to get one's needs met. Likely stemming from reinforced tantrum behavior in childhood or behavior modeled by parents, it continues unabated into adulthood. The therapist may end up being the target of the anger and needs to be prepared to stand fast. An equally common response is sadness and upset. When not getting one's way or not having one's demands met, tears may be the way in which the individual has learned to cope. The schema may be, "unless you meet my wishes I will be sad and you are guilty of victimizing me." Here too, the therapist must be able to avoid being victimized by the victim. Identifying the schema, helping the client to understand the way in which the schema operate, noting the effect of the victimized behavior on self and others, are all useful. However, unless the client has more to gain by changing than by maintaining the schema and the resulting behavior, little will change. The motivation to change will be an ongoing issue in couples and family work.

A common assumption in most psychotherapy literature is that most individuals have the ability or skills to change. Nothing can be further from reality. Not everyone has the same intellectual skills, problem-solving skills, self-calming skills, self-energizing skills, impulse-control skills, or verbal ability. Given that, the clinician must assess skills and strengths along with the areas of skill deficit. As we look at the contributions in both Parts II and III, the issue of skills looms large. To return to the couples and family treatment issue, we see that often the couples and families mean well in their actions and want the best for themselves, their partner, and their family. They may be motivated to change but lack the basic skills. The case is then made for the importance of psychoeducational interventions. These may be focused and manualized (Chapter 15), or taken from a repertoire of psychoeducational interventions applied to the individual.

The anxious client, as described by Himle (Chapter 17), and the depressed and suicidal client, described by Daoud and Tafrate (Chapter 18), are clearly skill deficient. The suicidal client has a limited repertoire of responses. At the top of that list is the idea that killing oneself is a good way to cope with difficult situations. In a similar way, the depressed individual may have a pattern of waiting for the depression to lift as a major coping tool. The idea that they can act to reduce the frequency of their depressive episodes, shorten the duration of the depressive episodes, and reduce the depth of the depression are often seen as impossible goals. They are, however, the very goals that will empower and help the individual take control of his or her life. Teaching problem solving, whether in the individual session or in a group format, is the focus of therapy. The skill of problem solving per se can help the individual to cope more effectively with both internal and external stressors.

The need for systemic interventions cannot be overstated. Having families and significant others be a part of the treatment is essential. We saw this with treatment of children and adolescents (Chapters 12 and 13) and see it as an equally important issue with elders (Chapter 16) and those with severe mental illness (Chapter 15).

COMORBIDITY

Probably the only place that one sees a client with a "pure" disorder is in *DSM-IVTR*. Many case studies in texts emphasize the treatment of a specific disorder. Even the term *dual-diagnosis* is misleading. Finding a client with only two diagnoses may often seem like a gift from God. Most often, clients seek therapy for the treatment of multiple problems, across all five axes. They carry an Axis I diagnosis, a personality disorder on Axis II, significant medical problems on Axis III, severe psychosocial stressors on Axis IV, and poor adaptive function on Axis V. In addition, there are problems that may be socioculturally based. Bordelon (Chapter 20), Morgillo Freeman and Osborn (Chapter 22), and Roche (Chapter 25) describe and discuss the problems of comorbidity. The problems of obtaining accurate data, making accurate diagnoses, developing a problem list, developing an effective treatment conceptualization that accounts for the varied and various pieces, and coming up with a treatment plan are exponentially increased. Rather than looking for the problem that offers the lowest common denominator, what is recommended is making the multiple diagnoses, prioritizing them, identifying which interventions might have the greatest utility in helping the individual cope most effectively with the most difficult or dangerous problems (e.g., suicidality). The key for most problems is psychoeducational. This aspect of CBT is designed to help the individual gain the basic and requisite skills. Part of this might be didactic (i.e., gaining new information from the therapist or from a group). A second part of the treatment will focus on the individual's ability and motivation to change. A third part of the treatment would involve behavioral interventions that are described and practiced in the office and then used in the client's life as "homework." We would make the case that the more that the client is willing and able to do in their life, the more effective the therapy will be. It is not insight alone that brings about change, but rather the insight that one needs to change, the acquisition of the skills to change, an arena that encourages and supports change, and the personal gain from changing. If there is no gain for the individual, clearly, the motivation to change is lessened.

Tammie Ronen
Arthur Freeman

REFERENCES

Freeman, A. (2003). We're not as smart as we think we are. In J. A. Kottler, & J. Carlson (Eds.), *Bad therapy: Master therapists share their worst failures* (pp. 123–130). New York: Routledge.

Kernberg, P. F. (1983). Borderline conditions: Childhood and adolescent aspects. In K. S. Robson (Ed.), *The borderline child* (pp. 101–119). New York: McGraw-Hill.

Cognitive Behavior Therapy in Clinical Social Work Practice

PART I

The Basic Foundation

*Social Work, Cognitive Behavior Therapy,
Evidence-Based Developmental
Characteristics*

CHAPTER 1

Clinical Social Work and Its Commonalities With Cognitive Behavior Therapy

Tammie Ronen

INTRODUCTION

Social workers are committed to the protection and empowerment of weak populations, of those people who are least powerful. Members of this profession struggle to help their clients improve their physical as well as mental well-being, within a society characterized by great economic inequality and a high potential for vulnerability (Bateman, 2002). During the past two decades, social workers have been facing a sorrowful reality depicted by the emergence of new generations of needy families on the one hand and significant cuts in resources on the other hand. Daily, social workers face the busy and complex world of human behavior in social contexts, a world in which relationships break down, emotions run high, and personal needs go unmet. Some people have problems with which they cannot cope and need intervention to overcome their difficulties or to learn to cope and live with them. Other people are the cause of their own problems and need intervention to change their own destructive behavior toward themselves and others (Howe, 2004).

Broadly, the goals of social work have been defined by the National Association of Social Work as follows: to assist individuals and groups to identify and resolve or minimize problems arising out of disequilibrium between themselves and their environment . . . to prevent the occurrence of disequilibrium and . . . to seek out, identify and strengthen the maximum potential in individuals, groups and communities. Social workers must therefore look for patterns and order behind societal changes, human functioning, and human experiences, and they must try to make sense of the people and situations in which they find themselves.

The wish to make the world a better place to live is common to all social workers. However, the view of the root cause of problems and therefore the ensuing focus of intervention and problem resolution differ between social workers. Social workers move between two diverse trends. The first highlights social influences and social processes as the major source of problems and thus as the target of intervention. The second trend views the individual, family, or group as the direct clients of clinical social work.

The first trend upholds that society is responsible for the distress that clients experience. Proponents of this approach explain difficult life situations in terms of society's inability to supply equal opportunities, equal rights, and minimal living standards for weak populations. These social workers hold the inequalities in society accountable for increased client vulnerability (Bateman, 2002). This trend emphasizes the need for social workers to concentrate on social and political advocacy and policy modification as means of changing society in order to help people improve their quality of life. Supporters of this trend also underscore their empowering and protecting roles *vis-à-vis* persons who live in poverty and their roles as advocates to procure social security, debt, and housing rights on behalf of service users (Bateman, 2002; Jones, 2002). While this first trend is indeed a valid, effective way of intervention in social work— it is not the main subject of this book. This book is directed to social workers who belong to the second group and their main interest is in clinical application of the profession.

Proponents of the second trend draw attention to clients themselves as the source of their own problems. This trend attributes problems to clients' ineffective ways of coping with distressing and stressful life conditions. Vulnerability, weakness, and skill deficits are seen as responsible for clients' inadequacies. Consequently, supporters of this trend conduct direct interventions with clients, who may be individuals, couples, families, groups, or systems. These interventions aim to help clients overcome difficulties, cope with stress, and improve their subjective well-being. Professionals who accentuate client interventions must act clearly, competently, and usefully in practical situations; must think theoretically; must retain a deep interest in people; and must wish to understand behavior and relationships, actions and decisions, attitudes and motivations (Howe, 2004). Clinical social workers who espouse direct intervention with clients are continually attempting to construct a unique and respected body of knowledge concerning the effectiveness of various services for suffering persons.

One of the main deficiencies in social work as an academic profession lies in the fact that it has not succeeded in developing its own theory and unique intervention modes. Rather, its basic theory comprises a mixture of theories taken from sociology, policy making, economy, psychology, psychiatry, and philosophy. From its early days, basic theory in social work leaned on psychodynamic conceptual models and intervention methods. Over the years, changes in society, in social work clients, and in the profession's goals and aims have also necessitated practical and theoretical modifications. Psychoanalysis has declined dramatically as a source of practical knowledge in social work, as it is seen as irrelevant to the dilemmas and conflicts faced by mainstream practitioners in their everyday work (Nathan, 2004). Rather, it has become more of a conceptualization that provides a fundamentally psychosocial knowledge base. Howe (1998) defined social work intervention as "that area of human experience which is created by the interplay between the individual's psychological condition and the social environment" (p. 173). Gradually, social work started to rely more on problem-solving methods, client-focused therapy, family theories, and, more recently, cognitive behavior theories, constructivist theories, and positive psychology developments.

CHANGES AND PROCESSES INFLUENCING SOCIAL WORK

Modern society has brought major changes to people's lives as outcomes of social, political, economic, and technological developments. Social workers today must reckon with multicultural societies, consumerism and communication explosions, personal expectations for empowerment and activism, slashed social welfare budgets, and the frequency and increasing severity of impoverished and multiproblem clients. Over the last decade, prompted by its continual search for effective, applicable modes of intervention, the social work profession has evolved to meet some of these changes head-on. Three main processes can be noted: a shift in the profession's view of clients from passive recipients to active partners, a new demand to focus on diversity that necessitates modifications in intervention strategies, and a mandate to apply evidence-based practice.

The Client's Shift From Passive Recipient to Active Partner

The first process affecting social work has been the radical change in the profession's view of the client's role, which in part stemmed from societal changes regarding human rights and equality. In the past, adopting the traditional medical model, clinical social workers viewed clients as passive recipients who needed to accept the therapist, the treatment, and the structure of intervention outright. Client responses such as objections, rejection, and noncompliance received central attention in intervention. Over the past decades, this shift in the role of clients has enabled interventionists to look at clients as equal partners and active participants in the intervention process, and the concepts of rejection and objection have been replaced by concepts like learning from clients, learning from success, empowerment, and so forth (Rosenfeld, 1983, 1985).

The mass media explosion has played a major part leading to this shift in client roles. Knowledge that was previously accessible only to professionals is now utterly available to everyone via computer, Internet, television, and radio. Encouraged by the mass communication's appeals for people to "take control of their lives" and to become more assertive, clients nowadays behave more and more as active consumers of their own treatment. This change is apparent in medicine, in which clients are more involved today in deciding how they should be treated, are now entitled to receive diagnoses, and make decisions regarding their wish to live or die, to take the proposed treatment or not. Clients wish to be involved and possess more knowledge than ever before about treatments and methods. They can learn independently about their problems and possible solutions even before they approach professionals, and they may continue to gather knowledge from other sources while they are involved in treatment. They know to ask: "How are you going to treat me? How long will it take? What proof do you have that the intervention will really make a difference?" Aware of the phenomenon of malpractice, they also want to be sure they are putting themselves in the hands of a reliable and effective practitioner.

These developments in client behavior all contribute to the increasing recognition on the part of social workers that clients are capable of making decisions about themselves and their treatment and can become active participants in the process of their own change (Ronen, 1997; Rosenbaum & Ronen, 1998). Modern life has reinforced the idea that people are capable, have strengths, and are entitled to be involved in a process concerning themselves and their own lives. Thus, clients are no longer passive recipients of help but rather active partners in decision making.

This movement toward clients' increased involvement, knowledgability, and activism is expected to continue in the next decades and to render an impact on the social work services offered (Gambrill, 2004). Individuals will probably have growing access to the same knowledge and information as available to professionals (Silagy, 1999). Hence, social workers must become increasingly expert in direct intervention, in selecting the treatment of choice for clients with diverse needs, and in the ability not only to apply intervention but also to explain treatment decisions satisfactorily to the client and to take responsibility for the outcomes.

Incorporation of Diversity Issues Into Intervention

The second process of change with major implications for the application of clinical social work has been the changing reality of increasingly diverse cultures in the United States and the global community (Anderson & Wiggins-Carter, 2004). A focus on diversity—of any kind—has become an integral part of social work profession standards (Council on Social Work Education, 2002; National Association of Social Work, 1996). In its code of ethics, the National Association of Social Work has added the need to understand culture and its function in human society. Diverse populations, diverse problems, and diverse situations have elicited social work commissions' recognition of diversity as a central concept (Dorfman, Meyer, & Morgan, 2004).

Social workers view themselves as competent to practice with and on behalf of diverse populations (Council on Social Work Education, 2002; National Association of Social Work, 1996). Such competence requires more than just adaptations of existing practice frameworks (Anderson & Wiggins-Carter, 2004). It necessitates an expansion of theory and the learning of new models of practice. To practice with and on behalf of diverse populations, social workers must adhere to a strength paradigm and to concepts that "facilitate the inherent capacity of human beings for maximizing both their autonomy and their independence, as well as their resourcefulness" (National Association of Social Work, 1996, p. 9). The strength perspective encompasses a collation of principals, ideas, and techniques that enable resources and resourcefulness of clients (Saleebey, 1997). Social workers thus should learn direct, structured, skills–directed therapy based on positive psychology, behavioral and cognitive therapies, and the search for empowerment. The empowerment approach (strengths perspective) in social work increases personal and interpersonal or political power and involves the creation of positive perceptions of personal worth; resources and skills; recognition that many of one's views do matter; connections with others; critical analysis; and strategies for social action on behalf of oneself and others.

Along with the strength paradigm that assumes and promotes client competence, two other perspectives have been proposed to facilitate practitioners who need to address diversity: methods and interventions that address the central components of individual and family resiliency (Fraser, 1985) and a focus on solutions rather than on problems (deShazer, 1985).

The Call for Evidence-Based Practice

The third process influencing changes in social work has been the growing call for social workers to apply evidence-based practice. This process has derived from diminished mental health budgetary resources and the ensuing need for intervention efficiency, as well as from accumulating frustration due to the continued suffering of constantly new generations of needy and multiproblem families. From its early stages, even when social work was not yet defined as a profession but rather comprised voluntary action or semiprofessionalism side by side with the need to help people change and cope with problems, social work has emphasized the scientific base underlying intervention. In his book *The Nature and Scope of Social Work*, Cheney (1926) related to social work as "all voluntary efforts to extend benefits which are made in response to a need, are concerned with social relationships, and avail themselves of scientific knowledge and methods" (p. 24) (see details in Chapter 3). Early on, Reynolds (1942) emphasized the need to base social work on a scientific foundation:

> The scientific approach to unsolved problems is the only one which contains any hope of learning to deal with the unknown . . . however, only in recent years, in line with the increasing demand to apply effective interventions, a trend has emerged to ground intervention in theory and to link the treatment's theoretical background to assessment and intervention. (p. 24)

Evidence-based practice has been defined as "the integration of best research evidence with clinical expertise and client values" (Sackett, Straus, Richardson, Rosenberg, & Hanyes, 2000, p. 1). In Chapter 3, Thyer and Myers state that almost all social work practice, dating back for decades, can reasonably be said to have involved clinical expertise and a judicious consideration of value-related issues. They emphasize that evidence-based intervention brings to the table the crucial additional or supplemental voice of giving weight to scientific research, alongside traditional clinical and value-related considerations. In applying evidence-based practice, decision making is transparent, accountable, and based on the best currently available evidence about the effects of particular interventions on the welfare of individuals (Macdonald, 2004).

Myers and Thyer (1997) offered clinicians several ways to facilitate effective interventions. For example, practitioners may use criteria from the Task Force on Promotion and Dissemination of Psychological Procedures (1995), employ stages to categorize empirical validation, base treatments on outcome studies (Chambless, 1996; MacDonald, Sheldon, & Gillespie, 1992), or learn from metaanalyses (Gorey, 1996; Kazdin, 1988).

Howe (2004) emphasized that evidence-based intervention requires social workers to become clearer about their theoretical assumptions and to induce theory from practice and observation. He proposed five key areas for doing so:

1. Observation, as a basis for making assumptions and determining the client's baseline functioning and environment.
2. Description, to help understand the situation in which the observation occurred.
3. Explanation, to link possible influences, relationships, and processes to the occurrence.
4. Prediction of future process, to help make decisions about what might happen.
5. Intervention, to help and change the proposed described situation.

Within this climate of enhancing efficacy, an important contribution of academic schools of social work lies in their shift in focus toward teaching and training students in how to design effective interventions through a clearer and more concrete definition of target problems (Stein & Gambrill, 1977), a greater willingness to pursue goals of a modest scope (Reid, 1978), the institution of baseline and outcome measures (Kazdin, 1988), and the inclusion of all of the aforementioned in social work education and professional training (MacDonald et al., 1992).

In sum, all three recent processes of change in social work—viewing the client as an active equal partner, focusing on diversity, and teaching and training to apply evidence-based practice—have become an integral part of modern social work.

THE BASIC VIEW OF CLINICAL SOCIAL WORK

Clinical social work today operates in a variety of settings in the statutory, voluntary, and private sectors. Social workers apply their practice in hospitals, physicians' clinics, schools, nurseries, prisons, institutions, as well as in a wide variety of primary social work agencies and welfare services. Cree (2004) argued that no clear definition exists concerning how social workers apply interventions to help clients in these varied settings, and that current definitions continue to raise questions about social work and postmodern society. Mostly, an acceptance of the notions that postmodern society is a "risk society" (Beck, 1992) and that social work cannot be separated from society (Cree, 2004) implies that the goals of social work comprise coping with risk and practicing effective means to help clients cope.

Clinical social workers adequately help meet client needs (Wodarski, 1981). Their multitarget and multimethod approaches are directed toward the achievement of positive change and the resolution of human problems (Schinken, 1981). In addition, clinical social workers aim to embrace shaping, educating, and teaching roles, for example, to implement self-help skills or problem-solving models. Another distinctive component of clinical social work is its development of innovative prevention programs to foster clients' ability to cope and manage better in the future (Hardiker & Barker, 1981; Wodarski, 1981).

Clinical social workers have always been interested in helping clients change effectively. The evolution of new intervention modes has permitted the achievement of rapid outcomes on the one hand (Marks, 1987; Ost, Salkovskis, & Hellstrom, 1991) and an increasing emphasis on valuative and comparative studies of treatment efficacy on the other hand (Garfield, 1983; Kazdin, 1982, 1986). The issues of the client's right to effective treatment and the therapist's responsibility to provide that efficacy have started gaining crucial attention in psychotherapy in general, and in social work in particular (Alford & Beck, 1997; Bergin & Garfield, 1994; Giles, 1993).

The importance of empirical study, valid information, and intervention effectiveness has always been accentuated by the social work field's central objectives of increasing accountability, maintaining exemplary ethics and norms, and establishing clear definitions and goals (Gambrill, 1999; Rosen, 1994, 1996; Thyer, 1996). Thyer has emphasized that the contemporary movement toward empirical clinical practice has ample historical precedent, referring to the theme of unifying social work science and practice, which appeared 40 years ago. Social work has been exerting considerable effort to realize its commitment to effective and accountable practice (Rosen, 1994, 1996). Many in the profession believe that effective practice will be enhanced through focused efforts to develop scientifically valid and practice-relevant knowledge for professional decision making.

Until the last decade, only a few interventions based on evidence appeared in Israel. In 1994, Rosen studied the sources of knowledge used to guide Israeli social workers' decisions in actual practice. He found that "value based" normative assessment was the most frequently used rationale in decision-making tasks. Other sources for decision making were theoretical, conceptual, or policy issues. Almost no decisions were made based on empirical outcomes. Thus, according to Rosen's study from a decade ago, practice was generally carried out in Israel on the basis of social workers' beliefs, training, and code of ethics, and only rarely based on valid empirical knowledge.

As previously described, recent processes of change in clinical social work in the United States in general, and in Israel in particular, have been leading to a shift toward the application of evidence-based practice. Nevertheless, most social work research studies continue to be conducted by individual faculty members from university schools of social work, and some are undertaken by independent research institutes and government-affiliated departments (Auslander, 2000). This situation implies that the main interest for research ordinarily does not originate from the service agencies themselves, and often the researcher is even considered an "outsider" who disrupts the agency's routine and whose presence spurs much complaining from the social work practitioners.

The existing gap between psychotherapy researchers and field clinicians resists closure and even threatens to widen (Greenberg, 1994). Clinicians are personally committed to creating a particular sort of intimate relationship with their clients. Researchers, on the other hand, are personally committed to asking difficult, sometimes provocative questions about those relationships. I believe that the only way to create a meaningful change in this discord and friction would be for local service providers to decide to employ researchers as members of their regular staff and to integrate research evaluation into their basic intervention processes. One of the most important foreseeable changes in social work intervention will be collaboration between researchers and clinicians, who will share a common view that evidence should serve as the basis for practice and that effective intervention applications should be rooted in everyday practice.

Social workers started focusing on planning interventions, in order to seek out the most effective methods for change, and also to evaluating the intervention process and its achievement of goals (Bloom & Fischer, 1982; Gambrill, 1990). Toward this end, social workers should look for short-term, concrete, operational, and effective treatment methods. They should also learn to routinely apply initial assessment tools as well as evaluation methods to research their own treatment outcomes. They need to enhance their awareness that solving a client's specific problem (whether personal or familial) cannot suffice. Rather, a powerful need exists to teach clients specific skills that will enable them to resolve and cope with their own problems in the future. In other words: The client must be taught to become his or her own change agent. Social workers need to shift the weight of their interventions from reliance on therapeutic skills to an approach that is based more on teaching, educating, and training people in skills for helping themselves.

This description sets the stage for understanding the new trends characterizing clinical social work: understanding that clients are equal beings and have the right to intervene in the process of change, focusing on diversity and therefore on strengths and solutions rather than on problems, basing practice on evidence about efficacy, planning and evaluating treatments, and looking to positive psychology when planning intervention. All of these trends likewise characterize cognitive behavior therapy (CBT).

THE BASICS OF CBT

The dynamic nature of CBT can be understood by reviewing its developments over the last 50 years (Ronen, 2002). Basic behavior theory focused on learning modes. Stimuli, response, and conditioning depicted classical conditioning (Wolpe, 1982), whereas operant conditioning utilized concepts such as behavior, outcomes, extinction, and reinforcement (Skinner, 1938). Social learning employed constructs such as modeling, environment, and observation (Bandura, 1969). Altogether, these constructs pinpointed the role of the environment in conditioning one's behavior and the links between stimuli and responses; behaviors and outcomes; and expectancies, behaviors, and environments.

These main concepts and explanations also manifested themselves in the six thinking rules developed by Kanfer and Schefft (1988) to direct the cognitive behavior therapist in conducting treatment:

1. *Think behavior.* Action should comprise the main dimension on which to focus interchanges in therapy.
2. *Think solution.* Attention should be directed toward determining which problematic situation needs resolving, what is the desirable future, and some indication of how to achieve it.
3. *Think positive.* Focus should be directed toward small changes and positive forces rather than on difficulties, and toward constantly reinforcing positive outcomes.
4. *Think small steps.* The targeting of small gradual changes reduces fears, motivates clients, and helps therapists observe and pinpoint difficulties. An accumulation of many small changes constitutes one final, large, and significant change.
5. *Think flexible.* Therapists should look for disconfirming evidence that points to alternatives. They should try to understand other people's points of view and to adapt treatment to the client's needs.
6. *Think future.* CBT challenges therapists to think toward the future, predicting how their client will cope and how they themselves would like to be different or better in the future.

The addition of cognitive components brought about a major change in the basic behavior model of therapy, creating CBT. As a way of thinking and perceiving human functioning and needs, CBT offers a way of operating within the environment in order to achieve the most effective means for accomplishing one's aims (Beck et al., 1990; Ronen, 1997, 2002). The cognitive theory of psychopathology and psychotherapy considers cognition as the key to psychological disorders. Cognition is defined as the function that involves inferences about one's experiences, occurrences, and control of future events.

Cognitive behavior theory emphasizes several components. First, as mentioned before, human learning involves cognitive mediational processes. Therefore, thoughts, feelings, and behaviors are causally interrelated. The thought is responsible for information processing relating to the world and to oneself, and that information influences emotions, behaviors, and physiology in reliable, predictable ways. Also, this theory highlights activities such as expectations, self-statements, and attributions, which are seen as important in understanding and predicting psychopathology and psychotherapeutic change.

An important theoretical concept comprises irrational or dysfunctional thought. Human problems derive from persons' irrational, dysfunctional, and inadequate way of thinking (Beck, Rush, Shaw, & Emery, 1979). CBT attributes problems either to thinking style (irrational or distorted) or to deficiencies such as a lack of skills that impedes clients from behaving as they should. Hence, skills acquisition is conceived both as a major, crucial component in human functioning and as an important therapeutic technique.

The underlying theoretical rationale of CBT upholds that human beings' affects and behaviors are largely determined by the way in which they structure the world (Beck, 1963, 1976; Beck, Emery, & Greenberg, 1985). From birth, humans start to develop their personal cognitions—verbal or pictorial "events" in the stream of consciousness—that derive from attitudes or assumptions developed from previous experiences (Alford & Beck, 1997). This personal interpretation creates the human being's personal repertoire of cognitions and reflects individuals' personal schemata toward themselves and the world around them. The schemata evolve from life experiences, personal nature, and environmental components. Personal repertoire and schemata reflect human beings' basic belief systems and manifest themselves in their automatic self-talk. Over the last few years, a wide range of research studies and applications of schema-focused therapy have emerged, as described in detail in Chapter 20.

The addition of constructivist components to CBT highlighted the role of change. Human beings are always in a process of change (Cull & Bondi, 2001). In directing intervention, therapists should therefore consider the fact that clients change and will continue to change in the future. Constructivism also focuses on personal constructs (Mahoney, 1991), emphasizing the role of human beings as architects, with responsibility for creating their own lives and experiences (Kelly, 1955). People make their own realities by constructing, reconstructing, and construing their life events and by attributing personal meanings to their experiences (Mahoney, 1991, 1993, 1999). Thus, problems do not constitute objective events themselves (e.g., death, depression, sickness) but rather how one subjectively interprets such events and how this specific interpretation gives rise to particular emotions and behaviors (Beck, 1976).

Over the past decades, other developments in CBT have included techniques emphasizing the need for acceptance of problems rather than a focus on overcoming and coping (Hayes, Jacobson, Follette, & Dougher, 1994). In addition, mindfulness techniques have been integrated into the process of intervention (Hayes, Follette, & Linehan, 2004).

Rosenbaum and Ronen (1998) summarized the seven basic, key features of CBT:

1. *Meaning making processes.* These processes help clients develop a new and more suitable way of understanding and accepting their behavior.
2. *Systematic and goal-directed processes.* The therapist plans and executes treatment and designs the therapeutic hour (Beck, 1976), with an emphasis on the need to define problems, goals, expectations, means to achieve these goals, assessment, and evaluation of the process.
3. *Practicing and experiencing.* CBT constitutes not a talking therapy but rather a doing therapy that encompasses practicing and experiencing as central components. Interventions vary and can be verbal or nonverbal, using experiential methods such as role assignments, imagery training, metaphors, writing methods, and so on (Mahoney, 1991; Ronen & Rosenbaum, 1998).
4. *Collaborative effort.* Therapist and client must enter into an alliance and collaborate on joint work in order to achieve the goals of therapy.
5. *Client-focused intervention.* CBT should aim at treating the person, rather than treating the problem. This view focuses on the person as a whole, and concentrates on the client's feelings, thoughts, and way of living, not only on the client's problem.
6. *Facilitating change processes.* This component emphasizes the important role of the therapist in pursuing effective strategies and techniques to help the client change (Rosenbaum & Ronen, 1998).
7. *Empowerment and resourcefulness.* All of the previous features aim to empower clients by training them in self-control skills for self-help and independent functioning.

CBT is not a method that is administered to the client, but rather a method that is designed in collaboration with the client. Therefore, intervention varies from one client to another. No one technique or means is essential for achieving change, but rather the therapist must design an appropriate intervention that suits each individual client, based on that client's unique nature, hobbies, particular problem, strengths and resources, and motivation for change (Ronen, 1997; Rosenbaum & Ronen, 1998). Therapists maintain a constant state of decision making, always asking themselves what the best intervention is with this specific client, with this specific problem, in this specific situation (Paul, 1967; Ronen, 2001).

Treatment is planned, structured, and goal directed. Yet, no rigid rules predetermine the length of therapy, the frequency of sessions, or the treatment location. These, too, encompass part of the decision-making process regarding the treatment of choice for each client. Treatment may begin with more frequent sessions, which lessen in frequency as the client progresses. Phone calls can provide between-session contact with the client. For example, asking a socially rejected child to call the therapist on each day that he was able to talk with children without them laughing at him may increase the boy's confidence, motivation, and awareness about his ability to carry on a conversation. Therapy generally transpires in the clinic but may make use of outdoor walks or natural settings for exposure exercises, or may shift to a basketball court to promote a child's motivation or practice new skills in a concrete context (Ronen, 2003).

CBT can be applied to various populations such as families, couples, adults, children, individuals, groups, and communities, with an emphasis on the unique nature and needs of each setting (Alford & Beck, 1997; Cigno & Bourn, 1998; Graham, 1998), as can be found in this book. Both verbal and nonverbal therapy can be used to achieve the most effective change possible (Freeman & Boyll, 1992), and some examples of the variety of techniques can be found in the various chapters in this book. Creative indirect techniques can assist therapists in overcoming difficulties in the treatment process, facilitating their clients to surmount obstacles in therapy, and applying more effective treatments to suit their clients' specific life purposes.

The best technique will be the one that is feasible for the therapist to use; suits the client's language, interests, and way of thinking; and enables the client to understand and change the present problem (Ronen, 2001). Decisions about the treatment of choice must be based on assessment of the client's characteristics, the severity of the problem, and the client's ability for change.

Concepts and Components Common to Both Social Work and CBT

Many of the basic concepts underlying social work interventions are shared by CBT. These similarities are not casual. Social work is a practical profession with practically defined goals and concrete techniques, based on structured intervention and goal-directed processes, and emphasizing the social workers' role as a change agent. CBT aims to resolve the problems of the individual and improve that person's quality of life. This section focuses on several additional concepts that demonstrate similarities between clinical social work and CBT: individualism; rational thinking; clearly defined objects for change; assessment, evaluation, and intervention planning; prediction; developing skills for behavior change; and empowerment.

Individualism

In its early days, social work emphasized the importance of focusing on the individual and on "individualism." Loewenberg (1998) emphasized the importance of individual differences as a notion that should guide social workers in their everyday functioning. Likewise, CBT approaches look for the person behind the problem and the special way in which the problem presents itself in each specific case. CBT focuses on how the person thinks, feels, or acts and what forces maintain his or her behavior. Individual differences also constitute the main concept underlying the approach advocating a focus on cultural diversity in social work. Understanding that every individual is unique, and that every person possesses strengths if only the therapist will look for them, is a common feature in social work as well as in CBT. This issue shifts the focus from diagnosis (e.g., depression) and from generalizations (e.g., depressive people act in a way . . .) to a focus on learning about the individual person and his or her strengths and resources.

Rational Thinking

Rosenfeld (1983) underscored the importance of rational thinking for social workers. He pointed out that the theory of social work stresses the need for awareness of both thoughts and emotions as the main determinants of people's behavior. Rational thinking is also the basis of CBT. Ellis (1973) viewed all problems that people experience as related to irrational thinking, and, therefore, he directed treatment toward changing irrational to rational thought. CBT looks at the person's behavior as an outcome of his or her thinking processes, which affect emotional states and direct the person to take specific actions. Rational thinking, therefore, plays a necessary part of social work as well as CBT.

Clearly Defined Objects for Change

Perlman (1953), Loewenberg (1998), Gambrill (1983, 1990), and others have emphasized that no intervention can be carried out in social work unless values and targets are very clear, concrete, and well-defined. These three features are at the basis of every cognitive and behavioral intervention, in contrast with the psychodynamic branches of therapy.

Assessment, Evaluation, and Intervention Planning

These components are central features of CBT. Therapy is based on careful assessment, intervention is directly linked to assessment and followed by evaluation. Social workers also recognize the need to evaluate and set criteria for change. One of the unique features of social work is its consistent need for planned intervention in all four systems: the change-agent system, the client system, the target system, and the problem system. Loewenberg (1984) emphasized the need for professionals to use explanation, prediction, practical guidance, and application of practical knowledge. All of these should be accompanied by assessment and evaluation methods to examine the efficacy of interventions.

Prediction

Loewenberg (1998) argued that social work applications should rely on two kinds of prediction: the way the client will act without intervention, and the way intervention might change the nature of the problem. Prediction encompasses an important part of the overall treatment (Bandura, 1969; Kanfer & Schefft, 1988), as a base for choosing the optimal techniques (Gambrill, 1983), and as a means whereby the client takes responsibility for his or her own change (Ronen, 2001).

Developing Skills for Behavior Change

Social work as a profession is built on the notion that theoretical knowledge can be translated into skills and practical know-how in order to achieve change (Beckerman, 1978; Kondrat, 1992). Thus, Schinken (1981) suggested that social workers should translate abstract theory into concrete methods for analyzing and alleviating personal and societal stresses. Skills-directed therapy is also a very important part of CBT in general and with children in particular (Ronen, 1994). For example, see Chapter 13 on children's problem solving and group social skills training. The conceptualization of the nature of the learning process within CBT theories emphasizes each individual's ability to learn and acquire new skills. Like any other type of learning, individual differences determine the amount of time and effort necessary to invest in learning, but there is no question that everyone is capable of learning.

Empowerment

As social work involves weak populations, empowerment constitutes an important interventional goal. Instead of instituting long-term dependent relationships between therapist and client, social workers aim to assist clients to become independent and to help themselves. Likewise, the purpose of CBT theories is to aid individuals, groups, and families to find their own resources, learn to recognize and use their own wisdom, and discover personal methods for self-help. These are expected to lead clients toward greater independence, self-trust, and capability for self-change (Rosenbaum & Ronen, 1998).

Considering the common base shared by social work and CBT, Rosen and Livne (1992) argued that social workers who subscribe to a psychodynamic orientation are more likely to emphasize the unity of personality and to view their own personality, intuition, and spontaneity as critical in treatment, focusing on personal rather than environmental features. They suggested that social workers who adopt a more planned, systematic, and research-oriented approach to treatment are less likely to formulate clients' problems in this way.

BRIDGING THE GAP BETWEEN CLINICAL SOCIAL WORK AND CBT

CBT is based on working toward an understanding of the client and then intervening in how that client anticipates experiences by creating an intervention appropriate for that one human being. Inasmuch as such therapy constitutes a planned, designed process, clinical researchers have given much attention to the construction of the intervention process. The most familiar procedure providing guidelines for conducting the process of intervention comprises Gambrill's 12 steps (Gambrill, Thomas, & Carter, 1971). Gambrill, who is one of the founding figures in behavior therapy, is also a well-known social worker. Although she proposed her intervention procedures many years ago, in the 1970s, they are amazingly relevant today, and I urge all my social work students to learn to use them. These 12 structured phases enable clinical social workers to check and recheck the intervention process, identify their current stage, and clarify what is missing.

1. *Inventory of problem areas.* Aims at collecting information about the whole spectrum of presented problems.
2. *Problem selection and contract.* Raises clients' motivation by collaborating with them and achieving their agreement on problem areas selected for change.

3. *Commitment to cooperate.* Aims to facilitate compliance and motivation by obtaining the client's agreement with the process.
4. *Specification of target behaviors.* Defines and analyzes each behavior to decide what maintains and reinforces the problem.
5. *Baseline assessment of target behavior.* Collects data about the frequency and duration of the problem, to provide a concrete foundation on which to evaluate change.
6. *Identification of problem-controlling conditions.* Identifies the conditions preceding and following the problem's occurrence.
7. *Assessment of environmental resources.* Uncovers possible resources in the client's environment.
8. *Specification of behavioral objectives.* Specifies the behavioral objectives of the modification plan, and elicits the client's terminal behavioral repertoire.
9. *Formulation of a modification plan.* Selects an appropriate technique for applying the most efficient program for change.
10. *Implementation of modification plan.* Modifies behavior and focuses effort on change.
11. *Monitoring of outcomes.* Collects information concerning the effectiveness of intervention.
12. *Maintenance of change.* Works to achieve maintenance and stabilization, to help prevent relapses.

INTEGRATING CBT INTO CLINICAL SOCIAL WORK: LOOKING TOWARD THE FUTURE

Social workers must first address their clients' high-risk, urgent situations, and only then can they free themselves to concentrate on preventive programs. CBT is a treatment of choice not only for decreasing immediate, hazardous problems but also for preventing future difficulties. Practitioners trained in CBT techniques are expected to be able to not only use the acquired skills directly but also to generate and generalize skills for future reference. Hence, one intervention may possibly facilitate the achievement of primary, secondary, and tertiary prevention goals.

Social workers need to look for effective methods for change, and CBT methods are very promising in this respect. CBT is not the only effective method for change but, at least, offers a well-grounded theory, together with clearly defined techniques and suggestions for assessment and evaluation of the change process. CBT has been proven effective for resolving concrete problems as well as for working on future goals. Moreover, inasmuch as CBT is anchored in skills acquisition and learning, it may be viewed as a nonstigmatic way to help normal, regular people.

As educators, teachers, and practitioners, social workers' main roles can be to educate clients for self-help, teach them needed skills, train them in practicing and applying those skills, and then supervise them in generalizing the acquired skills into other areas and problems. By imparting clients with skills and methods through such interventions, social workers can help clients to become their own change agents who are in charge of their self-help processes and who improve the quality of their own lives. CBT training should therefore be recommended as a helpful, effective, and empowering method both for social workers and for their clients.

Social workers practice interventions with different problems spanning a large range of social classes and cultures. It is impossible to design intervention without being familiar with the client's own socioeconomic class, culture, and way of life. The intervention should be adapted to fit the client's familiar way of behaving and only then should the attempt be made to slowly achieve change. Like in a good tennis game, the social worker should learn to meet the ball wherever it arrives and to try and raise it up. Only by so doing can CBT training be adapted to different cultures and problem areas. Concepts and techniques should be designed together with the client, to fit the client's own familiar language, outlook, and lifestyle.

Social workers, schools of social work, agencies, and clients alike need to be sure that social work has something important to offer them. It is time to return to our basic goals and aims. Social workers need to help people help themselves, fulfill their own wishes, and improve their own quality of life.

REFERENCES

Alford, B. A., & Beck, A. T. (1997). *The integrative power of cognitive therapy.* New York: Guilford.

Anderson, J., & Wiggins-Carter, R. (2004). Diversity perspectives for social work practice. In R. A. Dorfman, P. Meyer, & M. L. Morgan (Eds.), *Paradigms of clinical social work, Vol 3. Emphasis on diversity* (pp. 19–33). New York: Brunner-Routledge

Auslander, G. K. (2000). Social work research and evaluation in Israel. *Journal of Social Work Research and Evaluation, 1,* 17–34.

Bandura, A. (1969). *Principles of behavior modification.* New York: Holt, Rinehart & Winston.

Bateman, N. (2002). Welfare rights practice. In M. Davies (Ed.), *The Blackwell companion to social work* (2nd ed., pp. 132–140). Oxford: Blackwell.

Beck, A. T. (1963). Thinking and depression. *Archives of General Psychiatry, 9,* 324–333.

Beck, A. T. (1976). *Cognitive therapy and the emotional disorders.* New York: Meridian.

Beck, A. T., Emery, G., & Greenberg, R. L. (1985). *Anxiety disorders and phobias*. New York: Basic Books.

Beck, A. T., Freeman, A., & Associates. (1990). *Cognitive therapy of personality disorders*. New York: Guilford.

Beck, A. T., Rush, A. J., Shaw, B. F., & Emery, G. (1979). *Cognitive therapy of depression*. New York: Guilford.

Beck, U. (1992). *Risk society: Towards a new modernity*. London: Sage.

Beckerman, A. H. (1978). Differentiating between social research and social work research: Implications for teaching. *Journal of Education for Social Work, 14*, 9–15.

Bergin, A. E., & Garfield, S. L. (1994). *Handbook of psychotherapy and behavior change* (4th ed.). New York: Wiley.

Bloom, M., & Fischer, J. (1982). *Evaluating practice: Guidelines for the accountable professional*. Englewood Cliffs, NJ: Prentice Hall.

Chambless, D. L. (1996). An update on empirically validated therapies. *The Clinical Psychologist, 49*, 5–18.

Cheney, A. (1926). *The nature and scope of social work*. New York: D. C. Heath.

Cigno, K., & Bourn, D. (1998). (Eds.). *Cognitive-behavioural social work in practice*. Aldershot, UK: Ashgate/Arena.

Council on Social Work Education. (2002). CSWE *educational policy and accreditation standards*. Washington, DC: Author.

Cree, V. E. (2004). Social work and society. In M. Davies (Ed.), *The Blackwell companion to social work* (2nd ed., pp. 276–287). Oxford: Blackwell.

Cull, J., & Bondi, M. (2001). Biology/psychology of consciousness: A circular perspective. *Constructivism, 6*, 23–29.

deShazer, S. (1985). *Keys to solutions in brief therapy*. New York: Norton.

Dorfman, R. A., Meyer, P., & Morgan, M. L. (Eds.). (2004). *Paradigms of clinical social work, Vol. 3. Emphasis on diversity*. New York: Brunner-Routledge

Ellis, A. (1973). *Humanistic psychotherapy: The rational-emotive approach*. New York: McGraw-Hill.

Fraser, M. W. (Ed.). (1985). *Risk and resiliency in childhood: An ecological perspective*. Washington, DC: National Association of Social Work Press.

Freeman, A., & Boyll, S. (1992). The use of dreams and the dream metaphor in cognitive behavior therapy. *Psychotherapy in Private Practice, 10*(1-2), 173–192.

Gambrill, E. (1983). *Casework: A competency based approach*. Englewood Cliffs, NJ: Prentice Hall.

Gambrill, E. (1990). *Critical thinking in clinical approach*. San Francisco: Jossey-Bass.

Gambrill, E. (1999). Evidence-based clinical behavior analysis, evidence-based medicine and the Cochrane collaboration. *Journal of Behavior Therapy and Experimental Psychiatry, 30*, 1–14.

Gambrill, E. (2004). The future of evidence-based social work practice. In B. A. Thyer, & M. F. Kazi (Eds.), *International perspectives on evidence-based practice in social work* (pp. 215–234). London: Venture.

Gambrill, E., Thomas, E. J., & Carter, R. D. (1971). Procedure for sociobehavioral practice in open settings. *Social Work, 16*, 51–62.

Garfield, S. L. (1983). Effectiveness of psychotherapy: The perennial controversy. *Professional Psychology, 14,* 35–43.

Giles, T. R. (1993). *Handbook of effective psychotherapy.* New York: Plenum.

Gorey, K. M. (1996). Effectiveness of social work interventions: Internal versus external evaluations. *Social Work Research, 20,* 119–128.

Graham, P. (Ed.). (1998). *Cognitive behaviour therapy for children and families.* Cambridge, UK: University Press.

Greenberg, G. (1994). Psychotherapy research: A clinician's view. In P. F. Talley, H. H. Strupp, & S. F. Butler (Eds.), *Psychotherapy research and practice* (pp. 1–18). New York: Basic Books.

Hardiker, P., & Barker, M. (1981). *Theories of practice in social work.* London: Academic Press.

Hayes, S. C., Follette, V. M., & Linehan, M. M. (2004). *Mindfulness and acceptance: Expanding the cognitive behavioral tradition.* New York: Guilford.

Hayes, S. C., Jacobson, N. S., Follette, V. M., & Dougher, M. J. (1994). *Acceptance and change: Content and context in psychotherapy.* Reno, NV: Context Press.

Howe, D. (1998). Psychosocial work. In R. Adams, L. Dominelli, & M. Payne (Eds.), *Social work: Themes, issues and critical debates.* London: MacMillan.

Howe, D. (2004). Relating theory to practice. In M. Davies (Ed.), *The Blackwell companion to social work* (2nd ed., pp. 82–87). Oxford: Blackwell.

Jones, C. (2002). Poverty and social exclusion. In M. Davies (Ed.), *The Blackwell companion to social work* (2nd ed., pp. 7–18). Oxford: Blackwell.

Kanfer, F. H., & Schefft, B. K. (1988). *Guiding the process of therapeutic change.* Champaign, IL: Research Press.

Kazdin, A. E. (1982). *Single case research designs.* New York: Oxford University Press.

Kazdin, A. E. (1986). The evaluation of psychotherapy: Research design and methodology. In S. L. Garfield, & A. E. Bergin (Eds.), *Handbook of psychotherapy and behavior change* (3rd ed., pp. 23–68). New York: Wiley.

Kazdin, A. E. (1988). *Child psychotherapy: Developing and identifying effective treatments.* New York: Pergamon.

Kelly, G. A. (1955). *The psychology of personal constructs.* New York: Norton.

Kondrat, M. E. (1992). Reclaiming the practical: Formal and substantive rationality in social work practice. *Social Service Review, 66*(2), 237–255.

Loewenberg, F. M. (1998). Introduction: Fifty years of social work in Israel. In F. M. Loewenberg (Ed.). *Meeting the challenges of a changing society: Fifty years of social work in Israel,* pp. 7–19. Jerusalem: The Magnes Press, The Hebrew University.

MacDonald, G. M. (2004). The evidence-based perspective. In M. Davies (Ed.), *The Blackwell companion to social work* (2nd ed., pp. 425–430). Oxford: Blackwell.

MacDonald, G. M., Sheldon, B., & Gillespie, J. (1992). Contemporary studies of the effectiveness of social work. *British Journal of Social Work, 22,* 615–643.

Mahoney, M. J. (1991). *Human change processes: The scientific foundations of psychotherapy.* New York: Basic Books.

Mahoney, M. J. (1993). Introduction to special section: Theoretical developments in the cognitive psychotherapies. *Journal of Consulting and Clinical Psychology, 61,* 187–193.

Mahoney, M. J. (1999). *Constructive psychotherapy: Exploring principles and practical exercises.* New York: Guilford.

Marks, I. (1987). *Fears, phobias and rituals.* New York: Oxford University Press.

Myers, L. L., & Thyer, B. A. (1997). Should social work clients have the right to effective treatments? *Social Work, 42,* 288–298.

Nathan, J. (2004). Psychoanalytic theory. In M. Davies (Ed.), *The Blackwell companion to social work* (2nd ed., pp. 183–190). Oxford: Blackwell.

National Association of Social Workers. (1980). Code of ethics. *NASW News, 25,* 24–25.

National Association of Social Workers. (1996). *Code of ethics.* Silver Spring, MD: Author.

Ost, L. G., Salkovskis, P. M., & Hellstrom. K. (1991). One-session therapist-directed exposure vs. self-exposure in the treatment of spider phobia. *Behavior Therapy, 22,* 407–422.

Paul, G. L. (1967). Outcome research in psychotherapy. *Journal of Consulting Psychology, 31,* 109–118.

Paul, R. J. (1993). *Critical thinking: What every person needs to survive in a rapidly changing world* (3rd ed.). Sonoma, CA: Foundation for Critical Thinking.

Perlman, H. (1953). The basic structure of the casework process. *Social Service Review, 27,* 308–315

Reid, W. J. (1978). *The task centered system.* New York: Columbia University Press.

Reynolds, B. C. (1942). *Learning and teaching in the practice of social work.* New York: Farrar & Rinehart.

Ronen, T. (1997). *Cognitive developmental therapy with children.* Chichester, UK: Wiley.

Ronen, T. (2001). Collaboration on critical questions in child psychotherapy: A model linking referral, assessment, intervention, and evaluation. *Journal of Social Work Education, 1,* 1–20.

Ronen, T. (2002). Cognitive-behavioural therapy. In M. Davies (Ed.), *The Blackwell companion to social work* (2nd ed., pp. 165–174). Oxford: Blackwell.

Ronen, T. (2003). *Cognitive constructivist psychotherapy with children and adolescents.* New York: Kluwer/Plenum.

Ronen, T., & Rosenbaum, M. (1998). Beyond verbal instruction in cognitive behavioural supervision. *Cognitive & Behavioural Practice, 5,* 3–19.

Rosen, A. (1994). Knowledge use in direct practice. *Journal of Social Service Review, 68,* 561–577.

Rosen, A. (1996).The scientific practitioner revisited: Some obstacles and prerequisites for fuller implementation in practice. *Social Work Research, 20,* 104–113.

Rosen, A., & Livne, S. (1992). Personal versus environmental emphases in social workers' perceptions of client problems. *Social Service Review, ,* 87–96.

Rosenbaum, M., & Ronen, T. (1998). Clinical supervision from the standpoint of cognitive-behavioral therapy. *Psychotherapy, 35,* 220–229.

Rosenfeld, J. M. (1983). The domain and expertise of social work: A conceptualization. *Social Work, 28,* 3–5.

Rosenfeld, J. M. (1985). Learning from success. *Changing family patterns and the generation of social work practice.* Paper presented at the Workshop on the Family in the City, University of Witwatersrand, Johannesburg.

Sackett, D. L., Straus, S. E., Richardson, W. S., Rosenberg, W., & Hanyes, R. B. (2000). *Evidence-based medicine: How to practice and teach EBM* (2nd ed.). New York: Churchill-Livingstone.

Saleebey, D. (Ed.). (1997). *The strength perspective in social work practice* (2nd ed.). New York: Longman.

Schinken, S. P. (1981). *Behavioral methods in social welfare.* New York: Adline.

Silagy, C. (1999). Introduction to the new edition: The post-Cochrane agenda: Consumers and evidence. In A. L. Cochrane (Ed.), *Effectiveness and efficiency: Random reflections on health services.* Nuffield Trust, Royal Society of Medicine Press.

Skinner, B. F. (1938). *The behavior of organism.* New York: Appleton-Century-Crofts.

Stein, J., & Gambrill, E. (1977). Facilitating decision making in foster care. *Social Services Review, 51,* 502–511.

Task Force on Promotion and Dissemination of Psychological Procedures. (1995). Training in and dissemination of empirically-validated psychological treatments: Report and recommendations. *The Clinical Psychologist, 48,* 3–23.

Thyer, B. A. (1996). Forty years of progress toward empirical clinical practice? *Social Work Research, 20,* 77–81.

Wodarski, J. S. (1981). *The role of research in clinical practice: A practical approach for the human service.* Baltimore: University Press.

Wolpe, J. (1982). *The practice of behavior therapy* (3rd ed.). New York: Pergamon.

CHAPTER 2

Cognitive Behavior Therapy Model and Techniques

Catherine MacLaren

Arthur Freeman

INTRODUCTION

A number of terms have come to the fore in recent years as representative or descriptive of the direction of psychotherapy and have been generally taken as a reflection of the *zeitgeist*. Therapy forms that use terms such as *brief*, *short-term*, *problem-focused*, or *time-limited* as part of their name abound in the literature. Sometimes these terms are related to or connected with a particular theoretical orientation, for example, short-term psychodynamic psychotherapy (Davenloo, 1978, 1980; Sifneos, 1972; Said & Worchel, 1986; Worchel, 1990), interpersonal psychotherapy (Klerman, Weissman, Rounsaville, & Chevron, 1984; Weissman, 1995). Other models may be short-term by the very construction of the therapy, for example, cognitive therapy (Beck, Rush, Shaw, & Emery, 1979, Freeman, Pretzer, Fleming, & Simon, 1990, 2005).

Over the years, cognitive behavior therapy (CBT) has been applied to a variety of client populations (crisis problems, couples, children, suicidal clients) in a range of treatment settings (inclient, outclient, hospital, university counseling centers) and to the range of clinical problems.

CBT originally evolved out of two traditions, the behavior therapy tradition and the psychodynamic tradition. It has become increasingly popular in recent decades and stands as a meeting point for therapists from many different models.

This chapter provides a general overview of the cognitive behavior history, model, and techniques and their application to clinical social work practice. We begin with a brief history and description, provide a basic conceptual framework for the approach, highlight the empirical base of the model, and then discuss the use of cognitive, behavior, and emotive/affective interventions. An essential part of the model is the rationale and importance of homework or assigned activities between therapy sessions. It is hoped that this chapter will present the reader with a basic framework for understanding the content of the chapters that follow, which outline the tailored use of CBT with specific groups, clinical problems, and populations.

BRIEF HISTORY

Cognitive behavior therapy serves as an umbrella term that encompasses aspects of a number of specific approaches including Beck's Cognitive Therapy, McMullin's Cognitive Restructuring, Ellis' Rational Emotive Behavior Therapy, Goldfried's Systematic Rational Restructuring, Haley's Problem-Solving Therapy, Lazarus's Multimodal Assessment, Linehan's Dialectical Behavior Therapy, Meichenbaum's Self-Instructional Training or Stress Innoculation Training, Young's Schema-Focused Therapy, and others. Rather than present the specifics of each of these models (a task that would be far too lengthy and unwieldy for this single chapter), we will focus on the common elements that constitute a broad CBT approach.

Jones (1955) states that much of Freud's early work was in fact very short term, and has documented some of his early cases. Some of these cases include the famous conductor Bruno Walter, who Freud successfully treated in six sessions, or that of conductor, Gustav Mahler, whom he treated in one four-hour session. Alfred Adler, a member of the early psychoanalytic circle, was also a proponent of short-term therapy. Typically, Adler informed his clients at the beginning of therapy that the process would take 8 to 10 weeks. He recommended that with more difficult cases the client be told the following about the length of therapy; "I don't know. Let us begin. In a month I shall ask you whether we are on the right track. If not, we shall break it off" (Ansbacher & Ansbacher, 1964, p. 201).

Behavior Therapy

Behavior therapy was one of the first major departures from the more traditional, psychodynamically oriented approaches to therapy. Instances of the use of unofficial behavior therapy can be traced back to the 1800s, but in the early 1900s there are documented discoveries and hypotheses that formed the basis of behavior therapy. The early experiences of Pavlov, Skinner, Watson, Wolpe, and others helped to shape the behavior therapy tradition that emerged in the early to mid 1900s and into the 1950s to become quite popular with a segment of the psychology world.

Behavior therapy is based on both the classical (Pavlovian) and operant conditioning models (Skinnerian). Pavlov, a Russian physiologist, hypothesized that the simultaneous introduction of a bell (a learned or conditioned stimulus, the CS) and food (an unlearned or unconditioned stimulus, UCS) created an association between the two stimuli. The dogs would, naturally, salivate to the food. This was an unlearned or unconditioned response (UCR). Using dogs as subjects, Pavlov demonstrated that with sufficient pairings of the UCS and the CS, dogs would learn to salivate to the CS, yielding a conditioned response (CR). After enough exposure to the food and the bell simultaneously, the sound of the bell alone would cause the dogs to salivate, a reaction that had not existed previously and is certainly not a natural reaction. So while a dog might instinctively salivate when exposed to food, it can *learn* to salivate at the sound of a bell if a strong enough association is created between the two. This association was *reinforced* by the repeated pairing of the bell and food so that the salivation became a *conditioned response* to the bell with or without the food. However, Pavlov also discovered that if he introduced the bell too often without the food this would ultimately cause the *extinction* of the previously learned salivation. Extinction occurs when a conditioned reaction is no longer reinforced. This learning is automatic and nonconscious and Pavlov used this experiment as an example of what happens in everyday life. One common real-life example of classic conditioning is taste aversion. People sometimes develop aversions to certain food or drink if they've had a negative experience associated with them such as nausea, food poisoning, or a hangover. The consumption becomes associated with the negative consequences and an aversion is formed.

John B. Watson, a pioneer behaviorist, used the case of Little Albert (pseudonym) to illustrate this point as well. While the child played with a rabbit, Watson made loud noises behind the child's back by banging two metal poles together. Ultimately the child came to fear the rabbit (or other furry objects) because of the association between the rabbit and the loud, presumably extremely disconcerting and scary noises.

B. F. Skinner was the father of operant conditioning. He discovered that a behavior followed by a reinforcing stimulus results in an increased probability of that behavior occurring in the future and that a behavior no longer followed by a reinforcing stimulus results in a decreased probability of that behavior occurring in the future. So if a rat in a so-called

Skinner Box accidentally presses a bar and a food pellet is released it will likely continue to push the bar because there is a reward or a reinforcement in it for him. However, if pushing the bar no longer supplies a food pellet then the bar pushing behavior will likely be extinguished because the rat is no longer getting a reward for the behavior (i.e., there is lack of reinforcement for the behavior). Later on, if the bar pushing results in a food pellet, once again the behavior will increase much more quickly because of the history involved. Similarly, if a behavior results in a negative consequence (aversive stimulus) then there is a decreased probability of that behavior occurring again in the future but if the aversive stimulus is removed then there is an increased probability of that behavior occurring in the future.

These theories were used to explain and develop strategies for helping people overcome problems in the therapeutic setting and enjoyed a great deal of success. Joseph Wolpe reported and emphasized the obvious. When individuals were anxious they could not, by definition, be calm. Conversely, when they were calm and relaxed, they could not be anxious. He focused on two models. The first was the treatment of anxiety by the use of reciprocal inhibition. The second, and related treatment, was systematic desensitization. He worked with the client to create a systematic hierarchy of increasingly anxiety-producing experiences. These were then ranked in order of strength from low to high. Through the use of relaxation techniques the person is able ultimately to associate a relaxed state with the situations that had previously been anxiety-provoking. The person is able to relearn a more appropriate, functional association and subsequent response to the situation/experience.

The behavior therapy approach was a significant change in the field of psychotherapy for a number of reasons. Rather than seeking insight and understanding about a problem in order to indirectly cause change, specific symptoms or behaviors were targeted outright for intervention and change. A client's early life was largely ignored except inasmuch as it might provide some clues to work in the here and now. It was the first time that intervention methods shifted from the laboratory to the clinic and then back to the lab so that empirical research was informing practice and vice versa. There was now hard data to reinforce what was being done in the therapy office. In addition, behavior therapy called for the use of concrete, planned interventions, and monitored progress continuously and often quantitatively. It also moved away from the "disease" conceptualization of psychological problems due to early faulty personality development and focused instead on the target behavior as a learned response. Problem behaviors were no longer seen as symptoms of an underlying process such as an unconscious expression of a blocked desire but were deemed the actual problems.

However, by the end of the 1960s it became apparent that there was growing dissatisfaction among some with the behavior therapy model as a comprehensive approach to change (Mahoney, 1974). While behavior therapy had proven to be extremely helpful with some problems, there were issues such as obsessional thinking and other clinical concerns that highlighted a need for an approach that could address more than problem behaviors. A small group of clinicians such as Aaron T. Beck and Albert Ellis, both earlier trained as psychoanalysts, had already been suggesting in their writing and lectures that thinking played a large mediating role in behavioral and emotional reactions to the world. This concept of a mediational model began to take shape (Dobson, 2001). This mediational model was the beginning of cognitive behavior therapy.

Short-term Models

Recent trends in the field have made the need for short-term models of therapy an increasing necessity. There have been multiple factors that have driven this increased interest and necessity in short-term models. Some of these factors have included practical issues. For example, the nature of client problems will often dictate a short-term model for treatment of specific disorders. Based on empirical studies, a number of disorders have been clearly demonstrated to be treated in several sessions. Clearly, some client problems do not require long-term therapeutic intervention. Also, clients now seek quick, directive, symptomatic relief. Their motivation for extended therapy based on the erroneous but oft quoted adage that problems took a long time to form so will now need a long time for amelioration is gone. The wish to feel better quickly, rid oneself of long-standing thoughts, actions, or behaviors is not the result of a pathological need for instant gratification, but is motivated by the desire to quickly and reasonably address a specific symptom. Consumer/clients have been empowered to ask for what they want without being intimidated by interpretations.

Another factor that has increased the need for short-term models is institutional or administrative constraints. Both inclient and outclient programs have shortened lengths of available treatment/services so as to be able to provide services to a broader number of individuals with static or shrinking funding. This phenomenon has also been seen in community mental health centers where resources are often limited. (This has been particularly true since the deinstitutionalization of the chronically mentally ill.)

Sweeping changes in health care reimbursement procedures have also impacted on the need for short-term models. With the proliferation of health maintenance organizations (HMOs) and Preferred Provider

Programs (PPOs) has come an increased demand for accountability and a drive to contain health care costs. Behavioral health benefits were the first to be scrutinized, and were required to demonstrate this accountability. This has made short-term therapeutic models a financial necessity for many agencies, institutions, and clients.

BASIC CONCEPTUAL FRAMEWORK

CBT has several defining elements. They are:

Active: The client must be involved in the therapeutic process not as an observer or as an occasional visitor, but as a core and key participant. If the client cannot (or will not) be part of the process, therapy goals must be limited and even shortened.

Motivational: The therapist needs to take responsibility for helping to motivate the client toward a change in behavior, affect, or thinking. The therapist must be able to set up the format, setting, and rationale for the client to consider change of value.

Directive: The therapist must be able to develop a treatment plan and then to help the client to understand, contribute to, and see the treatment plan as a template for change. In effect, the therapist must have an idea of what the finished product subsequent to therapy will look like so as to use the optimal interventions, time them well, and choreograph the therapy.

Structured: CBT is structured in two ways. First, the overall therapy follows a structure that approximates the treatment plan. The individual session is structured so that every session has an identifiable beginning, middle, and end. This is especially useful for those clients who come to therapy because their lives are confused and disorganized.

Collaborative: Therapeutic collaboration cannot be 50/50. For the severely depressed client, the possibility to generate 50% of the therapeutic effort is an impossible dream. Initially, the collaboration may be 90/10, with the therapist doing 90% of the work. For each client, the therapist must evaluate the client's ability and motivation for the therapy and then supply the balance of collaboration needed. Any therapist who has worked with adolescents has learned that the expectation or demand that the adolescent provide at least 50% of the energy and motivation for therapy has most often been disappointed.

Psychoeducational: The therapist works as a change agent. Many of the problems that bring (or drive) people to therapy involve skill deficits. These skills might include self-soothing (anxiety), taking a forward rather than backward view of experience (depression), problem solving (substance abuse), anger management (partner abuse), or increased ability to tolerate frustration. The therapist may have to teach by direct instruction, modeling, role playing, guided practice, or *in vivo* experience.

Problem-oriented: CBT focuses on discrete problems rather than vague and amorphous goals of feeling good, getting better, or increasing self-esteem. The issues that bring people to therapy are more often complaints (depression) rather than the problems that comprise the depression (difficulty sleeping, low libido, apathy, etc.).

Solution-focused: The CBT therapist works with the client on generating solutions, not simply gaining insight into the problems. The CBT therapist uses the Socratic dialogue to move the client toward a more problem-solving focus.

Dynamic: The dynamic level of CBT is to help clients to identify, understand, and modify their schema. The schema are the basic templates for understanding one's world. Schema may be personal, religious, cultural, age-related, gender-related, or family-based. These so-called rules learned in one's family of origin are then modified throughout life by the interaction with family, friends, or institutions. The schema would encompass what was termed *superego* by the analysts.

Time-limited: Each therapy session should, ideally, stand alone. A time-limited focus is not a number of sessions, but rather way of looking at therapy. Ellis has, on many occasions, in his weekly demonstrations of REBT demonstrated that a single session can have a marked positive effect on an individual.

Cognitive behavior therapy is based on several principles:

- Cognitions affect behavior and emotion (the way we think affects what we do and how we feel).
- Certain experiences can evoke cognitions, explanation, and attributions about that situation.
- Cognitions may be made aware, monitored, and altered.
- Desired emotional and behavioral change can be achieved through cognitive change.

What does this really mean? Two people can be in the exact same situation but have very different reactions to it based on their idiosyncratic internal dialogue, that is, what they are telling themselves about the situation. In fact, the same person can be in similar situations and react differently to them at different times. This indicates that there is a filter through which we process experiences and that determines how we react to them. These mediating or filtering factors are what are termed *cognitions* (specifically) or *belief systems* (more broadly). Our beliefs about the world, other people, ourselves, and the potential for the future greatly influence our behavioral and emotional reactions. These activating events or triggers can be actual events, experiences, thoughts, memories, and anything else that causes a reaction. For example, reviewing past hurts and perceived injustice will likely lead to depression. If the individual views the world as dangerous or threatening, anxiety would result. If there is some specific object or situation that is perceived as dangerous, the result would be a phobic response. When an individual maintains a negative view of the future, hopelessness and possible suicide are possible. If an individual has thoughts of having been cheated or humiliated, anger is the common reaction. Or, thoughts of being abandoned will often lead to dependent feelings, thoughts, and behavior. From a behavioral perspective, the activating event is a stimulus (S).

For example, Jane recalls the painful ending to a romantic relationship, feels anger and frustration, goes home and drinks four glasses of wine, and then feels depressed. Sherrie has a similar relationship memory and when she thinks about it feels disappointed and chooses one self-care ritual to engage in (e.g., taking a long walk, bath, journaling, etc.). The difference in the way that these women respond to the initial S stimulus (the "A" or activating event) is in the way each of these women views and interprets the experience.

Thinking can be divided into two types. There is thinking that is helpful, reasonable, and useful to us and then there is the thinking that tends to be rigid and dogmatic and gets in our way by generating feelings and behaviors that do not serve us well. The helpful, flexible thinking is *rational* and *functional* and tends to be our preferences, wants, and desires about ourselves, the world, and other people. The unhelpful, inflexible thinking is *irrational* and *dysfunctional* and is largely made up of our demands about how we, the world, and others *should* be (Ellis & MacLaren, 2005). CBT advocates for the careful evaluation of our cognitions, behaviors, and emotions so that we can determine what is helpful and useful to us and what is self-defeating. The therapeutic goal is to work to change what is necessary in order to live full and satisfying lives. In this respect, CBT can also be seen as promoting a healthy philosophy of living. It is educative in that one goal is to help clients operate as their own therapists so that they are able to work through problems ultimately without the aid of a professional.

In Jane's case from the previous example, she may become angry and frustrated about the end of the relationship because she thinks, "my partner shouldn't have ended things that way, it was wrong, I should be treated better and I can't stand that I was treated that way." Note the rigidity and the "should" statements in her thinking combined with her belief that she "can't stand it." The discomfort of thinking and feeling this way may then lead to the alcohol consumption because she believes she "can't stand it" and "needs to feel better now" and she knows that she will feel better temporarily if she drinks. Later and the next day she feels depressed because drinking that much is not something she wants to do and she thinks of herself as a failure for having indulged and for still being consumed with the end of the relationship. On the other hand, when Sherrie recalls the end of the relationship she thinks, "I'm sorry it ended the way it did and I wish my partner had treated me better but at the very least it shows that it wasn't the right relationship for me and I have to take good care of myself so that I'm open to the next relationship that comes my way," which leads her to engage in a self-care behavior. Note that Sherrie's thinking consists of preferences and wants with an eye toward moving forward in her life. CBT does not mandate what is best for clients but asks them to clarify who and how they want to be and helps them strive toward their personal goals.

CBT is based on some general assumptions about human disturbance and change. The first is that cognitions are one of the most important determinants of human emotion and behavior so that dysfunctional thinking is a major determinant of emotional and behavioral distress. Therefore, one of the best ways to conquer distress is to evaluate the content, frequency, and strength of one's thoughts, and, as necessary to modify one's thinking. There are multiple factors that act as antecedents to dysfunctional or irrational thinking including biology, family of origin environment, developmental experiences, as well as others but people maintain a great deal of their disturbance through self-indoctrination. We are largely creatures of habit and practice ways of thinking, feeling, and behaving that can be problematic and may begin to feel automatic if we've been practicing them long enough. Our behaviors and feelings also influence our thinking. For example, we sometimes feel a certain way and then look for evidence to support what we feel in our thinking. Or we behave a certain way and then think and feel things about that behavior. The good news is that thinking, behaving, and feeling can be changed so that distress can be decreased and/or alleviated depending on what is deemed appropriate by the client for the situation and energy can be refocused in useful, productive ways.

The power of the mind is incredible and we look for evidence to support what we believe. If the evidence is not readily apparent we will sometimes make it up or skew existing information in support of what we believe, for better or for worse. There are some standard cognitive distortions that are typical (Beck, 1995; Burns, 1980; Freeman, Pretzer, Fleming, & Simon, 1990, 2005):

- **All-or-none thinking** (polarized or dichotomous thinking): You see a situation in terms of two mutually exclusive categories instead of a continuum with a spectrum of possibilities.
  Example: "If don't succeed at this I am a total and complete failure."
- **Catastrophizing/Awfulizing:** When thinking about situations you assume the worst will happen and that it will be intolerable.
  Example: "If this relationship doesn't work out then I'll never find anyone and will be miserable and alone for the rest of my life."
- **Emotional Reasoning:** Assuming that because you feel something it must be true without actually scrutinizing the validity of the thinking/evidence that caused the emotion in the first place.
  Example: "I'm anxious about this situation therefore I know it will end in disaster."
- **"Should," "Must," "Have to," and "Ought to" Statements:** Making and holding onto rigid demands about how you, the world, and others have to be despite evidence to the contrary making it sometimes difficult to cope with the reality of a situation.
  Example: "He should never act that way."
- **Personalization:** Attributing others' perceived negative behavior to yourself without considering the possibility of alternative explanations for the behavior.
  Example: "She was cold to me because she's upset by something I did."
- **Mind reading:** Believing we know without being told what other people are thinking and what their motivations are for behaviors.
  Example: "She thinks I'm a superficial flake."
- **Overgeneralization:** Jumping to broad negative conclusions based on one experience or a series of experiences.
  Example: "I didn't get this job just like I never get anything that I want."
- **Labeling:** Globally putting labels on ourselves as opposed to labeling and rating specific behaviors or experiences.
  Example: "I'm a complete failure," instead of "I failed to accomplish this."

- **Disqualifying/Discounting the Positive:** Positive experiences or behaviors that don't support our negative outlook on a situation are automatically discounted, ignored, or explained away.
  Example: "I only did well on the test because it was easy."
- **Selective Abstraction:** Paying close and generally irrational attention to one or a couple negative details in a situation or experience and virtually ignoring all other data.
  Example: "I received high grades in all of my classes but one which means I'm a terrible student."
- **Minimization:** Positive experiences or characteristics are acknowledged but generally treated as unimportant or insignificant.
  Example: "My professional life is going well but it doesn't matter because my personal life is a disaster."

Clients are asked to be as specific and concrete about their goals as possible based on the belief that we stand a better chance of getting where we want to go if we know what that looks like. While the goal of being happier is perfectly legitimate, it is important to break it down into what will increase and decrease behaviorally, emotionally, and cognitively that will indicate the person has made strides toward this goal. This also allows the therapist and client to monitor progress during therapy.

Once therapy goals are identified, agreed upon, and prioritized the therapist sets about helping the client start to identify and evaluate his or her thinking, behaving, and feeling that may be helpful and unhelpful. Through the use of Socratic questioning, CBT involves an ongoing assessment of the person and the problems throughout the therapy experience and is very sensitive to the idiosyncratic nature of an individual's problems (Beck, 1995). Once cognitive, behavioral, and emotive patterns are identified for change, the CBT therapist begins to introduce a variety of focused techniques to facilitate this process. These techniques are discussed later in this chapter.

CONCEPTUAL SHIFTS FOR CBT

CBT requires several conceptual shifts or practice modifications. It would be rare that a therapist wanting to use CBT would have to totally abandon what they do therapeutically, the knowledge base for that practice, or the conceptual basis for their work. It is, in our experience, the case that the therapist will often be practicing much of the CBT work.

The first shift is that the presenting symptom is viewed as a target for change, rather than a symptom of intrapsychic conflict or as a result of unresolved conflicts. Symptoms are typically viewed from the psychodynamic perspective as resulting from unresolved conflicts. Utilizing this construct would then direct the therapist to first identify the conflict and to then direct and focus the therapy toward eventually and finally resolving the myriad conflicts stemming from earlier years, interactions, and persons.

The early conflict theory would posit that by addressing the symptom as a target one could possibly expect some change. This change would be conceptualized as a transference cure or flight into health. These changes would be seen as more indicative of an escape and resistance to change. The therapist practicing CBT sees changing or even removing the symptoms as the chosen goal for therapy.

A second shift relates to the role of the therapist. The shift for CBT is away from seeing the therapist as priest, shaman, or healer. The idea of therapy as an art form is, in fact, dangerous. It suggests that there are those therapists who are magical and blessed with some artistic powers (the Rembrandts) and others who are not artistic and must be content to spread the paint in a mechanical manner without the same panache (the draftsperson).

The role of the therapist doing CBT is more of a consultant, a resource, and a catalyst for change. This does not mean that the therapy process does not have a calming, healing, or salutary effect. It means that the therapist is not a magician.

The third shift is the conflict of therapy goals. Do therapists cure people, or do they help them to cope more effectively? CBT is a coping model as opposed to a mastery model. A cure model suggests to clients that the result of the therapy will be that they will be cured of their depression, anxiety, panic, obsessive compulsive disorder, or borderline personality.

An issue often raised relative to requirements for the practice of short-term therapy is that CBT is the enemy that prevents cures. The argument is that were the therapist to have unlimited sessions with a client, the result would be better, more enduring cures. Sadly, the empirical evidence for therapeutic cures is poor or lacking, whether as a result of long-term or short-term therapies.

A fourth factor for consideration, related to the previous factor, is that CBT follows the principle of parsimony. This principle states that the preferred intervention is the intervention that is least intrusive, least aggressive, least expensive, with the greatest demonstrated effectiveness. Long-term therapies, which for many years were the predominant model, have taken on the cachet of higher value and importance. This came about for several reasons. First and foremost is that the senior faculty in most academic settings were psychoanalytic or psychodynamically-oriented. The psychodynamic faculty were in positions of power and prestige so that the normal student response of emulating teachers and mentors was to follow the more dynamic work. To not do so would likely have been seen as disloyal or even negative. If, indeed, long-term therapy was seen as the Rolls Royce of therapies, other therapies were acceptable, but not of the same position and power. The analogy has come to have a different meaning in contemporary practice in that very few can afford a Rolls Royce. CBT is seen as the effective but more economical alternative.

A fifth conceptual shift represents a difference between models that are reactive (i.e., the therapist follows the lead of the client), as is seen in free-association, and the CBT model, which requires that the therapy be a planned, focused, and directive endeavor. Planning, focus, and direction are the watchwords of the CBT model.

A sixth factor, related to the previous, is the CBT expectation that there be specified outcome protocols for the therapy. By setting specific goals, the therapist and the client can work toward those goals and be able to plan the expected outcome. At the conclusion of the therapy, the outcome is evaluated against the expectations. This allows the CBT practitioner to evaluate the efficacy of the therapy.

Seventh is the shift from the success of therapy being a matter of vague statements about feeling better to more specific empirically validated measures. This need for empirical validation is not a new idea and is hand-in-hand with the accountability that therapy has lacked and avoided for the last 100 years.

An eighth conceptual shift has to do with the guiding question for therapy. The traditional therapeutic question has been, "Why does this individual do what he does?" The implication of this question is that once the client recognizes the "Why," or gains insight, the problems will be attenuated or ameliorated. The notion seems to be that with insight or understanding the client's skills, motivation, and family will all change.

The questions that are central to CBT are, what keeps therapists using it and how do clients change? The "what" question address the reinforcers that maintain patterns of thought, affect, and behavior. The "how" question relates to skill building.

Ninth shift is the need for an established theoretical orientation. The buzzwords for the millennium have become *eclecticism* or *integration.* Too often they have been used to denote a lack of a theory rather than the mastery of many theories.

The tenth shift is between a goal of the client feeling better and actually getting better. What are the goals of therapy? Pipal (1995) offers the following statement, critical of a CBT orientation:

Absent is any reference to living fuller, more satisfactory lives. Yet who among us learned in graduate school that our task was to return people to their premorbid levels of functioning? I cannot re-call a single instance in my psychological training when I was taught that the mission of my profession was anything less than helping people become as happy and whole as life and effort will allow. (p. 326)

This message, all too often offered as the focus of therapy, has happy and vague goals for therapy.

The CBT practitioner's goal is to help the client to achieve higher levels of functioning. Whether these are to the premorbid level of function (which may have been quite high) or to a level that is higher than the baseline of what the client brings to therapy.

EMPIRICAL BASE OF CBT

CBT has been and will likely continue to be at the forefront of empirically supported therapies. In a large number of controlled studies, CBT has proven to be highly effective in treating a number of problems including depression, anxiety, eating disorders, substance abuse, anger management, personality disorders, and in facilitating relapse prevention.

The CBT model is usually explained to clients at the beginning of therapy so that they understand the reasons behind the questioning and interventions and sometimes the empirical data that will be offered to them if therapists believe clients will be compelled by it.

COGNITIVE INTERVENTIONS

Cognitive interventions represent one of the cornerstones of CBT. As we noted earlier, cognitions, behaviors, and emotions are interconnected so an intervention focused on one component is bound to influence the others but therapists have tried to organize a presentation of the major interventions based on where their primary focus lies.

Once the client's unhelpful and self-defeating thinking is identified it usually becomes an important focus of therapy. Two of the main goals of CBT are to help clients examine, challenge/dispute the current beliefs and thinking that causes them to have self-identified undesirable reactions, and then to aid them in developing new, more useful and helpful ways of thinking so as to further their goals. Some of these ways are:

"Thought" or "Self-help" Forms: These forms are employed in the identification of dysfunctional thinking. Clients are asked to write down the activating situation, their emotional and behavioral responses, and what they were thinking. They are then asked to identify their irrational thinking and potential rational responses that would have allowed them to respond in the way they would like to respond to this type of situation.

Disputing/Challenging Beliefs: Once a dysfunctional belief has been identified the therapist sets about helping the client challenge it. The therapist asks the following questions.

Functional: How is it helping you to believe this? Does it further your goals? Are there any negative consequences to thinking this way?

Empirical: Where is the evidence this is true?

Logical: How does it follow?

Friend: What advice would you give a friend in this situation?

Philosophical: Despite this can you still lead a satisfying life?

Alternative: Is there an alternative explanation or way of thinking about this that is equally viable?

Rational Coping Statements/Writing an Alternative Assumption: People are most likely to give up an irrational or dysfunctional belief when they can see that it is not helping them and they have an alternative that they see as more adaptive and functional. So after disputing or challenging a client's belief, it is crucial to help the client develop a self-statement that is in his or her words preferably. Writing it down is helpful in terms of remembering and practicing it.

Referenting: Have a client make a list of the real advantages and disadvantages of keeping his or her thinking the way it is and the advantages and disadvantages of working to change it. The purpose is to keep the client fully aware of the reasons he or she has chosen to attempt the change so that if he or she starts to relapse the list can be used to shore up their motivation.

Stop and Monitor: This method is for clients who are struggling with identifying their thinking. Have the client set up an innocuous cue that he or she will notice at least a few times a day. Each time they notice the cue they are instructed to write down their thoughts in that moment. They bring their journal of the week's thoughts in for the next session and review the thinking for helpful and unhelpful content.

Role Reversal: This intervention is for clients who have an especially challenging time disputing their own thinking. The therapist and client switch roles. The client is the therapist and the therapist is the client. Present him or her with the same thoughts and beliefs he or she has been presenting and see if they can argue the "client" out of them. This gives the therapist an idea of how entrenched they are in their unhelpful thinking.

Recording Therapy Sessions: Having clients listen to their therapy session provides them that one degree of separation that sometimes allows them to develop more insight and understanding about themselves. Clients will often come back to therapy after having listened to the previous session and feel they've discovered something about themselves in the process.

Proselytizing: Therapists often have an easier time identifying others' irrational or dysfunctional thinking than their own so if a client is struggling with identifying his or her own you might try having him or her choose a person in their life and identify their unhelpful thinking.

Reframing: Asking a client to identify what the opportunities may be in a situation rather than solely focusing on the inherent threats and problems can often bring clarity to a solution.

Bibliotherapy/Psychoeducational Assignments: Often CBT therapists will assign to the client as outside work books, tapes, workshops, lectures or anything else that's relevant and will supplement the work being done in therapy.

BEHAVIORAL INTERVENTIONS

Behavioral interventions can be especially helpful in promoting change in individuals who have a harder time making elegant core belief changes through cognitive methods. Clients may be limited by their intelligence or developmental level or there may be communication problems that get in the way of using cognitive interventions. For example, CBT work with younger children often focuses more on behavioral than cognitive interventions. Other interventions are:

Role Playing/Behavioral Rehearsal: Clients may find it helpful to practice situations such as discussions with co-workers or family members in the therapy session. This allows clients to receive coaching from the therapist and also to think through what they want to say in a potentially emotional conversation.

Skills Training: Clients may lack some life skills either on interpersonal or practical levels that are blocking their ability to reach their goals. Supplementing therapy with training in social skills, assertiveness skills, anger management skills, relaxation skills, computer skills, or other related areas may be especially helpful.

Modeling: Ask clients if they can identify someone in their life who they believe has a better way of handling a specific situation that they've identified they want to work on. Once they've identified that person, ask clients why they think the other person is better able to handle these situations. Then ask them to act the way that person would in the situation and see what happens in their thinking and feeling. Have them report back at the next session.

In Vivo Desensitization: This generally involves creating a "hierarchy of pain" to deal with an anxiety-provoking situation. Through repeated, systematic exposure to increasingly provocative situations, clients are asked to stay with the discomfort toward the ultimate goal of becoming desensitized to the triggers.

Graded Task Assignments: Clients break large, potentially overwhelming tasks into smaller pieces that feel more manageable with each step helping the client move toward their ultimate goal.

Activity Scheduling: An actual form can be used in which clients schedule their daily activities on an hour-by-hour basis to aid them in using their time more productively and effectively and reap the cognitive and behavioral benefits of doing so.

Reinforcements and Penalties: These interventions are used mostly to supplement homework assignments with motivated and compliant clients. Clients are instructed that if they comply with the primary assignment then they may enjoy a mutually agreed upon and appropriate reinforcement. A reinforcement is typically something the client enjoys doing such as reading a book, taking a walk, watching television, and so on. However, if the client does not comply with the primary assignment then a penalty is introduced, which is typically something the client does not enjoy such as washing dishes, cleaning, writing a small check to an organization he or she does not support, and so on.

Shame Attack/Behavioral Experiment: This intervention is used in an effort to help clients behaviorally test out the validity of beliefs they hold. Often used with people who are overly concerned with what other people think of them and fear appearing foolish or being evaluated negatively to the point where it is dysfunctional and holding them back from what they want. Clients may be asked to do something out of the ordinary (for them) in order to evaluate the results and their ability to handle the potential disapproval of others.

Acting on Rational Beliefs/Fixed Role Therapy: The best way to describe this intervention is by using Nike's campaign slogan: "Just do it." People often wait to feel motivated or hopeful or happy before engaging in behaviors that support those thoughts and feelings. With some clients it is possible to jump-start those thoughts and feelings by having clients agree to engage in some of the behaviors that would indicate success in those areas *whether or not* they feel like it.

EMOTIVE/AFFECTIVE INTERVENTIONS

Forceful Coping Statements: As noted earlier in the chapter, people become habituated to certain ways of thinking, feeling, and behaving through practice. Once a client has identified his or her own coping statements it can be useful to have him or her practice them forcefully (i.e., loudly and strongly) so as to reinforce them. This can be done in the session by the individual as a between-session assignment and can also be taped for the client to listen to as a homework assignment.

Humor: Appropriate humor can be very helpful in the therapeutic setting as people sometimes take ourselves and our problems too seriously. Making light of an aspect of a client's problem can serve to help him or her gain perspective and also develop the therapeutic relationship.

Unconditional Acceptance by Therapist: No matter how badly a client behaves we try to offer unconditional acceptance of the person. It is appropriate to take issue with specific client behaviors when appropriate without condemning the client as an entire person. This models the unconditional acceptance that we advocate for clients.

Encouragement: Therapists sometimes become focused on improvements clients want to make and may neglect to encourage and recognize the successes they have experienced along the way. Providing positive support and encouragement is a vital part of the CBT.

THE USE OF HOMEWORK BETWEEN SESSIONS

The use of homework or between-session assignments is essential to CBT and is viewed as equally important as anything that happens in the therapy office. Since the main objective of the approach is to help clients make effective and lasting changes in their lives, it is crucial that whatever is being discovered in the sessions be applied in the client's life.

Homework allows clients to test out what they are learning in therapy and creates additional material as grist for the therapeutic mill. The homework also becomes the thread that connects the different sessions. By specifically having clients do something between sessions, they are being educated to become their own therapist. After all, when therapy ends, everything is homework.

The therapist can greatly increase the likelihood that clients will comply with homework assignments by making sure that they understand the important role of homework in CBT. In addition, it is crucial that the therapist makes sure clients understand the relevance of each assignment, asks them to anticipate anything that might get in the way of completing the assignment, and follows up on the homework at the beginning of the next session. Collaborating with clients on assigning the homework can be another way to increase compliance once they have become accustomed to the process.

CONCLUSION

CBT employs a number of distinct and unique therapeutic strategies in its practice. It is a collaborative effort and process between therapist and client relying heavily not on the therapist's agenda but rather on the client's goals for therapy and in his or her life. All assessment and interventions are geared toward helping clients identify and achieve desired goals based on many years of research and practice that has informed the way that CBT is implemented today.

CBT is a dynamic and exciting approach to therapy that can be tailored to every client. Generally, a variety of methods are strategically employed so as to maximize desired change and establish the types of interventions that prove to be most effective to the individual. It is a process of trial and error but therapists are often able to reduce the degree of error through a careful assessment of past efforts toward change. By building on past successful efforts and avoiding avenues that have proved ineffective, we stand a better chance of helping our clients and establishing credibility with them.

REFERENCES

Ansbacher, H., & Ansbacher, R. (1964). *The individual psychology of Alfred Adler.* New York: Harper & Row.

Beck, A. T., Rush, A. J., Shaw, B. F. & Emery, G. (1979). *Cognitive therapy of depression.* New York: Guilford.

Beck, J. S. (1995). *Cognitive therapy: Basics and beyond.* New York: Guilford.

Burns, D. D. (1980). *Feeling good: The new mood therapy.* New York: Harper Collins.

Dobson, K. S. (Ed.). (2001). *Handbook of cognitive-behavioral therapies* (2nd ed.). New York: Guilford.

Ellis, A., & MacLaren, C. (2005). *Rational emotive behavior therapy: A therapist's guide* (2nd ed.). San Luis Obispo, CA: Impact.

Freeman, A., Pretzer, J., Fleming, B., & Simon, K. M. (1990). *Clinical applications of Cognitive Therapy.* New York: Plenum Press.

Freeman, A., Pretzer, J., Fleming, B., & Simon, K. M. (2005). *Clinical applications of cognitive therapy* (2nd ed.). New York: Kluwer Academic Press.

Mahoney, M. J. (1974). *Cognition and behavior modification.* Cambridge, MA: Ballinger.

Pipal, J. E. (1995). Managed care: Is it the corpse in the living room? *Psychotherapy Theory, Research, Practice, Training, 32,* 323–332.

CHAPTER 3

Research in Evidence-Based Social Work

Bruce A. Thyer
Laura L. Myers

INTRODUCTION

Evidence-based practice (EBP) is a model initially developed within medicine that provides helpful guidance to practitioners who have to make important decisions regarding the selection of assessment methods and interventions to be provided to individuals and to larger groups of clients. The major authoritative reference describing EBP is *Evidence-based Medicine: How to Practice and Teach EBM* by Sackett, Strauss, Richardson, Rosenberg, and Haynes (2000), but the near-universal applicability of this model has generated a very large number of spin-off texts in virtually all of the health and human professions, including clinical social work (e.g., Briggs & Rzepnicki, 2004; Corcoran, 2000, 2003; Cournoyer, 2004; Drake, Merrens, & Lynde, 2005; Gibbs, 2003; Mattaini & Thyer, 1996; Springer, McNeece & Arnold, 2003; Thyer & Kazi, 2004). A Google search conducted using *evidence-based practice* as a search term generated over 3.3 million hits on 22 June 2005. In contrast, *psychoanalysis* and *cognitive behavior therapy* yielded 1.4 and 1.3 millions hits respectively, on the same date. While a Google search is admittedly a blunt instrument to assess the impact of these various approaches to practice, clearly EBP is attracting a lot of attention. In this chapter we review the basic tenets of EBP, and discuss the potential applications of this model of practice and training for the field of clinical social work. We also present some actual illustrations of its use.

Evidence-based practice can be simply defined as "the integration of best research evidence with clinical expertise and client values" (Sackett et al., 2000, p. 1). Notice the triune nature of the definition involving research, clinical skills, and values. This should belie any notion that the only important factor in EBP relates to scientific research. Almost all social work practice, dating back for many decades, can reasonably be said to have involved clinical expertise and a judicious consideration of values-related issues. What the definition of EBP brings to the table is the crucial *additional* or *supplemental* voice of giving weight to scientific research *alongside* traditional clinical and value-related considerations. One cannot practice EBP without due consideration to all three elements. However, in traditional clinical social work practice, one could be said to be acting competently and ethically while applying interventions to clients that lacked any degree of rigorous scientific support. This is not the case within the EBP model. Nor, may we add, within the behavior or cognitive behavioral (CB) perspectives, which have always stressed basing practice on the findings of experimental research (both basic and applied). Thus there is a compelling congruity between EBP and CB therapy (CBT).

Sackett et al. (2000, p. 1) define *best research evidence* as "clinically relevant research . . . especially from patient-centered clinical research into the . . . efficacy and safety of therapeutic, rehabilitative and preventive regimens." *Clinical expertise* refers to the "ability to use our clinical skills and past experience," and *patient values* involve "the unique preferences, concerns and expectations which each patient brings to a clinical encounter and which must be integrated into clinical decisions if they are to serve the patient." EBP is operationalized by engaging in the following steps (from Sackett et al., pp. 3–4):

Step 1: Converting the need for information (about prevention, diagnosis, prognosis, therapy, causation, etc.) into an answerable question.

Step 2: Tracking down the best evidence to answer that question.

Step 3: Critically appraising that evidence for its validity . . . impact . . . and applicability.

Step 4: Integrating that critical appraisal with our clinical expertise and our patient's unique . . . values and circumstances.

Step 5: Evaluating our effectiveness and efficiency in executing steps 1–4 and seeking ways to improve them both for next time.

Subsequent chapters in Sackett et al. (2000) are devoted to an elaboration of each of these five steps. While the original EBP model is structured for the field of medicine, these steps have obvious applicability to the practice of clinical social work as well as that for CBT. Indeed, there are considerable historical antecedents to EBP within both fields. For example, within social work, Jayaratne and Levy's (1979) text, *Empirical Clinical Practice*, made case that the selection of interventions should be based on prior scientific research demonstrating positive outcomes, and these writers also devoted considerable attention to clinical variables and ethical considerations in the selection of social work treatments. There were numerous voices, dating back to the beginning of the social work profession, calling for the greater integration of scientific research findings and social work intervention. For example:

> Social work was *defined* as "All voluntary efforts to extend benefits which are made in response to a need, are concerned with social relationships, *and avail themselves of scientific knowledge and methods.*" (Cheney, 1926, p. 24, italics added)

> [T]he scientific spirit is necessary to social work whether it is a real profession or only a go-between craft . . . The elements of scientific approach and scientific precision must be back of all social reform. . . . (Todd, 1920, p. 66, 75, italics in original)

> Employment of scientifically approved and tested techniques will ensure the profession the confidence and respect of clients and the public, for increasingly the social casework process will operate more certainly for known and desired ends in the area of social adjustment. (Strode, 1940, p. 142)

> The scientific approach to unsolved problems is the only one which contains any hope of learning to deal with the unknown. . . . (Reynolds, 1942, p. 24)

These early exhortations have been at least somewhat listened to, to the extent that contemporary accreditation standards for social work education (Council on Social Work Education, 1991, italics added) assert that:

> Social work education combines *scientific inquiry* with the teaching of professional skills to provide *effective and ethical* social work services. (p. 3)

> Qualitative and quantitative research content provided understanding of a scientific, analytic, and ethical approach to building knowledge for practice. The content prepares students to develop,

use, and effectively communicate, empirically-based knowledge, including *evidence-based knowledge.* (p. 12)

While it is obvious to both academics and therapists that these noble sentiments do not always match treatments, the relationship between EBP and at least some of the historical current developments of clinical social work suggests that the match is not entirely preposterous.

WHAT IS CONSIDERED EVIDENCE IN EBP?

EBP avails itself of all scientifically credible sources of information which may assist practitioners in making decisions about the care of individual clients. However, it is certainly stressed that not all forms of evidence are equivalent, or capable of providing unambiguous findings. Sometimes research from basic science are helpful in this regard, but more often studies directly involving the clinical issue at hand are more relevant. Of highest utility are well-crafted *outcome studies*, which provide some meaningful scientific assessment of the efficacy of a given treatment in helping clients with a specific problem. Outcome studies themselves are a specialized form of scientific inquiry, in many ways more challenging than basic science-types of research. When research involves real-life clients with real and complex problems (often many of them at the same time), and is conducted in the messy, natural environments in which people live, the vagaries of the research process are exponentially expanded inasmuch as the possibility of adequately *controlling* for this multiplicity of factors (such *control* being seen as an essential component of really exemplary clinical research studies) is rendered so much more difficult (but not impossible). Before delving into the various forms of clinical outcomes studies that provide the bedrock of a clinician's ability to engage in EBP, it is nonetheless important to note that many other forms of research inquiry can be valuable in informing EBP, studies such as correlational observations (e.g., early studies showing that smokers were more likely to contract lung cancer than nonsmokers), epidemiological investigations, econometric and cost-benefit analyses, survey studies, and various forms of qualitative inquiry (Green & Britten, 2005). The following are the major forms of clinical outcome study that comprise the priority sources of information underpinning EBP.

Anecdotal Case Reports

These types of studies, abbreviated ACRs, are narrative reports of how one or more individual clients apparently responded to a given treatment.

These, like all outcome studies, can have positive (the client got better) or negative (the client worsened) results. Such studies continue to be published on a regular basis in mainstream scientific journals, and have a valuable role in bringing attention to the profession of potentially important new observations. Most major schools of psychotherapy such as psychoanalysis and behavior therapy originally appeared in print via ACRs. Their major limitation lies in their simplicity. While one may accurately report in an ACR that a client improved after receiving Treatment X, and while it is tempting to conclude that Treatment X *caused* this improvement, clients can improve for a variety of reasons, many unrelated to the *Xs* of the world, and also, clinicians themselves may not be the most unbiased assessors of a client's response to treatment.

Single-System Designs With Weak Internal Validity

A considerable improvement over the anecdotal case study is the single-system design, which incorporates the features of the ACR, with the addition of reporting empirical data on client functioning, using some reliable and valid appraisal of functioning. In one of its simplest configurations, a clinician could assess a client's functioning *one time* before the client receives treatment X, and again one time after X. But more commonly, client functioning is measured several times before client receipt of X, and several times during or after X. Such pretreatment measures are called a *baseline* (also known as an *A* phase), and measures taken during or after X is provided is known as the *B* or treatment phase. This is thus called an *AB* single-case design. If pretreatment measures are of sufficient duration and stability, and the *B* phase data are also stable and well-maintained over time, one can be more confident that X really did cause these apparent changes, given the lessened likelihood that the problem spontaneously remitted. The incorporation of *AB* and similarly simple single-system designs into routine clinical practice has long been advocated within clinical social work (e.g., Jayaratne & Levy, 1979; Stuart, 1973; Thomas, 1975), and other disciplines such as psychology and education (e.g., see Hawkins & Mathews, 1999; Morgan & Morgan, 2001), although one's ability to make strong causal inferences is limited. For example, the client may have had another important change in his or her life occur, about the same time the clinician applied X, or he or she may have sought some other form of help. Thus the role of *coincidence* in accounting for observed changes cannot usually be ruled out with this *AB* design. If a finding from a single *AB* design is successfully replicated across a number of clients, and the results reported together, the capability of causal inference can be enhanced somewhat (see an example by Bradshaw & Roseborough, 2004).

Single-System Designs With Strong Internal Validity

There are various modifications that can be added to single-system designs, which under circumscribed circumstances, *do* permit causal inferences to be made, as in *It is very clear that X caused this client's improvements.* This is can be accomplished through the planned and systematic *withdrawal* of a treatment. For example, visualize an *ABAB* design. In this idealized design, following lengthy and stable appraisals of client functioning (the first *A* phase), posttreatment observations (the first *B* phase), reflect immediate and durable improvements. The clinician deliberately discontinues the treatment for a period of time (the second *A* phase), and the client is seen to quickly relapse to initial-baseline levels of functioning. Then the same treatment is reinstated, and meaningful improvements are immediately evident (the second *B* phase). It is generally seen as quite unlikely that three successive coincidences transpired in the client's life, about the same time as *X* was begun or discontinued, to account for these changes (e.g., improvement from the first *A* phase to the first *B* phase, deterioration from the first *B* to the second *A*, *and* regained improvements from the second *A* to the second *B*). An *ABABAB* can provide even stronger evidence, as can replicating an *ABAB* design with different clients with the same problem, who received clinical social work intervention *X*.

Another way single-system studies can be designed with strong internal validity is using *multiple-baseline designs*, wherein, in one approach, two clients with the same problem are tracked concurrently during an *A* phase, but where the second client's baseline is longer than the first client's. If the first client improves following receipt of *X*, but the second client (still in the baseline phase) does not, only to improve when he or she received *X* sometime after the first client got *X*, then the role of coincidence is also reduced. Applying this strategy with three or more clients, and obtaining clear-cut data, can enhance the extent to which a clinician can conclude that *X* can cause improvements among clients with a given problem. Integrating an *ABAB* design within a multiple-baseline study can further strengthen the internal validity of single-system designs.

A variation of single-system designs, called N-of-1, trials is described in Sackett et al. (2000, pp. 150–153), and is highly recommended by these authors. Most single-system designs have their data displayed on line graphs and visual inspection of the graphed data is the main tool used to infer any changes. This is a rather insensitive way of detecting change, and largely limits conclusions to those that are strikingly obvious (and presumably clinically important), as opposed to those that are reliable but trivial.

Preexperimental Group Outcome Studies

When a clinician or researcher has access to a sizable group of clients with a similar problem, it becomes possible to implement relatively simple group outcome studies. Among the easiest is the single-group pretest-posttest design, wherein a number of clients with a given problem are assessed or observed using a reliable and valid measure of client functioning (this is called an O or observation phase). Treatment X is then provided to everyone, and sometime later a second assessment of functioning is given, a second O phase. This design is called an OXO group design, and remains a widely used and published evaluation method (e.g., Grote, Bledsoe, Schwartz, & Frank, 2004; Ronen, 2005), with particular utility in investigating novel treatments, or in applying well-established interventions to new client groups. Like the AB design with an individual client, the OXO remains vulnerable to the possibility that something significant happened in the lives of clients about the same time they received X, thereby compromising the therapist's ability to conclude that X caused any observed changes. Other possible explanations for changes observed in an OXO study include spontaneous remission, placebo influences, or the reactive effects of simply being in a study or of being assessed.

Quasi-Experimental Group Outcome Studies

Usually, in group research designs, some form of control group is needed to begin to control for rival explanations for positive changes seen after a group of clients receives a treatment. For example, it may be that clients are assessed on intake at an agency, using a reliable and valid indicator of functioning, and some are treated immediately, while others, due to the vagaries of agency resources, are placed on a waiting list. After some time, the first group completes treatment and is assessed again, and it so happens that the delayed treatment group is reassessed, just prior to treatment. Using our shorthand of O referring to an observation or assessment phase, and X referring to receipt of a treatment, this design, thus far, could be depicted as follows:

Group 1 or the Immediately Treated Group	O	X	O
Group 2 or the Wait-listed Group	O		O

The dashed line indicates that the groups were *not* created using random assignment. Logically, if Groups 1 and 2 were roughly equivalent at the first assessment, and at the second assessment Group 1 had improved and Group 2 had not, this could be seen as tentative evidence that X *causes* improvements. This type of design controls for some rival hypotheses, such as the passage of time, or the reactive effects of being assessed, since *both* groups received equal exposure to these factors (e.g., these were *controlled* for). This type of design was used by Vonk and Thyer (1999) in their assessment of the efficacy of services provided at a university-based student counseling center. What it does not control for are the nonspecific effects of being in *any* type of treatment, including placebo factors, so it is not really possible to claim in an unqualified manner that it is the unique and special features of X that are responsible for any improvements in Group 1.

Single, Randomized Controlled Trial

This type of design, abbreviated an RCT, is a quantum leap forward in terms of being able to make a clear and compelling conclusion about the possible effects of X. It too uses control groups but these are constructed using the process of *random assignment* of clients into the group to receive active, real treatment, and to any control groups, such as a no-treatment or delayed-treatment control group, to a group that will receive standard care or treatment-as-usual, or to one that receives placebo therapy. In one example, this design can be diagrammed as:

Group 1, or Active Treatment Group	R	O	X	O
Group 2, or Standard Care Group	R	O	Y	O
Group 3, or No-Treatment Group	R	O		O

with R indicating that the groups were created using random assignment. In this manner, assuming an adequate sample size (generally around 20 or more participants per group), these groups will be roughly equivalent in every respect (age, race, gender, severity of problem, etc.), thus *controlling* for these potentially confounding factors. If Group 3 does not improve, Group 2 gets a bit better, but Group 1 improves a great deal, then one can be pretty confident that it was the active ingredients of X that were responsible for the superior performance of Group 1.

RCTs can be difficult to implement in practice settings, and can be very expensive in terms of time and resources. Often they are supported through the practitioner-researcher's receipt of external research funding. Larkin and Thyer (1999) used such a design to evaluate cognitive behavior group therapy with elementary school children.

Sometimes in an RCT the pretreatment assessment is omitted, an approach called a posttest-only control group study, and was used by Bordnick, Elkins, Orr, Walters, and Thyer (2004) to evaluate three cognitive behavior treatments for drug addiction and a control condition (labeled here as *W*, *X*, *Y*, and *Z*), among inpatient cocaine addicts. Their design could be diagrammed as follows:

Group 1, Faradic Aversion Therapy	W	O
Group 2, Emetic Aversion Therapy	X	O
Group 3, Covert Sensitization Therapy	Y	O
Group 4, Relaxation Control Group	Z	O

The fact that the groups were created using random assignment means that at the time of pretreatment, the groups were very likely similarly composed, including along such dimensions as severity of drug abuse. Any posttreatment differences can thus be ascribed to the different treatment each group received.

Multisite Randomized Controlled Trials

The results of a single RCT can be very persuasive indeed, but they are not exempt from their own problems. For example, the prestigious *Journal of Reproductive Medicine* published a RCT involving over 200 women seeking assistance in becoming pregnant. All the patients reportedly received standard *in vitro fertilization* (IVF) therapy, and of these, one-half were unknowingly randomly assigned to be the subject of prayer on their behalf from Christian prayer groups (Cha, Wirth, & Lobo, 2001). A coauthor of this study was the Chair of the Department of Obstetrics and Gynecology at Columbia University, a very reputable institution and a position that added to the credibility of this report. According to this published article, the patients who were assigned to the prayer group experienced a pregnancy rate *double* that experienced by the patients receiving standard IVF without the benefits of prayer. This was a miraculous study indeed, and one that received widespread positive attention in the national media. Perhaps regrettably, it now appears that this supposedly well-designed RCT possessed significant flaws, and may even be completely fraudulent (see Flamm, 2002). This extreme example illustrates the importance of having initially positive findings regarding any treatment *X*, replicated by presumably disinterested and independent research teams. This is particularly called for when the apparent results are so unusual, strong, or counterintuitive. As scientific skepticism puts it, *Extraordinary claims require extraordinary evidence.* One strong approach is the multisite RCT, where a RCT's experimental protocol is prospectively replicated at a number of different research sites, and by different research teams, with the logic being that if similar results are obtained across these groups of researchers, then there is an enhanced protection against fraud or other scientific misconduct. To date there do not seem to have been any multisite RCTs conducted in the field of clinical social work.

Metaanalyses

As quasi-experimental studies and RCTs begin to accumulate evaluating a treatment X, it becomes possible to aggregate the findings of these disparate studies, even those using different outcome measures, using a statistical technique called metaanalysis (MA). One of the earlier MA in the field of psychotherapy research was conducted in 1977 by Smith and Glass, and since then MAs have proliferated across professional psychology and the human services. Typically the reviewers establish some inclusionary criteria, such as the type of study design to be included, over a given time frame, a minimum number of participants per study, and so on. Then the literature (sometimes only articles published in peer-reviewed journals, sometimes including unpublished workers, dissertations, books, etc.) is reviewed, and the relevant studies retrieved and reviewed. These studies are reliably coded along various pertinent dimensions, and an effect size can be calculated for each outcome measure. By aggregating the effect sizes obtained from different studies, even among those using different outcome measures, it becomes possible to make global claims about the effects obtained from *all* the surveyed studies, as opposed to the individual studies alone. Effect sizes can be calculated in various ways but one common approach results in an estimate of how much more the average client receiving treatment X improved, relative to the average client who received another treatment, placebo therapy, or no treatment. As in (hypothetically), *The average client receiving X improved more than 1.3 standard deviations than the average client who received credible placebo therapy.*

Gorey (1996), for example, conducted a MA involving some 88 social work outcome studies published from 1990 to 1994, and found that about 78 percent of clients who received social work intervention were better off than the average client who did not receive social work treatment. Gorey, Thyer, and Pawluck (1998) also conducted a MA on 45 social work outcome studies published between 1990 and 1994, appearing in 8 different social work journals. It emerged that cognitive behavior therapies (CBTs) were the most commonly represented approach to clinical social work (49% of the studies), a finding that is generally true across all psychotherapies. MA possess the virtues of representing a large number of quantitative studies, and of presenting them in a digestible form.

Systematic Reviews

A systematic review (SR) may include the results of MAs (which typically are limited to reporting the results of RCTs) but are more aggressive and inclusive in the types of studies they summarize, especially by including quasi-experimental studies, qualitative research, single-system designs, and other "shakier" forms of research inquiry, in order to capture as much as possible of the available, relevant evidence. SRs are not limited to condensing results down into some common quantified metric. Instead, SRs also report results narratively. Increasingly, SRs are not initially published in peer-reviewed journals, but are posted on the websites of organizations devoted to the design and reportage of SRs in various fields of practice (more on these groups later). This permits their more rapid dissemination and updating, as well as accessibility.

The previous discussion of research strategies appears in their approximate order as potentially valuable sources of information to guide clinician's seeking to adopt EBP as their orientation to clinical social work. The term *approximate* is deliberate in that this hierarchy is not a rigid caste system. A really good quasi-experimental study may far surpass a weak RCT, for example, in terms of its ability to provide credible answers. EBP practice suggests that clinical social workers keep abreast with the latest developments in services research, in whatever area of practice they are engaged. While this can be an intimidating task, especially in prolific areas of study, there are a few shortcuts which may be helpful. A few are described next.

WHAT ARE SOME USEFUL SOURCES OF INFORMATION ON EBP?

Here the issue is not how to locate information describing EBP, but rather on how to locate well-conducted narrative reviews of the literatures, metaanalyses, and systematic reviews, which address effective interventions for clients with a given problem. This is a rapidly churning area as scientific advances render the first-choice therapies of yesterday into the outmoded practices of today. Sackett and colleagues (2000), tongue in cheek, recommend burning your textbooks, because even the most recent of them are terribly out of date, and Sackett and co-authors are not even enamored with clinician consulting the latest issue of professional journals due to their staleness for the same reason. Instead, for clinicians active in the field of health care, the website of the Cochrane Collaboration (CC) is highly praised (www.cochrane.org), and for those more involved in the fields of social welfare, criminal justice, and education, the website of the Campbell Collaboration (C2) is recommended (www.campbellcol-laboration.org). Both groups are similarly organized. The CC is an "international nonprofit and independent organisation, dedicated to making up-to-date, accurate information about the effects of healthcare readily available worldwide. It produces and disseminates systematic reviews of healthcare interventions" (retrieved on 27 June 2005 from www.cochrane.org/docs/descrip.htm). It is these comprehensive reviews, conscientiously assembled following investigatory protocols as free from bias as possible, which can be extremely helpful to practitioners seeking guidance about what seems to work best with clients (and what does not seem to work well).

Apart from devising rigorous scientific protocols for conducting systematic reviews, the Cochrane Collaboration is organized into Review Groups, international groups of professionals with a common interest. Current CC Review Groups relevant to clinical social work and CBT include the Cochrane Schizophrenia Review Group, and the Cochrane Depression, Anxiety and Neurosis Group, among others. CC systematic reviews within the Cochrane Schizophrenia Group deal with topics such as *Assertive Community Treatment for People with Severe Mental Disorders, Case Management for People with Severe Mental Disorders, Cognitive Behaviour Therapy for Schizophrenia, Crisis Intervention for People with Severe Mental Illnesses, Life Skills Programmes for Chronic Mental Illnesses, Psychoeducation for Schizophrenia, and Token Economy for Schizophrenia.* Cochrane systematic reviews in the general areas of depression, anxiety, and neuroses include *Cognitive Behaviour Therapy for Chronic Fatigue Syndrome, Interventions on Preventing Eating Disorders in Children and Adolescents, Psychological and/or Educational Interventions for the Prevention of Depression in Children and Adolescents, Psychological Treatment of Post-Traumatic Stress Disorder, Psychotherapy for Bulimia and Binging, and Psychosocial and Pharmacological Treatments for Deliberate Self-Harm.* Protocols are in process to complete CC systematic reviews on topics such as *Behavioral and Cognitive Behavioral Therapy for Obsessive Compulsive Disorder in Children and Adolescents, Brief Cognitive Behavioral Therapies versus Other Brief Psychological Therapies for Depression, Cognitive Behavioral Therapy for Bipolar Disorder, Marital Therapy for Depression, and Psychotherapy for Generalized Anxiety Disorder.* Clearly the work of the Cochrane Collaboration has the potential to inform much of clinical social work practice.

An examination of the webpages of the Campbell Collaboration is also very informative. The social welfare coordinating group within C2 has reviews completed or in process on topics such as *Solution-focused Therapy, Cognitive Behavioral Interventions for Sexually Abused Children,*

Cognitive Behavioral Training Interventions Designed to Assist Foster Careers in the Management of Difficult Behavior, Cognitive Behavioral Therapy for Violent Men Who Batter Female Partners, Cognitive Behavioral Therapy for Physically Abused Children and Their Families, and *Cognitive Behavior Programs in Residential Treatment of Antisocial Behavior in Youth.* Obviously the work of the CC and C2 is a rich mine for the clinical social worker interested in learning about the latest evidence-based developments in cognitive behavioral therapy.

In the United States, the federal Agency for Healthcare Research and Quality (AHRQ) has established 13 practice centers to promote evidence-based practice in everyday care, especially among patients enrolled in the Medicare and Medicaid insurance programs (see www.ahrq.gov). Similar in spirit to the CC or C2, AHRQ practice guidelines have been developed in areas such as the treatment of depression, postmyocardial depression, and attention-deficit hyperactivity disorder. The AHRQ supports a National Guidelines Clearinghouse (www.guideline.gov), which contains, among others, about 87 guidelines on different types of psychotherapy, covering topics such as *Anxiety Disorders, Depression, Bipolar Disorder, Borderline Personality Disorder, Schizophrenia,* and *Enuresis.* There are 59 guidelines dealing with behavior therapy alone, so this too is a potentially valuable resource for clinicians. Most such guidelines are interdisciplinary and cover much of the available research evidence of good quality. The impression is that the AHRQ reviews are not quite as current or updated as frequently as those of the CC or C2, and are formatted more as practice guidelines than as systematic reviews.

WHAT ARE THE IMPLICATIONS OF EBP TO SOCIAL WORK?

Slowly, the major U.S. professional social work associations are accepting some of the tenets of EBP (see the CSWE [1991] accreditation standards referenced earlier). The *National Association of Social Workers* is minimally participating in federal conferences dealing with "how to support use of evidence-based preventions, treatments, and services" (Staff, 2000). The *Society for Social Work and Research* (www.sswr.org) with over 1,700 members, explicitly states that one of its goals is to advance evidence-based practice, and its annual conference and sponsorship of the bimonthly peer-reviewed journal *Research on Social Work Practice* reflect this purpose. At least one educational program, the School of Social Work at Washington University, has adopted EBP as its curriculum's organizing framework (see Howard, McMillan, & Pollio, 2003). Thus far, this has clearly been an evolutionary change, given that behavioral and cognitive behavioral perspectives made their introduction to the clinical social work field in the mid-1960s (see Werner, 1965, 1982). But make no mistake, if fully realized, the implications of EBP are not merely evolutionary but revolutionary, effecting social work education, practice, research, and continuing education (see McNeece & Thyer, 2004; Thyer, 2002a, 2004). Many more BSW and MSW programs would be aligned like the one at Washington University, and our 70 plus Ph.D. programs would by necessity focus on teaching the design and conduct of intervention research (see Harrison & Thyer, 1988), as opposed to primarily being incubators of generic behavior and social science scholarship. Generic and nonspecific graduate courses on so-called *practice skills* would be replaced by intensive training seminars and practica devoted to acquiring skills in evidence-based interventions, and in systematically monitoring clinical outcomes. Clinical social work continuing education programs would be similarly restructured.

SOME SELECTED EXAMPLES OF EVIDENCE-BASED CBT IN CLINICAL SOCIAL WORK

EBP is almost by definition an interdisciplinary field, with no one profession having hegemony in terms of setting direction or having primacy. And while the perils of claiming the existence of a unique and specific domain of disciplinary knowledge are well known (Thyer, 2002b), it is nevertheless possible to illustrate some specific arenas in which clinical social workers employing a cognitive behavioral approach have made definite contributions to a field. Here are several that are most conspicuous.

Sheldon Rose and the Development of Cognitive Behavioral Group Therapy

Sheldon Rose is a Professor of Social Work at the University of Wisconsin, and was instrumental in extending the applications of CBT from the realm of one-to-one practice to that of group therapy (Rose, 1967, 1969, 1977). He was also very involved in development of the *Association for Advancement of Behavior Therapy*. Over the course of 11 years alone, Dr. Rose supervised 18 social work Ph.D. students through the completion of their dissertations, which involved some form of outcome study of social work practice and involved experimental research designs, usually an RCT (see Rose, 1988). A number of these projects tested assertiveness training provided in a group format, an intervention that was later expanded to social skills training involving both adults, children, and adolescents. Later studies tested cognitive behavioral group therapy to cope with stress, pain, and anger. So Professor Rose was a pioneer in at least two areas, promoting CBT in clinical social work, and in his advocacy for doctoral students to conduct experimental evaluations of social work services as their dissertation project.

Gerald Hogarty and the Psychoeducational Model of Assisting Persons With Schizophrenia

Gerald E. Hogarty, MSW, is a full Professor of Psychiatry with the University of Pittsburgh School of Medicine, and has been active for over 35 years in researching the effectiveness of various forms of psychosocial therapies and medications in the treatment of persons with chronic mental illnesses such as schizophrenia. Among his most recent articles is one titled "Cognitive Enhancement Therapy for Schizophrenia," for which he was first author and which appeared in the *Archives of General Psychiatry*, arguably the most prestigious psychiatric journal in North America (see Hogarty et al., 2004). This was an RCT with a 24-month long follow period involving 121 patients. Professor Hogarty's work on the contributions that cognitive and psychosocial treatment can have for persons with schizophrenia has been both ground-breaking and profound. Other examples of Professor Hogarty's senior-authored articles appearing in the *Archives of General Psychiatry* include Hogarty and colleagues (1974, 1979, 1986, 1992; Hogarty & Goldberg, 1973). A recent *Medline* search by the authors found over 50 articles authored by Professor Hogarty in mainstream psychiatric journals. The family psychoeducational model he pioneered for the care of persons with schizophrenia has entered the mainstream of evidence-based practice for cognitive behavior care for persons with schizophrenia, as supported by a 2005 Cochrane Review of this approach is an effective treatment (Pekkala & Merinder, 2005).

Gail Steketee and the Development of Exposure Therapy and Response Prevention in Obsessive-Compulsive Disorder

Gail Steketee, MSW, Ph.D., is a Professor of Social Work and Acting Dean with the Boston University School of Social Work. She has been active for over a quarter of a century in the design, conduct, and publication of clinical research studies on the treatment of obsessive compulsive disorder (OCD) and other anxiety-related conditions. She is the senior author of an early review article on the cognitive behavior treatment of OCD, appearing in the *Archives of General Psychiatry* (Steketee, Foa, & Grayson, 1982). Her major focus for many years was on the development and testing of an approach called *exposure therapy and response prevention* (ETRP) to care for persons with OCD, and she has published dozens of empirical research studies on the topic. ETRP is currently strongly supported as an evidence-based cognitive behavior approach to treatment for OCD (see Balkum et al., 1994; Franklin & Foa, 2002; Steketee, 1993), a development made possible to some significant degree by the research of clinical social worker Gail Steketee.

Myrna Weissman and Interpersonal Psychotherapy for Depression

Myrna Weissman, MSW, Ph.D., is a social worker with over 30 years of work in the development and testing of an approach to treating clinically depressed persons called *interpersonal psychotherapy* (IPT). She is a full Professor of Epidemiology in Psychiatry at the College of Physicians and Surgeons and the School of Public Health at Columbia University. The initial development of IPT was through a series of empirical articles in psychiatric journals and an influential psychotherapy textbook (Klerman, Weissman, Rounsaville, & Chevron, 1984), followed over the ensuing decades by an astonishing array of outcome studies testing and extending the applications of IPT. A *Medline* search using *Weissman* and *Interpersonal Psychotherapy* on 29 June 2005 revealed 31 records, almost all published in major psychiatry and clinical psychology journals, including, in just the *Archives of General Psychiatry* alone, DiMascio and colleagues (1979), Mufson and colleagues (1994, 1999, 2004), Rounsaville and colleagues (1981, 1983), Weissman (1979), Weissman & Markowitz (1994), Weissman and colleagues (1974, 1981). A recently published clinical trial on group IPT provided to depressed persons in Uganda co-authored by Weissman and appeared in the *Journal of the American Medical Association* (Bolton et al., 2003). Overall, Professor Weissman has authored over 450 journal articles and book chapters, and 10 books. Sufficient evidence has accrued in support of IPT so that it too can be considered to be an evidence-based treatment (Craighead, Hart, Craighead, & Ilardi, 2002), developed with substantial contributions by a social worker who received the 2001 American Psychiatric Association Award for Achievement in Research.

Space does not permit a comprehensive detailing of the contributions that many other clinical social workers have made to behavioral and cognitive behavioral research and practice, or to the work they have done in laying the foundations for evidence-based practice. Sometimes our disciplinary contributions get overlooked because some of our leaders in the field of clinical research are described as Ph.D., which of course fails to note their possession of the MSW or that their Ph.D. may be in the field of social work. It is hoped that by our highlighting three such distinguished and productive individuals, Professors Hogarty, Steketee, and Weissman, that the efforts of these and numerous others clinical social workers will be more widely recognized. I have stressed works that have appeared in one of the very best journals devoted to publishing research pertinent to evidence-based practice. Some readers may be shocked to find this surreptitious social work presence within the pages of the *Archives of General Psychiatry*. Hopefully the time will come when such publications are not such an unusual practice.

FUTURE DIRECTIONS FOR EVIDENCE-BASED PRACTICE AND CLINICAL SOCIAL WORK

As the human services increasingly develop robust evidence regarding the effectiveness of various psychosocial treatments for various clinical disorders and life problems, it becomes increasingly incumbent upon individual practitioners (and their major professional associations) to become proficient in, and to provide, as first choice treatments, these various forms of evidence-based practice (Myers & Thyer, 1997; Thyer, 1992, 1995). It is also increasingly evident that CBT and practice represents a strongly supported approach to social work education and practice (Thyer & Myers, 1997, 2000), one with widespread applicability across the many domains of social work practice and with disparate client groups (Arhin & Thyer, 2004; Thyer, 1994, 2001). With time, we hope, professional ethical and educational standards will strengthen the evidence-based content of social work training and practice, which will, *perforce*, result in an enhanced adoption of cognitive behavioral principles in clinical social work.

REFERENCES

Arhin, A., & Thyer, B. A. (2004). The causes of racial prejudice: A behavior-analytic perspective. In J. L. Chin (Ed.), *The psychology of prejudice and discrimination: Vol. 1, Racism in America* (pp. 1–19). Westport, CT: Praeger.

Balkum, A., van Oppen, P., van Vermeulen, A., Nauta, N., Vorst, H., & Dyck, R. (1994). A meta-analysis on the treatment of obsessive compulsive disorder: A comparison of antidepressant, behaviour and cognitive therapy. *Clinical Psychology Review, 14,* 359–381.

Bolton, P., Bass, J., Neuebauer, R. Verdeli, H., Clougherty, K. F., Wickramaratne, P., et al. (2003). Group interpersonal psychotherapy for depression in rural Uganda: A randomized controlled trial. *Journal of the American Medical Association, 289,* 3117–3124.

Bordnick, P. S., Elkins, R. L., Orr, T. E., Walters, P., & Thyer, B. A. (2004). Evaluating the relative effectiveness of three aversion therapies designed to reduce craving among cocaine abusers. *Behavioral Interventions, 19,* 1–24.

Bradshaw, W., & Roseborough, D. (2004). Evaluating the effectiveness of cognitive-behavioral treatment of residual symptoms and impairment in schizophrenia. *Research on Social Work Practice, 14,* 112–120.

Briggs, H. E., & Rzepnicki, T. L. (Eds.). (2004). *Using evidence in social work practice.* Chicago, IL: Lyceum.

Cha, K. Y., Wirth, D. P., & Lobo, R. A. (2001). Does prayer influence the success of in vitro fertilization-embryo transfer? *Journal of Reproductive Medicine, 46,* 781–787.

Cheney, A. (1926). *The nature and scope of social work.* New York: D. C. Heath.

Corcoran, J. (2000). *Evidence-based social work practice with families.* New York: Springer.

Corcoran, J. (2003). *Clinical applications of evidence-based family interventions.* New York: Oxford University Press.

Council on Social Work Education. (1991).

Cournoyer, B. R. (2004). *The evidence-based social work skills book.* Boston: Allyn & Bacon.

Craighead, W. E., Hart, A. B., Craighead, L., & Ilardi, S. S. (2002). Psychosocial treatments for major depressive disorder. In P. E. Nathan & J. Gorman (Eds.). *A guide to treatments that work* (2nd ed., pp. 245–261). New York: Oxford.

DiMascio, A., Weissman, M. M., Prusoff, B. A., Nev, C., Zwilling, M., & Khermn, G. L. (1979). Differential symptom reduction by drugs and psychotherapy in acute depression. *Archives of General Psychiatry, 36,* 1450–1456.

Drake, R. E., Merrens, M. R., & Lynde, D. W. (Eds.). (2005). *Evidence-based mental health practice.* New York: Norton.

Flamm, B. (2002). Faith healing by prayer: Review of Cha, K. Y., Wirth, D. P., Lobo, R. A. Does prayer influence the success of in vitro fertilization-embryo transfer? *The Scientific Review of Alternative Medicine, 6,* 47–50.

Franklin, M. E., & Foa, E. B. (2002). Cognitive behavioral treatments for obsessive compulsive disorder. In P. E. Nathan & J. Gorman (Eds.), *A guide to treatments that work* (2nd ed., pp. 367–386). New York: Oxford.

Gibbs, L. E. (2003). *Evidence-based practice for the helping professions.* Pacific Grove, CA: Thompson.

Gorey, K. M. (1996). Effectiveness of social work interventions: Internal versus external evaluations. *Social Work Research, 20,* 119–128.

Gorey, K. M., Thyer, B. A., & Pawluck, D. E. (1998). Differential effectiveness of prevalent social work practice models: A meta-analysis. *Social Work, 43,* 269–278.

Green, J., & Britten, N. (2005). Qualitative research and evidence based medicine. *British Medical Journal, 316,* 1230–1232.

Grote, N. K., Bledsoe, S. W., Schwartz, H. A., & Frank, E. (2004). Feasibility of providing culturally relevant, brief interpersonal psychotherapy for antenatal depression in an obstetrics clinic: A pilot study. *Research on Social Work Practice, 14,* 397–407.

Harrison, D. F., & Thyer, B. A. (1988). Doctoral research on social work practice. *Journal of Social Work Education, 24,* 107–114.

Hawkins, R. P., & Mathews, J. R. (1999). Frequent monitoring of clinical outcomes: Research and accountability for clinical practice. *Education and Treatment of Children, 22,* 117–135.

Hibbs, E. D., & Jensen, P. S. (Eds.). (2005). *Psychosocial treatments for child and adolescent disorders: Empirically based strategies for clinical practice.* Washington, DC: American Psychological Association Press.

Hogarty, G. E., & Goldberg, S. C. (1973). Drug and sociotherapy in the aftercare of schizophrenic patients: One year relapse rates. *Archives of General Psychiatry, 28,* 54–64.

Hogarty, G. E., Goldberg, S. C., & Schooler, N. R. (1974). Drug and sociotherapy in the aftercare of schizophrenic patients. Vol. III. Adjustment of nonrelapsed patients. *Archives of General Psychiatry, 31,* 609–618.

Hogarty, G. E., Schooler, N. R., Ulrich, R., Mussare, F., Perro, P., & Herron, E. (1979). Fluphenazine and social therapy in the aftercare of schizophrenic patients: Relapse analysis of a two-year controlled study of fluphenazine decanoate and fluphenazine hydrochloride. *Archives of General Psychiatry, 36,* 1283–1294.

Hogarty, G. E., Anderson, C. M., Reiss, D. J., Kornblith, S. J., Greenwald, D. P., & Javna, C. D. (1986). Family psychoeducation, social skills training, and maintenance chemotherapy in the aftercare treatment of schizophrenia. Vol. I. One-year effects of a controlled study on relapse and expressed emotion. *Archives of General Psychiatry, 43,* 633–642.

Hogarty, G. E., Anderson, C. M., Reiss, D. J., Kornblith, S. J., Greenwald, D. P., Ulrich, R. F., et al. (1992). Family psychoeducation, social skills training, and maintenance chemotherapy in the aftercare treatment of schizophrenia. Vol. I. Two-year effects of a controlled study on relapse and adjustment. *Archives of General Psychiatry, 48,* 340–347.

Hogarty, G. E., Flesher, S., Ulrich, R., Carter, M., Greenwald, D., Pogue-Geile, M., et al. (2004). Cognitive enhancement therapy for schizophrenia: Effects of a 2-year randomized trial on cognition and behavior. *Archives of General Psychiatry, 61,* 866–876.

Howard, M. O., McMillan, C. J., & Pollio, D. E. (2003). Teaching evidence-based practice: Toward a new paradigm for social work education. *Research on Social Work Practice, 13,* 234–259.

Jayaratne, S., & Levy, R. L. (1979). *Empirical clinical practice.* New York: Columbia University Press.

Klerman, G. L., Weissman, M. M., Rounsaville, B. J., & Chevron, E. S. (1984). *Interpersonal psychotherapy of depression.* New York: Basic Books.

Larkin, R., & Thyer, B. A. (1999). Evaluating cognitive-behavioral group counseling to improve elementary school students' self-esteem, self-control, and classroom behavior. *Behavioral Interventions, 14,* 147–161.

Mattaini, M. A., & Thyer, B. A. (1996). *Finding solutions for social problems: Behavioral strategies for change.* Washington, DC: American Psychological Association Press.

McNeece, C. A., & Thyer, B. A. (2004). Evidence-based practice and social work. *Journal of Evidence-based Social Work, 1,* 7–25.

Morgan, D. L., & Morgan, R. K. (2001). Single-participant research design: Bringing science to managed care. *American Psychology, 56*, 119–127.

Mufson, L., Weissman, M. M., Moreau, D., & Garfinkel, R. (1999). Efficacy of interpersonal psychotherapy for depressed adolescents. *Archives of General Psychiatry, 56*, 573–579.

Mufson, L., Dorta, K. P., Wickramaratne, P., Nomura, Y., Olfson, M., & Weissman, M. M. (2004). A randomized effectiveness trial of interpersonal psychotherapy for depressed adolescents. *Archives of General Psychiatry, 61*, 577–584.

Mufson, L., Weissman, M. M., Moreau, D., & Garfinkel, R. (1994). Efficacy of interpersonal psychotherapy for depressed adolescents. *Archives of General Psychiatry, 56*, 573–579.

Myers, L. L., & Thyer, B. A. (1997). Should clients have the right to effective treatment? *Social Work, 42*, 288–298.

Pekkala, E., & Merinder, L. (2005). Psychoeducation of schizophrenia. Retrieved from *The Cochrane Database of Systematic Reviews, Issue 2*, (CD002831. DOI:10.1002/14651858.CD002831).

Reynolds, B. C. (1942). *Learning and teaching in the practice of social work.* New York: Farrar & Rinehart.

Ronen, T. (2005). Students' evidence-based practice intervention for children with oppositional defiant disorder. *Research on Social Work Practice, 15*, 165–179.

Rose, S. D. (1967). A behavioral approach to the group treatment of children. In E. J. Thomas (Ed.), *The socio-behavioral approach and applications to social work* (pp. 39–58). New York: Council on Social Work Education.

Rose, S. D. (1969). A behavioral approach to the group treatment of parents. *Social Work, 14*, 21–29.

Rose, S. D. (1977). *Group therapy: A behavioral approach.* Englewood Cliffs, NJ: Prentice-Hall.

Rose, S. D. (1988). Practice experiments for doctoral dissertations: Research training and knowledge building. *Journal of Social Work Education, 24*, 115–122.

Roth, A., & Fonagy, P. (2005). *What works for whom?* (2nd ed.). New York: Guilford.

Rounsaville, B. J., Klerman, G. L., & Weissman, M. M. (1981). Do psychotherapy and pharmacotherapy for depression conflict: Empirical evidence from a clinical trial. *Archives of General Psychiatry, 38*, 24–29.

Rounsaville, B. J., Glazer, W., Wilber, C. H., Weissman, M. M., & Kleber, H. D. (1983). Short-term interpersonal psychotherapy in methadone-maintained opiate addicts. *Archives of General Psychiatry, 40*, 629–636,

Sackett, D. L., Strauss, S. E., Richardson, W. S., Rosenberg, W., & Haynes, R. B. (2000). *Evidence-based medicine: How to practice and teach EBM* (2nd ed.). New York: Churchill-Livingstone.

Smith, M. L., & Glass, G. V. (1977). Meta-analysis of psychotherapy outcome studies. *American Psychologist, 32*, 752–760.

Springer, D. W., McNeece, C. A., & Arnold, E. M. (2003). *Substance abuse treatment for criminal offenders: An evidence-based guide for practitioners.* Washington, DC: American Psychological Association Press.

Staff. (2000). Surgeon General Convenes Experts. *NASW News, 45*, p. 9.

Steketee, G. S. (1993). *Treatment of obsessive compulsive disorder.* New York: Guilford.

Steketee, G. S., Foa, E., & Grayson, J. (1982). Recent advances in the behavioral treatment of obsessive-compulsives. *Archives of General Psychiatry, 39,* 1365–1371.

Strode (1940). *Introduction to social casework.* New York: Harper and Brothers.

Stuart, R. B. (1973). Research in social work: Social casework and social group work. In R. E. Morris (Ed.), *Encyclopedia of social work, 16th edition* (vol. 2, pp. 1106–1122). Washington, DC: NASW Press.

Thyer, B. A. (1992). Should all social workers be well trained in behavioral principles? In E. Gambrill & R. Pruger (Eds.), *Controversial issues in social work* (pp. 79–84, 89–91). New York: Allyn & Bacon.

Thyer, B. A. (1994). Social learning theory: Empirical applications to culturally diverse practice. In R. R. Greene (Ed.), *Human behavior theory: A diversity framework* (pp. 113–146). New York: Aldine de Gruyter.

Thyer, B. A. (1995). Promoting an empiricist agenda in the human services: An ethical and humanistic imperative. *Journal of Behavior Therapy and Experimental Psychiatry, 26,* 93–98.

Thyer, B. A. (2001). Evidence-based approaches to community practice. In H. Briggs & K. Corcoran (Eds.), *Social work practice: Treating common client problems* (pp. 54–65). Chicago: Lyceum.

Thyer, B. A. (2002a). Evidence-based practice and clinical social work. *Evidence-based Mental Health, 6,* 6–7.

Thyer, B. A. (2002b). Developing discipline-specific knowledge for social work: Is it possible? *Journal of Social Work Education, 38,* 101–113.

Thyer, B. A. (2004). What is evidence-based practice? *Brief Treatment and Crisis Intervention, 4,* 167–176.

Thyer, B. A., & Kazi, M. A. F. (Eds.). (2004). *International perspectives on evidence-based practice in social work.* London: Venture Press.

Thyer, B. A., & Myers, L. L. (1997). Behavioral and cognitive theories for clinical social work. In J. Brandell (Ed.), *Theory and practice in clinical social work* (pp. 18–37). New York: Free Press.

Thyer, B. A., & Myers, L. L. (2000). Approaches to behavioral change. In P. Allen-Meares & C. Garvin (Eds.), *The handbook of direct social work practice* (pp. 197–216). Thousand Oaks, CA: Sage.

Thomas, E. J. (1975). Uses of research methods in interpersonal practice. In N. A. Polansky (Ed.), *Social work research* (pp. 254–283). Chicago: University of Chicago Press.

Todd, A. J. (1920). *The scientific spirit and social work.* New York: Macmillan.

Vonk, E. M., & Thyer, B. A. (1999). Evaluating the effectiveness of short-term treatment at a university counseling center. *Journal of Clinical Psychology, 55,* 1095–1106.

Weissman, M. M. (1979). The psychological treatment of depression: Evidence for the efficacy of psychotherapy alone, in comparison with, and in combination with pharmacotherapy. *Archives of General Psychiatry, 36,* 1261–1269.

Weissman, M. M., Klerman, G. L., Paykel, E. S., Prusoff, B., & Hanson, B. (1974). Treatment effects on the social adjustment of depressed patients. *Archives of General Psychiatry, 30,* 771–778.

Weissman, M. M., Klerman, G. L., Prusoff, B. A., Sholmskas, D., & Padian, N. (1981). Depressed outpatients: Results one year after treatment with drugs and/or interpersonal psychotherapy. *Archives of General Psychiatry, 38,* 51–55.

Weissman, M. M., & Markowitz, J. C. (1994). Interpersonal psychotherapy: Current status. *Archives of General Psychiatry, 51,* 599–606.

Werner, H. D. (1965). *A rationale approach to social casework.* New York: Association Press.

Werner, H. D. (1982). *Cognitive therapy.* New York: Free Press.

CHAPTER 4

Critical Thinking, Evidence-Based Practice, and Cognitive Behavior Therapy

Choices Ahead

Eileen Gambrill

Cognitive behavior therapists assume that a person's thoughts contribute to problems such as depression, anxiety, and anger. They emphasize that fallacies in thinking and distortions of reality, such as exaggerating perceived slights by others, can create such troubling reactions. In some approaches, such as rational emotive therapy developed by Albert Ellis, the influence of the Greek philosopher, Epictetus, is acknowledged: "Men are disturbed not by things, but the views they take of them" (www.nacbt. org, on 11 June 2005). Clients are encouraged to recognize the relationship between what they think and feel and what they do. Assignments are used to facilitate this aim. Clients are guided in examining the evidence for and against dysfunctional thoughts such as catastrophizing ("If I don't get a raise, I will die") and replacing such thoughts with realistic appraisals. Behavioral methods are added as needed, such as social skills training. This chapter describes the relevance of critical thinking and the related process and philosophy of evidence-based practice to cognitive behavior therapy and suggests choices that lie ahead in integrating these areas.

CRITICAL THINKING: RELATED VALUES, KNOWLEDGE, AND SKILLS

Critical thinking in the helping professions involves the careful appraisal of beliefs and actions to arrive at well-reasoned ones that maximize the likelihood of helping clients and avoiding harm. It involves reasonable and reflective thinking focused on deciding what to believe or do (Ennis, 1987). Viewed broadly, the process is part of problem solving—for example, providing strategies to check intuitive assumptions (Hogarth, 2001). Critical thinking skills involves more than the mere possession of related knowledge and skills; it requires using them in everyday situations and acting on the results (Paul, 1993). It requires clarity of expression, critical appraisal of evidence and reasons, and consideration of well-argued alternative points of view. Critical thinkers question what others take for granted. They ask questions such as: Could I have been wrong? Have there been any critical tests of this claim? If so, what are the results? How representative were the samples used? Were studies relatively free of bias? Are the presented facts correct? Has counterevidence been presented? Are weak appeals used, such as to emotion or to special interests? Critical thinking involves the accurate presentation of well-argued alternative perspectives and attention to the process of reasoning, not just the product. Critical thinking and scientific reasoning are closely related. Both value clarity and the critical appraisal of claims. Only by thinking critically about practice- and policy-related claims can we maximize the services that are effective in achieving outcomes that clients value and minimize ineffective and harmful ones. Critical thinking encourages professionals to think contextually, to consider the big picture, and to connect personal troubles to social issues. The National Association of Social Workers' Code of Ethics states that "Fundamental to social work is attention to the environmental forces that create, contribute to, and address problems-in-living" (National Association of Social Workers, 1996, Preamble). This requires social workers to be aware of conceptual concerns associated with the framing of problems such as depression and social anxiety as biologically based, with no attention to related psychological and environmental circumstances. Examples of attitudes involved in critical thinking suggested by Paul (1993) include:

> **Intellectual courage:** Critically assessing viewpoints regardless of negative reactions. It takes courage to tolerate ambiguity, and to face ignorance and prejudice in our own thinking. The penalties for nonconformity are often severe.
> **Intellectual curiosity:** An interest in deeply understanding, figuring things out, and in learning.

Intellectual humility: Awareness of the limits of our knowledge, sensitivity to bias and prejudice and limitations of one's viewpoint. No one should claim more than he or she actually knows. Lack of pretentiousness and conceit, combined with insight into the strengths and weaknesses of the logical foundations of one's views.

Intellectual integrity: Honoring the same standards of evidence to which we hold others, practicing what we advocate, and admitting discrepancies and inconsistencies in our own thought and action.

Intellectual perseverance: The pursuit of accuracy despite difficulties, obstacles, and frustration; adherence to rational principles despite irrational opposition to others: recognizing the need to struggle with confusion and unsettled questions to pursue understanding. This trait is undermined when others provide the answers, or do our thinking for us. (pp. 470–472)

THE NEED FOR CRITICAL THINKING

Professionals are required to be familiar with and honor professional codes of ethics. Examples of obligations described in such codes include drawing on practice and policy-related research, accurately informing clients about the risks and benefits of recommended procedures and alternatives, treating clients with respect, and acting with integrity. Research regarding the extent to which those in the helping profession honor such obligations shows that the rhetoric in such codes does not match reality. For example, many helpers do not honor requirements for informed consent (e.g., Braddock, Edwards, Hasenberg, Laidley, & Levinson, 1999) and do not draw on practice-related research findings to inform practice decisions (e.g., see Rosen, Proctor, Morrow-Howell, & Staudt, 1995). Not keeping up with practice-related research findings makes it impossible to honor informed-consent obligations and may result in decisions that harm rather than help clients (e.g., Jacobson, Foxx, & Mulick, 2005).

Fallacies in thinking are by no means confined to clients and their significant others (those who influence them). They are also prevalent among researchers and professionals as illustrated by the extensive literature describing pseudoscience and fads in the helping professions (e.g., see Lilienfeld, Lynn, & Lohr, 2003; Sarnoff, 2001; Jacobson, Foxx, & Mulick, 2005). Indeed, flaws in the professional literature such as biased presentation of findings (e.g., hiding methodological limitations) were a key reason for the development of evidence-based practice (Gray, 2001a, b). We continue to see such flaws (Altman, 2002) and increasing attention is being paid to them as well as to the negative influence of related industries such as the pharmaceutical industry (Angell, 2004; Kassirer, 2004). Research shows that a variety of biases come into play that dilute the quality of decisions (e.g., Gambrill, 2006). Examples include the *fundamental attribution error* (the tendency to attribute the cause of behaviors to personal characteristics of people and to overlook environmental factors) and the *confirmation bias* (the tendency to search for data that support favored positions and to ignore data that do not). Practitioners are influenced by the availability of material such as vivid case examples that may be misleading rather than informative. Such biases have been found not only in the helping professions but in a wide range of other contexts as well (Dawes, 2001; Hastie & Dawes, 2001). Confirmation biases may result in overlooking contradictory data (Nickerson, 1998). Failure to ask, "Is there a better alternative?" and "What are problems with my view?" encourages justification of favored views and ignoring of well-argued alternative accounts that may be more accurate. The emphasis on gathering evidence in support of a favored position rather than exploring alternative views may hinder the discovery of valuable options. Base-rate data are often ignored. A social worker who sees many parents who sexually abuse their children may overdiagnose this event because of his or her unique situation; the social worker may overestimate the true prevalence of sexual abuse. Resemblance criteria—the extent to which a characteristic seems to resemble or be similar to another characteristic—can also lead those in the helping profession astray (e.g., Gilovich, Griffin, & Kahneman, 2002; Nisbett & Ross, 1980). The social worker may assume that effects resemble their causes when, in fact, causes and effects may bear little or no resemblance to each other.

Increasing attention is being given to the prevalence of bogus and grandiose claims in the helping professions. Such claims may result (and have resulted) in harming clients in the name of helping them. Harm includes removing valued opportunities that do not harm others, stigmatizing people by applying negative diagnostic labels of dubious value in understanding or minimizing problems, and not fully informing clients with the result that they make decisions they otherwise would not make. The history of the helping professions reveals the frequency of harm in the name of helping (e.g., Scull, 2005; Sharpe & Faden, 1998; Valenstein, 1986). Blenkner, Bloom, and Nielson (1971) found that intensive case management *increased* mortality for older clients. Common practices thought to help people were found to harm them. Consider the blinding of 10,000 children by use of oxygen at birth (Silverman, 1980) and the death of a child by "rebirthing" therapy. Professionals should fully inform clients about the risks and benefits of recommended services. Books such as *Science and Pseudoscience in Clinical Psychology* (Lilienfeld, Lynn, & Lohr, 2003) and *Controversial Therapies for Developmental*

Disabilities: Fad, Fashion, and Science in Professional Practice (Jacobson, Foxx, & Mulick, 2005) remind us that the follies and fallacies that occur in the area of health care (e.g., Skrabanek & McCormick, 1998) also occur in our field.

Errors in judgment may result in incorrect assumptions about the causes of problems and inaccurate predictions about suicidal potential, need for hospitalization, future recurrence of violent acts, or the results of a new service policy. Only if practitioners are aware of common biases and fallacies and develop skills and related values to counter them, such as questioning their assumptions, may biases be minimized (see, e.g., Skrabanek & McCormick, 1998). Critical-thinking knowledge, skills, and values can help professionals critically appraise claims and arguments, use language clearly, recognize affective influences on decisions, avoid cognitive biases that interfere with sound decision making, and spot pseudoscience and quackery and thus help avoid their influence. Critical-thinking skills are of value in avoiding reliance on questionable grounds for accepting claims about what may be true or false, such as authority, popularity, or tradition (Gambrill & Gibbs, 2002). Although intuition is an invaluable source of ideas, it is not a sound guide for testing beliefs.

Critical thinking encourages deep rather than superficial appraisal. There is a subtext of problem definition and explanation in helping professions such as social work, psychology, and psychiatry that is often unquestioned but questionable (e.g., Szasz, 1987). This is the age of biomedical approaches to personal problems. In the United States, we have just come out of the decade of the brain. This approach has been carried to such excess, especially on the part of the pharmaceutical industry, that there is a vigorous counterreaction (e.g., Angell, 2004; Kassirer, 2004). Those who assume that problems have a biochemical or genetic cause may overlook well-argued critiques (see, e.g., Leo & Cohen, 2003). Critical thinking can be of value in spotting and avoiding informal fallacies (such as straw-man arguments and ad hominem appeals) and in discovering methodological and conceptual problems related to common assertions. It is an antidote to mystification that may harm clients, such as assuming uncritically that an entity called schizophrenia is responsible for a variety of troubling behaviors when there may be no evidence for this (Boyle, 2002). The history of the mental health industry reveals a long list of false causes for personal troubles and social problems, as well as harmful interventions to cure "mental illnesses" (e.g., Ofshe & Watters, 1994; Scull, 2005; Valenstein, 1986). Costs of premature acceptance of inaccurate views of problems include neglecting promising alternatives, and wasting money on ineffective and harmful services at the cost of not fully funding programs found to be effective.

CRITICAL THINKING: INTEGRAL TO
EVIDENCE-BASED PRACTICE

Evidence-based practice (EBP) arose as an alternative to authority-based practice in which decisions are based on criteria such as consensus, anecdotal experience, and tradition (see e.g., Chalmers, 1983; Sackett, Richardson, Rosenberg, & Haynes, 1997). Although the philosophical roots of evidence-based practice are old, its blooming as a process attending to evidentiary, ethical, and application issues in all professional venues (education, practice and policy as well as research) is fairly recent—facilitated by the Internet revolution. It is designed to break down the division between research, practice, and policy—emphasizing the importance of attention to ethical issues. Codes of ethics call on professionals to consider practice-related research findings and inform clients about them. Evidence-based practice involves "the conscientious, explicit and judicious use of current best evidence in making decisions about the care of individual [clients]" (Sackett et al., 1997, p. 2). Best available external clinical evidence refers to practice-related research on the accuracy and precision of assessment, risk measures and descriptive data, and the efficacy and safety of treatment and preventative services. "Without clinical expertise, practice risks becoming tyrannized by evidence, for even excellent external evidence may be inapplicable to or inappropriate for an individual [client]. Without current best evidence, practice risks becoming rapidly out-of-date, to the detriment of [clients]" (Sackett et al., 1997, p. 2). Steps in evidence-based practice include the following:

1. Converting information needs related to practice decisions into answerable questions.
2. Tracking down, with maximum efficiency, the best evidence with which to answer questions.
3. Critically appraising that evidence for its validity, impact (size of effect), and applicability (usefulness in practice).
4. Applying the results of this appraisal to practice and policy decisions. This involves deciding whether evidence found (if any) applies to the decision at hand (e.g., Is a client similar to those studied? Is there access to services described?) and considering client values and preferences, as well as other applicability concerns, in making decisions.
5. Evaluating the effectiveness and efficiency in carrying out steps 1–4 and seeking ways to improve them in the future (Sackett, Straus, Richardson, Rosenberg, & Haynes, 2000, pp. 3–4).

Evidence-based practice is an evolving process designed to attend to interrelated evidentiary, ethical, and implementation concerns. It "is the integration of best research evidence with clinical expertise and [client] values" (Sackett et al., 2000, p. 1). It describes a philosophy and process designed to forward effective use of professional judgment in integration of information about each client's unique characteristics, circumstances, preferences, and actions with external research findings. "It is a guide for thinking about how decisions should be made" (Haynes, Devereaux, & Guyatt, 2002). Although the term *evidence-based practice* can be mistaken to mean only that the decisions made are based on evidence of their effectiveness, its use does call attention to the fact that available evidence may not be used or the current state of ignorance in the field may not be shared with clients. It is hoped that professionals who consider related research findings regarding decisions and inform clients about them will provide more effective and ethical care than those who rely on criteria such as anecdotal experience, available resources, or popularity.

Evidence-based practice (EBP) requires professionals to search for research findings related to important practice and policy decisions and to share what is found (including nothing) with clients. It highlights the uncertainty involved in helping clients, and it attempts to give those in the helping profession the knowledge and skills they need to handle this constructively and to help clients handle it. Evidence-based practice is designed to break down the division between research and practice, for example, emphasizing the importance of clinicians' critical appraisals of research reviews and developing a technology to help them to do so; "the leading figures in EBM [evidence-based medicine] . . . emphasized that clinicians had to use their scientific training and their judgment to interpret [guidelines] and individualize care accordingly" (Gray, 2001a, p. 26). Clinical expertise includes the use of effective relationship skills and the experience of individual helpers to rapidly identify each client's unique circumstances, characteristics and "their individual risks and benefits of potential interventions and their personal values and expectations" (p. 1). It is drawn on to integrate information from these varied sources (Haynes, Devereaux, & Guyatt, 2002). Client values refer to "the unique preferences, concerns and expectations each [client] brings to an . . . encounter and which must be integrated into . . . decisions if they are to serve the [client]" (p. 1).

Evidence-based practice draws on the results of systematic, rigorous, critical appraisal of research related to important practice questions such as, Is this assessment measure valid? and Does this intervention do more good than harm? (see, e.g., Sackett et al., 1997). Such rigorous searches and appraisals decrease the likelihood that professionals pose as "false prophets" (Popper, 1992, p. 128). A major contribution of EBP is encouraging preparation of *systematic* reviews that are based on an exhaustive search for research findings related to a specific practice or policy question, rigorous critical appraisal of each study located, and complete transparency of criteria used to carry out this critical appraisal (see, e.g., Cochrane Collaboration Guidelines; Egger, Smith, & Altman, 2001). EBP is closely tied to the Cochrane Collaboration, a worldwide network of centers designed to prepare, maintain, and disseminate high-quality reviews of the effects of health care. The Campbell Collaboration has been formed to prepare and disseminate systematic reviews in the areas of social welfare, crime and justice, and education. Preparing fragmented (incomplete) uncritical research reviews regarding practice and policy questions may result in inflated claims of effectiveness that provide misleading conclusions. Indeed, systematic reviews typically suggest less positive effects compared to traditional narrative reviews. Different questions require different kinds of tests to critically appraise them (see, e.g., Gambrill, 2005; Gibbs, 2003; Gray, 2001b). Each method is subject to certain biases. The Cochrane Collaboration has developed guidelines for locating and critically appraising research related to specific questions. Reviews are based on a hand (as opposed to computer) search for all material, both published and unpublished and in all languages, related to a question (see, e.g., Bero & Rennie, 1995).

Evidence-based practice and health care originated in medicine in part because of variations in services offered and their outcomes (Wennberg, 2002). In discussing the origins of EBP, Gray (2001a) notes the increasing lack of confidence in data of potential use to clinicians: peer review, which he refers to as "feet of clay," and flaws in books, editorials, and journal articles. Examples include submission bias, publication bias, methodological bias, abstract bias, and framing bias. This remains a problem (Altman, 2002). There are biased estimates of the prevalence of concerns in the professional literature; there is often propagandistic advocacy in place of careful weighing of evidence and reporting of related facts and figures (e.g., Sarnoff, 2001). For example, recommendations regarding practice guidelines may not be sound. In place of critical, systematic reviews of research, there are often fragmented, uncritical ones (e.g., Oxman & Guyatt, 1993). Books with titles such as *What Works* (without a question mark) may not describe search procedures used or criteria used to critically appraise research (Kluger, Alexander, & Curtis, 2001).

RELEVANCE OF CRITICAL THINKING AND EVIDENCE-BASED PRACTICE FOR COGNITIVE BEHAVIOR METHODS

Both critical thinking and EBP emphasize the ethical obligations of professionals in making decisions. These include drawing on practice and policy-related research and involving clients as informed participants in decisions made. They highlight the importance of being honest concerning the evidentiary status of claims forwarded. A key implication of critical thinking and EBP is an openness to and welcoming of criticism. Feedback that facilitates learning is vital. A critical attitude, which Karl Popper (1972) defines as a willingness and commitment to open up favored views to severe scrutiny, is basic to science, which distinguishes it from pseudoscience. If we think critically about cognitive behavior therapy (CBT), we ask questions like:

1. Are related methods informed by well-argued related theories?
2. Are related methods informed by empirical findings regarding the interaction among behaviors, thoughts, and feelings, and environmental events?
3. What is the evidentiary status of related claims? Are there systematic (compared to narrative) reviews? (see, e.g., Egger, Smith, & Altman, 2001).
4. Do we find excessive claims of effectiveness, that is, claims that are not compatible with related research findings?
5. Have the effective ingredients of particular cognitive behavior methods been identified?
6. Have moderating factors been identified such as certain qualities of the therapist–client relationship?
7. With what percentage of clients with a certain kind of problem (e.g., depression, anxiety) are cognitive behavior methods effective?
8. How long do positive effects last? Have there been follow-up studies and what is their quality?
9. Has the possibility of negative effects been investigated and what has been found?
10. What training programs are most effective in developing related values, knowledge, and skills that contribute to successful outcomes?

When are cognitive behavioral methods most helpful? If a claim is made that they are most helpful for a given kind of problem, on what basis is this claim made? Hopefully the content in this book can be used to accurately inform readers about the evidentiary status of the use of cognitive behavior methods. Our ethical obligations to critically assess knowledge claims and the reflection of this in EBP require us to ask probing questions. The very origins of EBP highlight the need for this (e.g., flaws in the professional literature such as hiding methodological limitations and fragmented, uncritical literature reviews). Let us say that we read, "A review of studies regarding ADHD (attention deficit hyperactivity disorder) shows that x is most effective." We should raise the following questions: Were Cochrane and Campbell review guidelines followed? For example, was the search for relevant studies exhaustive? Was it a hand search of all relevant journals in all languages? Were unpublished reports sought and critically appraised as relevant? Do authors include in their research review studies in which findings were negative or no effects were found? Were criteria used to review individual studies rigorous? For example, do we know for each study whether ratings of outcome were blinded (see CONSORT guidelines, Altman et al., 2001)? Were the studies randomized controlled trials of high quality in which there was an intention to treat analysis? Were search procedures clearly described? We do not want to get caught up in yet another fad. A fad has been defined as: "a therapy that is not supported by scientific evidence and that has a fairly rapid rise and fall" (Vyse, 2005, p. 5).

We live in a society in which grandiose claims are the rule-of-day, even in publications that portend to critically appraise claims such as the *Evidence-Based Practice Manual* edited by Alberts and Greene (2002). (See critique by Carlstedt, 2005.) Thus we cannot rely on the words used to describe an endeavor. We must look more carefully. To what extent are cognitive behavior methods based on empirical research concerning the relationship between behavior, thoughts, feelings, and environmental contingencies? For example, in June 2005, on the NACBT Online Headquarters (National Association of Cognitive-Behavior Therapists) we read the following: "Cognitive-behavior therapy is based on the scientific fact that our thoughts cause our feelings and behaviors, not external things, like people, situations, and events." Is this true? Is this a "scientific fact"? The term *cognitive behavior methods* suggests that both cognitive and behavior methods are used as needed. This would imply that theory related to both are drawn on. But is this so? If we look at the website of the National Association of Cognitive-Behavioral Therapists, we find the following statement: "Cognitive behavior methods are based on cognitive theory." If this is so, why not call the methods "cognitive therapies"?

Critical thinking is integral to the practice of cognitive behavior methods. Cognitive behavior therapy emphasizes the role that thoughts play in creating and maintaining anxiety, anger, depression, and related behaviors. Fallacies in thinking are given special attention. Examples include the following:

- All-or-nothing thinking
- Overgeneralization
- Mental filter—filtering out positives, focusing on negatives
- Discounting positives—downplaying or ignoring accomplishments or positive qualities and emphasizing negative qualities or failures

- Jumping to conclusions (mind reading and fortune telling)
- Magnification or minimization (blowing things out of proportion or discounting their importance)
- Emotional reasoning—reasoning based on feelings
- Should statements ("I should, must, ought to _____")
- Labeling (using negative labels to describe oneself)
- Blame (self-blame for events for which we are not responsible or blaming others).

Such distortions may be related to core beliefs such as "I must always succeed in whatever I try; I should never feel angry, anxious or sad; Others won't love or respect me unless I am perfect" (see, e.g., Burns, 1999). Therapists who practice cognitive behavior methods should be experts in identifying fallacies in thinking. Is such expertise generalized to scholarly writing and research? Would we for example find a high correlation between accurate identification of certain fallacies in clients' thinking with fallacies avoided in one's own professional writing and research? Let's say that a cognitive behavior therapist is skilled in helping clients to alter troubling feelings by helping them to identify post hoc ergo propter hoc reasoning (after this therefore because of this). This refers to the incorrect belief that if event A precedes event B in time, then event A has caused B (Gibbs & Gambrill, 1999). If we examine her research and writing, would we find that she has avoided this fallacy (e.g., avoided claims that CBT methods are effective based on a pre-post study with no control group)? Does specializing in the identification of flaws in clients' thinking increase the likelihood of identifying flaws in one's own work such as faulty assumptions and flaws in research conducted and reported concerning cognitive behavior methods? Does such specialization encourage honest brokering of knowledge, ignorance and uncertainty on the part of related professional organizations such as the National Association of Cognitive-Behavior Therapists? What do we find for example when we examine this website?

CHOICES THAT LIE AHEAD

Values, knowledge, and skills related to critical thinking including related literature on judgment and decision making (e.g., Gilovich et al., 2002) as well as the process and philosophy of evidence-based practice suggest a number of inter related choices that lie ahead for cognitive behavior therapists.

How to Define Evidence-Based Practice

Earlier in this chapter the process and philosophy of EBP was described as this is envisioned by its originators and is evolving in original literature. EBP is often defined in a much narrower fashion in the professional literature (Gambrill, 2003). Consider the following: "We use evidence-based practice here primarily to denote that practitioners will select interventions on the basis of their empirically demonstrated links to desired outcomes" (Rosen & Proctor, 2002). In a state directive in Oregon, an evidence-based program is defined as one that: "(a) incorporates significant and relevant practices based on scientifically based research, and (b) is cost effective" (www.namiscc.org/news/spring/, 1 July 2005). Such views ignore ethical obligations such as involving clients as informed participants—sharing ignorance and uncertainty as well as knowledge. Such views also typically ignore the unique *process* for helping practitioners to integrate research and practice (see list of steps in EBP on page 72). What will be the choice of cognitive behavior therapists and related organizations? Will we take advantage of the *process* of EBP and related tools? Evidence-based practice describes a *process* via which practitioners can discover the evidentiary status of a claim such as "Cognitive behavioral methods are effective in decreasing anxiety." Tools have been created such as systematic reviews to help practitioners and clients discover the results of related research.

How Rigorous to Be in Assessing Claims of Effectiveness

The rigor with which practice-related research should be appraised is controversial. Consider controversies regarding the effectiveness of multisystem therapy (Henggeler et al., 2005; Littell, 2005a, 2005b). Indicators used to assess whether content is scientifically oriented include whether well-argued alternative views are accurately presented, whether limitations of research are candidly described and whether negative outcomes are searched for and noted. The invention of the process and philosophy of EBP has encouraged probing questions concerning not only the evidentiary status of claims (e.g., "cognitive behavior therapy is effective"), but also of ethical aspects of services (has there been informed consent, are clients involved as informed participants). The history of harming in the name of helping in the helping professions should encourage us to err on the cautious side when making claims. Otherwise, we may initiate or continue services that are ineffective or harmful and lose opportunities to critically evaluate new methods. Systematic reviews differ greatly from narrative review in their rigor of appraisal (see previous discussion). Here too, as in other areas, "weasel" words (those that are misleading) may be used to obscure important differences between rigorous reviews of research and traditional narrative reviews. To protect clients from bogus claims and their consequences (such as ineffective or harmful services) we should be informed about the differences between systematic and fragmentary uncritical review. For example, narrative reviews usually report more positive findings.

How Transparent to Be Regarding Evidentiary Status

Respect, integrity, and self-determination called for in professional codes of ethics require being honest with clients—for example, sharing the evidentiary status of services (which is often none). Both critical thinking and EPB encourage clear description of what is done to what effect, including mistakes and errors. Such transparency may help practitioners to avoid inflated claims of knowledge that mislead clients (impede informed consent) and hinder the growth of knowledge. Terms such as *well established*, and *validated* convey a certainty that is not possible (see Popper, 1972). Self-determination and empowerment involve giving clients real (rather than merely perceived) influence over the quality of their lives and involving clients in making decisions that affect them. They require a focus on outcomes that clients value (whenever they do not compromise the rights of others) and a candid recognition and discussion of any coercive aspects of contact between social workers and clients. Although there is a great deal of talk about empowerment in social work, when we examine what is actually done in everyday practice, this often reveals little assessment followed by a biomedical recommendation—medication. Considering client values and expectations and involving clients as informed participants in decision making are hallmarks of EBP as envisioned by its originators (see, e.g., Edwards & Elwyn, 2001; O'Conner, Stacey, Rovner, Holmes-Rovner, Tetoe, Llewellyn-Thomas, et al., 2002; Sackett et al., 1997). In the public social services, conflicts between individual and state rights (as reflected in legislation and public policies) limit the self-determination both of social workers and clients. Hiding coercive elements may result in professionals misleading both themselves and clients about what they can offer and how effective it is likely to be.

There are many opportunities to honor components of informed consent even in nonautonomous (coercive) situations (Faden & Beauchamp, 1986). For example, staff could be required to give clients a written description of the evidentiary status of recommended services, the agency's record of success in achieving related outcomes and the record of success of the staff member who will offer this service (Entwistle, Sheldon, Sowden, & Watt, 1998). Clearly describing goals and methods (including their risks and benefits as well as alternative options) and any

coercive aspects of meetings (including unapparent negative consequences dependent on the amount of participation), provide a degree of
self-determination that contrasts with the pursuit of vague goals and
vaguely described methods. Ongoing monitoring of valid progress indicators allows timely, informed decisions and keeps clients informed about degree of progress. The National Association of Social Workers' Code of
Ethics calls for social workers to "monitor and evaluate policies, the implementation of programs and practice interventions" (section 5.02). (It
does not, but should, call for social workers to share this information with
clients.)

How Systemic to Be in Providing Services

Evidence-based practice involves a systemic approach to improving quality of services, including attending to educating professionals who are lifelong learners, involving clients as informed participants in decision
making, attending to management practices and policies that influence
services offered such as agency culture and climate, and considering application challenges such as scarce resources (e.g., Gray, 2001a; Sackett et
al., 2000). A systemic approach includes helping practitioners to acquire
the knowledge, skills, and tools needed to deliver services within a helping framework in which research findings related to decisions are actively
sought and critically appraised. Quality of service is unlikely to improve
in a fragmented approach, that is, without attending to *all* links in the system of service provision. Only by considering the interlinked contingencies related to a problem may a professional accurately understand it and
estimate the degree to which it is solvable and, if so, how. Many problems
clients confront are not solvable by social workers (e.g., lack of well-
paying unskilled jobs, poor-quality education, lack of health care). This
highlights the need for a functional analysis (Haynes & O'Brien, 2000).

Integrating Research Findings and Practice in Care

An extensive literature in EBP addresses challenges of integrating research
findings and practice decisions, including description of tools of value in
locating relevant research and critical appraisal of these tools, such as
valuable websites and systematic reviews. A key focus in EBP is helping
practitioners to develop skills in critically appraising research findings related to practice and policy questions, including the adequacy of research
reviews (e.g., Geddes, Tomlin, & Price, 1999; Greenhalgh, 2001). In addition, there is a focus on helping clients to develop such skills and on giving them access to needed resources such as relevant databases (e.g.,
Edwards & Elwyn, 2001). Keep in mind that misleading claims in the

professional literature on the part of academics and researchers was a key reason for the development of EBP (Gray, 2001a, b). Sources such as *Bandolier* produce a steady stream of material that reviews the effectiveness of common practices and highlights common methodological concerns in practice-related research such as unblinded rating of outcomes and lack of random assignment of subjects (see CONSORT guidelines; Altman et al., 2002). Helpers cannot empower clients if they are not empowered themselves (e.g., are not informed about research findings related to practice and policy decisions that must be made, or do not have the knowledge or resources needed). Social workers cannot inform clients about the risks and benefits of recommended methods (including assessment, intervention, and evaluation methods), unless they are well informed. The degree to which social workers "empower" clients thus depends partly on the extent to which their knowledge, skills, and other resources match what is needed to help clients attain outcomes they value. Accurately estimating this match is one important way that social workers take responsibility for their decisions.

How Much Attention to Give to Individual Differences

Decisions must be made, together with the client, about whether research findings apply to a particular client, considering the client's values and expectations. Different clients may weigh potential risks and benefits differently. "Expertise [proficiency and judgment that individual practitioners acquire through experience and practice] is reflected in many ways, but especially in more effective and efficient [assessment] and in the more thoughtful identification and compassionate use of individual [clients'] predicaments, rights, and preferences in making . . . decisions about their care" (Sackett et al., 1997). Evidence-based practitioners transform information needs related to decisions about a particular client into answerable questions that guide a literature search (see, e.g., Gambrill, 2006a, 2000b; Gibbs, 2003).

How Much Attention to Pay to Minimizing Harming in the Name of Helping

Identifying and minimizing errors, accidents, and mistakes will decrease harm. There is remarkably little systemic study of errors, accidents, and mistakes in social work (for an example see, Munro, 1996). If, indeed, professionals learn through their mistakes, they are forgoing many opportunities to learn. By trying to solve a problem and failing, they may learn a little more about a client's problem (problems, theories, criticisms, new problems) (Popper, 1994, p. 159). A careful review of the circumstances related to mistakes allows us to plan how to minimize avoidable ones. Research regarding errors in medicine shows that latent causes (e.g., quality of staff training, agency policy) contribute to mistakes and errors (Reason, 2001). Each agency should have a system for identifying, tracking and reporting errors, identifying their causes and consequences, and using the information gained to minimize avoidable errors that diminish quality of services.

Whether to Blow the Whistle on Pseudoscience, Quackery, Fraud, and Related Propaganda Tactics

Transparency of what is done to what effect, critical appraisal of claims, and honoring ethical obligations to clients call for blowing the whistle on pseudoscience, fraud, quackery, and propaganda in professional contexts. Censorship of competing views and critiques of preferred views misleads rather than informs. It prevents discovery of promising alternatives. Propaganda is designed to encourage beliefs and actions with the least thought possible (Ellul, 1965). Common propaganda methods include suppression of well-argued alternative views and glittering generalizations, including inflated claims of effectiveness. Some medical schools now include courses designed to alert students to propaganda methods that pharmaceutical companies use to promote drugs (Wilkes & Hoffman, 2001). Pseudoscience (material with the trappings of science without the substance), quackery, and fraud take advantage of propaganda methods. Quackery refers to the for-profit promotion and marketing of untested, often worthless, and sometimes dangerous health products and procedures, by either professionals or others (Young, 1992). Indicators include the use of anecdotes and testimonials to support claims and secrecy (claims are not open to objective scrutiny). Fraud is the intentional misrepresentation of the effect of certain actions to persuade people to part with something of value (e.g., money). Fraudulent claims (often appealing to the trappings of science) may result in overlooking effective methods or being harmed by remedies that are supposed to help.

SUMMARY

Critical-thinking values, skills and knowledge, and EBP are suggested as guides to making ethical, professional decisions. Both encourage basing decisions on well-reasoned judgments in which the interests of all parties are considered. Advantages of both in relation to ethical practice include an emphasis on transparency of what is done to what effect and encouraging integration of research and practice. Sources such as the Cochrane and Campbell Collaborations and other avenues for diffusion, together with helping practitioners and clients to acquire critical appraisal skills, will make it increasingly difficult to mislead people about "what we know." It will be more difficult to ignore questions and well-argued alternative views, lack of evidence regarding services used and harming in the name of helping. It may be easier to locate programs that have been critically tested and found to help clients with particular problems. Cognitive behavior therapists should be especially skilled in identifying faulty beliefs and distortions in thinking. It is hoped that such skills and knowledge will be drawn on in appraising their own work. Cognitive behavior methods are described as those of first choice regarding effectiveness in many sources. Such sources differ in the rigor of critical appraisal ranging from Cochrane reviews to less critical narrative reviews. Values, skills, and knowledge related to both critical thinking and EBP such as valuing honest brokering of knowledge, ignorance and uncertainty is and will be reflected in literature describing cognitive behavior methods to different degrees. As always, the future offers further choices.

REFERENCES

Altman, D. G. (2002). Poor-quality medical research. What can journals do? *Journal of the American Medical Association, 287,* 2765–2767.

Altman, D. G., Schulz, K. F., Moher, D., Egger, M., Davidoff, F., Elbourne, D, et al. for the CONSORT Group. (2001). The Revised CONSORT statement for reporting randomized trials: Explanation and elaboration. *ANNALS of Internal Medicine, 134,* 663–694. Available at www.consort-statement.org.

Angell, M. (2004). *The truth about drug companies: How they deceived us and what to do about it.* New York: Random House.

Bero, L., & Rennie, D. (1995). The Cochrane Collaboration. Preparing, maintaining, and disseminating systematic reviews of the effects of health care. *Journal of the American Medical Association, 274,* 1935–1938.

Boyle, M. (2002). *Schizophrenia: A scientific delusion?* (2nd ed.). London: Routledge.

Braddock, C. H., Edwards, K. A., Hasenberg, N. M., Laidley, T. L., & Levinson, W. (1999). Informed decision making in outpatient practice. Time to get back to basics. *Journal of the American Medical Association, 282,* 2313–2320.

Burns, D. D. (1999). *Feeling good: The new mood therapy* (2nd ed.). New York: Avon.

Carlstedt, R. A. (2005). Toward evidence-based practice: Perfunctory pursuits or potent paradigms? A review of *Evidence-based practice manual:* Research and outcome measures. In A. R. Roberts & K. R. Yeager (Eds.), *Health & human services.* New York: Oxford.

Chalmers, I. (1983). Scientific inquiry and authoritarianism in perinatal care and education. *Birth, 10*, 151–155.

Critical Appraisal of Skills Program (CASP). Institute of Health Services. Old Road, Headington, OX3 7LF casp@earthlink.com.

Dawes, R. M. (2001). *Everyday irrationality: How pseudo-scientists, lunatics and the rest of us systematically fail to think rationally.* Boulder, CO: Westview Press.

Edwards & Elwyn. (2001). *Evidence-based patient choice: Inevitable or impossible?* New York: Oxford.

Egger, M., Smith, G. D., & Altman, D. G. (Eds.). (2001). *Systematic reviews in health care: Meta-analysis in context* (2nd ed.) London: BMJ Books.

Ellis, A. (1996). *Better, deeper, and more enduring brief therapy: The rational emotive behavior therapy approach.* New York: Brunner/Mazel.

Ellul, J. (1965). *Propaganda: The formation of men's attitudes.* New York: Vintage.

Ennis, R. H. (1987). A taxonomy of critical thinking dispositions and abilities. In J. B. Baron & R. J. Sternberg (Eds.), *Teaching thinking skills: Theory and practice* (pp. 9–26). New York: W. H. Freeman.

Entwistle, V. A., Sheldon, T. A., Sowden, A. J., & Watt, I. A. (1998). Evidence-informed patient choice. *International Journal of Technology Assessment in Health Care, 14*, 212–215.

Faden, R. R., & Beauchamp, T. L. in collaboration with King, N. M. P. (1986). *A history and theory of informed consent.* New York: Oxford University Press.

Gambrill, E. (2003). Evidence-based practice: Sea change or the Emperor's new clothes? *Journal of Social Work Education, 39*, 3–23.

Gambrill, E. (2006a). *Critical thinking in clinical practice: Improving the quality of judgments and decisions* (2nd ed.). New York: Wiley.

Gambrill, E. (2006b). *Social work practice: A critical thinker's guide* (2nd ed.). New York: Oxford.

Gambrill, E., & Gibbs, L. (2002). Making practice decisions: Is what's good for the goose good for the gander? *Ethical Human Sciences and Services, 4*, 31–46.

Geddes, J., Tomlin, A., & Price, J. (1999). *Practicing evidence-based mental health.* Abingdon, Oxon, UK: Radcliffe Medical Press.

Gibbs, L. E. (2003). *Evidence-based practice for the helping professions.* Pacific Grove, CA: Thompson/Brooks/Cole.

Gibbs, L., & Gambrill, E. (1999). *Critical thinking for social workers: Exercises for the helping professions* (2nd ed.). Thousand Oaks, CA: Sage.

Gibbs, L., & Gambrill, E. (2002). Evidence-based practice: Counterarguments to objections. *Research on Social Work Practice, 12*, 452–476.

Gilovich, T., Griffin, D., & Kahneman, D. (Eds.). (2002). *Heuristics and biases: The psychology of intuitive judgment.* New York: Cambridge.

Gray, J. A. M. (2001a). The origin of evidence-based practice. In A. Edwards & G. Elywn (Eds.), *Evidence-informed client choice* (pp. 19–33). New York: Oxford.

Gray, J. A. M. (2001b). *Evidence-based health care: How to make health policy and management decisions* (2nd ed.). New York: Churchill Livingstone.

Greenhalgh, T. (2001). *How to read a paper: The basis of evidence-based medicine* (2nd ed.). London: BMJ Publishing Group.

Hardin, R. (1990). The artificial duties of contemporary professionals. *Social Service Review, 64,* 528–541.

Hastie, R., & Dawes, R. M. (2001). *Rational choice in an uncertain world* (2nd ed.). Thousand Oaks, CA: Sage.

Haynes, R. B., Devereaux, P. J., & Guyatt, G. H. (2002). Clinical expertise in the era of evidence-based medicine and patient choice. [Editorial] *ACP Journal Club,* March/April, 136: A11, pp. 1–7.

Haynes, S. N., & O'Brien, W. H. (2000). *Principles and practice of behavioral assessment.* New York: Kluwer Academic/Plenum.

Henggeler, Schoenwald, Borduin, & Swenson (in press). *Children and Youth Services Review.*

Hogarth, R. (2001). *Educating intuition.* Chicago: University of Chicago Press.

Houts, A. (2002). Discovery, invention, and the expansion of the modern diagnostic and statistical manuals of mental disorders. In L. E. Beutler & M. L. Malik (Eds.), *Rethinking the DSM: A psychological perspective* (pp. 17–65). Washington, DC: American Psychological Association.

Jacobson, J. W., Foxx, R. M., & Mulick, J. A. (Eds.). (2005). *Controversial therapies for developmental disabilities: Fad, fashion, and science in professional practice.* New York: Erlbaum.

Kassirer, J. P. (2004). *On the take: How medicine's complicity with big business can endanger your health.*

Kluger, M. P., Alexander, G., & Curtis, P. A. (Eds.). (2001). *What works in child welfare.* Washington, DC: CWLA Press.

Kutchins, H., & Kirk, S. A. (1997). *Making us crazy: DSM: The psychiatric bible and creation of mental illness.* New York: Free Press.

Leever, M. G. (2003). Conflicts of interest in the privatization of child welfare. *Philosophy in the Contemporary World, 10,* 55–60.

Leo, J., & Cohen, D. (2003). Broken brains or flawed studies? A critical review of ADHD neuroimaging research. *Journal of Mind and Behavior, 24,* 29–56.

Lilienfeld, S. O., Lynn, S. J., & Lohr, J. M. (2003). *Science and pseudoscience in clinical psychology.* New York: Guilford.

Littell, J. (2005a). Lessons from a systematic review of multisystemic therapy. *Children and Youth Services Review, 27,* 445–463.

Littell, J. (2005b). The case for multisystemic therapy: Evidence or Orthodoxy. *Children and Youth Services Review.*

Moynihan, R., Heath, I., & Henry, D. (2002). Selling sickness: The pharmaceutical industry and disease mongering. *British Medical Journal, 324,* 886–891.

Munro, E. (1996). Avoidable and unavoidable mistakes in child protection work. *British Journal of Social Work, 26,* 793–808.

Munz, P. (1985). *Our knowledge of the growth of knowledge: Popper or Wittgenstein.* London: Routledge & Kegan Paul.

National Association of Social Workers. (1996). Code of ethics. Silver Spring, MD: NASW.

Nickerson, R. S. (1998). Confirmation biases: ambiguous phenomenon in many guises. *Review of General Psychology, 2,* 175–220.

Nisbett, R., & Ross, L. (1980). *Human inference: Strategies and shortcomings of social judgement.* Englewood Cliffs, NJ: Prentice-Hall.

O'Conner, A. M., Stacey, D., Rovner, D., Holmes-Rovner, M., Tetoe, J., Llewellyn-Thomas, H., et al. (2002). Decision aids for people facing health treatment or screening decisions. [Cochrane Review]. *The Cochrane Library Issue 2.* Oxford: Update Software.

Ofshe, R., & Watters, E. (1994). *Making monsters: False memories, psychotherapy, and sexual hysteria.* New York: Charles Scribner's.

Oregon Adopts Evidence-based treatment requirement. *Mental Health Weekly,* 5/2/04. Downloaded 7/1/05.

Oxman, A. D., & Guyatt, G. H. (1993). The science of reviewing research. In K. S. Warren & F. Mosteller (Eds.), *Doing more good than harm: The evaluation of health care interventions* (pp. 125–133). New York: New York Academy of Sciences.

Paul, R. (1993). *Critical thinking: What every person needs to survive in a rapidly changing world* (3rd ed.). Sonoma, CA: Foundation for Critical Thinking.

Popper, K. R. (1972). *Conjectures and refutations: The growth of scientific knowledge* (4th ed.). London: Routledge and Kegan Paul.

Popper, K. R. (1992). *In search of a better world: Lectures and essays from thirty years.* New York: Routledge.

Popper, K. R. (1994). *The myth of the framework: In defense of science and rationality.* Edited by M. A. Notturno. New York: Routledge.

Reason, J. (2001). Managing the risks of organizational accidents. In C. Vincent (Ed.), *Clinical risk management* (2nd ed.). London: BMJ Press.

Roche, T. (Nov. 13, 2000). The crisis in foster care. *Time,* 156, p. 74.

Rosen, A., & Proctor, E. K. (2002). Standards for evidence-based social work practice. In A. R. Roberts & G. J. Greene (Eds.), *The social worker's desk reference* (pp. 743–747). New York: Oxford University Press.

Rosen, A., Proctor, E. E., Morrow-Howell, N., & Staudt, M. (1995). Rationales for practice decisions: Variations in knowledge use by decision task and social work service. *Research on Social Work Practice, 15,* 501–523.

Sackett, D. L., Richardson, W. S., Rosenberg, W., & Haynes, R. B. (1997). *Evidence-based medicine: How to practice and teach EBM.* New York: Churchill Livingstone.

Sackett, D. L., Strauss, S. E., Richardson, W. S., Rosenberg, W., & Haynes, R. D. (2000). *Evidence-based medicine: How to practice & teach EBM* (2nd ed.). New York: Churchill Livingstone.

Sarnoff, S. K. (2001). *Sanctified snake oil: The effects of junk science and public policy.* Westport, CT: Praeger.

Scull, A. (2005). *Madhouse.* New Haven: Yale University Press.

Sharpe, V. A., & Faden, A. I. (1998). *Medical harm: Historical, conceptual, and ethical dimensions of iatrogenic illness.* New York: Cambridge University Press.

Silverman, W. A. (1980). *Retrolental fibroplasias: A modern parable.* New York: Grunne & Stratton.

Skrabanek, P. (1994). *The death of humane medicine and the rise of coercive healthism.* The Social Affairs Unit. Bury St. Edmunds, Suffolk: St. Edmundsbury Press.

Szasz, T. (1987). *Insanity: The idea and its consequences.* New York: John Wiley & Sons.

Valenstein, E. S. (1986). *Great and desperate cures: The rise and decline of psychosurgery and other medical treatments for mental illness.* New York: Basic Books.

Vyse, S. (2005). When do fads come from? In J. W. Jacobson, Foxx, R. M., & J. A. Mulick (Eds.), *Controversial therapies for developmental disabilities: Fad, fashion, and science in professional practice* (pp. 3–17). New York: Erlbaum.

Wennberg, J. E. (2002). Unwarranted variations in healthcare delivery: Implications for academic medical centres. *British Medical Journal, 325,* 961–964.

Wilkes, M. S., & Hoffman, J. R. (2001). An innovative approach to educating medical students about pharmaceutical promotion. *Academic Medicine, 76,* 1271–1277.

Young, J. H. (1992). *American health quackery.* Princeton: Princeton University Press.

CHAPTER 5

Developmental Factors for Consideration in Assessment and Treatment

A Review of the Aging Process in the Domains of Cognition and Emotion

Amy Carrigan

INTRODUCTION

Let us suppose that you are asked to see a client for whom thought and action are virtually identical. The client spends great amounts of time experiencing guilt and ruminating over what he has done in deed and in thought. He is in a constant state of agitation inasmuch as he fears the real or imagined loss of a relationship or supportive other. If his significant other does not call him frequently, he assumes the worst—that the significant other has left him forever. These characteristics are frequently interpreted as part of a borderline personality. It is also significant that these are descriptive aspects of Piaget's sensorimotor stage.

Another client seems to be resistant. No matter what the therapist's interpretation, the client just doesn't seem to "get it." The client, though intelligent, seems to be unable to problem solve, generalize thoughts or actions, or to test hypotheses. These are all characteristics of Piaget's formal operational ability, a stage that adults are expected to attain by age 11 or 12.

It is significant that many of the disorders that are seen for therapy have clear developmental issues embedded within them. Issues of separation, attachment, individuation, development of identity, and many other factors must be addressed and worked through as part of the therapeutic collaboration. This chapter offers a brief and focused review of human development, with specific emphasis on cognition and emotion. It is essential that the reader distinguishes between cognitive development (a facet of overall development), cognitive psychology (the study of the broad range and role of cognition in relation to affect, behavior, and understanding), and cognitive therapy (the psychotherapeutic treatment modality that emphasizes the role and function of cognition in the development and maintenance of psychological disorders). This chapter focuses on the first two areas, and only minimally of the therapeutic aspect. That is left for the rest of the contributors to this volume.

INFANCY (BIRTH THROUGH 24 MONTHS)

Cognitive Development

Research indicates that infants are able to discriminate sounds, sights, and tactile stimulations. Babies are able to scan their world around them, rather roughly, even in the dark. When there is a sharp contrast in light and dark, they stop scanning and begin to focus on the object. Babies also become bored with certain objects that become too familiar which is referred to as habituation, indicating the need for continuous stimulation. Depth perception develops during the first 12 months. Depth perception requires that babies integrate visual information from both eyes at the same time. According to Bornstein (1992), babies possess some degree of depth perception fairly young, but don't use information from both eyes in a coordinated way until they are about 7 months old.

Piaget (1977), a developmental psychologist, was struck by the fact that all children seem to go through the same sequence of discoveries about their world making the same mistakes and arriving at the same solutions. Piaget introduced four stages of cognitive development; sensorimotor, preoperational, concrete operational, and formal operational. During the first 18 months of life, the baby experiences the sensorimotor stage. The baby understands the world through her senses and her motor actions. She begins to use simple symbols such as single words and pretend play (Piaget, 1977).

Object permanence is another concept gradually developed during the sensorimotor stage. Object permanence, which usually begins to develop around 2 months of age, is the understanding that objects continue to exist even when they can't be seen. An example of this concept can be illustrated when an infant loses a toy in her crib. She does not search for it under the blankets but simply assumes that it has disappeared. But when object permanence begins to develop, the infant can be observed sifting through her blankets looking for her lost toy.

Can infants learn? From the first moments following birth, babies are capable of learning. Classical conditioning occurs by the presence of the caregiver, thus contributing to the child's attachment. Operant conditioning is demonstrated by the sucking response and head turning behaviors through the use of reinforcements such as familiar sounds like the mother's voice.

Through operant conditioning, it is possible to support the idea that infants do have memory. According to Bhatt and Rovee-Collier (1996), babies as young as 3 months can remember specific objects and their interactions with those objects over periods of 7 days. This can be demonstrated using a mobile and how the baby reacts by kicking her feet at different frequencies and time frames throughout a week-long period.

Spoken communication begins at birth through crying. Crying can signal a wet diaper, pain, and so forth. There are also other sounds such as gurgling, and satisfied sounds that are a form of communication. Between 1 to 2 months, an infant can express herself through laughing and cooing (vowel sounds). Around 6 or 7 months, the infant begins to display consonant and vowel sounds combined that sound like a syllable. The repetition of these consonant and vowel sounds is referred to as *babbling*, which continues through approximately 12 months of age. In addition to the babbling, around 10 months of age, the infant begins to use gestures indicating her wants. Typically, by the time the child is 1 year old, she can begin to produce one-word sounds that have meaning. This telegraphic speech begins to develop into two-word sentences and eventually by the time the child reaches 16 months, new words develop rapidly. According to Fenson, Dale, Reznick, Bates, Thal, & Pethick (1994), the average 16-month-old has a vocabulary of 50 words and a 24-month-old has about 320 words. Casasola and Cohen (2000) report that infants lack the ability to consistently associate words with actions until around 18 months of age.

Cross-cultural studies of early language development find that children learn words for people or things before they learn words for actions. This is very similar in children who are learning two languages (Oller, Cobo-Lewis, & Eilers, 1998).

EMOTIONAL DEVELOPMENT

The physical closeness between parent and infant is the strongest during the first 12 months of life than any other time frame. The attachment theory described by Bowlby (1988) explains that the ability and need to form an attachment relationship early in life are genetic characteristics of all human beings. Attachment is the emotional tie to a parent experienced by an infant from which the child derives security. For parents to form a strong attachment with their infant, synchrony must be developed. This is a set of mutually reinforcing and interlocking behaviors that characterize the interactions of parent and child. Both parents do form strong bonds with their children, but fathers are more physical with their attachment, displaying a more playful behavior compared to mothers.

Bowlby (1988) identifies three stages of attachment. Stage one, the infant displays indiscriminate attachment to anyone within reach. Stage two involves attachment to more than one person, and finally stage three, beginning around 6 months, in which clear attachment is evident. Securely attached children appear to have increased social skills, are not hesitant being introduced to new tasks, and are more mature.

According to Bowlby (2005), the ability to regulate one's feelings develops through the attachment between the infant and the caregiver. The emotional interplay between the caregiver and the infant predicts emotional regulation later in life. If the experience is negative, deviant and unhealthy patterns for emotions can develop during the adult years. The adult may be very sensitive to criticism and have difficulties in accepting his negative feelings toward attachment figures.

The infant also begins to develop a sense of self, which includes the awareness of a separate self and the understanding of self-permanence (subjective self) and an awareness of herself as an object in the world (objective self). An emotional self also develops during the first year, shown in facial expressions and the ability to make use of information about emotions (Haviland & Lelwica, 1987).

Freeman et al. (2004) also explains that beginning in the early stages of development, the child organizes her self according to proximity to the caregiver and attachment figure. If the child is aroused, then the child will share her interest with that person if attachment has occurred.

EARLY CHILDHOOD (TWO YEARS TO SEVEN YEARS)

Cognitive Development

Piaget refers to early childhood as the preoperational stage, which is the second major stage of cognitive development (Piaget, 1977). Children become more sophisticated in their use of symbolic thought but are not yet able to use logic. There are many cognitive advances during this stage of development. The child begins to use symbols, the ability to think of something without needing to see it in front of them. They see the world as more orderly and predictable. The child is aware that superficial alterations do not change the nature of things. While understanding that the world is orderly, the child also realizes that they can cause events to happen. The child is also finding it possible to organize objects, people, and events into meaningful categories and at the same time begin to count and deal with quantities. Their ability to develop relationships with others becomes possible because they are able to imagine how others might feel. They begin to develop the ability to explain and predict other people's actions by imagining their beliefs, feelings, and thoughts.

The limitations of Piaget's preoperational thought is very obvious compared to the level of concrete operations in the middle child. The child experiences centration, which is when the child focuses on one aspect of a situation and neglects others. Another limitation is irreversibility. The child fails to understand that an operation or action can go both ways such as two halves of a broken cookie can be put back together to make a whole cookie. The child fails to understand the significance of the transformation between states such as a deflated balloon. Transductive reasoning is another limitation where the child does not use deductive or inductive reasoning; instead, she jumps from one particular to another and sees cause where none exists. Egocentrism is when the child assumes everyone else thinks as they do. They also think in animistic style, which is giving life to objects not alive. And finally, the child confuses what is real with outward appearance (Piaget, 1977).

During early childhood, the vocabulary increases tremendously and grammar and syntax become fairly sophisticated. By the time the child is 6 years old, there are approximately 14,000 words in his or her vocabulary, which is about nine new words per day since age 18 months (Rice, 1982). Talking aloud to oneself is normal and usually disappears by the time the child is nine years old. Between the ages of four and five years, the child averages four- to five-word sentences. Between six and seven years of age, the child begins to speak in compound and complex sentences and uses all the parts of speech in her communication. Young children are interested in the great big world and ask questions about anything and everything, improving their linguistic skills.

Studies of memory development indicate that recognition is better than recall, but both will increase during early childhood. Recognition is the ability to identify a previously encountered stimulus and recall is the ability to reproduce material from memory (Lange, MacKinnon, & Nida, 1989). The inability to remember in early infants is called infantile amnesia. Piaget (1969) explains that early events are not stored in memory at all as compared to Freud, who believed that early memories are repressed because they are emotionally troubling. Other theorists feel that early memories become inaccessible because they are not encoded with that which is being prepared for storage. More recent research indicates that children can remember things that happened to them, the same as adults do (Nelson, 1992).

There are different kinds of memories encoded in different ways. Memories that people know they have (facts, names, and so forth) are encoded in a way that allows for intentional or explicit memory. Other memories such as throwing a ball seem to be encoded in a way that can produce a behavioral change through implicit memory. This type of memory seems to exist before the brain structures necessary for explicit memory have formed.

Emotional Development

The self-concept becomes more understandable and more compelling as a person ages and takes on the tasks of childhood, adolescence, and adulthood. By the time the child is 18 months old, he has self-recognition; when he looks into the mirror, he realizes the face in the mirror is his face. This continues with self-description and self-evaluation. Children around four years of age describe themselves mostly about concrete, observable behaviors such as physical features, preferences, possessions, skills, and members in their household. By the time they are five or six years of age, they begin to formulate future tasks based on their present skills such as being a pro-football player some day.

Emotions directed toward oneself (such as shame and pride) do not develop until around 36 months, after the child gains self awareness (Garner & Power, 1996). Erikson (1950) identifies this stage of personality development as initiative versus guilt. The conflict arises from the growing sense of purpose, which allows a child to plan and carry out activities, and the guilt the child has of the conscience to carry out these plans. The preschool child is becoming aware that they are learning that some of the things they want to do need to meet social approval, while others do not. Self-esteem, the judgment a person makes about her self-worth cannot be expressed until around 8 years old. They do not have the cognitive and social skills to compare themselves accurately with others (Harter, 1990).

They are few gender differences in early childhood. Boys and girls play together not recognizing gender typing. All societies hold beliefs about appropriate behaviors and attitudes for both sexes and these gender stereotypes can restrict the development of both sexes. According to the social learning theory, gender identity develops through observing and imitating models and through reinforcement of gender appropriate behavior. According to Fagot and Hagan (1991), research suggests that both biological and environmental factors, such as the influence of parents and the media, affect gender typing.

Parten (1932) classifies types of social and nonsocial play in early childhood into six types. *Unoccupied play* is when the child does not seem to be playing, but watches anything of momentary interest. In *onlooker play*, the child spends most of the time watching others play. The onlooker may communicate with the other children but does not engage in actual play with the children. *Solitary independent play* is when the child plays alone with toys that are different from those used by nearby children and makes no effort to join the others' play. *Parallel play* is when the child plays independently, but among other children, playing with toys like those used by the other children, but not playing with them in the same way. *Associative play* involves the child playing with other children, talking about their play, borrowing from others, following one another, and trying to control who can play in the group. Finally, *cooperative play* is when the child's play is in a group that is organized for some goal, to make something, play a game, or dramatize a situation (Parten, 1932).

Discipline is considered a tool for socialization. Punishment is effective when it is delivered immediately after the undesirable behavior, is consistent, explained why it is being delivered, and served by someone who has a positive relationship with the child. Harsh, physical punishment such as spankings and beatings can have damaging effects. Discipline based on induction is the most effective. Showing feelings of hatred toward the child is not effective (Grusec & Goodnow, 1994). Baumrind (1996) identifies three child rearing styles: *authoritative*, *permissive*, and *authoritarian*. Authoritative parents maintain control but seek their children's opinions and input. Permissive parents lack control of their children and maintain a poorly structured discipline policy. Authoritarian parents are very strict, are in control continuously, and they lack flexibility.

Children whose parents practice the authoritative style display more responsibility, are able to develop friendships, and are liked by their peers. Children who experience permissive parents lack control in social situations with their peers, display irresponsible behaviors, and tend to perform poorer academically. Authoritarian parents tend to have children who display more aggressive behaviors with their peers, have difficulty making and keeping friends, and have difficulty adjusting to new situations.

MIDDLE CHILDHOOD (10 TO 11 YEARS)

Cognitive Development

School-age children develop concrete operational thinking or reasoning that focuses on real, tangible objects. Concrete operations cause important transformations in the cognitive skills children develop in the preoperational period. In classifying objects, children can group things in more than one way at a time by about age 7. They know that a person can be both a parent and a teacher at the same time. They understand that some classifications are inclusive of others such as, that a particular animal can be both a dog and a pet. Conservation develops early during middle childhood. This is a realization that certain properties of an object necessarily remain constant despite changes in the object's appearance. For example, like amounts of clay can be formed into different shapes but each still remains the same amount or weight (Piaget, 1983).

During middle childhood, children are able to seriate, or arrange objects in sequence according to some dimension such as length or size. They understand temporal relations, or the nature of time, better than they did in early childhood. They understand calendars, clocks, holiday event timings such as Christmas or their birthday. They also understand spatial relationships and their surroundings. They can make maps and models of familiar places such as their home, their bicycles, and so forth (Piaget, 1983).

Both short-term and long-term memory improve, partly as a result of other cognitive developments such as learning strategies. Improvement in logical reasoning sometimes helps the development of long-term memory as does increasing richness or familiarity of knowledge. School-age children are skillful with language but continue to have difficulties with certain subtle features of syntax. During middle childhood, children are better able to understand metaphors. Telling a child that the teacher is sick of picking up their messes no longer represents that the teacher is physically ill and that he/she is going to vomit.

Emotional Development

During middle childhood, children face challenges concerning the development of an identity or a sense of self, achievement, peer relationships, family relationships, and school.

During middle childhood, children develop a sense of self. They have a more intensive understanding of who they are and what makes them different from others or unique. But this is not yet finalized. The challenge to achieve is another challenge in which the child is growing in awareness that they must do well in their performance because they are judged by others according to their outcome. The challenge with peers is even more important than younger years because they choose to spend more time in peer related activities. Family relationships are still important especially with the changing of the traditional family. Often times, children must share the challenge of holding a family together. In middle childhood, school is second to the family in influencing the child's social and emotional development. School requires the child to interact with a large number of children and adults giving them the opportunity to learn new social skills, values, beliefs, and a stronger sense of identity.

Children are influenced by their school's culture. The environment teachers create and their expectations of students shape children's school experiences. From the student's perspective, school is often a place where they may encounter denial of needs, interruptions, delays, and social distractions.

ADOLESCENCE (12 TO 18 YEARS)

Cognitive Development

There are many stereotypes of adolescents, usually portraying them as rebellious, negative toward authority, and irresponsible. Most adolescents are able to successfully transfer from childhood to adulthood. But there are some adolescents who are not provided adequate opportunities and support to become competent adults. It is important to view adolescents as a heterogeneous group, decreasing the mislabeled stereotype.

Piaget's fourth stage of cognitive development is formal operational thought. This stage is more abstract, idealistic, and logical than the other stages. *Hypothetical deductive* reasoning is a term used to describe adolescents' more logical reasoning. Adolescents have the cognitive ability to develop hypotheses, or guesses, about how to solve problems (Piaget, 1983).

Elkind (1976) defines adolescent egocentrism as the heightened self-conscious experienced in this age group. Adolescent egocentrism can be divided into two types of social thinking—imaginary audience and personal fable. An imaginary audience involves adolescents' belief that others are as interested in them as they themselves are, displaying attention-getting behaviors to be noticed. A personal fable involves an adolescent's sense of uniqueness and invincibility. He feels that no one understands how he feels, which contributes to the increase in risk-taking behaviors such as reckless driving.

Changes in information processing involve decision making and critical thinking in adolescence. Compared to younger age groups, adolescents generate options in decision making based on a variety of perspectives, weigh the consequences of their decisions, and question the credibility of their resources (Jacobs & Klaczynski, 2002).

According to Klaczynski & Narasimham (1998), cognitive changes that improved critical thinking in adolescence are: increased speed, automaticity, and capacity of information processing; more breadth of content knowledge in a variety of domains; increased ability to construct new combinations of knowledge; and a greater range and more spontaneous use of strategies or procedures for applying or obtaining knowledge such as planning, considering alternatives, and cognitive monitoring.

The transition from elementary school to middle school coincides with many social, familial, and individual changes in the adolescent's life and can often times be stressful. Successful schools for young adolescents take individual differences seriously, show a deep concern for what is known in early adolescence, and emphasize socio-emotional as well as cognitive development (Lipsitz, 1984).

Emotional Development

Some researchers have found that self-esteem drops in early adolescence, and the decline is greater for girls. This decline in both sexes can possibly be explained because of body image as pubertal change occurs and their interest in social relationships that is not adequately rewarded by society (Baldwin & Hoffman, 2002).

Erikson (1968) identifies this stage of development as identity versus identity confusion. It is a time of being interested in finding what one is all about and where the future leads. This is when there is a gap between the security of childhood and the autonomy of adulthood. Adolescents who do not successfully resolve this identity crisis are unsettled and experience identity confusion. Behaviors identified with this crisis are withdrawing, isolating themselves from peers and family, or losing their identity in the crowd.

Many parents have a difficult time dealing with their adolescent's need to become more independent or autonomous. Adolescents do not simply move into a world where their parents disappear. Attachment to parents increases the probability than an adolescent will be socially competent. Parent and adolescent conflicts increase and the conflicts are usually moderate rather than severe. A small percentage of adolescents experience high parent-adolescent conflicts that can be linked to negative outcomes.

Sullivan (1953) believed that there is a dramatic increase in the psychological importance and intimacy of close friends in early adolescence. Developmentally, the adolescent depends on friends rather than family to satisfy social needs. Sullivan believed that the need for intimacy intensifies during early adolescence, motivating teenagers to seek out close friends. He felt that if the teenager fails at this task, she may fail to have close friendships, have feelings of loneliness, and a reduced sense of self-worth.

According to Brown (2003), cliques and crowds assume more important roles in the lives of adolescents than children. Cliques are small groups that range from two to twelve individuals, averaging about five to six individuals, and can form because adolescents engage in similar activities. A crowd is a larger group structure than a clique. A crowd is usually formed based on reputation and members may or may not spend much time together.

Dating begins during this age and it can have many functions. Younger adolescents often begin to hang out together in heterosexual groups. If an adolescent begins dating too soon, it sometimes can be associated with developmental problems. Male dating scripts are proactive, and female reactive. Emotions are heavily involved in adolescent dating and romantic relationships.

EARLY ADULTHOOD (20 YEARS TO 40 YEARS)

Cognitive Development

Intellectual processes are at their peak in early adulthood. The pattern of cognitive decline varies widely and the differences can be related to environmental factors, lifestyle factors, and heredity. Piaget's view of formal thought continues strongly in early adulthood and is strongly tied to experiences. Adults are quantitatively more knowledgeable than adolescents, but they do not enter a new stage of cognitive development. Young adults engage in reflective, relativistic thinking. This post-formal thought process involves the understanding that the correct answer might require reflective thinking but might vary from one situation to another. In addition, the search for truth is often never ending. In addition, the post-formal stage includes the understanding that solutions to problems often need to be realistic and that both subjective and emotional factors can be involved in thinking (Perry, 1999).

In one's forties, creativity is at its highest, and then declines, but this decline is slight. There are also vast differences in creativity levels throughout life (Csikszentmihalyi, 2000). Csikszentmihalyi identifies several ways to increase creativity in one's life. He suggests that one try to be surprised by something every day; try to surprise at least one person per day; write down the surprise experienced each day and the surprise reciprocated to another person and responses; follow interests that are sparked; have a goal identified every morning to accomplish; master personal scheduling; and spend time in creative settings that are stimulating.

Researchers look at different components of intellectual abilities across the adult years. *Crystallized intelligence* is knowledge and judgment acquired through education and experience. *Fluid intelligence* is the aspect of intelligence that reflects fundamental biological processes and does not depend on specific experiences (Cattell, 1963; Horn, 1982). Memory skills remain stable during early adulthood, but with age, memory processes become both slower and less efficient. Memory differences between younger and older adults are usually restricted to tasks involving speed of processing.

Emotional Development

Erikson (1968) proposed that young adults face the crisis of intimacy versus isolation. Young adults who do not establish a stable relationship with an intimate partner or a network of friends become socially isolated. Levinson (1978) felt that adult development involves alternating periods of stability and instability, through which adults construct and refine life structures.

Many people are involved in intimate relationships and many of those people wish their relationship might be better. Most adults do succeed in establishing some kind of close relationship. Not all marry, and intimate relationships can develop through friendships. Stack (1998) finds that those adults who are not able to establish an intimate relationship experience more loneliness and depression than the average adult and suffer from a variety of mental health problems. Married adults are generally happier and healthier than single adults; however, psychologists believe that it is a relationship quality that is associated with both mental and physical health.

A life structure is the underlying pattern or design of a person's life at a given time, which includes roles, relationships, and behavior problems (Levinson, 1978). As adults enter a period in which a new life structure is required, there is a period of adjustment called the *novice phase*. In the mid-era phase, adults become more competent at meeting the new challenges through reassessment and reorganization of the life structure they created during the novice phase. Stability returns in the *culmination phase*, when adults have succeeded in creating a life structure that allows them to manage demands of the new developmental challenges with more confidence and less distress (Levinson, 1978).

During early adulthood, the person is making choices for future career endeavors, possibly becoming parents, and becoming more financially in debt. The financial debt is associated with becoming independent from the nuclear household in terms of transportation, health care insurance, mortgage/rent, and so on. Many men and women want to become parents because they view raising children as a life-enriching experience. This transition to parenthood can be stressful and can lead to dissatisfaction with the partner. This is possibly due to the division of increased labor, individual personality traits, and the available help from the extended family.

The specific job a young adult chooses is paralleled by her education, intelligence, family background and resources, family values, personality, and gender. The majority of adults have chosen jobs that fit into their cultural norms for their social class and gender (Bachman, Segal, Freedman-Doan, & O'Malley, 2000).

MIDDLE ADULTHOOD (40 YEARS TO 65 YEARS)

Cognitive Development

During middle adult years, some cognitive abilities improve and some show declines. Schaie's (1983) longitudinal study of changes in memory and cognition found that lack of mental exercise tends to be correlated with declines in memory and cognitive skills. Subjective responses from middle-aged adults feel that forgetfulness increases with age. However, memory demands of middle-aged adults' everyday lives are greater than those of young adults. Working memory is limited and the more it is put to task, the more that is forgotten (Commissaris, Ponds, & Jolles, 1998). Performance on more complex memory tasks, such as remembering lists of words also declines with age but usually not until after 55 years of age. Recognition of words and texts appears to remain stable throughout adulthood (Zelinski & Burnight, 1997).

Verbal abilities continue to grow in middle age. Creative productivity also appears to remain high during middle adulthood for those who are in challenging jobs (Simonton, 2000).

Emotional Development

Erikson (1968) felt that middle-aged adults face a significant issue in life: generativity versus stagnation. Generativity is the need to leave behind a legacy of one's self, but if this cannot be accomplished, stagnation is experienced. This is where the individual feels the sense that they have nothing for the next generation.

According to Kotre (1984), middle-aged adults can develop generativity in many ways. Through biological generativity, adults conceive and give birth. Through parental generativity, adults provide nurturance and guidance to children. Through work, the adult develops skills that are passed down to others. Cultural generativity involves adults creating, renovating, or conserving some aspect of culture that ultimately survives.

Levinson (1978) suggests that the change to middle adulthood in males lasts about five years, between the ages of 40 to 45 years. This requires the adult male to come to grips with four major conflicts: (1) being young versus old, (2) being destructive versus being constructive, (3) being masculine versus being feminine, and (4) being attached to others versus being separated from them. Levinson feels that midlife is a crisis point where the middle-aged adult is suspended between the past and the future; trying to resolve this crisis and to cope with this event can threaten life's continuity. . . (i.e.), things change.

During middle adulthood, parents find themselves launching their children into adult life. Parents can face new adjustments as disequilibrium occurs because of the child's absence. Empty nest syndrome is a decrease in marital satisfaction after children leave home, because parents derive considerable satisfaction from their children. Middle-aged parents may find themselves at the dinner table with nothing to discuss when previously the time spent there was filled with parent–child interaction. Parents who live their lives through their children may have difficulties with this transition, but most parents' marital satisfaction increases during the years after child rearing finding more time for career development and more time with each other.

Sibling relationships continue throughout life, some being close and some being distant. Friendships continue to be important during middle age. Mothers and daughters typically have the closest relationship in middle adulthood. This age group is also referred to as the middle generation squeeze. Adult children are caught between obligations to children and obligations to parents. The middle-aged generation plays an important role in linking generations.

LATE ADULTHOOD

Cognitive Development

During the young-old (aged 65–75 years), cognitive changes are still fairly small. The old-old (75 years plus) show average declines on all measures of intellectual skills with the highest decline in speed and unexercised abilities (Giambra, Arenberg, Zonderman, Kawas, & Costa, 1995).

Late adulthood may have some advantages over young adulthood because of the accumulation of knowledge and skills. Wisdom is a hypothesized cognitive characteristic of older adults that includes accumulated knowledge and the ability to apply that knowledge to practical problems of living (Baltes & Staudlinger, 2000).

Enhanced creativity may also be an element of cognition in older adults. Some highly creative composers and artists reach their peak in late adulthood. Cohen (2000) developed a four-stage theory of mid- to late-life creativity. Cohen believes that these phases apply to ordinary people who are more creative than others in their everyday lives as well as to professional creators.

According to Cohen (2000), at around age 50, creative individuals enter a reevaluation phase, during which they reflect on past accomplishments and formulate new goals. This reevaluation process leads to the increase in the need to create and produce. Around age 60, the person enters the liberation phase where they feel freer to create because most have retired from their work (Cohen, 2000). At this age, more are willing to take risks because they are tolerant of their own failures. By 70 years of age, the person is entering the summing-up phase and they want to "knit" their accomplishments together into a meaningful story. The last phase is the encore phase experienced by the 80 years-plus group. This is when there is a desire to complete unfinished works or to fulfill desires that have been put aside (Cohen, 2000).

Emotional Development

The last of Erikson's (1968) stages of life crises is the ego-integrity-versus-despair crisis experienced during late adulthood. Ego integrity is the feeling that one's life has been worthwhile. To achieve ego integrity, the older adult must come to terms with who she is and has been, how her life has been lived, choices that she has made, and the opportunities gained and lost. This process also involves coming to terms with death and accepting its imminence. If the older adult does not achieve ego integrity, feelings of hopelessness and despair would result because there would be too little time to make changes before death. Disengagement has been found not to be essential in old age; high life satisfaction and good mental health are found most often among elders who disengage the least (Erikson, 1968).

Another theory focuses on the question of whether it is normal, necessary, or healthy for older adults to remain active as long as possible, or if it is normal for the older adult to gradually turn inward. Activity theory says that it is normal and healthy for older adults to try to remain as active as possible for as long as possible. The disengagement theory states that it is normal and healthy for older adults to slow down their social lives and to separate themselves from others to a certain degree (Adlemann, 1994; Zimmer, Hickey, & Searle, 1995).

Among unmarried elders in the United States, living alone is the most common and preferred living arrangement. Marriages in late adulthood are on the average highly satisfying for both spouses. They exhibit strong loyalty and mutual affection. Married elders as a group are somewhat healthier and more satisfied with their lives than are single elders (Larsen, Mannell, & Zuzanek, 1986).

The majority of older adults has at least one living child and takes pleasure in seeing their children regularly. The quality of relationships with siblings increase as well. The degree of contact with friends is correlated with overall life satisfaction among older adults (Pinquart & Soerensen, 2000).

SUMMARY

It would be impossible to try to deal with an individual in any venue without addressing how they receive, process, and understand the data coming from the environment or that which is internally generated. The way in which information is manipulated is developmentally related. As individuals work toward establishing an adaptive position within their world, they are impacted by the experiences that they have had and the meanings that they give to experiences.

Cognitive style and format make the mysterious understandable for the individual. Equally, an understanding of an individual's cognitive style and content help the clinician better understand the client and structure therapeutic experiences that have the greatest likelihood of success.

REFERENCES

Adelmann, P. (1994). Multiple roles and physical health among older adults: Gender and ethnic comparisons. *Research on Aging, 16,* 142–166.

Bachman, J., Segal, D., Freedman-Doran, P., & O'Malley, P. (2000). Who chooses military service? Correlates of propensity and enlistment in the U.S. Armed Forces. *Military Psychology, 12,* 1–30.

Baldwin, S., & Hoffman, J. (2002). The dynamics of self-esteem: A growth curve analysis. *Journal of Youth and Adolescence, 31,* 101–113.

Baltes, P., & Staudlinger, U. (2000). Wisdom. *American Psychologist, 55,* 122–136.

Baumrind, D. (1996). The discipline controversy revisited. *Family Relations, 45,* 405–414.

Bhatt, R., & Rovee-Collier, C. (1996). Infants' forgetting of correlated attributes and object recognition. *Child Development, 67,* 172–187.

Bornstein, M. (1992). Perception across the life span. In M. Borstein & M. Lamb (Eds.), *Developmental psychology: An advanced textbook* (3rd ed., pp. 155–210). Hillsdale, NJ: Erlbaum.

Bowlby, J. (1988). *A secure base.* New York: Basic Books.

Bowlby, J. (2005). The role of childhood experience in cognitive disturbance. In A. Freeman, M. J. Mahoney, P. Devito, & D. Martin (Eds.), *Cognition and Psychotherapy* (2nd ed., pp. 101–122).

Brown, B. (2003). Crowds, cliques, and friendships. In G. Adams & M. Berzonsky (Eds.), *Blackwell handbook of adolescence*. Malden, MA: Blackwell.

Casasola, M., & Cohen, L. (2000). Infants' association of linguistic labels with causal actions. *Developmental Psychology, 36*, 115–168.

Catell, R. (1963). Theory of fluid and crystallized intelligence: A critical experiment. *Journal of Educational Psychology, 54*, 1–22.

Cohen, G. (2000). *American Academy of Pediatrics guide to your child's sleep: Birth through adolescence*. New York: Villard Books.

Commissaris, C., Ponds, R., & Jolles, J. (1998). Subjective forgetfulness in a normal Dutch population: Possibilities of health education and other interventions. *Patient Education & Counseling, 34*, 25–32.

Csikszentmihalyi, M. (2000). Creativity: An overview. In A. Kazdin (Ed.), *Encyclopedia of psychology*. Washington, DC, & New York: American Psychological Association and Oxford University Press.

Elkind, D. (1976). *Child development and education: A Piagetian perspective*. New York: Oxford University Press.

Erikson, E. (1950). *Childhood and society*. New York: Norton.

Erikson, E. (1968). *Identity: Youth and crisis*. New York: W.W. Norton.

Fagot, B., & Hagan, R. (1991). Observations of parent reactions to sex-stereotyped behaviors: Age and sex effects. *Child Development, 62*, 617–628.

Fenson, L., Dale, P., Reznick, J., Bates, E., Thal, D., & Pethick, S. (1994). Variability in early communication development. *Monographs of the Society for Research in Child Development, 59* (5, Serial No. 242).

Freeman, A., Mahoney, M., Devito, P., & Martin, D. (2004). *Cognition and psychotherapy*. New York: Springer.

Garner, P., & Power, T. (1996). Preschoolers' emotional control in the disappointment paradigm and its relation to temperament, emotional knowledge, and family expressiveness. *Child Development, 67*, 1406–1419.

Giambra, L., Arenberg, D., Zonderman, A., Kawas, C., & Costa, P. (1995). Adult life span changes in immediate visual memory and verbal intelligence. *Psychology and Aging, 10*, 123–139.

Grusec, J., & Goodnow, J. (1994). Impact of parental discipline methods on the child's internalization of values: A reconceptualization of current points of view. *Developmental Psychology, 30*, 4–19.

Harter, S. (1990). Processes underlying adolescent self-concept formation. In R. Montemayor, G. R. Adams, & T. P. Gullotta (Eds.), *From childhood to adolescence: A transitional period?* (pp. 205–239). Newbury Park, CA: Sage.

Haviland, J., & Lelwica, M. (1987). The induced affect response: 10-week-old infants' responses to three emotional expressions. *Developmental Psychology, 23*, 97–104.

Horn, J. (1982). The aging of human abilities. In B. B. Wolman (Ed.), *Handbook of developmental psychology* (pp. 847–870). Englewood Cliffs, NJ: Prentice-Hall.

Jacobs, J., & Klaczynski, P. (2002). The development of judgment and decision making during childhood and adolescence. *Current Directions in Psychological Science, 11*, 145–149.

Klaczynski, P., & Narasimham, G. (1998). Development of scientific reasoning biases: Cognitive versus ego-protective explanations. *Developmental Psychology, 34,* 175–187.

Kotre, J. (1984). *Outliving the self: Generativity and the interpretation of lives.* Baltimore: Johns Hopkins University Press.

Lange, G., MacKinnon, C., & Nida, R., (1989). Knowledge, strategy, and motivational contributions to preschool children's object recall. *Developmental Psychology, 25,* 772–779.

Larsen, R., Mannell, R., & Zuzanek, J. (1986). Daily well-being of older adults with friends and family. *Psychology and Aging, 1,* 117–126.

Levinson, D. (1978). *The seasons of a man's life.* New York: Knopf.

Lipsitz, J. (1984). *Successful schools for young adolescents.* New Brunswick, NJ: Transaction.

Nelson, K. (1992). Emergence of autobiographical memory at age 4. *Human Development, 35,* 172–177.

Oller, D., Cobo-Lewis, A., & Eilers, R. (1998). Phonological translation in bilingual and monolingual children. *Applied Psycholinguistics, 19,* 259–278.

Parten, M. (1932). Social play among preschool children. *Journal of Abnormal and Social Psychology, 27,* 243–269.

Perry, W. (1999). *Forms of critical and intellectual development in the college years.* New York: Holt, Rinehart & Winston.

Piaget, J. (1969). *The child's conception of time.* (A. J. Pomerans, Trans.). London: Routledge & Keegan Paul.

Piaget, J. (1977). *The development of thought: Equilibrium of cognitive structures.* New York: Viking.

Piaget, J. (1983). Piaget's theory. In P. Mussen (Ed.), *Handbook of child psychology: Vol. 1.* New York: Wiley.

Pinquart, M., & Soerensen, S. (2000). Influences of socioeconomic status, social network, and competence on subjective well-being in later life: A meta-analysis. *Psychology & Aging, 15,* 187–224.

Rice, M. (1982). Child language: What children know and how. In T. M. Field, A. Huston, H. Quay, L. Troll, & G. Finley (Eds.), *Review of human development research.* New York: Wiley.

Schaie, K. (1983). The Seattle longitudinal study: A 21-year exploration of psychometric intelligence in adulthood. In K. Schaie (Ed.), *Longitudinal studies of adult psychological development* (pp. 64–135). New York: Guilford.

Simonton, D. (2000). Creativity: Cognition, personal, developmental, and social aspects. *American Psychologist, 55,* 151–158.

Sullivan, H. (1953). *The interpersonal theory of psychiatry.* New York: W.W. Norton.

Zelinski, E., & Burnight, K. (1997). Sixteen-year longitudinal and time lag changes in memory and cognition in older adults. *Psychology & Aging, 12,* 503–513.

Zimmer, Z., Hickey, T., & Searle, M. (1995). Activity participation and well-being among older people with arthritis. *The Gerontologist, 35,* 463–471.

PART II

Methods of
Intervention
Theory and Techniques

CHAPTER 6

Cultural Diversity and Cognitive Behavior Therapy

Jordana Muroff

INTRODUCTION

A hallmark of the social work profession is its work with diverse client populations. Many social work services are specifically aimed to serve "marginalized communities and special population groups that typically include disproportionately high numbers of people of color, elderly people, people with disabilities, and clients of lower socioeconomic status" (National Association of Social Workers [NASW], 2001, p. 26). A main tenet of social work practice is cultural sensitive and cultural competent assessment and intervention. As defined by the NASW, culture "implies the integrated pattern of human behavior that includes thoughts, communications, actions, customs, beliefs, values, and institutions of a racial, ethnic, religious, or social group" to include people with disabilities, people of various religious backgrounds, and/or people who are gay, lesbian, transgender (NASW, 2000, p. 61). Although sometimes viewed as a "separate category of human experience" that is better "left out" (Hays, 1995, p. 309), it is the role of social work to centralize culture. Culture by its very nature influences behavioral outcomes and cognitions (McNair, 1996; Purcell, Campos, & Perilla, 1996). "The primary mission of social work profession is to enhance human well-being and help meet the basic human needs of all people, with particular attention to the needs and empowerment of people who are vulnerable, oppressed, and living in poverty" (NASW, 2001, p. 9).

109

The mosaic of the U.S. population is approximately 12.6% Hispanic/Latino, 0.89% American Indian/Alaskan Native, 3.62% Asian, 14 percent Native Hawaiian or Other Pacific Islander, 12.33% Black or African American, 75.16% White, 5.47% Other or Unknown, and 2.42% Two or more races (U.S. Census Bureau, 2000), with innumerable subgroups. Estimates of the U.S. population that are gay or lesbian ranges from 10% (Binson, Michaels, & Stall, 1995; Kinsey, Pomeroy, & Martin, 1948) to 5% (Smith & Gates, 2001). Another study reports 6.2% of men and 3.6% of women in the United States, reported having had same-sex sexual contact in the past 5 years; when attraction to same sex persons was included, the numbers climbed to 20.8% of men and 17.8% of women (Sell, Wells, & Wypij, 1995). Additionally, the median age of the U.S. population in 2000 was 35.3 (U.S. Census Bureau, 2000). The average life span is cited as 72.1 years for men and 78.9 years for women, in 1993 (Zeiss & Steffen, 1996). Furthermore, approximately 19% of the U.S. population has a disability (U.S. Census Bureau, 2000).

The composition of the U.S. population is continually changing. By the year 2050, it is estimated that 50% of the population will be non-Hispanic White Americans, a reduction from 75% of the population in 2001 (U.S. Census Bureau, 2001). The older population is rapidly growing larger as well (Zeiss & Steffen, 1996).

Mental health services utilization patterns differ across populations. Group comparisons reveal that African Americans, Latinos, and Asian Americans are less likely to seek mental health services than Whites (Neal & Turner, 1991; Snowden, 1999; Tracey, Leong, & Glidden, 1986). Studies show that African Americans are more likely to seek help from general physicians, ministers, and hospital emergency rooms than from mental health professionals (Neighbors, 1985, 1988; Neal & Turner, 1991, p. 401). If mental health professionals are sought, African Americans more frequently go to private psychotherapists or local community mental health centers over university or medical school settings (Neighbors, 1988; Weiss & Kupfer, 1974). Asian Americans tend to rely on family and community care exhausting all other resources before assessing the mental health system (Lin & Cheung, 1999). The tendency for many cultural groups to seek services other than university or medical school settings has significant implications for clinical research and the treatment of these populations, since a large proportion of research is conducted at university medical centers and medical schools (Weiss & Kupfer, 1974). Despite their growing numbers, members of "racial/ethnic minority populations are vastly underrepresented in both efficacy and effectiveness studies" (Alvidrez, Azocar, & Miranda, 1996; Vera, Vila, & Alegria, 2003, p. 8). Thus, little is known as to whether current treatments are helpful or about the culturally specific needs of diverse social groups.

Due to the social work mission and the growing diversity among the U.S. population, social workers are more and more likely to work with clients of diverse backgrounds. Therefore, it is increasingly important to understand the relevance of culture and the applicability of treatment methods across diverse groups. There are many different types of mental health interventions, some of which are empirically supported as effective. The focus of this chapter is on one such treatment modality, cognitive behavior therapy (CBT). CBT (along with many other prominent therapeutic modalities such as psychodynamic, behavioral, humanistic, existential, and family systems) was first conceived and validated in the treatment of White, middle-class, and educated clients, with little to no consideration of the diversity of client characteristics with regards to race/ethnicity, nationality, gender, sexual orientation, age, religion/spirituality, or disability (Friedman, Paradis, & Hatch, 1994, p. 144; Hays, 1995).

However, research also suggests that CBT may be "applied successfully to people of various ethnic, racial, or socioeconomic backgrounds" with appropriate adaptations, as well (Friedman et al., 1994, p. 144), though studies in this area are scant. The field of cognitive behavior therapy acknowledges that it needs to continue to build its cultural competence. As treatment providers of diverse populations who have a particular awareness and focus on cultural responsiveness, it is important for social workers to be able to apply CBT with cultural proficiency and develop original strategies within the context of the client's culture.

This chapter reviews relevant theoretical frameworks, existent empirical studies on CBT with diverse cultural groups, strengths and limitations of this modality across cultures, and suggestions for culturally responsive CBT practice, in order to better inform social work practice.

Imagine the following scenarios:

You are a social worker, and have recently been contacted about a new client that has an appointment with you.

The client is a 28 year old female.

She has three children; two girls and a boy.

She presents with what appear to be obsessive compulsive disorder (OCD) symptoms such as "contamination" worries and excessive concerns around her son being harmed.

She is an Orthodox Jew.

What other information would you seek?

Study the picture in your mind.

Clear it.

You have another new client.
   The client is a 28 year old male.
   He has three children; two girls and a boy.
   He presents with what appear to be obsessive compulsive disorder symptoms such as "contamination" worries and excessive concerns around his son being harmed.
   He is an African American.
   What other information would you seek?

Study the picture in your mind.

Ask yourself, is the cultural background of the client relevant to cognitive behavioral therapy? What may be the potential impact of culturally relevant factors on cognitive behavioral treatment for OCD (and/or other disorders)?

THE QUESTION OF UNIVERSALITY

The movement toward multiculturalism, cultural understanding, and so on called into question the generalizability and universality of theory and practice methods. The majority of psychological theory was based on "universal assumptions," which emphasized group similarities and minimized culturally based differences, by applying virtually the same "methods, constructs, measures, and treatments across cultural groups" (Vera et al., 2003, p. 2). On the other extreme, particularists emphasize individual differences and experiences, discounting the value of generalizations (Vera et al., 2003). Neither really addresses the "cultural context" of culturally diverse clientele (Falicov, 1998; Vera et al., 2003, p. 2). The culture-specific perspective accentuates the client's cultural characteristics related to race, ethnicity, gender, but may overemphasize such factors leading to homogenizing and/or stereotyping (see Vera et al., 2003).

   The multidimensional ecosystemic comparative approach integrates these three perspectives by promoting the universal perspective regarding human similarities that unify people (etic characteristics), respecting cultural differences inherent to the culture specific perspective (emic characteristics), and also considering the individual experience of each client through the particularist perspective (Vera et al., 2003). This approach emphasizes three main components: (1) the multiple contexts around language, ethnicity, gender, religion, socioeconomic status . . . that compose a culture, (2) the individual's ecological field including his or her experiences interacting with his or her environment (i.e., discrimination, support system), and (3) the importance of similarities and differences in the contexts and experiences between a clinician and client (Vera et al., 2003).

CBT AND CULTURE

While cognitive behavior therapy was developed with universal assumptions and without consideration to the diversity of the cultural contexts of consumers, it is grounded in theory that is likely to have "some universal basis across populations" (Hansen, Zamboanga, & Sedlar, 2000, p. 56). Contemporary CBT methods have been described as heterogeneous in approach; meanwhile the field is said to still be growing and maturing (Dobson & Shaw, 1995). The literature is still limited, yet there is a growing amount of research exploring CBT with clients of various cultural backgrounds that traditionally have not been included in CBT research. Research spans a number of CBT skill areas and contexts (e.g., schools) as well. The following section identifies numerous studies; while it is comprehensive, it is not all-inclusive.

Race/Ethnicity

There are a number of studies that examine CBT with specific non-White racial and ethnic groups. Several studies present cases including a Native American female child with selective mutism (Conrad, Delk, & Williams, 1974), a 17-year-old Indian male with Dhat Syndrome (Raj, Prasadarao, & Raguram, 1998), a Portuguese woman with anxiety (Diaz-Martinez, 2003), and an Asian Indian male with a driving phobia (Brink, 2003). Additionally, a number of studies support the use of CBT with clientele of diverse cultural backgrounds with anxiety and depression symptoms. Some of these studies include older Chinese Americans with minor symptoms of depression (Dai, et al., 1999), Cambodian refugees with posttraumatic stress disorder (PTSD) (Otto, et al., 2003), an ethnically diverse sample with panic disorder (Sanderson, Raue, & Wetzler, 1998), group therapy with African American women with panic disorder (Carter, et al., 2003), exposure response prevention (ERP) with Hispanic/Latinos youth with phobic and anxiety disorders (Pina, et al., 2003), group treatment with Puerto Rican women with depressive symptoms (Comas-Díaz, 1981), and in vivo exposure with African Americans with agoraphobia (Chambless & Williams, 1995). Other studies discuss specific CBT skills with particular racial/ethnic groups, such as social skills training (including bicultural competence skills); assertiveness with Native Americans (LaFromboise & Rowe, 1983) and other ethnic minority clients (Wood & Mallinckrodt, 1990); parenting skills for Mexican American adolescents who are pregnant or parents (Harris & Franklin, 2003). Still other research addresses particular cultural influences on CBT such as the influence of Chinese culture on rational emotive therapy (RET) (Chen, 1995) or biculturalism among Hispanic CBT clients (Valdez, 2000).

Income

A number of studies have also examined CBT with clients of lower income levels. These include a pilot study investigating CBT for depression with low-income minority clients (Satterfield, 1998; 2002), a randomized CBT control trial including depressed young minority women (Miranda et al., 2003), and a randomized CBT depression prevention intervention with low-income single mothers (Peden, Rayens, & Hall, 2005). Other studies show positive effects of using culturally responsive CBT with depressed low-income African American women (Kohn, Oden, & Muñoz, 2002) and depressed Latino primary care patients (Organista & Dwyer, 1996).

Gender

Gender and feminist (Kantrowitz & Ballou, 1992) issues in CBT practice are addressed in a number of research studies and theoretical pieces. Davis and Padesky (1989) review specific content areas that may be particularly relevant to cognitive therapy with women (e.g., physical and social experiences, parenting) while O'Kelly (2002) examines how CBT promotes women's health. Another study focuses on issues specifically relevant to men in cognitive therapy (CT) (Mahalik, 2005). Research has also been done on gender issues related to specific CBT skills such as assertiveness and social skills training (Gambrill & Richey, 1983; 1986).

Sexual Orientation

Several book chapters focus on CBT with gay, lesbian, and bisexual adults (Kuehlwein, 1992; Wolfe, 1992) and couples (Martell & Land, 2002). Case examples of gay, lesbian and/or bisexual youth (Safren, Hollander, Hart, & Heimberg, 2001), and adults (Safren & Rogers, 2001; Wolfe, 1992), discuss how CBT may be helpful to issues concerning "coming out" and same-sex sexuality.

Spirituality/Religion

Religion and spirituality has also been integrated with CBT. Case studies include discussion of religiously sensitive (Nielsen, Ridley, & Johnson, 2000) and spiritually oriented (Tan & Johnson, 2005) CBT practice. Specifically the use of rational emotive therapy has been examined with religious Christian clients (Ivey, Ivey, & Simek-Morgan, 1993; Johnson & Ridley, 1992; Robb, 2002).

Age

Furthermore, studies discuss CBT treatment issues with older people (Zeiss & Steffen, 1996) and common concerns among this population (e.g., death, reduced abilities and independence) to be incorporated into CT. A number of case studies also illustrate specific clinical problems and considerations for CBT practice with older adults (Silven & Gallagher, 1987; Thompson, Davies, & Gallagher, 1986) including the chronically ill (Rybarczyk, Gallagher-Thompson, & Rodman, 1992). Cognitive therapy for older people with depression (David & Gallagher-Thompson, 2001) has also been examined. Another study combined operant and cognitive therapy in treating older clients (Hussian, 1983). Additionally, CBT has also been shown to be effective with children and adolescents with anxiety, depression, aggression, and attention deficit hyperactivity conditions (Kendall, 1993; Werry & Wollersheim, 1989).

Physical Disability

Finally, numerous studies demonstrate support for CBT with people with physical disabilities to address social-emotional issues (Sweetland, 1990) and loneliness (Hopps, Pepin, & Boisvert, 2003). Studies demonstrate benefits of rational emotive behavior therapy (REBT) (Yankura & Dryden, 1997) and problem-solving skills (Frieden & Cole, 1984). Some include individual case studies (Yankura & Dryden, 1997) or protocols including patient samples with conditions like chronic pain (Skinner, Erskine, & Pearce, 1990).

Many of the studies noted are case studies, preliminary studies, or theoretical and educational pieces of work in contrast to random clinical trials. More studies are needed to test the efficacy and effectiveness of CBT with persons of diverse backgrounds.

WHAT ARE SOME OF THE STRENGTHS OF CBT IN ITS APPLICATION ACROSS CULTURES?

CBT has a number of strengths that may make it useful across diverse populations. CBT is a goal-oriented, skill-based, and time-limited therapy that focuses on conscious processes and specific behavior changes. Fitting with social work theory, CBT aims to empower the client to gain control over his own thoughts, behaviors, and feelings and modify them (Dobson & Block, 1988) in order to improve functioning, mood, and/or some other symptoms. Strategies are personalized to the client's specific circumstances, considering contextual factors (Hays, 1995). CBT is also considerate of time and cost of treatment (Hays, 1995).

A critical aspect of CBT is its ongoing collaborative and inclusive focus. This method places significant value on the client's viewpoints and outlook. It emphasizes continuous assessment and documentation throughout the therapeutic process of events, behaviors, and so on, including various measures, such as the client's own account, information from family, significant others, or teachers (Hansen et al., 2000). Other outcome and symptom scales may be used in combination. These recurrent assessments of specific behaviors and events also provide an opportunity to consider and incorporate the client's cultural context and experiences and reduce potential for bias (a specific assessment type called functional analyses, which will be discussed again later in the section on culturally responsive practice). This may include one's "broader culture of origin, [cultural] identification, the more immediate family and community cultures, as well as other influential 'cultures' (i.e., peer culture)" (Hansen et al., 2000, p. 56). Its specificity in focus as compared to therapies based on more abstract theory (Casas, 1988) may reduce cultural misunderstanding between clinician and client in the therapeutic process, strengthening the therapeutic alliance. CBT was ranked the least likely to be culturally biased among the treatment assessment approaches (Paniagua, 1998).

A client's culture may affect whether treatment methods are a good fit and accepted by the individual (e.g., Kazdin, 1980; Hansen et al., 2000). It appears that this approach may be compatible with the cultural beliefs, preferences, and expectations of some ethnic minority groups about therapy (Hansen et al., 2000; Paniagua, 1998). Clients may prefer skill-based and tool-oriented therapies that encourage acquiring healthy coping methods in contrast to methods that emphasize insight and resolving particular problems (Thompson, Bazile, & Akbar, 2004).

Finally, CBT techniques support methodological theories of scientific method, and evidence-based practice.

WHAT ARE SOME OF THE LIMITATIONS OF CBT IN ITS APPLICATION ACROSS CULTURES?

There are some limitations to the application of CBT across diverse populations. Although the CBT approach may consider the cultural context of the client, it has been critiqued for being subtly biased (Hays, 1995, p. 311) toward White American middle-class "mainstream" values (i.e., futuristic orientation) and emphasizing adaptation to the environment

(Casas, 1995). Such an approach may seem to buttress the status quo and insufficiently acknowledge the negative impact of societal injustices and oppression, while placing the burden of change on the individual. Thus, the degree to which diverse perspectives and worldviews are included in CB treatment can be quite variable, and may depend of the therapist's sensitivity and cultural competence (Hays, 1995), therapeutic alliance, issues of trust/mistrust, and so on. Another critique of CBT is that it places less emphasis on the client's history than other psychotherapy methods. This method is more oriented toward future goals; viewing time in a linear fashion that is also associated with values of "White American middle class" (Casas, 1995; Vera et al., 2003). Additionally, there is concern around assessment measures used to monitor outcomes and symptoms utilized in CBT methods being valid and reliable for treating clients of diverse backgrounds (Hays, 1995; Vera et al., 2003). Finally, CBT's underpinnings are linked to the "rational thinking," "scientific method," and evidence-based practice that may be value-laden as well (Hays, 1995, p. 311). CBT's empirical support is predominantly based on research of White middle-class clients.

(Mis)perceptions of CBT

The literature speaks to some misperceptions and distrust of CBT methods in communities of color (Neal-Barnett, 2003). Behavior therapy has been erroneously confused with behavior modification, which has negative associations because it was applied inappropriately to limit the freedoms of persons in prisons during the 1960s. In contrast, CBT is more collaborative, whereby the client has the "freedom of choice" and is not coercive. Misperceptions and stigma inhibit persons from seeking mental health services (Neal-Barnett, 2003).

Such strengths, limitations, and (mis)perceptions point to complexities in the therapeutic process, underscore the influence of sociocultural factors (e.g., therapeutic alliance, stigma, finances, etc.) and highlight aspects of CBT strategies that may be modified to improve cultural responsiveness.

SOCIOCULTURAL FACTORS AFFECTING CBT TREATMENT

Sociocultural factors are highly relevant to the field of cognitive behavioral practice and the social workers who work with these methods. How sociocultural factors interact with the mental disorder (Smith, Friedman,

& Nevid, 1999) affects presentation, response to treatment, outcomes, and so on. Mental disorders may not manifest uniformly across all patient populations, despite the existence of formal diagnostic criteria (Renfrey, 1992). The diagnostic criteria cited in the Diagnostic Statistical Manual (*DSM-IV-TR*; APA, 2000) were developed with mostly White, middle-class, heterosexual males. A client's clinical presentation of some mental health condition may include or exclude "classical" diagnostic symptoms of a disorder, and the nature and number of those symptoms may vary across cultures. For example, African Americans experience a greater number of symptoms (8.0) during panic attacks as compared to Whites (6.9) (Horwath, Johnson, & Hornig, 1993). Tingling feet or fingers and hot and cold flashes were reported significantly more frequently by African Americans as compared to Whites, even when controlling for socioeconomic status (SES) (Horwath, Johnson, & Hornig, 1993). Additionally, depressed African American patients tend to present with more somatic complaints while depressed White patients endorse cognitive disturbances and depressed mood (Raskin, Crook, & Herman, 1975; Simon, 1973). Asian patients are also more likely to present with somatic or physical complaints in contrast to psychological symptoms (Leong, 1986). Furthermore, pediatric depression can be expressed as irritability, in contrast to low or sad mood (Dulcan & Martini, 1999). Psychiatric symptoms may be expressed variably across cultures and thus may be misinterpreted, misdiagnosed, and/or treated with inappropriate intervention methods. Reasonable behaviors may also be misperceived as evidence of mental illness, when none is present. *For Example:* A 23-year-old African American male presents to you for treatment. He responds to your questions with brief one to two word responses. His voice is barely audible. He avoids eye contact. He does not display much affect. These behaviors initially appear to evidence mistrust and suspiciousness.

These symptoms may be a form of cultural suspiciousness, yet may be misinterpreted by a clinician as a sign of paranoia. Thus, the behaviors may be unremarkable as evidence for depression; however, if the influence of culture is not considered a clinician may erroneously treat them as psychosis (Whaley, 1997, p. 16). This example demonstrates how sociocultural factors may interact with clinical presentation.

Given that CBT is a symptom-focused and skill-based therapy, it is of critical importance that clinicians heed the clinical presentations and understand them within the client's cultural context. Understanding the norms and rules that govern the client's behavior also can help determine whether behavior is outside the bounds of healthy and appropriate behavior, expose cultural variations in symptom expression, and inform cognitive behavioral treatment. For example, it is critical to understand the cultural factors associated with verbal and nonverbal communication (e.g., personal space, facial expression, gestures, eye contact, voice), when working on social skill building, as will be discussed in more detail later in the chapter.

Additionally, sociocultural factors may affect the type of problems for which mental services are sought, and therefore the focus of the CBT treatment. For example, African American men are more likely to seek services because of the death of a spouse or close friend or relative (Neighbors, 1988). Additionally, persons of color, gay and lesbians, may also present with problems around discrimination. It is key that clinicians initiate conversations about experiences of discrimination with the "supposition" that the client has been discriminated against and emphasize the importance of comprehending the process of discrimination (McNair, 1996, p. 344). This would include discussing what occurred, who else was involved, and what were the client's responses (McNair, 1996, p. 344). This may help to determine whether the client's rights have been violated, their cognitive and affective tendencies (i.e., internalization and externalization), and their coping abilities (McNair, 1996).

Again, one must be mindful of heterogeneity within cultural groups as well, and how "germane" are issues to each client of a particular category. As Renfrey (1992) stated, members of cultures (i.e., Native Americans) "are not members of a common culture, [but] represent a "diverse cultural collage" (Renfrey, 1992, p. 328). As another example, persons with diverse sexual orientations, may or may not identify with the gay/lesbian community, and may be of various ethnic, racial, religious, spiritual, socioeconomic backgrounds (Purcell et al., 1996).

The next section on culturally responsive CBT practice will illustrate the significance of sociocultural factors, and attempt to address how to integrate such factors with CBT practice methods.

CULTURALLY RESPONSIVE CBT PRACTICE

Culturally responsive practice is for all clients, not just clients of marginalized or disadvantaged groups. The following discussion and suggestions are organized into several main aspects of practice: general structure and content (including assessment, plan, and treatment).

General Structure

As with any intervention, clients should be well informed of the type of treatment that they are receiving (in this case CBT). It is important to convey the purpose and general process of CBT, its relevance to the client's presenting problems, and time frame. It is also critical to emphasize that the client plays an active role in identifying and elucidating the problems, collaborating to develop the intervention plan, practicing methods with therapist's assistance and through individual between-session assignments (Hays, 1995; Thompson et al., 1986).

Various methods may facilitate clients' engagement and involvement in the therapeutic process. Some methods may be more or less helpful or appropriate to clients with specific characteristics than others. Audiotaping sessions, taking notes, and requesting that the client summarize the session at the end of session to review and clarify the information can be helpful especially with older clients (Hays, 1995; Silven & Gallagher, 1987) and persons with limited English proficiency. Framing CBT sessions as classes may reduce concerns around stigma (Gallagher & Thompson, 1983). Technical language and lingo associated with CBT may confuse, intimidate, or offend clients so it's more effective to use language that is simple, direct, and understandable for all; for example, "unhelpful thoughts," instead of "cognitive distortions" or negative thoughts in contrast to irrational thoughts (Gallagher & Thompson, 1983; Hays, 1995, p. 312; Thompson et al., 2004).

Integrating a number of other general cultural elements may demonstrate a CBT therapist's competence, sensitivity, and responsiveness as well as enhance client adherence and satisfaction. While findings are inconclusive regarding the importance of cultural matching (e.g., gender, ethnicity, sexual orientation) between clinicians and clients (Chambless & Williams, 1995; Jenkins-Hall & Sacco, 1991; Sue, 1988; Sue, Fujino, Hu, Takenchi, & Zane, 1991), a multicultural and multilingual mental health services staff may demonstrate a more culturally responsive and inviting environment (Satterfield, 1998). Reading materials, artwork, or furnishings that depict persons or elements reflecting diverse cultures may offer more appeal and awareness as well (Satterfield, 1998). Additionally, sensitive use of language related to sociodemographic descriptors is important (e.g., "Black" may be preferable to "African American," "gay man" and "lesbian" may be preferable to "homosexual") (Purcell et al., 1996). Genderless language (e.g., partner, significant other versus boyfriend, girlfriend) may also demonstrate cultural competence. Clinicians may refrain from greeting an individual with a handshake and/or may leave the office door slightly ajar, when interacting with a client of the opposite sex who ascribes to particular cultural observances (e.g., Orthodox Judaism, Islam) (Margolese, 1998).

Certain services such as intake may be performed in the client's home, which may serve as an interpersonal bridge. Other suggested strategies include reminder phone calls the night before to problem solve potential transportation issues, or other barriers to attendance, more lenience regarding "no shows," with a follow-up letter or phone call, and contact with case managers and/or primary care health providers (Satter-field, 1998).

Besides structural improvements, there are a number of content specific changes that may be made to make CBT more culturally responsive.

Content (Culturally Responsive Practice)

Assessment:

Although CBT is a skill-based intervention, it is critical that assessments go beyond discrete behaviors and identify and examine potential contextual factors and "environmental contingencies" (Fudge, 1996, p. 332) that might facilitate and/or inhibit CBT skill acquisition, utilization, and motivation (Bhugra & Bhui, 1998). "Culture reflects the overarching context within which learning takes place for members of a given community" (McNair, 1996, p. 338). As mentioned earlier, evaluating client's problems within their sociocultural context has been referred to as a "functional analysis" (in Hansen et al., 2000, p. 56; see Tanaka-Matsumi, Seiden, & Lam, 1996) and may include numerous measures, methods, and sources of information (e.g., family, peers).

Clients arrive at mental health professionals' (i.e., social workers') offices through many different paths of health care utilization, which may or may not be voluntary. It is essential to understand how persons arrived at your office, how they feel about it, and who, if anyone, made the referral and/or did the client consult with prior to their visit with you. Clinicians may "learn what the client has already tried in her or his attempts to solve the problem, what has worked and what has not worked, what conditions (intrapersonal, interpersonal, and environmental) might be reinforcing and maintaining the problem, and what consequences result from the particular strategies being used" (from Hays, 1995, p. 312). Assessing client's attitudes about mental health services and concerns regarding stigma are likely to impact treatment engagement and improve the cultural responsiveness of clinicians, as well (Hansen et al., 2000).

During the initial cognitive behavioral assessment, it is critical for clinicians to explore and observe cultural factors affecting the client's life including details of his/her interaction with the environment, norms, values, beliefs, strengths, coping strategies, connection to cultural group(s), and so on, in order to be more culturally responsive. The client's environment may include their living conditions and acute and chronic stressors (Hansen et al., 2000) around poverty, racism, sexism, homophobia/heterosexism (Kuehlwein, 1992, p. 249). Lesbians and gays (Herek & Berrill, 1992; from Purcell et al., 1996) and members of other specific cultural groups are more likely to be victims of trauma and violence

(Snowden, 1999). Other negative life events such as incarceration, substance abuse, divorce, parental loss are more common among specific racial/ethnic groups of color and low-income persons (Smith et al., 1999). Acute and chronic stressors may also include acculturative stress (Smith et al., 1999) and immigration (Diaz-Martinez, 2003). These stressors and cultural adjustments may be assessed by evaluating migration history and recentness, language abilities and preferences, acculturation, ethnic-racial identity, perceived group status, family and community relationships and influence, relationships with people of different cultural backgrounds, most recent involvement in traditional versus nontraditional religious/ spiritual affiliations, ceremonials, and other cultural commitments, sociographic location, and degree of formal education (Alvidrez et al., 1996; Hall, 2001, p. 504; Renfrey, 1992, p. 334). Thus, the assessment process should not exclusively focus on helping the client simply adjust to his or her conditions, but instead examine social and political factors relevant to the client's distress (McNair, 1996).

Being a member of a specific group may suggest that the individual possesses particular cultural values and traditions, but not necessarily (McNair, 1996). Determining how clients identify culturally during the assessment process may preclude erroneous assumptions, prompt more client disclosure, and convey the clinician's openness. Some clinicians may be uncomfortable addressing cultural identity issues directly due to concerns of incompetence or offensiveness. Cardemil and Battle (2003) recommend neutral questioning such as "How do you identify your racial or ethnic background?" Clients may vary in their comfort level in discussing identity issues with the therapist; thus, demonstrating respect for whatever level of disclosure may strengthen the therapeutic alliance, as well.

The client's own strengths and assets including coping strategies, problem-solving capacity, and ability to manage stress are very important to identify during assessment (Lum, 1996, p. 228). For example, if an individual is spiritual or religious, then this might be considered a strength and be incorporated into his/her coping strategies (McNair, 1996). Identifying and accessing community-based resources and other positive social networks may be of great benefit as well (Lum, 1996).

Developing, validating, and using culturally competent assessment instruments and scales with diverse populations may improve assessments and enhance culturally responsive practice. Several studies have included culturally specific components in their assessment processes. One study incorporated an engagement interview including an ethnographic and a psycho-education interview, in-between sessions phone calls, and assistance in accessing social services into an Interpersonal Therapy (IPT) protocol (Grote, Bledsoe, & Swartz, 2004). The engagement interview used in this study explored "clients perceptions of their conditions, social problems and stressors, practical and psychological barriers associated with obtaining care, attitudes toward mental health services, including perceptions of institutional racism; treatment desires beliefs and practices related to health, including the importance of spirituality and prayer in her life" (Grote et al., 2004, p. 399). Positive results were found for adherence and patient satisfaction. Such methods may be applied with CBT protocols, as well.

Finally, clinicians may consider the benefits and importance examining their own cultural history (e.g., their own ethnocultural assessment) (Diaz-Martinez, 2003), as well. This is likely to help clinicians gain insight into and awareness of their own biases, beliefs, and stereotypes (McCarthy, 1988; Bhugra & Bhui, 1998, p. 318). Clinicians need to be aware of and monitor their cultural assumptions and reactions. As described by Sue (1988, 1998), cultural misunderstandings may occur when a clinician and patient's styles of verbal and nonverbal communication "including proxemics (perception of personal and interpersonal space), kinesics (facial expressions, posture, movement, gestures, eye contact), and paralanguage (vocal cues such as loudness of voice, use of silence and pauses)" (from Cardemil & Battle, 2003, p. 281; Renfrey, 1992) differ and are misinterpreted. For example, members of some cultures (e.g., Mexican, Japanese) avoid eye contact to show respect, however, a White therapist may misperceive this as an indication of mistrust, timidness, or low mood (from Cardemil & Battle, 2003). Members of some ethnic/racial groups are also more accustomed to less personal space (e.g., African Americans, Hispanic/Latinos) and may be offended if a White therapist who is used to more physical interpersonal space appears to retreat inadvertently (from Cardemil & Battle, 2003). As described by Dwairy and Van Sickle (1996), cultural misunderstandings may occur between a Western trained psychotherapist and Arabic clients, due to contrasting styles related to eye contact, concepts around time, verbal communication, openness, and self-disclosure.

Treatment Plan:

Information gleaned from the assessment phase may be integrated into the CBT planning and treatment phases, in a culturally responsive manner. The relationship between the diagnosis(es) and intervention plans are to be explained in a straightforward, comprehensible, and sensitive manner. An explicit treatment contract including therapeutic goals, rationale and benefits, time frame with specified ending date or review dates, and treatment outline or manual is helpful to clarify expectations and services to be delivered (Satterfield, 1998).

It is important that treatment maintains a strength-based approach as compared to a deficiency-based orientation. CBT treatments may improve stress tolerance and management, coping, and support. Specific self-monitoring methods such as logging and recording narratives, commonly practiced in CBT, generate information that clinicians and clients may draw from as they collaborate to choose "social" and "physical" stimuli (Hansen et al., 2000, p. 59). Clinicians and clients are to work together to choose stimuli that are culturally relevant and appropriate and incorporate individuals that are part of the persons social network (e.g., family, peers) into treatment to address enablement, social support, and enhance skill development (from Stokes & Osnes, 1989; Hansen et al., 2000). When including others, attempts should be made to select people that the client can relate and/or identify with. In working with some cultures whereby the family is more "hierarchical" and "authoritarian" (e.g., traditional Arab culture), family support may be more critical to therapeutic success (Dwairy & Von Sickle, 1996, p. 244). Additionally, other "self-mediated physical and verbal stimuli (e.g., self-instruction, problem-solving strategies)" (Hansen et al., 2000, p. 59) may be integrated into treatment, as well. The application of such stimuli and contextual influences may be beneficial in augmenting the "generalization and maintenance of treatment" (Hansen et al., 2000, p. 60).

When clinician and client define problems and goals, it's critical to consider the behavior within the norms of the client's culture and the dominant culture (if they differ) and take into account implications for targeting and/or modifying a specific behavior and cognition in both contexts (Hays, 1995; Tanaka-Matsumi & Higginbotham, 1989). For example, assertiveness, or talking out conflicts could be dangerous in some environmental conditions . . . Additionally, examining thoughts to identify distortions and modify them should also be done within the context of the expectations of the client's culture(s) (Diaz-Martinez, 2003). The inclusion of values, beliefs, and cultural narratives in the therapeutic process allows for a degree of cultural specificity that can increase the effectiveness of treatment with [various social groups including] Hispanics, the poor and other minorities" (Inclan & Hernandez, 1992, p. 252). In this collaborative treatment process, the clinician's role is a consulting expert and guide, helping the client expand his/her skill set (i.e., coping strategies) and contextualizing how client behaviors may be interpreted by the dominant culture (Hays, 1995; Wood & Mallinckrodt, 1990). For example, in some cultures, staring may be an indication of flattery and admiration; in other cultures it may be interpreted as rude, intimidating, and aggressive. However, the client has ultimate choice and control, making determinations as to "which behaviors and when and where to use them" (Hays, 1995, p. 313; Wood & Mallinckrodt, 1990).

Thus, therapists must familiarize themselves with the client's culture, including beliefs, practices. Social workers may avail themselves of numerous resources including books, film, lectures, or community events. Active clarification is critical. Therapists may utilize phrases such as: "What is it that you mean by that?" "Please help me to understand," or "Please explain this to me" (Dwairy & Van Sickle, 1996, p. 245). Such clarification enhances consideration of "individual client variability" (Hall, 2001, p. 503).

Due to the complexities inherent to the therapeutic process, it may be best to begin with CBT methods for general stress management such as deep breathing and progressive muscle relaxation, to give time for the development of rapport while improving symptom management (Diaz-Martinez, 2003). Additionally, motivational techniques are important to use early on, in order to engage the individual and build therapeutic alliance and trust (Thompson et al., 2004).

It is essential to allow for some modifications and moderate flexibility in the completion of behavioral tasks; however, too much flexibility may be interpreted as disinterest, incompetence, and or internalized as an indication of the clinician's lack of confidence in the client (Bhugra and Bhui, 1998). Bhugra and Bhui (1998) cite deadlines as an example that could be viewed as "intrusive and pushy" if enforced too severely. The client is to be involved in his/her own "self-instruction, self-monitoring, and problem-solving strategies" (Hansen et al., 2000, p. 59). Several studies have also shown that adding a group component to the treatment protocol may be particularly helpful (Freidman, Paradis, & Hatch, 1994; Wolfe, 1992).

Finally, it is critical that traditional methods of healing are treated with respect and not condemned (Dwairy & van Sickle, 1996). Social workers and clients may work together to integrate scientific methods such as CBT and traditional interventions (Renfrey, 1992, p. 332). However, when combining natural healing methods and psychotropic medications may be harmful, it should be addressed sensitively and earnestly.

CULTURAL ISSUES AND SPECIFIC CBT SKILLS

For the most part "Euro-American norms and values have dominated CBT practice" (Hays, 1995, p. 313). The following sections describe culture-based modifications to CBT and cultural issues affecting particular CBT skills. Not all adaptations and strategies will be appropriate or fitting to the individual client, with their diverse strengths and weaknesses (Zeiss & Steffen, 1996). CBT skills also may be developed within the context of the client's life context, with specific considerations, adaptations, and modifications to better fit their diverse needs.

Because of space limitations, only several broad categories of social groups (i.e., religious/spiritual, age, gay/lesbian clients) and CBT skills (i.e., social skills training, behavior management parent training, exposure/response prevention) will be addressed here. This section serves to demonstrate a few of the numerous ways culture may be integrated into CBT and how CBT can be shaped by culture from the "bottom up" and "top down."

CBT Modifications With Religious/Spiritual Clients

Religious or spiritual faith may be incorporated into CBT methods. CBT interventions may include religious/spiritual elements including prayer, scriptures, meditations, psalms, quotations, song, and so on. Beliefs and behaviors may be significantly influenced by religious/spiritual beliefs and rules, and become part of one's schema. A client's repertoire of coping strategies may include prayer, song, rehearsal of religious readings, requests to a higher power or religious figure for strength in addressing problematic thoughts and behaviors, as a few examples. Additionally, negative automatic (or irrational) thoughts may be challenged with evidence from scriptures, which may provide a standard of "truth" (Johnson & Ridley, 1992, p. 225; Hays, 1995, p. 312). Such treatments have been adopted for Christian clients (Johnson & Ridley, 1992, p. 225; Hays, 1995, p. 312). Additionally, a therapist may suggest to a religious or spiritual client who engages in prayer to include particular concerns and issues in their prayer (McNair, 1996, p. 345). By doing so, "the therapist validates his/her religious perspective, and gives the client the opportunity to reflect on the issue at hand" (McNair, 1996, p. 345). Prayer may be an alternative to the written prose, in order to explore thoughts and feelings and find the answer within (McNair, 1996, p. 345). The clinician may share the client's religious or spiritual beliefs and/or background, but it is not necessary for the clinician to pray with the client. Such expectations should be discussed to preclude potential misunderstandings. Collaborations with members and/or leaders of the same religious community may be valuable as well.

CBT Modifications With Older Adults

"Because learning is seen as a lifelong process in the philosophical underpinnings of CB therapy, it is expected that therapy can be helpful for people of any age" (Zeiss & Steffen, 1996, p. 372). However, older clients may have reservations about receiving mental health care for concerns of being perceived as "old and useless" or "mentally incompetent" (Zeiss & Steffen, 1996, pp. 379–380). Therefore, the more collaborative approach of CBT may be especially helpful with engaging this population. Sessions may be framed as "classes" to reduce stigma. The distinction between mental health and physical health problems may need to be clarified. Materials may be presented at a slower pace, with the treatment goals, process, and distinction between mental health and physical health clearly defined and elucidated (Zeiss & Steffen, 1996, p. 377).

Several CBT adaptations methods can be considered when working with older adults. First, older clients have a lot of life experience, which is valuable and needs to be respected and solicited. They are likely to have lived in multiple contexts and recognize how complex and indeterminate life can be. Such experiences and challenges may impart wisdom, personal skills, and factual knowledge. Older clients may have achieved more extensive self-knowledge so that they may be better able to identify their strengths and how such strengths have been helpful in the past and may be applied to some current therapeutic objective (Zeiss & Steffen, 1996, pp. 376–377). Specific issues such as "limited financial resources and transportation, grief and loss, health problems which may affect cognitive status and cognitive capacities, and caregiving for demented loved ones" (Zeiss & Steffen, 1996, p. 378) may be particularly relevant to older clients.

Using multimodalities ("say it, show it, do it") can be helpful to surmount any losses in sensory functioning while the repetition may facilitate memory encoding and storage (Zeiss & Steffen, 1996, p. 376). Because memory difficulties may also inhibit generalization, skills must be presented repetitively in multiple contexts. Other memory aids may include tapes from sessions, printed handouts, folders, and notebooks for assignments and therapy materials, and the verbal confirmation of the key points and assignments at the conclusion of a session. To assist older clients to stay focused on the session topics, social workers may need to redirect conversation or gently remind clients of the focal point of the discussion.

Zeiss and Steffen (1996) refer to the mnemonic MICKS (Multimodal Interdisciplinary awareness, Clearer, Knowledge of aging challenges and strengths, Slower) to capture these specific principles for adapting CBT to older adults (p. 379). Finally, CBT may be a good fit for older adults, because it is relatively easy to adapt to individual developmental changes, and is time-limited, which may also make it more economically feasible (Zeiss & Steffen, 1996, p. 380).

CBT Modifications With Gay and Lesbian Clients

Several studies have described the use of cognitive behavior methods with gay and lesbian clients, particularly the use of rational emotive therapy, cognitive restructuring, and behavior experiments. Such methods may be used to address dysfunctional cognitive schema and thoughts such as internalized homophobia, anger and depressive responses to societal oppression and discrimination, and/or issues and emotions surrounding the "coming out" process, as depicted in several case studies (Kuehlwein, 1992; Safren & Rogers, 2001; Wolfe, 1992).

Rational emotive therapy (RET) has been described as "a pioneering cognitive-behavioral therapy," which emphasizes the identification of "client's dogmatic, unconditional musts and differentiating them from mere preferences" (Wolfe, 1992, p. 258). Cognitive distortions—such as, people's "shoulds" (i.e., "the demands for approval, success, fair treatment, and comfort")—may trigger " 'awfulizing' about what one needs," "I can't stand it"—like responses, and condemning behavior of others and/or the self, causing emotional difficulties (p. 258). RET applies the ABC model, to examine and explicitly identify activating events and the connection between irrational beliefs and emotional consequences related to ego anxiety (arising from fear of failure and rejection) and discomfort anxiety (which involves fear of fear and fear of discomfort) (Wolfe, 1992, p. 258). By doing so, the client gains skills in problem solving to resolve unconstructive behaviors and negative emotions (e.g., anxiety depression, anger). Such strategies may assist a lesbian/gay client who is dealing with discrimination and rejection from societal and/or family and significant others, due to his sexual orientation.

Mental health professionals may also collaborate with their lesbian/gay clients who are struggling with internalized homophobia (or internalized "heterosexism"), by using cognitive restructuring methods in combination with behavioral tests and exposure response methods (Kuehlwein, 1992; Safren & Rogers, 2001). Internalized homophobia is a "conditioned negative emotional response to lesbians and gay men," which likely occurs among lesbians and gay clients, as well, causing psychological distress (Purcell et al., 1996, p. 402). Some helpful techniques may include exploring origins of heterosexist beliefs (i.e., where they gleaned them from, at what age, the meaning of being gay/lesbian according to prominent figures in client's life). Additionally, free associations about homosexuality and heterosexuality may reveal assumptions; generating various levels of evidence in favor and against these ideas may uncover the client's possible distortions in what it may be to be gay/lesbian (Kuehlwein, 1992). Cognitive restructuring and behavioral experiments are helpful techniques for testing automatic negative thoughts and assumptions, gathering evidence to counter such thoughts, and developing effective and constructive methods of coping (Safren & Rogers, 2001).

Internalized heterosexism may be exacerbated by other mental health conditions such as social anxiety, as described in Safren and Rogers

(2001). CBT treatment for social anxiety with a gay or lesbian client with internalized heterosexism includes development of a fear hierarchy, cognitive restructuring, role playing, and exposure exercises involving general and "gay-related" anxiety producing thoughts and situations (Safren & Rogers, 2001).

It is most important that the CBT focuses on cognitions that are relevant to the individual, to enhance its effectiveness and value. Mental health professionals must take heed not to overemphasize or downplay the role of sexual orientation in the client's problems (Safren & Rogers, 2001). Given that being a sexual minority can be isolating, clinicians should inquire about the social supports that may exist in their gay and lesbian clients' lives (Safren & Roger, 2001). Regardless, being gay, lesbian, transgender, or heterosexual should not be pathologized (and clinicians should remain sensitive to clients' concerns regarding clinical bias due to the pathologizing of "homosexuality" by the Diagnostic Statistical Manual ([DSM,] APA) in the recent past).

Additionally, CBT should not be used to change one's sexual orientation; this is likely to be very harmful (Safren & Rogers, 2001).

CULTURAL ISSUES AND SPECIFIC CBT SKILLS

Because cultural factors influence behavioral, cognitive, and affective outcomes it is essential that they be considered when applying particular CBT strategies. There are a great number of CBT skills including social skills and assertiveness training, relaxation training, parent behavior management training, cognitive restructuring, exposure/response prevention (ERP), exposure to external/situational cues, exposure to internal cues, and coping statements. This section discusses cultural issues and implications relevant to social skills and parent management training, and exposure/response prevention (ERP), specifically.

Social Skills and Parenting

The culture and environmental context must be considered when deciding which competencies to include in CBT skill development such as parent behavior management, social skills and assertiveness training. Life circumstances, the neighborhood, socioeconomic class, or race/ethnicity may influence the skills that are most needed and deemed appropriate. It will also influence which behaviors to target, "the shaping of behavioral contingencies," and the specific types of reinforcements and punishers (McNair, 1996, p. 339).

For instance, due to differences in environment, poor urban parents tend to value different "competencies" and behaviors than parents of higher socioeconomic position (Ogbu, 1985; Forehand & Kotchick, 1996, p. 193). Compliance tends to be stressed among persons who are underprivileged and faced with economic hardship, while independence and assertiveness are emphasized among persons with circumstances characterized as more affluent and stable (Forehand & Kotchick, 1996). Additionally, parenting styles may also reflect cultural and environmental disparities. African American parents, as compared to White parents, tend to adopt a more authoritarian approach, monitoring their children's activities and peer relationships more closely (Gilmore, Catalano, Morrison, Wells, Iritani, & Hawkins, 1990; Giordano, Cernkovich, & Demaris, 1993; Peterson, Hawkins, Abbott, & Catalano, 1994; Wallace & Muroff, 2002) and being more likely to use disciplinary measures such as physical punishment and emotional withdrawal (Forehand & Kotchick, 1996; McGoldrick, Giordano, & Pearce, 1996). African Americans tend to live in poorer and crime-ridden areas. Such parental practices may stem from strong parental concerns regarding children's well-being and beliefs that such practices will deter misbehavior and be protective (McGoldrick & Giordano, 1996). Consequently, African American parents may be more apprehensive about adopting specific types of behavioral management plans, for example, a rewards and privileges focused plan, for fear that their child would be less protected and more likely to get in harm's way (Himle, Fischer, & Muroff, 2004). Thus, clinicians and clients must collaborate to ensure that cultural and environmental factors are being considered.

Additionally, it is critical that clinicians and clients work together to determine which of the client's skills are maladaptive and adaptive, and which should be incorporated into CBT skills development. Therapists must also evaluate whether a client's behaviors might endanger the individual himself, given his environment. For example, social behavior that tends to provoke others ought to be targeted for change, in an environment characterized by violence (e.g., high crime neighborhood). Furthermore, social skills appropriate in mainstream culture may vary from social skills that are more culturally specific to the family, neighborhood, peer-group, individual's identity, and so on. Moreover, individuals are likely to have multiple characteristics with which they identify (e.g., being Latina and lesbian). Thus, the individual may need a range of social skills to effectively communicate and manage social expectations across various domains (Hays, 1995; LaFromboise & Rowe, 1983). Social skills training may integrate bi- or multicultural competencies (Renfrey, 1992) and help the individual balance and appropriately apply such skills that may contradict each other (Himle et al., 2004).

Finally, social supports are important to discern, because they may be helpful role models and motivators. Social supports may include a diverse network (e.g., family, friends, religion/spirituality, community). Clinicians should be familiar with their client's culturally specific social network characteristics and determine who (if anyone) resides in the same home with the client.

CASE STUDY

Jackie, a 10-year-old African American female came in with her mother presenting with difficulties with anger, low mood, suicidal thoughts, and family discord. She has always been a stellar student but her grades have begun to fall from straight As to Bs and Cs. Jackie notes that she is "not smart enough to keep up with the other kids."

Because of her mother's own mental health problems and financial difficulties, they had moved in recently with Jackie's grandmother. According to Jackie's mother, her grandmother indulges Jackie with clothing, toys, and is lax with whatever rules the mother tries to establish and reinforce. She feels that Jackie does not respect or obey her. Jackie's grandmother has been unwilling to attend a session with Jackie and her mother, since she "does not believe in therapy."

As noted earlier, it is important that the clinician explore contextual issues surrounding Jackie's mood and behavior. Clinician and client may examine specific episodes of low mood or anger that are likely to disclose several automatic thoughts and core beliefs, revealing potential cultural factors and environmental contingencies. For example, Jackie's negative automatic thoughts including "I'm not smart enough to keep up with the other kids" may reveal perceptions of discrimination, internalized racism, and negative ethnic identity and consciousness (Fudge, 1996; McNair, 1996).

Furthermore, a part of the intervention may include collaborating with Jackie, her mother, and grandmother to develop a behavioral contract to improve parental consistency and better manage Jackie's behavior. When formulating behavioral contracts to manage a child's behavior, in a home with numerous adults (e.g., mother, grandmother, cousin), it is recommended that the agreement specify who is the parental authority figure(s) (Himle et al., 2004). Too many "managers" may lead to inconsistent behavioral reinforcement. Additionally, behavioral reinforcements determined by the parent and child should be culturally relevant and motivating.

Finally, if Jackie's grandmother does not wish to attend the sessions, then the clinician may attempt to contact her by telephone, in order to gather more information. Framing the initial contact with the grandmother as an opportunity (for the social worker) to learn about the family environment and how she perceives her grandchild's behavior, is likely to lead to more valuable information to be incorporated into the intervention plan and help build rapport. The mutual goal is Jackie's well-being and that there be less family conflict. Social workers ought to be careful not to dispense too much advice during this first contact; but rather gather information. If the mother, grandmother, and Jackie each feel that their perspectives are being acknowledged and attended to, collaboration may be more feasible.

Exposure: Specific CBT Skills and Cultural Issues

Cultural factors may manifest in other CBT treatment methods, for example in vivo exposure exercises (Fink, Turner, & Beidel, 1996; Williams, Chambless, & Steketee, 1998). In vivo exposure (exposure to external/situational cues) is an effective CBT technique particularly when working with clients with anxiety disorders.

In vivo exposure activities may bring the clinician and client outside the office, to capture "real-live" anxiety-producing stimuli. Members of racial and ethnic minorities (e.g., African American clients) with obsessive compulsive disorder (OCD) have been reported to experience extreme shame and fear that members of their community would discover their behavior (e.g., compulsions) and judge them as "crazy" (Williams et al., 1998). These concerns can lead to self-consciousness about their mental health condition, and a preoccupation with it being obvious to others. Thus, there may be some reluctance to engage in even discrete exposure in public settings. In a case study by Williams and colleagues (1998), an African American client with OCD was unwilling to participate in any type of exposure that brought her into a public arena including riding a public bus with her therapist, because she felt that the other passengers would be able to discern the true reason for her presence on the bus (p. 166).

CASE STUDY

A 25-year-old Dominican male presents with panic disorder. His panic attacks first occurred at a fair and then a shopping mall. As a result, he has been avoiding large shopping areas and crowds. His CBT intervention plan included exposure to situational cues including stores. However, the client quickly dropped out of treatment when behavioral assignments were initiated whereby the client was to challenge his anxiety by spending approximately an hour at a store several times a week.

Due to experiences with racism and discrimination, clients of color may be more concerned that others may monitor or scrutinize them generally; and thus, during their in vivo exposure practice, as well. In the case study, the client may have been unwilling to engage in an exposure exercise whereby he was to browse around a store for about an hour, for fear of being perceived as a shoplifter and monitored by the store personnel. This concern has been depicted in other studies as well (Chambless & Williams, 1995). CBT interventions that do not consider such societal-based stressors impede progress, distract the client from focusing all their attention on treatment, and may lead to premature treatment termination, as it did in this case.

Furthermore, the selected stimuli applied in exposure activities may be influenced by race/ethnicity related issues and the social contextual issues. A case study examining the behavioral treatment of an African American female diagnosed with chronic and severe social phobia, indicated that the triggers of social-evaluative fear may be related to race-related experiences (Fink et al., 1996, p. 208). The client was an African American female physician who had developed an intense fear of hospitals and stuttering behavior during her residency training that seemed to be exacerbated by encounters with White males. Such "racially relevant cues [that] enhanced [her] social-evaluative fear" were incorporated into her in vivo exposure assignments. For example, she introduced herself to White medical professionals whom she did not know, invited a White physician to lunch, and "initiated a set number of conversations and outings with her White neighbors and coworkers each week" (Fink et al., 1996, p. 205).

Racial or other sociocultural factors must be taken into consideration when applying CBT methods. It is critical that clinicians are culturally sensitive and aware of these issues when discerning the triggers for symptoms of distress (e.g., anxiety) and in negotiating assignments. Noncompliance and/or dropout may not be a result of disinterest or avoidance, but rather inappropriate assignments and/or the client's distrust of the practitioner.

In working with CBT skills such as social skills, assertiveness, parent behavior management trainings, and in vivo exposure with diverse clientele, it is also recommended that materials such as video, audio, media, and motivational speakers feature individuals who are of similar backgrounds to the client, or are models to which the client (and his family) can relate (Neal-Barnett & Smith, 1996). Hatch, Friedman, and Paradis (1996) discuss how their clinic, the Anxiety Disorders Clinic at the Health Sciences Center of the State University of New York at Brooklyn, has developed a series of videotapes of African American clients with OCD talking about their symptoms and treatment. Some of the individuals featured in the videos also agreed that clients could contact them by phone, creating a social network (p. 312). These efforts have helped reduce feelings of isolation and stigma, and help educate and motivate African American clients in OCD (Hatch et al., 1996, p. 312).

DIFFERENTIAL OUTCOMES OF CBT ACROSS DIVERSE GROUPS

While study findings suggest that CBT interventions are associated with positive outcomes across diverse social groups, the results may not be equivalent across groups. For example, CBT treatment outcomes for persons of color (e.g., African Americans) may not be as successful as compared to Whites (Chambless & Williams, 1995; Friedman & Paradis, 1991; Sue et al., 1991).

Race/ethnic differences in treatment outcomes may be explained by discrepancies in socioeconomic status, stressors, and stigma. Clients of lower socioeconomic status seem to benefit less from treatment than individuals of middle- and upper-class status (Wade, Monroe, & Michelson, 1993; Carter, Sbrocco, & Carter, 1996, p. 454). These treatment outcomes may result due to inadequate access to transportation back and forth from therapy sessions and lack of child care support. Another study shows that people who experience chronic stress have less success with behavior treatment than people who experience less stress (Wade et al., 1993). A greater proportion of the non-White (i.e., African American) population is of lower economic status and may experience more stress, as compared to Whites (Carter et al., 1996), which may help explain disparities in treatment outcome. Stressors may impede non-White clients from concentrating fully on treatment and having sufficient time to dedicate to time-consuming homework assignments. Higher treatment dropout rates among specific cultural groups (i.e., African Americans) may also contribute to the poorer treatment outcomes.

Studies also indicate that treatment outcome is also affected by fear of stigma, sense of isolation, and therapists' expectations of therapeutic success (Hatch et al., 1996, p. 308; Williams et al., 1998). Several studies show that non-White clients often feel excessively shameful, have concerns that family, community members, and therapists will view them as crazy, hopeless, and not wish to work with them, feel unique, isolated, and view their condition as undermining their racial identity (Hatch et al., 1996; Williams et al., 1998). Furthermore, disparate outcomes may stem from therapists' expectations regarding clients therapeutic progress. It has been suggested that therapists have lower expectations of poorer and non-White clients, which may become a self-fulfilling prophecy (Garvin & Seabury, 1997). Finally, disparate outcomes may be due to inadequate consideration and attention to cultural relevant factors.

CONCLUSION

The universality of CBT and other psychotherapies has been called into question as the composition of the U.S. population continues to diversify. It has become increasingly important to understand how applicable and beneficial CBT is across social groups. There exists substantial empirical support for CBT; however, it mainly applies to a specific cultural group (i.e., the White, middle class). The efficacy of CBT has not yet been adequately determined with other racial/ethnic and social groups (Sue, 1998; Hall, 2001). It is critical to determine whether culture moderates outcomes of CBT (Hall, 2001; Kendall, Flannery-Schroeder, & Ford, 1999) to ensure the delivery of quality mental health care across all subgroups of client populations. As mental health professionals, social workers tend to be at the forefront of mental health service delivery to underserved communities, including poor and non-White social groups. It is important for social workers to critically consider the influence of clients' (and their own) social contexts including specific sociocultural issues (e.g., finances, stigma) on the CB treatment process. Social workers have a vital role in making culture-based modifications to extant CBT methods and developing and applying CBT models that integrate general, universal strategies with techniques that are more relevant to specific cultural groups and the needs of the individual client. This chapter discussed some of the critical issues surrounding culture and cognitive behavioral methods in order to better inform the advancement of culturally responsive social work practice.

The idea of being culturally proficient in all cultures can be overwhelming and intimidating; the task is unachievable (Hong, Garcia, & Soriano, 2000). As a result, some clinicians reject notions of multiculturalism and culturally competent services. However, general labels depicting broad social groups (e.g., racial categories such as Asian American, Latino, African American, Native American, White) capture a myriad of cultures and subcultures (Hong et al., 2000, p. 462). While there are many group distinctions, it may also be helpful to identify "commonalities among diversities" (Hong et al., 2000, p. 461). Therefore, being a culturally competent CBT social worker does not necessitate experience and expertise with persons of every culture and subculture. Instead it may entail an integrated etic-emic approach including mastery of general universal techniques, combined with skills that are critically relevant to members of specific social groups, and likely to be encountered in the therapeutic process (Hong et al., 2000).

More research is needed to determine which CBT techniques are most relevant to diverse clientele and to develop more culturally responsive CBT skills, including new CBT skills that emerge from a broader cultural base. There are specific challenges that are associated with these goals. For instance, there is an underrepresentation of persons from non-White racial/ethnic groups, poorer persons . . . in efficacy studies (Hall, 2001). Members of numerous social groups (e.g., African Americans) do not tend to seek treatment in research settings (Neal & Turner, 1991) commonly located in university environments, but instead consult ministers, physicians, or emergency rooms within their own communities (Neighbors, 1985, 1988). In fact, persons of color and the poor underutilize mental health services (Cheung & Snowden, 1990; Sue et al., 1991); this has been attributed to a lack of available culturally responsive therapists and services (Lee & Ramirez, 2000) among other factors. Thus, a preliminary step may be to include more diverse populations in CBT research (Hall, 2001; Sue, 1999). Additionally, while the benefit of cultural matching is debatable (Chambless & Williams, 1995; Jenkins-Hall & Sacco, 1991; Sue, 1988; Sue et al., 1991), increasing the diversity of mental health professionals and staff trained in cognitive behavioral methods may attract a more diverse clientele and elevate cultural competence (Caraway, 2001).

As noted by Hall (2001), it is important that the cultural phenomena of interest are conceptualized and examined within their cultural context and using measures that assess such constructs" (Betancourt & Lopez, 1993; Hall, Bansal, & Lopez, 1999; Lewis-Fernández & Kleinman, 1994). When CBT interventions and assessment instruments based on research and treatment with White middle class people are applied to other diverse groups, findings will primarily inform "universal" behavioral phenomena and persons who are most similar to White middle-class individuals (Hall, 2001). Thus, emic constructs must be developed and assessed in order to gain additional information about CBT with a more culturally diverse population. Other steps include developing and validating scales for use with these diverse populations (Renfrey, 1992) to capture more culturally relevant factors. For example, assessments measuring acculturation and identity may be important in efforts to make CBT skills more culturally congruent (Friedman et al., 2003).

The recent recognition and commitment of the field of CBT to the importance of cultural factors, has stimulated much critical thought and debate across the mental health community. Social workers have a lot to offer this burgeoning area while continuing to hone their own CBT skills to make them more culturally responsive, in the process.

REFERENCES

Agras, W. S., Walsh, B. T., Fairburn, C. G., Wilson, G. T., & Kraemer, H. C. (2000). A multicenter comparison of cognitive-behavioral therapy and interpersonal psychotherapy for bulimia nervosa. *Archives of General Psychiatry, 57*, 459–466.

Alvidrez, J., Azocar, F., & Miranda, J. M. (1996). Demystifying the concept of ethnicity for psychotherapy researchers. *Journal of Consulting and Clinical Psychology, 6*, 903–908.

American Psychiatric Association. (June, 2000). *Diagnostic Statistical Manual of Mental Disorders DSM-IV-TR* (4th ed.). Washington, DC: Author.

Bell, D. C., Richard, A. J., & Dayton, C. A. (1996). Effect of drug user treatment on psychosocial change: A comparison of in-treatment and out-of-treatment cocaine users. *Substance Use & Misuse, 31*, 1083–1100.

Betancourt, H., & Lopez, S. R. (1993). The study of culture, ethnicity, and race in American psychology. *American Psychologist, 48*, 629–637.

Bhugra, D., & Bhui, K. (1998). Psychotherapy for ethnic minorities: Issues, context and practice. *British Journal of Psychotherapy, 14*, 310–326.

Binson, D., Michaels, S., & Stall, R. (1995). Prevalence and social distribution of men who have sex with men. *Journal of Sex Research, 32*, 245–254.

Brink, N. E. (2003). Imagination, cognition and personality. *Imagination, Cognition & Personality, 23*, 89–96.

Caraway, S. J. (2001). Toward increasing the number of behavioral and cognitive-behavioral ethnic minority therapists. *The Behavior Therapist, 24*, 210–211.

Cardemil, E. V., & Battle, C. L. (2003). Guess who's coming to therapy? Getting comfortable with conversations about race and ethnicity in psychotherapy. *Professional Psychology: Research and Practice, 34*, 278–286.

Carter, M. M., Sbrocco, T., & Carter, C. (1996). African Americans and anxiety disorders research: Development of a testable theoretical framework. *Psychotherapy: Theory, Research, Practice, Training, 33*, 449–463.

Carter, M. M., Sbrocco, T., Gore, K. L., Marin, N. W., & Lewis, E. L. (2003). Cognitive-behavioral group therapy versus a wait-list control in the treatment of African American women with panic disorder. *Cognitive Therapy and Research, 27*, 505–518.

Casas, J. M. (1988). Cognitive behavioral approaches: A minority perspective. *Counseling Psychologist, 16*, 106–110.

Casas, J. M. (1995). Counseling and psychotherapy with racial/ethnic minority groups in theory and practice. In B. M. Bongar & L. E. Beutler (Eds.),

Comprehensive textbook of psychotherapy (pp. 311–335). London: Oxford University Press.

Chambless, D. L., & Williams, K. E. (1995). A preliminary study of African Americans with agoraphobia: Symptom severity and outcome of treatment with in vivo exposure. *Behavior Therapy, 26,* 501–515.

Chen, C. P. (1995). Counseling applications of RET in a Chinese cultural context. *Journal of Rational-Emotive & Cognitive Behavior Therapy, 13,* 117–129.

Chorpita, B. F., Taylor, A. A., Francis, S. E., Moffitt, C., & Austin, A. A. (2004). Efficacy of modular cognitive behavior therapy for childhood anxiety disorders. *Behavior Therapy, 35,* 263–287.

Chorpita, B. F., Daleiden, E. L., & Weisz, J. R. (2005). Identifying and selecting the common elements of evidence based interventions: A distillation and matching model. *Mental Health Services Research, 7,* 5–20.

Comas-Díaz, L. (1981). Effects of cognitive and behavioral group treatment on the depressive symptomatology of Puerto Rican women. *Journal of Consulting & Clinical Psychology, 49,* 627–632.

Conrad, R. D., Delk, J. L., & Williams, C. (1974). Use of stimulus fading procedures in the treatment of situation specific mutism: A case study. *Journal of Behavior Therapy and Experimental Psychiatry, 5,* 99–100.

Dai, Y., Zhang, S., Yamamoto, J., Ao, M., Belin, T. R., Cheung, F., et al. (1999). Cognitive behavioral therapy of minor depressive symptoms in elderly Chinese Americans: A pilot study. *Community Mental Health Journal, 35,* 537–542.

Davis, D., & Padesky, C. (1989). Enhancing cognitive therapy with women. In A. Freeman & K. M. Simon (Eds.), *Comprehensive handbook of cognitive therapy* (pp. 535–557). New York: Plenum.

Diaz-Martinez, A. M. (2003). The case of Maria: Cultural approaches. *Clinical Case Studies, 2,* 211–223.

Dobson, K. S., & Block, L. (1988). Historical and philosophical bases of the cognitive-behavioral therapies. In K. S. Dobson (Ed.), *Handbook of cognitive-behavioral therapies* (pp. 3–38). New York: Guilford.

Dobson, K. S., & Shaw, B. F. (1995). Cognitive therapies in practice. In B. Bongar & L. E. Beutler (Eds.), *Comprehensive textbook of psychotherapy: Theory and practice* (pp. 159–172). New York: Oxford University Press.

Dulcan, M. K., & Martini, D. R. (1999). *Concise Guide to Child and Adolescent Psychiatry* (2nd ed.). Washington, DC: American Psychiatric Press.

Dwairy, M., & Van Sickle, T. D. (1996). Western psychotherapy in traditional Arabic societies. *Clinical Psychology Review, 16*(3), 231–249.

Falicov, C. J. (1998). *Latino families in therapy.* New York: Guilford.

Ferrell, C. B., Beidel, D. C., & Turner, S. M. (2004). Assessment and treatment of socially phobic children: A cross-cultural comparison. *Journal of Clinical Child and Adolescent Psychology, 33,* 260–268.

Fink, C. M., Turner, S. M., & Beidel, D. C. (1996). Culturally relevant factors in the behavioral treatment of social phobia: A case study. *Journal of Anxiety Disorders, 10,* 201–209.

Forehand, R., & Kotchick, B. A. (1996). Cultural diversity: A wake-up call for parent training. *Behavior Therapy, 27,* 187–206.

Friedman, S., & Paradis, C. (1991). African-American patients with panic disorder and agoraphobia. *Journal of Anxiety Disorders, 5*, 35–41.

Friedman, S., Paradis, C. M., & Hatch, M. (1994). Characteristics of African-American and white patients with panic disorder and agoraphobia. *Hospital and Community Psychiatry, 45*, 798–803.

Friedman, S., Paradis, C. M., & Hatch, M. L. (1994). Issues of misdiagnosis in panic disorder with agoraphobia. In S. Friedman (Ed.), *Anxiety disorders in African Americans* (pp. 128–146). New York: Springer.

Friedman, S., Smith, L. C., Halpern, B., Levine, C., Paradis, C., Viswanathan, R., et al. (2003). Obsessive-compulsive disorder in a multi-ethnic urban outpatient clinic: Initial presentation and treatment outcome with exposure and ritual prevention. *Behavior Therapy, 34*, 397–410.

Fudge, R. C. (1996). The use of behavior therapy in the development of ethnic consciousness: A treatment model. *Cognitive and Behavioral Practice, 3*, 317–335.

Gallagher, D., & Thompson, L. W. (1983). Depression. In P. M. Lewisohn & L. Teri (Eds.), *Clinical geropsychology: New directions in assessment and treatment* (pp. 7–37). New York: Pergamon.

Gambrill, E., & Richey, C. A. (1983). Gender issues related to group social skills training. *Social Work with Groups, 6*, 51–66.

Gambrill, E. D., & Richey, C. A. (1986). Criteria used to define and evaluate socially competent behavior among women. *Psychology of Women Quarterly, 10*, 183–196.

Garvin, C. D., & Seabury, B. A. (1997). *Interpersonal practice in social work: Promoting competence and social justice* (2nd ed.). Boston: Allyn & Bacon.

Gilmore, M., Catalano, R., Morrison, D., Wells, E., Iritani, B., & Hawkins, J. (1990). Racial differences in acceptability and availability of drugs and early initiation of substance use. *American Journal of Drug and Alcohol Abuse, 16*, 185–206.

Giordano, P., S., C., & A., D. (1993). The family and peer relations of Black adolescents. *Journal of Marriage and the Family, 55*, 277–287.

Goldfein, J. A., Devlin, M. J., & Spitzer, R. L. (2000). Cognitive behavioral therapy for the treatment of binge eating disorder: What constitutes success? *The American Journal of Psychiatry, 157*, 1051–1056.

Grote, N. K., Bledsoe, S. E., & Swartz, H. A. (2004). Culturally relevant psychotherapy for perinatal depression in low-income ob/gyn patients. *Clinical Social Work Journal, 32*, 327–347.

Gupta, R. (2003). Cognitive behavioral treatment on driving phobia for an Asian Indian male. *Clinical Gerontologist, 26*, 165–170.

Hall, G. C. N. (2001). Psychotherapy research with ethnic minorities: Empirical, ethical, and conceptual issues. *Journal of Consulting and Clinical Psychology, 69*, 502–510.

Hall, G. C. N., Bansal, A., & Lopez, I. R. (1999). Ethnicity and psychopathology: A meta-analytic review of 31 years of comparative MMPI/MMPI-2 research. *Psychological Assessment, 11*, 186–197.

Hansen, D. J., Zamboanga, B. L., & Sedlar, G. (2000). Cognitive-behavior therapy for ethnic minority adolescents: Broadening our perspectives. *Cognitive and Behavioral Practice, 7*, 54–60.

Harper, G. W., & Iwamasa, G. Y. (2000). Cognitive-behavioral therapy with ethnic minority adolescents: Therapist perspectives. *Cognitive and Behavioral Practice, 7,* 37–53.

Harris, M. B., & Franklin, C. G. (2003). Effects of a cognitive-behavioral, school-based, group intervention with Mexican American pregnant and parenting adolescents. *Social Work Research, 27,* 71–83.

Hatch, M. L., Friedman, S., & Paradis, C. M. (1996). Behavioral treatment of obsessive-compulsive disorder in African Americans. *Cognitive and Behavioral Practice, 3,* 303–315.

Hays, P. A. (1995). Multicultural applications of cognitive-behavior therapy. *Professional Psychology: Research and Practice, 26,* 309–315.

Herek, G. M., & Berrill, K. T. (1992). *Hate crimes: Confronting violence against lesbians and gay men.* Thousand Oaks, CA: Sage.

Himle, J. A., Fischer, D. J., & Muroff, J. (2004). Behavioral child therapy: Emphasis on an African American family living in a high-risk community. In R. A. Dorfman, P. Meyer, & M. L. Morgan (Eds.), *Paradigms of clinical social work: Emphasis on diversity* (Vol. 3). New York: Taylor & Francis.

Hong, G. K., Garcia, M., & Soriano, M. (2000). Responding to the challenge: Preparing mental health professionals for the new millennium. In I. Cuellar & F. A. Paniagua (Eds.), *Handbook of multicultural mental health* (pp. 455–476). San Diego, CA: Academic Press.

Hopps, S. L., Pepin, M., & Boisvert, J.-M. (2003). The effectiveness of cognitive-behavioral group therapy for loneliness via inter-relay-chat among people with physical disabilities. *Psychotherapy: Theory, Research, Practice, Training, 40,* 136–147.

Horwath, E., Johnson, J., & Hornig, C. D. (1993). Epidemiology of panic disorder in African-Americans. *American Journal of Psychiatry, 150,* 465–469.

Hussian, R. A. (1983). A combination of operant and cognitive therapy with geriatric patients. *International Journal of Behavioral Geriatrics, 1,* 57–61.

Inclan, J., & Hernandez, M. (1992). Cross-cultural perspectives and codependence: The case of poor Hispanics. *American Journal of Orthopsychiatry, 62,* 245–255.

Ivey, A. E., Ivey, M. B., & Simek-Morgan, L. (1993). *Counseling and psychotherapy: A multicultural perspective.* Boston: Allyn & Bacon.

Jenkins-Hall, K., & Sacco, W. P. (1991). Effect of client race and depression on evaluations by White therapists. *Journal of Social & Clinical Psychology, 10,* 322–333.

Kantrowitz, R. E., & Ballou, M. (1992). A feminist critique of cognitive-behavioral therapy. In L. S. Brown & M. Ballou (Eds.), *Personality and psychopathology: Feminist reappraisals* (pp. 70–87). New York: Guilford.

Kaufman, D. (2005). *Cultural understanding vital to treat patients from diverse ethnic backgrounds.* Retrieved February 16, 2005

Kazdin, A. E. (1980). Acceptability of alternative treatments for deviant child behavior. *Journal of Applied Behavior Analysis, 13,* 259–273.

Kendall, P. C. (1993). Cognitive-behavioral therapies with youth: Guiding theory, current status, and emerging developments. *Journal of Consulting & Clinical Psychology, 61,* 235–247.

Kendall, P. C., Flannery-Schroeder, E. C., & Ford, J. D. (1999). Therapy outcome research methods. In P. C. Kendall, J. N. Butcher, & G. N. Holmbeck (Eds.), *Handbook of research methods in clinical psychology* (2nd ed., pp. 330–363). New York: John Wiley & Sons.

Kinsey, A. C., Pomeroy, W. B., & Martin, C. E. (1948). *Sexual behavior in the human male.* Philadelphia: W. B. Saunders.

Kohn, L. P., Oden, T., & Muñoz, R. F. (2002). Adapted cognitive behavioral group therapy for depressed low-income African American women. *Community Mental Health Journal, 38,* 497–504.

Kuehlwein, K. T. (1992). Working with gay men. In A. Freeman & F. M. Dattilio (Eds.), *Comprehensive casebook of cognitive therapy* (pp. 249–255). New York: Plenum.

LaFromboise, T. D., & Rowe, W. (1983). Skills training for bicultural competence: Rationale and application. *Journal of Counseling Psychology, 30,* 589–595.

Lee, R. M., & Ramirez, M. I. (2000). The history, current status, and future of multicultural psychotherapy. In I. Cuellar & F. A. Paniagua (Eds.), *Handbook of multicultural mental health* (pp. 279–305). San Diego, CA: Academic Press.

Leong, F. T. (1986). Counseling and psychotherapy with Asian-Americans: Review of the literature. *Journal of Counseling Psychology, 33,* 196–206.

Lewis-Fernández, R., & Kleinman, A. (1994). Culture, personality, and psychopathology. *Journal of Abnormal Psychology; Special issue: Personality and psychopathology, 103,* 67–71.

Lin, K.-M., & Cheung, F. (1999). Mental health issues for Asian Americans. *Psychiatric Services, 50,* 774–780.

Lum, D. (1996). *Social work practice and people of color* (3rd ed.). Pacific Grove, CA: Brooks/Cole.

MacCarthy, B. (1988). Clinical work with ethnic minorities. In F. N. Watts (Ed.), *New developments in clinical psychology* (Vol. 2, pp. 122–139). Oxford, England: British Psychological Society John Wiley and Sons.

Mahalik, J. R. (2005). Cognitive therapy for men. In G. E. Good & G. R. Brooks (Eds.), *New handbook of psychotherapy and counseling with men: A comprehensive guide to settings, problems, and treatment approaches* (pp. 217–233). San Francisco, CA: Jossey-Bass.

Margolese, H. C. (1998). Engaging in psychotherapy with the Orthodox Jew: A critical review. *American Journal of Psychotherapy, 52,* 37–53.

Martell, C. R., & Land, T. E. (2002). Cognitive-behavioral therapy with gay and lesbian couples. In F. W. Kaslow & T. Patterson (Eds.), *Comprehensive handbook of psychotherapy: Cognitive-behavioral approaches* (pp. 451–468). New York: John Wiley & Sons.

McGoldrick, M., Giordano, J., & Pearce, J. K. (1996). *Ethnicity and family therapy* (2nd ed.). New York: Guilford.

McNair, L. D. (1996). African American women and behavior therapy: Integrating theory, culture, and clinical practice. *Cognitive and Behavioral Practice, 3,* 337–349.

Miranda, J., & Munoz, R. (1994). Intervention for minor depression in primary care patients. *Psychosomatic Medicine, 56,* 136–142.

Miranda, J., Chung, J. Y., Green, B. L., Krupnick, J., Siddique, J., Revicki, D. A., et al. (2003). Treating depression in predominantly low-income young minority women: A randomized controlled trial. *Journal of the American Medical Association, 290*, 57–65.

National Association of Social Workers [NASW]. (2000). Cultural competence in the social work profession. In *Social work speaks: NASW policy statements* (pp. 59–62). Washington, DC: Author.

National Association of Social Workers. (2001). *NASW standards for cultural competence in social work practice.*

National Association of Social Workers. (2002). Cultural Competence. *Equity: Practice update from the National Association of Social Workers, 1*(3), 1–4.

Neal-Barnett, A. (2003). *Soothe your nerves: The Black woman's guide to understanding and overcoming anxiety, panic, and fear.* New York: Fireside.

Neal, A. M., & Turner, S. M. (1991). Anxiety disorders research with African Americans: Current status. *Psychological Bulletin, 109*, 400–410.

Neal-Barnett, A. M., & Smith, J. M. S. (1996). African American children and behavior therapy: Considering the Afrocentric approach. *Cognitive & Behavioral Practice; Special issue: Ethnic and cultural diversity in cognitive and behavioral practice, 3*, 351–369.

Neal-Barnett, A. M., Ward-Brown, B. J., Mitchell, M., & Krownapple, M. (2000). Hair pulling in African Americans—only your hairdresser knows for sure: An exploratory study. *Cultural Diversity and Ethnic Minority Psychology, 6*, 352–362.

Neal-Barnett, A. (2004). Orphans no more: A commentary on anxiety and African American youth. *Journal of Clinical Child and Adolescent Psychology, 33*, 276–278.

Neighbors, H. W. (1985). Seeking help for personal problems: Black Americans' use of health and mental health services. *Community Mental Health Journal, 21*, 156–166.

Neighbors, H. W. (1988). The help-seeking behavior of Black Americans. *Journal of the National Medical Association, 80*, 1009–1012.

Nielsen, S. L., Ridley, C. R., & Johnson, W. B. (2000). Religiously sensitive rational emotive behavior therapy: Theory, techniques, and brief excerpts from a case. *Professional Psychology: Research & Practice, 31*, 21–28.

O'Kelly, M. (2002). How can cognitive-behaviour therapy contribute to the promotion of women's health? *Behaviour Change, 19*(1), 1–.

Ogbu, J. U. (1985). A cultural ecology of competence among inner-city blacks. In M. B. B. Spencer & Geraldine Kearse (Ed.), *Beginnings: The social and affective development of black children* (pp. 45–66). Hillsdale, NJ: Lawrence Erlbaum Associates.

Organista, K. C., & Dwyer, E. V. (1996). Clinical case management and cognitive-behavioral therapy: Integrated psychosocial services for depressed Latino primary care patients. In P. Manoleas (Ed.), *Cross-cultural practice of clinical case management in mental health* (pp. 119–143). New York & England: Haworth.

Otto, M. W., Hinton, D., Korbly, N. B., Chea, A., Ba, P., Gershuny, B. S., et al. (2003). Treatment of pharmacotherapy-refractory posttraumatic stress disorder among Cambodian refugees: A pilot study of combination treatment with cognitive-behavior therapy vs. sertraline alone. *Behaviour Research and Therapy, 41,* 1271–1276.

Paniagua, F. A. (1988). *Assessing and treating culturally diverse clients: A practical guide* (2nd ed.). Thousand Oaks, CA: Sage.

Paradis, C. M., & Friedman, S. (2005). Sleep paralysis in African Americans with panic disorder. *Transcultural Psychiatry, 42,* 123–134.

Peden, A. R., Rayens, M. K., & Hall, L. A. (2005). A community-based depression prevention intervention with low-income single mothers. *Journal of the American Psychiatric Nurses Association, 11,* 18–25.

Perez, J. E. (1999). Integration of cognitive-behavioral and interpersonal therapies for Latinos: An argument for technical eclecticism. *Journal of Contemporary Psychotherapy, 29,* 169–183.

Peterson, P., Hawkins, J., Abbot, R., & Catalano, R. (1994). Disentangling the effects of parental drinking, family management, and parental alcohol norms on current drinking by African American and European American Adolescents. *Journal of Research on Adolescents, 4,* 203–227.

Pina, A. A., Silverman, W. K., Fuentes, R. M., Kurtines, W. M., & Weems, C. F. (2003). Exposure-based cognitive-behavioral treatment for phobic and anxiety disorders: Treatment effects and maintenance for Hispanic/Latino relative to European-American youths. *Journal of the American Academy of Child and Adolescent Psychiatry, 42,* 1179–1187.

Pina, A. A., Silverman, W. K., Weems, C. F., Kurtines, W. M., & Goldman, M. L. (2003). A comparison of completers and noncompleters of exposure-based cognitive and behavioral treatment for phobic and anxiety disorders in youth. *Journal of Consulting and Clinical Psychology, 71,* 701–705.

Propst, L. R., Ostrom, R., Watkins, P., Dean, T., & Mashburn, D. (1992). Comparative efficacy of religious and nonreligious cognitive-behavioral therapy for the treatment of clinical depression in religious individuals. *Journal of Consulting and Clinical Psychology, 60,* 94–103.

Purcell, D. W., Campos, P. E., & Perilla, J. L. (1996). Therapy with lesbians and gay men: A cognitive behavioral perspective. *Cognitive and Behavioral Practice, 3,* 391–415.

Raj, A. J., Prasadarao, P. S. D. V., & Raguram, R. (1998). Cognitive behaviour therapy in Dhat Syndrome: A case study. *Indian Journal of Clinical Psychology, 25,* 211–217.

Raskin, A., Crook, T. H., & Herman, K. D. (1975). Psychiatric history and symptom differences in black and white depressed patients. *Journal of Consulting & Clinical Psychology, 32,* 643–649.

Renfrey, G. S. (1992). Cognitive-behavior therapy and the Native American client. *Behavior Therapy, 23,* 321–340.

Richard, A. J., Montoya, I. D., Nelson, R., & Spence, R. T. (1995). Effectiveness of adjunct therapies in crack cocaine treatment. *Journal of Substance Abuse Treatment, 12,* 401–413.

Robb, H. (2002). Practicing rational emotive behavior therapy and religious clients. *Journal of Rational-Emotive & Cognitive Behavior Therapy, 20,* 169–200.

Rybarczyk, B., Gallagher-Thompson, D., & Rodman, J. (1992). Applying cognitive-behavioral psychotherapy to the chronically ill elderly: Treatment issues and case illustration. *International Psychogeriatrics, 4,* 127–140.

Safren, S. A., Hollander, G., Hart, T. A., & Heimberg, R. G. (2001). Cognitive-behavioral therapy with lesbian, gay, and bisexual youth. *Cognitive and Behavioral Practice, 8,* 215–223.

Safren, S. A., & Rogers, T. (2001). Cognitive-behavioral therapy with gay, lesbian, and bisexual clients. *Journal of Clinical Psychology/In Session: Psychotherapy in Practice, 57,* 629–643.

Sanderson, W. C., Raue, P. J., & Wetzler, S. (1998). The generalizability of cognitive behavior therapy for panic disorder. *Journal of Cognitive Psychotherapy: An International Quarterly, 12,* 323–330.

Sapp, M. (1996). Irrational beliefs that can lead to academic failure for African American middle school students who are academically at-risk. *Journal of Rational-Emotive & Cognitive-Behavior Therapy, 14,* 123–134.

Satterfield, J. M. (1998). Cognitive behavioral group therapy for depressed, low-income minority clients: Retention and treatment enhancement. *Cognitive and Behavioral Practice, 5,* 65–80.

Satterfield, J. M. (2002). Culturally sensitive cognitive-behavioral therapy for depression with low-income and minority clients. In F. W. Kaslow & T. Patterson (Eds.), *Comprehensive handbook of psychotherapy: Cognitive-behavioral approaches* (Vol. 2, pp. 519–545). New York: John Wiley & Sons.

Sell, R. L., Wells, J. A., & Wypij, D. (1995). The prevalence of homosexual behavior and attraction in the United States, the United Kingdom and France: Results of national population-based samples. *Archives of Sexual Behavior, 24,* 235–248.

Shannon, H. D., & Allen, T. W. (1998). The effectiveness of a REBT training program in increasing the performance of high school students in mathematics. *Journal of Rational-Emotive & Cognitive-Behavior Therapy, 16,* 197–209.

Silven, D., & Gallagher, D. (1987). Resistance in cognitive-behavioral therapy: A case study. In T. L. Brink (Ed.), *The elderly uncooperative patient* (pp. 75–78). New York: Haworth.

Simon, R. F. J. (1973). Depression and schizophrenia in hospitalized patients. *Archives of General Psychiatry, 14,* 475–481.

Skinner, J. B., Erskine, A., & Pearce, S. A. (1990). The evaluation of a cognitive behavioural treatment programme in outpatients with chronic pain. *Journal of Psychosomatic Research, 34,* 13–19.

Smith, L. C., Friedman, S., & Nevid, J. (1999). Clinical and sociocultural differences in African American and European American patients with panic disorder and agoraphobia. *Journal of Nervous and Mental Disease, 187,* 549–560.

Smith, D. M., & Gates, G. J. (2001). *Gay and Lesbian Families in the United States: Same-Sex Unmarried Partner Households: A Preliminary Analysis of 2000 United States Census Data.* Washington DC: Human Rights Campaign Urban Institute.

Snowden, L. R. (1999). African American service use for mental health problems. *Journal of Community Psychology, 27,* 303–313.

Snowden, L. R., & Cheung, F. K. (1990). Use of inpatient mental health services by members of ethnic minority groups. *American Psychologist, 45,* 347–355.

Stokes, T. F., & Osnes, P. G. (1989). An operant pursuit of generalization. *Behavior Therapy, 20,* 337–355.

Sue, S. (1988). Psychotherapeutic services for ethnic minorities: Two decades of research findings. *American Psychologist, 43,* 301–308.

Sue, S. (1998). In search of cultural competence in psychotherapy and counseling. *American Psychologist, 53,* 440–448.

Sue, S. (1999). Science, ethnicity, and bias: Where have we gone wrong? *American Psychologist, 54,* 1070–1077.

Sue, S., Fujino, D. C., Hu, L., Takeuchi, D. T., & Zane, N. W. (1991). Community mental health services for ethnic minority groups: A test of the cultural responsiveness model. *Journal of Consulting and Clinical Psychology, 59,* 533–540.

Sweetland, J. D. (1990). Cognitive-behavior therapy and physical disability. *Journal of Rational-Emotive & Cognitive Behavior Therapy; Special issue: Cognitive behavior therapy with physically ill people, 8,* 71–78.

Tan, S.-Y. J., W. Brad. (2005). Spiritually oriented cognitive-behavioral therapy. In L. Sperry & E. P. Shafranske (Eds.), *Spiritually oriented psychotherapy* (pp. 77–103). Washington, DC: American Psychological Association.

Tanaka-Matsumi, J., & Higginbotham, H. N. (1989). Behavioral approaches to counseling across cultures. In P. B. Pedersen & J. G. Draguns (Eds.), *Counseling across cultures* (3rd ed., pp. 269–298). Honolulu, HI: University of Hawaii Press.

Tanaka-Matsumi, J., Seiden, D. Y., & Lam, K. N. (1996). The Culturally Informed Functional Assessment (CIFA) Interview: A strategy for cross-cultural behavioral practice. *Cognitive and Behavioral Practice, 3,* 215–233.

Thompson, L. W., Davies, R., & Gallagher, D. (1986). Cognitive therapy with older adults. *Clinical Gerontologist, 5,* 245–279.

Thompson, E. E., Neighbors, H. W., Munday, C., & Jackson, J. S. (1996). Recruitment and retention of African American patients for clinical research: An exploration of response rates in an urban psychiatric hospital. *Journal of Consulting and Clinical Psychology, 64,* 861–867.

Thompson, L. W. C., David W., Gallagher-Thompson, Dolores. (2001). Comparison of desipramine and cognitive/behavioral therapy in the treatment of elderly outpatients with mild-to-moderate depression. *American Journal of Geriatric Psychiatry, 9,* 225–240.

Thompson, V. L. S., Bazile, A., & Akbar, M. (2004). African Americans' perceptions of psychotherapy and psychotherapists. *Professional Psychology: Research and Practice, 35,* 19–26.

Tracey, T. J., Leong, F. T., & Glidden, C. (1986). Help seeking and problem perception among Asian Americans. *Journal of Counseling Psychology, 33,* 331–336.

U.S. Census Bureau. (2000). *Census 2000 United States fact sheet—American fact finder,* from http://factfinder.census.gov.

Valdez, J. N. (2000). Psychotherapy with bicultural Hispanic clients. *Psychotherapy: Theory, Research, Practice, Training, 37,* 240–264.

Vera, M., Vila, D., & Alegria, M. (2003). Cognitive-behavioral therapy: Concepts, issues, and strategies for practice with racial/ethnic minorities. In G. Bernal, J. E. Trimble, A. K. Berlew & F. T. Leong (Eds.), *Handbook of racial and ethnic minority psychology* (pp. 1–15). Thousand Oaks, CA: Sage.

Wade, S. L., Monroe, S. M., & Michelson, L. K. (1993). Chronic life stress and treatment outcome in agoraphobia with panic attacks. *American Journal of Psychiatry, 150,* 1491–1495.

Wallace, J. M., & Muroff, J. R. (2002). Preventing substance abuse among African American children and youth: Race differences in risk factor exposure and vulnerability. *The Journal of Primary Prevention, 22,* 235–261.

Weiss, B. L., & Kupfer, D. J. (1974). The Black patient and research in a community mental health center: Where have all the subjects gone? *American Journal of Psychiatry, 131,* 415–418.

Werry, J. S., & Wollersheim, J. P. (1989). Behavior therapy with children and adolescents: A twenty-year overview. *Journal of the American Academy of Child & Adolescent Psychiatry, 28,* 1–18.

Whaley, A. L. (1997). Ethnicity/race, paranoia, and psychiatric diagnoses: Clinician bias versus sociocultural differences. *Journal of Psychopathology & Behavioral Assessment, 19,* 1–20.

Williams, K. E., Chambless, D. L., & Steketee, G. (1998). Behavioral treatment of obsessive-compulsive disorder in African Americans: Clinical issues. *Journal of Behavior Therapy and Experimental Psychiatry, 29,* 163–170.

Williams, J. W., Barrett, J., Oxman, T., Frank, E., Katon, W., Sullivan, M., et al. (2000). Treatment of dysthymia and minor depression in primary care: A randomized control trial in older adults. *Journal of the American Medical Association, 284,* 1519–1526.

Wolfe, J. L. (1992). Working with gay women. In A. Freeman & F. M. Dattilio (Eds.), *Comprehensive casebook of cognitive therapy* (pp. 257–265). New York: Plenum.

Wood, P. S., & Mallinckrodt, B. (1990). Culturally sensitive assertiveness training for ethnic minority clients. *Professional Psychology: Research and Practice, 21,* 5–11.

Yankura, J., & Dryden, W. (1997). *Special applications of REBT: A therapist's casebook.* New York: Springer.

Zeiss, A. M., & Steffen, A. (1996). Treatment issues with elderly clients. *Cognitive and Behavioral Practice, 3,* 371–389.

CHAPTER 7

Using Dialectical Behavior Therapy in Clinical Practice

Client Empowerment, Social Work Values

Susan Dowd Stone

INTRODUCTION

When Charles, a 46-year-old divorced male with an extensive psychiatric history of depression, substance abuse, and disordered eating resulting in a suicide attempt, erratic employment, and two failed marriages, began treatment with a clinical social worker trained in dialectical behavior therapy (DBT), he was an angry, dysphoric individual beginning yet another cycle of destructive behavior. The recent loss of several landscaping clients due to his increasingly volatile outbursts at work, the return of urges to use and self-harm, and his parent's threat to evict him from their home led him to seek treatment again.

Skeptical during the initial interview due to a past treatment record that failed to sustain minimal gains, Charles warily considered the demanding requirements of the DBT program to which he had applied, that is, daily homework, individual and group therapy, strict attendance, shared responsibility for progress, and coaching calls.

As the discussion of recent behaviors commenced, Charles expected to feel the usual shame of his psychiatric label subsume his identity as a talented human being who had published writings and survived a traumatic, tragic life including sexual abuse and the shooting death of his twin brother. Instead, this DBT therapist was explaining the Biosocial theory—that biological vulnerabilities activated by an invalidating or stressful environment can trigger neurochemical changes leading to engagement in impulsive often self-defeating behavioral choices seeming to offer the quickest relief.

The therapist suggested that his previous behavioral remedies may have seemed the only effective solutions to his suffering at the time. She stated how hard it must have been to live with such pain all these years and how glad she was he had made it to her office today. She described the positive resources she noted from Charles's history as a creative survivor with talents and strengths. She asked about his motivation to give up those behaviors and asked him if he could eliminate the option of suicide and make a commitment to live so that new behavioral strategies and skills could be learned.

The therapist offered Charles new ways of thinking about his life, presenting an overview of the dialectic process and applying it to a current presenting problem, which demonstrated how skillful negotiation of environmental transactions could lead to less painful encounters with self and others. Together they would prioritize behavioral goals according to those threatening his life (as treatment was not possible if he was not alive), therapy and quality of life. By her acknowledgement of his suffering, acceptance of those past solutions to his pain, her genuine belief that her client could make new behavioral choices given options and presentation of a therapeutic blueprint, she elicited Charles's curiosity and hope. Feeling he had nothing to lose, Charles agreed to the treatment.

This engaging and powerfully validating client introduction and cross-examination "is a signature technique of what has become one of the most popular new psychotherapies in a generation" (Carey, 2004), embodying the DBT perspective, which extends its cognitive behavioral base to include dialectic thinking as a powerful support to the change process. Dialectic behavior therapy, initially developed by Marsha Linehan for borderline personality disorder (Linehan, 1993a) with its emphasis on radical self/other/and situational acceptance while fostering change; achievement of a Wise Mind through the balancing of practical and emotional needs; and tolerance for the consideration of multiple, sometimes polarized truths; both distinguishes DBT from its cognitive behavioral rootedness and intensifies CBT's efficacious legacy.

To practitioners utilizing CBT in the treatment of emotion regulation disorders, DBT's attention to dichotomous thinking, assignment of client-specific homework and acknowledgment that analysis of deeply held schema cannot occur until skills acquisition takes place and a therapeutic relationship develops (Beck, Freeman & Davis, 2004), seems to offer a natural theoretical extension. Levendusky (2000) notes that DBT may be the first cognitive behavioral therapy approach that is designed to treat complex and multifaceted clinical conditions.

As social workers are increasingly charged with treatment of complex multi-axis cases, DBT is highlighted as it offers an efficacious and therapeutic dialectic deeply syntonic with social work values. Its acknowledgment of the environmental/biological role in impulse disorders removes client blame while empowering them through a didactic multimodal process vigorously generalized to their environment. DBT's dialectic view that "while patients may not have caused their problems, they are responsible for solving them" (Linehan, 1993a), encourages client autonomy, self-actualization and use of resources to gain independence while respecting the inherent dignity and worth of the person, important social work principals (National Association of Social Workers [NASW], 1999). Additionally the DBT perspective that clients cannot fail, only treatment can, places equal focus on therapist competency, collaborative responsibility for outcomes and the need for ongoing education and supervision, important social work practice considerations that are built into the model.

The Biosocial theory—that biology and environment are co-conspirators that can overwhelm coping systems in vulnerable individuals when perceived or actual invalidation produces sufficient tension—also aligns itself with the biopsychosocial perspective associated with social work. By assigning a biological/environmental rather than amotivational or personality genesis to dysregulatory disorders, the Biosocial perspective may serve to moderate the pervasive shame often felt by these clients that can further handicap treatment.

Nathanson (1992) speaks of a shame-based psychopathology prevalent in severe personality disorders that can interrupt affective communication limiting intimacy and empathy and interfering with neocortical cognition. Schore (1994), who proposes that early disruptions in effective maternal child exchanges affecting the neurochemical environment of an infant's developing brain can permanently alter self-regulatory capacities suggests that unregulated shame and socioemotional psychopathology are fundamental attributes of both borderline and narcissistic disorders.

And, current research in trauma that traces both the etiology of profound regulatory disorders and explains their impact on client's ability to correctly perceive and respond to environmental stimulants (Van der Kolk, McFarlane, & Weisaeth, 1996) also offers theoretical and practical support to the model by offering biological evidence (i.e., limbic system abnormalities found in brain images of clients suffering from posttraumatic stress disorder, or PTSD) supporting DBT's mandate to first bolster client ability to manage increased arousal before initiating trauma-focused treatment (Becker & Zayfert, 2001).

Offering a full frontal attack on the constellation of symptoms associated with the dysregulatory process, DBT includes: methods to alter client perceptions of precipitating events (dialectics), methods to dissipate a threatened escalation before chemical changes reinforce the intensity of the response or tolerate present affect (skills), and ways to empower clients to build skills outside the office (coaching calls, homework, focus on skills generalization). Finally methods to sustain and support the highly interactive therapist involvement are also a crucial model component (the use of a consultation team to support the therapist).

DBT appears to be imbued with the social work principals: that educate (skills training), advocate (insistence that change is possible amidst a population previously associated with poor outcomes), and intervene (active social worker involvement). Its dialectic view helps deepen clinicians' respect for the life that came before the current intervention and for client ingenuity in designing methods of survival. While validating the suffering that led to previous behavioral choices, DBT respectfully submits new options, helps clients locate, and apply their own skills sets, offers new skills sets, and most importantly, offers a new way of thinking about self and situations that can reduce anxiety and enhance problem solving. DBT's components, together and separately actualize many of social works most important ethical principals.

This chapter provides the reader with an overview of the standard DBT model as developed by Linehan. Through a review of current literature, discussion of model components and presentation of case studies, responsible implementation of nonstandard DBT is considered.

REVIEW OF LITERATURE

Originally developed for treatment of borderline personality disorder (covered elsewhere in this text), DBT has demonstrated success in reducing self-harm, inpatient days, and treatment attrition in outpatient settings for this population (Dimeff, Koerner, & Linehan, 2001). These early victories led to program modifications for other populations in which behavioral containment was indicated, such as eating disorders and substance abuse. Findings suggest that DBT may be adapted for other disorders in which dysfunctional behaviors serve to regulate emotions (Koerner & Dimeff, 2000). Outcome studies for these populations applying either the full or partial program (i.e., DBT skills training group without DBT individual therapy; individual DBT therapy without DBT skills training group) consistently yield positive, if uneven results.

In two full model studies for women with BPD co morbid with substance abuse referred to in Scheel (2000), reduction of substance abuse was superior to treatment as usual (TAU) in the first study and resulted in a lower percentage of opiate positive UA's in the second), (Linehan, et al., 1999; Linehan, et al., 2002).

In another pre-post test study of women diagnosed with binge eating disorder, (Telch, Agras, & Linehan, 2000) participants attended the DBT skills group only but still achieved significant decreases in binge days and binge episodes that were maintained six months after treatment. In a study seeking to evaluate the contributions of individual program components, clients who perceived their DBT treatment to have been of value most emphasized the importance of the working client/therapist relationship citing the nonjudgmental and validating qualities of their therapist as helping to create the environment for change (Cunningham, Wolbert, & Lillie, 2004). While the importance of this relationship, including the therapist's willingness to self-disclose was also emphasized in Araminta's thesis (2000), *Dialectic Behavior Therapy: A Qualitative Study of Therapist and Client Experience,* clients in this study most frequently cited the skills training group as an important source of educational support, validation, and peer socialization.

In an article considering adaptations of DBT for BPD or suicidal behavior, Robins and Chapman (2004) noted a study (Turner, 2000) that compared DBT to client-centered therapy in a community mental health setting over a period of one year for 24 clients. In this setting, the DBT skills training was incorporated into individual therapy in one group, but not the other. Results showed improvement in both groups, yet participants in the DBT-oriented individual therapy demonstrated greater improvement on variables such as reduction of suicide attempts, suicidal ideation, self-harm, anger, depression, impulsivity, and global mental health.

While the absence of sustained long-term changes (one year after treatment) in client cognitions/self-perceptions noted in some studies was presented as a cautionary point in considering the model's effectiveness (Scheel, 2000), this early benchmark may be unrealistic when considering the inherent biological etiology of such disorders. It may be that behavioral management and increased ability to moderate affect would be the more realistic and optimal achievement of Stage I DBT treatment rather than permanent changes in biologically stimulated cognitions that may require completion of all four suggested treatment stages to moderate.

An analogous comparison could be the daily insulin shot that is not rejected as ineffective because it does not cure diabetes after one year, but rather allows client independence and self-management of the illness and fewer medical interventions. For clients suffering from regulatory deficits, daily applications of skills and dialectic techniques that reduce in-patient days and increase client independence and self-esteem may be the most reasonably set measurable treatment goal at Stage I. And dialectical behavior therapy consistently improves client capacity for self-management.

In conclusion, while Peck and Smith (2004) have ventured that applying only individual aspects of DBT could be inconsistent with the principles of wholeness and relatedness inherent in the theory, it appears that responsible integration of individual program components can also lead to improved treatment outcomes. While attempts to analyze the efficacy of partialized DBT yield inconsistent results when modularized, more consistent findings emerge when key philosophies are implemented across treatment contexts. As suggested by Linehan (2000a) in her article *Commentary on Innovation in Dialectical Behavior Therapy* the importance of principal-driven treatments, which include the following elements noted by Fruzetti and Levensky (2000), can contribute to successful program adaptations: expansion of client capabilities, attending to client motivation while engaging in new behaviors, generalization of new behaviors, a treatment environment that does not inadvertently reward reinforce dysfunctional behaviors and punish progress, and maintaining the motivation and skills of therapists. Balance and change can take many forms, limited perhaps only by the ingenuity and creativity of the therapeutic community.

To these factors could be added the importance of the dialectic thought process in reducing shame and client self/other situational acceptance, thereby engaging the didactic and therapeutic process more fully; the consistency offered by rigorous application of homework, long a cognitive behavioral standard emphasized in this model; the staging and setting of reasonable therapeutic goals to empower client success and minimize treatment failure; and the importance of ongoing peer consultation and supervision to maintain therapist competence and the nonpejorative spirit of DBT.

DBT PROGRAM COMPONENTS

The DBT Consultation Team

Deemed essential by program therapists and Linehan, the treatment team offers support, validation, education, and supervision to participating members who also "apply the treatment to each other" (Swenson, 2000). Meetings may begin with Mindfulness exercises or other soothing meditations for practice and eventual inclusion in client treatment. Araminta (2000) notes the frequency with which participating therapists mentioned DBT's positive impact on their own lives in addition to those of their clients by providing structure, support, and a nonpathologizing way to deal with severe behaviors.

In the standard model, team members undergo intensive DBT training; five to ten days of thorough immersion in the model's philosophy, components, and application offered by Linehan's group, Behavioral Technology (www.behavioraltech.com). The team may include all staff members involved in client treatment such as psychologists, social workers, nurses, psychiatrists, occupational and recreational therapists, but could minimally include the client's individual therapist and skills group trainer. The groups' responsibilities may cover the discussion of proposed candidates, case presentations, administrative considerations, and ongoing education and supervision of members.

The treatment unifying features of the consultation team help discourage staff splitting, manipulation, and inadvertent reinforcement of therapy interfering behaviors by therapist or client. Because DBT clients cannot fail, only the treatment itself can fail, the consultation team can help monitor early warnings that the treatment is inappropriate for a particular client or being improperly delivered by a therapist. DBT's insistence on regular consultation for the most experienced therapists can help prevent burnout and head off potentially problematic therapist and client behaviors (Peck & Smith, 2004).

DBT Pretreatment Interview

This initial client interview is meant to elicit the serious commitment from program applicants necessary to maintain motivation in such a rigorous program. Candidates must make a commitment to life that includes refraining from suicidal attempts and best efforts to avoid hospitalization while in treatment. The Biosocial theory is introduced, the difficulty of program adherence is emphasized; clients are challenged to consider their own expectations and why they would wish to change current patterns. Agreements between therapist and client may be put in writing, covering attendance, homework, behavior in group, confidentiality, appropriate avenues for crisis management, and clearly delineated contingencies for noncompliance.

The DBT Skills Training Group

This group is responsible for the delivery of didactic program components and meets weekly for up to two hours (sometimes billed as two groups although some insurance companies now reimburse for the skills training group). The skills group is co-led and gains its structure and direction from the text's companion skills training manual, which includes modules on Core Mindfulness, Emotion Regulation, Interpersonal Effectiveness, and Distress Tolerance. Co-leaders support each other, helping to prevent burnout with one therapist assuming responsibility for group structure and content while the other may focus more on individual group dynamics thereby providing balance and synthesis to members (Linehan, 1993b).

Group time is generally divided between discussion of the previous week's homework, including successes or difficulties encountered when attempting skills application and the didactic portion in which new skills are taught. Group members are encouraged to review homework and offer feedback. Noncompletion of assigned homework is considered to be a therapy interfering behavior, reducing opportunity for group participation and addressed in the individual session.

The skills training group is not a psychotherapy group and redirection of participant content may be necessary among clients unused to a didactic context. Discussion of suicidal ideation, specific descriptions of destructive behaviors, and interpersonal judgments are not permitted. The total focus is on learning and applying new skills and validation of progress. Enthusiastic recognition from peers and co-leaders for small but significant gains, like avoiding a potentially distressing phone call when vulnerable, is extremely validating to group members (Araminta, 2000). For many, the replacement of shame with pride in accomplishments is a new and welcome experience.

Core Mindfulness

The concept of Core Mindfulness introduces the dialectic thinking including Wise Mind in which practical and emotional needs negotiate a satisfactory solution to a problem and can lead to a fascinating discussion for clients not used to "holding" multiple truths. For example, the client's view of his therapist might be positive when the session is perceived to go well and angrily negative when gains seem lacking. The Wise Mind view validates the emotional discomfort of such an impasse, but logically argues that the therapeutic process is inherently uneven as the relationship consists of two imperfect individuals influenced by multiple factors on any given day. Thus, neither client nor therapist is seen as "good" or "bad." (For a further discussion of Mindfulness, see Koons, this volume.)

Along with the dialectic thought process, the attention to transaction details (observe, describe, participate) is explored in the Mindfulness module. The emphasis is on the achievement of situational objectivity prior to action by learning to watch events unfold without attributing judgment. Through exercises and discussion, participants are made aware of the ongoing presence of triggering cognitions and distracting environmental factors and how they could choose to be nonreactive to such stimulus. At the same time, the dialectic encourages full participation in events. These are not easy concepts to grasp and much practice through offered examples in group or individual therapy is important to client retention and application of these important program tenets.

Emotion Regulation

Another component is Emotion Regulation. It offers skills to decrease suffering, reduce vulnerability, and understand emotional interplay with the environment (Linehan, 1993b). Clients frequently ask when and how they should use skills. An Emotion Regulation Handout offers a Model for Describing Emotions, offers clients an excellent roadmap of how environmental factors trigger impulses to engage in destructive behaviors, and where on the continuum those skills might be best applied to reverse or contain an event. Acting opposite to current emotion produces some lively discussion due to its seeming incongruity with staying in the moment, but it can be a powerful antidote to escalation.

Interpersonal Effectiveness

This module teaches methods of negotiating with self or situations and others, challenging clients to tolerate the discomfort of assertion or the receipt of a disappointing response through the mastery of Wise Mind. It offers a hierarchy for determining the value of keeping relationships and self-respect while achieving situational objectives. It asks participants to consider the consequences of action or inaction. For example, my mother makes constant demands on my time after treatment when I am exhausted and that makes me angry. Yet, if I refuse her requests, I will feel guilty as she is supporting me through this treatment cycle. The client's choices include doing nothing or staying miserable, finding another way to think about the situation that allows it to be tolerated, negotiating for a better situation, or leaving the situation entirely. One suggestion in this case might be to agree to spend one hour helping with chores on some days, while seeking permission to focus on recovery needs on alternate days.

Distress Tolerance

Sometimes the first module selected for treatment after Mindfulness due to the need for immediate alternatives to previously destructive behaviors, Distress Tolerance helps clients develop a "DBT toolbox" of skills that may be resourced during emotional emergencies. Clients are taught that the more senses a self-soothing activity engages, that is, sight, smell, taste, sound, and touch, the more impact its effect. Examples may include physically leaving a discomforting situation to go for a walk, watching a movie, eating a favorite food, sharing affection with a pet, listening to music, or asking for assistance through a coaching call. Throughout the treatment, clients are encouraged to experiment with and list specific activities that best respond to a particular situation developing their own guide for such emergencies.

Coaching Calls

This client resource, which is rarely abused when the format is carefully outlined and maintained, greatly assists with skills generalization. When DBT clients feel they cannot manage a present situation or feel a crisis may be imminent, they may call for coaching. Clients may be unable to recall skills during moments of emotional distress, but may react with relief when the skill is reintroduced. Directing clients to attempt skills application prior to the call can reduce feelings of helplessness and set up the call's framework. Lasting no more than a few moments, the purpose of the call is to review the current issue, identify skills that may be applied, and construct a containment plan. The call does not offer therapy and the client is assured that further discussion will take place during individual session. Coaching calls are not a suicide hotline and clients are given alternate direction for life-threatening emergencies. In situations in which destructive action or hospitalization has already occurred, the client may not place coaching calls for 24 hours. In this way, therapist attention rewards attempts at skillful adaptation while discouraging the association between destructive behaviors and therapist response (Ben-Porath, 2004).

Individual DBT Therapy

Individual sessions supplement the skills training group by offering more personal focus on skills application and current concerns. Treatment decisions, including contingency management of noncompliance, are tasks assigned to an individual DBT therapist who agrees to be accountable for role fulfillment and qualitative elements such as client respect, flexibility, and balance.

Target behaviors that may be the focus of treatment for 1 week or several are prioritized according to those behaviors affecting life, interfering with therapy, and interfering with quality of life. Examples may include the behavior itself, such as binge eating or thoughts of self-abuse, or an associated ancillary behavior, such as driving down the street where drugs were purchased, conversing with an ex-spouse which elicits feelings of failure and rage, or listening to a particular song associated with self-harm.

Treatment is staged according to: basic skills acquisition, that may take a year or longer to complete (Stage I); the reduction of posttraumatic stress disorder (PTSD) symptoms, which does not commence until Stage I has been successfully completed (Stage II); increasing self-respect and achievement of individual goals (Stage III); and the integration of self with past, present, and future (Stage IV) (Linehan, 1993a). Clients may move among treatment stages if the client lapses and current challenges reverse previous gains.

Two important tools introduced by the individual therapist are the *diary card* and the *chain analysis*. The diary card assists clients in defining and numerically rating their emotional states, destructive urges, response to therapy, attempts to use skills, and efforts to increase or reduce target behaviors. Joy is among the emotions listed, which is initially perplexing to some clients, but reinforces the dialectic that moments of joy can exist even while suffering continues. The daily identification and rating of emotions reinforces the didactic material included in the skills training manual and enhances self-assessment. Beck (1995) notes the difficulty that some clients have identifying and rating their emotional states can lead them to erroneous assumptions about potential escalations. The diary card helps clients become expert on their own emotional life, empowering them to take appropriate action with an effective corresponding skill.

The chain analysis is a cognitive behavioral assessment tool that seeks to specifically identify and evaluate each factor contributing to behavioral urges or relapses. Requiring thoughtful review of all environmental and cognitive precipitants that negatively impact recovery goals, the chain analysis, along with the diary card, is an empowering tool that greatly assists in skills generalization by helping clients to correctly identify and respond to situational triggers. The chain leans the client along the path noting which action, thought, or feeling leads to other thoughts, feelings, and actions.

MODIFYING DBT FOR DIFFERENT PRACTICE SETTINGS

The full DBT program as previously described exacts a high commitment from clients, therapists, and agencies alike but can be a deeply rewarding practice experience for all. Solo or small-group practitioners wishing to adapt the model must analyze current client needs to assess for appropriateness of treatment and determination of which aspects of the treatment model are most likely to be important for that population (Robins, 2000).

The method of delivery (individual, group, or both), staff availability, financial resources to administer and maintain the program, and the possibility that investments of time may not be reimbursed are all important considerations.

In addition, qualitative factors such as therapist/agency readiness to embrace the dialectic philosophy must be considered as this may vary greatly from previous therapeutic strategies. These include therapist/client boundaries, such as self-disclosure, responsibility for therapist-interfering behaviors, the context of client contact (such as coaching calls), the sharing of responsibility for treatment outcomes, the therapist/client equality inherent in a behavioral model, and the high level of therapist activity necessary to sustain and deliver the treatment. DBT's cognitive behavioral basis may necessitate further formal study if there has not been prior clinical experience with CBT.

The textbook, *Cognitive Behavioral Treatment of Borderline Personality Disorder* (Linehan, 1993a) and its accompanying skills manual should be thoroughly absorbed. In one study set in a state mental health department attempting to determine if line clinicians could master the conceptual complexities of dialectical behavior therapy (Hawkins & Sinha, 1998), it was determined that combinations of study groups, thorough familiarity with Linehan's texts and peer support led to solid knowledge development.

The optimal resource for DBT staff training continues to be the intensive 5 or 10 day training offered by the Behavioral Technology Group. This resource is not available to solo practitioners or small agencies unwilling to commit to the development of the consultation team. However, numerous other workshops addressing skills acquisition, individual and group therapy application, advanced techniques, and diagnostic specific adaptations of DBT are periodically available nationwide. In addition, many excellent resources can be found online at www.behavioral-tech.com.

While the development of the non-negotiable treatment team component can present a challenge to the solo or small-group practitioners, solutions can be found. Joining the consultation team of an agency offering the full program may be possible if working on an individual basis with their clients. Creating a consultation team or minimally a DBT study group with other solo or small-group practitioners in the area may be another avenue. Available technology such as teleconferencing through bridge lines may connect geographically distant solo practitioners for the purposes of consistent consultations, collaborative support, and ongoing education.

Despite these challenges, the emerging data warrants consideration of DBT's inclusion for a variety of treatment populations when its guiding principals can be responsibly operationalized. Sheel (2000), after analysis of outcome studies offering full or partial model modifications, suggests that "if any partial incorporation of DBT concepts is made, adopting the empathic client conceptualization of DBT and providing therapist support would seem to be among those aspects that most safely and profitably could occur outside the standard DBT model" (p. XX).

CLINICAL EXAMPLES

Two case presentations are offered; first, one in which the client participated in a full outpatient DBT program at a teaching hospital and the second in which DBT skills training alone was incorporated into individual therapy. Clinical issues and resolutions in both contexts are discussed.

Charles, the client described at the beginning of this chapter, agreed to participate in the full DBT program and was assigned to a female clinical social worker for twice monthly individual sessions and a weekly skills training group. He understood that his individual therapist would attend weekly consultation team meetings in which his case might be discussed and signed all relevant consents. Most fortunately, Charles's insurance company certified his treatment throughout much of the first 8 months, including group and individual therapy, medication management, consultation with the agency nurse, and intermittent consults with a nutritionist. The only program modification was that Charles was assigned to the DBT group for eating disorders that additionally included participation in a therapeutic meal (a group dining experience in which participants weigh and measure their foods and eat in a calm environment).

Target behaviors selected and listed on the client's diary card include reduction of suicidal ideation (considered life-threatening as it had led to previous suicide attempts) and medication compliance (that was deemed to be a contingency for continued program enrollment). As these goals were achieved, secondary targets were introduced including reducing the quantity of food ingested during a binge and avoidance of a route home that passed by several fast food establishments.

CHARLES:

Clinical Issues

Therapy-interfering behaviors during initial treatment months included noncompletion of homework, medication noncompliance, and two consecutive absences from the skills training group. Each was addressed

during individual therapy with some resolution, but homework completion continued to be erratic. Contingencies initially set in place for noncompliance, such as forfeiture of individual session, were not immediately
resourced as the therapist was reluctant to affect perceived treatment mo-
mentum. Ultimately, however, the therapist presented the case to the consultation team who disagreed and supported the therapist to activate the
client's agreed upon contingencies. While the client felt angry at the removal of individual session or complained that taking a whole session to
complete his diary card was "stupid," the therapist took responsibility for
having allowed the situation to continue; subsequent attendance at group
and diary card completion became more consistent.

Outcome

After three months, Charles appeared to enjoy reciting his homework
and became an active and highly regarded group member whose input
was eagerly solicited. After 8 months, Charles's symptoms greatly improved; his depression had stabilized, incidents of binging were reduced,
substance use was eliminated, and patient reported full medication compliance. Charles developed a "tool box" of DBT skills that included skills
and behaviors from all four DBT modules. For Mindfulness, client used
the assistance of musical meditations, which he greatly enjoyed. For interpersonal effectiveness, client was able to apply radical acceptance at
times, for example, his landscaping customer who was never satisfied
with his services was eventually seen as someone with a need for power
instead of a person out to get him; Emotion Regulation skills included
writing about his feelings, physically leaving the situation if needed, or
acting opposite to emotion: Distress Tolerance skills included watching
movies, going for a drive, hitting a punching bag, or making a coaching
call. The acquisition of skills and more effective interpersonal transactions resulted in increased socialization and more stability in his business
and parental relationship.

Client Perspective

By client's report, important factors in his progress were prioritized as:
his close alliance with his individual therapist, skills group co-leaders and
members, his successful and carefully titrated prescription for skills incorporation, the consistency of the treatment, the quantity of the treatment
(2 to 3 hours per week including coaching calls), and the nonpejorative
DBT philosophy, which was syntonic with client's belief system. Charles
liked the empowering therapeutic independence fostered by the model
and appreciated coaching calls, which he appropriately utilized. While
Charles readily acknowledged that past therapies had not led to present

gains, his complaints included a wish for a more "talking time" in session and the extent of the time commitment necessary to complete all program mandates.

Therapist Perspective

From the therapist's perspective, all DBT's modalities were required to stimulate and sustain cumulative client gains that averaged three agency hours per week, including phone contact. The consultation team was essential in supporting Charles's process offering both nonjudgmental validation of application difficulties and getting the therapist back on track when treatment stalled. It is doubtful that the therapist could have sustained high levels of enthusiasm and client confidence without this important resource.

KAREN

Nonstandard DBT Case Presentation

Karen, a 34-year-old married mother of a healthy infant son born by unexpected Caesarian section after 2 years of in vitro fertilization, was referred to the agency by her obstetrician for postpartum depression. An Axis II diagnosis was deferred, but interpersonal difficulties and "going off," were a self-reported problem throughout her adult life. Karen reported having anxiety attacks and flashbacks in college emanating from an attempted rape at age 15. She remained physically scarred from a knife wound sustained in the struggle, but never sought treatment as the perpetrator was a friend's brother. Her present depression was described as alternating between tearfulness and inability to properly care for her infant for whom she felt "nothing" and angry outbursts at her husband including profane language and throwing/breaking household objects. This behavior did little to solicit her husband's support and resulted in, "I am a horrible mother; I have lost my best and only friend." She felt she could not adequately communicate her feelings to her husband and was irritated by her family's attempts to intervene, describing them as intrusive and overly involved despite her current need of their practical assistance. She reported having felt unprepared for the possibility of Caesarian section about which she was angry at her doctor and exhausted by recovery from major surgery, which she felt had compromised the bond with her newborn son.

Karen was asked to consider the introduction of DBT skills training to her individual therapy. She expressed enthusiasm for "anything" that might help repair her marital relationship and contain her tirades. An antidepressant had been prescribed and although its effects were initially subtle, she was able to determine that she was feeling better by comparing diary cards that served to instill a sense of hope and progress in those early murky weeks of recovery. Karen also willingly completed a chain analysis and verbalized shock and a sense of empowerment when discovering "apparently unimportant" factors in the environment that triggered outbursts. As Karen's mood stabilized, she was more able to engage in the skills training necessary to negotiate tasks related to infant care and the setting of boundaries for her family's support so that she felt in control of their intercessions.

Clinical Issues

Implementation of skills training could not be initiated until affective crisis was stabilized, but even early in treatment, strategies for self and other acceptance offered through the dialectic perspective helped Karen to reduce self-blame and allowed her to consider strategies to improve her mood, for example, getting more sleep, accepting help from family on her terms.

Outcome

Karen's symptoms resolved over the course of several months after which time she was demonstrating consistent application of new skills, affect stabilization, and verbalizing hope for a full recovery. She expressed interest in continuing treatment, which would eventually include focus on her earlier trauma.

Client Perspective

Karen became an enthusiastic proponent of skills training and purchased the skills training manual; she attributed the skills training as an important factor in her recovery. While client only made one coaching call, she stated that knowing she could call for help made her feel important, supported, and connected to her therapist.

Therapist Perspective

While Karen received individual DBT skills training only, the introduction and application of skills greatly assisted the recovery process, offering client concrete activities to incorporate at home even during the affective crisis. The individual therapist remained part of the DBT consultation team throughout Karen's treatment, which helped the therapist monitor the appropriateness and effectiveness of skills training inclusion in this alternate context and determine client readiness for Stage II treatment.

SUMMARY

Dialectic behavior therapy is an empowering form of treatment for clients and therapists alike, imbued with qualities that support the values and ethics of the social work profession. Based in the cognitive behavioral tradition, the introduction of dialectic thinking seeks to foster acceptance balanced with change and enhances the cognitive behavioral association. Its biosocial theory parallels that of the biopsychosocial social work perspective and is supported by research in the etiology of emotion dysregulation disorders including PTSD. This nonblaming view helps reduce client shame, often a latent but treatment disruptive emotion experienced by this population, thereby increasing potential for the strong therapeutic alliance needed to affect change. Client retention for DBT participants tends to be high and reductions in suicidal behaviors, inpatient hospitalizations, and para suicidal behaviors have been repeatedly observed.

Dialectical behavior therapy, which engages vulnerable individuals early in its treatment cycle by acknowledging suffering and the intensity of the biosocial forces to be overcome and then attending to resulting symptoms, appears to be the model most congruent with and responsive to the cumulative scientific and theoretical research indicating the need for the development of self-regulatory abilities prior to discussions of traumatic material or deeply held schema.

The emergence of DBT as an efficacious treatment for complex and multiply diagnosed clients has led to attempted incorporation of the model across treatment populations. While empirical validation for nonstandard, partialized DBT is uneven, it becomes more consistent when qualitative or philosophical program elements are considered, such as the unique dialectic perspective, the use of multimodal efforts to acquire and generalize skills, and the emphasis on therapist support and supervision through formation of the consultation team.

DBT's engaging dialectic perspective encourages clients to renew recovery efforts by seeing themselves as creative survivors in the context of their own often traumatic histories. Blame, but not responsibility, is removed from the client/therapist transactions reducing shame and fostering self-respect. Through its acceptance of clients as whole individuals with certain regulatory deficits or biological vulnerabilities, but not lacking in courage or character, DBT helps clients supersede the discriminatory psychiatric labels with which they have lived, delivering a comprehensive and

empowering roadmap to self-discovery, self-management, and enrichment of life.

REFERENCES

Araminta, T. (2000). Dialectical Behavior Therapy: A Qualitative Study of Therapist and Client Experience. Unpublished doctoral dissertation, California
School of Professional Psychology, San Diego. Obtained from UMI Micro-
form: 9958971. Ann Arbor MI: Bell & Howell Information and Learning
Company.

Beck, A. T., Freeman, A., & Davis, D. D. (2004). *Cognitive therapy of personality disorders.* New York: Guilford.

Beck, J. S. (1995). *Cognitive therapy: Basics and beyond.* New York: Guilford.

Becker, C. B., & Zayfert, C. (2001). Integrating DBT-based techniques and concepts to facilitate exposure treatment for PTSD. *Cognitive & Behavioral
Practice, 8,* 107–122.

Ben-Porath, D. D. (2004). Intersession telephone contact with individuals diagnosed with borderline personality disorder: Lessons from dialectical behavior therapy. *Cognitive & Behavioral Practice 11,* 222–230.

Carey, B. (2004, July 13). With toughness and caring, a novel therapy helps tor-
tured souls. *New York Times,* p. F1.

Cunningham, K., Wolbert, R., & Lillie, B. (2004). It's about me solving my problems. *Cognitive & Behavioral Practice, 11,* 248–256.

Dimeff, L., Koerner, K., & Linehan, M. M. (2001). Summary of research findings
in DBT. Retrieved from www.behavioraltech.org.

Hawkins, K. A., & Sinha, R. (1998). Can line clinicians master the conceptual
complexities of dialectical behavior therapy? An evaluation of a state department of mental health training program. *Journal of Psychiatric Research, 32,*
379–384.

Koerner, K., & Dimeff, L. A. (2000). Further data on dialectical behavior therapy. *Clinical Psychology: Science and Practice, 7,* 104–112.

Levendusky, P. G. (2000). Dialectical behavior therapy; so far so soon. *Clinical
Psychology: Science and Practice, 7,* XXX–XXX.

Linehan, M. M. (1993a). *Cognitive-behavioral treatment of borderline personality disorder.* New York: Guilford.

Linehan, M. M. (1993b). Skills training manual for treating borderline personality disorder. New York: Guilford.

Linehan, M. M. (2000a). Commentary on innovations in dialectical behavior
therapy. *Cognitive & Behavioral Practice, 7,* 478–481.

Linehan, M. M. (2000b). The empirical basis of dialectical behavior therapy:
Development of new treatments versus evaluation of existing treatments.
Clinical Psychology: Science and Practice, 7, 113–119.

Nathanson, D. L. (1992). *Shame and pride: Affect, sex and the birth of the self.*
New York: W.W. Norton & Company.

National Association of Social Workers [NASW]. (1999). *Code of ethics.*

Palmer, R. L., Birchall, H., D., Amani, S., Gatward, N., McGrain, L., & Parker, L. (2003). A dialectical behavior therapy program for people with an eating disorder and borderline personality disorder—description and outcome. *International Journal of Eating Disorders, 33,* 281–286.

Peck, P. L., & Smith, L. D. (2004). Dialectical behavior therapy: A review and a call to research. *Journal of Mental Health Counseling, 26,* 25.

Robins, C. J. (2000). Expanding applications of dialectical behavior therapy: Prospects and pitfall. *Cognitive and Behavioral Practice, 7,* 481–484.

Robins, C. J. (2002). Zen principles and mindfulness practice in dialectical behavior therapy. *Cognitive and Behavioral Practice, 9,* 50–57.

Robins, C. J., & Chapman, A. L. (2004). Dialectical behavior therapy: Current status, recent developments and future directions. *Journal of Personality Disorders, 18,* 73–89.

Scheel, K. R. (2000). The empirical basis of dialectical behavior therapy: Summary, critique, and implications. *Clinical Psychology: Science and Practice, 7,* xxx.

Schore, A. N. (1994). *Affect regulation and the origin of the self.* Hillsdale, NJ: Lawrence Erlbaum Associates.

Swenson, C. R. (2000). How can we account for DBT's widespread popularity? *Clinical Psychology: Science and Practice, 7,* 87–91.

Swenson, C. R., Torrey, W. C., & Koerner, K. (2002). Implementing dialectical behavior therapy. *Psychiatric Services, 53,* 171–178.

Telch, C. F., Agras, W. S., & Linehan, M. M. (2001). Dialectical behavior therapy for binge eating disorder. *Journal of Consulting and Clinical Psychology, 69,* 1061.

Van der Kolk, B. A. (1994). The body keeps the score: Memory and the emerging psychobiology of post traumatic stress. *Harvard Review of Psychiatry, 1,* 253–265.

Van der Kolk, B. A., McFarlane, A. C., & Weisaeth, L. (1996). *Traumatic stress: The effects of overwhelming experience on mind, body and society.* New York: Guilford.

Wisniewski, L., & Kelly, E. (2003). The application of dialectical behavior therapy to the treatment of eating disorders. *Cognitive & Behavioral Practice, 10,* 131–138.

CHAPTER 8

The Use of Mindfulness Interventions in Cognitive Behavior Therapies

Cedar R. Koons

INTRODUCTION

Social workers deal with human suffering daily. Whether they are arranging a kidney transplant, placing children in foster care, or treating chronic depression, social workers encounter situations in which their clients face uncertainty, loss, and pain. They also encounter clients who need to make a change in their lives but are full of fear, anger, and impatience about the change process. Social workers need tools to help their clients accept pain, loss, and the change process itself, in a moment-by-moment way.

Acceptance has traditionally been the province of religion, and different religions have employed similar kinds of activities to promote acceptance, including ritual, prayer, chanting, and scriptural study. In most of the major world religions some attention is also given to meditation or contemplation as a means of understanding and accepting human life and its difficulties. For example, Christianity offers centering prayer, Islam has the practices of Sufism, Hinduism provides various meditations and yogas, and Judaism has the Kaballah. These activities place emphasis on experiencing and accepting the present moment as it is, an awareness that has been termed *mindfulness*.

Buddhism is the tradition most commonly associated with mindfulness practices. Buddhism offers several strong traditions of mindfulness practices including Zen, Tibetan, and Vipassana traditions. Mindfulness is also a strong feature of many practices that are not considered religious, including athletics, music, and the martial arts.

Mindfulness at its most basic is awareness in the present. This awareness is not evaluating in nature but is directed toward the ongoing experience of thoughts, emotions, and sensations observing with one's full attention. For example, Thich Nat Hahn, a Buddhist monk and teacher, said there are two ways to wash the dishes. One is to get the task done; the other is to wash the dishes *to wash the dishes* (Hahn, 1976). According to Jon Kabat-Zinn, developer of Mindfulness-Based Stress Reduction, "mindfulness means paying attention in a particular way: on purpose, in the present moment and nonjudgmentally" (Kabat-Zinn, 1990).

THE CORE MINDFULNESS SKILLS OF DIALECTICAL BEHAVIOR THERAPY

Dialectical behavior therapy (DBT) was developed by Marsha Linehan and colleagues at the University of Washington in the 1980s and described in a book and treatment manual in 1993. DBT is based on three very different foundations; behaviorism, dialectics, and Zen. The primary change strategies come from behaviorism. The primary acceptance strategies come from Zen and the principles of dialectics provide for the balance of the two. As taught in the skills curriculum that comprises a key component of the treatment, the Core Mindfulness Skills provide easy to understand principles that clinicians can teach to clients or use themselves as a foundation for improved coping or practice. Linehan's principles are simple and practical and do not require the practice of sitting meditation. Instead, they emphasize being aware in the present moment, whatever the circumstances, and therefore can be practiced by anyone, anytime. These seven skills are presented here to afford the social worker with a ready-to-use toolkit for understanding and implementing mindfulness in practice.

States of Mind

Linehan (1993b) first describes three "states of mind" common to all people. At any given time, when awake, an individual is primarily experiencing one of these three states of mind. The first is *reasonable mind*, a state of mind that is concerned mainly with the facts such as how to get from point A to point B, how to add up a column of figures, or what ingredients are needed to cook a stew. Reasonable mind is by nature cool and nonurgent. It is task oriented and not focused on feelings.

A second state of mind is *emotion mind* that is characterized by whatever emotions are currently activated. Emotion mind by nature is "hotter" and more insistent than reasonable mind. Emotions activate the entire body with sensations and urges. This activation is part of our survival. For example, when fear is aroused the heart rate speeds up, blood rushes to the extremities in preparation for flight, and the person feels a sensation in the body of fear. If the emotion of joy is activated, the physiological changes and sensations are less extreme, but still noticeable, involving increased heart rate and a sensation of well-being. Emotion mind is also urgent. All emotions have action urges associated with them and when those emotions are aroused the action urge begins to be felt as a more or less insistent drive to act in concert with the emotion. For example, when one is angry, the urge is to attack, when one feels love, the urge is to approach. In contrast to the reasonable mind, emotion mind is focused on feeling and not as concerned with the facts.

The third state of mind delineated by Linehan is termed *wise mind*. Wise mind is depicted as being in touch with both the facts of a situation and the feelings involved. In addition, wise mind, as a synthesis of the two other states of mind, has something more than the sum of its parts. Wise mind "adds intuitive knowing to emotional experiencing and logical analysis" (Linehan, 1993b). The goal of the skills of mindfulness is to reach wise mind, which is described as a quiet and peaceful knowing that everyone can access through simple (not easy) practice. Wise mind is the place from which anyone who is struggling to deal with pain and suffering can make a skillful choice for themselves.

The following six skills are some of the main means of reaching wise mind, those that comprise the core skills.

The Skills

Observe, Describe, Participate

These first three skills are called the "what" skills and describe actions to undertake in order to begin to enter into a mindful experience of the present moment. The "what" skills can only be done one at a time. Observing is simple noticing, without putting words on the experience. Clients are instructed to notice the sensation of their feet on the floor, for example, or to place their hand on a nearby surface and notice the feeling. The skill of observe requires that a person step back and notice without evaluating the experience, talking to oneself about the experience, dissociating or allowing distractions to take one's attention. At times, observing alone can be helpful to help an individual in distress notice impulses for what they are and employ skills to avoid acting upon them.

The skill of describing is simply putting to words what is observed. One has stopped observing and now can respond to and label what is observed. Using the skill of describe one sticks to the simple facts, leaving out inferences, suppositions, and conclusions. One describes a thought as a thought for example, or an emotion as an emotion, describing what has been observed, with the same detachment that characterizes the use of the observe skill. Use of the describe skill is valuable both in self-talk and in talk with others. It can lower the emotional impact of what is said by removing unhelpful inferences and assessments. Used together in sequence, observe and describe allow the practitioner to stay connected moment by moment to his or her experience as it unfolds rather than veer off into thoughts or emotions about the experience. The skills also help one to gather more information about how to handle complex situations. Used together these skills, also prepare one to enter fully into the experience of life, to participate mindfully, which is the third "what" skill.

To participate is to step into the game and play. Participate is described as "acting intuitively from wise mind" in contrast to acting impulsively from emotion mind. Utilizing the skill of participate one "throws oneself into" the experience, rather than hanging back fearfully or willfully, and rather than avoiding, ruminating or otherwise stepping out of the moment. Moments of participation are "flow" moments. The mind is focused, the attention is on what is at hand, and one acts as skillfully as possible. This state is what one achieves through practicing observe and describe long enough that a certain amount of comfort with the activity is possible. For example, in learning to drive a car, it is first necessary to observe all the elements of its operation including the accelerator, brake, steering wheel, and gear shift. In order to back up or parallel park, new drivers must carefully observe the steps in the process and describe them to themselves or an instructor. Only when driving is fully learned does the process become automatic. Then one must still pay attention during the operation of the vehicle, but a level of skill is attained so that one can participate in driving without needing to observe and describe. However, there are times when a return to observe and describe may be necessary, such as when beginning to drive on the right in a different country.

Nonjudgmentally, One-mindfully, Effectively

In addition to observe, describe, and participate, Linehan also delineates three "how" skills that accompany the "what" skills and describes how they must be done to remain mindful. The "how" skills, can be used simultaneously, just as three adverbs can modify the same verb. The first skill of this group is nonjudgmentally. The practitioner of DBT mindfulness skills is instructed to adopt a nonjudgmental stance toward the self and others. Judging in this case is labeling as good or bad rather than describing a situation using "just the facts." Instead of judging, the client is instructed "to unglue your opinions from the facts." Focusing on the facts of a situation does not preclude one from attending to the consequences of a situation that might be judged. For example, saying if you smoke you are likely to damage your health is not the same as saying if you smoke you are stupid. The former statement focuses on the consequences and provides more information than the judgment in the second sentence. A crucial element of adopting a nonjudgmental stance is to also adopt it toward oneself. For example, rather than saying "I am a jerk," this skill would have its practitioner reflect on and state the facts, such as "I forgot to call my best friend on her birthday and I feel regret about that." Finally, a corollary to the skill of nonjudgmentally is not to judge one's own judging.

The second "how" skill is one-mindfully, which is to focus one's attention on only one activity at a time. The skill of one-mindfully requires having undivided attention. This skill is in contrast to distracted attention. Distracted attention is doing one thing while thinking of something else, such as driving while talking on the phone. One-mindfully is a description of many formal religious activities such as observing one's breath, counting the breath, saying the rosary or davening. It is also useful in playing golf or tennis. It has even been used to deal with the problem of worry. Borkevec (cited in Linehan, 1993b) suggests setting aside 30 minutes a day for focused worrying and then during the rest of the day reminding oneself as worries arise that there will be time to attend to them during the formal worry time.

The skill of effectively is the last of the "how" skills. To use the skill of effectively one must first focus on what is the goal of any given situation and then decide what will work to get that goal. Use of the skill of effectively requires that one focus on *what is* rather than on *what should be* and therefore letting go of imposing one's sense of righteousness and fairness on others when that gets in the way of one's goal. The skill of effectively is the opposite of "cutting off your nose to spite your face." For example, if a prisoner wants to get certain privileges he or she must play by the rules. A prisoner who becomes irate and demanding when another inmate gets "undeserved" privileges is not likely to be effective.

The three "what" skills and three "how" skills are all proceed from and lead to wise mind. They focus the mind, allow emotional urges to be contained, and contribute to acceptance of what is in the moment. Use of any of these skills can reduce distress and allow a person to begin making better choices. Learning about wise mind and how to access it can be helpful to children, adolescents, adults, and elders. These skills are especially helpful with people who must accept much that is painful and limiting, such as people in prison, people with chronic physical or mental illness, people who are in recovery from addiction, and couples in conflict.

Using Linehan's Core Mindfulness Skills to Improve Social Work Practice

How can social workers use the skills of mindfulness to improve their social work practice and why would an individual choose to do so? As already mentioned, social workers deal daily with human suffering, often with little possibility of immediately relieving that suffering. In addition, social workers sometimes work in large and intractable systems, in stressful working conditions, and with burned out colleagues. In such situations, the ability to remain present with the client, and to be able to focus on the tasks at hand, is paramount. First of all, clinicians need to know when their own emotions are interfering, that is, when they are in emotion mind. Emotion mind will tinge assessments with the clinician's emotions and interfere with generating effective solutions. On the other hand, if clinicians are stuck in reasonable mind, focusing on certain facts without access to the emotions involved, they are unlikely to have the information they need to empathize with the client. As much as possible, social workers want to be able to integrate the facts of a situation with the emotions involved and arrive at wise mind, or at the very least arrive in the present moment knowing their current state of mind.

The skills of observe and describe are extremely useful in allowing clinicians to stick with the facts in the situation while also noticing emotions, judgments, inferences, and other influences that could detract from accurate assessments. Observe, describe, and participate are invaluable in any crisis situation, in which the social worker is required to intervene without falling into an emotion-driven response. Using these skills, clinicians may find themselves more alert, more relaxed, and less subject to the stress surrounding them.

Practicing a nonjudgmental stance is in harmony with social work values and supports good assessment skills. Judgment is the basis of prejudice, stigma, and discrimination that are adversaries of social work practice. When social workers adopt a nonjudgmental stance toward clients, colleagues, and systems, they may be able to achieve more understanding and empathy that can contribute to more effective helping. Focusing on one thing in the moment helps the practitioner avoid feeling overwhelmed at the many problems and issues that need to be addressed. Finally, using the skill of effective, the social worker keeps an eye on the client's goals at all times rather than getting lost in what he or she thinks *should* be going on. When dealing with poverty, injustice, and discrimination it can be easy to become distracted from the simple goal of helping a client get visitation with her children *this week*.

Mindfulness skills as described by Linehan are helpful in many ways as social workers interact with clients and colleagues. In addition, the practice of mindfulness can be useful in an individual clinician's life to help maintain balance, avoid burnout, and increase the capacity for acceptance of the profession's joys and burdens. In order to teach mindfulness, it would seem clear that a clinician would have to practice mindfulness. In some treatments, a daily sitting practice is required of all clinicians. In others, formal daily practice is highly recommended. For the social worker in a hectic work setting, daily formal and informal mindfulness practices can provide a basis of centered awareness from which to approach their work.

MEDITATION AND MINDFULNESS IN THEORETICAL PSYCHOLOGY

Interest in Eastern meditation has long been associated with theoretical psychology and there has been debate about whether meditation states are beneficial. Freud wondered if the "oceanic feeling" of meditation was regressive, while Jung was more complimentary and even wrote a commentary on the *Tibetan Book of the Dead* (in Germer, 2005). Psychologist Eric Fromm compared notes with Zen scholar and roshi, Dr. T. Suzuki in the early 1960s. Former Harvard psychologist Ram Dass introduced many to ideas of meditation and enlightenment in his book *Be Here Now* (1971). Meanwhile, some studies were undertaken, such as that by Herbert Benson on the role of relaxation to treat heart disease (Benson, 1975). In 1977, the American Psychiatric Association first called for an examination of the clinical effectiveness of meditation. (For a history of mindfulness in psychotherapy, see Germer, 2005.)

Prior to 1991, a confluence of meditation practice and psychotherapy was already emerging in popular and academic psychology (Bogart, 1991). Scholars noted that there are many forms of meditation that have been developed over millennia. Their physiological, cognitive, and psychological effects may be quite different one from another and in novice and experienced practitioners. Some practices, such as Transcendental Meditation (TM), focus the attention on one point to approach a state of absorption and tranquility, and others, such as Vipassana, encourage the practitioner to notice all thoughts, feelings, and sensations exactly as they occur in an attempt to become more familiar with one's mental processes and thereby learn to step aside from them (Bogart, 1991). Until the mid-nineties, theoretical formulation and clinical investigation into mindfulness as a psychotherapeutic intervention was still in its early development. Nonetheless, interest in and controversy about the intersection of psychotherapy and various differing meditations was strong in many psychotherapeutic traditions, including cognitive behavior therapies (Bogart, 1991).

Mindfulness and Cognitive Behavior Therapy

Traditionally, cognitive behavior therapy (CBT) has been focused on getting clients to change: to give up maladaptive behaviors and thoughts that lead to pain and suffering and learn new ways of thinking and behaving. However, no one is able to stay the course of behavioral change without first accepting their present circumstances. Through accepting that in the present they are depressed, anxious, obese, or a single parent, conditions that rarely change overnight, clients can begin to tolerate the pace and pain of change. Additionally, some circumstances, such as a history of abuse, will never change. As stated by Marsha Linehan (1993b),

> Suffering is pain plus nonacceptance of the pain. Suffering comes when people are unable or refuse to accept pain. Suffering comes when people cling to what they want, refusing to accept what they have. Suffering comes when people resist reality as it is in the moment. Pain can be difficult or almost impossible to bear, but suffering is even more difficult. Refusal to accept reality and the suffering that goes along with it can interfere with reducing pain. It is like a cloud that surrounds pain, interfering with the ability to see it clearly. Radical acceptance transforms suffering into pain. (p. 000)

Mindfulness and other acceptance strategies have begun to emerge in CBT to augment technologies of change with an experiential technology of acceptance.

Mindfulness as practiced in CBT is separate from any religious beliefs and represents a new area of exploration in the field. Hayes (2004) characterizes three waves of CBT. The first wave, which began in the 1950s, countered the prevailing mainly symbolic psychoanalytic interpretations of behavior with an alternative view that was "direct, humble, rational, and empirical." Early behaviorism focused on symptom relief and "first-order change," meaning that the targets were often direct behavioral change rather than "unconscious interests or conflicts." The focus was on the stimulus-response association. There was an emphasis on social skills training, through instruction and feedback. The second wave, begun in the 1960s, brought cognitive methods to bear, introducing a central focus on language and thoughts. At first, cognitive therapy struggled with behavior therapy for who would lead the field, and the cognitivists, like the behaviorists before them, also addressed first-order change, but by focusing primarily on dysfunctional beliefs and faulty thinking. Gradually, the cognitive and behavioral camps have begun to unite, combining some of their targets and strategies. This combination greatly strengthened the field, which still primarily focused on the forms of behavior and on first-order change. Researchers in the 1980s began to question some assumptions made by earlier manualized models especially when those manuals lacked pragmatic means of generalization. How well could these models make the jump from the academic laboratories to large public agencies and hospitals where most treatment was delivered? Beginning in the 1990s a new wave of exploration, while still solidly governed by the empirical principles of CBT, became focused on broader, more experiential and flexible solutions that addressed the contexts and functions of behavior. Hayes (2004) defines the third wave thusly:

> the new behavior therapies carry forward the behavior therapy tradition but they 1) abandon a sole commitment to first-order change, 2) adopt more contextualistic assumptions, 3) adopt more experiential and indirect change strategies in addition to direct strategies and 4) considerably broaden the focus of change. (p. 6)

The incorporation of mindfulness practices into CBT is central to the third wave. Mindfulness practices not only help clients make first-order change, such as letting go of ruminative thinking, but also help them *accept* that certain thought patterns are likely to emerge and recur during a depressive episode. Similarly, a client seeking "freedom *from* her anxiety" may actually discover "freedom *in* her anxiety" through the use of mindfulness and acceptance strategies (Germer, 2005). Finally, individuals seeking treatment for posttraumatic stress must experience emotions, thoughts, memories, and behavioral predispositions that are highly unpleasant. The more these unwanted experiences are avoided, the more they occur. The well-described CBT tool of exposure is useful here. But in the meantime, clients need to learn to tolerate the experience of the present. For these clients, mindfulness introduces a more experiential and accepting focus, significantly broadening the basis of the intervention.

Four Examples of Cognitive Behavior Therapies That Employ Mindfulness

In order to explore how mindfulness is used in current CBT practice, we turn our attention to four treatments that have been shown to be effective. These treatments address important treatment areas that are highly likely to be encountered by the practicing social worker, including 1) chronic pain and disability, 2) alcohol and drug use disorders, 3) borderline personality disorder, and 4) recurrent major depression. We examine Mindfulness-Based Stress Reduction (MBSR), and Vipassana Meditation for Alcohol and Drug Use Disorders, where mindfulness practice is the main or only treatment, and a complex, principal-driven treatment, Dialectical Behavior Therapy (DBT), which employs mindfulness as a theoretical underpinning and as a skill. In DBT, mindfulness is a smaller portion of the overall treatment, which also employs standard CBT and other innovations. Mindfulness-Based Cognitive Therapy for depression (MBCT) mixes almost equal parts mindfulness training with standard cognitive therapy.

Mindfulness-Based Stress Reduction

A pioneer in the introduction of mindfulness and meditation into behavioral medicine, Jon Kabat-Zinn founded the Stress Reduction Center at the University of Massachusetts in 1979. Working with patients referred to him because traditional medicine could not help them, Kabat-Zinn became interested in whether the meditation and mindfulness he had been practicing since his years as a graduate student could help patients with chronic pain and disability achieve better coping. Together with colleagues, Kabat-Zinn developed a protocol that introduced patients to meditation, yoga, and an opportunity to develop a new awareness through practice and discussion. The class, known as Mindfulness-Based Stress Reduction, consists of eight 150-minute classes that include guided and silent meditations, yoga stretching, instructor-led discussions, and extensive homework practice using audiotapes. Participants sit on meditation mats if possible and recline on mats for the practice of the body scan and for some of the guided meditations. The classes are large in size, including as many as 30 participants at a time. Participants share their experiences of the exercises with the group as part of the class. The meditation taught in MBSR emphasizes acceptance of all thoughts, emotions, and sensations as they arise and bringing an attitude of detached interest and nonstriving to the practice. Participants are strongly encouraged to continue their daily meditation practice after the class is completed and are invited to yearly reunion meditation retreats.

Thousands of patients have completed MBSR, and research has demonstrated that a majority of participants experience a lasting decrease in physiological and psychological symptoms, reduction in pain levels and improvement in the ability to cope with pain, an increased capacity to relax, improvement on measures of self-esteem, enthusiasm for life, and improvement in the ability to cope with stress. MBSR has become an area of interest in behavioral medicine and has also inspired the work of cognitive behavioral scientists to apply some of its techniques to the treatment of chronic depression (Center for Mindfulness, 2005).

Vipassana Meditation as a Treatment for Alcohol and Drug Use Disorders

The most widely disseminated models for the treatment of alcohol and drug use disorders are CBT and the 12-step models of Alcoholics Anonymous (AA) and Narcotics Anonymous (NA). CBT attempts to address environmental, emotional, and cognitive precursors and consequences to substance abuse, and address these with skills training, exposure training, marital therapy, and other interventions. AA and NA focus on the peer support, reliance on a higher power, prayer, and spiritual awakening. AA and NA are more widely available and lower in cost than CBT, but may not be preferred by treatment seekers, particularly those belonging to Eastern religions, or to atheists (Marlatt et al., 2004). Some treatment seekers also experience embarrassment or a stigma associated with the use of terms such as "alcoholic" or "addict" in 12-step programs (Sobell, Ellingstad, & Sobell, 2000, in Marlatt et al., 2004).

These two approaches differ in many significant ways, nevertheless, they appear to have similar outcomes and mechanisms of action (Moos, Finney, Ouimette, & Suchinsky, 1999, reported in Marlatt et al., 2004, and Morganstern, Labouvie, McCrady, Kahler, & Frey, 1997, reported in Marlatt et al., 2004).

The noted researcher and treatment developer Alan Marlatt first became interested in meditation when, as an assistant professor, he was diagnosed with borderline hypertension. He took a TM course and began meditating on a regular basis (Marlatt, 2002). Later, as he explored the treatment of high-risk drinkers, Marlatt became interested in whether meditation might have a role. In his first study, Marlatt and colleagues randomly assigned college students who met criteria for heavy drinking to one of three conditions: a mantra-based meditation, deep muscle relaxation, or daily periods of quiet, recreational reading. A control group did no relaxation, but monitored their drinking daily. Compared to those in the control group, all of those in the relaxation groups showed significant improvement. But those in the meditation group showed the most reductions in drinking over the six-week intervention period, with an average decrease of 50% in daily alcohol consumption (Marlatt, Pagano, Rose, & Marques, 1984). The findings were replicated in another study 2 years later, also with heavy drinkers that compared meditation with aerobic exercise. Both were significantly associated with drops in daily drinking (Murphy, Pagano, & Marlatt, 1986). These studies prompted Witkiewitz and Marlatt to focus on meditation and exercise as crucial components of his relapse prevention model, MBRP, which combines mindfulness skills with standard CBT for relapse prevention (Witkiewitz, Marlatt & Walker, in press).

Marlatt reports on two studies of an intervention that assigns individuals with significant substance abuse histories to a 10-day Vipassana meditation course that included approximately 11 hours of sitting meditation, plus didactic presentations and meetings with the instructors. Participants were housed in the silent retreat center and provided with two vegetarian meals, and snacks. The first study participants were incarcerated individuals and the second study was a community sample. The studies are ongoing, but preliminary findings indicated support for reducing alcohol and drug as well as improving drinking-related cognitions, optimism, self-regulation, and readiness to change in both samples (in Marlatt, 2004).

While both CBT and AA/NA directly address the first-order change goal of reducing substance use, Vipassana gives no specific instruction as how to apply the mindfulness skills learned to specific problems such as craving for drugs. Vipassana, like many other traditions, assumes that mindfulness is useful in reducing all kinds of suffering brought on by thoughts, emotions, and sensations. Marlatt hypothesizes that mindfulness effects the "meta-cognitive processes" by changing one's relationship with urges and cravings. With extended practice, the meditator observes the intervals between the otherwise lock-step process of stimulus-response, and pauses to choose an alternative response to the habitual and maladaptive ones, such as focusing on the breath, a choice that can make the difference between staying clean and sober and relapsing (Marlatt et al., 2004).

Dialectical Behavior Therapy

Zen practitioner Marsha Linehan was treating chronically suicidal and self-injurious women in the early 1980s using behavior therapy. She found that standard cognitive behavioral methods were not enough to engage this population, many of whom had borderline personality disorder. Linehan came to recognize that as much as her patients needed to change behavior they also needed help accepting themselves in the present moment. In her efforts to teach them the skills they needed to take control of their attention and tolerate the moment, Linehan turned to her Zen training and introduced mindfulness, awareness, breathing, and radical acceptance into her skills curriculum. These skills focused on accepting the moment and acted as a balance for the more change-oriented skills in the emotion regulation and interpersonal effectiveness modules.

Linehan wove acceptance strategies into her treatment at many levels. To balance the emphasis on change in behaviorism, Linehan added validation strategies for the therapist to use, strategies more familiar in humanistic than behavioral therapies. Validation addresses the difficulty a client perceives in accepting current reality, a difficulty that can prompt hopelessness, shame, and suicidal ideation. When the therapist validates the client, he or she acknowledges that given past learning or current circumstances, everything is as it should be. This is also an important Zen principle. It does not mean that the therapist or the client approves of how things are, only that they both recognize that for conditions to change in the moment, one would need to address each of the myriad factors that have contributed to the current conditions. Therefore, the therapist communicates, in the moment, how a certain behavior, such as binge-eating, has been learned by the client as a way to cope since she gave up methamphetamine. The therapist further communicates that given the current level of stress, the presence of the binge food, and in the absence of other skills she can use, it is understandable that the client would binge-eat. Robins (2002) points out how Zen principles contribute to the stated assumptions Linehan makes about borderline clients, particularly the idea of inherent wisdom in each individual. The skill of radical acceptance, taught in the most acceptance based module, "Distress Tolerance" employs the Zen principles of seeing reality as it is and accepting reality without judgment (Robins, 2004). This skill can be very difficult for borderline individuals, especially those who have suffered great injustices in life such as sexual abuse and have spent many years refusing to accept what happened to them. Linehan says that "acceptance is the only way out of hell" (1993b) and that "accepting something is not the same as saying it is good" (1993). One of Linehan's many great contributions to the field is her delineation of the "core skills" of mindfulness, presented earlier. She took the specific mindfulness practices of her own spiritual training in Zen, and defined them as the specific skills, thereby breaking mindfulness down into its component parts for ease of teaching to clients and to therapists.

Randomized controlled trials of DBT have been conducted for its efficacy for borderline personality disorder and also for the treatment of eating disorders. In addition, it has been adapted for various populations, including suicidal adolescents and depressed elders. Since DBT is a complex treatment, which has not been dismantled into its component parts and studied, it is difficult to know what role mindfulness plays in its efficacy.

Mindfulness-Based Cognitive Therapy for Depression—
Relapse Prevention

Following in the footsteps of Jon Kabat-Zinn, three researchers in the field of cognitive therapy for depression began an exploration of what factors contribute to depression becoming a chronic, relapsing condition for many patients and what if anything could be done about the problem.

How could relapse into depression be prevented, especially for individuals who had experienced three or more episodes of depression? Could this treatment act as a "maintenance dose" of therapy, similar to maintenance doses of antidepressant medication?

In the 1960s and 1970s the emphasis of cognitive and behavioral treatments for depression was on the acute phase of the illness. In the 1980s, researchers became more aware of the chronic nature of the disorder and that the individuals who had experienced three or more episodes were at risk for a lifetime of chronic depression. At the same time, gains in the pharmacological treatment of depression offered hope, and many patients now expect to be on a maintenance dose of antidepressant medication for their lifetimes. However, there were still many patients who declined to take antidepressants, or for whom antidepressant medication was not indicated, or for whom the side effects were unacceptable. In their efforts to develop a maintenance version of cognitive therapy for depression, researchers Zindel Segal, Mark Williams and John Teasdale (2002) turned to mindfulness as a therapeutic tool to address relapse.

Segal, Williams, and Teasdale studied Kabat-Zinn's 8-week MBSR model as well as the structures used by Marsha Linehan in DBT and developed the Mindfulness-Based Cognitive Therapy (MBCT) for Depression Relapse Prevention program. Like MBSR, MBCT is an 8-week class with much guided meditation, silent meditation, didactic presentation, discussion, and homework practice. Like MBSR, MBCT emphasizes the 8-week class as the beginning of a daily practice that is to be maintained as a bulwark against depressive relapse. And, like MBSR, MBCT has some data demonstrating results, specifically, a significant reduction in relapse of depression for the target group, namely those with three or more episodes of major depression as compared with treatment as usual (Segal, Teasdale, & Williams, 2004).

MBCT differs from MBSR in some significant ways. The most obvious difference is in the focus on depression in the handouts and didactic presentations. Additionally, MBCT uses many of the standard tools of the cognitive therapy tradition, including a thorough orientation to the treatment, a written relapse prevention plan, and handouts/homework such as an automatic thought questionnaire, pleasant and unpleasant events calendar, and suggestions for how to see your thoughts differently. Borrowing from Linehan, Segal, Williams, and Teasdale suggest two clinicians lead the class together, and the classes are smaller, involving 8 to 12 participants rather than the 30 in the Kabat-Zinn model.

MBCT seeks to prevent relapse by preventing the establishment of a negative thinking patterns that lead to depression. Examples of these patterns include constantly monitoring one's current state and comparing it to a desired state, or being on "automatic pilot" and going through life unaware. The experiential part of the class teaches concentration, awareness of thoughts, emotions and bodily sensations, being in the moment, and being rather than doing. Leaders deemphasize evaluation of one's experience, attachment to doing it right, and attempting to achieve a certain state of relaxation, peace, happiness, and so on.

The format of the classes first introduces concentration slowly with shorter exposures and more clinician-led experiences. Participants are encouraged to close their eyes and pay attention but not to pursue any specific state of being. Gradually, exposure is increased as more sitting meditations are introduced, and participants are encouraged to notice thoughts as thoughts, emotions as emotions, and so on, without defaulting to their characteristic thoughts and reactions to them. Clients are also encouraged to describe their experiences without referencing inferences, ideas, evaluations of judgments and are encouraged to adopt an attitude of "gentle curiosity" to whatever occurs. Leaders are encouraged to ask open-ended questions and pose back to client many of the questions they ask in order to keep the class as focused as possible on the experience as it is. In this way, MBCT is truly representative of the "third wave" mentioned by Hayes, in that it helps patients "to sidestep the content of their thoughts and focus instead on the process" (Segal et al., 2004).

MBCT has data from two randomized controlled trials. The two trials show that for patients with recurrent major depression, participation in the MBCT course contributed on average to a 50% reduction in their relapse to depression, as compared with a 20% reduction in relapse for treatment as usual during the follow-up period. The program appears to be especially effective with a history of three or more episodes of major depressions. And, because the treatment is administered in a group, it is considered cost efficient (Segal et al., 2004).

There are many other CBT treatments that employ mindfulness including treatments for trauma and generalized anxiety disorder, acceptance and commitment therapy, functional analytic psychotherapy, and others worthy of exploration for the student but beyond the scope of this chapter. The following is an example of how mindfulness, combined with good social work and other treatments, succeeded with a depressed veteran with chronic pain and a history of heroin dependence.

PUTTING MINDFULNESS INTERVENTIONS TO WORK— A CLINICAL CASE EXAMPLE

Luke is a 37-year-old single white male with a history of heroin dependence, chronic pain, and major depression. Luke had his first major depressive episode at age 19, after breaking up with his girlfriend of 5 years.

He did not recognize what he was feeling as depression and describes his symptoms as, "I just felt like hell. I felt like I lost who I was. I used to have a backbone. I just went limp. I hated myself." He did not receive treatment but instead entered the Marines to "put it all behind me." He did two tours but never saw combat. He reached the rank of ensign and considered a longer commitment to the Marines, when he learned he was being demobilized. Not long after that Luke was critically injured on base in a motor vehicle accident.

Luke was treated at a military hospital and then discharged from the Marines. He returned to his home city to live with his parents, retired school teachers. Luke's pain from his injury was constant and his mobility was restricted. Formerly quite active and fit, Luke became sedentary, overweight, and addicted to Vicodin and eventually heroin. Luke's relationship with his parents deteriorated as his addiction progressed. He worked intermittently at a video rental facility owned by a friend of the family, lived in his parents' basement, and became more and more depressed and hopeless. Finally, about 3 years post-discharge, Luke attempted suicide with a drug overdose. During the hospitalization that followed, Luke was assigned to a social worker, Joan, who linked him to a pain clinic with good results treating formerly addicted patients. Joan also helped Luke apply for a VA service-connected disability and for social security disability. With his own income, Luke was able to rent a duplex near the VA Medical Center where he received his treatment. He volunteered for the Disabled American Veterans (DAV) office 3 days a week. The rest of the time he isolated in his apartment, watched television, and smoked and drank three to six beers most nights. Joan encouraged Luke to consider attending NA or AA, in order to address the issues of his addiction and to avoid becoming an alcoholic, but Luke refused. "I can't handle all the God-bothering," he said.

Though better off than at any time since his discharge from the Marines, Luke still described himself as "lonely, angry, and hopeless." His only relationships were with his parents, the DAV representative who tolerated his moodiness and absenteeism, and Joan, who cared deeply for him, but did not know how to help him any more than she already had. The VA considered Luke a real success story, and in some ways he was. He had stayed out of the hospital and off heroin. But he was still deeply miserable.

Joan thought Luke would benefit from the DBT program offered in the Mental Health Clinic. It took her 6 weeks to get him to consider trying DBT and another 6 weeks to get him into the skills training group. Joan joined the DBT consultation group and introduced a diary card, behavior analysis, and other standard DBT protocols into their work.

Through practicing the DBT skills and with Joan's help, Luke began to address his mood dependent behaviors, especially by reducing and eliminating alcohol, increasing his attendance at his volunteer job, and changing his habits of isolation. Over the 18 months he attended skills training, Luke found that when he worked with the skill of "Radical Acceptance" regarding his accident and chronic pain, he began to feel less hopeless and angry. This also helped him reduce the alcohol, which he was using to numb himself emotionally. By practicing observe, describe, and participate, Luke was able to overcome his social anxiety and begin to engage in relationships and even begin dating. Adopting a nonjudgmental stance was most helpful to Luke in reducing his self-blame and self-loathing. Reducing these and other ruminative behaviors improved his mood. Through informal and formal exposure techniques, Joan helped Luke work through the lingering distress regarding his accident. Exposure helped Luke reduce his emotional avoidance and increase the range of emotions he could comfortably feel.

After completing stages one and two of DBT, Luke became interested in the MBSR class offered at a local college. With Joan's encouragement he enrolled in the 8-week class and found that the mindfulness skills he learned in DBT were very congruent with the curriculum. He had worried that the 30- and 45-minute meditation sessions would prove too difficult for him but found that, while they were a challenge, he actually enjoyed them. Luke experienced a reduction in the feeling that he could not cope with his pain and an increase in his sense of mastery. He decided to make sitting meditation for at least 15 minutes a day a part of his daily routine and had started attending the Quaker meeting his parents had joined. He found that he no longer wanted to drink alone in the evenings, although he still occasionally had a beer or two with friends. He continued to use his prescription pain medication compliantly. For the next 6 to 8 months he continued to work with Joan on his goals of finding meaningful work he could handle and having a successful dating relationship.

Now 33-years-old, Luke is enrolled in an associate's degree program at the community college and has a steady girlfriend he met at Quaker meeting. He is on good terms with his parents and continues to volunteer two afternoons a week at the DAV office. He sees Joan once a month and participates in a veterans' drop-in support group every other week. He is considering becoming a drug and alcohol counselor. Most days, he continues his sitting meditation practice. He has not relapsed on drugs, uses alcohol moderately, and has not experienced a depressive episode in over a year. His chronic pain remains a problem for him, but he describes himself as "really enjoying his life" for the first time since the accident.

FUTURE DIRECTIONS

Initial data on the use of mindfulness interventions in treatment development are promising, but further study is clearly needed. In complex treatments such as DBT or Acceptance and Commitment Therapy (ACT), dismantling studies are needed to determine what the "active ingredients" are that make the treatments effective and if mindfulness is one of those ingredients. And for mindfulness as an intervention it remains unclear what the specific effects are, how they can be measured and what is the underlying mechanism of change (Baer, 2003).

Questions arise about the overlap of certain mindfulness interventions and interventions used in standard cognitive behavior therapy. For example, what are the differences in mindfulness and relaxation, exposure, self-monitoring, and cognitive change? On the question of relaxation and mindfulness, EEG patterns appear to be quite different in the two practices, with slow wave activity associated with relaxation and fast wave activity associated with mindfulness but more study is needed to know whether the psychological effects are different (Dunn, Hartigan, & Mikulas, 1999, in Roemer & Orsillo, 2003). Linehan and Kabat-Zinn have posited a relationship between the mechanism of mindfulness and that of exposure (in Roemer & Orsillo, 2003), which both encourage direct experiencing of internal states. The goals of the two interventions are quite different in that exposure aims at a reduction of distress and mindfulness emphasizes acceptance of what is. However, both interventions may lead to more capacity to fully experience the moment. Also, the moment-to-moment self-awareness of mindfulness has been compared to the self-monitoring in CBT, but the latter is much more structured and goal-oriented than the former. As regards the cognitive changes associated with cognitive therapy versus those associated with mindfulness, the former are more directed toward the content of cognition and the latter focuses more on the relationship of the thinker to the thoughts, seeing thoughts as thoughts rather than reality (Roemer & Orsillo, 2003).

Finally, study is needed to determine the best way to deliver mindfulness training. What is the needed dose, 3 minutes or 8 hours? Is a daily sitting practice required, or does practicing observe, describe, and participate throughout the day suffice? Do the effects of mindfulness increase or decrease over time? Is mindfulness training in a mental health clinic preferable to attending an ashram or zendo? While these and other questions remain unanswered, social workers can still benefit from familiarity with the tools of mindfulness in their work with clients.

SUMMARY

In this chapter we have explored how and why mindfulness has emerged in recent years as an important intervention in cognitive behavior therapy both as a stand alone treatment and woven into more complex treatments. Mindfulness, a nonjudgmental awareness of moment-to-moment experiencing, has moved from a province of religion and philosophy to a part of effective treatments for borderline personality disorder, chronic pain, depression, generalized anxiety, posttraumatic stress disorder, and substance abuse. In some treatments in which mindfulness is a part, effectiveness has been demonstrated, but dismantling studies are needed. Data on treatments in which mindfulness is the primary intervention are promising, but questions about the mechanism of change and optimal type of delivery need to be addressed. Research is also needed to measure and distinguish between the effects of standard cognitive behavior interventions and mindfulness effects.

In this chapter also, we have introduced the core skills of mindfulness as described by Linehan and discussed how they are useful to clients and to social workers. In cognitive behavior theory and research treatment development will continue. How mindfulness is incorporated into existing treatment will change according to the research and new treatments will emerge. The principles of mindfulness, however, will remain. They are ancient and changeless and will always be of use to those seeking shelter from the suffering of life. They are good tools to have in the expanding kit of social work.

REFERENCES

Baer, R. A. (2003). Mindfulness training as a clinical intervention: A conceptual and empirical review. *Clinical Psychology: Science and Practice 10*, 125–142.

Benson, H. (1975). *The relaxation response.* New York: Avon.

Bogart, G. (1991). The use of meditation in psychotherapy: A review of the literature. *American Journal of Psychotherapy, XLV*, 383–413.

Center for Mindfulness at University of Massachusetts Medical Center, website, 2005.

Germer, C. K. (2005). Mindfulness: What is it? What does it matter? In *Mindfulness and Psychotherapy* (pp. 3–27). New York: Guilford.

Hahn, T. N. (1976). *The miracle of mindfulness.* Boston: Beacon Press.

Hayes, S. C. (2004). Acceptance and commitment therapy and the new behavior therapies. In *Mindfulness and acceptance* (pp. 1–29). New York: Guilford.

Hayes, S. C., Strosahl, K. D., & Wilson, K. G. (1999). *Acceptance and commitment therapy.* New York: Guilford .

Kabat-Zinn, J. (1990). *Full catastrophe living.* New York: Dell Publishing.

Kumar, S. M. (2002). An introduction to Buddhism for the cognitive-behavioral therapist. *Cognitive and Behavioral Practice, 9,* 40–43.

Linehan, M. M. (1993a). *Cognitive-behavioral treatment of borderline personality disorder.* New York: Guilford.

Linehan, M. M. (1993b). *Skills training manual for treating borderline personality disorder.* New York: Guilford.

Marlatt, G. A. (2002). Buddhist philosophy and the treatment of addictive behavior. *Cognitive and Behavioral Practice, 9,* 50–57.

Marlatt, G. A., Witkiewitz, K., Dillworth. T. M., Bowen, S. W., Parks, G. A., Macpherson, L. M., et al. (2004). Vipassana meditation as a treatment for alcohol and drug use disorders. In *Mindfulness and acceptance* (pp. 261–287). New York: Guilford.

Murphy, T. J., Pagoso, R. R., & Marlatt, G. A. (1986). Lifestyle modification with heavy alcoholic drinkers: Effects of aerobic exercise and medication. *Addictive Behaviors, 11,* 175–186.

Robins, C. J. (2002). Zen principles and mindfulness practice in dialectical behavior therapy. *Cognitive and Behavioral Practice, 9,* 50–57.

Robins, C. J. (2004). Dialectical behavior therapy: Synthesizing radical acceptance with skillful means. In *Mindfulness and Acceptance.* New York: Guilford.

Roemer, L., & Orsillo, S. M. (2003). Mindfulness: A promising intervention strategy in need of further study. *Clinical Psychology: Science and Practice, 10,* 172–178.

Segal, Z., Williams, M., & Teasdale, J. (2002). Mindfulness-based cognitive therapy for depression: A new approach to preventing relapse. New York: Guilford.

Segal, Z., Teasdale, J., & Williams, M. (2004). Mindfulness-based cognitive therapy: Theoretical rationale and empirical status. In *Mindfulness and Acceptance.* New York: Guilford.

Witkiewitz, K., Marlatt, G. A., & Walker, D. D. (in press). Mindfulness-based relapse prevention for alcohol use disorders: The meditative tortoise wins the race. *Journal of Cognitive Psychotherapy.*

PART III

Focus on Children

CHAPTER 9

Cognitive Behavior Therapy With Children and Adolescents

Tammie Ronen

INTRODUCTION

One of the largest populations at the center of social workers' attention is that of children (including adolescents), who constitute more than 50% of referrals to social welfare services. Epidemiological studies indicate that from 17% to 22% of children under 18 years of age suffer from developmental, emotional, or behavioral problems, most of which are long lasting and predictive of problems in adulthood (Kazdin, 1993, 2000).

As a profession whose primary obligation consists of intervening for the welfare of weak and vulnerable populations, social work by definition must engage in child-focused intervention. Social workers must help children who live under dangerous conditions, whether at risk, abused, or neglected. However, children also present a large range of other disorders necessitating intervention, whether with the individual child or with the child as part of the family or peer group.

Children's disorders relate to all areas of life, starting at a young age with educational problems that involve eating, toileting, sleep, and dis-

The author would like to express her appreciation to Dee B. Ankonina for her editorial contribution.

cipline, or with developmental problems such as pervasive developmental disorder, attention deficit/hyperactivity disorder, Asperger syndrome, autism, and so on. Childhood disorders may also concern emotional problems like anxiety, depression, and stress or social problems such as loneliness and social phobia.

Social workers meet children in various settings such as schools, welfare services, physical and mental health agencies, and private practice. Referrals vary in the identified source of the child's problems: Children may be the cause of their own problems, as in the case of aggressive or violent behavior disorders, or may be a victim of an environmental problem, as in cases of abuse or neglect (see Chapter 11 by Rene Mason). Alternatively, children's problems may stem from the presence of various disorders such as attention deficit/hyperactivity (ADHD), anxiety, stress, depression, or school difficulties (see Chapter 12 by Stewart Barbera and Chapter 10 by Bert Alian and Catherine Lemieux). In other cases, the child may be playing the role of identified client for a family problem (see Chapter 15 by Susan Gingerich on working with families).

In light of the range of problem areas and types exhibited by children, social workers should be able to work with the individual child, the group, the family, and the wider environment. At the same time, when working with children, social workers must maintain awareness of developmental, emotional, cognitive, social, and communicational problems, as well as to the question of who is really in focus of intervention: the child, the family, or the environment.

In view of the fact that one of the critical predictors for adult mental health problems is childhood disorder (Kazdin, 1993), the issue of applying effective intervention in childhood and adolescence becomes crucial. Kazdin's review of over 230 different techniques for child and adolescent therapy revealed that the great majority of these techniques has never been studied and, therefore, has never been shown to be effective. An effective intervention is one that links developmental components (see Chapter 5 by Amy Carrigan) with evidence-based practice (see Chapter 3 by Bruce Thyer and Laura Myers) to help enable clients to live with, accept, cope with, resolve, and overcome their distress and to improve their subjective well-being (Kazdin & Weisz, 2003).

Cognitive behavioral therapy (CBT) offers a promising approach to address such needs for treatment efficacy, on the condition that social workers adapt basic CBT to the specific needs of children and design the intervention holistically to foster change in children (Ronen, 1997, 2003). This chapter suggests a route for applying effective interventions in the day-to-day work of social workers who are primarily involved in direct interventions with children and their families.

MAIN GOALS OF CHILD INTERVENTION

CBT with children addresses four main aims: to decrease behavior, to increase behavior, to remove anxiety, and to facilitate development (Mash & Terdal, 1988; Ronen, 2001). Each of these aims targets one of the four main groups of children commonly referred to treatment.

For many years, most cognitive behavioral child studies and treatments have focused on children who reveal acting-out, externalizing disorders such as aggressiveness, delinquency, negativism, disobedience, hyperactivity, or impulsivity (Durlak, Fuhrman, & Lampman, 1991)—mainly because these problems disturb adults, and adults are those who refer children to therapy. Children suffering from externalizing disorders act without thinking or planning and lack careful information processing in situations in which thinking would be beneficial. They demonstrate difficulties in tolerating frustration, delaying gratification, and keeping attention on target (Barkley, 1997; Kendall, 1993; Kendall & Braswell, 1993; Ronen, 1997, 2001). Therapy for these children should aim to decrease their undesired behaviors (Achenbach, 1985; Mash & Terdal, 1988) and to train them in the skills needed to use problem-solving skills and change their impulsive manner of thinking and acting.

Less attention and knowledge have related to a second group of children who need to increase specific behaviors and stop their avoidance (Achenbach, 1985; Mash & Terdal, 1988). These children exhibit acting-in, internalizing disorders such as anxiety, depression, somatic complaints, and social loneliness. The main feature of such disorders comprises fear of new and unknown experiences and of disturbing or disconcerting emotions. Characterized by emotional dysfunction, these children demonstrate low self-confidence, self-acceptance, and self-esteem. Inasmuch as these children often overemphasize self-evaluations, they frequently establish unrealistic goals or harsh criteria for themselves and thereby underappreciate their own achievements (Kendall, 1993). Kendall suggested that such children are limited to distorted thinking, in which they misconstrue and misconceive social situations. Thus, interventions with these children should address distortions in their self-concept and should challenge them to do more, with a focus on experiencing and practicing.

Children who suffer mainly from anxiety—the third type of treatment goals—cannot achieve their potential capabilities due to avoidance and regression caused by their fears, anxieties, and trauma. Unlike the second group, these children's difficulties do not stem from overly high expectations, low self-evaluations, and distorted thoughts, but rather from overwhelmingly anxious feelings. They need to acquire a wider repertoire of coping skills and to practice exposure assignments in order for them to try out new experiences.

For the last group of children, whose development needs to be facilitated due to their immaturity, treatment should promote the acquisition of new skills such as to refrain from or cease crying, to restrain themselves in various situations, or to take on responsibilities. To facilitate change for this fourth group, treatment should also offer practice in new tasks and provide new models for change both for the children themselves and for their environments. For example, a child's immature behavior may root in a lack of skills but also could result from an absence of family encouragement to the child to become more independent or to take on responsibility. Knowing the aim of therapy for a specific child will enable a better selection of intervention setting and treatment techniques.

THE BASICS OF CBT WITH ADULTS

CBT comprises a longstanding treatment of choice with adults, offering an empirically based, integral, holistic therapy that targets improvement in people's way of thinking, feeling, and acting. CBT views thoughts, emotions, and behaviors as interlinked and as influencing coping. In this therapeutic approach, cognitive factors relating to how humans process information play a central role in conceptualizing maladaptive behavior, stress, and distress (Alford & Beck, 1997; Beck, Freeman, & Associates, 1990).

Human beings' behavior relates to their basic cognitive schemata (attitudes and beliefs). As an outcome of their schema, humans develop cognitive products such as thoughts and images that influence how they process information and how they manifest problematic behavior (Grave & Blissett, 2004; Powell & Oei, 1991). For more details on CBT with adults, see Chapter 2 by Catherine MacLaren and Art Freeman in this book.

ADAPTATION OF CBT BASICS TO CHILDREN

To apply CBT with children, the basic adult CBT model should be adapted to a child's way of thinking and understanding. The therapist should recognize that children often express their thoughts through actions, images, or feelings rather than through thinking per se (Powell & Oei, 1991). Thus, the therapist should translate treatment techniques, concepts, and goals into children's day-to-day language. This will facilitate the involvement of children in therapy, and increase the motivation and the collaboration of the child in therapy as active participants in the process of learning and change. For example, by using Kelly's (1955) concept of the client as an architect who is involved in designing his or her own life or as a scientist who study and research his or her own life, the child can be empowered and encouraged to collaborate.

Unlike CBT with adults, CBT with children consists of an umbrella term encompassing different treatment techniques offered in many different sequences and permutations. It is not restricted to one theoretical tenet or single-minded applied technique, but rather consists of a set of interrelated strategies for providing new learning experiences (Kendall & Braswell, 1993). As an outcome, there is no one integrated theory for children but a collection of specific techniques each directed for solving a specific problems.

The therapist should also take into account the importance of applying evidence-based practice. Research evidence suggests that CBT comprises an effective treatment for children with externalizing behavior problems such as disruptive, attention, and conduct disorders (Kazdin, 1994; Southam-Gerow & Kendall, 2000) as well as with internalizing problems such as anxiety, depression, and fears (Southam-Gerow & Kendall, 2000). However, Durlak, Fuhrman, and Lampman (1991) proposed that CBT is mainly effective with children 11 years and over. Grave and Blissett (2004) recently asked if CBT can benefit young children. Do they possess the needed skills to gain from CBT? I believe the question should not be whether CBT is indicated for young children but rather what efforts and modifications therapists should undertake to adapt CBT to young children (Ronen, 2003).

ADVANCES IN CBT WITH CHILDREN

Modern studies of emotional processes and social relationships have contributed to a recent shift of interest from externalizing disorders to internalizing ones. Research on affective processes has underscored the role of emotions for human development in general (Greenberg & Safran, 1987; Hayes, Jacobson, Follette, & Daugher, 1994; Mahoney, 1991; Neimeyer & Mahoney, 1995; Safran & Segal, 1990) and for children's development in particular (Shirk & Russell, 1996). This body of research underscores the risk of future impairment among children with internalizing disorders. Researchers have proposed that such children must not merely learn to actively resolve their problems but rather must become able to accept difficulties as well, and to live with ambiguities and insecurities. Advances in studies relating to social influences have emphasized the importance of interpersonal relationships and peer activity for children's growth (Schaffer, 1996). Much of children's normal behavior, as well as much of their distress, can be attributed to social relationships and therefore to emotional responses.

Over the last decade, impressive progress has occurred in the application of CBT for children. This important change results from several trends. First, social processes have elicited interest in children's abuse, neglect, and distress that in turn, have triggered interest in developing effective interventions. Concurrently, research outcomes have pinpointed the lasting effects of childhood disorders such as loneliness, depression, and aggression, and their impact on adults' adjustment and adaptation to society. Also, the notion of linking cognitive, emotional, social, and developmental components with information processing models and with the basics of adult CBT has permitted the formation of a unified theoretical framework for working with children. Another important development consisted of the emergence of studies about emotions and about the role of therapeutic relationships that are crucial for child therapy. All of these trends, together with the recent call for evidence-based therapy and the emphasis on outcome studies, goal-directed treatment, and data-based knowledge, have enabled new and groundbreaking applications of CBT with children (Thyer & Kazi, 2004).

A NEW MODEL FOR APPLYING CBT WITH CHILDREN: SKILLS-DIRECTED THERAPY

As an example to a model that relates to children developmental issues, that enable integrating behavioral versus emotional problems and apply evidence-based practice, I will describe our SDT model.

Together with Michael Rosenbaum, I developed a new model for children's disorders and treatment that emphasizes skill acquisition (learning and training) as the main feature responsible for children's change, within the framework of the CBT approach. Skills-directed therapy (SDT) is an integrative child CBT model that combines an array of developmentally significant features, including the child's age and gender, cognitive development, linguistic and information processing, emotional, and social development, peers and family. First, the rationale for incorporating all of these developmentally linked components into the SDT model are described, and followed by a specific application for children who demonstrate aggressive behavior, based on this model for learning self-control skills.

THE IMPORTANCE OF INTEGRATING
DEVELOPMENTAL COMPONENTS IN CBT
WITH CHILDREN

Throughout childhood, children experience changes in all areas of life, from physical and motoric changes, through cognitive and emotional changes, to social changes. These changes indicate not only differing degrees of organismic complexity but also alterations in the biological and psychological substructures that emerge and unfold within the child's social surroundings (Shapiro, 1995; see also Chapter 5 by Amy Carrigan). Effective intervention with children should, therefore, directly relate child disturbances to developmental considerations. Only through knowledge of normal developmental processes can one begin to understand deviations in development and their importance for assessment and intervention (Forehand & Weirson, 1993).

At different ages and stages of development and differentially for boys and girls, specific processes and opportunities may emerge, in domains such as cognitive comprehension, exposure to new experiences, establishing relationships, perceiving and expressing emotions, and so forth (Ronen, 1997). Research on cognitive development, the influence of peers, and transition periods (e.g., transferring schools) suggests the need for varied sorts of interventions to effectively achieve change (Kazdin, 1993).

Age as Mediator in Child Therapy

Age is an important component while relating to child therapy. Dush, Hirt, and Schroeder (1989) found a positive relationship between age and treatment outcome in cognitive therapy with children, in which older children having more advanced cognitive skills benefited more from treatments. The best results emerged for adolescents (aged 13 to 18 years), and good outcomes also emerged for preadolescents (aged 11 to 13), but younger children (aged 5 to 11) demonstrated only one-half the success rate as compared to adolescents. This outcome elicits the question of what kind of CBT has been applied to children and whether the therapist tried to adapt therapy to the child developmental stage.

The integration of developmental theory into CBT implies that the therapist's understanding of normal development should be considered critical for the child assessment process. First, placing symptoms into a developmental context can determine whether a specific behavior is age-normal or age-deviant. Second, knowledge of developmental tasks facing children may help explain the etiology of the referred problem, as well as the need to adapt assessment considerations to the child's age (Forehand & Weirson, 1993).

Age criteria are often crucial in determining when a behavior previously considered normal becomes maladaptive. For example, a child who wet the bed at the age of 1 year old is merely manifesting normal behavior that typifies infants and young children. At the age of 3, a child may already have a bedwetting habit but this is not yet defined as a problem. At the age of 5, however, the child already presents a problem that needs to be addressed. Similar age criteria can be applied to eating habits, sleeping habits, aggressive behaviors, and so on.

Age is crucial not only in determining whether to treat the problem but also for decision making as to who should be treated. Children develop different roles at each childhood age or stage, requiring a specific treatment plan best suited to facilitating the new roles (Forehand & Weirson, 1993). For example, when children are very young and depend on the caregiver, therapy usually has primary prevention aims, that is, preventing future risk and reducing the incidence of disorder (Graham, 1994). Treatment of young children from birth up through preschool also takes the form of counseling and supervising parents in child rearing and education (Ronen, in press). As children grow up and begin school, therapy should be directed to the child within his or her natural environment of parents, teachers, and friends, and also toward educational-therapeutic assignments. These comprise secondary prevention that prevents existing problems from worsening and reduces the duration of the disorder (Graham, 1994). As children enter adolescence, therapy should be directed toward the child herself and focus on tertiary prevention. That is, therapy should aim to solve an already existing problem, prevent future risks, and impart skills for decreasing its frequency. Adolescent therapy covers rehabilitative activities and reduces the disability arising from an established disorder (Graham, 1994).

Sensitivity to developmental issues is critical not only for assessment but also for intervention. Age should be a primary consideration in identifying the best technique for a specific child. Different techniques in cognitive therapy should be considered for children of different ages. Young children need simple, concrete instructions and can enjoy more behavioral or cognitive techniques based on simple instructions. For example, while trying to teach young children about the link between thoughts and behavior, the therapist can use concrete play and art methods, such as utilizing a commander and a soldier to demonstrate how the brain executes a command to the body. Another illustration would be while trying to teach a young child how to change automatic thoughts into mediated ones: Therapists can draw a river and show the child how to change the direction of its flow by blocking the old waterway with a dam and digging a new one. While attempting to design the goals for therapy or to show how therapy is an outcome of small gradual steps, the therapist can present a life-size ladder and talk about climbing it.

Gender as Mediator in Child Therapy

Basic cognitive and social learning research findings suggest that biological elements (genes and hormones) set the process of sex differentiation into motion but that environmental conditions, information-processing models, and parental influences maintain this process (Vasta, Haith, & Miller, 1995). Gender differences may be explained by multiple factors such as social norms or variations in maturation processes. Gender differences are important while considering assessment and evaluation.

Gender influences development and renders an impact on behavioral dysfunction. For example, in general, patterns of play and social relations differ among boys and girls (Raviv, Keinan, Abazon, & Raviv, 1990). Girls stay close to one or two significant friends of their own age and sex, whereas boys tend to play in large same-sex groups. Girls find it more difficult to make new friends than do boys. Thus, loneliness among girls will be assessed differently than among boys, treatment goals with the lonely girl will differ than that of a boy, and treatment outcomes will evaluate differently for the two.

Another example relates to the fact that girls, like women, reveal a greater willingness to seek and receive help than do boys/men in times of crisis (Nadler, 1986). In addition, girls' greater expressiveness and ability to share feelings with others may have important ramifications in the planning of treatments for both sexes.

The cognitive approach to gender-role development focuses not so much on the sociobiological differences between the genders as on the kind of gender schemata each child develops (Ronen, 2003).

Cognitive Stage as a Mediator in Child Therapy

General agreement exists about the need for a good match between the child's developmental level and the complexity level of the selected intervention. Questions arise, however, concerning how therapists can assess the child's cognitive level and what cognitive considerations should be taken into account. An awareness of the child's cognitive level, strengths, and limitations enables the therapist to devise the treatments' cognitive processes and techniques in a way that will appropriately meet the child's developmental needs (Knell, 1993)

The traditional view of child cognitive development derived from Piaget's (1924) description of cognitive developmental stages (see Amy

Carrigan Chapter 5 on developmental components). Focusing on children's cognitive development in the light of developmental tasks, Forehand and Weirson (1993) delineated the most appropriate cognitive interventions for each age. Their approach linked cognitive stage-dependent problems to the kind of settings, strategies, and techniques most suited for children of different ages. During infancy, the developmental task consists of shifting from dependence on the caregiver to increased independence and self-regulation. It follows that an infant's problems in gaining initial achievements in autonomy at this stage usually relate to how the parent is educating the child and must therefore focus on the parents as the clients. During early childhood, the major developmental task is to begin mastery of academic and social situations. Hence, interventions at this age should involve parents' and teachers' supervision in how to use behavioral principles with children, as well as social skills training and group intervention. From middle childhood to early adolescence, the main task consists of individual identity development and acquisition of self-control. Therefore, therapy should directly treat the child and be based on social skills training, problem-solving skills, and training in self-control methods (i.e., self-talk, self-reinforcement). Finally, in middle adolescence, the task of individuation from the family and moving toward independence requires interventions based on problem-solving skills (see Chapter 13 by LeCroy in this book) and self-control training.

Identification of the child's cognitive level will foster the therapist's decision making with regard to the kinds of skills that a child needs to acquire and the best ways to teach these skills. For example, younger children exhibit a limited appreciation of time; therefore, distant goals and long-term benefits will seem incomprehensible, whereas short-term gratification and displeasure will be vivid in comparison, shaping the design of treatment objectives. Older children have already acquired abstract thinking; therefore they can work on changing automatic thoughts into mediated ones. The important component of practicing newly learned skills can be facilitated with children by explaining how therapy is analogous to sports. Just like athletes in world competitions need to train, practice, and work toward improving their physical and mental skills, the child should practice to win the medal for improving behavior.

Information Processing as a Significant Component in CBT With Children

A significant aspect of cognitive development that deserves particular elaboration comprises children's unique way of processing information. Processing of information influences how children think, feel, and behave, and therefore, how therapists should help them (Crick & Dodge, 1994).

The Dodge model presents the way children process information and relate it to social events (Crick & Dodge, 1994; Dodge & Pettit, 2003). According to this model, children engage in four main steps before enacting competent behavior. In the first step, the child encodes information about a particular situation. The way a child thinks is influenced not by reality, but by what the child encodes from that reality. After encoding situational cues, the child's second step is to construct an interpretation of the situation. The third step entails a mental search for possible responses to the situation, and the last step consists of selecting a response. Thus, a child accesses possible responses to the situation from long-term memory, evaluates those responses, and then selects the most favorable one for enactment. This information-processing model has successfully predicted a child's social adjustment and may contribute considerably to understanding how cognitive development influences a child's behavior. For example, a child with social phobia who avoids going to a friend's birthday party is not reacting to a single element, such as the child's inferences about being rejected or prediction about standing alone in a corner at the party. Rather, the child's behavior stems from a multivariate, contingent, and nonlinear aggregation of numerous factors related to any of the four processing steps (Crick & Dodge, 1994).

Therapists must consider how children process information in order to assess their problems, behavior, and treatment goals and to plan appropriate interventions. CBT with children, therefore, should start from the very beginning of the encoding process by first training the child in "how to collect information" before beginning to guide the child in working toward various interpretations of social scenarios.

Language Skills as Crucial Components in Child's Therapy

Another important component of child intervention is the development of linguistic skills. Based on Vygotzky's (1962) and Luria's (1961) theories about how language evolves in childhood, Mischel (1973, 1974) explained children's processes of development and learning how to control themselves. Mischel (1973) described the development of internalizing self-talk as the prerequisite for children's shift from being directed by adult external control to individual internal control. Children move from talking aloud to internal self-talk that actually constitutes a state of self-control that enables children to use cognitive thinking, stop automatic negative thoughts, and start using mediated dialogue (Meichenbaum, 1979; Meichenbaum & Goodman, 1971; Ronen, 1997).

Self-talk is grounded in linguistic skills and encompasses a crucial component in developing self-control and in being able to enjoy cognitive therapy. Children with behavior problems often have difficulties in using self-talk, and they act before thinking. The ability to use language as a self-control mechanism starts with experiencing adults' attempts to utilize language to instruct the child in what to do and adults' demonstrations of the role of instruction and self-talk in everyday life. Children then learn to imitate adults and talk to themselves (Ronen, 1997). Self-talk is a necessary skill for CBT and a basic component for delaying gratification, coping with temptation, and mediating and controlling behavior (Meichenbaum & Goodman, 1971; Mischel, 1974; Ronen, 1997).

The SDT model focuses on assessing first whether children possess basic linguistic skills. If skills are absent, children first need to learn the appropriate words, terms, and methods of thinking aloud, using language spoken aloud as self-instruction to guide their behavior. Once these skills have been acquired, therapy should focus on teaching children how to utilize the skills of silent self-talk and self-instruction as a means for guiding their behavior. In the SDT model, training in these key linguistic skills encompasses an important part of self-control intervention.

Emotional Components as Crucial Skills in Child Therapy

Until recently, children's feelings were not regarded as central to CBT. For example, an aggressive child would certainly have been taught in therapy to control behaviors such as hitting (e.g., using self-talk or imagination), but the child's frustration, anger, and helplessness that underlie and elicit the aggressiveness were not usually addressed. The last few years have seen a dramatic increase of interest in the role of emotion in therapy in general, and in CBT in particular, bringing affective issues into clear focus in therapy. Emotions are no longer considered to be a byproduct or outcome of other phenomena but rather to be a necessary and integral human function. They are both the cause and the outcome of cognition (Mahoney, 1991). The human mind is no longer conceived only as an information processing organ (as described in the previous section) but rather as actively constructing reality through its interaction with impinging stimuli and its interpretation and classification of these stimuli based on one's perception of the world (Guidano, 1995).

Children are frequently referred for psychotherapy because of problems with emotions, and many childhood disorders can be viewed as involving difficulties with the experience, expression, or regulation of affects (Shirk & Russell, 1996). To help children cope with, experience, and be able to express emotions, therapists must thoroughly understand the role of emotion in general behavior, and its specific role in the processes of acquiring and maintaining change.

Emotions are elicited through the development of an attachment to significant figures from the first few months; through the second year of life when specific attachment bonds become clearest and fear begins to emerge as a dominant emotion, including wariness of strangers and separation protests; and up to the age of 11 years and higher, when children are already more likely to attribute emotional arousal to internal causes rather than to external events (Thompson, 1989). Thus, with increasing age, children not only develop a broader range of emotional concepts but also increasingly appreciate the psychological dimensions of emotional experience that help them to interpret their own emotional experiences in more sophisticated ways.

Young children are likely to rely on cognitively uncomplicated outcome-dependent emotions such as happiness or sadness that are developed early and easily understood (e.g., "I hurt my knee, so I'm sad"). Not long afterwards, children begin mastering more complex concepts of emotion related to attributional understanding (Thompson, 1989) (e.g., "Mother must be feeling sad and scared right now because she hurt herself as I did"). As cognitive functions mature, new emotions emerge and become available to the child as experiences, and the child can comprehend differential attributions (e.g., "Maybe my mother feels differently from me when she gets hurt—maybe she's angry," or "Look, Mom feels sad and scared, and she didn't even hurt herself—there's another reason"). Psychologists identify cognitive-developmental transitions as preconditions for a child to be able to think about emotion (Gordon, 1989).

In order for children to be able to control emotions, they first need to be able to express emotions, an ability that appears a few days after birth. Later, they should learn to identify simple emotions such as happiness and sadness. Only after achieving this can children begin to understand other and more complex emotions, to accept their emotions, and to recognize emotions in other persons. These all comprise preliminary stages for controlling emotions.

Control of emotion cannot be learned by means of trial and error but rather requires modeling, reinforcing, and mirroring. Children need knowledge of when to control and how to control emotions. Young children are rigid in the extent of control they apply, often demonstrating overcontrol or undercontrol in emotional functioning. Reinforcement, cognitions, and knowledge obtained throughout the childhood years influence the process of appraising, dealing with, and regulating emotions.

Therapists cannot expect emotions to change without teaching the child how to change them and without training the child in emotional skills. Treating emotions therefore necessitates, first of all, assessment of the emotional skills that the child possesses, the emotional skills that the child lacks, and the way to help the child acquire those skills. The SDT model also targets this important issue of emotional skills through an understanding of the child's developmental stages. Determination of the child's affective stage of development comprises a prerequisite for any efficient treatment. The child's emotional stage significantly shapes decision making about the kind of therapy that the child needs and about the most favorable means to achieve the therapeutic goals.

As an example, let us look at children of different ages who exhibit disobedient disorders. A 4-year-old boy who rejects his parents' authority and presents defiant behavior can cry, shout, kick, and refuse to obey his parents' demands. Assessment will probably yield the conclusion that the child is practicing self-control and independence skills in an attempt to test his parents' ability to limit his behavior and control him, and that the child lacks more appropriate ways to express his ability to control himself. Therapy should focus on shifting the child's desire for independence and self-control toward more positive behaviors such as trying to express his refusal in words, standing up for his wishes, and using speech to express what he actually wants. Training will help the child practice self-talk and behavior change, without focusing to a great extent on emotion.

Similar defiance in a boy at 7 years of age may represent his attempt to manipulate his environment and obtain what he wishes, while exploring his own strengths and his parents' weaknesses. This child can still be a happy, well-functioning child. Assessment would pinpoint the need to address emotions, but mainly to focus on linking what the child thinks ("I don't want you to tell me what to do") to what he feels (disappointed because he did not get what he wanted), and to how he makes his parents feel, and how his feelings and thoughts affect his behavior.

At the age of 9, however, similar conduct may already indicate that the child has developed a consistent negative way of expressing anger toward authority figures. This behavior is liable to evolve into a more serious disorder accompanied by negative hostile thoughts and emotions toward himself and the world around him. At this stage, to help the child overcome his disobedient behavior, therapy should facilitate the boy's ability to express and identify negative emotions and to learn how to cope with and accept emotions.

The SDT therapist should ask: Does the child possess the needed emotion-related skills: the ability to express, identify, understand, accept, and control feelings? If a skill is insufficient, is it absent altogether or is it deficient or distorted? Does the child possess the skill but find it difficult to practice it in vivo? The SDT model thus views emotions as a set of skills enabling children to socialize and adjust to the world.

Social Components as Crucial Skills in Child Therapy

Schaffer (1996) emphasized that social development is an outcome of early attachment, awareness of the self (self-awareness, self-concept, self-esteem, and self-emotion), and socialization with parents, siblings, and the environment. Social development therefore encompasses the acquisition of skills relating to *behaviors* (participating in the environment and learning social competencies), skills relating to *thoughts* (accepting and understanding social norms and rules and thinking it is important to be a part of society, comprehending what another person may be feeling or thinking), and skills relating to *emotions* (the wish to be a part of society, the feeling of belonging, feelings of empathy). Social experiences and social interactions critically influence the child's ability to become an integral part of society and to develop self-concept, self-identity, and self-control (Harter, 1983; Ronen, 2003).

CBT relates to social skills, prosocial values, positive communication, self-efficacy, and social efficacy as crucial for human adjustment to society (Bandura, Caprara, Barbaranelli, & Pastorelli, 2001; Gambrill & Richey, 1988; McGinnis & Goldstein, 1997). Studies have also highlighted the role of social support as an important resource for helping children cope with life distress (Baumeister, 1999; Hamama, Ronen, & Feigin, 2000; Schaffer, 1996).

Social development is an outcome of the child's process of learning how to be social, how to take others' perspectives into account, and how to acquire social skills, prosocial behaviors, and values. Experience encompasses a chief part of this process. New circumstances and developmental changes contribute to the need to develop social abilities (Davies, 1999).

Children develop different social roles at each childhood stage (Forehand & Weirson, 1993). The SDT therapist should identify the child's social roles and social developmental stage to understand what kinds of skills the child possesses and what kinds of skills the child lacks, thereby permitting the design of a specific treatment plan best suited to facilitating the new roles.

The Role of Family Environment

Whenever a child is concerned, the parents must be involved. CBT has always focused on treating children within their natural environment (Bandura, 1997). Parents play a vital role in the development, maintenance, and resolution of their children's disorders. The interpersonal role of the child's pathology is inseparable from the familial influence that helped elicit this pathology. Research has underscored this link between parents' problems and those of their children (Kazdin, 2000). This link can be seen not only in terms of the parents' history of problems and frequency of disorders but also in terms of belief systems and behavioral development. Research outcomes, for example, have presented a correlation between parents' self-control and children's self-control and also between parents' lack of self-control and children's high frequency of disorders.

Parents are not only responsible for the child's learning and normal development but are also important change agents for the child, facilitating the child's ability for change (Patterson, 1982; Webster-Stratton, 1993, 1994). Among all their other roles, parents act as role models and direct trainers, which both hold significant implications for children's skills acquisition (Patterson, 1982; Webster-Stratton, 1993, 1994).

The SDT therapist should assess parental skills and pinpoint crucial skills that parents lack. The SDT therapist should then train the parents in the identified skills—both those necessary to help their children grow up and adjust to society and acquire the skills conducive to better functioning, and also those skills that parents need in order to help themselves cope better as parents of children at a specific stage and with particular problems (Ronen, 1997, 2001, 2003).

In sum, SDT therapy must consider age and gender and cognitive, linguistic, information processing, emotional, and social development, together with family components. The integrative child SDT model described next blends all these components to form the foundation for devising a new broad theoretical and applicative treatment model focusing on skills acquisition.

THE SDT MODEL FOR CHILDREN

In one of his latest studies, Bandura proposed that self-efficacy and self-control skills constitute the most important factors predicting adjustment in children (Bandura et al., 2001). Ronen and Rosenbaum (2001) recently extended the self-control intervention model, which applies the self-control intervention developed by Ronen to treat various children's disorders (Ronen, 1997, 2003). The model aims to impart children with both self-control skills and also with self-help methods to facilitate their future independent functioning. Enhancing children's self-help skills enables them to maintain treatment outcomes, continue treating themselves in daily life after successfully being treated by the therapist, generalize and transfer their basic learning, and facilitate self-change. The self-control intervention model contains four modules.

1. Cognitive Restructuring

This module aims to teach the child that a behavior can be changed and that, like many other kinds of behavior, this change depends on the child. The therapist elicits cognitive restructuring by increasing children's self-efficacy about their ability to achieve change (Bandura, 1997), as well as by utilizing redefinition, changing attributional styles, and reframing the child's present functioning (Beck, Emery, & Greenberg, 1985; Kanfer & Schefft, 1988; Meichenbaum, 1979).

2. Problem Analysis

This module trains the child to observe the link among the brain, body, and final problematic behaviors. The therapist teaches the child to notice the links among thoughts, emotions, and behaviors and to observe the link between cause and effect (Beck, 1963; Ronen, 1997). The therapist helps the child accept responsibility for behaviors by learning to change the brain's commands. The child practices identifying automatic thoughts and using self-talk and self-recording to change unmediated thoughts into mediated ones.

3. Attentional Focus

This module aims to increase the child's awareness of behavior and internal stimuli, raise sensitivity to the body, and particularly learn to identify internal cues related to the specific problem (Bandura, 1997; Mahoney, 1991, 1995). The therapist uses relaxation, concentration, and self-monitoring to promote achievement of these targets.

4. Self-Control Practice

This module trains the child in self-control techniques such as self-talk, self-evaluation, self-monitoring, thinking aloud, and problem-solving skills (Ronen, 1997). In the first stage of general skills training, the therapist assigns various kinds of practicing. Practice includes using self-instruction, both in the sessions and in homework assignments, to overcome disappointments. Through practice, the child learns that as confidence grows, the chances of success also increase (Bandura, 1997). The self-control techniques include physical as well as emotional exercises such as resisting temptation, self-talk, self-reward, problem solving, and imagery exercises (Meichenbaum, 1979; Ronen, 1997).

SDT Application to Children With Aggressive Behavior

In recent years, the skills-directed self-control intervention model has been applied both as individual therapy and as small group courses conducted by social work students at the Bob Shapell School of Social Work in the ongoing *Empowering Children and Adolescents* project, established in 2000 and supported by the JDC (Jewish Federation) and the Pratt Foundation. The project was founded to establish a clinical research center for study and intervention targeting children with oppositional defiant disorder and for training professionals in this area. Within the empowerment project, children participate in a 12-session course in a small group (of six children) that is homogenous in terms of age and problems. Each 75-minute session presents new knowledge and combines demonstrations, practice, discussion, and homework assignments. During this course, children learn what a behavior is, how to look at their aggression as a behavior, how their behavior is connected to their thoughts and emotions, what kinds of techniques can help them change their behavior, and so on. They learn to assess, evaluate, and plan the change process; they establish criteria and expectations for change; they learn to observe, evaluate, and reinforce themselves; and they learn to identify their internal cues and to replace automatic thoughts with mediated ones (Ronen, in press).

Each of the developmental and environmental components previously described contributed to the design of this self-control–based SDT intervention. The *cognitive* components, with their developmental stages, influenced the intervention's design as a learning course for children. Utilization of imagery, metaphors, exercises, drawing, sculpturing, and so forth served to adapt the intervention to children's cognitive ability to understand the treatment's concepts. The *information-processing* model was incorporated in the self-control training program by targeting the child's ability to look at an event, interpret and encode it, seek out alternatives, select the optimal option, and try to apply the learning process. *Language* is taken into account both by assessing the linguistic skills that the child possesses and by teaching the child how to use self-talk to control and direct his or her own behavior. This SDT model emphasized the role of *emotion* by pinpointing the children's ability to express, identify, accept, understand, and control affects. The treatment design worked directly toward those emotional goals, teaching and training children in the needed emotions, and practicing the skills in group interventions. Children's *social* development influenced the decision, first of all, to work with children in groups and to target the social interaction in vivo, and second, to introduce features concerning social values, prosocial values, and social skills training into our training programs. The self-control intervention model emphasized the role of *families* by designing parent supervision groups. Parents of each of the involved children participated in a parent group and underwent a program similar to the children's, relating first of all to the parents themselves and how they can acquire skills, and then to their children and how to educate their children using appropriate skills (Ronen, in press).

Preliminary outcomes from the first four years of conducting the treatment course in small children's groups reveal a very high percentage of change. That is, children attending these groups significantly improved their self-control skills and significantly reduced their aggressive behavior according to children's, parents', and teachers' assessments. The treatment boasted a very low dropout rate and a very high rate of maintaining treatment outcomes at the 2-year follow up. I believe this success can be attributed to our integration of the following components:

1. A *developmental approach* to the child, blending cognitive, emotional, linguistic, and social developmental issues with the child's information-processing models and relate it to the child's age, gender, and cognitive skills.
2. A *family approach* emphasizing relationships between the child and the family and also designing contracts pertaining to the involvement of each.
3. *Theoretical grounding* that integrates the basics of CBT with information-processing models and self-control interventions.
4. *Cognitive constructivist techniques* both for verbal and nonverbal intervention modes (Ronen, 2003).

Thus, learning was preconstructed and gradual, included training and applications, integrated developmental and environmental components, derived from a broad theoretical model, and focused on skills training within one systematic self-control intervention.

The proposed model is an example to the way I believe CBT should be applied to children. It is an educational therapeutic intervention that is characterized by a nonstop process of making decisions about the optimal treatment for the specific client, with the specific problem, at the specific stage of development, in the specific environmental context.

Like other therapies, treating children necessitates the client's active participation and therefore, an important task of therapies is to elicit motivation. Kanfer and Schefft (1988) stated that everyone is motivated, and that it is our responsibility as therapists to find out what they are motivated toward, and to develop and work toward increasing that motivation.

The advantages of SDT lie in its ability to relate to all areas of children's functioning—thoughts, emotions, and behaviors. It aims to empower clients and develop self-control and self-help. CBT looks for and increases clients' support systems, strengths, and resources and helps them to help themselves.

REFERENCES

Achenbach, T. M. (1985). *Assessment and taxonomy of child and adolescent psychopathology.* Beverly Hills, CA: Sage.

Alford, B. A., & Beck, A. T. (1997). *The integrative power of cognitive therapy.* New York: Guilford.

Bandura, A. (1997). *Self-efficacy: The exercise of control.* New York: W. H. Freeman.

Bandura, A., Caprara, G. V., Barbaranelli, C., & Pastorelli, C. (2001). Sociocognitive self-regulatory mechanisms governing transgressive behavior. *Journal of Personality and Social Behavior, 80,* 125–13

Barkley, R. A. (1997). Behavioral inhibition sustained, attention, and executive functions: Constructing a unifying theory of ADHD. *Psychological Bulletin, 121,* 65–94.

Baumeister, R. F. (1999). *The self in social psychology.* Philadelphia: Taylor & Francis.

Beck, A. T. (1963). Thinking and depression. *Archives of General Psychiatry, 9,* 324–333.

Beck, A. T., Emery, G., & Greenberg, R. L. (1985). *Anxiety disorders and phobias.* New York: Basic Books.

Beck, A. T., Freeman, A., & Associates. (1990). *Cognitive therapy of personality disorders.* New York: Guilford.

Crick, N. R., & Dodge, K. A. (1994). A review and reformulation of social information-processing mechanisms in children's social adjustment. *Psychological Bulletin, 115,* 74–101.

Davies, D. (1999). *Child development: A practitioner's guide.* New York: Guilford Press.

Dodge, K. A., & Pettit, G. (2003). A biopsychosocial model of the development of chronic conduct problems in adolescence. *Developmental Psychology, 39,* 1–41.

Durlak, J. A., Fuhrman, T., & Lampman, C. (1991). Effectiveness of cognitive-behavior therapy for maladaptive children: A meta-analysis. *Psychological Bulletin, 110,* 204–214.

Dush, D. M., Hirt, M. L., & Schroeder, H. E. (1989). Self-statement modification in the treatment of child behavior disorders: A meta-analysis. *Psychological Bulletin, 106,* 97–106.

Forehand, R., & Weirson, M. (1993). The role of developmental factors in planning behavioral intervention for children: Disruptive behavior as an example. *Behavior Therapy, 24,* 117–141.

Gambrill, E., & Richey, C. (1988). *Taking charge of your social life.* Berkeley, CA: Behavioral Options.

Gordon, S. L. (1989). The socialization of children's emotions: Emotional culture, competence, and exposure. In C. Saarni & P. L. Harris (Eds.), *Children's understanding of emotion* (pp. 319–344). New York: Cambridge University Press.

Graham, P. (1994). Prevention. In M. Rutter, E. Taylor, & L. Hersov (Eds.), *Child and adolescent psychiatry: Modern approaches* (3rd ed., pp. 815–828). Oxford: Blackwell.

Grave, J., & Blissett, J. (2004). Is cognitive behavior therapy developmentally appropriate for young children? Review of the evidence. *Clinical Psychology Review, 24,* 399–420.

Greenberg, L. S., & Safran, J. D. (1987). *Emotion in psychotherapy*. New York: Guilford.

Guidano, V. F. (1995). A constructivist outline of human knowing processes. In M. J. Mahoney (Ed.), *Cognitive and constructive psychotherapies: Theory, research, and practice* (pp. 89–102). New York: Springer.

Hamama, R., Ronen, T., & Feigin, R. (2000). Self-control, anxiety, and loneliness in siblings of children with cancer. *Social Work in Health Care, 31,* 63–83.

Harter, S. (1983). Developmental perspectives on the self-system. In P. H. Mussen (Series Ed.) & E. M. Hetherington (Vol. Ed.), *Handbook of child psychology: Vol. 4. Socialization, personality, and social development* (pp. 275–386). New York: Wiley.

Hayes, S. C., Jacobson, N. S., Follette, V. M., & Daugher, M. J. (Eds.). (1994). *Acceptance and change: Content and context in psychotherapy*. Reno, NV: Context Press.

Kanfer, F. H., & Schefft, B. K. (1988). *Guiding the process of therapeutic change*. Champaign, IL: Research Press.

Kazdin, A. E. (1993). Psychotherapy for children and adolescents: Current progress and future directions. *American Psychologist, 48,* 644–656.

Kazdin, A. E. (1994). Psychotherapy for children and adolescents. In A. E. Bergin & S. L. Garfield (Eds.), *Handbook of psychotherapy and behavior change* (4th ed., pp. 543–594). New York: Wiley.

Kazdin, A. E. (2000). *Psychotherapy for children and adolescence: Directions for research and practice*. New York: Oxford University Press.

Kazdin, A. E., & Weisz, J. R. (Eds.). (2003). *Evidence-based psychotherapies for children and adolescents*. New York: Guilford.

Kelly, G. A. (1955). *The psychology of personal constructs*. New York: Norton.

Kendall, P. C. (1993). Cognitive-behavioral therapies with youth: Guiding theory, current status, and emerging developments. *Journal of Consulting and Clinical Psychology, 61,* 235–247.

Kendall, P. C., & Braswell, L. (1993). Cognitive behavioral therapy for impulsive children (2nd ed.). New York: Guilford.

Knell, S. M. (1993). *Cognitive behavioral play therapy*. Northvale, NJ: Jason Aronson.

Luria, A. R. (1961). *The role of speech in the regulation of normal behaviors*. New York: Liverwright.

Mahoney, M. J. (1991). *Human change processes: The scientific foundations of psychotherapy*. New York: Basic Books.

Mahoney, M. J. (1995). Continuing evolution of the cognitive sciences and psychotherapies. In R. A. Neimeyer & M. J. Mahoney (Eds.), *Constructivism in psychotherapy* (pp. 39–67). Washington, DC: American Psychological Association.

Mash, E., & Terdal, L. G. (1988). Behavioral assessment of child and family disturbance. In E. J. Mash & L. G. Terdal (Eds.), *Behavioral assessment of childhood disorders* (2nd ed., pp. 3–65). New York: Guilford.

McGinnis, E., & Goldstein, A. (1997). *Skillstreaming the elementary school child*. Champaign, IL: Research Press.

Meichenbaum, D. H. (1979). Teaching children self-control. In B. Lahey & A. Kazdin (Eds.), *Advances in clinical child psychology* (Vol. 2, pp. 1–30). New York: Plenum.

Meichenbaum, D. H., & Goodman, J. (1971). Training impulsive children to talk to themselves: A means of developing self-control. *Journal of Abnormal Psychology, 77*, 115–126.

Mischel, W. (1973). Toward a cognitive social learning reconceptualization of personality. *Psychological Review, 80*, 252–283.

Mischel, W. (1974). Processes in delay of gratifications. In L. Berkowitz (Ed.), *Advances in experimental and social psychology.* New York: Academic Press.

Nadler, A. (1986). Self-esteem and the seeking and receiving of help: Theoretical and empirical perspectives. *Experimental Personality Research, 14*, 115–163.

Neimeyer, R. A., & Mahoney, M. J. (Eds.). (1995). *Constructivism in psychotherapy.* Washington, DC: American Psychological Association.

Patterson, G. R. (1982). *Coercive family process: A social learning approach.* Eugene, OR: Castalia.

Piaget, J. (1924). *The language and thought of the child.* London: Routledge & Kegan Paul.

Powell, M. B., & Oei, T. P. S. (1991). Cognitive processes underlying the behavior change in cognitive behavior therapy with childhood disorders: A review of experimental evidence. *Behavioural Psychotherapy, 19*, 247–265.

Raviv, A., Keinan, G., Abazon, Y., & Raviv, A. (1990). Moving as a stressful life event for adolescents. *Journal of Community Psychology, 18*, 130–140.

Ronen, T. (1997). *Cognitive-developmental therapy with children.* Chichester, UK: Wiley.

Ronen, T. (2001). Collaboration on critical questions in child psychotherapy: A model linking referral, assessment, intervention, and evaluation. *Journal of Social Work Education, 1*, 1–20.

Ronen, T. (2003). *Cognitive constructivist psychotherapy with children and adolescents.* New York: Kluwer/Plenum.

Ronen, T. (in press). Cognitive behavior therapy with children: Skills directed therapy. *Hellenic Journal of Psychology.*

Ronen, T., & Rosenbaum, M. (2001). Helping children to help themselves: A case study of enuresis and nail biting. *Research in Social Work Practice, 11*, 338–356.

Safran, J. D., & Segal, Z. V. (1990). *Interpersonal process in cognitive therapy.* New York: Basic Books.

Schaffer, H. R. (1996). *Social development.* Oxford: Blackwell.

Shapiro, T. (1995). Developmental issues in psychotherapy research. *Journal of Abnormal Child Psychology, 23*, 31–44.

Shirk, S. R., & Russell, R. L. (1996). *Change process in child psychotherapy.* New York: Guilford.

Southam-Gerow, M. A., & Kendall, P. C. (2000). Cognitive-behavior therapy with youth: Advances, challenges and future directions. *Clinical Psychology and Psychotherapy, 7*, 343–366.

Thompson, R. A. (1989). Causal attributions and children's emotional understanding. In C. Saarni & P. L. Harris (Eds.), *Children's understanding of emotion* (pp. 117–150). New York: Cambridge University Press.

Thyer, B., & Kazi, M. A. F. (2004). (Eds.). *International perspectives on evidence-based practice in social work*. Birmingham: Venture Press.

Vasta, R., Haith, M. M., & Miller, S. A. (1995). *Child psychology: The modern science*. New York: Wiley.

Vygotsky, L. (1962). *Thought and language*. New York: Wiley.

Webster-Stratton, C. (1993). Strategies for helping early school-aged children with oppositional defiant and conduct disorders: The importance of home-school partnerships. *School Psychology Review, 22*, 437–457.

Webster-Stratton, C. (1994). *Trouble families—problem children. Working with parents: A collaborative process*. Chicester, UK: Wiley.

CHAPTER 10

The Use of Metaphorical Fables With Children

Application of Cognitive Behavior Therapy to Prevention Interventions

G. Bert Allain

Catherine M. Lemieux

INTRODUCTION

Delinquency and drug-using behavior in adolescence is usually preceded by a number of risk factors that present themselves early on in a child's development such as acting-out behavior and impulsivity, and problems in school such as aggressiveness with peers and academic underachievement (Hawkins, Catalano, & Miller, 1992). It is often these problematic behaviors that precipitate referrals to social workers or other mental health specialists in school and community-based settings. Current research shows that prevention interventions with young, school-age children should mobilize protective factors such as impulse control, parental support, and social and academic competence, and reduce the risk factors just described before problem behaviors develop (Hawkins, Catalano, Kosterman, Abbott, & Hill, 1999). This chapter describes one such intervention, the Coping Skills Program, an innovative school-based prevention curriculum that uses metaphorical fables, in-class problem solving, social skill-building exercises, modeling, and reinforcement to identify, challenge, and modify young children's negative or faulty cognitions.

Rooted in cognitive behavior theory, the Coping Skills Program consists of carefully constructed metaphorical fables that are designed to teach children about their thinking; about the connections among their thoughts, feelings, and behavior; and about how to change what they are thinking, feeling, and doing when their behavior causes them problems. In this chapter, a thorough description of the Coping Skills Program and how it is implemented is framed by a discussion of relevant research-based literature, and the theoretical underpinnings underlying this cognitive behavior approach with school-aged children. This chapter also includes the results of preliminary testing of the Coping Skills Program.

The Coping Skills Program, which will be described in greater detail in the following text, is composed of a multilevel prevention intervention that targets students' strengths, engages parent support, focuses on the classroom culture and learning environment, and helps teachers manage students' behaviors in the classroom. As such, the multisystem focus of the Coping Skills Program is consistent with the social work ecological approach, which, according to noted experts in the field (Allen-Meares; 2004; Germain, 2002) is the most desirable theoretical framework to guide social work practice in school settings.

An ecological approach to practice is heavily contextualized, in that it directs attention away from individuals to the various systems that affect individuals. Because of its preventive, strengths-based, and multisystem focus, the Coping Skills Program satisfies the programmatic criteria recently endorsed by Frey and Dupper (2005) as "a broader and more flexible clinical approach to school social work practice" (p. 41). These experts argue that school social workers should market themselves as prevention, as opposed to mental health specialists, in order to keep pace with the changes created by contemporary education reform efforts. Consistent with Frey and Dupper's proposed conceptualization, the Coping Skills Program is illustrative of the type of intervention that school social workers could and should implement and evaluate in order to advance the field of school social work practice in the future.

Although the Coping Skills Program is implemented by teachers who are trained by practitioners, social workers have long been at the forefront of children's behavioral and other problems in the school setting. A recent review of all school social work intervention studies published between 1999 and 2003 ($N = 32$) indicated that school social workers do, in fact, seek to improve specific outcomes related to children's symptoms such as self-esteem, behavior problems, anger, aggressiveness, impulsivity, loneliness, and substance use; and problems with functioning such as attendance, academic performance, social problem solving, assertiveness, and health and well-being (Staudt, Cherry, & Watson, 2005). Further, these authors' research demonstrated that a cognitive behavior intervention component was used for 3 of the 7 studies addressing children's symptoms and for 3 of the 11 studies investigating problems with functioning. Among the 32 studies reviewed, the interventions were administered most frequently in groups at the elementary school level (Staudt et al., 2005). This suggests that the Coping Skills Program is a prevention intervention consistent with those described in school social work studies that have been published in the major social work journals to date.

Unlike approaches undertaken by well-established prevention researchers in the field (Greenberg, Kusche, Cook, & Quamma, 1995; Ialongo, Poduska, Werthamer, Kellam, 2001), however, the Coping Skills Program relies on the use of metaphorical fables to teach students about their thinking and how their thinking influences their feelings and subsequent actions. Each fable in the Coping Skills Program corresponds to one or more faulty or distorted cognitions. Delivering a problem-solving curriculum in this manner diverges considerably from the sequentially staged, unit-based approaches of classroom-based programs with which social worker may be familiar, such as the Interpersonal Cognitive Problem-Solving Program (ICPS) (Shure, 2001), Making Choices (MC) (Fraser, Nash, Galinsky, & Darwin, 2001), and Promoting Alternative THinking Strategies (PATHS) (Greenberg & Kusche, 1993). In the Coping Skills Program, the fable's characters think irrationally (such as Stinky), their emotions are too intense or inappropriate, and their behavior is self-defeating (such as Thumbs Down). The fables enable children to see a sequence of events from start to finish, and allow for different thinking by the characters that can then change emotional responses and behavioral reactions. Thus, the fables provide students with metaphors for pursuing rational alternatives in a manner that is more accessible to children than rules, expectations, and someone in authority pointing out individual, Thumbs-Down behavior. This innovative, cognitively based approach to problem solving with young children is supported by the research-based literature in three broad substantive areas: childhood risk and protective factors, intervention studies of classroom-based curricula with children, and cognitive-behavioral methods with children.

REVIEW OF THE LITERATURE

Early Childhood Protective and Risk Factors

Although the trajectories are decidedly complex and multifactorial, the risk factors present in children in the early elementary grades (e.g., aggressive behavior, academic problems, and social rejection) are appropriate targets of interventive efforts, for which the overall goal is to alter the developmental course that places children at greater risk for adolescent drug involvement. Thus, the prevention of adolescent substance abuse among young, school-age children focuses on mobilizing protective factors (e.g., impulse control, parental support, social and academic competence) and reducing risk factors before problem behaviors develop (Hawkins et al., 1999).

The behavioral antecedents to adolescent substance abuse, antisocial behavior, and other disorders often appear early in life when children transition to school, where they are challenged to meet the demands of new social and academic experiences (Ialongo et al., 2001). It is in the ecology of the school setting that the problems of interpersonal aggression and peer rejection manifest themselves. These are the two predictors of adolescent substance abuse and related disorders that have received the most empirical attention in the developmental literature (Loeber, 1990; Loeber & Farrington, 2001; Reid, Patterson, & Snyder, 2002). Enhancing children's interpersonal problem-solving abilities and social adjustment, therefore, is a strategy that can reduce the risk factors and bolster protective mechanisms associated with bonding to school and developing prosocial competencies. Such early prevention and intervention efforts have the potential to alter a critical developmental pathway to substance abuse and delinquency.

The empirically verified link between children's cognitive-affective processes and their behavior (see e.g., Crick, Grotpeter, & Bigbee, 2002) has important implications for developing preventive interventions that target individual-level risk factors. School-based interventive efforts that have targeted the interpersonal skills and social problem solving of aggressive and non-aggressive children emphasize both cognitive and affective components that are thought to maintain aggressive behavior (Conduct Problems Prevention Research Group, 2002; Fraser et al., 2001; Greenberg et al., 1995; Shure & Spivack, 1980). This focus is consistent with research demonstrating that children's cognitions, especially their processing of social information (Crick & Dodge, 1994; Pakaslahti, 2000) and their capacity to regulate emotions (Eisenberg, Fabes, Guthrie, & Reiser, 2002; Lengua, 2002), serve as the foundational features of adaptive interpersonal problem solving and social competence.

School-Based Universal Prevention Curricula for Young Children

Developmental risk factors usually present themselves by the third grade (Fraser, 2004; Patterson, Dishion, & Yoerger, 2000), and according to Patterson (2002), prevention initiatives should target children at "some point prior to Grades 4 or 5" (p. 10). Effective, universal drug prevention programs consist of multiple components that provide family support to enhance parenting skills and to strengthen parent-school collaboration, thereby targeting a broader array of individual- and family-level risk and protective factors. (Ialongo et al., 2001; Greenberg et al., 1995). The results across these and other studies of selective elementary school prevention programs (e.g., Conduct Problems Prevention Research Group, 2002; Fraser, Day, Galinsky, Hodges, & Smokowski, 2004) indicate that well-timed and carefully constructed interventions can positively influence the developmental trajectories of young children.

Well established universal classroom-based programs that target young children's cognitions, such as ICPS (Shure, 2001), MC (Fraser et al., 2001), and PATHS (Greenberg & Kusche, 1993); share the commonality of a classroom curriculum that is presented to students via sequentially staged, unit-based lessons (at 77, 28, and 60 lessons, respectively). All three programs begin with a unit on recognizing, labeling, and managing feelings that is then followed by specific skills training to help students identify and interpret what is occurring in any given interpersonal or social situation. Subsequent units in the PATHS and MS programs focus on setting goals, making choices, and evaluating the outcomes; whereas the ICPS program teaches a set of problem-solving skills (alternative solutions, consequences, solution-consequence pairs, means-end thinking) (Shure, 2001).

Cognitive Behavior Methods With Children

A dynamic relationship exists between children's cognitive-affective understanding of social situations and their intrapersonal and real-world interpersonal experiences. Cognition refers to both cognitive contents (e.g., thoughts, tacit beliefs, and self-statements) and cognitive processes (e.g., the way information is represented in memory and the procedures by which information is used) (Kendall, 2000). Thus, cognition is a set of complex skills that incorporates problem-solving strategies, communication, and interpersonal abilities.

The idea that children's immature or irrational thinking is meaningfully related to their emotions and behavior is a plausible way of recasting the cognitive-affective link to behavior. Since the mid-1980s, developmental researchers have amassed a considerable body of evidence demonstrating the association between children's cognitions and important developmental outcomes, such as interpersonal problem-solving skills and social competence. Research has shown that children displaying behavioral and emotional concerns engage in various forms of negative thinking (Crick & Dodge, 1994), and researchers (Rudolph, Hammen, &

Burge, 1997) have identified interconnections between these negative cognitive representations and children's social worlds. Cognitive restructuring is a cognitive behavior method widely used with children that helps them recognize and modify self-statements, expectancies, or beliefs that create emotional distress. Children exhibiting subjective distress, problematic behaviors, or both have been treated effectively with a variety of cognitive approaches that specifically target cognitive and affective components and the links between them that underlie child psychopathology. For example, research shows that children can learn rational analysis of cause-effect links to understand how thoughts are connected to behavior, thereby learning self-control skills and subsequently improving their behavior (Ronen, 1994; Ronen & Rosenbaum, 2001). According to Kendall (2000), the outcome literature examining cognitive behavior interventions with children provides evidence that specific applications, all of which incorporate a pronounced cognitive restructuring component, can be recommended with confidence to treat youth experiencing psychosocial difficulties such as aggression, depression, and anxiety.

THE COPING SKILLS PROGRAM: APPLICATION OF COGNITIVE BEHAVIOR THEORY

Description of the Coping Skills Program

The Coping Skills Program is a school-based prevention curriculum that incorporates metaphorical fables, in-class problem solving and social skill-building exercises, modeling, and reinforcement to teach children about the connections between their thoughts feelings, and behaviors. The program is universal in that it is taught by classroom teachers to the entire classroom of regular education students. The multigrade curriculum consists of 48 culturally and developmentally appropriate fables and accompanying worksheets. Fables of increasing complexity are sequentially presented to second-, third-, and fourth-grade students. Each of the 48 fables corresponds to one or more of the following faulty or distorted cognitions commonly held by children (Waters, 1982, p. 572):

1. I'm bad if I make a mistake.
2. Things should come easily to me.
3. It's awful if others don't like me.
4. There is only one right answer.
5. I shouldn't show my feelings.
6. I shouldn't have to wait for anything.

7. Everything should go my way, and I should always get what I want.
8. The world should be fair, and that bad people should be punished.
9. I must win.
10. Adults should be perfect.

The learning content of each fable consists of a multistep lesson that is taught in the classroom for about one hour, every other week. The goals of the Coping Skills Program are to (a) increase students' understanding of the relationship among their thoughts, emotions, and behaviors; (b) increase their sense of personal responsibility for their thinking, feelings, and actions; (c) increase students' knowledge of the faulty or distorted cognitions that are linked to emotional distress and maladaptive behaviors (with emphasis on antisocial behaviors and substance abuse); (d) increase students' capacity for rational thinking; (e) increase the extent to which students exhibit adaptive behavior (i.e., coping skills) in the classroom environment; and (f) create a culture of coping in the classroom. These goals are accomplished with a set of carefully constructed lessons in the form of metaphorical stories, in-class exercises, and ongoing reinforcement to promote generalization to school and home situations.

Each fable, which is narrated by Cosmos Crow, has colorful characters that exhibit irrational beliefs (Stinky Thinking), negative emotions (Not OK Emotions), and maladaptive (Thumbs Down) behaviors, and, as a result, the characters incur unpleasant life consequences. The characters maintain the students' interest and the stories have the metaphorical qualities that enable students to accept that the characters should try alternative ways of thinking, feeling, and behaving. Cosmos Crow launches the Coping Skills Program with the Grizzly Bear story that illustrates how children can react differently to the same situation based on whether their thinking is Good (rational) or Stinky (irrational). The use of metaphors is an important strategic device that can offer new choices and new perspectives to change fixed and rigid patterns of behavior (Otto, 2000). Further, storytelling with children engages them and sustains their interest in difficult or complex material by providing accessible cues that can be easily recalled (Barker, 1996). As such, metaphorical storytelling buttresses the range of narrative therapies used with young children (Smith & Nyland, 1997).

Description of the Lesson Phases

During the first phase of the lesson, the teacher reads the fable aloud in an animated manner while the students follow along. With the visual aid of a 20- by 30-inch storyboard, the instructor reads the story one more time. This time, the instructor teaches students about the characters' irrational thinking and its consequences using laminated representations of the characters, situations, Good and Stinky Thinking, OK and Not OK Emotions, and Thumbs Down and Thumbs Up Behavior. After students have identified the irrational thinking, negative emotions, and problem behaviors, the instructor then asks the students to rewrite the story.

Using the storyboard and laminated representations, the students are encouraged to identify the links between the characters' more rational thinking and the emotions, functional behaviors, and more satisfying outcomes that likely would follow. The workbook contains a section for students to write down both the rational and irrational thinking, along with the emotions, behaviors, and social and interpersonal consequences that follow each line of thinking. This latter exercise uses the metaphorical story situation to help students conceptualize alternative ways of thinking, feeling, and acting in social and interpersonal situations.

Following completion of the workbook, the teacher asks students to describe situations in which they behaved like the main supporting characters in the particular fable. The teacher encourages students to identify what their thinking was at the time they behaved like the characters. The class is then encouraged to offer alternative (rational) thinking and to anticipate what types of emotions and behavior might accompany this new line of thinking. This latter component is a cognitive restructuring technique that is used effectively with young children who demonstrate aggressive, depressed, and anxious behaviors (Kendall, 2000).

The fourth phase of the lesson consists of a 10-question, multiple-choice test that covers factual information about the fable and assesses students' understanding of the thinking-feeling-behaving links demonstrated by the story's characters. The tests are designed to provide immediate, positive reinforcement because they are constructed to result in high rates of successful responding by students. The test results provide information to the instructor about students' understanding of the material.

Following the test portion, a workbook section explains the real-world meaning of the fable, and how the experiences of the fable's characters relate to those of the students. The purpose of this exercise is to demonstrate the connection between the characters' thinking and the students' thinking, and to help students understand how they could expect similar consequences to those endured by the fable's characters if the students don't change their Stinky Thinking. One final component concludes the lesson that can be undertaken at home or in the class. This final exercise is designed such that parents, who maybe unfamiliar with the specific story, can reinforce the content and underlying message of the fable and its application to real-world problem solving and social situations. At the conclusion of the fable, students are given colorful bookmarks imprinted with pictures of the characters and highlights of the lessons for that story. This multistep process is repeated for each fable. Through repetition, students are taught to recognize the association among their thoughts, emotions, and behaviors and that they likely can feel and do better by modifying their faulty thinking. Over the course of the program, students develop alternatives to their habitual ways of thinking about and reacting to various situations, thereby expanding their repertoire of effective and adaptive coping skills.

Case Illustration 1

Timmy's behavior was the most difficult to manage among all of the children in Ms. Smith's homeroom of third graders. Although Timmy participated in the Coping Skills during the school year, his most problematic behaviors endured. He frequently was in fights with other children and he was suspended numerous times during the school year for various disciplinary infractions. He refused to take responsibility for any of the problems that he was experiencing with his peers. Timmy's academic performance was well below his estimated capability, and he ultimately failed the third grade. Timmy participated in the Coping Skills Program again during his second, third-grade year. Early on in the year, Ms. Smith observed improvements in Timmy's behavior, noting that his changes paralleled the lessons of the Coping Skills fables. In class, he demonstrated understanding of the thinking-feeling-behaving links and he was encouraged to articulate the similarities between the consequences of the Stinky Thinking used by the characters in the Coping Skills fables and his own experiences in the classroom. With increased exposure to the program, Timmy began to take responsibility for his emotional upsets and he controlled his behavior to the point of having no fights and few suspensions over the year. Timmy's academic performance also improved. The most notable change observed by Ms. Smith and his other teachers was his willingness to say, "I'm sorry," and mean it.

The Classroom Environment as the Target of Intervention

In order to create a classroom culture of coping, the teacher uses the characters from the stories as cues when a student is exhibiting inappropriate or disruptive classroom behavior. When this occurs, students are challenged to recognize their self-defeating behaviors and underlying irrational thoughts. This is accomplished with the use of a cue poster that pictures the characters of the relevant fable. Cue posters are used to reinforce the lessons of current and previous fables. For example, a student may repeatedly fail to complete his or her homework. The teacher asks the student, while pointing to the appropriate cue poster, "Is your behavior similar to that of Jeff the Monkey?" The teacher asks the student to describe the Stinky Thinking that Jeff the Monkey told himself to avoid some of the tasks that were necessary for him to succeed. Next, the teacher asks the student to describe his or her thoughts had during the previous night about the homework assignment and whether the student's thinking was Good or Stinky. Finally, the teacher asks the student to describe the kind of self-talk that would have resulted in the homework getting done (Thumbs Up Behavior), and asks whether the student would be feeling better or worse today if the student had used Good Thinking. In this example the teacher is using Jeff the Monkey as a cue to help a student recognize how his or her thinking is causing problems (i.e., in this case, incomplete homework), that this thinking is changeable, and that changed (Good) thinking will result in more positive (OK) emotions and adaptive (Thumbs Up) behavior. The use of the fable character to illustrate the cause of the problem behavior is less threatening and is, therefore, less likely to elicit a habitually used defense mechanism such as denial or avoidance. With practice, students learn to use and apply these cues with minimal prompting from the teacher to identify and modify a faulty or distorted line of thinking.

As students learn to recognize the relationship between their thoughts, feelings, and behaviors, the teacher introduces incentive tokens that picture the characters from the relevant fable, to reward the Good Thinking underlying students' adaptive coping skills. The teacher makes a determined effort to observe and subsequently reinforce behaviors associated with rational thinking, behaviors incompatible with inappropriate behavior (and attendant irrational thinking), and spontaneously occurring behavior that the teacher wants to encourage. In order to generate a large number of positive behaviors and to maintain them long enough for them to become habituated, students are rewarded with tokens using a variable-ratio schedule. Thus, a teacher may decide to reinforce an appropriate behavior the first time it occurs for all students and then occasionally for some students, but more frequently for other students for whom the behavior is out of character. The teacher also can vary the type of reward by changing the number of tokens rewarded to particular students for certain types of behaviors. For example, some behaviors may be worth one token with one child but worth ten with another, because the behavior is so out of character for this latter student. A large body of research has established the effectiveness of developmentally appropriate behavioral contingencies for increasing the desired behaviors of children experiencing a variety of behavioral disorders (Kendall, 2000).

Case Illustration 2

This case shows how unexpected issues can arise when using a program that involves rewarding children with behavioral incentives. In one of the more rural schools, Ms. Brown was concerned about one child and the tokens she was receiving for her appropriate, Thumbs Up behavior. According to Ms. Brown, Margaret's classroom behaviors were extremely problematic and disruptive prior to her participation in the Coping Skills Program. Margaret actively participated in the program and her class-room behavior improved such that she was receiving more tokens than any other child in the class. However, Margaret refused to redeem any of her tokens for the prizes that were available to her. As the school term ended, the teacher was concerned that Margaret, who had "double fists full" of tokens, simply refused to give them up for the prizes. Ms. Brown was concerned that she was doing something inappropriate or wrong by encouraging Margaret to turn in her tokens for prizes. In an interview with Margaret at the end of the school year, Ms. Brown realized that to Margaret, the tokens were a very tangible way of knowing that she was "okay." In a real-world environment that had focused consistently on her mistakes and limitations, the tokens represented a real reward for appro-priate behaviors that were never acknowledged prior to the Coping Skills Program.

As appropriate behaviors become habituated, teachers can incorpo-rate more verbal praise and encourage more peer praise to gradually replace the token economy. The process of token redemption depends upon individual students' needs, the nature of the reward, and how much teacher involvement it requires. Because the Coping Skills Program teaches students to delay gratification, the teacher is encouraged to delay the re-ward as long as possible. The teacher can use group contingencies or class-oriented rewards (e.g., no-homework day, ice cream party) to gradually shift the students from an individual token economy and to reward all stu-dents for working together to contribute to a positive classroom coping culture.

Case Illustration 3

Ms. Clark found that delivering the Coping Skills Program to the entire classroom of third-grade students was one of its most powerful features for modifying the group culture of that class. Instead of focusing on only those children who engaged in Thumbs Down behavior, the program taught all of the children about the consequences of Stinky Thinking. Ms. Clark addressed the problem of name calling in her classroom by asking students aloud, whenever the problem came up, if name calling was the result of Good Thinking or Stinky Thing. This strategy eventually defused the negative situations that arose in class due to the name calling. Students began to see the behavior as silly and unimportant, and the behavior subsequently lost its ability to generate a strong emotional reaction within the class.

In addition to reinforcing students' appropriate behaviors and rational thinking, the teacher models effective coping skills by behaving in a way that conveys underlying rational thinking, by articulating thoughts behind certain actions, by saying out loud for the rest of the class the rational thinking that is presumably behind a student's or group of students' appropriate behaviors, and by exposing students to other adults who convey rational thinking. In sum, the components of the Coping Skills Program integrate storytelling, visual cues, in-class exercises, structured discussion, modeling, reinforcement, and generalization to achieve proximal goals for students and for the classroom as community.

Case Illustration 4

This case illustrates how the teachers of an entire K–8 school borrowed concepts underlying the Coping Skills Program to address students' ineffective coping skills and disruptive classroom behaviors. In hearing about the positive behavioral changes occurring among third-graders who were participating in the Coping Skills Program, teachers in the other grades began the practice of reinforcing and validating students' positive responses and behaviors rather than the negative ones. Teachers throughout the school began to "catch" students demonstrating positive behaviors. The school created an "OK Wall" in the school's main hallway, and the names of children who were "caught" doing something positive were displayed on the wall. The teachers in this school observed that the "OK Wall" served to increase pride among children whose names were listed, as well as to encourage other students to earn a place on the wall.

Teacher Training, Treatment Fidelity, and Parent Involvement

Teachers whose classes have participated in the Coping Skills Program have received, on average, four hours of manual-based, didactic and experiential training from the project consultant on the following topics: (a) risk factors for adolescent substance use and abuse; (b) basic tenets of cognitive-behavior therapy; (c) research-based knowledge describing the relationship between children's cognitions, emotions, and behaviors; (d) description of and rationale behind development of the Coping Skills Program, (e) detailed instructions for completing the multi-step lesson of each fable; (f) instructions and training for reinforcing, modeling, and generalizing the curriculum; (g) strategies for encouraging parental involvement; and (h) project evaluation methods. Each teacher receives a training manual, cue posters, and a CD-ROM that contains the exercises, handouts, brochures, tokens, and visual representations used in the students' workbooks. Teachers are supervised over the course of the school year via telephone consultation and site visits, as needed. The project consultant also observes Coping Skills Program lessons as requested by teachers to ensure that curricular content is being properly delivered.

Parents whose children participate in the Coping Skills Program are encouraged to attend a two-hour didactic workshop at the onset of the program that covers the following material: (a) risk factors for adolescent substance use and abuse; (b) basic tenets of rational emotive behavior therapy; (c) description of and rationale behind development of the Coping Skills Program, and (d) ways in which parents can reinforce application of the material at home. Very few parents have attended the workshop since the program's inception. In order to address the problem of minimal parental involvement, the project consultant developed a 32-page manual entitled, *Good Thinking* that describes the fables covered in the children's workbook and how these stories are used to encourage children to change their irrational thinking to address life's difficulties. *Good Thinking* has been distributed to parents since 2004.

PRELIMINARY EVALUATION OF THE COPING SKILLS PROGRAM

The Coping Skills Program curriculum was developed in 1998 by the project consultant. Prior to school year 2001–2002, the Coping Skills Program was a voluntary, afterschool program offered to third and fourth graders. In 2001, data gathered with the statewide *Communities That Care Survey* showed that middle-school children residing in rural and impoverished, southern areas of the state were engaging in disproportionately high levels of delinquent behavior. These findings, along with recommendations from teachers who had delivered the afterschool curriculum for three years, resulted in substantive revisions to the Coping Skills Program such that the material could be delivered in regular education classrooms over the entire school year. The behavioral incentive program was added in 2001, along with the manual-based teacher-training component. Since 2001, approximately 2000 second-, third-, and fourth-grade children in 10 elementary schools have participated in the Coping Skills Program.

Curriculum Pretest-Posttest

Curriculum pretest-posttest evaluation data have been gathered regularly from students since the inception of the program. The project consultant developed the pretest-posttest instrument, and it consists of ten multiple-choice questions with three response options. Four questions measure students' knowledge of the thinking-feeling-behaving links covered in the curriculum ("If you get angry with someone, what caused you to get angry?" "Your emotions are the result of what?" "Sometimes people are mean to you and you get upset. What causes you to be upset?" "When we find ourselves very angry, sad, or scared, what is the first thing we should ask ourselves?"). The remaining six questions ask students to apply the curricular content by indicating how they would handle real-life school and home situations (e.g., "Your teacher is giving the class a lot of homework on the night of your favorite TV show. What should you do?" "You want a new toy or some clothes, but your parents tell you that they can't afford it. What should you do?"). The scenarios described in the behavioral-situational questions are not taught in the curriculum, and students are not told either the correct answers or their test scores. The amount of time from pretest to posttest is approximately 5 to 7 months, with lower scores reflecting less knowledge and less understanding of the curriculum content.

Pretest-posttest data were gathered from students who participated in the Coping Skills Program during the time in which it was a voluntary afterschool program consisting of 9, 1-hour sessions. The average pretest and posttest scores for 315 third-grade participants during the 1999–2000 school year were 44% and 57%, respectively, a 13% increase. The pretest and posttest scores for 210 third-grade students during the 2000–2001 school year were 41% and 56%, respectively, a 15% increase. In 2001 the Coping Skills program was delivered as a universal, classroom-based program, consisting of 18 lessons (presented over a 9-month time period) and a behavioral incentive program. The average pretest and posttest scores for 365 third-grade students during the 2001–2002 school year were 44% and 75%, respectively, a 31% increase, which is approximately twice as much improvement as indicated in previous years. Approximately equal proportions of African-American and White students and boys and girls comprised the above samples.

Additional longitudinal pretest-posttest data were gathered recently from 86 second grade students in a rural public school, over a 2-year time period. The sample was composed of roughly equal proportions of African-American and White students and equal proportions of boys and girls. The curriculum test was administered at five different time periods: a second-grade pretest was administered before students began the Coping Skills Program in 2003, a second-grade posttest was administered at the end of the 2003–2004 school year, a third-grade pretest was administered at the beginning of the school year (in 2004) prior to the second year of the Coping Skills Program, a third-grade posttest at the end of the 2004–2005 year, and a fourth-grade pretest at the beginning of the school year (in 2005). Students' test scores were ranked as either in the low, average or high range, with scores in the low range falling below 40%, scores in the average range between 50% and 70%, and scores in the high range between 80% and 100%.

As seen in Table 10.1, the proportion of second-grade students whose scores were in the low range decreased by 26% from pretest to posttest. One year later, the proportion of students with scores in the low range decreased from 35% at pretest to 5% at posttest (See Table 10.1). During the period of time from the second-grade pretest to the third-grade posttest, the proportion of students whose scores were in the average range doubled (from 20% to 40%) (See Table 10.1). The proportion of second-grade students whose scores fell in the high range doubled from pretest to posttest. As seen in Table 10.1, the proportion of students whose scores fell in the high range increased from 12% at second-grade posttest to 23% at third-grade pretest, an 11% increase over the summer months. From third-grade pretest to posttest, the proportion of students whose scores fell in the high range increased by 32% (See Table 10.1). These data show the improvements gained with increased exposure to the program.

Social Skills Rating System-Teacher Form

In 1999 and 2000, longitudinal data were gathered from four classes in one school to assess students' social skills, academic competence, and problem

TABLE 10.1   Curriculum Pretest–Posttest Scores: Proportions of Students Scoring in the Low, Average, and High Ranges from Second Through Fourth Grade (N = 86)[a]

Grade and Test Type	Low	Average	High
2 Pretest	74%	20%	6%
2 Posttest	48%	40%	12%
3 Pretest	35%	42%	23%
3 Posttest	5%	40%	55%
4 Pretest	2%	46%	52%

Note: Low Range = 0–40%, Average Range = 50–70%, and High Range = 80–100%.
[a]Minimal attrition and few class composition changes occurred over the 2-year time period.

behaviors. Approximately equal proportions of African American and White students and boys and girls comprised the sample. The *Social Skills Rating System-Teacher Form* (*SSRS-T*) (Gresham & Elliott, 1990) was administered at two points in time to one group of students who received the Coping Skills Program and to one group of students who did not. *SSRS-T* is a 57-item teacher-completed scale that rates students in three domains: Problem Behaviors (externalizing, internalizing, hyperactivity), Social Skills (cooperation, assertion, self-control), and Academic Competence (intellectual functioning, classroom behavior, academic performance, motivation and family support for academic success) (Gresham & Elliott, 1990). The *SSRS-T* Problem Behaviors, Social Skills, and Academic Competence scales for elementary school students demonstrate adequate internal consistency (coefficient alpha = .94, .88, and .95, respectively), and test-retest reliability (.85, .84, and .93, respectively) (Gresham & Elliott, 1990).

Teachers used the *SSRS-T* to rate 91 second-grade students who had not received the program at the conclusion of the 1999 school year. The following year in the third grade, 46 did not participate in the Coping Skills Program and 45 participated in the program. Third-grade teachers evaluated these same 91 third-grade students approximately 9 months later at mid-semester in 2000. Because the Coping Skills Program was a voluntary afterschool program at the time, teachers did not know which students in their classes had participated in the program and which students had not. Among those who did not receive the Coping Skills Program ($n = 46$), the proportion of students who were rated above the national norm on social skills decreased from 30% in second grade to 10% in third grade, a 20% decrease. The proportion of students in this group who were rated above the national norm on academic competence decreased from 10% to 8% (a 2% decrease), and the proportion of students who were rated above the national norm on problem behaviors increased from 7% to 22% (indicating that 15% more students were demonstrating this degree of problem behaviors). Among the 45 third-graders who participated in the program, the proportion of students who were rated above the national norm on social skills rose from 12% in second grade to 43% in third grade, a 31% increase. The proportion of students in this group who were rated above the national norm on academic competence rose from 17% to 35% (an 18% increase), and the proportion of students who were rated above the national norm on problem behaviors decreased from 52% to 30% (indicating 22% fewer students were demonstrating this degree of problem behaviors).

Although the sample size is small and the data are not linked to curriculum pretest-posttest scores, the results show that teachers reported change in a positive direction among program participants on measures of student outcomes targeted by the Coping Skills Program. Among students who participated in the program, the proportion rated above the norm on social skills and academic competence increased, whereas the proportion rated above the norm on problem behaviors decreased. Further, the Coping Skills Program was delivered after school when *SSRS-T* data were gathered. Thus, these students received a relatively low dosage of the curriculum.

Program Satisfaction

Program satisfaction data have been collected from the parents of all Coping Skills Program participants at the end of the school year with an eight-item instrument developed by the project consultant. The instrument includes four items about the curriculum (i.e., age appropriateness, ability of material to keep child interested, overall quality of the materials, likelihood that material will help the parent with parenting), one item about the teacher, and one item assessing the child's ability to retain the material. Two final items ask parents about the likelihood of reviewing stories with the child in the future and about the likelihood of attending a workshop on parent coping. Response options include "Very Good," "Good," "Fair," and "Poor." In 2000 (during the time in which the program was delivered as an afterschool program), 130 parents were surveyed, with 96 completing and returning the questionnaire (a 73.8% response rate). Most parents ($N = 91, 95\%$) rated the Coping Skills Program as "Very Good" or "Good" on all items, except for the question about the likelihood of attending a workshop on parent coping. The response rate for this survey dropped precipitously in 2001 when teachers began to deliver the program in the classroom. Parents presumably were less aware of the program because children were not staying after school to participate and because it carried no study or grading requirements. In 2002, 380 parents were surveyed, with 64 returning completed questionnaires (a 16.8% response rate). Again, most ($N = 61, 96\%$) parents rated the Coping Skills Program as "Very Good" or "Good" on all items, except for the item about attending a workshop. These data were no longer collected after 2002 because of the low response rate.

In 2000, program satisfaction data were gathered from 525 third graders who participated in the afterschool format of the Coping Skills Program, with a brief, five-item instrument required of all state-funded substance abuse programs. Although the reliability of this survey for children is questionable, most students ($N = 483, 92\%$) rated the Coping Skills Program as "Excellent" or "Very Good." This survey was no longer used when the program was changed to an in-class format because teachers were consistently reporting high levels of student enjoyment, and also because it became too unwieldy to collect the data as the number of sites increased. Although the process is not formalized, teachers often ask students to provide feedback about the program. The following representative student comments collected in 2002 from third graders, who were in the second year of the program, are offered as testimonials of the Coping Skills Program: "I like coping skills. It is fun to do. Because you get books and stuff. We read a lot. And on the bus I read it over again. That's why I like coping skills." "What I like about Coping Skills is that it is very fun to me. Coping Skills have very beautiful stories. My favorite was the young girl because she made her village more richer. I love the story the Collard Green but the girl used stinky thinking b/c she let the animals tell her what to do." "I like coping skills very much. It helps me learn a lot of stuff. It help me keep away from stuff I am not suppose to do. Just like smoking. And a lot of other stuff, too. I wish we could do this every day."

Students' comments broadly reflect positive appraisals of the fables used in the Coping Skills Program curriculum as well as the way that teachers use the stories in the classroom. Although the Coping Skills Program targets the classroom environment, evaluation data on classroom-level variables have not been systematically gathered.

SUMMARY

This chapter describes the Coping Skills Program, an innovative, school-based, universal curriculum for elementary-school aged children that is rooted in cognitive behavior theory. Although more rigorous testing is warranted, preliminary uncontrolled evaluation results show that participation in the Coping Skills Program is associated with increases in measures of rational thinking from pretest to posttest; improved independent teacher ratings on measures of problem behaviors, social skills, and academic competence over time; and self-reported student satisfaction with the curriculum.

The Coping Skills Program is a multigrade prevention intervention that is supported by the research-based literature on children's developmental risk and protective factors. Research shows that universal, school-based prevention programs that target children's social and problem-solving competencies should be implemented early on in order to positively influence the developmental trajectories of young children (Patterson, 2002). Unlike other classroom-based curricula, the Coping Skills Program relies on the use of metaphorical fables to teach students about their thinking and how their thinking influences their feelings and subsequent actions. The Coping Skills Program is rooted in a substantial body of outcome research demonstrating the effectiveness of cognitive behavior treatment applications with children experiencing a variety of psychosocial difficulties (Kendall, 2000).

In addition to being well grounded in the research-based literature, the Coping Skills Program is a prevention intervention that is well-suited to contemporary school social work practice. Frey and Dupper (2005), noted experts in the field, took stock of the complex knowledge and skills required for effective school social work practice in the 21st century, and they urged school social workers to respond to this changing landscape by marketing themselves as prevention specialists. The Coping Skills Program is representative of a multisystem and strength-based prevention intervention that is consistent with a broader clinical approach to school social work recommended by Frey and Dupper.

It is worth noting that Staudt and colleagues (2005) recently took the first step toward developing practice guidelines for school social workers by reviewing all school social work intervention studies ($N = 32$) published from 1999 though 2003. According to these authors, most of the studies did not employ rigorous designs or standardized outcome measures. Fewer than half (44%) referenced a treatment manual, and only 19% addressed treatment fidelity issues (Staudt et al., 2005). In this context, the information provided about the Coping Skills Program in this chapter addresses some of the limitations noted by Staudt and colleagues. The use of a comparison group, multiple measures of important system-level variables, and longitudinal outcome data would strengthen future evaluations of the Coping Skills Program.

The research-based literature shows that cognitive behavior approaches are among the interventions commonly used by social workers to help young children in school settings (Ronen, 1994; Staudt et al., 2005). Clinicians are therefore encouraged to continue applying and testing theoretically grounded and evidence-based approaches to their work with young children in school settings to advance knowledge regarding the prevention of risk factors that predict adolescent substance abuse and other forms of delinquency. The results of uncontrolled evaluations of the Coping Skills Program have been favorable, and ongoing testing of this universal school-based curricula is warranted.

REFERENCES

Allen-Meares, P. (2004). An ecological perspective of social work services in the schools. In P. Allen-Meares (Ed.), *Social work in schools* (4th ed., pp. 71–94). Boston: Allyn & Bacon.

Barker, P. (1996). *Psychotherapeutic metaphors: A guide to theory and practice.* Bristol, PA: Brunner/Mazel.

Conduct Problems Prevention Research Group. (2002). Predictor variables associated with positive FAST Track outcomes at the end of third grade. *Journal of Abnormal Child Psychology, 30,* 37–52.

Crick, N. R., & Dodge, K. A. (1994). A review and reformulation of social information-processing mechanisms in children's social adjustment. *Psychological Bulletin, 115,* 74–101.

Crick, N. R., Grotpeter, J. K., & Bigbee, M. A. (2002). Relationally and physically aggressive children's intent attributions and feelings of distress for relational and instrumental peer provocation. *Child Development, 73,* 1134–1142.

Eisenberg, N., Fabes, R. A., Guthrie, I. K., & Reiser, M. (2002). The role of emotionality and regulation in children's social competence and adjustment. In L. Pulkkinen & A. Caspi (Eds.), *Paths to successful development: Personality in the life course* (pp. 46–70). New York: Cambridge University Press.

Fraser, M. W. (2004). *Risk and resilience in childhood: An ecological perspective* (2nd ed.). Washington, DC: NASW Press.

Fraser, M. W., Day, S. H., Galinsky, M. J., Hodges, V. G., & Smokowski, P. R. (2004). Conduct problems and peer rejection in childhood: A randomized trial of the Making Choices and Strong Families programs. *Research on Social Work Practice, 14,* 313–324.

Fraser, M. W., Nash, J. K., Galinsky, M. J., & Darwin, K. E. (2001). *Making choices: Social problem-solving skills for children.* Washington, DC: NASW Press.

Frey, A. J., & Dupper, D. R. (2005). A broader conceptual approach to clinical practice for the 21st century. *Children & Schools, 27,* 33–44.

Germain, C. B. (2002). An ecological perspective on social work in the schools. In R. Constable, S. McDonald & J. P. Flynn (Eds.), *School social work: Practice, policy and research perspectives* (5th ed., pp. 33–44). Chicago: Lyceum.

Greenberg, M. T., & Kusche, C. A. (1993). *Promoting social and emotional development in deaf children: The PATHS project.* Seattle, WA: University of Washington Press.

Greenberg, M. T., Kusche, A., Cook, E T., & Quamma, J. P. (1995). Promoting emotional competence in school-aged children: The effects of the PATHS curriculum. *Development and Psychopathology, 7,* 117–136.

Gresham, F. M., & Elliott, S. N. (1990). *Social Skills Rating System manual.* Circle Pines, MN: American Guidance Service, Inc.

Hawkins, J. D., Catalano, R. F., & Miller, J. Y. (1992). Risk and protective factors for alcohol and other drug problems in adolescence and early adulthood: Implications for substance abuse prevention. *Psychological Bulletin, 112,* 64–105.

Hawkins, J. D., Catalano, R. F., Kosterman, R., Abbott, R., & Hill, K. G. (1999). Preventing adolescent healthy-risk behaviors by strengthening protection during childhood. *Archives of Pediatric Adolescent Medicine, 153,* 226–234.

Ialongo, N., Poduska, J., Werthamer, L., & Kellam, S. (2001). The distal impact of two first-grade preventive interventions on conduct problems and disorder in early adolescence. *Journal of Emotional and Behavioral Disorders, 9,* 146–160.

Kendall, P. C. (2000). *Child and adolescent therapy: Cognitive-behavioral procedures* (2nd ed.). New York: Guilford.

Lengua, L. J. (2002). The contribution of emotionality and self-regulation to the understanding of children's response to multiple risk. *Child Development, 73,* 144–161.

Loeber, R. (1990). Development and risk factors of juvenile antisocial behavior and delinquency. *Clinical Psychological Review, 10,* 1–42.

Loeber, R., & Farrington, D. P. (Eds.). (2001). *Child delinquents.* Thousand Oaks, CA: Sage.

Otto, M. W. (2000). Stories and metaphors in cognitive-behavioral therapy. *Cognitive and Behavioral Practice, 7,* 166–172.

Pakaslahti, L. (2000). Children's adolescents; aggressive behavior in context: The development and application of aggressive problem-solving strategies. *Aggression and Violent Behavior, 5,* 467–490.

Patterson, G. R. (2002). The early development of coercive family process. In J. B. Reid, G. R. Patterson, & J. Snyder (Eds.), *Antisocial behavior in children and adolescents* (pp. 25–44). Washington, DC: American Psychological Association.

Patterson, G. R., Dishion, T. J., & Yoerger, K. (2000). Adolescent growth in new forms of problem behavior: Macro- and micro-peer dynamics. *Prevention Science, 1,* 3–13.

Reid, J. B., Patterson, G. R., & Snyder, J. (2002). *Antisocial behavior in children and adolescents.* Washington, DC: American Psychological Association.

Ronen, T. (1994). Imparting self-control skills in the school setting. *Child and Family Behavior Therapy, 16*(1), 1–20.

Ronen, T., & Rosenbaum, M. (2001). Helping children to help themselves: A case study of enuresis and nail biting. *Research on Social Work Practice, 11,* 338–356.

Rudolph, K. D., Hammen, C., & Burge, B. (1997). A cognitive-interpersonal approach to depressive symptoms in preadolescent children. *Journal of Abnormal Child Psychology, 25,* 33–45.

Shure, M. B. (2001). *I can problem solve: An interpersonal cognitive problem-solving program* (2nd ed.). Champaign, IL: Research Press.

Smith, C., & Nyland, D. (1997). *Narrative therapies with children and adolescents.* New York: Guilford.

Staudt, M. M., Cherry, D. J., & Watson, M. (2005). Practice guidelines for school social workers: A modified replication and extension of a prototype. *Children & Schools, 27,* 71–81.

Waters, V. (1982). Therapies for children: Rational Emotive Therapy. In C. R. Reynolds & T. B. Gutkin (Eds.), *Handbook of school psychology.* New York: Wiley & Sons.

CHAPTER 11

Working With Abused Children and Adolescents

Rene Mason

INTRODUCTION

Social workers have a long history of working with abused children and adolescents. It would be safe to say that most social work professionals have had contact with children at some point in their careers. Child welfare agencies, schools, hospitals, and private practice are just some of the settings in which the lives of children are our primary concern. Even in our work with adults, we are often confronted with issues that are related to our clients' children. The social worker's responsibilities range from identification and reporting of abuse, to providing court testimony, to treatment and prevention. This chapter focuses primarily on the clinical treatment of the abused child or adolescent using a cognitive behavior approach (CBT). More often than not, these clients have experienced repeated episodes of traumatic stress in addition to the physical and/or sexual abuse that led to the referral for treatment (Cloitre, Farina, Davis, Carr, & Brown, 2005; Chaffin & Hanson, 2000). The conceptualization of symptoms of child abuse as a form of posttraumatic stress disorder (PTSD) provides a framework for implementing cognitive behavioral interventions that can be modified according to developmental and cognitive needs in order to help clients understand their experience and develop appropriate coping skills that can be utilized throughout their lifespan.

As clinical social work practice continues to advance, increased emphasis is being placed on the validity and utility of social work interventions. Schools of social work are emphasizing the importance of developing a research base for the work that we do. Empirically based treatments offer our patients the best possible opportunity for healing through proven interventions. Although social work practice is more typically associated with psychodynamic theories, CBT is well suited to the mission of social work practice. CBT builds on the patient's strengths by allowing the patient to work collaboratively with the therapist toward measurable goals thereby reducing symptoms and enhancing functioning. Certainly, CBT is consistent with the social work ideal of client self-determination.

Based on social learning theory, the basic premise of CBT is that one's thoughts, feelings, and behaviors are connected, and that by manipulating one's thoughts and/or behaviors, one has the ability to reduce symptoms, cope with difficult feelings, and improve overall functioning. CBT is quite structured, goal oriented, and solution focused. Problems are identified and solved by means of a collaborative relationship between the patient and the therapist. The patient is educated about the nature of his problems and is invited to attempt and evaluate different strategies to cope with or solve these problems. The goal of treatment, in addition to developing insight by challenging irrational beliefs, is the reduction of symptoms through the development of coping strategies and problem-solving techniques. The therapeutic process of guided discovery mirrors the developmental tasks that children should accomplish, making it an ideal modality for the treatment of children.

This chapter familiarizes the reader with the treatment of children and adolescents who are experiencing impairment as a result of post-traumatic stress associated with their history of abuse. A brief discussion of the literature in the fields of abuse and trauma in children provides information regarding the consequences of physical and sexual abuse, and the results of treatment. The components of the CBT model and the conceptualization of childhood trauma as a form of PTS, as evidenced by the literature, are defined in order to facilitate the clinician's understanding of how to apply these concepts to practice and provide the rationale for the CBT approach to treatment. The specific criteria for PTSD diagnosis in children and adolescents will be reviewed with consideration of developmental and cognitive traits. Assessment of abused children utilizing clinical interviews and standardized assessment tools will be discussed with regard to the development of an appropriate treatment plan.

Detailed information will be provided on the adaptation of CBT techniques to different age groups. Session structure, collaborating with parents, coping skills, cognitive restructuring, the use homework, and the use of exposure are described theoretically and illustrated with case material.

THE SCOPE OF THE PROBLEM

The term *child maltreatment* includes neglect as well as physical, sexual, and emotional abuse. Neglect refers to the failure of a parent or caregiver to provide adequately for the needs of a child. It includes the neglect of physical needs, such as food, shelter, and clothing, as well as educational needs, medical care, and supervision. Abuse can be defined as deliberate actions that result in physical or emotional harm to a child. It can occur chronically over a period of time or acutely in a specific instance. It should be noted that the term *child abuse* or *maltreatment* does not constitute a specific diagnosis, but describes an event or series of events. This chapter focuses on the treatment of children who have been victims of physical and/or sexual abuse.

The National Child Abuse and Neglect Data System (NCANDS) collects data on all children that were the subject of an investigation or assessment by a child protective service agency. According to the NCANDS, approximately 906,000 children were determined to be victims of abuse or neglect in the United States in 2003. An estimated 19% of these children were physically abused and 10% were sexually abused (U.S. Department of Health and Human Services, 2003). It is important to note that these estimates are based on the number of incidents *reported* and do not take into consideration the significant number of cases that may not have been reported. The National Incidence Study-3 (1996) collected data from a nationally representative sample of approximately 5,000 professionals employed in public schools, hospitals, day care centers, and law enforcement agencies in the United States in addition to data from child protective services on children who experienced abuse perpetrated by their parents or caretaker. The study found that girls are three times as likely to be sexually abused as boys. Twenty percent of parents who were abused as children abuse their own children. The NIS-3 reported an increase in cases of sexually abused children in 1986 from 119,200 to approximately 217,700 in 1993, an 83% increase while the number of cases of physically abused children increased from 269,700 to 381,700, a 42% increase (Sedlak & Broadhurst, 1996). Data collection is currently underway for the NIS-4. Annual surveys conducted by the National Committee to Prevent Child Abuse indicate a 49% increase in reports of maltreatment between 1986 and 1995 (Prevent Child Abuse America, 2001). NCANDS reported

1,500 children died as a result of abuse or neglect and approximately 79% of those children were less than 4 years old. Child abuse and neglect impacts children of all races. Approximately 54% of the victims of child abuse and neglect in 2002 were White, 26% were African American, and approximately 10% were Hispanic. Certainly these statistics give emphasis to the magnitude and gravity of the crisis.

SOCIAL WORKERS: CHILD THERAPISTS VERSUS INVESTIGATORS

Social workers find themselves in many roles in their work with children. As mandated reporters, all social workers share in the responsibility to protect children by reporting any suspicion of child abuse or neglect. Despite this professional obligation, it is not unusual for social workers to feel personal discomfort and role confusion when confronted with the disclosure of childhood trauma. Ideally, the social worker's role should be clearly defined as investigator or therapist. The social worker as investigator (employed by child protective services) serves to verify if abuse actually occurred and takes the necessary steps to ensure the child's safety. The investigation and intervention of child protective services may require the involvement of legal, medical, and mental health professionals and often requires multiple interviews. The confidentiality that is so essential to the therapeutic relationship is not a requirement of forensic investigation as it is understood that the investigator is gathering information for the purpose of reporting to the court (Mannarino & Cohen, 2001). The social worker as therapist works with the child after abuse has been founded to help the child and family cope with the emotional ramifications of the trauma and its disclosure. The therapist provides education to the child and family about the investigative process, normalizes reactions to the abuse, and models appropriate support of the child for the custodial parent. Treatment goals may include reduction of symptoms, development of appropriate coping mechanisms, and family resolution.

LITERATURE REVIEW

Several research studies have documented the long-term consequences of abuse on children (Kelly, Thornberry, & Smith, 1997; Kendall-Tackett, Williams, & Finkelhor, 1993; Silverman, Reinherz, & Giaconia, 1996). Difficulties may include physical, emotional, developmental, cognitive, and social impairments within the child as well as the costs to society as a whole. The 2001 report by Prevent Child Abuse America estimates the costs of maintaining the child welfare, judicial, law enforcement, health and mental health systems to respond to the impact of child abuse to be approximately $24 billion each year. Long-term indirect costs of abuse, estimated at more than $69 billion per year include the cost of criminal activity, substance abuse, domestic violence, special education, and loss of productivity due to unemployment and underemployment (Prevent Child Abuse America, 2001).

The physical effects of abuse range from minor injuries to severe damage that may have long lasting impact on the child's developing brain; in some cases this damage results in a failure of certain areas of the brain to form properly (Perry, 2001; Shore, 1997). Decreased physical, mental, and emotional development and increased hyperarousal response have been noted. Physically abused children may demonstrate impairment in interpersonal functioning due to deficits in social competence, problem-solving skills, and increased levels of aggression as compared to nonabused children (Swenson & Kolko, 2000). These difficulties may persist into adolescence and adulthood jeopardizing long-term functioning with regard to interpersonal relationships and overall functioning. Attachment theory stipulates the necessity of a trusting relationship during infancy for normal development. In addition to the development of PTSD, anxiety or depression, exposure to violence may interrupt the tasks of normal development having effects that persist into adulthood (Margolin & Gordis, 2000). Early attachment to caretakers has a direct impact on how children integrate and process sensory information in order to cope with experiences without undue distress. Predictability and continuity is central to the development of the children's understanding of the rules of cause and effect and the development of their ability to influence and control the outcome of events. The caretaker's capacity to respond to distress provides a model for the child to build his own capacity for dealing with stress. When a child is abused, this predictability and continuity is tragically disrupted and tasks of normal development may not be accomplished. The result: The child's ability to self sooth and establish trusting relationships later in life is impaired. A diagnosis of PTSD by the age of 18 was shown to significantly increase the risk of diagnoses of depression, anxiety, and substance dependence in a study of more than 300 youths (Pfefferbaum, 1997). Research indicates that a history of child maltreatment significantly increases the risk of problematic behaviors in adolescence. Kelly and colleagues (1997) drew a sample of 1,000 students in public school in seventh and eighth grade and then collected data through eleventh and twelfth grades with regard to their history of maltreatment and involvement in delinquency, academic achievement, illegal drug use, teen pregnancy, and mental health problems. In a comparison of maltreated children to nonmaltreated children, the maltreated subjects demonstrated significantly increased levels of risk for illegal drug use, development of mental health problems, teen pregnancy, and problematic behaviors.

There is increasing evidence supporting the efficacy of CBT for children experiencing difficulties associated with abuse (Cohen & Mannarino, 1996, 1998; Cohen, Deblinger, Mannarino, & Steer, 2004; Deblinger, Lippmann, & Steer, 1996; King, et al., 1996). Using a sample of 209 children, 8 to 14 years old and their primary caretakers, Cohen and colleagues (2004) compared the efficacy of trauma-focused CBT treatment to child-centered psychotherapy in children experiencing emotional and behavioral problems related to sexual abuse at two sites. The children randomized to the CBT group showed significant improvement in PTSD symptoms, depression, shame, and misattributions. Additionally, the caretakers assigned to the CBT group reported improvement in their own depression, ability to provide support to the child, and parenting skills. In addition to replicating the results of earlier findings regarding PTSD symptoms in children (Cohen & Mannarino, 1996, 1998), this study demonstrated a reduction in nonoffending levels of parental distress associated with the abuse. King and colleagues (2000) randomized 36 children, 5 to 17 years old, to a child-alone CBT treatment, a family CBT treatment or a wait list control condition and found that the children who received treatment reported significant reductions in levels of anxiety and improvement in PTSD symptoms; however, no significant difference in symptoms was noted between the children randomized to the child-alone versus the child and family CBT conditions.

THE CBT MODEL

In the CBT model thoughts, feelings, and actions are thought to be intrinsically connected in such a way that they have the power to influence one another. The idea being that one can generate overall improvement by targeting the symptoms in any of these areas. Cognitions or thoughts influence the way we feel and the way we behave. Consider the anxiety a child might experience in anticipation of giving an oral report in class. The child might have fears that she will forget what she is going to say or make mistakes. As she continues to ruminate about possible negative outcomes, she feels increasingly anxious; perhaps the hands start to perspire and the heart rate increases. Underlying these thoughts and physiological reactions is a fundamental psychological premise or core belief that steers her to these negative automatic thoughts, and colors her perceptions. The core beliefs permit the negative thoughts to spring forth automatically and usually imperceptibly, so that the feelings and behaviors associated with these thoughts manifest. Perhaps, she tries to avoid school that day by feigning illness. In the case of this anxiety-ridden student, the underlying core belief could be "I'm not good enough" or "I'm stupid." If the child, however, could recognize the unhelpful negative thoughts and restructure them, reasoning perhaps that, "I've given presentations before, it went well, it's likely that it will go well this time" or "I know a lot of things so I can't be stupid," it stands to reason that feelings of anxiety could be replaced with feelings of competence and a reduction in the physical indications of anxiety. The ability to identify irrational automatic thoughts, question their validity, and restructure cognitions can precipitate change in feelings and thereby change in behavior. The connection between cognitions, behaviors, and thoughts is deceptively simple. The challenge for the clinician is to help the patient recognize and challenge her unhelpful thoughts by leading the patient through a process of guided discovery enabling the patient to come to her own conclusions about what is helpful. The clinician does not lecture the patient but instead provides education about the nature of the disorder, questions the patient to elicit irrational thoughts, and provides homework assignments to help the patient discover and challenge irrational beliefs, and alter behavior. Coping skills are practiced in session and for homework in order to help the patient learn to manage distressing symptoms. Imagined exposure allows the child to reexperience the emotions associated with the trauma and master them in a safe environment. The patient practices behavioral and cognitive strategies, and evaluates and modifies them accordingly with the help of the therapist. The patient works collaboratively with the therapist to identify the targets of treatment.

Anxiety disorders are essentially a misfiring of the innate flight-or-fight response. When threatened with danger, one's body prepares physiologically, as well as mentally, to self-protect in an attempt to ensure safety. An anxiety disorder ensues when there is no real danger or threat and the flight-or-flight response is activated unnecessarily, causing distress and interfering with functioning. Perceived threats and physical reactions interact with negative thoughts, creating a chain reaction of fear and avoidance. Treatment focuses on managing the physical sensations, identifying the thoughts associated with those feelings, and challenging the irrational thoughts that contribute to the distress and avoidant behavior. Imagined exposure desensitizes the child to the trauma and provides an opportunity to practice coping strategies.

In PTSD, intrusive thoughts and reminders of traumatic events stimulate a conditioned anxiety response to the extent that it interferes with normal functioning. Neutral stimuli associated with the trauma, such as scents or sounds, produce the same negative emotional response even though the circumstances may be benign. Consequently, the victim learns to avoid the neutral stimuli in order to avoid experiencing the habituated fear (Deblinger & Heflin, 1996). These symptoms may persist for months or years. Diagnosis of PTSD is contingent upon exposure to a traumatic event that is outside of the range of normal experience and potentially life threatening. Physical abuse, sexual abuse, kidnapping, accidents, community violence, and acts of terrorism all qualify as traumatic events. The exposure may be directly experienced or witnessed by the patient; or in some cases the patient may have learned about the trauma experienced by a family member or close associate. The response to the traumatic stressor must involve intense fear, helplessness, or horror. The cluster of symptoms associated with PTSD in children fall into the same categories as PTSD symptoms associated with adults: avoidance, reexperiencing, and hyperarousal. These symptoms, however, often manifest themselves differently in children than in adults. Children with PTSD will try to avoid reminders of the trauma, but may not be able to connect their distress to traumatic events. Avoidance may be evidenced as feelings of detachment, numbing or a general lack of responsiveness, diminished interest in activities, or an inability to recall aspects of the trauma. Children may also experience a foreshortened sense of the future feeling that they may not grow up and become adults. *Omen formation* refers to a child's prediction that negative events will occur in the future and the belief that there were signs that the impending trauma could or should have been recognized (American Psychiatric Association, 1994). Such misattributions are a primary target of CBT. Teenagers may engage in risk-taking behaviors feeling that life is hopeless and their behavior is inconsequential, thereby distracting themselves from the distressing feelings associated with the abuse. Reexperiencing may take the form of repetitive play, intrusive nightmares, acting or feeling as though the abuse is reoccurring, or experiencing physical symptoms when exposed to reminders of the trauma. Stomachaches and headaches are common. In order for a child to meet criteria for a diagnosis of PTSD, three symptoms of avoidance, two symptoms of hyperarousal, and at least one reexperiencing symptom must be evident at least 1 month after the trauma causing impairment to functioning. Evidence of these symptoms within 1 month of the trauma, with minimal functional impairment, may be considered a normal reaction to an abnormal event and could be classified as an adjustment disorder.

ASSESSMENT

It is important for the clinician to consider the child's developmental stage and cognitive ability when determining the level of functional impairment and embarking on a course of treatment. Both the presentation of symptoms and the treatment process are influenced by developmental and cognitive abilities. The clinician must be able to distinguish between developmental or cognitive deficits and symptoms related to the abuse in order to identify appropriate treatment goals and methods. Specific symptoms seem to be observed with different age groups. Younger children in particular are less likely to connect their behaviors to the abuse and may present with generalized anxiety symptoms: fear of strangers, fear of the dark or monsters, separation anxiety, and avoidance of triggers that have no apparent connection to the abuse. Sexually abused children may demonstrate sexualized behaviors that are inappropriate for their age group. Regressive symptoms, such as enuresis encopresis, and magical thinking may manifest. Children with severe PTSD from abuse may present with transient psychotic symptoms when they are confronted with fear-provoking situations (Cohen & Mannarino, 2004). Younger children may engage in traumatic play that repeatedly depicts aspects of the traumatic experience. This demonstration of reexperiencing is often an attempt to manage traumatic anxiety and related affect and not necessarily a precise account of the abusive experience (Pynoos & Nader, 1992).

Irritability, social withdrawal, separation anxiety, memory, and attention problems have been observed in children and adolescents who have been abused (Drake, Bush, & von Gorp, 2001). Latency-aged children and adolescents often struggle with feelings of guilt associated with the abuse and the life changes that can occur following disclosure. As children become increasingly independent during adolescence, they are more likely to accept blame for the abuse and its aftermath. Self-blame has been associated with more negative symptoms in sexually abused girls (Mannarino & Cohen, 1996). Blaming the perpetrator has been associated with more anger and disruptive behavior (Chaffin & Hanson, 2000).

Assessment should include separate interviews with the child, as well as the nonoffending parent. Parents are more likely to focus on externalizing behavioral symptoms and be less aware of internalizing symptoms (Cohen & Mannarino, 1988). Social workers employed in research settings may be familiar with the utility of standardized measures and structured questionnaires. Standardized measures are very helpful in determining the level of severity of symptoms and reducing the chance of diagnostic error due to clinician bias. Measures may also be used throughout the course of treatment to monitor progress toward treatment goals. Questionnaires, however, should not be used in place of a clinical interview as they may yield false positive results and are best utilized in conjunction with a clinical interview. In research, assessment usually takes place after the validity of abuse has been established. In practice, this may not be the case and measures that include scales of validity, such as the Trauma Symptom Checklist for Children, may be useful (Briere, 1996a). Structured interviews allow the clinician to screen for a variety of disorders in order to differentiate between PTSD and other disorders with similar presentation. In the absence of a structured interviewing tool, the social worker should a conduct complete clinical interview by gathering information on the child's functioning prior to the abuse, current functioning, history of previous psychiatric and medical treatment, peer relationships, developmental history, school functioning, family functioning and disciplinary strategies, substance use and legal involvement, ethnocultural and religious background, and the child's and parent's reactions to the disclosure of abuse and its impact on the family.

Evaluation should also include assessment of suicidal risk. Children feeling excessive self-blame, guilt, anxiety, and sadness or those unable to find resolution to these feelings may consider suicide a viable alternative. Assessment should include consideration of levels of hopelessness, depression, and impulsivity. In the parent interview, the social worker should inquire about access to lethal means and any history of prior suicide attempts or self-injurious behavior. In the interview with the child, it is important to determine if the child has genuine intention to die versus a desire to escape distress. A high level of intent is an indication of significant distress. The therapist should work with the child and the parent to develop a safety plan. In the event that such a safety plan cannot be developed, steps should be taken to ensure the child's safety.

There is considerable overlap in the diagnoses of PTSD, depression, and attention deficit hyperactivity disorder (ADHD). Irritability, loss of interest in activities, sleep and appetite disturbances, difficulty with concentration, impulsivity, and increased aggression are common manifestations of these disorders. Hyperarousal may be articulated in children as disorganized or agitated behavior, similar in presentation to ADHD (American Psychiatric Association, 1994). Research has documented frequent comorbidity of depression and other anxiety disorders in children with PTSD. ADHD is frequently diagnosed in children exposed to trauma regardless of whether they meet criteria for a diagnosis of PTSD (Cohen & Mannarino, 2004; Weinstein, Staffelbach, & Biaggio, 2000). ADHD may be diagnosed with mood disorders, anxiety disorders, learning disabilities, and PTSD. It is important to determine if the child has any psychiatric conditions predating the abuse that may have been exacerbated by trauma. Examining the context in which the symptoms occur, and obtaining a thorough history should help the clinician to differentiate PTSD from ADHD and other psychiatric disorders.

Not all children exposed to child abuse develop PTSD. There is some controversy as to whether children develop behavioral problems to the extent that they meet criteria for PTSD diagnosis after trauma or whether they are resilient and exhibit some increase in behavioral difficulties before returning to normal functioning (Ronen, 2002). Pynoos (1994) identified family functioning, developmental stage, and coping skills as influences in the reaction of children to traumatic events. In addition to exposure, vulnerabilities for the development of PTSD in children and adolescents include: level of violence, coercion or deceit, and relationship to the abuser with regard to the level of betrayal. In a study comparing sexually abused PTSD positive children to PTSD negative children, Wolfe and colleagues (1994) found that the feelings of guilt, the level of violence associated with the trauma, and the relationship the child had with the abuser were also significant factors in the development of PTSD. PTSD positive children were more likely to have experienced abuse over a period of time and were more likely to have experienced threat or coercion. Children who have been both physically and sexually abused seem to be at the highest risk of psychiatric disturbance (Ackerman, Newton, McPherson, Jones, & Dykman, 1998).

PSYCHOEDUCATION AND PREVENTION

A significant number of children remain asymptomatic and develop no apparent symptoms. Others become symptomatic at some point in the future or develop some PTSD-related symptoms, but not enough to meet criteria for a clinical diagnosis. Treatment for these children should focus on psychoeducation and skill building that will develop the child's ability to self-protect and avoid becoming a victim in the future. Parents should be educated about the nature of child abuse and its impact on children. Developing the parent's coping strategies is an essential part of treatment as children's responses are often influenced by their parent's reaction to the abuse (Foy, Madvig, Pynoos, & Camilleri, 1996). Treatment should include helping the parent identify a support network, education about the nature of abuse, parent training about behavior management and age appropriate expectations, and the development of a contingency plan in the event that the child is at risk.

CASE CONCEPTUALIZATION

Case conceptualization provides the underlying reasoning for the course of treatment and enables the social worker to create a treatment plan that is tailored to the patient's needs. Conceptualization should begin with the first session and continue throughout treatment, disallowing a mechanical approach to treatment by taking into consideration the specific psychological, cultural, developmental, behavioral, and environmental issues contributing to the presenting problems of the patient's unique situation. It differs from diagnosis in that, instead of merely describing symptoms, it provides a hypothesis for the probable cause of symptoms and anticipates the possible obstacles that may be encountered in treatment. The case conceptualization guides the choice of interventions, and the execution and timing of these interventions. In addition, case conceptualization is a key factor in evaluating the patient's progress. Data obtained from standardized measures can provide additional information for conceptualization. Consideration is also given to how the antecedents and consequences maintain problematic behaviors, as these may be possible targets of intervention. The case conceptualization should be continually revised as the therapeutic relationship develops and the social worker develops increased understanding of the patient's distinctive needs.

Conceptualization begins with a definition of the presenting problems in specific terms. It is helpful to break down the presenting problem into behavioral, emotional, interpersonal, physiological, and cognitive components in order to identify specific treatment goals (Friedberg & McClure, 2002). For example, if Sara's presenting problem is that she is afraid to be away from her mom, we can identify behavioral components as clinging to mom and crying, emotional components as sadness and anxiety, interpersonal components as not having friendships with peers, physiological components as stomachaches and increased heart rate, and cognitive components as automatic thoughts that it is "not safe without mom," and a core belief that "I am unable to protect myself from harm." These components help identify specific goals of treatment. Once the list of problems has been delineated, the therapist considers how the patient's history, the antecedents and consequences of negative behaviors, cognitions, and cultural factors contribute to the maintenance of the problems and determines what interventions are appropriate and when they should be implemented. The therapist makes an attempt to anticipate obstacles to treatment in order to plan accordingly. For instance, if Sara's mother is overprotective and always rescues Sara from anxiety-provoking situations, this reinforces Sara's feelings of incompetence. The social worker may provide psychoeducation for the mother on the need for children to separate from parents in order to develop autonomy and help develop behavioral strategies that can be used to address Sara's tantrums.

Family practices, beliefs, symptom presentation, and responses to treatment are strongly influenced by the patient's ethnic and cultural background. In some instances these influences are readily apparent while in others they may be less obvious or imperceptible. Chances are that these influences are least apparent when the culture of the patient and family is similar to the clinician's background. It is important to consider how ethnicity and cultural issues contribute to the development and maintenance of symptomotology and how these factors may present obstacles (as well as opportunities) in the implementation of interventions in treatment. The culture of both the social worker and the family colors perceptions and impacts treatment. Similarities and differences between the social worker, the family, and the victim with regard to culture and personal experience can have a powerful influence on how treatment is conceptualized, implemented, and received. The therapist must remain vigilant about how his own experiences, cultural background, and expectations impact the treatment process and should be particularly mindful of how his comfort level with sensitive material influences his ability to approach these issues in a constructive manner. When conceptualizing a case, the social worker should ask himself what factors contributed to the development of the disorder, how these factors have impacted the patients beliefs about herself, the world and others, how these difficulties have been maintained, and what obstacles may be anticipated in treatment (Beck, 1995).

CBT TREATMENT: USEFUL TECHNIQUES AND STRATEGIES

Collaboration is a key aspect in CBT treatment. The therapist and patient work as a team through the process of guided discovery to test the validity of the patient's beliefs. The therapist uses empathy, Socratic questioning, behavioral experiments, problem solving, and homework assignments to help the patient shed doubt on her unhelpful thoughts and discover alternative strategies that may be more helpful to them. Children and adolescents are often unaccustomed to having this type of relationship with an adult where their point of view is seen as essential to the course of action. The level of collaboration varies in accordance with the ability of the child to participate. Early in treatment the therapist may take a more active role in the collaboration. Age, motivation, frustration tolerance, impulsivity, cognitive and developmental abilities, as well as cultural considerations are additional factors that may influence the child's ability to collaborate (Friedberg & McClure, 2002). Younger children may require more direction from the therapist while older, more autonomous youngsters may be able to collaborate to a greater degree. Passive patients and those who come from cultures where there is an expectation of obedience to authority figures may also expect more guidance from the clinician.

As treatment progresses and the child becomes familiar with the expectations of therapy, increased collaboration should occur. The premise of collaboration enhances the therapeutic relationship and empowers the child to progress in treatment by building on many of the tasks associated with normal development.

Providing the rationale for treatment is an essential component of the collaborative process. It indicates the clinician's respect for the patient by empowering the patient with knowledge of how the therapeutic process works and serves to provide motivation for increased involvement. Anxiety can be lessened by the demystification of the therapeutic process. The therapist may provide information on the connections between thoughts, feelings, and behaviors using concrete examples from the child's experience, storytelling, or drawings. Friedberg and McClure (2002) involve the young patient in illustrating a very simple story about a girl who loves balloons, receives a balloon, and loses the balloon when it accidentally bursts to educate the child about the connection between thoughts, feelings, and behaviors. Initial discussion of an abusive experience can be quite anxiety provoking for a child. At times it may be helpful to demonstrate the connection between thoughts, feelings, and actions by eliciting a more benign experience from the patient to illustrate the concepts. For example, the therapist might describe a situation where a child has been pushed by another child. The therapist might ask for all the possible reasons why the other child pushed. Once the patient has listed the possible reasons, the therapist can elicit thoughts about possible explanations: "he hates me" or "it was an accident." Once the alternative explanations have been elicited, the therapist can help the patient explore how the alternative explanations might change how she feels and how she reacts. Once the patient understands the connections between thoughts, feelings, and behaviors, the therapist can explain how they will be working together to investigate ideas and discover things that can help to make the patient feel better. Describing the thoughts and feelings that other children in similar situations have experienced can help lessen the stigma associated with abuse and acclimate the child to the model of treatment. The therapist should use age-appropriate language to orient the patient to the structure and expectations of the sessions. By establishing predictability and clear expectations about session structure, homework, and the limits of confidentiality, the patient is better prepared to collaborate in the treatment process. Engaging the child in a discussion of her thoughts and feelings about the treatment session contributes to the collaborative process.

Sessions follow a structured format. The session typically begins with a mood check in, homework review, and agenda setting. Younger children may have difficulty articulating their feelings and may need assistance from the therapist to describe mood and intensity of mood. It may be helpful for a child to draw a face that describes her mood and use a diagram of a thermometer to indicate how intense the feeling is. The therapist can also help clarify generalized responses by providing choices, or using self-report measures. During homework review, the social worker elicits the patient's response regarding the helpfulness and utility of the assignment. If the assignment was not completed, the therapist works with the patient to come up with ways to overcome obstacles to homework completion. It is often helpful to begin work on the assignment in session, ensuring that the patient understands what is expected and has a model to work from.

The therapist and the patient collaboratively set the agenda for the session by deciding what items will be discussed. In this way, important items are not overlooked and are given priority. Throughout the session, the therapist elicits feedback from the child in order to strengthen the collaborative nature of the relationship and empower the child. Summarizing session content encourages feedback and asking the patient to summarize information makes the patient an active participant in the therapeutic process.

Working With Parents

Parents can be valuable partners in the therapeutic process, but they require support during this very stressful time. The life they have known is being challenged and it is not uncommon for parents to experience a wide range of emotions as well as disruptions to the household that interfere with their ability to provide the necessary support to their abused children. The clinician must thoroughly assess the ability of parents to participate in treatment in addition to determining the level of anxiety the child will experience with joint sessions, and the possible repercussions when the family leaves the session. Children who have experienced physical abuse are more likely to remain in the care of their parents than victims of sexual abuse. These parents may exhibit impaired parenting skills, poor problem-solving abilities, unrealistic expectations of their child's behavior, and a greater tendency to judge their child's misbehavior as deliberate (Runyon, Deblinger, Ryan, Thakkar-Kolar, 2004). In some cases, parents may benefit from individual therapy. Both physical and sexual abuse present immediate concerns about the safety of the child that require crisis management, but the clinician should consider long-term outcomes when the abuse occurs within a family. Parameters for maintaining safe contact (when appropriate), addressing cognitive distortions within the family, and the response of the nonoffending parent and siblings are some of the enduring term issues to be considered during the course of treatment. The coexistence of parent-child, as well as perpetrator-victim bonds, necessitates the construction of a framework that ensures safety while taking into consideration the reality that family relationships will continue to exist after crisis intervention has ended, requiring new ways of functioning (Saunders & Menig, 2000).

Building Coping Skills

Skills training provides the child with the necessary tools to cope with the distressing feelings associated with the abuse in a positive manner. By providing psychoeducation to the patient and the nonoffending parent about the symptoms commonly associated with trauma and its consequences, the therapist develops rapport and helps to normalize reactions the child is experiencing. Patients and parents may recognize their own symptoms within the contexts of psychoeducation and the rationale for treatment. For example, Cynthia may recognize her unexplained stomachaches on school mornings as a physiological trauma reaction and identify it as a target for treatment.

CBT is an active treatment that engages the patient in the practice of interventions in and out of session. It is more likely that a patient will attempt a technique if she has had an opportunity to rehearse it in a safe therapeutic environment with the support of the therapist. The therapist should inquire about the specifics of a given situation in order to make the role play as realistic as possible and provide the patient with a genuine opportunity to practice the skills learned. Once anxiety-provoking situations have been identified, role play provides experience that the patient can draw on when confronted with similar situations in real life.

Stress inoculation provides the patient with the necessary tools to combat the physical symptoms of PTSD. Deep breathing and progressive muscle relaxation are techniques that can reduce physical symptoms of anxiety that patients often experience when confronted with reminders of their traumatic experience. Using age-appropriate language, the therapist provides a rationale for breathing from the diaphragm in an effort to calm the patient down when she is experiencing stress thereby relaxing uncomfortable physical sensations. During progressive muscle relaxation, the patient tenses and relaxes muscles groups in sequence to gradually let go of muscular tension. The two techniques may be combined or used separately. For example, a therapist might explain to a 7 year old how breathing deeply through the belly can help the body to slow down and relax so she can feel better when she gets scared or angry. These skills should be practiced in and out of session to develop effective skill levels. Patients are taught to label and rate their feelings using a numeric scale that describes the intensity of a particular emotion. By connecting feelings to the scale in specific situations, patients develop their awareness of stressful circumstances and useful strategies for coping with them.

Homework

Homework is an essential component of CBT treatment. It develops the skills taught in session, provides an opportunity for practical application of skills in real-life situations, and affords a basis for evaluation of how useful the skills are to the patient. Homework assignments should be created in response to the issues presented in session so that the patient is more likely to find the assignment relevant. The therapist must ascertain if the child has the level of skill required to complete the assignment. Sufficient time must be allowed to explain the homework and ensure that the patient understands its purpose. Homework is a tool used in therapy to gain insight and discover what is helpful. It can be helpful to begin an assignment in session in order to provide a model for its completion. Noncompliance with homework is a common dilemma in treatment with children and adolescents. Reasons for noncompliance include anxiety, depression, rebelliousness, lack of environmental support, and assignment of tasks that exceed the patient's ability. Noncompliance issues are addressed in session by brainstorming ways to overcome obstacles to homework completion.

COGNITIVE RESTRUCTURING

Cognitive restructuring is the process whereby useful alternative thoughts replace maladaptive thoughts that contribute to distress. The therapist facilitates this process by means of Socratic questioning, self-instruction, and questioning the evidence. Socratic questioning makes it possible for children to question and evaluate their unhelpful thoughts. The therapist begins the discussion by extracting the automatic thoughts: "What was going through your mind when that happened?" Once the thoughts have been articulated, the therapist attempts to ascertain how that thought makes the child feel or behave in order to connect thoughts to behaviors and feelings by asking, "How did you feel?" or "What did you do then?" It may be difficult for a child to differentiate a thought from a feeling. The therapist can help the child distinguish between thoughts and feelings by asking, "What were you saying to yourself when this happened?" or "What pictures were going through your mind when you felt that way?" The therapist continues the discussion by questioning the patient to discover what verification she is using to support her thoughts. Helping the patient to search for the evidence to confirm or shed doubt on the irrational thought, consider alternative explanations, decatastrophize, and problem solve allows the patient to contemplate more helpful, rational explanations resulting in improved mood, affect, and behavior. The case conceptualization should provide the necessary guidelines for the therapist's use of Socratic questioning with regard to the patient's developmental stage, cognitive functioning, cultural background, and emotional state. The therapist must use his clinical expertise to assess the ability of the patient to reason, and determine if the irrational thoughts are due to cognitive distortion or cognitive deficiency. Children at lower stages of developmental and cognitive functioning may not have the capacity to engage in abstract discussions and may become frustrated or seem resistant. When children are in severe distress, they may not be able to engage in protracted exploration and may benefit from more support and direction. These children may find rehearsal of self-instruction techniques in session advantageous. Self-instruction teaches children to prepare themselves for stress by anticipating difficulties, using prepared internal dialogues to replace unhelpful thoughts with more beneficial thoughts when confronted with a stressor, and complimenting themselves for using self-instruction techniques.

Imaginal Exposure

Gradual exposure is used in trauma-focused CBT to help children reduce the symptoms of avoidance associated with the trauma and gain control over their feelings. In PTSD, children connect the feelings of fear they experienced with the abuse to the neutral stimuli surrounding the abuse. As a result, the child becomes conditioned so that the previously neutral stimuli have the power to bring forth the same physical and emotional reactions as the traumatic events. In an effort to cope, the child attempts to avoid reminders of the abuse. When the avoidance response results in temporary relief, the behavior is reinforced. Unfortunately, although the child may experience short-term relief, this is not an effective coping mechanism in the long term as the child does not have control over the presentation of reminders or his response to them. Ultimately, avoidance can impede the victim's ability to function normally. Exposure treatment takes place after psychoeducation, goal setting, and skills acquisition have been accomplished. During exposure, the clinician assists the child to repeatedly confront his fears by using his imagination to re-create the abusive events, endure the accompanying negative affect, and practice the coping skills learned earlier in treatment. By repeatedly recalling the trauma and associated affect, and utilizing his coping skills, the child becomes habituated to the anxiety-provoking stimuli and gradually experiences less distress. Deblinger and colleagues (1996a,b) found that exposure was the technique that produced the most improvement in PTSD symptoms. Recollection may be accomplished through creative means such as storytelling, drawing, or the creation of a book, according to the needs and capabilities of the child. While adults may be able to tolerate the discomfort of intense exposure treatment (flooding) in view of the fact that treatment will ultimately serve to improve their symptoms, children and adolescents are typically more fearful of being overwhelmed by the experience and require a more gradual approach. Utilizing a numeric scale (referred to as SUDS, subjective units of discomfort) the therapist and patient create a hierarchy of anxiety-provoking situations associated with abuse. Beginning with the most benign memories, the clinician assists the child to recall the event in. The therapist supports the recollection by eliciting sensory details and helping the child remain focused on the emotions he is experiencing. Periodically the therapist will ask the child for a subjective units of distress (SUD) rating to ascertain the patient's level of arousal and coaches the child to use his coping skills should the affect become overwhelming. It is crucial that the exposure never becomes so aversive that the fear is reinforced (Kendall, Chu, Pimentael, & Choudhury, 2000). The therapist notes when cognitive distortions are apparent during the recollection of the memory. For instance, if the child says, "I should have known better than to make him mad," the therapist should note that the child is assuming blame for what happened and address the issue in treatment Once the child has recalled the memory, the therapist debriefs with the patient and praises the patient's efforts.

Termination

Termination marks the end of the therapeutic relationship. The child and therapist go over the skills learned and review the progress that was made during the course of treatment. The therapist acknowledges the child's hard work and efforts using concrete examples of accomplishments. For example, the therapist might say, "When you started treatment, you always felt really scared when you had to get home on your own after school, now you have ways to feel safe like walking with friends or taking the city bus, and you can calm yourself down by practicing controlled breathing." The therapist should address the patient's feelings about ending treatment. Often children are saddened at the prospect of the relationship ending and doubtful about their ability to maintain their progress. The patient should be encouraged to continue to practice the skills learned to maintain accomplishments. Additionally, the family should be referred to resources should they require addition services.

DESCRIPTION OF LIFE SKILLS/LIFE STORY

Life Skills/Life Story is a 16-week manualized cognitive behavioral treatment that was designed to address the emotional, functional, and interpersonal difficulties that are typical of adolescents who have experienced sexual and/or physical abuse (Cloitre, Farina, Davis, Carr, & Brown, 2005). These youth have often been exposed to multiple traumatic experiences, such as domestic and community violence. This treatment has been tested on inner city females between the ages of 13 and 21 who indicated a history of physical and/or sexual abuse in addition to other traumas. The components of the manual are easily adapted to the cognitive abilities and emotional needs of adolescents. It consists of two phases: skills training in emotion regulation and imagined exposure. During the first phase of treatment, the therapist establishes rapport, orients the patient to the rationale and structure of the treatment, and provides skills training. The patient is educated about the impact of trauma and works to monitor her own feelings, and develop the emotion regulation skills for coping with these difficult feelings. In the second phase of treatment, the patient processes her memories of trauma through narrative storytelling. The patient gradually integrates the memories and feelings associated with the abuse utilizing the coping skills developed in the first phase of treatment. Through repeated narration, the patient develops an understanding of how these physical and emotional reactions are triggered and gains control over the feelings she has been trying to avoid.

CASE PRESENTATION

Sheila W. is a 15-year-old girl referred for treatment following an investigation by child protective services that found she had been sexually abused by her adult stepbrother several times. Sheila remained in the home since her stepbrother was not a resident of the household, but the disclosure caused significant difficulty in the relationship between the parents. Evaluation indicated that Sheila was experiencing the following PTSD symptoms: physical symptoms of anxiety in response to reminders, intrusive thoughts, trying to avoid thinking about the abuse, avoidance of reminders of the abuse, increased irritability, and difficulty sleeping. Sheila reported that she had recently started to use marijuana and alcohol to help her "relax."

During the first session, the therapist focused on establishing rapport, providing an overview of what treatment would be like, and helping Sheila develop personal goals. Sheila was educated about the typical reactions to trauma that teenagers often experience when they are exposed to interpersonal violence and sexual or physical abuse. It was explained that the treatment was designed to help teenage girls cope with their feeling without getting overwhelmed and help them improve their relationships with others. Sheila was told that she would learn coping strategies to help her deal with the uncomfortable feelings she experienced in upsetting situations in the first phase of treatment and that the second phase of treatment would involve talking about the abuse. Sheila expressed anger about having to talk about the details of the abuse again and said that talking about it made her feel bad and didn't help. The therapist explained to Sheila that the purpose of telling her story was to gain control of the thoughts and feelings that were upsetting and assured her these discussions would proceed at a comfortable pace when she would have several coping skills within her repertoire to assist her.

THERAPIST: I notice that you really haven't said very much and I'm wondering what's going through your mind.

SHEILA: Nothing really. I'm just wish I wasn't here, because this is stupid.

THERAPIST: What's stupid?

SHEILA: Being here. None of this ever helps anything.

THERAPIST: What do you mean "this never helps"?

SHEILA: Just this therapy stuff. I've had it before and I just don't like it. Talking about things just makes me feel worse, I don't want to talk about it!

THERAPIST: Well, it's really good that you told me that. The whole idea of therapy is for us to find ways for you to feel better. A lot of people feel upset when they talk about difficult things. There are skills that I can teach you that can help you remain in control when you start to feel upset. Would you be willing to try some of them and let me know how they work for you?

SHEILA: I guess that would be okay.

THERAPIST: Talking about things can be hard, but it can help you feel better and not feel overwhelmed when you don't expect it. First we'll work on some of the coping skills and see what works for you, and then we can discuss things when you have the skills to help you deal with your feelings. Does that sound like something you could try?

SHEILA: Well, maybe I could try.

THERAPIST: Good. It takes a lot of courage to face these kinds of issues. I'm glad you're going to give it a try.

The therapist has started to develop rapport by empathizing with Sheila and addressing her concerns. Collaboration was facilitated by eliciting Sheila's agreement to the treatment plan and provided verbal reinforcement for Sheila's efforts. During the remainder of the session the therapist helped Sheila identify some goals for treatment and the limits of confidentiality were explained. Sheila was advised that the therapist would meet with her parents to talk about treatment goals, the effects of trauma, and confidentiality.

The first phase of treatment focused on labeling of feelings and development of coping skills to regulate emotions. Sheila practiced relaxation skills to help regulate her emotions and learned to apply these skills as an alternative to alcohol and marijuana use. A number of strategies were developed collaboratively to help Sheila manage upsetting social situations and communicate assertively about her feelings. Strategies included the use of self-talk, visualization, strengthening communication skills, and challenging cognitions and core beliefs. The therapist met with the parents to ensure that an appropriate safety plan was in place and to enlist their support in Sheila's treatment.

CONCLUSION

Child abuse is a widespread problem that impacts society on a variety of levels having long lasting effects on the child, the family, and the community. As clinicians providing cognitive behavior treatment for abused children and adolescents, social workers have the opportunity to act as agents of social change at the most primary level. CBT uses a collaborative approach that is consistent with traditional social work practice and the principal of self-determination. CBT is based on the premise that thoughts are connected to behaviors and feelings in a reciprocal way. By learning to change irrational thoughts, the patient can reduce negative feelings and behaviors, thereby improving overall functioning.

PTSD is the result of exposure to a traumatic event (or series of events) that leads the patient to ineffectively cope with the associated distress by attempting to avoid and protect themselves from trauma reminders to the extent that normal functioning is impaired. Symptoms are classified as avoidance, hyperarousal, or reexperiencing, and present differently based on developmental stage. Utilizing a PTSD framework for understanding the symptoms associated with abuse allows the social worker to build on the client's strengths to foster healing by building coping strategies, increasing understanding of abuse and its impact, and developing the client's social competence and self-advocacy skills. The essential components of a CBT treatment for children experiencing symptoms of

PTSD are: education and goal setting, skills development, exposure, and cognitive restructuring. These components are presented in treatment in a structured, yet flexible, manner in an effort to maximize patient collaboration, and attend to the needs of the patient toward the realization of specific goals. The therapist conceptualizes the case throughout the course of treatment by considering the psychological, environmental, cultural and developmental issues that cause and maintain the symptoms. This conceptualization guides the choice, timing, modification, and implementation of interventions.

In CBT, problems are not simply discussed but are addressed in a hands-on manner. Homework assignments are used to build skills and provide an opportunity for the patient to discover effective strategies for coping. Imagined exposure desensitizes the patient to anxiety-provoking stimuli by allowing confrontation of fears in a safe environment. The focus of treatment is the resolution of current problems.

The use of CBT in clinical social work with abused children and adolescents offers an opportunity to utilize treatment that has been shown to be effective in reducing PTSD symptoms. The flexibility of CBT allows treatment to be appropriate for children of all ages and can be effectively modified in response to cognitive limitations and the presentation of symptoms. In addition, children in treatment have the opportunity to develop practical skills that will continue to be of value as they mature. As advocates for children and agents of change committed to serving the underserved, CBT offers the clinical social worker tools to promote child welfare and have significant impact on one of the most deleterious issues facing our society.

REFERENCES

Ackerman, P. T., Newton, J. E. O., McPherson, W. B., Jones, J. G., & Dykman, R. A. (1998). Prevalence of post traumatic stress disorder and other psychiatric diagnoses in three groups of abused children (sexual, physical, and both). *Child Abuse & Neglect, 22*, 759–777.

American Psychiatric Association. (1994). *Diagnostic and statistical manual of mental disorders* (4th ed.). Washington, DC: Author.

Beck, J. S. (1995). *Cognitive therapy: Basics and beyond.* New York: Guilford.

Briere, J. (1996a). Trauma Symptom Checklist for Children (TSCC). Odessa, FL: Psychological Assessment Resources.

Briere, J. (1996b). Trauma Symptom Checklist for Children (TSCC), Professional Manual. Odessa, FL: Psychological Assessment Resources.

Chaffin, M., & Hanson, R. F. (2000). Treatment of multiply traumatized abused children. In R. M. Reece (Ed.), *Treatment of child abuse: Common ground for mental health, medical & legal practitioners.* Baltimore: Johns Hopkins University Press.

Cohen, J. A., Deblinger, E., Mannarino, A. P., & Steer, R. (2004). A multisite, randomized controlled trial for children with sexual abuse-related PTSD symptoms. *American Academy of Child and Adolescent Psychiatry, 43,* 393–402.

Cohen, J. A., & Mannarino A. P. (1996). A treatment outcome study for sexually abused preschool children: Initial findings. *Journal of the American Academy of Child and Adolescent Psychiatry, 35,* 42–50.

Cohen, J. A., & Mannarino, A. P. (1998). Interventions for sexually abused children: Initial treatment outcome findings. *Child Maltreatment, 3,* 17–26.

Cohen, J., & Mannarino, A. P. (2004). Posttraumatic stress disorder. In *Phobic and anxiety disorders in children and adolescents: A Clinician's Guide to*

Cloitre, M., Farina, L., Davis, L., Carr, D., & Brown, J. (2005). Life Skills/Life Story: Joining skills training in affective regulation with narrative story telling. Unpublished manuscript.

Deblinger, E., & Heflin, A. H. (1996). Treatment of an adolescent survivor of child sexual abuse. In M. A. Reinecke, F. Datillo, & A. Freeman (Eds.), *Cognitive therapy with children and adolescents* (pp. 199–226). New York: Guilford.

Deblinger, E., Lippman, J., & Steer, R. (1996a). Sexually abused children suffering posttraumatic stress symptoms: initial treatment outcome findings. *Child Maltreatment, 1,* 310–321.

Deblinger, E., Lippman, J., & Steer, R. (1996b). *Treating sexually abused children and their nonoffending parents: A cognitive-behavioral approach.* Thousand Oaks, CA: Sage.

Drake, E. B., Bush, S. F., & von Gorp, W. G., (2001). Evaluation and assessment of PTSD. In S. Eth (Ed.), *PTSD in children and adolescents* (pp. 1–31). Washington, DC: American Psychiatric Publishing.

Foy, D., Madvig, B., Pynoos, R., & Camilleri, A. (1996). Etiologic factors in the development of posttraumatic stress disorder in children and adolescents. *Journal of School Psychology, 34,* 133–145.

Friedberg, R. D., & McClure, J. M. (2002). *Clinical practice of cognitive therapy with children and adolescents: The nuts and bolts.* New York: Guilford.

Kelly, B. T., Thornberry, T. P., & Smith, C. A. (1997). In the wake of childhood maltreatment. U.S. Department of Justice. Juvenile Justice Bulletin. Retrieved May 20, 2005 from www.nejrs.org/pdffiles//165257.pdf

Kendall, P. C., Chu, B. C., Pimentael, S. S., & Choudhury, M. (2000). Treating anxiety disorders in youth. In P. C. Landall (Ed.), *Child and Adolescent Therapy* (pp. 235–287). New York: Guilford.

Kendall-Tackett, K. A., Williams, L. M., & Finkelhor, D. (1993). Impact of sexual abuse on children: A review and synthesis of recent empirical studies. *Psychological Bulletin, 113,* 164–180.

King, N. J., Tonge, B. J., Mullen, M. P., Meyerson, N. M., Heyne, D., Rollings, S. M., Martin, R. M., & Ollendick, T. H. (2000). Treating sexually abused children with posttraumatic stress symptoms: A randomized clinical trial. *Journal of the American Academy of Child & Adolescent Psychiatry, 39,* 1347–1355.

Kolko, D. J. (1996). Individual cognitive behavioral treatment and family therapy for physically abused children and their offending parents: A comparison of clinical outcomes. *Child Maltreatment, 1,* 322–342.

Mannarino, A. P., & Cohen, J. A. (1996). Abuse-related attributions and perceptions, general attributions and locus of control in sexually abused girls. *Journal of Interpersonal Violence, 11,* 162–180.

Mannarino, A. P., & Cohen, J. A. (2001). Treating sexually abused children and their families: Identifying and avoiding professional role conflicts. *Trauma, Violence & Abuse, 2,* 331–342.

Margolin, G., & Gordes, E. B. (2000). The effects of family and community violence on children. *Annual Review Psychology, 51,* 445–479.

Perry, B. D. (2001). The neurodevelopmental impact of violence in childhood. In D. Schetky & E. Benedek (Eds.), *Textbook of child and adolescent forensic psychiatry.* Washington, DC: American Psychiatric Press.

Pfefferbaum, B. (1997). Posttraumatic stress disorder in children: A review of the past 10 years. *Journal of the American Academy of Child & Adolescent Psychiatry, 36,* 1503–1511.

Prevent Child Abuse America. (2001). *Total estimated cost of child abuse and neglect in the United States.* Retrieved July 1, 2005, from www.prevent childabuse.org/learn more research_docs/cost_analysis.pdf

Pynoos R. S., & Nader, K. (1992). Issues in the treatment of posttraumatic stress in children and adolescents. In J. P. Wilson & B. Raphael (Eds.), *International handbook of traumatic stress syndromes.* New York and London: Plenum Press.

Runyon, M., Deblinger, E., Ryan, E., & Thakkar-Kolar, R. (2004). An overview of child physical abuse: Developing an integrated parent-child cognitive-behavioral approach. *Trauma, Violence & Abuse, 5,* 65–85.

Saunders, B. E., Menig, M. B. (2000). Immediate issues affecting long-term family resolution in cases of parent-child sexual abuse. In R. M. Reece (Ed.), *Treatment of child abuse common ground for mental health, medical & legal practitioners.* Baltimore: Johns Hopkins University Press.

Sedlak, A. J., & Broadhurst, D. D. (1996). Third National Incidence Study of child abuse and neglect: Final report. Washington, DC: U.S. Department of Health and Human Services.

Shore, R. (1997). *Rethinking the brain.* New York: Families Work Institute.

Silverman, A. B., Reinherz, H. Z., & Giaconia, R. M. (1996). The long-term sequelae of child and adolescent abuse: A longitudinal community study. *Child Abuse & Neglect, 20,* 709–723.

Swenson, C. C., & Kolko, D. J. (2000). *Long-term management of developmental consequences of child abuse.* In R. M. Reece (Ed.), *Treatment of child abuse: Common ground for mental health, medical & legal practitioners* (pp. 135–154). Baltimore, MD: Johns Hopkins University Press.

U.S. Department of Health and Human Services. (1996). Administration for children youth and families. *National Incidence Survey.* Washington DC: Author.

U.S. Department of Health and Human Services. (2003). Administration for children youth and families. *Child Maltreatment 2003*. Washington DC: Author.

Weinstein, D., Staffelbach, D., & Biaggio, M. (2000). Attention-deficit hyperactivity disorder and posttraumatic stress disorder: Differential diagnosis in childhood sexual abuse. *Clinical Psychology Review, 20,* 359–378.

Wolfe, D. A., Sas, L., & Wekerle, C. (1994). Factors associated with the development of posttraumatic stress disorder among child victims of sexual abuse. *Child Abuse & Neglect, 18,* 37–50.

CHAPTER 12

Social Work Practice in the Schools

L. Stewart Barbera, Jr.

INTRODUCTION

The societal requirement that all children, from age 5 through adolescence (the age depending on the state), must attend school makes the school one of the most important and powerful forces in socialization. Children are a captive audience, and the school is a microcosm of the external world. There are groups, subgroups, prejudice, love, power struggles, power differentials, demands for conformity, rewards for positive performance, punishment for perceived misdeeds, and the explicit demand that the child acquire a number of skills as part of their experience in the school system.

The "front-line" troops in the schools are the teachers. It is their charge to educate the child, imbue him or her with an appreciation of the learning process, and guide him or her through the multitude of life experience, developmental milestones, and social interactions that make up the educational process. The vast majority of children and adolescents navigate the educational system with little difficulty, causing little difficulty. For those children for whom the educational content, process, or procedures are difficult or overwhelming, the comprehensive educational system must offer opportunities for remediation, amelioration, and for moderation. Social work practice has long been associated with individuals, institutional systems, and the interaction of the individual within the system. It is therefore reasonable that the key professional working within the school system be trained in the philosophy and theory of social work practice.

School social workers provide direct treatment for a multitude of problems that affect child and adolescent development and learning; these problems include mood disorders (e.g., anxiety, depression), attention deficit hyperactive disorder (ADHD), disruptive behavior disorders, and learning disorders, as well as child abuse and neglect, foster care, poverty, school drop out, substance abuse, and truancy, to name but a few (Dupper, 2003). They may also serve as the integrating professional that brings together the child, the family, the school psychologist, school counselor, and possibly medical personnel. Although the challenges and problems that children and adolescents face may vary, the goal of school social workers remains the same; that is, "to promote the healthy social functioning of pupils" (Allen-Meares, 2004, p. 91). As part of an interdisciplinary team, school social workers are uniquely positioned to address these complex problems because of their clinical training and because of the various roles they hold within the school setting (e.g., administrator, advocate, clinician, or consultant) (Bowen, 2004; Constable, Kuzmickaite, Harrison, & Volkmann, 1999).

Since its inception nearly a century ago, school social work has evolved into a specialized area of practice (Allen-Meares, 2004; McCullagh, 2002). Contemporary school social work practice incorporates empirically based forms of treatment including cognitive behavior therapy (Franklin, 2004).

Cognitive behavior therapy (CBT), which can be considered an important adjunct to social work treatment, has been found to be an effective form of treatment for a wide variety problems facing children and adolescents (Erickson & Achilles, 2004). By integrating the principles and practices of cognitive behavior therapy, school social workers can enhance their conceptualization of complex problems presented by children and adolescents and can provide more effective treatment.

Using the problem of academic underachievement as a focal point, this chapter examines four constructs that are important when working with students. These constructs include: (1) assessment and cognitive case conceptualization, (2) the working alliance, (3) self-regulated learning, and (4) social problem solving. The concepts may be generalized beyond the problem of academic underachievement and provide social workers with a practical approach to working with children and adolescents in school settings.

REVIEW OF THE LITERATURE

It is widely accepted that students may be referred to mental health clinicians because of concerns related to academic problems (Ducey, 1989; Green, 1989; Jongsma, Peterson, & McInnis, 2000; Mandel & Marcus, 1988). For example the *Diagnostic and Statistical Manual of Mental Disorders Fourth Edition Text-Revision (DSM-IV-TR)* (American Psychiatric Association, 2000) includes the diagnosis of academic problem (V62.3) and defines it as "a pattern of failing grades or of significant underachievement in a person with adequate intellectual capacity in the absence of a Learning or Communication Disorder or any other mental disorder that would account for the problem" (p. 741).

Academic underachievement is a global phenomenon. As the legislation No Child Left Behind Act of 2001 demonstrates, the topic of academic achievement is a problem that continues to capture the attention of clinicians, communities, educators, families, governmental officials, and social scientists (Borkowski & Thorpe, 1994; Herbert, 2001; Mandel, 2004; Mason, Mendez, Nelsen, & Orwig, 2005; National Commission of Excellence in Education, 1983; Rimm, 1997; Zosky & Crawford, 2003). Academic underachievement can be described as

> a severe discrepancy between expected achievement (as measured by standardized achievement test score or cognitive or intellectual ability assessments) and actual achievement (as measured by class grades and teacher evaluations). To be classified as an underachiever, the discrepancy between expected and actual achievement must not be the direct result of a diagnosed learning disability and must persist over an extended period of time. (Reis & McCoach, 2000, p. 157)

Incidence of Underachievement

Although it is difficult to estimate precisely how many students might be considered as achieving below their potential, it is widely recognized that "many students within the educational system do not meet the expected academic gains in the regular instructional setting" (Shapiro & Bradley, 1996, p. 344). Researchers estimate that approximately 16 percent of all learners might be considered to be academically underachieving (Mandel, 2004; McCall, Evahn, & Kratzer, 1992). Underachievers are a heterogeneous population comprising every economic, ethnic and social class, attending private, public and parochial schools in urban, suburban and rural settings (Butler-Por, 1987; Mandel, Marcus, & Dean, 1996; McCall et al., 1992; Sikorski, 1996).

Etiology

Academic underachievement is correlated with a myriad of variables that seem to affect people idiosyncratically (Baker, Bridger, & Evans, 1998; Butler-Por, 1987; Mandel et al., 1988). For example, it seems that a significant portion of a student's failure or success in school could be affected by variables related to the environment, family, and personality (Baker et al., 1998; Bronfenbrenner, 1994; Griffin, 1988; Lantieri & Patti, 1996; Mandel et al., 1988; Okagaki, 2001; Rimm, 1995, 1997). Based on an exhaustive review of the literature, McCall and colleagues (1992) produced a list of 23 factors that researchers found to be related to underachievement. They arranged these characteristics according to the following domains: (a) self-perception, (b) goal orientation, (c) peer relations, (d) authority relationships, (e) locus of control, and (f) emotional expression. Other researchers have suggested that deficiencies in academic skills and self-control may also contribute to underachievement (Borkowski et al., 1994; Herbert, 2001; Mandel et al., 1988). Others, however, have noted that poor problem-solving skills and self-regulated learning may place a student at risk for developing academic problems (Bradley-Klug & Shapiro, 2003; Elias & Butler, 1999).

Typically, the onset of underachievement occurs during elementary school, however, it may not be recognized until high school, college, or beyond (Baker et al., 1998; Ducey, 1989; Krouse & Krouse, 1981). It has been reported that academic underachievement may be more prevalent among boys than among girls at an approximate ratio of 2:1 (Griffin, 1988; Herbert, 1998, 2001; McCall et al., 1992; Rimm, 1982). The duration of underachievement may be present for only a relatively short duration of time or it may span a student's entire academic career (McCall et al., 1992). The scope of underachievement may be isolated to a specific subject or it may span the curriculum (Borkowski & Thorpe, 1994). Finally, the severity of the underachievement may also vary from mild to severe (McCall et al., 1992).

Students who are underachieving may present with a variety of symptoms such as "procrastination, incomplete assignments, disorganization, and careless work" (Rimm, 1997, p. 418). However, one of the cardinal features of underachievement is the *lack* of perseverance in academic tasks (Butler-Por, 1987; McCall et al., 1992). These students may also have beliefs and cognitions that interfere with academic success (e.g., a student may believe that to try and fail is worse than not trying at all). Therefore, these students may not even attempt to put forth their efforts because of the possibility of failure (Butler-Por, 1987; Griffin, 1988). Some of the other factors that may be correlated with underachievement include a negative self-concept, "perfectionism," poor study and organizational skills, and procrastination (Butler-Por, 1987; Baker et al., 1998, Mandel, 2004).

The adverse consequences of academic underachievement can be profound both for the individual and for society (Butler-Por, 1987; Green, 1989; Richman, Rosenfeld, & Bowen, 1998). McCall and colleagues (1992) studied a sample of 6,720 male and female junior and senior high school students. Data from this study suggested that high school underachievers may (a) think less about future careers, (b) earn less money, (c) choose less challenging courses, (e) have lower educational and professional goals, (f) have a higher rate of divorce, (g) enter the military at a higher rate, (h) have lower self-esteem, (i) have a lower sense of self-efficacy, and (k) change jobs more frequency than a matched control group who had similar mental abilities (McCall et al., 1992). Furthermore, Sikorski (1996) noted that underachievement and school failure are associated with such negative events as "teen pregnancy, substance abuse, conduct disorder, and delinquency and adult criminal behavior and un-employability" (p. 393).

To summarize, academic underachievement is a serious problem affecting a significant number of children and adolescents. Cognitive behavior therapy can provide school social workers with an empirically based orientation to facilitate the conceptualization of the problem, strengthen the working relationship, and guide treatment (e.g., improve social problem-solving skills and self-regulated learning).

ASSESSMENT AND CONCEPTUALIZATION OF ACADEMIC PROBLEMS

A robust assessment is a critical component in the diagnosis and treatment of academic underachievement (Mandel & Mandel, 1995; Rimm, 1997). According to the cognitive behavior model, the assessment is structured using the cognitive case conceptualization (Beck, 1995, 1996; Needleman, 1999, 2003), which can enhance the psychosocial assessment by providing the clinician with a systematic approach to understanding the client's problematic behavior, beliefs, and cognitions. Although formulated during the initial assessment, the cognitive case conceptualization is revised throughout treatment as more information is gathered and hypotheses are tested (Beck, 1995; Needleman, 1999, 2003). The cognitive case conceptualization includes information about the client's automatic thoughts (e.g., thoughts or images that influence how the student would feel and behave), situations that trigger automatic thoughts and core beliefs (e.g., those fundamental beliefs that the student believes about himself, the world, and his future), and intermediate beliefs (e.g., assumptions and values that the student possesses) (Needleman, 1999, 2003). The cognitive case conceptualization also identifies compensatory strategies (e.g., how the student copes with problems) as well as those behaviors and cognitions that maintain the problematic behavior (Needleman, 1999, 2003). The cognitive case conceptualization ought to be sensitive to the child's age, to his cognitive and developmental stage and gender in order that an accurate assessment be made and appropriate interventions set in place, which are tailored to the needs of the particular child (Ronen, 1998; Wong, Harris, & Graham, 1991).

Cognitive behavior therapy is a collaborative approach to treatment. Therefore, it is important that cognitive case conceptualization is discussed with the client. Reviewing this information promotes the working alliance of child and therapist, as well as providing and allowing for the opportunity to revise the accuracy of the conceptualization as needed. Discussing the cognitive case conceptualization also serves to socialize the client to cognitive behavior therapy and to assess, among other things, the reciprocal relationship between the environment (e.g., situations) and thoughts, feelings, and behaviors. Discussing the cognitive case conceptualization can help the client to better understand how his beliefs and behaviors are associated with the problem. By reviewing the cognitive case conceptualization, the client can begin to recognize factors that seem to maintain the problem, and to identify possible interventions that may be used to address the problem (Beck, 1995, 1996; Needleman, 1999; see Needleman, 1999, for a description of cognitive case conceptualization).

When working with underachieving students, a comprehensive psychoeducational evaluation that includes a developmental history and social/emotional assessment is recommended. The psychoeducational evaluation is a diagnostic tool that can identify learning disorders as well as provide a valid and reliable measure of academic achievement, including an estimate of a student's intellectual capacity and expected school performance (Green, 1989; Mandel et al., 1995; Rimm, 1997).

Cognitive behavior therapy incorporates an ecological and general systems perspective (Allen-Meares, 2004; Dupper, 2003; Erickson et al., 2004; Ronen, 1998; Zarb, 1992). Therefore, the information contained in the assessment should be obtained from multiple sources, including: (a) a review of the student's educational records, (b) an interview with the student's parents/caretakers, and (c) teachers and school personal (e.g., guidance counselor) (Butler-Por, 1987; Herbert, 1998; Mandel et al., 1995; Mandel et al., 1988; Sattler, 1992; Zarb, 1992). In addition, when working with children in school settings, the following factors should be considered as part of the assessment: (a) the community (Bowen, 2004; Bronfenbrenner, 1994; Green, 1989), (b) socioeconomic status (e.g., poverty) (Herbert, 2001), (c) the school environment (e.g., assessing whether it is a safe and secure environment, has supportive teachers, utilizes a curriculum that is challenging, flexible, and perceived by students as interesting, and meeting individual educational needs of students) (Baker et al., 1998; Butler-Por, 1987; Herbert, 1998, 2001; Lantieri et al., 1996; Mandel et al., 1988; Rimm, 1982, 1995, 1997). Because it seems to play an important role in the development and maintenance of academic performance, the family system should be included in the assessment (Butler-Por, 1987; Green, 1989; Mandel et al., 1988; Rimm, 1995, 1997). Similarly, the client's culture and ethnicity should also be examined, and consideration should be given to how this might influence the client's academic performance (Mandel et al., 1988; Okagaki, 2001; Reis et al., 2000). Peer relationships should also be assessed because they may also influence academic achievement (Herbert, 2001; Rimm, 1997; Woodward & Fergusson, 2000). Together, this information can then be synthesized and integrated as part of the cognitive case conceptualization and social work assessment.

Finally, the conceptualization should also identify the client's readiness for change (Freeman & Dolan, 2001). According to the transtheoretical model developed by DiClemente and Prochaska (1988, 2005), the process of change can be conceptualized as occurring along a continuum that comprises five distinct stages: (1) precontemplative, (2) contemplative, (3) preparation, (4) action, and (5) maintenance. As with developmental tasks, each stage is composed of processes and tasks that need to be completed in order to move on to the next stage. Although the process of change occurs in a predictable series of steps it is rarely linear (Freeman et al., 2001). DiClemente and Prochaska (2005) identified the following five levels at which change can occur: (1) symptoms/situational problems, (2) maladaptive cognitions, (3) current interpersonal conflicts, (4) family/system conflicts, and (5) intrapersonal conflicts. When working with clients, it is important to assess their stage of change (e.g., precontemplative or contemplative), the level of change that will be addressed in treatment (e.g., symptoms/situations such as failing in a particular academic subject), as well as the processes that can facilitate the movement through the stages of change (e.g., from contemplation to preparation to action) (DiClemente et al., 2005). As Needleman (2003) noted, it is important to assess a client's readiness for change because "a growing body of research suggests that, for a wide variety of mental health problems, therapeutic effectiveness increases when therapists match interventions to clients' stage of change" (p. 5). When working with academic underachievers there frequently are expectations for an immediate improvement in students' behavior; this may include such behaviors as increasing homework time. Yet, if interventions are not congruent with a client's stage of change, these efforts may not be effective.

For example, the social worker, teachers, and parents may want a student to change his behavior and complete homework assignments. However, if the student is in the precontemplative stage he may not even recognize that not completing homework is a problem. According to the transtheoretical model of change, the intervention needs to be instituted from "where the client is at." As Freeman et al. (2001) indicated, treatment interventions need to fit the particular client's "level of motivation, interest, and readiness for change" (p. 224). The transtheoretical model is a vital part of the case conceptualization so that interventions are congruent with the client's readiness for change.

THE WORKING ALLIANCE

The working alliance is critically important when working with children and adolescents. Indeed, it is the sine qua non of effective psychotherapy (Bordin, 1979, 1994). The *working alliance*, which refers to the relationship that exists between the therapist and the client, consists of the bond between the therapist and the client and the mutually agreed upon goals and tasks of therapy (Alford & Beck, 1997; Bordin, 1979, 1994; Goldfried & Davison, 1994). As Ronen (1998) noted, according to the cognitive behavior therapy model, "the child is seen as someone who can be an active partner in decision making concerning the aims of therapy, establishing criteria for target behaviors, and making decisions about the kinds of techniques to be used" (p. 3).

The Bond

The "bond" can be defined as the collaborative relationship between the therapist and the client; it is dynamic, developing, and changing over time (Schulman, 1992). Sometimes the bond becomes resilient and strong, but at other times it can become ruptured or strained (Arnkoff, 2000). Both the client and the therapist contribute to or inhibit the development of the bond. The bond reflects qualities such as "mutual liking, attachment, and trust between the client and therapist" (Raue & Goldfried, 1994, p. 141). Bordin (1994) described the bond within the context of the working alliance cogently when he wrote:

> The bonding of the persons in a therapeutic alliance grows out of their experience of association in a shared activity. Partner capability (bonding) is likely to be expressed and felt in terms of liking, trusting, respect for each other, and a sense of common commitment and shared understanding in the activity. (p. 16)

A strong and well-developed bond is important to the alliance because it can provide the client the opportunity to participate more fully in the process of therapy (Bordin, 1994). This aspect of the alliance seems relevant when working with underachieving students. By developing an authentic sense of collaboration, based on the aforementioned characteristics, the underachieving students may perceive a sense of encouragement, empathy, and support from the clinician as they strive to improve their academic performances.

The Goals

The goals of therapy are another aspect of the working alliance. The goals of treatment are the "purpose of therapy" (Horvath, 1994, p. 262). They are identified and agreed upon *collaboratively* both by the therapist and the client (Raue et al., 1994). Thus, the strength of the bond can facilitate the attainment of the treatment goals (Arnkoff, 2000). The development of attainable and realistic goals is a critical component both of self-regulated learning and social problem solving, which are discussed later in this chapter. The collaborative establishment of effective goals seems particularly important for underachieving students because such goals would seem to provide direction to their actions, support their motivation for change and promote their perceived self-efficacy. It also seems of equal importance that the students assume the responsibility for defining their goals. Instead of being "told" what they need to do to improve their academic situations, students who set their own goals are acting as self-directed learners in deciding what changes they would like to make.

The Tasks

The tasks of therapy, the third domain of the working alliance, are the means through which the client achieves the goals (Arnkoff, 2000; Raue et al., 1994). The tasks include the specific behaviors or interventions that the client performs in order to achieve the treatment goals. Like the goals of the working alliance, the therapeutic tasks are identified and implemented *collaboratively* by the therapist and the client. Establishing and enacting the tasks seems particularly relevant to reversing underachievement. By helping students to become the architects of their own success it seems that they may be more likely to implement those steps that are relevant to the remediation of their academic underachievement. As described previously, the tasks of therapy must be in concert with the client's readiness for change.

SELF-REGULATED LEARNING

Academic self-regulation is considered an integral aspect of successful learning (Bradley-Klug & Shapiro, 2003; Feldmann, Martinez-Pons, & Shaham, 1995; Gredler & Schwartz, 1997; Zimmerman, 1998; Zimmerman & Martinez-Pons, 1986; Schunk & Zimmerman, 1994). Academic self-regulation can be understood as self-directed behaviors, cognitions, and emotions that the student implements to achieve his learning goals. "Academic self-regulation is not a mental ability, such as intelligence, or an academic skill, such as reading proficiency; rather, it is the self-directive process through which learners transform their mental abilities into academic skills" (Zimmerman, 1998, pp. 1–2).

Zimmerman (1998) conceptualized the process of self-regulated learning as comprising three phases: forethought, performance, and self-reflection. The phases are cyclical, continuously influencing one another (Zimmerman, 1998). Each part of academic self-regulation comprises various subprocesses. For example, forethought is made up of: (a) goal setting (what is to be accomplished in the learning process), (b) strategic planning (the strategies employed to reach the goal), (c) self-efficacy (the belief that one is capable of performing a task), (d) learning goal orientation (focusing on the process of learning rather than on the outcome), and (e) intrinsic interest in the task (Zimmerman, 1998). The performance processes includes: (a) focusing attention on the learning task, (b) using self-instruction (telling oneself how to go about a task), (c) imagery ("forming mental pictures" to facilitate the learning process), and (d) self-monitoring (Zimmerman, 1998, p. 4). The self-reflection phase is made up of the following subprocesses: (a) self-evaluation (comparing information gathered from the self-monitoring phase to a particular outcome measure), (b) attributions (explaining what caused the particular outcome), and (c) self-reactions (to a particular learning task) (Zimmerman, 1998).

Self-regulated learning develops as the child matures (e.g., cognitively, emotionally, intellectually, and socially). Self-regulated learning seems to be influenced by many variables such as the student's ecological/systemic environment (e.g., interactions with others such as parents, peers, or teachers) as well as from personal experiences (affective, behavioral, and cognitive) as he or she directs and structures his or her own learning (Perry, 1998; Zimmerman, 1998).

Cognitive behavior therapy can facilitate the development of self-regulated learning (Bradley-Klug et al., 2003). Interventions associated with this therapy can be directed at the phases or subprocesses that compose self-regulated learning. For example, cognitive behavior interventions can be directed to addressing self-instruction (e.g., increasing the child's ability to understand what is required of him in the task and to monitor his strategies), self-management skills (how the individual controls his behaviors and cognitions relative to the environment and his goal) and/or increasing self-monitoring skills (e.g., being aware of the attention and concentration during a learning task, strategies, and tasks employed to reach a goal) (Belfiore & Hornyak, 1998; Bradley-Klug et al., 2003). Self-monitoring is one of the hallmark features of self-regulated learners because it enables students to be cognizant of their progress and overall learning (Schunk et al., 1994, 1998).

Other interventions that may improve self-regulated learning include modeling, rehearing and role-playing behaviors, increasing motivation, modifying maladaptive attributions and self-talk, strategy instruction (the strategies that are available, including ways to implement them), planning and problem-solving skills (Butler, 1998; Hofer, Yu, & Pintrich, 1998; Miller, 2000; Zimmerman, 1998; See also Graham, Harris, & Troia, 1998 and Zimmerman, Bonner & Kovach, 1996, for a description of interventions that seek to facilitate self-regulated learning). These interventions can be introduced to students either by being integrated into the curriculum, as a separate course (e.g., study skills course) or as part of an individual or group counseling session (Hofer et al., 1998; Mandel et al., 1995). By increasing their self-regulated learning, students may be able to improve academically. Another important aspect approach to reversing academic underachievement is social problem skills, discussed next.

PROBLEM SOLVING

Social problem solving (SPS) has been studied empirically as a treatment for a wide variety of problems including academic problems (Clabby & Elias, 1987; Elias & Tobias, 1990; See also Bedell & Lennox, 1997; D'Zurilla & Nezu, 1999; Nezu, Nezu, & Houts, 1993, for a more detailed description of social problem solving). In describing problem-solving training in the classroom Kendall and Bartel (1990) noted that the "ultimate goals of problem-solving training is the self-directed learner, who is able and willing to discern that it is that he or she who must learn or perform, and to identify and implement appropriate cognitive and behavioral strategies enabling the learning or performance to occur" (p. 13).

Conceptualizing Social Problem Solving

According to D'Zurilla et al. (1999) social problem solving can be divided into two parts. The first part is referred to as the problem orientation and the second part consists of the rational problem-solving skills. Rational problem-solving skills include four distinct skills (D'Zurilla & Nezu, 1990, 1999; Nezu et al., 1993). These are (a) problem definition and formulation, (b) generation of alternatives, (c) decision making, and (d) solution implementation and verification (Bedell & Lennox, 1997; D'Zurilla et al., 1999; Nezu et al., 1993).

Problem Orientation

Problem orientation is the first domain of the problem-solving process. It refers to the set of attitudes, beliefs, feelings, and perceptions that a student holds about the problem. Problem orientation is commonly considered the motivational aspect of the problem-solving process (D'Zurilla et al., 1990).

Problem orientation comprises five domains. These five parts are (1) problem perception, (2) problem attribution, (3) problem appraisal, (4) perceived control and (5) time and effort commitment. Problem orientation includes the ability to recognize that a problem exists. Detecting that a problem exists is the first and perhaps the most profound step because it gives rise to the subsequent problem-solving processes. Problem orientation also includes the student's beliefs, perceptions, and schema that he or she has regarding problems (e.g., why the problem occurred) and the ability to solve problems (D'Zurilla et al., 1999; Nezu et al., 1993). Underachieving students may believe that problems exist for a variety of reasons that may not be true. For example, these students could place the responsibility for their weaker than expected performance on their teachers or on other third parties or on distorted beliefs (e.g., that they will "never understand the material").

A third dimension of the problem orientation is referred to as problem perception. Problems can be perceived as opportunities or they may be viewed as threats. As a result, problem perception gives rise to emotions that accompany a problem. These subjective reactions can affect the student's level of motivation and perceived sense of efficacy. Thus, the problem perception prompts a person to approach or to avoid the problem. Some underachieving students seem to perceive their academic difficulties negatively, as situations over which they have little control. It seems that viewing problems negatively would contribute to the underachieving students' avoidance of those subjects in which they are experiencing difficulties; this can further diminish motivation and problem-solving skills.

Another aspect of problem orientation is the concept of perceived control, or the extent to which the person feels capable of solving the problem effectively. Time and effort are other aspects of problem orientation. These concepts refer to the student's estimate of the energy, resources, and time that are necessary to resolve the problem, including the probability that the problem solver will invest these resources (D'Zurilla et al., 1999).

Problem Definition and Formulation

When the problem is recognized, it is important that it is operationally defined (D'Zurilla et al., 1999). Typically when problems are initially identified they are often described in generalities (D'Zurilla et al., 1999). For example, students who are underachieving in school may recognize that they are struggling and comment that, "I'm failing in school and I've got to do better." To address this, D'Zurilla and Nezu (1999) identified the following four recommendations for this stage of effective problem solving. First, gather as much factual information about the problem as possible. Second, clearly define the problem. Third, establish realistic goals in relation to the problem. Fourth, determine the degree of significance that the problem and its resolution hold for the individual. A concise definition of a problem is important because it helps to ensure that the solutions that are developed are relevant and effective (Bedell et al., 1997; D'Zurilla et al., 1999).

Understanding the Problem

When conceptualizing the problem it is useful to understand not only what aspect of the situation is "unacceptable" to the student but also what changes are sought (D'Zurilla et al., 1999, p. 24). For example, it may be beneficial for the underachieving student to refine the definition of his or her problems from "doing better in school" to "understanding my Spanish vocabulary." In addition, when conceptualizing the problem it is important to consider what obstacles might get in the way of resolving the problem (D'Zurilla et al., 1999). By anticipating obstacles, preparations may be made about how to negotiate obstacles if they arise. For instance, students who may require a balance between involvement in school activities and school work may need to develop a schedule that affords them adequate time for involvement in extracurricular activities as well as adequate time for studying.

Setting Goals

Goal setting is another important aspect of problem definition and formulation. As with each of the earlier steps, the goal should be operationally defined (D'Zurilla et al., 1999). It is also important that the goal be "realistic or attainable" (D'Zurilla et al., 1999, p. 25). Students who are underachieving in school might initially state that they need to "get their act together" or that they need to "ace" the next test. It is helpful for these students to establish goals in terms that are clearly defined (e.g., earn an 85% on the next math quiz). Also, these students should select goals that are attainable, given their current level of achievement and expected potential. Using the previous example, establishing a goal to earn an 85% on next math quiz may be more realistic then earning a 100%.

When the problem is operationally defined and the goals are made explicit, the next step, according to D'Zurilla and Nezu (1999), is for the problem solvers to reappraise the significance of the problems. In so doing, the problem solvers are clarifying the reasons why the problems are important. It is here that the persons revisit the question about whether the problems are opportunities or threats toward their well-being. Helping students perceive problems as challenging opportunities that are important to them and to their lives may develop their commitment toward resolving the problems. Also, helping students to identify why they believe their goal is important may also help to motivate them to achieve their goals.

Generation of Alternatives

The next step in the problem-solving model is generation of alternatives, commonly referred to as "brainstorming" (D'Zurilla et al., 1999). There are two guiding principles that govern the generation of alternatives. The first is the deferment of judgment (D'Zurilla et al., 1999; Parnes, 1988) and the second is the quantity of possible alternatives. Deferring of judgment enables the problem solver to develop a greater quantity of possible solutions because the person is not critiquing each alternative. As more ideas are generated, the probability that there will be effective ideas contained within the list of possible alternatives increases (Parnes, 1988). Students who are underachieving in a particular subject may find it useful to brainstorm a list of alternative solutions that they can implement to achieve their goals. In essence, the students are asking themselves to search for specific steps to reach their academic goals.

There are two types of alternatives (D'Zurilla et al., 1999). The first is known as a strategy, which may be understood as a general approach to solving a problem. The second type of alternative is known as a tactic. Tactics, which make up the strategies, are the specific actions that lead to the achievement of goals (D'Zurilla et al., 1999). When gathering information about the problem, it is important to identify what strategies and tactics need to be implemented in order to solve the problem. It is also important to identify what might be some of the obstacles that may impact the problem-solving process just as the problem should be operationally defined into measurable and objective tactics. The underachieving students who want to earn 85% on the next Spanish quiz can strive to memorize the vocabulary terms (strategy) and to develop a vocabulary flash card (tactic) for each of the terms they are memorizing as ways in which to implement this strategy.

Decision Making

The next step in the problem-solving process is reviewing the alternatives and deciding which alternatives will be most efficacious (D'Zurilla et al., 1999). There are several procedures that can be used to facilitate decision making (D'Zurilla et al., 1999). For example, a cost benefit analysis of the various alternatives can be useful in determining which alternative is most effective. This process allows the problem solver to examine the advantages and disadvantages of a particular alternative. Another consideration that can be helpful for decision making is considering the likely outcome of the various alternatives, as well as the likelihood that the problem solver will implement the plan (Parnes, 1988). When selecting the alternatives to choose, it is often useful to consider not only the effect the alternative will have on personal well-being, but also the time and effort required in implementing the alternative (D'Zurilla et al., 1999). For the underachieving student, decision making includes reviewing the strategies and tactics that were previously developed and then deciding which alternatives to implement.

Solution Implementation and Verification

Solution implementation and verification is the last stage of the problem-solving process. Solution implementation and verification occurs after an alternative has been selected, allowing for an evaluation of the outcome. As a result, this step helps to guide behavior by allowing for self-correction. There are several aspects of solution implementation and verification that can enhance problem-solving effectiveness. These include: (a) self-monitoring, (c) self-evaluation, and (d) self-reinforcement.

Self-monitoring, which allows the problem solver to become aware of the way in which the alternative was implemented, also allows the opportunity for him to identify which behavior and thoughts affected this alternative. *Self-evaluation* allows the problem solver to reflect on the effort and manner in which the alternative was implemented. In addition, self-evaluation also allows one to judge the overall effectiveness of the strategy (Kendall et al., 1990).

Finally, *self-reinforcement* refers to the internal and/or external rewards the persons experience as a result of their problem-solving behavior; this step is critical to facilitating problem-solving behavior and maintaining this behavior. By reflecting on how effective the implementations of the alternatives are working, students can devise and improve their strategies and tactics to meet the demands of their subjects.

To summarize, as this discussion of problem solving demonstrates, each aspect of the problem-solving model can be applied to the intervention of academic underachievement. Collectively and individually, each aspect of the problem-solving model plays a unique role in the resolution of academic underachievement. Depending on whether students view problems as challenges or threats (problem orientation), to defining the problem operationally, to the selection of realistic problem-focused goals that are attainable and realistic, to the generation of alternatives (strategies and tactics) and the selection of alternatives to implement (decision making) to the final step of problem-solving model (solution implementation and verification), the problem-solving model seems to be a paradigm that is congruent with understanding and treating underachievement.

CASE STUDY

The following clinical example provides an overview of some of the seminal topics discussed in this chapter, namely the importance of a comprehensive assessment, the working alliance, self-regulated learning, and social problem solving.

Terry, age 16, was referred for counseling near the end of the school year because he was underachieving academically—specifically he was failing geometry. Terry met with his counselor after school twice a week for 45 minutes, for approximately 4 weeks. Shortly before meeting with his counselor, Terry had completed a psychoeducational assessment by the school psychologist. A review of the psychoeducational report and his educational records indicated that Terry did not have learning disability, behavioral or mood disorder. However, he had been struggling academically in several classes throughout the school year. Terry's underachievement seemed to be chronic and generalized to several subjects. The counselor then met with Terry and his parents to discuss their perception of the problem. With their permission the counselor met with Terry's geometry teacher to gather more information, including any specific recommendations that teacher had to improve the young man's academic performance.

During the initial session, the working alliance was formulated. Terry and the clinician began to establish a collaborative working relationship. Terry was asked to select one academic subject in which he would like to improve; his reply indicated that he would like to improve his geometry grade. Asked to describe what he wanted to accomplish by working together with the counselor, Terry said that he wanted "to do well in math class." With the assistance of his counselor, Terry operationally defined his goal so that it was attainable, realistic, measurable, and time limited. His goal became identified as earning a grade of 83% or greater in geometry by the end of the marking period.

Terry stated that he *wanted* to earn better grades and was willing to participate in counseling in order to learn new strategies to improve his schoolwork. In terms of the readiness for change model, Terry seemed to be in the preparation stage (DiClemente et al., 2005). Each session was to be structured using a cognitive behavior therapeutic treatment format that included: (1) brief check-in/update, (2) bridge from previous session, (3) setting the agenda, (4) review of the homework, (5) discussion of the agenda items, (6) assigning new homework, and (7) summary and feedback (Beck, 1995). The overall goal of therapy was to increase both Terry's self-regulated learning and social problem-solving skills relevant to geometry.

During the subsequent sessions, the concepts of social problem-solving were introduced. For example, having reframed the problem as a challenge rather than a threat, Terry was asked to brainstorm a list of alternatives (e.g., actions) that he could take to achieve his goal. Terry said that he could achieve his goal by: meeting with his teacher for extra help, asking to review the teacher's notes, collaborating with a classmate for homework help and tutoring, improving his note-taking in class, reading over notes each evening and reviewing notes on the way into school, participating more in class (asking and answering more questions during class), and making up flashcards that described key math concepts.

One of the interventions that had been made to facilitate self-regulated learning included a homework assignment that Terry complete a self-monitoring sheet each time he studied geometry. The self-monitoring sheets, which provided Terry with a structured approach to ways in which he would achieve his goal, directed Terry to focus on the *process* of his learning and to evaluate his efforts (e.g., were the tasks he identified

(continues)

helpful in learning the material?). The self-monitoring sheets were discussed at the beginning of each session. This allowed the counselor and Terry to evaluate the tactics and to add, delete, or modify them. The self-monitoring sheets also allowed Terry to identify any automatic thoughts he might have while implementing the steps and to begin to modify those thoughts that were accurate and adaptive.

Although Terry's academic grades were mixed (Terry had a decrease in quiz scores and increase in test scores while in counseling) he noted that he was approaching his studies in a more confident and organized manner. He seemed to have begun the process of facilitating his social-problem solving and his self-regulated learning.

SUMMARY

School social work has evolved into a highly specialized practice that incorporates empirically based forms of intervention, such as cognitive behavior therapy, to treat a variety of problems that affect children and adolescents (Allen-Meares, 2004; Dupper, 2003; Franklin, 2004). Cognitive behavior therapy can provide school social workers with a paradigm to enhance their conceptualization of child and adolescent problems and offer effective treatment interventions.

This chapter examined the problem of academic underachievement and four constructs that are critically important when working with children and adolescents in school settings. These constructs included: (1) the need for a robust assessment and cognitive case conceptualization, (2) the importance of the working alliance, and facilitating, (3) self-regulated learning, and (4) social problem-solving skills.

Academic underachievement is a serious problem affecting the lives of many children. The adverse consequences of academic underachievement can be profound both for the individual and for society. Underachieving students, for example, not only perform below the potential in school but they may also think less about the future; that is, they may be satisfied with lower educational and professional goals, and among other drawbacks, earn less money, have lower self-esteem and self-efficacy (Borokowski et al., 1994; Butler-Por, 1987; Herbert, 2001; Mandel, 2004; Mandel et al., 1996; McCall et al., 1992; Richman et al., 1998).

As part of an interdisciplinary team, school social workers can offer a unique perspective regarding the conceptualization and treatment of academic problems such as underachievement. By integrating cognitive behavior principles school social workers can augment the efficacy of their practice and further the healthy development of children and adolescents in school settings.

REFERENCES

Alford, B. A., & Beck, A. T. (1997). *The integrative power of cognitive therapy.* New York: Guilford.

Allen-Meares, P. (Ed.). (2004). *Social work services in schools* (4th ed.). Boston: Pearson.

American Psychiatric Association (2000). *Diagnostic and statistical manual of mental disorders (DSM-IV-TR).* Washington, DC: Author.

Arnkoff, D. B. (2000). Two examples of strains in the therapeutic alliance in an integrative cognitive therapy. *Journal of Clinical Psychology, 56,* 187–200.

Baker, J. A., Bridger, R., & Evans, K. (1998). Models of underachievement among gifted preadolescents: The role of personal, family and school factors. *Gifted Child Quarterly, 44,* 5–15.

Beck, J. (1995). *Cognitive therapy: Basics and beyond.* New York: Guilford.

Beck, J. (1996). Cognitive therapy of personality disorders. In P. M. Salkovskis (Ed.), *Frontiers of cognitive therapy* (pp. 165–181). New York: Guilford.

Bedell, J. R., & Lennox, S. S. (1997). *Handbook for communication and problem-solving skills training: A cognitive-behavioral approach.* New York: John Wiley & Sons.

Belfiore, P. J., & Hornyak, R. S. (1998). Operant theory and application to self-monitoring in adolescents. In D. H. Shunk & B. J. Zimmerman (Eds.), *Self-regulated learning: From teaching to self-reflective practice* (pp. 184–202). New York: Guilford.

Bordin, E. S. (1979). The generalizability of the psychoanalytic concept of the working alliance. *Psychotherapy: Theory, Research, and Practice, 16,* 252–260.

Bordin, E. S. (1994). Theory and research on the therapeutic working alliance: New directions. In A. O. Horvath & L. S. Greenberg (Eds.), *The working alliance: Theory, research, and practice* (pp. 13–37). New York: John Wiley & Sons.

Borkowski, J. G., & Thorpe, P. K. (1994). Self-regulation and motivation: A lifespan perspective on underachievement. In D. H. Schunk & B. J. Zimmerman (Eds.), *Self-regulation of learning and performance* (pp. 45–71). Hillsdale, NJ: Erlbaum.

Bowen, G. L. (2004). Social organization and schools: A general systems theory perspective. In P. Allen-Meares (Ed.), *Social work services in schools* (4th ed., pp. 53–70). Boston: Pearson.

Bradley-Klug, K., & Shapiro, E. S. (2003). Treatment of academic skills problems. In M. A. Reinecke, F. M. Dattilio, & A. Freeman (Eds.), *Cognitive therapy with children and adolescents: A casebook for clinical practice* (2nd ed., pp. 281–303). New York: Guilford.

Bronfenbrenner, U. (1994). Ecological models of human development. In M. Gauvain & M. Cole (Eds.), *Readings on the development of children* (2nd ed.). New York: W. H. Freeman & Co.

Butler, D. L. (1998). The strategic content learning approach to promoting self-regulated learning: A report of three studies. *Journal of Educational Psychology, 90,* 682–697.

Butler-Por, N. (1987). *Underachievers in school: Issues and Intervention.* Chichester, NY: John Wiley & Sons.

Clabby, J., & Elias, M. J. (1987). *Teach your child decision making: An effective 8 step program for parents to teach children of all ages to solve everyday problems and make sound decisions.* Garden City NJ: Double Day.

Constable, R., Kuzmickaite, D., Harrison, W. D., & Volkmann, L. (1999). The emergent role of the school social worker in Indiana. *School Social Work Journal, 24*(1), 1–14.

DiClemente, C. C., & Prochaska, J. O. (1998). Toward a comprehensive transtheoretical model of change: Stage of change and addictive behaviors. In W. R. Miller & N. Heather (Eds.), *Treating addictive behaviors* (2nd ed.). New York: Plenum.

DiClemente, C. C., & Prochaska, J. O. (2005). The transtheoretical approach. In J. C. Norcross & M. R. Goldfried (2nd ed.), *Handbook of psychotherapy integration.* New York: Oxford University Press.

Ducey, C. P. (1989). Academic underachievement. In P. A. Grayson & K. Cauley (Eds.), *College psychotherapy* (pp. 166–192). New York: Guilford.

Dupper, D. R. (2003). *School social work: Skills and interventions for effective practice.* New York: John Wiley & Sons.

D'Zurilla, T. J., & Nezu, A. M. (1990). Development and preliminary evaluation of the Social Problem-Solving Inventory. *A Journal of Consulting and Clinical Psychology, 2,* 156–163.

D'Zurilla, T. J., & Nezu, A. M. (1999). *Problem-solving therapy: A social competence approach to clinical intervention* (2nd ed.). New York: Springer.

Elias M. J., & Butler, L. B. (1999). Social decision making and problem solving: Essential skills for interpersonal and academic success. In J. Cohen (Ed.), *Educating minds and hearts: Social emotional learning and the passage into adolescence* (pp. 74–94). New York: Teachers College Press.

Elias, M. J., & Tobias, S. E. (1990). *Problem Solving/Decision Making for social and academic success.* Washington, D.C.: National Education Association.

Erickson, S. J., & Achilles, G. (2004). Cognitive behavioral therapy with children and adolescents. In H. Steiner (Ed.), *Handbook of mental health interventions in children and adolescents: An integrated developmental approach* (pp. 525–556). San Francisco: Jossey-Bass.

Feldmann, S. C., Martinez-Pons, M. & Shaham, D. (1995). The relationship of self-efficacy, self-regulation, and collaborative verbal behavior with grades: Preliminary findings. *Psychological Reports, 77,* 971–978.

Franklin, C. (2004). The delivery of school social work services. In P. Allen-Meares (Ed.), *Social work services in schools* (4th ed., pp. 295–326). Boston: Pearson.

Freeman, A., & Dolan, M. (2001). Revisiting Prochaska and DiClemente's stages of change theory: An expansion and specification to aid treatment planning and outcome evaluation. *Cognitive and Behavioral Practice, 8,* 224–234.

Goldfried, M. R., & Davison, G. C. (1994). *Clinical behavior therapy* (exp. ed.). New York: John Wiley & Sons.

Graham, S., Harris, K. R., & Troia, G. A. (1998). Writing and self-regulation: Cases from the self-regulated strategy development model. In D. H. Shunk & B. J. Zimmerman (Eds.), *Self-regulated learning: From teaching to self-reflective practice* (pp. 20–41). New York: Guilford.

Gredler, M. E., & Schwartz, L. S. (1997). Factorial structure of the self-efficacy for self-regulated learning scale. *Psychological Reports, 81,* 51–57.

Green, R. J. (1989). "Learning to Learn" and the family system: New perspective on underachievement and learning disorders. *Journal of Marital and Family Therapy, 15,* 187–203.

Griffin, R. S. (1988). *Underachievers in secondary school: Education off the mark.* Hillsdale, NJ: Lawrence Erlbaum Associates.

Herbert, T. P. (2001). "If I had a new notebook, I know the things I would change": Bright underachieving young men in urban classrooms. *Gifted Child Quarterly, 45,* 174–194.

Herbert, T. P. (1998). Gifted black males in an urban high school: Factors that influence achievement and underachievement. *Journal for the Education of the Gifted, 21,* 385–414.

Hofer, Yu, & Pintrich (1998). Teaching college students to be self-regulated learners. In Schunk & Zimmerman (Eds.), *Self-regulated learning: From teaching to self-regulated practice* (pp. 57–85). New York: Guilford.

Horvath, A. O. (1994). Research on alliance. In A. O. Horvath & L. S. Greenberg (Eds.), *The working alliance: Theory, research, and practice* (pp. 259–286). New York: John Wiley & Sons.

Jongsma, A. E., Peterson, M. L., & McInnis, W. P. (2000). Academic underachievement. In *The adolescent psychotherapy treatment planner* (2nd ed., pp. 12–22). New York: John Wiley & Sons.

Kendall, P. C., & Bartel, N. R. (1990). *Teaching problem solving: A manual for classroom teachers.* Unpublished manuscript.

Krouse, J. H., & Krouse, H. J. (1981). Toward a multimodal theory of academic underachievement. *Educational Psychologist, 16,* 151–163.

Lantieri, L., & Patti, J. (1996). *Waging peace in our schools.* Boston: Beacon Press.

Mandel, H. P. (2004). Constructive confrontation: Cognitive-behavioral therapy with one type of procrastinating underachiever. In H. C. Schouwenburg, C. H. Lay, T. A. Pychyl, & J. R. Ferrari (Eds.), *Counseling the procrastinator in academic settings* (pp. 119–131). Washington, DC: American Psychological Association.

Mandel H. P., & Mandel, D. E. (1995). *Along the path: Case histories of differentially diagnosed underachievers* (Rev. ed.). Toronto: Institute on Achievement and Motivation, York University.

Mandel, H. P., & Marcus, S. I. (1988). *The psychology of underachievement: Differential diagnosis and differential treatment.* New York: John Wiley & Sons.

Mandel, H. P., Marcus, S. I., & Dean, L. (1996). *Could do better: Why children underachieve and what to do about it.* Toronto: HarperPerennial.

Mason, D. A., Mendez, M., Nelsen, G., & Orwig, R. (2005). Effects of top-down and bottom-up elementary school standards reform in an underperforming California district. *The Elementary School Journal, 105*, 353–376.

McCall, R. B., Evahn, C., & Kratzer, L. (1992). *High school underachievers.* Newbury Park, CA: Sage.

McCullagh, J. G. (2002). The inception of school social work in Boston: Clarifying and expanding the historical record. *School Social Work Journal, 26*, 58–67.

Miller, J. W. (2000). Exploring the source of self-regulated learning: The influence of internal and external comparisons. *Journal of Instructional Psychology, 27*, 47–52.

National Commission of Excellence in Education. (1983). *A nation at risk: The imperative for educational reform.* Washington, DC: United States Department of Education.

Needleman, L. D. (1999). *Cognitive case conceptualization: A guidebook for practitioners.* Mahwah, NJ: Lawrence Erlbaum Associates.

Needleman, L. D. (2003). Case conceptualization in preventing and responding to therapeutic difficulties. In R. L. Leahy (Ed.), *Roadblocks in cognitive-behavioral therapy: Transforming challenges into opportunities for change* (pp. 3–23). New York: Guilford.

Nezu, C. M., Nezu, A. M., & Houts, P. S. (1993). Multiple applications of problem-solving principles in clinical practice. In K. T. Kuehlwein & H. Rosen (Eds.), *Cognitive therapies in action: Evolving innovative practice* (pp. 353–378).

Okagaki, L. (2001). Triarchic model of minority children's school achievement. *Educational Psychologist, 36*, 9–20.

Parnes, S. J. (1988). *Visualizing: State of the art processes for encouraging innovative excellence.* East Aurora, NY: D.O.K. Publishers.

Perry, N. E. (1998). Young children's self-regulated learning and contexts that support it. *Journal of Educational Psychology, 90*, 715–729.

Raue, P. J., & Goldfried, M. R. (1994). The therapeutic alliance in cognitive-behavioral therapy. In A. O. Horvath & L. S. Greenberg (Eds.), *The working alliance: Theory, research, and practice* (pp. 131–152). New York: John Wiley & Sons.

Reis, S. M., & McCoach, D. B. (2000). The underachievement of gifted students: What do we know and where do we go? *Gifted Child Quarterly, 44*, 152–170.

Richman, J. M., Rosenfeld, L. B., & Bowen, G. L. (1998). Social support for adolescents at risk of school failure. *Social Work, 43*, 309–323.

Rimm, S. B. (1982). *The underachieving gifted child: Definition and home etiologies. WAEG/T Journal, 4*, 11–22.

Rimm, S. B. (1995). *Why bright kids get poor grades: And what you can do about it. A six-step program for parents and teachers.* New York: Three Rivers Press.

Rimm, S. B. (1997). Underachievement syndrome: A national epidemic. In N. Colangelo & G. A. Davis (Eds.), *Handbook of gifted education* (2nd ed., pp. 416–434). Boston: Allyn & Bacon.

Ronen, T. (1998). Linking developmental and emotional elements into child and family cognitive-behavioural therapy. In P. Graham (Ed.), *Cognitive-behaviour therapy for children and families* (pp. 1–17). Cambridge: Cambridge University Press.

Sattler, J. M. (1992). *Assessment of children* (3rd ed.). San Diego: Author.

Schulman, L. (1992). *The skills of helping: Individuals, families and groups* (3rd ed.). Itasca, IL: F. E. Peacock.

Schunk, D. H., & Zimmerman, B. J. (Eds.). (1994). *Self-regulation of learning and performance: Issues and educational applications.* Hillsdale, NJ: Lawrence Erlbaum Associates.

Schunk, D. H., & Zimmerman, B. J. (Eds.). (1998). *Self-regulated learning: From teaching to self-reflective practice.* New York: Guilford.

Shapiro, E. S., & Bradley, K. L. (1996). Treatment of academic problems. In M. A. Rineke, F. M. Dattilio, & A. Freeman (Eds.), *Cognitive therapy with children and adolescents: A casebook for clinical practice* (pp. 344–366). New York: Guilford.

Sikorski, J. B. (1996). Academic underachievement and school refusal. In R. J. DiClemente, W. B. Hansen, & L. E. Ponton (Eds.), *Handbook of adolescent health risk behavior* (pp. 393–411). New York: Plenum Press.

Wong, B. Y. L., Harris, K. R., & Graham, S. (1991). Academic applications of cognitive-behavioral programs with learning disabled students. In P. C. Kendall (Ed.), *Child and adolescent therapy: Cognitive-behavioral procedures* (pp. 245–275). New York: Guilford.

Woodward, L. J., & Fergusson, D. M. (2000). Childhood peer relationship problems and later risks of educational under-achievement and unemployment. *Journal Child Psychology and Psychiatry, 41,* 191–201.

Zarb, J. M. (1992). *Cognitive-behavioral assessment and therapy with adolescents.* New York: Brunner/Mazel.

Zimmerman, B. J. (1998). Developing self-fulfilling cycles of academic regulation: An analysis of exemplary instructional models. In D. H. Schunk & B. J. Zimmerman (Eds.), *Self-regulated learning: From teaching to self-reflective practice* (pp. 1–19). New York: Guilford.

Zimmerman, B. J., Bonner, S., & Kovach, R. (1996). *Developing self-regulated learners: Beyond achievement to self-efficacy.* Washington, DC: American Psychological Association.

Zimmerman, B. J., & Martinez-Pons, M. (1986). Development of a structured interview for assessing student use of self-regulated learning strategies. *American Educational Research Journal, 23,* 614–628.

Zosky, D. L., & Crawford, L. A. (2003). No Child Left Behind: An assessment of an afterschool problem on academic performance among low-income, at-risk students. *School Social Work Journal, 27,* 18–31.

The author would like to acknowledge and thank Sr. Joan Dugon, S.S.J., for her editorial review and support.

CHAPTER 13

Problem Solving and Social Skills Training Groups for Children

Craig Winston LeCroy

INTRODUCTION

Behavioral group therapy (BGT) is a major vehicle for the delivery of cognitive behavioral treatment to children and adolescents. Most BGT with children and adolescents include aspects of problem solving or social skills training or both. There are a number of advantages of working with children in groups. The peer group is a natural part of child and adolescent development and as such the treatment more nearly simulates their real world than the client-adult dyad. Groups also represent a more efficient way of delivering interventions than in dyads. Group membership commonly ends the sense of isolation and lack of understanding many clients experience since they are surrounded by other children who are dealing with similar issues and problems. Certain interventions are more accessible or more effective in the small group, for example, the use of brainstorming in teaching problem-solving skills. Feedback from other members following role playing and designing extra-group tasks and goals is another. Groups are an effective way of delivering information. Games and other recreational activities in groups can be used to build cohesion and can be adapted to encourage children to try new behaviors. Finally, groups enhance generalization of change since each member observes and helps solve a diversity of problems manifested by the other clients as well as his or her own.

Of course, groups are not without disadvantages. In groups it is more difficult to individualize treatment plans for each child in the group than in individual or family therapy. Stigma associated with therapy group membership can be a barrier to obtaining a child's interest in joining a group or in obtaining parental permission. Concerns about confidentiality is common, especially among older children and adolescents and can be a barrier to recruitment of members to groups. Confidentiality and the consequences of breaches need to be dealt with by the group therapist in pregroup screening and early in treatment.

Most therapy groups range in size from 5 to 15 members, although the norm is about 6 to 9. The therapy ranges in duration from 6 to 20 sessions depending on the complexity of the presenting problems. Most sessions last from 45 minutes to one and a half hours. There are either one or two therapists. One experienced therapist is more efficient, but two provide an opportunity for therapist training and provide the members with multiple adult roles. Most groups are closed and time limited with a fixed beginning and ending time ranging from 4 to 16 sessions. Open groups in which members are added and dropped periodically are more common in institutions. Most of these decisions regarding the previous issues mentioned are made for practical reasons. Although there is some data to support the use of smaller groups over larger groups and providing group structure that permits intense interaction by everyone in the group. The more complex the clients' problems the longer the length of time in each session and the larger the number of sessions required.

BGT is guided by several principles unique to group context. The first is that there is broad and active participation if the previous advantages are to be realized. The interaction should be characterized by its provision of support and reinforcement or mutual aid for each other. The second principle is gradual progress toward independence and autonomy. The therapist initially provides structure and gradually delegates or encourages responsibility for that structure to the members. The third principle is that the goals of treatment are formulated to promote the generalization of the behaviors and attitudes learned in the group. The fourth principle is that of gradually increased demand for self-disclosure. It is the clients' behavior and cognitions in these problem situations that become the target of the interventions. Interrelated to these principles is building the cohesion of the group. With children and youth, the therapy group should be both a work and fun experience.

The two most widely used group cognitive behavior group methods are problem solving and social skills training. Both of these methods are reviewed in the next section.

LITERATURE REVIEW

Problem Solving Training

Problem solving training grew out of early work that focused on training children in cognitive protocols for learning self-control. Indeed, the treatment was born out of a frustrated experience by George Spivak who was trying to understand why a child had left a residential center to go into town and not told anyone. As he inquired about why the child would do such a thing he was struck by the child's repeated assertions, "I don't know," "I just did it," "I didn't think about that," "It didn't occur to me," and "that is all I could think to do." Spivak began to wonder if the child just didn't have the needed social problem-solving skills to address difficult situations. These experiences lead to research to investigate what cognitive skills were needed to ensure adequate social adjustment. The classic study (Spivack & Shure, 1974) outlined social problem-solving skills that had been negatively correlated with adjustment. To begin with, children needed to become aware of social conflicts that might suggest the need for problem solving. Once aware of the need, it was hypothesized that generating a list of alternative solutions would be helpful. Evaluating the solutions is a further step and knowing the consequences of different actions (consequential thinking) is critical to good decision making. After children are taught to become aware of conflicts, generate alternative solutions, engage in consequential thinking, and select a solution they develop a plan to implement a solution.

These modest notions grew into a substantial treatment program that has been used across a wide variety of treatment problems. The largest application of problem solving has been with externalizing disorders, particularly conduct disorders. In a series of studies (see Kazdin, 2003 for a review) it was found that problem solving training reduced symptoms including behavior ratings at 1-year follow-up time periods. Perhaps most interesting in these studies was a comparison of problem-solving treatment with more conventional relationship therapy or "talk therapy" provided in an outpatient mental health setting. The findings showed that at 1 year, children in the problem solving group had improved on outcome measures but that the children in the relationship therapy were unchanged. Problem solving training for children in groups has also been combined with parent training and found positive results (Webster-Stratton & Taylor, 2001).

Other applications of problem solving include: attention deficit/hyperactivity disorder (ADHD) (Hinshaw, 2000), anxious children (Barrett & Shortt, 2003), anger management (Nelson & Finch, 2000), treating children with chronic health conditions (Varni, La Greca, & Spirito, 2000), and substance use and prevention (LeCroy & Mann, 2004) to name only a few. Because problem solving training has easy importability it is used in most cognitive behavior treatment programs at some level.

Social Skills Training

Social skills training grew out of the clinical observation and research that found a relationship between poor peer relationships and later psychological difficulties (Hartup & Abecassis, 2002). In fact, disturbances in peer relationships are among the best predictors of psychiatric, social, and school problems. Research strongly suggests that social competence is essential for healthy normal development. Child developmentalists stress that it is through a child's interactions with peers that many of life's necessary behaviors are acquired. For example, children learn sexual socialization, control of aggression, expression of emotion, and caring both from their families and through interaction with peers. When children fail to acquire such social skills, they are beset by problems such as inappropriate expression of anger, friendship difficulties, and an inability to resist peer pressure. It is this understanding that has led to the present focus on changing children's interpersonal behavior with peers (Ronen, 1997).

Social skills can be defined as a complex set of skills that facilitate successful interactions among peers, parents, teachers, and other adults. *Social* refers to interactions between people; *skills* refers to making appropriate discriminations—deciding what would be the most effective response and using the verbal and nonverbal behaviors that facilitate interaction. The conceptualization of social skills as training suggests that problem behaviors can be viewed as remediable deficits in a child's response repertoire (King & Kirschenbaum, 1992; LeCroy, 2002). This perspective focuses on building prosocial responses as opposed to eliminating excessive antisocial responses. Children learn new options in coping with problem situations. Learning how to respond effectively to new situations produces more positive consequences than using behaviors, which may have been used in similar situations in the past. This model focuses on the teaching of skills and competencies for day-to-day living rather than on understanding and eliminating defects. This model is an optimistic view of children and is implemented in an educative-remedial framework.

A classic social skills training study by Oden and Asher (1977) sought to improve the social skills and peer relationships of third- and fourth-grade children who were identified as not well liked by their peers. The social skills program taught the following four skills: participation, cooperation, communication, and validation/support. The intervention consisted of a 5-week program whereby each skill was (a) described verbally,

(b) explained with examples, (c) practiced using behavior rehearsal, and (d) refined through feedback, coaching, and review of progress. This study found that the children increased their social skills and that they had improved significantly more than a group of elementary schoolchildren who did not participate in the program. Particularly impressive was the finding at 1-year follow-up that the children showed gains in how their classmates rated them on play and peer acceptance.

Like problem solving training, social skills training has received widespread application across a number of problems. Social skills training has been used with conduct disorder and aggressive behavior (Larson, Lochman, & Lochman, 2001), depression (Clarke, Lewinsohn, & Hops, 2001), anxiety disorders (Kearney & Albano, 2000), substance abuse prevention (Botvin, 2000) and for children with disabilities (Weiss & Harris, 2001).

Problem solving training and social skills training methods do overlap. Many people consider problem solving to be one particular type of social skill. In practice, many treatment programs offer a combination of these treatments. Participants may learn specific social skills, for example, refusal skills, in substance abuse prevention, but also learn problem-solving skills in order for children to help manage difficult or problem situations in which a specific skill may not address the issue.

IMPLEMENTING BEHAVIORAL GROUP THERAPY

In this chapter, the focus is on the unique application of behavioral treatment using groups with an emphasis on assessment, principles of effective treatment, and guidelines for the practitioner. We shall focus primarily on the use of the group in describing these aspects of BGT.

Assessment in Groups

One important early step in the process of treatment is assessment of the presenting problems and the resources the child has for resolving them. In assessment BGT takes into consideration the environment in which the behavior and emotions occur. This includes each person's social support network. Most BGT models teach specific skills for coping with and resolving unique problem situations. Individual assessment and pregroup interviews are used for treatment planning within groups. But the group itself is also used for assessment by having the members observe each other's interactions, having members interview each other, and by member's observing role plays of others (Rose & LeCroy, 2005).

As part of assessment, long- and short-term goals are formulated (Rose, 1998). Each member negotiates his or her own goals with suggestions from the other group members and the therapist. Interviews with parent and teachers may contribute to the formulation of significant goals. For example, the goal of a child with a problem of excessive anger when criticized was to express his disagreement in a matter of fact tone of voice. For a child whose long-term goal was to make new friends, his short-term goal might be during the following week to ask another child to play with him. Extra-group tasks (which are often the same as short-term goals) to try out these behaviors are negotiated during the session with each member, and each reports back the results at the subsequent session (Rose, 1998b). Success or failure in accomplishing these tasks provides evidence of progress or lack of it.

Principles of Effective Group Treatment

In order to provide a better sense of how the group is conducted with children and adolescents some of the key group strategies for effective treatment are reviewed. These include building group cohesion, identifying and correcting group problems and using effective group interventions, and using individual treatment procedures in a way that is compatible with a group environment (Rose et al., 2005).

Building Group Cohesion

Group therapy research has supported the principle of group cohesion as an effective ingredient of group treatment (Rose, 1998a, b). Especially since most groups for children and adolescents are often involuntary, building cohesion can be a needed process in obtaining motivation and compliance with group tasks. Cohesion refers to the mutual liking of members for each other and the group therapist and their attraction to the program of the group. High cohesion tends to be correlated with high motivation to work on significant problems. As Rose (1998a, b) notes, the cohesion of the group can be enhanced by the use of group introductory exercises in which members interview each other in pairs and then partners introduce their partner to the group. It is also a safe way of increasing broad participation and is the first step in self-disclosure. With children and youth the use of games and other recreational activities at the end of a session dramatically increases the cohesion of the group (Rose, 1998). Cohesion is also enhanced by creating opportunities for continued broad participation, protecting members from premature and/or too harsh confrontation, keeping the interaction positive, using variation in the program, using humor, and developing opportunities for choice and self-decision making by the members. Finally, cohesion is enhanced by training the members in giving and receiving both positive and critical feedback.

Establishing Group Goals

Group goals in contrast to treatment goals refer to a future change in interactive phenomena that occur in the group. An example of one common group goal is to increase the attraction of group members to each other in order to build stronger cohesion. Or another group goal might be that everyone in the group participates actively in the group exercises or discussion. Most group goals are proposed to the group by the therapist. Group goals are important only insofar as their achievement facilitates the achievement of individual treatment goals. For example, in an anxiety group in which the group problem was that members would rarely provide each other with feedback, the group goal was to increase the feedback given to each other. This goal would enhance the members' learning the skills they needed if the goal was achieved.

Addressing Group Problems

The most common group problems are inattentiveness, low cohesiveness, and uneven distribution of participation and low self-disclosure all of which can be interrelated. The use of group exercises and self-disclosure can be used to increase cohesion and address some of these problems (Rose, 1998a, b). As members come to like and trust others in the group, they are increasingly willing to share with others their conflicts, their goals, their level of motivation, and their appraisal of problematic events and to accept feedback and suggestions.

Basic Group Interventions

Modeling and Rehearsal

The use of modeling and behavioral rehearsal by group members is a major group intervention because it involves many members in each role play. Although used in dyadic treatment, the group provides multiple roles and multiple models for each client. Modeling-rehearsal is a form of role playing used to demonstrate new behaviors by leaders or members (modeling) and to practice these behaviors (behavioral rehearsal). These plus group feedback and additional group tasks are the core of social skills training. In most children groups, group social skill training is a major component.

Brainstorming

Brainstorming is conducted by all the group members to help an individual discover alternative strategies for appraising situations and all possible interventions for resolving specific situations or difficulties. Because it involves all the members of the group, it is a true group procedure, which is in contrast with the treatment dyad. A group provides a richness of ideas based on the wide experience of all the members and the therapist.

Group Exercises

The use of group exercises involves the use of structured interactive activities as ways of teaching clients the skills that mediate the achievement of therapeutic goals. Introductory exercises to gradually increase group self-disclosure and to enhance cohesion have already been mentioned as have exercises in the use of positive and critical feedback in analyzing problematic situations. Some of the more commonly used group therapy exercises with children and adolescents are described in detail in Rose (1998a, b).

GUIDELINES FOR PRACTITIONERS

This section provides more details concerning how BGT procedures are typically used in groups. In conducting social skills and problem solving training there is a sequential process that can be followed. The following seven basic steps delineate the process (based on LeCroy, 1994). These guidelines were developed for social skills groups with middle school and high school students. Social skills groups with younger children would have to be modified. (See King and Kirschenbaum (1992) for guidelines with younger children.) Table 13.1 presents these steps and outlines the process for teaching social skills and problem solving. In each step there is a request for group member involvement. This is because it is critical that group leaders involve the participants actively in the skill training. Also, this keeps the group interesting and fun for the group members.

1. **Present the social skill being taught.** The first step for the group leader is to present the skill. The leader solicits an explanation of the skill, for example, "Can anyone tell me what it means to resist peer pressure?" After group members have answered this question, the leader emphasizes the rationale for using the skill. For example, "You would use this skill when you're in a situation where you don't want to do something that your friends want you to do and you should be able to say 'no' in a way that helps your friends to be able to accept your refusal." The leader then requests additional reasons for learning the skill.

TABLE 13.1   A Summary of the Steps in Teaching Social Skills Training

1. Present the Social Skills Being Taught
    *   Solicit an explanation of the skill
    *   Get group members to provide rationales for the skill
2. Discuss the Social Skill
    *   List the skill steps
    *   Get group members to give examples of using the skill
3. Present a Problem Situation and Model the Skill
    *   Evaluate the performance
    *   Get group members to discuss the model
4. Set the Stage for Role Playing the Skill
    *   Select the group members for role playing
    *   Get group members to observe the role play
5. Group Members Rehearse the Skill
    *   Provide coaching if necessary
    *   Get group members to provide feedback on verbal and nonverbal elements
6. Practice Using Complex Skill Situations
    *   Teach accessory skills, for example, problem solving
    *   Get group members to discuss situations and provide feedback
7. Train for Generalization and Maintenance
    *   Encourage practice of skills outside the group
    *   Get group members to bring in their own problem situations

2. **Discuss the social skills.** The leader presents the specific skill steps that constitute the social skill. For example, the skill steps for resisting peer pressure are: good nonverbal communication (includes eye contact, posture, voice volume), saying "no" early in the interaction, suggesting an alternative activity, and leaving the situation if there is continued pressure. Leaders then ask group members to share examples of when they used the skill or examples of when they could have used the skill but did not.
3. **Present a problem situation and model the skill.** The leader presents a problem situation. For example, the following is a problem situation for resisting peer pressure:

> After seeing a movie, your friends suggest that you go with them to the mall. It's 10:45 and you are supposed to be home by 11:00. It's important that you get home by 11:00 or you won't be able to go out next weekend.

The group leader chooses members to role play this situation and then models the skills. Group members evaluate the model's performance. Did the model follow all the skill steps? Was his or her performance successful? The group leader may choose another group member to model if the leader believes they already have the requisite skills. Another alternative is to present to the group videotaped models. This has the advantage of following the recommendation by researchers that the models be similar to the trainee in age, sex, and social characteristics.

4. **Set the stage for role playing of the skill.** For this step the group leader needs to construct the social circumstances for the role play. Leaders select group members for the role play and assign them their parts to play. The leader reviews with the role players how to act out their role. Group members not in the role play observe the process. It is sometimes helpful if they are given specific instructions for their observations. For example, one member may observe the use of nonverbal skills, another member may be instructed to observe when "no" is said in the interaction.

5. **Group members rehearse the skill.** Rehearsal or guided practice of the skill is an important part of effective social skills training. Group leaders and group members provide instructions or coaching before and during the role play and provide praise and feedback for improvement. Following a role play rehearsal the leader will usually give instructions for improvement, model the suggested improvements, or coach the person to incorporate the feedback in the subsequent role play. Often the group member doing the role play will practice the skills in the situation several times to refine his or her skills and incorporate feedback offered by the group. The role plays continue until the trainee's behavior becomes more and more similar to that of the model. It is important that "overlearning" takes place, so the group leader should encourage many examples of effective skill demonstration followed by praise. Group members should be taught how to give effective feedback before the rehearsals. Throughout the teaching process the group leader can model desired responses. For example, after a role play the leader can respond first and model feedback that starts with a positive statement.

6. **Practice using complex skill situations.** The last phase deals with more difficult and complex skill situations. Complex situations can be developed by extending the interactions and roles in the problem situations. Most social skills groups also incorporate the teaching of problem-solving abilities. Problem solving is a general approach to help young people gather information about a problematic situation, generate a large number of potential solutions, evaluate the consequences of various solutions, and outline plans for the implementation of a particular solution. Group leaders can identify appropriate problem situations and lead members through these steps. The problem-solving training is important because it prepares young

people to make adjustments as needed in a given situation. It is a general skill with large scale application. For a more complete discussion on the use of problem-solving approaches, see Elias and Clabby (1992) and Rose (1998a, b).

7. **Train for generalization and maintenance.** The success of the social skills program depends on the extent to which the skills young people learn transfer to their day-to-day lives. Practitioners must always be planning for ways to maximize the generalization of skills learned and promote their continued use after training. There are several principles that help facilitate the generalization and maintenance of skills. The first is the use of overlearning. The more overlearning that takes place the greater likelihood of later transfer of skills. Therefore, it is important that group leaders insist on mastery of the skills. Another important principle of generalization is to vary the stimuli as skills are learned. To accomplish this, practitioners can use a variety of models, problem situations, role play actors, and trainers. The different styles and behaviors of the people used produces a broader context in which to apply the skills learned. Perhaps most important is to require that young people use the skills in their real-life settings. Group leaders should assign and monitor homework to encourage transfer of learning. This may include the use of written contracts to do certain tasks outside of the group. Group members should be asked to bring to the group examples of problem situations in which the social skills can be applied. Lastly, practitioners should attempt to develop external support for the skills learned. One approach to this is to set up a buddy system in which group members work together to perform the skills learned outside the group (for examples, see Rose, a, b, 1998).

CASE STUDY

The following example demonstrates how the group therapy principles are used in a children's group. A description of what happens in the group is detailed and in italics is an explanation of the group leader's behavior that demonstrates some of the group strategies described in this chapter.

LEADER: Today we are going to talk about social skills and one important skill we want to learn is resisting peer pressure. What does it mean to resist peer pressure? *Explanation of the group therapist's behavior is in italics. The group therapist begins by soliciting an explanation of the skill and seeks to involve all group participants.*

(continues)

BETH: It's when your friends try to force you into things.

MARK: It's when other kids get you into trouble and it's not your fault.

LEADER: That's right, Beth and Mark; resisting peer pressure means other people are trying to get you to do something you don't want to do. So when you are in a situation where you don't want to do something that your friends want you to do, you need to be able to say no and do it in a way that your friends will leave you alone. *The leader points out the influence of peers and stresses the need to learn the skill.* What reasons can you think of for learning how to resist peer pressure? *Providing rationales for the skill.* I'll start—you resist peer pressure so that you'll feel better about yourself because you didn't get talked into doing something you might feel bad about later. *The leader begins by modeling the first response, and the group members follow in a similar manner.*

KEVIN: So you don't get into trouble with your parents.

LEADER: Good point, Kevin. *Encouraging and reinforcing the group members to share.*

WENDY: So you don't get talked into using drugs.

TOMMY: Your friends will listen to you and know you're not just saying things.

LEADER: Great, Wendy and Tommy. *Provides reinforcement for group members' participation.* As a number of you have pointed out, there are a lot of reasons to resist peer pressure. I think you have also talked about how hard it is to do. That's why we need to practice the skill. *Summarizes and emphasizes the difficulty in resisting peer pressure.* Let's go over the steps in doing a role play. Remember practice good nonverbal skills and start by saying a clear no early on, stick to your no, and if necessary leave the situation or suggest an alternative activity. *Reviews the skills steps that identify a sequence that the members should follow in learning the skill. The leader puts these on the board or provides students with handouts.* Here is a situation we can use: Two friends come up to you at recess and ask you to steal someone's homework as a joke. *The leader provides a situation for the group. This is provided to assure that the skills are understood and learned. Later, members can bring in their own situations to practice.* This is a person that gets picked on a lot, and he will probably feel picked on if you do it. Wendy, pick two people to do a role play of this situation. *The leader picks a member who can do a good job with the role play (that is, modeling the skill) since this is the first time through.* Ok, role players take a minute to think of what you want to say. Everyone else can watch to see if Wendy follows the skills steps. Kevin, will you also see if she uses good nonverbal behavior? Ok, let's start. *Finally, leader prepares the members to listen and observe so they can observe the model and give feedback. One member's attention is specifically directed to keep his attention focused.*

TOM: Hey, Wendy, go get Todd's homework; it's sitting right there.

KERRY: Yeah, he'll never know you did it.

WENDY: Uh . . . I . . . Uhmmmm . . . I don't think I better.

TOM: Come on Wendy, just do it.

WENDY: No, I can't—you do it if you want Todd's homework.

LEADER: Ok, break, let's give Wendy some feedback. Kevin, let's start with you; what nonverbal behavior did you observe? *The leader begins the process of feedback by asking group members to comment on Wendy's performance. The group members have been taught to use positive feedback at first before being critical, although here they move too quickly to the critical.*

KEVIN: Well she spoke up and looked Tom in the eye.

LEADER: Ok, good, what do you think she could have done better? *The leader encourages students to share observations and then asks for critical feedback.*

KEVIN: She tripped over her words at the beginning.

BETH: Yeah, she could have said no better at the beginning, but the second time was better.

LEADER: Beth, what do you think would be a better response when Tom asked her to take the homework? *The leader gets other members to model better responses to the situation.*

BETH: She could have said, no, I don't think that is right.

LEADER: Why isn't it right? *The leader uses role reversal or role taking to encouraging the members to think about what it is like when someone hurts your feelings.*

BETH: Because it would hurt his feelings.

LEADER: Yes, I think it would. Ok, any other feedback for Wendy? Well I have some. I think Wendy did a good job of being

(continues)

serious. I think the second time she spoke she could have suggested another activity like we learned. Any ideas of what she could have suggested? *The leader gives her feedback, making sure that the role play incorporates the skills needed to resist peer pressure.*

TOM: You mean she should have said let's go play outside?

LEADER: Yes, she could have suggested they go outside and forget about taking Todd's homework. Ok, we've got a good start; let's redo the role play, and Wendy, try to use the suggestions for improvements the group gave you. For example, how could you say "no" right away after Tom and Kerry put pressure on you?

WENDY: I could say, "No, I think it is mean and I don't want to do it."

LEADER: Good, that's better. Let's go ahead and try it out again. Remember to say no early on, be forceful, and suggest an alternative activity. *The leader summarizes the suggestions and then prepares the group to redo the role play and incorporate the ideas suggested by the group. Here it is important to make sure the role players understand how to incorporate the feedback for an improved performance. The remainder of the session is devoted to continued practice and feedback.*

The leader helps students to identify situations outside of the group where they can practice skills in the upcoming week and assigns homework practice using the "buddy system." The group closes with a brief fun game to increase group cohesion among the children and keep the group fun and interesting.

SUMMARY

The primary goal of using BGT with children is enhancing the socialization process of children, teaching social skills and problem solving, and promoting social competence. Group workers can make an important contribution to children, families, and schools through preventive and remedial approaches like those described in this chapter. Children's social behavior is a critical aspect of successful adaptation in society. The group represents an ideal place for children to learn and practice social behavior. It provides the needed multipeer context and offers multiple opportunities for newly learned behaviors to be generalized to other situations and circumstances.

Social skills and problem-solving training provide a clear methodology for providing remedial and preventive services to children. This direct approach to working with children has been applied in numerous problem areas and with many child behavior problems. It is straightforward in application and has been adapted so that social workers, teachers, and peer helpers have successfully applied the methodology. Although we have emphasized the group application, social skills training also can be applied in individual or classroom settings. In general, research has supported the efficacy of social skills and problem-solving training; it is one of the most promising treatment approaches developed for working with children and adolescents.

REFERENCES

Barrett, P. M., & Shortt, A. L. (2003). Parental involvement in the treatment of anxious children. In A. E. Kazdin & J. R. Weisz (Eds.), *Evidence-based psychotherapies for children and adolescents* (pp. 101–119). New York: Guilford.

Botvin, G. J. (2000). *Life skills training: Promoting health and personal development.* New York: Princeton Health.

Clarke, G. N., Lewinsohn, P. M., & Hops, H. (2001). Instructor's manual for the adolescent coping with depression course. Retrieved January 20, 2005 from www.kpchr.org/public/acwd/acwdl.html.

Elias, M. J., & Clabby, J. F. (1992). *Building social problem-solving skills.* San Francisco: Jossey-Bass.

Hartup, W. W., & Abecassis, M. (2002). Friends and enemies. In P. K. Smith & C. H. Hart (Eds.), *Blackwell handbook of childhood social development* (pp. 285–306). Malden, MA: Blackwell.

Hinshaw, S. P. (2000). Attention-deficit/hyperactivity disorders: The search for viable treatments. In P. C. Kendall (Ed.), *Child and adolescent therapy: Cognitive-behavioral procedures* (pp. 90–128). New York: Guilford.

Kazdin, A. E. (2003). Problem-solving skills training and parent management training for conduct disorder. In A. E. Kazdin & J. R. Weisz (Eds.), *Evidence-based psychotherapies for children and adolescents* (pp. 241–262). New York: Guilford.

Kearney, C. A., & Albano, A. (2000). *When children refuse school: A cognitive-behavioral therapy approach therapist guide.* New York: Academic Press.

King, C. A., & Kirschenbaum, D. S. (1992). *Helping young children develop social skills.* Pacific Grove, CA: Brooks/Cole.

Larson, J., Lochman, J. E., & Lochman, J. (2001). *Helping school children cope with anger: A cognitive-behavioral intervention.* New York: Guilford.

LeCroy, C. W. (1994). *Handbook of child and adolescent treatment manuals.* New York: The Free Press.

LeCroy, C. W. (2002). Child therapy and social skills. In A. R. Roberts & G. J. Greene (Eds.), *Social work desk reference* (pp. 406–412). New York: Oxford University Press.

LeCroy, C. W., & Mann, J. (2004). Preventing substance abuse among youth: Universal, selected and targeted interventions. In L. A. Rapp-Paglicci, C. N. Dulmus, & J. S. Wodarski (Eds.), *Handbook of preventive interventions for children and adolescents* (pp. 198–226). Hoboken, NJ: John Wiley & Sons.

Nelson, W. M., & Finch, Jr., A. J. (2000). Managing anger in youth: A cognitive-behavioral intervention approach. In P. C. Kendall (Ed.), *Child and adolescent therapy: Cognitive-behavioral procedures* (pp. 129–172). New York: Guilford.

Oden, S. L., & Asher, S. R. (1977). Coaching low accepted children in social skills: A follow-up sociometric assessment. *Child Development, 48,* 496–506.

Ronen, T. (1997). Cognitive developmental therapy with children. Chichester: Wiley.

Rose, S. D. (1998a). *Group therapy with troubled youth.* Thousand Oaks, CA: Sage.

Rose, S. D. (1998b). *Group therapy with troubled youth, A cognitive-behavioral interactive approach.* Thousand Oaks, CA: Sage.

Rose, S. D., & LeCroy, C. W. (2005). Behavioral group therapy with children. In M. Hersen (Ed.), *Encyclopedia of behavior modification and therapy: Volume I.* Thousand Oaks, CA: Sage.

Spivack, G., & Shure, M. B. (1974). *Social adjustment of young children.* San Francisco: Jossey-Bass.

Varni, J., La Greca, A. M., & Spirito, A. (2000). Cognitive-behavioral interventions for children with chronic health conditions. In P. C. Kendall (Ed.), *Child and adolescent therapy: Cognitive-behavioral procedures* (pp. 291–333). New York: Guilford.

Webster-Stratton, C., & Taylor, T. (2001). Nipping early risk factors in the bud: Preventing substance abuse, delinquency, and violence in adolescence through interventions targeted at young children (0–8 years). *Prevention Science, 2,* 165–192.

Weiss, M. J., & Harris, S. L. (2001). *Reaching out, joining in: Teaching social skills to young children with autism.* New York: Woodbine House.

PART IV

Focus on Couples
and Families

CHAPTER 14

Working With Couples

Donald K. Granvold

INTRODUCTION

The emotional pain and concomitant psychological and behavioral consequences of couple relationship distress are rivaled by few other life
crises and stresses. It is not surprising that people seek treatment for committed relationship problems more than for any other issue (Veroff,
Kulka, & Douvan, 1981). This finding is particularly relevant to social
workers inasmuch as social workers comprise a significant percentage of
the clinical practitioners who staff family treatment centers, employee assistance programs (EAPs), hospitals, community centers, counseling centers housed and operated under the auspices of religious organizations
(e.g., Jewish Family Services, Catholic Social Services, Lutheran Social
Services), university counseling centers, and other social agencies. In addition to agency-based service delivery, growing numbers of social workers are working in private practice, the setting in which most couples
treatment in the United States is provided. Collectively, social workers in
both public and private settings are providing a remarkable percentage of
couple treatment. Based on the evidence that social workers provide a
significant percentage of direct counseling services and that intimate relationship problems are often the issues for which treatment is sought,
it behooves social workers and social workers in training to develop
their knowledge and skills in couple treatment. The purpose of this chapter is to provide social workers with effective methods for the treatment

of problems in intimate committed relationships. The conceptualization of couple functioning and treatment and clinical procedures presented in this chapter are highly relevant for same gendered couples. As I have addressed elsewhere, same gendered couples are confronted with many of the same issues, frustrations, and problems as are heterosexual couples (Granvold & Martin, 1999).

The beginnings of marital and family therapy can be traced to the early thirties when several marital treatment centers were founded specifically for the treatment of couple relational problems (Olson, 1975). Through the decades, the couple treatment field has embraced a myriad of treatment approaches in search of effective methods to help couples attain levels of satisfaction worthy of maintaining their unions. The burgeoning divorce rate through the latter period of the 20th century is a powerful indicator that there has been a remarkable increase in couples' expectations of what it takes to remain committed. It could be hypothesized that many of the methods shown to be effective in the past would likely fall short of the clinical demands of contemporary couples.

The provision of effective treatment of couple distress has been more than a formidable challenge to couple therapists during all eras. Reporting on the effectiveness of marital therapy in the recent past, Gottman (1999) indicates that "the therapeutic effects of the therapies that have been scientifically evaluated are generally weak, and there is a very high relapse rate" (p. 5). He goes on to state that the results of his longitudinal studies show a strong positive correlation between couples treatment and divorce. Further research results indicate that approximately 35% of couples in marital treatment make immediate change. However, for many, those changes are relatively short-lived. Lasting clinically meaningful change has been found in only 11% to 18% of couples receiving treatment in controlled study programs.

These findings suggest that there is little likelihood of effective treatment of couple distress with the best of interventions. This said, it is even more critical that therapists select treatment methods with demonstrated effectiveness. Cognitive behavior methods have been highly scrutinized in their application to a myriad of clinical problems resulting in demonstrated treatment efficacy (Beck, J. S., 1995; Clark, Beck, & Alford, 1999; Granvold, 1997). It is the strength of treatment efficacy that has driven this widespread application of cognitive behavior interventions to diverse problems and populations. This chapter describes and depicts the use of cognitive behavior methods to ameliorate problems in intimate relationships.

REVIEW OF LITERATURE

History of Cognitive Behavior Couple Therapy

The evolution of cognitive behavior couple therapy (CBCT) can be traced to behavioral marital therapy (BMT), which was largely developed in the 1970s (Hurvitz, 1975; Jacobson & Margolin, 1979; Lieberman, 1975; Stuart, 1969, 1980; Weiss, 1978; Weiss, Hops, & Patterson, 1973). The focus of BMT intervention was on change in observable behavior. Treatment strategies utilized the application of reinforcement principles and operant conditioning, behavior exchange contracting, communication skills training, problem-solving skill training, and modeling and behavior rehearsal. BMT, characterized as a behavioral skills deficit model, ultimately was considered to be too restrictive in focus (Baucom & Epstein, 1990; Baucom, Epstein, & LaTaillade, 2002; Dattilio, Epstein, & Baucom, 1998; Epstein & Baucom, 2002; Jacobson & Christensen, 1996). It became increasingly evident that cognitive factors play a critical function in couple distress, dysfunction, and dissatisfaction. Expectations regarding intimate relationships; interpretations including causal attributions; beliefs, values, and moral perspectives; core beliefs about self (self-schemata); and other aspects of meaning making became recognized as viable elements in partners' views of their own and their mate's behaviors. Not only were cognitive factors viewed as meaningful in the assessment of relational problems, they were considered to be ripe targets for intervention. There is little doubt that couples receiving BMT experienced meaningful cognitive changes as byproducts of their behavioral change efforts. In essence, cognitive variables have always enhanced or deterred outcomes of behaviorally focused interventions. Isolating cognitions to help explain the etiology of couple distress and utilizing specific cognitive change methodologies represents a far more viable approach to treatment than focusing only on behavior change.

Although CBCT can be traced largely to BMT, independent efforts to treat couple distress through cognitive change were being made by cognitivists during the years BMT was enjoying success and popularity. As early as the late fifties and early sixties Ellis and his colleagues began applying Rational Emotive Therapy (RET) to treat couples (Ellis, 1977; Ellis & Harper, 1961; Ellis, Sichel, Yeager, DiMattia, & DiGiuseppe, 1989). During the seventies and eighties, based on their success with the application of cognitive methods to other disorders, a significant number of cognitivists developed, applied, and reported the application of cognitive methods for the assessment and treatment of couples (Abrahms, 1983; Dattilio & Padesky, 1990; Epstein, 1983; Granvold, 1988).

During the years that BMT and CBCT were developing, a parallel development was taking place in the marriage and family therapy (MFT) field. The early development of the MFT field "was spearheaded by theorists and clinicians who eschewed mental health models that focused on internal psychological processes and linear causality in favor of observable family interaction patterns and the circular causal concepts of systems theory (Nichols & Schwartz, 2001)" (Dattilio & Epstein, 2005, pp. 7–8). Only recently has CBCT received more widespread acceptance among MFT practitioners. Dattilio and Epstein (2005) identify a number of factors contributing to the enhanced appeal of cognitive interventions among MFTs. There has been a movement toward evidence-based practice within the MFT field in which treatment outcomes are empirically validated. Other factors include: (1) the proactive approach to relational issues, (2) emphasis on a collaborative relationship between clients and therapist characteristic of postmodern approaches, (3) the flexibility and integrative potential of CBCT methods facilitating their incorporation with other favored approaches among MFTs, and (4) the recent broadening of CBCT to include consideration of contextual factors that take into account "aspects of the couple or family's physical and interpersonal environment (e.g., extended family, the workplace, neighborhood violence, national socioeconomic conditions)" (p. 10). See Epstein et al., (2002) for a detailed presentation of enhanced cognitive behavior couples therapy in which broader contextual aspects of coupling are elements of assessment and couple treatment strategies.

Cognitive behavior couple treatment practiced 40 years ago has evolved through the innovative and creative efforts of many. The model of CBCT currently practiced by many contemporary practitioners is highly compatible with traditional social work principles involving more holistic views of the individual and with the person in social context perspective. The *reciprocal determinism* model, advanced by Bandura (1978), stipulates that behavior, cognition, and personal factors (emotion, motivation, physiology, and physical factors) and social/environmental factors are considered to be interactive, overlapping, and mutually influential. This model is more evident in the applications of cognitive behavior approaches to couple problems today in which the circularity of cognitive, emotive, and behavioral factors is recognized and addressed. Interaction *patterns* derived either from the current union or from the individual's family of origin, physical health and physical conditioning factors, and broader contextual factors may be evident in CBCT case conceptualizations and treatment plans. Contextual factors include such issues as work factors (stress, career goals, performance demands, support, socialization), spirituality and its social/community expression, economic success or inadequacy, and physical environmental comfort or inadequacy/vulnerability. In conceptualizing an enhanced approach to CBCT, Epstein and Baucom (2002) isolate the previous contextual factors for assessment and intervention. They note that cognitive behavior approaches "generally have emphasized detailed analyses of specific relationship events or microbehaviors without commensurate attention to couples' long-term, macrobehavioral patterns and the couple's experiences of relationship themes" (p. 13).

Another departure from early BMT and CBCT models is the emphasis on identifying and building on the couple's strengths. Epstein and Baucom (2002) note that traditionally there has been an emphasis on negative cognitions and behaviors in couple distress with little attention focused on the role of positive cognitions, behaviors, and emotions in the couple's relationship. The widespread adoption of the "strengths perspective" in social work (Saleebey, 2002b) and the movement advanced by postmodernists (and many others) throughout the helping professions away from the pathology model to empowerment and the enhancement of possibilities are evident in the treatment efforts of many CBCT therapists. (See the following for discussion of the depathologization of human distress and the promotion of empowerment and possibilities: Granvold, 2001; Mahoney, 2000; Raskin & Lewandowski, 2000; Saleebey, 2002a). While there is wisdom in teasing out flaws in cognitive, emotive, and behavioral functioning for which change strategies should be developed, there is great merit in defining and accentuating the many ways the couple effectively functions. Gottman (1999) notes that effective functioning is not represented in freedom from conflict and negativity but rather it is the couple's repair strategies facilitating dialogue about their differences that mark nondistressed couples. This research finding is one example demonstrating the potential pitfall in emphasizing the negativity of couple conflict (problem) instead of focusing on the couple's repair behaviors (strengths).

Status of Current Research

Cognitive behavior couple therapy has been researched extensively. Baucom and his colleagues conducted a comprehensive review of CBCT outcome studies and concluded that the approach is effective in reducing marital distress (Baucom, Shoham, Mueser, Daiuto, & Stickle, 1998). It is noteworthy that the interventions more focused on behavior change produced greater behavior change, while the interventions more focused on cognitive restructuring produced greater cognitive change. Gottman (1999) contends that "what we need is a real theory of how marriages work and fail to work, and that theory ought to emerge from a study of what real couples do to accomplish the everyday 'tasks' of being married"

(p. 7). To satisfy this objective, he developed a marriage laboratory at the University of Washington. This "up close and personal" assessment of couple interaction and individual physiological responses has produced a myriad of specific conclusions about coupling that Gottman has then used to predict divorce or sustained commitment.

When it comes to what works to produce significant, desirable change in human behavior, the status of CBCT research is no different than that of individual therapy research. We have yet to determine what specifically produces change (i.e., therapy process factors). It is my belief that intervention must be closely tailored to the idiosyncratic characteristics of the individual/couple rather than one-size-fits-all manualized procedures. CBCT meets this requirement inasmuch as a defining principle of cognitive therapy is the exposure of beliefs, values, information processing patterns, and other cognitive factors *unique* to the client. While cognitive behavior procedures continue to be promising, additional research is needed to explicate specific intervention elements, therapist behaviors, and treatment formats that promote efficacy.

FACTORS FOR CONSIDERATION IN CBCT

Providing a clear explanation of what CBCT therapists do to promote change in couple relationships forces a rather linear explanation of human functioning and human change best conceptualized with an atomic model. The aspects of the human condition one must consider (behavior, cognition, emotion, physical/physiological, social/environmental) are best understood in terms of the properties and interactions of the component elements. The specific properties of the component parts are highly variable from person to person and for each individual from occasion to occasion. Furthermore, the components are highly interactive and mutually influential (Bandura, 1985; Granvold, 1994). Although the descriptions of variables will be addressed separately, keep in mind that all components are highly interactive. In some measure, it is impossible to isolate specific contributions of component parts to human functioning. The following example may serve to illustrate this point. In their recent modification of traditional behavior couple therapy, Jacobson et al. (1996) proffered *acceptance* as the missing link in traditional behavior therapy. A key element of acceptance is the couple "letting go" of the effort to change one another. To do so is a *cognitive* activity—a decision must be made to abandon the expectation that one's partner will change. Furthermore, a concomitant behavior change takes place as a consequence (if "letting go" actually happened) and that is that behavioral efforts to promote partner change stop. There are likely to be emotional consequences that could take many forms. For example, the partner may experience frustration over the "undesirable" behavior of the mate while resigned to no change, or alternatively the partner could feel relief (emotional comfort) as a consequence of the "acceptance." What kind of change has taken place and why? It is obvious that change has taken place cognitively, emotionally, and behaviorally. Were we capable of tracking the partner physiologically, we would likely discover changes in physiology related to her acceptance as well.

As you read the remainder of this chapter, keep in mind the interactive nature of the components of the human condition. An intervention aimed at a change in one component will necessarily result in some degree of change in other components. The remainder of this section addresses specific considerations for implementing CBCT.

First, CBCT addresses both: (1) individual psychological factors contributing to the development and maintenance of relationship discord, and (2) interactional factors that influence couple functioning. While psychological problems may be the consequence of distress and unhappiness in an intimate relationship, one mate's psychological problems (e.g., depression, anxiety, grief and loss, posttraumatic stress disorder (PTSD), anger, childhood sexual abuse survivorship) may be in large part the cause of distress, dissention, and unhappiness in the couple's relationship. The co-occurrence of depression and marital discord is a useful case in point. Many studies have found that depression significantly contributes to marital unhappiness and often relationship unhappiness is the primary causal factor in depression (Beach, 2000; Beach, Sandeen, & O'Leary, 1990; Beach, Whisman, & O'Leary, 1994; Hickey et al., 2005; Karney & Bradbury, 1995). Although a reciprocal relationship exists between depression and relationship distress, intervention may be focused on depression. When intervention is biased toward individual change, the therapist may draw from cognitive behavior literature in selecting an efficacious treatment strategy. Many effective cognitive behavior interventions have been developed for the treatment of a broad range of emotional disorders and behavioral problems (Beck, J., 1995; Granvold, 1997).

Second, in CBCT cognitive and behavioral components of human functioning are targeted for change based on the view that these components are powerful interactively and in their impact on other components of human functioning. As noted earlier, a change in one aspect of the human system effects change in all others. Cognitive and behavioral change are emphasized with the expectancy that emotional change, in particular, will follow. Stated another way, emotional change in couples is typically accomplished through cognitive and behavioral change. Furthermore, although change in emotion may not be a stated goal, it is highly likely that emotional change will occur concomitantly with behavior and cognitive change. Altered ways of viewing one another and the modification of specific behaviors may effectively enhance individual emotional well-being and produce greater positive feelings toward the mate in specific areas as well as globally.

Third, consistent with the social work profession traditionally and the enhanced CBCT model of Epstein et al. (2002), environmental and social contextual factors are given consideration. The physical environment often contributes to the stressors experienced by the couple. Crowding, lack of privacy (individual/couple), inadequate climate control, lack of safety, and neighborhood conflict represent external demands that impact the couple's lives. Work requirements, parenting and extended family relationships and responsibilities (e.g., elderly parent living in the home), social priorities (e.g., friendships, volunteerism, clubs and organizations), and Internet activities take time and energy resources from the relationship. Social/environmental aspects of the couple's lives may serve as positive elements enhancing their relationship (assets) or, alternatively, may produce negative effects on the union.

Fourth, each partner's physical health, physical conditioning, and other embodiment aspects of their life routines (e.g., relaxation, meditation, touch) may have a significant impact on the couple's relationship. Mahoney (1991) notes that the techniques and domains most neglected by psychotherapy researchers are those involving human embodiment. Many physical illnesses and their treatments have emotional and physical limitation consequences potentially taxing to the relationship. Physical conditioning through exercise and sports programs and embodiment aspects of stress management efforts (e.g., deep muscle relaxation, nutrition, sleep) promote optimal personal preparation to meet the stress demands of contemporary living. Shared physical activities and touch are also effective ways for the couple to enhance intimacy in the relationship. Another common contributor to relationship problems is substance use/abuse by one or both partners. The couple should be assessed regarding the use of prescription drugs, illicit drugs, and alcohol. Particular attention should be given to the role these behaviors play in the couple's relationship. Substance abuse often produces erratic behavior, errors in judgement, and other cognitive processing impairment, poor impulse control, and impaired conflict management.

COGNITIVE FACTORS IN COUPLE RELATIONSHIPS

Most of us are socialized to process information in distorted ways. We learn to view the world from a "center of the universe" perspective and meaningful adults in our environment (parents, teachers, media models) teach us flawed ways of meaning making. We learn to perceive through biased and erroneous lenses, and to make causal connections (why actions take place) without adequate supportive evidence. I believe that a developmental challenge of adulthood is to unlearn the cognitive distortions that we have been taught and to replace them with more valid (verifiable) and viable (of positive consequence) ways of interpreting our world and other people's actions. Errors in cognitive processing (information processing errors) are often present in the interactions of distressed couples (Beck, 1988).

Each partner brings to the relationship a unique personal history, expectations or assumptions about relationships, and personal strengths and limitations. Family of origin experiences, prior relationship history, and other societal coupling models contribute to the development of relationship expectations and prepare the individual behaviorally to partner. Much of what individuals believe about commitment, expectations about specific ways of functioning as a couple, and expectancies about change and adaptation over time is retained consciously. Other cognitive processing, however, occurs at an abstract level, outside awareness boundaries. The products of this cognitive functioning are called *schemas*. These core beliefs have a profound impact on the individual's views of self, the world, and the future (Beck, Rush, Shaw, & Emery, 1979). In addition to self-schemas, in committed relationships schemas are formed and maintained about the partner and partnering (couple schemas). Schemas tend to be difficult to access and, once accessed, are change resistant. Surface held beliefs and schemas (both self-schemas and couple schemas) are tremendously influential in the development and maintenance of an intimate relationship. Normative and nonnormative relationship functioning may be traced to beliefs about the fulfillment of individual and relationship desires.

Cognitive Processing Errors

Cognitive processing may result in meaning distortion. Processing involves functions such as perception, selection, concentration, recall, coding, cognitive elaboration, reasoning, decision making, and impulse control. Beck (1988) notes that errors in cognitive processing typical of those with psychological disorders are frequently evident in distressed couples. Couples who seek therapy in crisis are even more likely to evidence cognitive distortions since extreme stress disrupts normative processing functions (Beck, 1993). The consequences of extreme stress

> are that the individual is highly vulnerable to cognitive distortions,
> the activation thresholds of dysfunctional schemata become lowered

significantly, voluntary control processes become impaired, and the individual becomes hypervigilant and hypersensitive to "threatening" stimuli. This erosion in cognitive functioning leaves the individual vulnerable to extreme emotional responses and the activation of uncharacteristic or dysfunctional behavior. (Granvold, 2000, p. 374)

Elsewhere, others and I have enumerated common errors in cognitive processing useful in working with couples (Beck, 1988; Dattilio & Padesky, 1990; Epstein et al., 2002; Granvold, 1988, 1998; Granvold & Jordan, 1994):

- *Absolutistic and dichotomous thinking.* Viewing experiences, objects, and situations in a polarized manner.
- *Overgeneralization.* Reaching a conclusion or drawing a general rule on the basis of minimal evidence and applying the concept across the board to all related and unrelated situations.
- *Selective attention.* Focusing on the negative in a situation, ignoring other positive (sometimes more salient) features, and viewing the entire experience as negative, based on the selective view.
- *Arbitrary inference.* Reaching a negative conclusion on the basis of minimal supportive evidence or in light of evidence to the contrary.
- *Magnification and Minimization.* Attaching a greater or lesser meaning than fits the circumstance.
- *Personalization.* Involves making a causal connection between a negative event or situation and oneself without adequate supportive evidence.
- *Negative attribution.* Reaching a conclusion about the cause or motivation behind a behavior or event.

Schematic Functioning

Underlying beliefs about oneself, one's mate, and about coupling serve as the basis upon which partners automatically evaluate the relationship in specific instances and generally. Meaning making is largely the consequence of these rapid cognitive transactions. Schemas "are relatively enduring internal structures of stored generic or prototypical features of stimuli, ideas, or experiences that are used to organize new information in a meaningful way thereby determining how phenomena are perceived and conceptualized" (Clark et al., 1999, p. 79). Identified in the etiology and treatment of various psychological disorders, schemas play a role in both normative and nonnormative couple functioning. Young has developed a schema model in which he describes and categorizes early maladaptive schemas, unconditional beliefs about self that form early in life, and has delineated the ways they function in human disturbance. Schemas develop early, are elaborated through life, and interrelate forming a meaning matrix. This schematic matrix serves as the basis for orienting oneself temporally—past, present, and future—and is reflected in pervasive themes about self and one's relationships with others (McGinn & Young, 1996). Maladaptive schemas are conceptualized as being responsible for interpreting life from a perspective of distrust, defective, emotionally needy, incompetent, and other disadvantageous states.

Gaining access to schemas may be accomplished through a Socratic dialogue starting with beliefs held at the conscious level. For example, a man reports being upset over his wife's plans to go out of town to a business meeting.

THERAPIST: What would it mean to you if your wife goes on the business trip?

CLIENT: She thinks more about work than she does me.

THERAPIST: What would it mean to you if work was more important to her than you at times?

CLIENT: I'm going to lose her. I was afraid that when we married, she'd end up divorcing me no matter how hard I tried.

This excerpt exposes an intimate relationship incompetency schema that is activated by his wife's situational priority on work. The exposed schema would become the focus of consideration therapeutically. Attention would be devoted to early life experiences that may have contributed to schematic formation and couple relationship history in which this view was reinforced (e.g., threats of divorce). Evidence contradictory to the client's schema would be sought and emphasized. It should be noted, however, that evidence that contradicts maladaptive schemas may have little initial impact on the reduction of their strength. It takes repetition to modify core beliefs and it is highly likely that they will never be eliminated. More realistic therapeutic goals are to reduce the strength of maladaptive schemas and to enhance the strength of competing beliefs. (See Neimeyer, 1993, for further explanation of the "downward arrow" procedure demonstrated in the dialogue.)

Expectations

Couples commit to a relationship with expectations about self as a mate and expectations about coupling. There are four types of expectations.

First, there are *explicitly stated and agreed upon* expectations. These expectations have been discussed by the couple and agreed upon or, alternatively, there is behavioral evidence of agreement. For example, if they both share the joys of playing co-ed softball, their behavior would support the expectation that playing softball together is desirable. There are two immediate flaws in explicitly held and agreed upon expectations. First, there is a tendency to generalize the expectation. Suppose Janie enjoys playing co-ed softball with Bill, but really prefers playing tennis with others. Bill may *generalize* the expectation that he and Janie play softball together to playing all sporting activities together. He may further assume that, since there is behavioral evidence that he and Janie play sports together, Janie is in agreement. Second, people *change!* A common eventuation about which many jokes have been made is that precommitment and early relationship behaviors modify greatly over time. Although the couple may have enjoyed playing softball together, other priorities may capture the desires of one or the other and displace the commitment to softball.

A second set of expectations is those that are *explicitly stated and agreed upon, but lack compliance*. Belief, attitude, and opinion are, at times, poor predictors of behavior. Due to human limitations, flaws, and shortcomings a mate may agree with an expectation but fail to satisfy it. Examples are anger control and controlled substance use. The mate may be highly committed to impulse control and demonstrate noncompliance. A further example of expectations in this category is the development of an extramarital relationship. The literature indicates that few who enter into such relationships believe that their behavior is desirable or appropriate. The relationship evolves in conflict with personal values and in violation of personal commitment.

The third set of expectations is those that are *explicitly stated with disagreement*. These expectations often form around issues of control. The desire of one is met with resistance or unwillingness from the other. Although this type of expectation may be evident during dating, they become more frequent later in relationships. Jeff wants Josie to call him if she is going to arrive home later than a half hour past her typical arrival time. Josie thinks that she should not have to be this "accountable" just because she is in a committed relationship with Jeff.

The fourth set of expectations is the most common. These are *implicitly held expectations* that require inferential reasoning for the mate to become aware. They frequently become evident as a mate is criticized by the partner for behavior committed or omitted. "If you loved me you'd know" represents expectations which, at least in the mind of one partner, do not require explication. Obviously, there are many expectations that reasonably belong in this category and for which one can expect little misunderstanding or noncompliance. However, should this category of expectation be significantly expanded or a partner function rather obtusely in relationship matters, the likely consequences are hurt, disappointment, dissatisfaction, and conflict.

It has been hypothesized that those who set expectations of their relationship too high are at risk of dissolving the relationship. Gottman (1999) found evidence to the contrary. Those couples who set their expectations high, including romantic ones, had better relationships than those who didn't. It follows that therapists would do well to encourage and support lofty expectations, facilitate the clear explication of these desires, and guide couples in realizing their dreams.

BEHAVIORAL FACTORS IN COUPLE RELATIONSHIPS

As indicated in the introduction to this chapter, CBCT evolved from behavioral marital therapy. The use of behavioral change methods to enhance relationship functioning has been extensively researched. The results indicate that behavior change is a viable avenue to modify couple functioning in specific areas such as communication, conflict management, and sexual functioning. In addition, behavior change in which there is an increase in the couple's positive behavior and pleasure activities tends to promote corresponding increases in subjective satisfaction with the relationship.

Cognitive, Emotive, and Behavior Reinforcement

It has long been recognized that learning theory provides a valid explanation of human behavior. People tend to behave in ways that are reinforcing. *Reinforcement* is defined as "any contingent event that alters the likelihood that a particular behavior will be emitted. *Motivation* describes the need state that increases the salience of a particular reinforcement" (Alexander, Jameson, Newell, & Gunderson, 1996, p. 180). It is not enough that a reinforcing consequence may be anticipated for a given behavior, the individual must exist with a desire for the consequence to demonstrate the behavior. Furthermore, in applying reinforcement principles to couples it should be emphasized that contingencies of reinforcement are variable from person to person, from occasion to occasion, and within a given social encounter.

The principles of reinforcement apply not only to overt behavior, but to cognition and emotion as well. As noted earlier, we learn ways of cognitive processing, develop beliefs, and form cognitive habits. The rules of learning that contributed to the development of cognition functioning may be applied to cognitive change. Cognitions can be modified through observation, modeling, shaping, reinforcement, conditioning, and counter-conditioning.

Emotions are also subject to reinforcement. The mate's responses to the partner's emotional expressions may serve to reinforce the affect state. The effect may be prolonged negative affect and an increased likelihood that similar emotional states will be expressed in the future. Some couples develop patterns in which a partner is emotionally coerced to behave in a "desired" way. The use of anger is a prime example of this phenomenon. "If you don't comply with my wishes, I'll get angry." Compliance on the part of the "coerced" partner inadvertently serves to reinforce this mal-adaptive pattern of emotional expressiveness.

Reinforcement Erosion or Increase?

Jacobson and Margolin (1979) hypothesized that partner behavior may decrease in reinforcement value over time. The meaning of shared experiences and behavior (e.g., interests, hobbies, talk time, sex) was considered to decrease in meaning the longer the couple are together. This phenomenon may actually characterize distressed couples. Gottman (1999) found evidence to the contrary in his research on older couples. Desire to spend time together and affection increased the longer the couple was married. Questions remain to be answered regarding the differences in marriages in which there is erosion in desire and frequency to spend time together and those in which there is not.

From Behavior Exchange to Noncontingent Positivity

In the early work in BMT, it was hypothesized that couple behavior is characterized by an approximately equitable behavior exchange of positives and negatives. The goal of "behavior exchange interventions" was to assist couples in reducing their negative behavior exchanges and increasing positive exchanges. This give-to-get model evolved over time to a noncontingent positivity approach promoting an overall increase in positive behavior routinely. Couples have been encouraged to engage in more positive behavior, random acts of kindness and caring, and expressions of positive feelings and affection toward their partner without expecting reciprocation. Such acts have been found to yield positive dividends. Increased levels of positivity leads to the creation of positive sentiment override (PSO). Weiss (1980) contended that responses to a negative gesture may be determined by the global positivity within a couple relationship, resulting in a neutral or positive response to a negative gesture. The potentially negative impact of the gesture is absorbed by

PSO. Alternatively, a partner in a relationship in which global positivity is absent is likely to evidence negative sentiment override (NSO). When NSO is active, positive behaviors are screened out, viewed neutrally, or ascribed negative attributions (e.g., "You are being nice to me just because my parents are visiting us").

Negative reciprocity has been found to exist to a degree in both distressed and nondistressed couples. Most couples respond to negative affect with negative affect. More important than stopping negative exchanges is to facilitate the development of effective repair strategies when negativity occurs. Even though the couple may not be able to resolve certain "perpetual" problems, maintaining an open dialogue about the conflict may allow them to forge some degree of progress over time. From his extensive research of couples, Gottman (1999) concluded that "the two necessary 'staples' of marriages that work (whatever their typology) are (1) an overall level of positive affect, and (2) an ability to reduce negative affect during conflict resolution" (p. 105). Treatment strategies should focus on ways that the couple can increase global positivity and the development of strategies to both remove barriers and build effective patterns of repair.

COGNITIVE INTERVENTION STRATEGIES

The initial goals of the therapist in cognitive intervention are: (1) to join the couple in their unique ways of meaning making, (2) to understand through cognitive conceptual lenses the specific cognitive elements that appear to promote personal and relationship well-being and those that do not, (3) to gain enough understanding through interviewing and Socratic questioning to make it possible to identify interaction patterns that appear to characterize their relationship, and (4) through the relationship with the couple to bring these insights into their awareness. The following information is important to learn from the couple:

- What are their expectations regarding problems and problem resolution?
- Does each partner appear to be open to change?
- Are cognitive distortions readily evident in their expressions or descriptions of problematic interactions?
- Do their explanations of the motive(s) or cause of their mate's behavior (attributions) tend to be negative? Do they seek to validate their views? Are causal beliefs retained even though there is evidence to the contrary?
- What beliefs support and promote effective couple functioning?

- What beliefs appear to interfere with effective couple functioning?
- How closely do their "realities" (meanings) match? Are their interpretations of life highly disparate/similar?
- What are their expectations about coupling in key areas? Are these expectations explicit and to what extent is there agreement/compliance?
- Is one or the other partner functioning with an active maladaptive schema that is influencing personal and/or relationship unhappiness?
- In conceptualizing the couple's relationship, are there patterns of interaction or relationship themes (e.g., togetherness/independency; intimacy/distance) that recur? In what areas of the relationship do these patterns surface?

There is an educational component to cognitive intervention. Early in treatment as part of role structuring, cognitive factors and behavior are identified as targets of change. Meanings of cognition and the impact of cognitive functioning on couple distress are discussed. If possible, specific examples are taken from the couple's interactions to explicate meanings and to determine the effects on their relationship. Cognitive change requires repetitive applications. The process is initiated in session but must be transferred to their daily interactions outside therapy. The objective is for the couple to modify cognitive functioning either privately through internal dialogue or interpersonally in their communication. It is the therapist's responsibility to guide the couple in becoming experts on the use of cognitive change uniquely tailored to them individually and as a couple.

Meaning Making

The predominant deficiency in couples cognitively is in their interpretation of meanings. Couples do not share reality, they share experiences. The meaning of a shared experience becomes each partner's personal "reality." The likelihood that the couple's meanings of shared experiences will consistently "match" is slim. Certainly, living together allows couples the opportunity to know one another better than others in their respective personal domains. Nevertheless, the margin for error is great. Some individuals become so confident in their knowledge of the mate that they express (and believe) that they know the mate better than the mate knows himself or herself! In these circumstances the strength of an objective perspective becomes pitted against self-awareness. In a therapy session, Alice expressed that she didn't mean to come across insensitively to her husband's boss at a recent social gathering. Alice's husband, Joe, said, "Bullshit, you knew exactly what you were doing. You were ugly!" Joe is either saying that he knows Alice better than she knows herself or he is implying that Alice is being untruthful. The therapeutic challenge is to determine if Joe's interpretation is cognitively distorted or if there is veracity to his meanings. Alice admitted to being in a "mood" that day. *Did she act with a lack of self-awareness at that moment?* To this point, Joe is interpreting (stated as *truth*) *what* took place (Alice was knowingly insensitive). Joe went on to angrily say, "You were moody with Sandy because you've never trusted her with me." This is a negative attribution, a statement of implied causality. Joe has shifted his interpretation of this experience from *what* took place to *why* Alice behaved as she did.

Much of the time I spend on cognitive aspects of couple interaction is devoted to the clarification of meanings, both *what* and *why*. The couple is encouraged to embrace the view that meanings are proprietary. Each is guided in the expression of his or her views and exploration of factors (e.g., personal history, beliefs, developmental stage) they consider to have contributed to the meaning. This presents the mate with an opportunity to better *understand* his or her partner. The following excerpt demonstrates this process. Doris and Larry went to their farm for the weekend. Doris arose early Sunday morning, did some chores, and returned to the bedroom to awaken Larry. Larry got angry with Doris for awakening him so early and Doris got angry with Larry for failing to welcome her "rise and shine" invitation with positiveness.

DON: What were you thinking, Doris, when you came to awaken Larry?

DORIS: First, I was thinking that it was nice of me to let Larry sleep in while I got up at 6:00 A.M. to do some chores. Then, at 8:00 A.M. I figured that since we agreed to get work done at the farm, I should get Larry up before it got too hot.

DON: Thank you for that explanation, Doris. Now Larry, what were your thoughts when Doris awakened you Sunday morning?

LARRY: I thought that we had an agreement that the one day I would sleep in is Sunday. I go to the farm for leisure, not just to work. I work hard all week in town. The last thing that I want to do is work all weekend. I mowed for 3 hours on Saturday. It is not like I don't *do* anything at the farm.

This served as a beginning of an exploration into several issues. Through further questioning Doris disclosed that she was ashamed of her household as an adolescent because it was in such a state of disarray. Furthermore, her mother was the only one who did any housework. Doris wants Larry to share in the work and to make the farmhouse "presentable" so that they can entertain. Larry was unaware of how strongly Doris felt about her family's "messy" house when she was growing up. Larry explained that he wants to improve the farm, but not at the *pace* that

Doris apparently wants it done (and he is *not* interested in entertaining). Doris agreed that she wants improvements to be made faster. The *meaning* of awakening Larry (being awakened by Doris) was expanded and clarified through this discussion. Further discussion exposed greater understanding of each mate's views about work, leisure, division of labor, having house guests, and timelines. Through therapist encouragement, before leaving the session the couple agreed on a specific project to improve the farm and set a target date for its completion.

Cognitive Restructuring

Cognitive processing errors, faulty attributions, and beliefs underlying couple conflict may be isolated for cognitive restructuring. The first step is to identify a specific cognitive phenomenon that is considered to be contributing to negative views of the mate, negative feelings, or conflict. Once isolated, the Socratic method is used to seek evidence to support the view, to identify evidence to the contrary, and to expose consequences. The goal is to collaborate with the client in seeking alternative ways of thinking that are more valid and of greater utility (Beck, J., 1995). *Validity* is the appraisal of how accurately the belief matches "objective" reality. "The *utility of a cognition* refers to how functional or adaptive it is in the individual's life and the couple's relationship" (Epstein et al, 2002, p. 348). In the following clinical example, a negative attribution is central to the couple's current conflict. Willie believes that Natasha came to his family reunion late out of disrespect for his family. Natasha explained that she had to stop by work the morning of the reunion and that she needed to stay at work longer than she had thought. Furthermore, she professed great love and respect for *most*, but not all, of Willie's family. Willie was asked by the therapist how he felt toward Natasha when he thinks that she doesn't respect his family. He said that he feels angry and somewhat hurt. The therapist explained the concept of negative attribution to Willie and Natasha. Then Willie was guided in determining other possible explanations for Natasha being late as alternatives to the belief that she was late due to disrespect for his family. He arrived at the conclusion that she is a very dedicated professional and she needed to continue working at the hospital until the staffing problem was handled. Willie was then asked to identify specific behavior on Natasha's behalf that showed respect for his family. Willie responded with a half dozen examples and Natasha chimed in with a couple more. Willie was then asked if he could find any evidence to support his initial conclusion other than Natasha's arrival at the reunion at 4:00 P.M. instead of noon. He could not. Based on the evidence, Willie was asked to consider modifying his thoughts about Natasha arriving late. "If you shift your view from, 'she was late out of disrespect for my family' to 'she was late because she had to work and she got there as soon as she could,' how do you feel toward Natasha?" Willie said that he didn't feel angry or hurt when he thought of it that way—that he actually realized how good he feels about her as a dedicated manager.

Following this cognitive restructuring, Willie was asked to monitor his negative attributions, seek evidence to support them and to think of competing explanations for the causal conclusions that he reaches in specific instances.

BEHAVIORAL INTERVENTION STRATEGIES

The two categories of behavior change that will be addressed here are: (1) increasing behaviors that are already in the couple's repertoire or that require little "technical" training to demonstrate, and (2) skills development.

Promoting Positive Behavior

The importance of markedly increasing positive behavior in the relationship without the expectation of reciprocation is emphasized. The couple is asked to identify the ways they showed kindness, caring, affection, and supportiveness to one another in the past. They are asked if there are any particular barriers that are interfering with the objective of greatly increasing positive behavior. If, for example, extreme emotional distance characterizes the current state of the relationship, the couple is asked what they are willing to do. Even though it may be minimal, the expectation of behavior change is maintained. Each partner is asked to express behaviors that they desire from the mate. Oftentimes it is at this juncture that a cognitive intervention is interjected. If one or both partners say that they don't *feel* like doing an activity or behavior desired by the spouse, like going out to dinner, they are gently challenged. After determining their objections, if it is really a matter that they would just as soon not go out to dinner, I proceed as follows:

DON: Do you mow your own lawn? (Hopefully you already know that they do. If they don't, select a task they do that has a low reward value associated with it.)

LOUIS: Yes I do, every Saturday morning during mowing season.

DON: Have you ever awakened Saturday morning with a burning desire to mow the lawn?

LOUIS: I can't say that I have.

DON: How is it that you do it, if you don't really want to.

LOUIS: I just do it.

DON: You have come to me with the desire to improve your marriage. You are willing to mow your lawn even though you really don't want to. Would you be willing to go to dinner with Tina even though you would just as soon not go? (The implication: Is your marriage as important to you as your lawn?)

I may suggest that they adopt the phrase, "I can't afford to wait for the want to!"

The partners are asked to be vigilant of the positive efforts that their mate is making and to acknowledge the specific behavior demonstrated. In this way, desired behaviors may be reinforced, raising the likelihood that they will be repeated.

Skills-Based Interventions

Initially or during the course of treatment it may become apparent that the couple lacks relationship skills that are considered essential in satisfying a deficiency or may greatly enhance the relationship. Communication problems have been identified as the greatest area of limitation among unhappy couples. Communication skills may be the focus of instruction in session. There are many healthy rules of communication, decision making, and conflict management for application to the major communication deficiencies apparent in couple's relationship. As extra session work, the couple may be asked to audiorecord their discussions as a means of getting a baseline assessment of their communication skills, to gain insight into specific communication flaws, and to track improvement as treatment progresses. As adjuncts to in-session didactic instruction, discussion, and rehearsal, the couple is encouraged to improve their communication skills through the use of books, videotapes, lectures, and seminars.

Other common skills deficit areas include parenting, anger control, and intimacy and sexuality. As with communication, both in-session and extra session approaches should be utilized. Materials recommended for extra session use should be reviewed by the therapist and tailored to the couple's specific skill development needs.

CONCLUSION

In this chapter, I have tried to provide a view of the evolution of CBCT identifying the predominant influence of BMT along with the work of early cognitivists. The progress has been shaped largely by the results of empirical research. Insights into significant differences between distressed and nondistressed couples and outcomes from rigorous evaluations of treatment procedures are evident in the form of CBCT presented here. The current model is broader in scope including consideration of environmental factors, places greater emphasis on the interactive effects among factors, and reflects a shift in emphasis from deficits to strengths. Cognitive and behavioral aspects of couple functioning have been described and CBCT intervention procedures have been presented.

Evidence-based practice is the standard for clinical social work practice today. The seventies marked the "age of accountability" in social work. The expectation was clearly sounded that practice at all levels (micro, mezzo, and macro) be evaluated. Clinically, the objective was to determine if interventions were effective in helping people change. Cognitive behavioral couple therapy is comprised of approaches that are compatible with evidence-based practice. The methods continue to undergo empirical scrutiny, the results of which can be expected to shape the next generation of this approach to helping couples change.

REFERENCES

Abrahms, J. L. (1983). Cognitive-behavioral strategies to induce and enhance a collaborative set in distressed couples. In A. Freeman (Ed.), *Cognitive therapy with couples and groups* (pp. 125–155). New York: Plenum.

Alexander, J. F., Jameson, P. B., Newell, R. M., & Gunderson, D. (1996). Changing cognitive schemas: A necessary antecedent to changing behaviors in dysfunctional families. In K. S. Dobson & K. D. Craig (Eds.), *Advances in cognitive-behavioral therapy* (pp. 174–192). Thousand Oaks, CA: Sage.

Bandura, A. (1978). The self system in reciprocal determinism. *American Psychologist, 33,* 344–358.

Bandura, A. (1985). Model of causality in social learning theory. In M. J. Mahoney & A. Freeman (Eds.), *Cognition and Psychotherapy.* New York: Plenum.

Baucom, D. H., & Epstein, N. (1990). *Cognitive-behavioral marital therapy.* New York: Brunner/Mazel.

Baucom, D. H., Epstein, N., & LaTaillade, J. J. (2002). Cognitive-behavioral couple therapy. In A. S. Gurman & N. S. Jacobson (Eds.), *Clinical handbook of couple therapy* (3rd ed., pp. 26–58). New York: Guilford.

Baucom, D. H., Shoham, V., Mueser, K. T., Daiuto, A. D., & Stickle, T. R. (1998). Empirically supported couples and family therapies for adult problems. *Journal of Consulting and Clinical Psychology, 66,* 53–88.

Beach, S. R. H. (2000). *Marital and family process in depression: A scientific foundation for clinical practice.* Washington, DC: American Psychological Association.

Beach, S. R. H., Sandeen, E. E., & O'Leary, K. D. (1990). *Depression in marriage: A model for etiology and treatment.* New York: Guilford.

Beach, S. R. H., Whisman, M. A., & O'Leary, K. D. (1994). Marital therapy for depression: Theoretical foundation, current status, and future directions. *Behavior Therapy, 25,* 345–371.

Beck, A. T. (1988). *Love is never enough.* New York: Harper & Row.

Beck, A. T. (1993). Cognitive approaches to stress. In P. M. Lehrer & R. L. Woolfolk (Eds.), *Principles and practice of stress management* (2nd ed., pp. 333–372). New York: Guilford.

Beck, A. T., Rush, A. J., Shaw, B. F., & Emery, G. (1979). *Cognitive therapy of depression.* New York: Guilford.

Beck, J. S. (1995). *Cognitive therapy: Basics and beyond.* New York: Guilford.

Clark, D. A., Beck, A. T., & Alford, B. A. (1999). *Scientific foundations of cognitive theory and therapy of depression.* New York: Wiley.

Dattilio, F. M., & Epstein, N. B. (2005). Introduction to the special section: The role of cognitive-behavioral interventions in couple and family therapy. *Journal of Marital and Family Therapy, 31,* 7–13.

Dattilio, F. M., Epstein, N. B., & Baucom, D. H. (1998). An introduction to cognitive-behavioral therapy with couples and families. In F. M. Dattilio (Ed.), *Case studies in couple and family therapy: Systemic and cognitive perspectives* (pp. 1–36). New York: Guilford.

Dattilio, F. M., & Padesky, C.A. (1990). *Cognitive therapy with couples.* Sarasota, FL: Professional Resource Exchange.

Ellis, A. (1977). The nature of disturbed marital interactions. In A. Ellis & R. Grieger (Eds.), *Handbook of rational-emotive therapy* (pp. 170–176). New York: Springer.

Ellis, A., & Harper, R. A. (1961). *A guide to rational living.* Englewood Cliffs, NJ: Prentice-Hall.

Ellis, A., Sichel, J. L., Yeager, R. J., DiMattia, & DiGiuseppe, R. (1989). *Rational-emotive couples therapy.* New York: Pergamon.

Epstein, N. (1983). Cognitive therapy with couples. In A. Freeman (Ed.), *Cognitive therapy with couples and groups* (pp. 107–123). New York: Plenum.

Epstein, N. B., & Baucom, D. H. (2002). *Enhanced cognitive-behavioral therapy for couples: A contextual approach.* Washington, DC: American Psychological Association.

Gottman, J. M. (1999). *The marriage clinic: A scientifically based marital therapy.* New York: W. W. Norton.

Granvold, D. K. (1988). Treating marital couples in conflict and transition. In J. S. McNeil & S. E. Weinstein (Eds.), *Innovations in healthcare practice* (pp. 68–90). Silverspring, MD: NASW Press.

Granvold, D. K. (1994). Concepts and methods of cognitive therapy. In D. K. Granvold (Ed.), *Cognitive and behavioral treatment: Methods and applications* (pp. 3–31). Pacific Grove, CA: Brooks/Cole.

Granvold, D. K. (1997). Cognitive-behavioral therapy with adults. In J. R. Brandell (Ed.), *Theory and practice in clinical social work* (pp. 164–201). New York: Free Press.

Granvold, D. K. (1998). Brief cognitive-behavioral couples therapy. *Crisis Intervention, 4,* 23–48.

Granvold, D. K. (2000). Divorce. In F. M. Dattilio & A. Freeman (Eds.), *Cognitive-behavioral strategies in crisis intervention* (2nd ed., pp. 362–384). New York: Guilford.

Granvold, D. K. (2001). Constructivist theory. In P. Lehmann & N. Coady (Eds.), *Theoretical perspectives for direct social work practice: A generalist-eclectic approach.* New York: Springer.

Granvold, D. K., & Jordan, C. (1994). The cognitive-behavioral treatment of marital distress. In D. K. Granvold (Ed.), *Cognitive and behavioral treatment: Methods and applications* (pp. 174–201). Pacific Grove, CA: Brooks/Cole.

Granvold, D. K., & Martin, J. I. (1999). Family therapy with gay and lesbian clients. In C. Franklin & C. Jordan (Eds.), *Family practice: Brief systems methods for social work* (pp. 299–320). Pacific Grove, CA: Brooks/Cole.

Hickey, D., Carr, A., Dooley, B., Guerin, S., Butler, E., & Fitzpatrick, L. (2005). Family and marital profiles of couples in which one partner has depression or anxiety. *Journal of Marital and Family Therapy, 31,* 171–182.

Hurvitz, N. (1975). Interaction hypotheses in marriage counseling. In A. S. Gurman & D. G. Rice (Eds.), *Couples in conflict* (pp. 225–240). New York: Jason Aronson.

Jacobson, N. S., & Christensen, A. (1996). *Acceptance and change in couple therapy: A therapist's guide to transforming relationships.* New York: W. W. Norton.

Jacobson, N. S., & Margolin, G. (1979). *Marital therapy: Strategies based on social learning and behavior exchange principles.* New York: Brunner/Mazel.

Karney, B. R., & Bradbury, T. N. (1995). The longitudinal course of marital quality and stability: A review of theory, methods, and research. *Psychological Bulletin, 118,* 3–34.

Lieberman, R. P. (1975). Behavioral principles in family and couple therapy. In A. S. Gurman & D. G. Rice (Eds.), *Couples in conflict* (pp. 209–224). New York: Jason Aronson.

Mahoney, M. J. (1991). *Human change processes: The scientific foundations of psychotherapy.* New York: Basic Books.

Mahoney, M. J. (2000). Core ordering and disordering processes: A constructive view of psychological development. In R. A. Neimeyer & J. D. Raskin (Eds.), *Constructions of disorder: Meaning-making frameworks for psychotherapy.* Washington, DC: American Psychological Association.

McGinn, L. K., & Young, J. E. (1996). Schema-focused therapy. In P. M. Salkovskis (Ed.), *Frontiers of cognitive therapy* (pp. 182–207). New York: Guilford.

Neimeyer, R. A. (1993). Constructivist approaches to the measurement of meaning. In G. J. Neimeyer (Ed.), *Constructivist assessment: A casebook* (pp. 58–103). Newbury Park, CA: Sage.

Nichols, M. P., & Schwartz, R. C. (2001). *Family therapy: Concepts and methods* (5th ed.). Boston: Allyn & Bacon.

Olson, D. H. (1975). A critical overview. In A. S. Gurman & D. G. Rice (Eds.), *Couples in conflict* (pp. 7–62). New York: Aronson.

Raskin, J. D., & Lewandowski, A. M. (2000). The construction of disorder as human enterprise. In R. A. Neimeyer & J. D. Raskin (Eds.), *Constructions of disorder: Meaning-making frameworks for psychotherapy*. Washington, DC: American Psychological Association.

Saleebey, D. (2002a). Introduction: Power to the people. In D. Saleebey (Ed.), *The strengths perspective in social work practice* (3rd ed.). Boston: Allyn & Bacon.

Saleebey, D. (Ed.). (2002b). *The strengths perspective in social work practice* (3rd ed.). Boston: Allyn & Bacon.

Stuart, R. B. (1969). Operant-interpersonal treatment for marital discord. *Journal of Consulting and Clinical Psychology, 33,* 675–682.

Stuart, R. B. (1980). *Helping couples change: A social learning approach to marital therapy*. New York: Guilford.

Veroff, J., Kulka, R. A., & Douvan, E. (1981). *Mental health in America: Patterns of helpseeking from 1957 to 1976*. New York: Basic Books.

Weiss, R. L. (1978). The conceptualization of marriage from a behavioral perspective. In T. J. Paolino & B. S. McCrady (Eds.), *Marriage and marital therapy: Psychoanalytic, behavioral, and systems theory perspectives* (pp. 165–239). New York: Brunner/Mazel.

Weiss, R. L. (1980). Strategic behavioral marital therapy: Toward a model for assessment and intervention. In J. P. Vincent (Ed.), *Advances in family intervention, assessment and theory* (Vol. 1, pp. 229–271). Greenwich, CT: JAI Press.

Weiss, R. L., Hops, H., & Patterson, G. R. (1973). A framework for conceptualizing marital conflict, a technology for altering it, some data for evaluating it. In L. A. Hamerlynck, L. C. Handy, & E. J. Mash (Eds.), *Behavior change: Methodology, concepts, and practice* (pp. 309–342). Champaign, IL: Research Press.

CHAPTER 15

Family Intervention for Severe Mental Illness

Susan Gingerich
Kim T. Mueser

INTRODUCTION

Over the past 25 years there has been a growing recognition of the importance of working with families of persons with severe mental illnesses such as schizophrenia, bipolar disorder, and treatment-refractory depression. A variety of different models of family intervention have been developed, and numerous research studies have shown that working with families can dramatically improve the outcome of these illnesses (see Literature Review section that follows). Family intervention can be provided by a wide range of professionals, including social workers, psychologists, nurses, psychiatrists, and counselors.

Social workers are often in a good position to provide family intervention because of the field's rich tradition of helping people in the context of their own environment. Social workers are well represented in inpatient and outpatient mental health facilities, and in many settings they outnumber other mental health professionals ("Social workers outnumber," 1999). They frequently work with people with severe mental illnesses and conduct individual, group, and family therapy. The caseload of a social worker is likely to contain a large number of clients who have active family involvement, since 40 to 60% of persons with schizophrenia or bipolar disorder live at home, and many others have regular contact with their family (Brown & Birtwistle, J., 1998; Carpentier, Lesage, Goulet, Lalone, & Renaud, 1992; Goldman, 1984). Because family interventions have been shown to improve outcomes of people with mental illnesses, it is important that social workers are familiar with effective treatment models for this population.

Professionals working with families of people with a severe mental illness should be aware of the stress that relatives experience (Hatfield & Lefley, 1987, 1993; Mueser, 2004). Family members often provide important emotional and concrete support to a relative with mental illness and face many challenges and strains. The burden of care can be high for family members, and it is more severe when they are not given support and practical information about the causes, symptoms, course, and treatment of their relative's disorder. An additional source of stress is that mental health professionals often fail to recognize the important role of the family in treatment, and exclude them from important meetings and discussions involving decisions that affect their relative.

The primary goals of family intervention for severe mental illness are to reduce the burden of care on families and educate them about the psychiatric illness and principles of treatment. Models of family intervention differ in terms of theoretical orientation, format, and location of treatment, but they share much in common. Effective family interventions are long term (9 months or longer), avoid blaming the family, provide education about the illness and its treatment, improve communication and problem-solving skills, teach strategies for decreasing stress, focus on the present and the future rather than the past, and aim to improve the quality of life of *everyone* in the family (Mueser, 2001). When family members are involved in treatment that includes these components, they are able to become members of the treatment team, monitor the course of their relative's illness, alert team members when their relative's symptoms worsen in order to prevent relapses and rehospitalizations, and use positive communication and problem-solving skills to help their relative take steps toward recovery.

In this chapter we provide an overview of two empirically supported family intervention models for major mental illness: behavioral family therapy (BFT; conducted with single families) and multifamily groups (MFGs), both of which employ a combination of education and cognitive behavior techniques such as problem solving training. In both BFT and MFGs, *family* is broadly defined to include the client and anyone with a caring relationship with him or her, such as parents, partners, siblings, other relatives, close friends, or an involved member of the community, such as clergy. It is helpful for clinicians to be familiar with providing both of these approaches in order to respond to the needs of a variety of families. For example, some families may be easier to engage in BFT, which can be individually tailored and provided in the home, whereas others may gain more from MFGs, where they can get support and suggestions from other families.

LITERATURE REVIEW

In the past, families were mistakenly blamed for causing severe mental illnesses such as schizophrenia (Bateson, Jackson, Haley, & Weakland, 1956; Fromm-Reichman, 1948; Sullivan, 1972), which led many mental health professionals to discourage family involvement in treatment and to resist their efforts to learn more about their relative's illness. Numerous studies over the course of the past 25 years, however, have consistently shown that family members do *not* cause mental illness and can play an important role in improving the course of the illness for their relatives. Extensive research on family interventions has included multiple randomized controlled trials, primarily focusing on schizophrenia and bipolar disorder (Dixon et al., 2001; Falloon, Held, Coverdale, Roncone, & Laidlaw, 1999; Pilling et al., 2002; Pitschel-Walz, Leucht, Bäuml, Kissling, & Engel, 2001). One of the most striking findings is that the risk of relapse following family intervention is reduced by approximately one-half compared to clients not receiving family intervention. Other key findings include that the most effective family intervention programs usually last between 9 months and 2 years, and that family intervention programs are associated with reduced burden and distress among relatives. Research also indicates that family therapy is cost effective, resulting in a net savings in total health care costs because of its effect on reducing relapses and costly rehospitalizations (Cardin, McGill, & Falloon, 1986; Tarrier, Lowson, & Barrowclough, 1991).

The strong evidence base for family intervention led the Schizophrenia Patient Outcomes Research Team (PORT) to recommend that clients with severe mental illness who have ongoing contact with their families should *routinely* be offered a family intervention (Lehman & Steinwachs, 1998). Family intervention was also selected by the Substance Abuse and Mental Health Services Administration (SAMHSA) as one of six evidence-based practices for severe mental illness to be developed into implementation resource kits to facilitate implementation in mental health centers throughout the United States ("Evidence-based mental health system transformation," www.samhsa.gov; Murray-Swank & Dixon, 2005).

Clinicians who plan to implement BFT or MFGs can find more detailed information by consulting Falloon, Boyd, and McGill (1984) for BFT for schizophrenia, Miklowitz and Goldstein (1997) for BFT for bipolar disorder, and Mueser and Glynn (1999) for BFT with families whose relatives have a range of severe mental illnesses, including schizophrenia, schizoaffective disorder, bipolar disorder, major depression, posttraumatic stress disorder (PTSD, and obsessive-compulsive disorder (OCD). Mueser and Glynn's book also includes multiple reproducible forms, such as educational handouts, assessment forms, communication skill sheets, and problem-solving records. McFarlane's book (2002) describes how to conduct MFGs for schizophrenia and includes chapters about other diagnoses, such as bipolar, major depression, borderline personality disorder, and OCD. *Integrated Treatment for Dual Disorders* (Mueser, Noordsy, Drake, & Fox, 2003) contains chapters about working with families of persons with substance abuse and mental illness using the BFT and MFG models, and includes a large number of reproducible handouts for clients and family members. Reading "Couples-Based Interventions for Schizophrenia-Spectrum Disorders" (Mueser & Brunette, 2003) will help clinicians tailor BFT to address specific issues for working with spouses and partners. SAMHSA's Family Psychoeducation Implementation Resource Kit (www.sahmsa.gov) provides instructions for conducting BFT and MFGs.

In addition to BFT and MFGs, support groups and educational groups conducted by relatives are widely available in many communities, and there is some evidence showing they are beneficial to families in terms of increased knowledge, self-confidence, and decreased burden of care (Dixon et al., 2004; Dixon et al., 2001; Solomon, Draine, Mannion, & Meisel, 1996). The Family-to-Family Education Program (Burland, 1998), sponsored by the National Alliance for the Mentally Ill (NAMI), is the most widespread and well-known family-led program (Murray-Swank et al., 2005). In this program, families, not including the consumer, attend a series of twelve weekly, 2 to 3 hour classes focusing on different topics about mental illness, including symptoms and treatment, problem solving, communication skills, self-care, and advocacy.

BEHAVIORAL FAMILY THERAPY (BFT)

Overview

BFT uses educational and social learning techniques to teach family members information about psychiatric disorders and their treatment, and communication and problem-solving skills aimed at lowering stress and promoting family cooperation. In addition, BFT facilitates the ability of the family to collaborate with the treatment team in the treatment of the psychiatric disorder and to support the client in pursuing personal goals. Thus, the overarching goals of BFT are improved illness management, through collaboration between the family and the treatment team, and reduced family stress.

BFT can be conducted either at a mental health agency or at the home of the family. Sometimes a combination approach works well, such as conducting sessions at the home to engage family members in treatment, and then shifting to sessions at the agency as therapy progresses. Sessions include the client and relatives who have regular contact. Weekly contact is preferred, though it is not required if a relative or significant other expresses a desire to be involved and a commitment to support the client in coping with his or her illness. Family members benefit from participating in all BFT sessions, although some, such as siblings who do not live nearby, may attend selected sessions. It is recommended that family sessions include members who are 16 years old or older, although the clinician may want to meet separately with children in the family to respond to their specific concerns (Mueser & Gingerich, in press).

BFT sessions last about 1 hour and are conducted on a declining contact basis, (e.g., weekly for 3 months, biweekly for 6 months and monthly for 3 to 6 months). BFT is a structured program aimed at teaching a specific curriculum, which is tailored to address the specific needs of the family, including the duration of sessions, the number of sessions spent on specific topic areas, and total length of the program. Most families take 9 months to 2 years to complete BFT.

BFT is divided into six stages, which build knowledge and skills in a step-by-step fashion. Table 15.1 lists the stages and general guidelines for the number of sessions.

Engagement

In this stage, the clinician reaches out to the family. The clinician first approaches the client to explain the importance of working with his or her

TABLE 15.1   Stages of BFT

BFT Stage	Approximate number of sessions
1. Engagement	1 session per family member; 1 family session
2. Assessment	1 session per family member; 1 optional family session
3. Psychoeducation	3 to 8 family sessions
4. Communication skills training (if needed)	4 to 8 family sessions
5. Problem solving training	5 to 15 family sessions
6. Termination	1 family session

family and to ask for permission to contact family members. It is useful to describe BFT as a program that helps family members work together to manage the psychiatric illness and achieve personal and shared goals. Clients are often reassured to hear that BFT is focused on the present and the future, and is intended to lower stress on everyone in the family.

With the client's permission, the clinician then gets in touch with family members to describe BFT and the benefits of working together. The clinician often describes BFT briefly in a phone call, followed up by a more detailed meeting in person. The clinician conveys that the overall goals of BFT are education, reducing hospitalizations, reducing stress, and promoting their relative's independence. Because family members may have had unpleasant experiences in the past with family therapy, or may have negative preconceptions about family therapy, it may be helpful for the clinician to point out how BFT differs from other approaches of working with families. If families are "burned out" due to the stress and burden of caring for their relative over a long period of time, the clinician can empathize with the challenges they have faced, let them know about families who have gone through similar experiences and have benefited from BFT, and encourage them that it is never too late to work together to improve things for the future. If family members are still hesitant about making a long-term commitment to BFT, they can be encouraged to "give it a try" for a few sessions, and then reevaluate whether they want to continue.

When the client and his or her family members have agreed to participate in BFT, the clinician schedules a family orientation meeting. The goals of this meeting are to explain the program in more detail and to set positive expectations for participating in it. The clinician can use an orientation sheet (see Mueser & Glynn, 1999; Mueser et al., 2003) that spells out the goals, format, and expectations of BFT to guide this session, which generally takes 20 to 30 minutes. After going over the orientation sheet and answering the family's questions, the clinician sets up appointments to complete individual assessments and a time to convene the whole family for the first BFT session.

Assessment

The individual assessment sessions with family members help the clinician establish a therapeutic relationship with each person, evaluate his or her knowledge about the client's mental illness, understand his or her perspective on the family (strengths and weaknesses), and identify personal goals for participating in BFT. Individual assessment interviews also allow family members to share information that they might not feel comfortable revealing during family sessions. Parents, for example, may talk more freely about past episodes of violence in the home or reveal that they are frustrated with their relative's not taking medication regularly. Clients may be more forthcoming about their desire to live independently or their use of drugs or alcohol to cope with symptoms such as hearing voices.

Some family members may find it difficult to identify personal goals to work on, because they see their participation strictly as a way to help their relative with mental illness. The clinician can point out that the personal well-being of every family member is important and has an effect on overall stress in the family, which in turn affects the course of their relative's mental illness. Family members may benefit from hearing examples of personal goals that others have identified, such as improving physical fitness, developing a hobby or interest (e.g., music, art, sports, crafts), socializing more often, learning ways to reduce stress, eating more nutritional meals, and going out more often as a couple. If goals are ambitious, the clinician can help break them down into small steps that can be accomplished one at a time.

Most individual assessments can be completed in a single interview. An additional session can be scheduled to assess family problem solving, which involves selecting a problem that the family is experiencing and asking them to work on it independently for 10 minutes while the family clinician observes and takes notes. This is an optional assessment and is described in detail in Mueser and Glynn (1999). Assessment is an ongoing process, however, with the clinician observing how family members communicate with one another and solve problems in later psychoeducational, communication skills, and problem-solving sessions. For example, do family members routinely express positive feelings such as affection? Do members criticize one another? Do they argue frequently? Is there a high level of tension? Does one family member tend to dominate the problem-solving discussions?

Psychoeducation

For this stage, the clinician meets with the family to educate them about the client's disorder and its treatment. The goals of psychoeducation are to legitimize the psychiatric disorder, reduce negative feelings in the family (e.g., guilt, anxiety, depression, and anger), enlist everyone in helping the client manage his or her illness, and increase the family's ability to monitor the disorder and communicate with the treatment team. Information about the illness is summarized in written handouts, which are used in an interactive way during sessions. The clinician and family members may take turns reading from the handouts, or the clinician may take the lead and summarize the contents, and suggest that family members read the handout at a later time as a home assignment. The clinician pauses frequently to ask questions to make sure family members understand and to help them apply the information to their own experiences. The client is connoted to the relatives as the "expert" in the psychiatric illness and is asked to share what he or she has experienced. The topics for psychoeducation in BFT sessions are summarized in Table 15.2.

In psychoeducational sessions, it is important for the clinician to create an atmosphere in which family members feel free to ask questions and express their opinions, even to disagree with one another. At this stage, however, the family has not yet been taught more effective communication and problem-solving skills, so it is important to avoid confrontation and conflict. The clinician can acknowledge significant differences of opinion and let family members know that these will be addressed later in BFT. Even if the client does not accept that he or she has a mental illness, psychoeducation can be provided, using words or phrases that the client finds acceptable. For example, some clients use terms such as *nervous condition, emotional disorder,* or *neurological problem* to describe their mental illness. Other clients simply refer to *the problems I've been having.*

In BFT sessions the clinician follows a structure that involves reviewing family members' goals (identified and broken down into steps during the assessment stage), teaching new material, and developing home assignments to follow up what they are learning in the sessions (see Table 15.3). A fundamental component of all home assignments is asking the family to conduct a weekly family meeting where they review information or practice skills taught in sessions. These family meetings may be

TABLE 15.2   Topics of Psychoeducational Sessions

Basic Topics*	• Basic Facts About Mental Illness (separate handouts for schizophrenia, schizoaffective disorder, bipolar disorder, major depression, obsessive compulsive disorder, posttraumatic stress disorder)
	• Medications (separate handouts for antipsychotics, antidepressants, mood stabilizers, and sedatives)
	• The Stress Vulnerability Model
	• Drug and Alcohol Use
	• Role of the Family
	• Keys to Good Communication
Additional Topics**	• Alcohol and Drugs: Motives and Consequences
	• Treatment of Dual Disorders
	• Infectious Diseases

* = Reproducible handouts available in Mueser and Glynn (1999) and Mueser et al. (2003)
** = Reproducible handouts available in Mueser et al. (2003)

TABLE 15.3   Structure of BFT Sessions

Activity	Time Period
Welcome family members to the session, socialize informally, review the family's week	2 to 3 minutes
Review individual family members' goals	5 minutes
Review home assignment and family meeting	5 to 15 minutes
Present psychoeducational topic or teach skill	20 to 30 minutes
Develop home assignment (including meeting together as a family) to follow up what was taught in session	5 minutes
Summarize session and thank members for their participation	2 to 3 minutes
Optional: If necessary, reserve time to problem solve urgent problems raised in the session (e.g., crises)	5 to 15 minutes at the end of the session

very short at first (15 minutes) as the members get comfortable talking to each other about mental illness. Later in BFT, weekly family meetings are typically longer as they involve practicing specific communication skills or solving problems together. In each session, the clinician follows up whether the family meeting was held and how it went. If the family has met, the clinician provides positive feedback, and if they did not meet, the clinician problem solves with them about any obstacles they encountered. If the clinician follows up routinely in this fashion, most family members will get in the habit of meeting together on their own in between sessions and doing home assignments.

Communication Skills Training

Some families have excellent communication skills and need only a brief review, as provided in the psychoeductional stage in the handout "Keys to Good Communication" (Mueser & Glynn, 1999). Other families need specific training in communication skills to reduce stress in the household and to prepare them for discussing and solving problems in the next phase of BFT. The clinician explains that good communication skills are helpful to any family, and are especially important when a family encounters stress or problems, such as those caused by mental illness. Communication skills are taught using the steps of social skills training (Bellack, Mueser, Gingerich, & Agresta, 2004; Gingerich, 2002; Liberman, DeRisi, & Mueser, 2001).

- Establish a rationale for learning the skill. Ask family members why they think it could be helpful to learn (or strengthen) the skill.

- Break down the skill into three to four steps.
- Demonstrate the skill in a role play. Ask the family for feedback regarding the specific steps of the skill.
- Ask a family member to practice the skill in a role play, while others observe.
- Elicit positive feedback about what was done well in the role play. Provide extra positive feedback as necessary.
- If needed, provide a suggestion about how the person could perform the skill even better.
- Ask the family member to repeat the role play, requesting that he or she implement the suggestion for improvement.
- Provide positive feedback and suggestions for additional improvement in the skill.
- Engage each family member in one or more role plays, providing positive feedback and suggestions for improvement after each role play.
- Develop a home assignment with family members to practice the skill in their everyday life.

Communication skills training focuses on six skills: expressing positive feelings, making a positive request, expressing unpleasant feelings (such as annoyance or sadness), active listening, compromise and negotiation, and requesting a time-out. Some families may need training in only one skill, whereas others may benefit from learning more skills. One or two training sessions (and occasionally more) are usually necessary for family members to learn a specific skill. An example of a skill broken down into steps is included in Table 15.4. Reproducible handouts of communication skills and home assignments (such as "Catch a Person Pleasing You" for practicing the skill of expressing positive feelings) are available in Mueser et al. (1999) and Mueser et al. (2003).

Problem Solving

One of the main goals of BFT is to teach families a systematic method of solving their own problems. The clinician emphasizes the importance of family members learning collaborative problem solving in order to solve problems on their own rather than relying on professionals. Learning how to solve problems empowers the family to be more self-sufficient and

---

TABLE 15.4   Steps of Expressing Unpleasant Feelings

- Look at the person.
- Tell the person what he or she did to displease you. Be specific.
- Tell the person the feeling it gave you. Be specific.
- Make a positive request for change, if possible, so that the situation can be prevented in the future.

---

able to deal with a variety of situations that may arise. The six steps of problem solving are summarized in Table 15.5.

In family problem solving, a "chairperson" is elected who guides the family through the steps and makes sure that everyone has input throughout the process. In addition, someone is usually asked to act as a "secretary," to write down the results of the problem solving on a summary sheet (see the Problem-Solving Record in Mueser et al., 1999) so that family members can refer back to it. The role of the chairperson and secretary can be combined.

At the beginning of teaching problem solving, the clinician first explains the steps and demonstrates them by working on a specific problem with the family. The clinician first chooses a problem or goal of the family that is not extremely difficult to solve, such as identifying an activity that the family could do together or selecting a consistent time for weekly family meetings. Initially, the clinician takes the role of chairperson, helping members go through all six steps. As the family members gain experience, they gradually take on the role of problem solving on their own, with less and less assistance from the clinician. As the family gets better at problem solving, they can tackle more challenging problems related to the client, such as finding a part-time job, reducing substance use, making friends, or developing coping strategies for persistent symptoms, as well as working on the goals of other family members.

Termination

When family members have gained an understanding of the mental illness and have made significant progress in their communication and

TABLE 15.5   Step-by-Step Problem Solving

Define the problem as specifically and simply as possible. Get everyone's opinion about the problem and find a definition that everyone agrees on.

Brainstorm possible solutions. Each family member suggests at least one potential solution. Avoid evaluating solutions during this step, and encourage brainstorming, even "wild ideas."

Evaluate the solutions. Briefly identify the advantages and disadvantages of each possible solution.

Select the best solution or combination of solutions. Choose the solution (or combination) that is most likely to solve the problem.

Plan the steps for carrying out the solution. Decide what steps are needed to implement the solution, including who will do what, when different steps should be completed, what resources are needed, and what problems could be encountered (and how to solve them) along the way.

Set a date for follow-up. At this follow-up meeting, give credit for what has been done, and problem solve to address any obstacles encountered.

---

problem-solving skills, the clinician works with them to plan for ending the intervention. Some families take longer than others to complete BFT, depending on the knowledge and skills with which they started and the complexity of problems they experience. Likewise, families vary in the supports they need to maintain the progress they have made. Most families benefit from a few planned booster sessions (either in person or by phone) to provide support and review information and skills they learned. Many also benefit from joining a family support group, where they can meet other families who are dealing with similar challenges.

CASE STUDY

Example of a Family Participating in BFT

Lorenzo began experiencing symptoms of schizophrenia at age 19, when he heard voices that told him he was "no good" and he thought that the television shows he watched were about his life and were revealing personal information to everyone in the audience. After much confusion on the part of his parents about what to do, they were finally able to convince Lorenzo to go to an emergency room, where he was diagnosed with schizophrenia and sent to an inpatient hospital. After his first admission, he was discharged with medication. He continued to live with his parents, who pressured him to go back to his job repairing cars. After several episodes of stopping taking medication, Lorenzo was readmitted to the hospital. This time, the social worker at the inpatient facility recommended BFT, and Lorenzo and his mother, father, sister, and brother, agreed to participate after hearing more about the program.

During the assessment stage, the family clinician found out that Lorenzo knew very little about schizophrenia, and had thought that he only needed to take medications until he felt better. He said there was considerable tension at home and that he wanted to get his own apartment. In Lorenzo's parents' session with the clinician, they reported that they had read some things about schizophrenia on the Internet, but did not understand the symptoms and thought that Lorenzo could overcome the illness if he would just go back to work. Lorenzo's siblings, who lived some distance away, had only recently learned about his diagnosis and were very concerned that he would be dependent on their parents for the rest of his life.

Lorenzo and his parents attended all five psychoeducational sessions, and his brother and sister attended the ones on "Basic Facts About Schizophrenia," "Medications," and "Role of the Family." At first the clinician noted that Lorenzo was very quiet, but after she explained to the family that he was "the real expert in the illness," and asked questions about his own experience, he gradually took a more active role in the sessions. As his parents and siblings learned more about the biological nature of the illness, they began to make fewer negative comments to Lorenzo and started to focus more on supporting his participation in treatment such as taking medication. Although the clinician asked them to start having weekly family meetings on their own, they repeatedly reported that they had been unable to do so because of being "too busy."

While Lorenzo's parents became less critical during the psychoeducational stage, the clinician noted several stressful communication patterns and initiated communication skills training. Lorenzo and his parents worked for two sessions each on the skills of "Expressing Positive Feelings," "Making Positive Requests," "Expressing Unpleasant Feelings." His brother and sister attended about half the sessions, often adding a welcome touch of humor to the learning of skills. The family became more successful at holding weekly family meetings on their own, which sometimes included the siblings when they visited on weekends or holidays.

During the problem-solving stage of BFT (15 sessions), Lorenzo and his parents were able to identify several problems to work on, such as Lorenzo finding an apartment, the parents planning a vacation on their own, Lorenzo developing a schedule for his days that included household chores, Lorenzo's parents and siblings becoming part of his relapse prevention plan, Lorenzo identifying recovery goals, including finding a volunteer job or part-time job, and everyone in the family developing strategies for dealing with stress. Over time, the family met more regularly for their family meetings and began to use problem solving on their own. Lorenzo's siblings continued to support the family by attending some of the problem-solving sessions and joining family problem-solving meetings on occasion.

After 1 year of BFT, Lorenzo and his family had developed a good knowledge of schizophrenia and its treatment, were communicating in a more positive way, and had developed skills for solving problems on their own. The clinician and family discussed termination for a few sessions and agreed that joining a multifamily support group would help the family continue the progress they had made. Lorenzo also asked to be referred to a supported employment program (Becker & Drake, 2003; Bond & Jones, 2005) to pursue his interest in a part-time job.

MULTIFAMILY GROUPS

Like BFT, multifamily groups (MFGs) teach families the knowledge and skills they need to manage psychiatric illness in one of their members. By bringing several families together on a regular basis, MFGs also provide social support, opportunities to learn from others' experience, and suggestions for solving problems from a variety of people outside of one's own family. Families can participate in MFGs as an alternative to BFT or in addition to it. We describe here two approaches to conducting MFGs that share much in common, but differ in their format for psychoeducation, the structure of group sessions, and the amount of formal problem solving conducted in group meetings.

Multifamily Support Group: Overview

The multifamily support group model was developed for the treatment strategies in schizophrenia study (Mueser et al., 2001; Schooler et al., 1997) and has been adapted for families of clients with other psychiatric disorders, including those with comorbid substance abuse (Mueser et al., 2003). Groups are conducted monthly or biweekly (every 2 weeks) for 1 hour or 90 minutes, and are provided on a time-unlimited basis. Groups are usually scheduled in the evening to accommodate family members who work. Groups should be held at a standard time and location, and sessions that land on holidays should be rescheduled for the next week. Projectors, blackboards, or flip charts are especially helpful in presenting educational topics to a large number of people. Both clients and family members are invited to attend the group, but if either declines, the others can still attend and benefit. It is recommended to start a group with at least 6 to 10 individuals (3 to 5 families) and to not allow group size to exceed more than 25. Clients with different diagnoses of severe mental illness and at different stages of recovery can join the group, as long as they are interested in participating. Co-leaders are highly recommended.

Reminders should be sent to group members a week or two prior to the next session, including the date, time, location, and planned topic. If members do not attend, group leaders should follow up with a phone call. To foster a relaxed atmosphere and encourage informal socialization, refreshments should be served at all meetings. When groups have met for several months, they may enjoy planning holiday potlucks or other celebrations.

Engagement

The group leaders should contact clients and family members (either in person or by phone) to let them know that a multifamily support group is being started and invite them to join. Scheduling a joint meeting with all family members, including the client, can be helpful. In talking with potential group members, the group leader explains that the goals of the group are education, reducing hospitalizations, and providing support for families who have gone through similar experiences, and that the group will meet regularly on an ongoing basis (give the specific day, time, and location). More than one contact may be necessary to orient family members to the group and to explore any concerns they have.

Psychoeducation

An educational topic of relevance to mental illness is included in each session of the group, followed by discussion. In the first months of the group, the leaders take turns presenting the topics, and later in the course of the group, outside speakers may be invited to present selected topics. For the first few months of the group, the leaders usually present basic educational topics, such as information on different psychiatric diagnoses, the stress-vulnerability model, and medications. Group leaders may find the BFT handouts useful for guiding the presentation of basic topics (refer back to Table 15.2). Ideas for additional educational topics for later group sessions are listed in Table 15.6.

Structure of Group Meetings

Meetings of the multifamily support group follow a regular pattern, which is summarized in Table 15.7.

Problem Solving

Leaders can use group-based problem solving to address a problem that several members experience or to address an urgent problem that has come up for one family. The same six-step method used in BFT can be

---

TABLE 15.6   Examples of Additional Topics for Multifamily Support Groups

- Managing stress
- Scheduling fun activities
- Coping with depression
- Meeting new friends
- Improving friendships
- Recovery from mental illness
- Positive communication skills
- Developing household rules
- New medications
- Hobbies
- Responding to crises
- Volunteering
- Finding jobs
- Problem solving
- Strategies for coping with symptoms
- Strengthening the family
- Managing money
- Coping with anxiety
- Effects of alcohol and drugs
- Resources available in the community
- Planning for the future
- Talking to the doctor

TABLE 15.7   Structure of Multifamily Support Group Meetings

Activity	Time
Welcoming to the group, introductions (as needed), sharing how things have been going since the last meeting	5 to 10 minutes
Presentation of educational topic by leader or outside speaker	20 to 35 minutes
Group discussion and sharing of coping strategies	20 to 35 minutes
Wrap-up, planning topics for future meetings	5 to 10 minutes

employed (refer to Table 15.5), with a group leader taking the role of chairperson, leading the group members through the steps and eliciting everyone's ideas. Many families have found group-based problem solving especially helpful because they get a chance to hear suggestions from outside their own family.

CASE STUDY

Roberta was a 38-year-old woman who had been diagnosed with bipolar disorder for 15 years. Roberta had long periods of taking her medication and functioning very well, including working at a series of part-time jobs, but had often stopped taking her lithium, which resulted in a return of her manic symptoms. She expressed interest in the multifamily support group after her last hospitalization, which was preceded by a manic episode when she quit her job, gave away all her clothing, and announced that she was going to teleport herself to heaven to be nearer to God, whom she described as "my best friend." During her hospitalization she confided in her social worker that she wanted to do something to avoid future relapses and wanted her family to understand her illness better. Although she lived independently, Roberta had regular contact with her widowed father and her cousin, whom she described as being like a sister to her. All lived within five miles of one another and usually spent time together on the weekends and holidays.

Roberta's father and cousin were interested in attending the group, which was scheduled monthly at the local community mental health center, saying that no one had reached out to them in all the years of Roberta's receiving treatment. Over the course of 2 years attending the group, Roberta and her family experienced several benefits. Roberta became more knowledgeable about bipolar disorder and the importance of taking medication even when she felt good. Although she experienced a relapse, she was able to seek help more quickly, which allowed her to stay out of the hospital, and afterward used the group to do problem solving to identify strategies for avoiding the kinds of stress that had contributed to the relapse. After a group discussion on employment, she decided to learn computer skills, which would allow her to obtain a more satisfying job. One of the other group members recommended a computer class that he had attended.

Her father enjoyed meeting other families, from whom he received support and validation. After talking several times to another father during the socialization period following the group, he joined a bowling league, renewing a hobby he had enjoyed in the past. Roberta's cousin had previously felt helpless about Roberta's illness, but after attending the group she was more confident that she could offer appropriate advice and assistance.

Psychoeducational Multifamily Groups: Overview

The psychoeducational multifamily group model was developed by William McFarlane and his colleagues (McFarlane, 2002; McFarlane, Link, Dushay, Marchal, & Crilly, 1995; McFarlane et al., 1995) for schizophrenia and has been adapted for families of clients with other psychiatric disorders, including bipolar disorder, depression, OCD and borderline personality disorder (McFarlane, 2002). In the psychoeducational multifamily group approach, families attend a one-day psychoeducational workshop before participating in regular group sessions, which focus primarily on problem solving.

The group sessions that follow the psychoeducational workshop are conducted by co-leaders for 90 minutes biweekly (every 2 weeks), sometimes decreasing to monthly sessions after 1 year or 18 months. The groups are provided on a time-unlimited basis. Single diagnosis, closed groups are recommended, although families can join ongoing groups that have shrunk in size. Clients and their family members are invited to join the group, but either may attend without the other. Five to eight families are recommended for starting the group. As in the multifamily support group model, co-leaders are encouraged to provide refreshments, send out reminders for each group, and to follow up with group members who do not attend.

The three stages of psychoeducational multifamily groups (joining, psychoeducational workshop, and problem-solving groups) follow.

Joining

Joining is the process of connecting, building rapport, and establishing a working alliance between the group leaders and clients and their families. Usually at least three joining meetings are held with a family before they attend the psychoeducational workshop. It is recommended that each co-leader join with half of the families scheduled to participate in the group. The client may attend the family joining sessions, or if he or she has difficulties with symptoms or concentration, the group leader may schedule separate joining sessions. All joining sessions begin and end with several minutes of socializing, in order to create a relaxed informal atmosphere and help people see themselves as separate from the mental illness.

The first joining session focuses on discussing the most recent crisis or episode of the illness and identifying precipitating events, prodromal symptoms, and early warning signs of relapse. The second joining session explores the family's feelings and reactions to the psychiatric disorder, how it has affected each of them, and the composition of their social network. In some cases, the consumer and his or her family members may feel more comfortable speaking openly about their feelings and reactions to the mental illness in separate sessions. The third joining session includes the identification of the family members' personal strengths, hobbies, interests, and experience with work and school. In addition, the family members identify goals for treatment and learn more about the psychoeducational workshop and ongoing group sessions that will follow. The group leaders may schedule additional joining sessions if needed.

Psychoeducational Workshop

In this model, the preponderance of psychoeducation is provided in the format of a one-day workshop attended by all the families who are scheduled to join the multifamily group. Clients are invited to attend the workshop, although some choose not to or attend part of the day because of problems with concentrating for long periods of time. The workshop is usually scheduled for a weekend day, from 9 A.M. to 4 P.M., with breakfast and lunch provided. The co-leaders are the hosts, and promote a relaxed, friendly atmosphere where questions and interactions are encouraged. The workshop begins and ends with several minutes of informal socializing. The co-leaders present much of the information of the workshop, but may invite other professionals to help present topics. For example, it can be helpful to have a doctor present information about medications. The workshop includes the following major topics: the biology of mental illness, diagnosis, treatment and rehabilitation, family reactions, relapse prevention, and family guidelines (see McFarlane, 2002). The family guidelines are a list of 12 specific recommendations, which are summarized in Table 15.8. The co-leaders often return to these guidelines in the multifamily group sessions that follow the workshop.

Group Sessions

After the psychoeducational workshop, families begin to attend biweekly multifamily group meetings. The theme of the first meeting is "Getting to Know Each Other," in which group members are encouraged to talk about topics unrelated to mental illness, such as hobbies, interests, and daily activities. The group leaders model sharing information by taking the lead in telling things about themselves. The theme of the second multifamily meeting is "How Mental Illness Has Affected Our Lives," which involves group members talking about their own experiences. Again, the

TABLE 15.8   Family Guidelines

1. GO SLOW. Recovery takes time. Rest is important. Things will get better in their own time.
2. KEEP IT COOL. Enthusiasm is normal. Tone it down. Disagreement is normal. Tone it down, too.
3. GIVE EACH OTHER SPACE. Time out is important for everyone. It's OK to reach out. It's OK to say "no."
4. SET LIMITS. Everyone needs to know what the rules are. A few good rules keep things clear.
5. IGNORE WHAT YOU CAN'T CHANGE. Let some things slide. Don't ignore violence.
6. KEEP IT SIMPLE. Say what you have to say clearly, calmly, and positively.
7. FOLLOW THE DOCTOR'S ORDERS. Take medications as they are prescribed. Take only medications that are prescribed.
8. CARRY ON BUSINESS AS USUAL. Reestablish family routines as quickly as possible. Stay in touch with family and friends.
9. NO STREET DRUGS OR ALCOHOL. They make symptoms worse, can cause relapse, and prevent recovery.
10. PICK UP ON EARLY SIGNS OF RELAPSE. Note changes. Consult with your family clinician.
11. SOLVE PROBLEMS STEP-BY-STEP. Make changes gradually. Work on one thing at a time.
12. LOWER EXPECTATIONS, TEMPORARILY. Use a personal yardstick. Compare this month to last month rather than last year or next year.

Source: From Family Psychoeducation Implementation Resource Kit, www.samhsa.gov.

co-leaders model by sharing their experiences with mental illness, which may include having a friend or relative with a psychiatric disorder, how they became interested in working in mental health, or how they have been personally affected by their professional work with people with mental illness. In the third meeting, the leaders teach the step-by-step model of solving problems (see Table 15.5) and lead the group members through an example of solving a problem volunteered by someone in the group. One leader is the "chairperson" who leads the group through the six steps, and the other leader encourages group participation. The leaders select a "recorder" to write down the steps on a chalkboard or note pad or both. The recorder can be a co-leader or a family member. The leaders and the family whose problem was being worked on should receive copies of the results of problem solving.

The remaining multifamily group sessions follow the structure outlined in Table 15.9. Common categories of problems that are addressed in psychoeducational multifamily groups include finding and keeping employment, difficulties with daily living skills, substance abuse, and problems related to medication.

TABLE 15.9   Structure of Multifamily Psychoeducational Group Sessions

Activity	Time
Initial socializing	15 minutes
"Go-round," where group members review the week's events, advice is given as needed, and problems are identified	20 minutes
Selection of a problem to work on	5 minutes
Problem solving, using the six-step model	45 minutes
Final socializing	5 minutes

CASE STUDY

Nick was 18 years old when he was diagnosed with schizophrenia, and 30 years old when he moved into a supervised apartment. He and his parents found this move to be a challenging transition and after witnessing several family arguments at the supervised apartment, his case manager suggested they join a psychoeducational multifamily group at the outpatient clinic where Nick went for medication visits. He and his parents started by meeting for three joining sessions with one of the co-leaders of the group. They all attended the psychoeducational workshop for the morning. Nick said that he was tired after lunch and returned to his apartment while his parents stayed for the afternoon. On the way home, his parents talked about the different people they had met, and discussed some of the "Family Guidelines" that were presented during the workshop.

During the first multifamily group meeting, the family initially had difficulty staying on the topic of "Getting to Know Each Other" without talking about problems related to schizophrenia, and the co-leaders gently guided them to talk about their interests and hobbies. At the second group meeting, they joined in the topic "How Mental Illness Has Affected Our Lives" by sharing what they had experienced in regards to Nick's symptoms of schizophrenia, especially the distress of the first few years of the illness before he received an accurate diagnosis. They expressed surprise that other families had much in common with theirs. In the third group meeting they learned about solving problems with the step-by-step method, and over the course of attending groups for the next 2 years participated in helping several families solve problems. Nick frequently received praise from other group members for the creative solutions he offered during problem solving.

The family found the overall atmosphere friendly and supportive, and especially enjoyed the socializing at the beginning and end of every group. Nick and his family used the group to help them resolve a conflict about how often his parents should visit and how much they should be involved with cleaning his apartment. With the help of other families, they came up with the solution that Nick would do his dishes every other day and his laundry once a week. Nick and his parents agreed that they would visit him once a week, beginning each visit by finding something to compliment in his apartment and offering their help only if Nick asked them. Nick and his family found the input of other clients and family members very helpful.

SUMMARY

Behavioral family therapy (BFT) and multifamily groups (MFGs) provide family members with the knowledge, strategies, and skills that are needed to help their relative manage severe mental illnesses, such as schizophrenia, bipolar disorder, and major depression. Both models have been shown to improve outcomes for the client (most notably reduced relapses and rehospitalizations) and the family (reduced burden and distress). Each model of family intervention has its advantages, and some families may benefit from participating in a combination of both approaches. BFT is provided in a single-family format and can be tailored to meet the needs of individual families with a wide range of different problems associated with their relative's illness, including families who cannot or will not attend clinic-based sessions, but who can be engaged in their homes. BFT can be initiated relatively quickly because it does not require gathering several families who can meet for group sessions at the same time. The MFG model, however, provides unique opportunities to families through validation, social support, and the chance to learn from other families' experiences. Conducting MFGs also allows clinicians to provide assistance to several families concurrently. Being knowledgeable about both models of family intervention will help clinicians respond to the needs of a variety of families.

Social workers often find that conducting BFT and MFGs fits naturally with their training and orientation. Social work has a long history of working with families (Solomon, Marshall, Mannion, & Farmer, 2002), providing education (Lukens & Prchal, 2002), building on strengths (Rapp, 1997), and developing support networks within the community (Tracy, 2002). These traditions provide a strong foundation for working with families collaboratively in order to improve the outcome of severe mental illness and enhance the quality of all family members' lives.

REFERENCES

Bateson, G., Jackson, D. D., Haley, J., & Weakland, J. (1956). Toward a theory of schizophrenia. *Behavioral Science, 1,* 251–264.

Becker, D. R., & Drake, R. E. (2003). *A working life for people with severe mental illness.* New York: Oxford University Press.

Bellack, A. S., Mueser, K. T., Gingerich, S., & Agresta, J. (2004). *Social skills training for schizophrenia: A step-by-step guide* (2nd ed.). New York: Guilford.

Bond, G. R., & Jones, A. (2005). Supported employment. In R. Drake, M. Merrens, & D. Lynde (Eds.), *Evidence-based mental health practice: A textbook* (pp. 367–393). New York: W. W. Norton.

Brown, S., & Birtwistle, J. (1998). People with schizophrenia and their families: Fifteen-year outcome. *British Journal of Psychiatry, 173,* 139–144.

Burland, J. (1998). Family-to-Family: A trauma and recovery model of family education. *New Directions in Mental Health Services, 77,* 33–44.

Cardin, V. A., McGill, C. W., & Falloon, I. R. H. (1986). An economic analysis: Costs, benefits and effectiveness. In I. R. H. Falloon (Ed.), *Family management of schizophrenia* (pp. 15–123). Baltimore: Johns Hopkins University Press.

Carpentier, N., Lesage, A., Goulet, I., Lalone, P., & Renaud, M. (1992). Burden of care of families not living with a young schizophrenic relative. *Hospital and Community Psychiatry, 43,* 38–43.

Dixon, L., Lucksted, A., Stewart, B., Burland, J., Brown, C. H., Postrado, L., et al. (2004). Outcomes of the peer-taught 12-week family-to-family education program for severe mental illness. *Acta Psychiatrica Scandinavica, 109,* 207–215.

Dixon, L., McFarlane, W., Lefley, H., Lucksted, A., Cohen, C., Falloon, I., et al. (2001). Evidence-based practices for services to family members of people with psychiatric disabilities. *Psychiatric Services, 52,* 903–910.

Dixon, L., Stewart, B., Burland, J., Delahanty, J., Lucksted, A., & Hoffman, M. (2001). Pilot study of the family-to-family education program. *Psychiatric Services, 52,* 965–967.

Falloon, I. R. H., Boyd, J. L., & McGill, C. W. (1984). *Family care of schizophrenia: A problem-solving approach to the treatment of mental illness.* New York: Guilford.

Falloon, I. R. H., Held, T., Coverdale, J. H., Roncone, R., & Laidlaw, T. M. (1999). Family interventions for schizophrenia: A review of long-term benefits of international studies. *Psychiatric Rehabilitation Skills, 3,* 268–290.

Fromm-Reichman, F. (1948). Notes on the development of treatment of schizophrenics by psychoanalytic psychotherapy. *Psychiatry, 1,* 263–273.

Gingerich, S. (2002). Guidelines for social skills training for persons with mental illness. In A. R. Roberts & G. J. Greene (Eds.), *Social workers' desk reference.* New York: Oxford University Press.

Goldman, H. H. (1984). The chronically mentally ill: Who are they? Where are they? In M. Mirabi (Ed.), *The chronically mentally ill: Research and services* (pp. 33–44). New York: Spectrum.

Hatfield, A. B., & Lefley, H. P. (Eds.). (1987). *Families of the mentally ill: Coping and adaptation.* New York: Guilford.

Hatfield, A. B., & Lefley, H. P. (1993). *Surviving mental illness: Stress, coping and adaptation.* New York: Guilford.

Lehman, A. F., & Steinwachs, D. M. (1998). At issue: Translating research into practice: The Schizophrenia Patient Outcomes Research Team (PORT) treatment recommendations. *Schizophrenia Bulletin 24,* 1–9.

Liberman, R. P., DeRisi, W. J., & Mueser, K. T. (2001). *Social skills training for psychiatric patients.* Boston: Allyn & Bacon.

Lukens, E. P., & Prchal, K. (2002). Social workers as educators. In K. J. Bentley (Ed.), *Social work practice in mental health: Contemporary roles, tasks, and techniques* (pp. 122–142). Pacific Grove, CA: Brooks/Cole.

McFarlane, W. R. (2002). *Multifamily groups in the treatment of severe psychiatric disorders.* New York: Guilford.

McFarlane, W. R., Link, B., Dushay, R., Marchal, J., & Crilly, J. (1995). Psychoeducational multiple family groups: Four-year relapse outcome in schizophrenia. *Family Process, 34,* 127–144.

McFarlane, W. R., Lukens, E., Link, B., Dushay, R., Deakins, S. A., Newmark, et al. (1995). Multiple-family groups and psychoeducation in the treatment of schizophrenia. *Archives of General Psychiatry, 52,* 679–687.

Mental Health System Transformation/Evidence-based Practices. From www.samhsa.gov.

Miklowitz, D. J., & Goldstein, M. J. (1997). *Bipolar disorder: A family-focused treatment approach.* New York: Guilford.

Mueser, K. T. (2001). Family treatment of schizophrenia and bipolar disorder. In M. M. MacFarlane (Ed.), *Family therapy and mental health: Innovations in theory and practice.* New York: Haworth Press.

Mueser, K. T. (2004). Families and major mental illness. In D. R. Craine & E. S. Marshall (Eds.), *Handbook of families and health: Interdisciplinary perspectives.* Newbury Park, CA: Sage.

Mueser, K. T., & Brunette, M. F. (2003). Couples-based interventions for schizophrenia-spectrum disorders. In D. K. Snyder & M. A. Whisman (Eds.), *Treating difficult couples: Helping clients with coexisting mental and relationship disorders.* New York: Guilford.

Mueser, K. T., & Gingerich, S. (in press). *Family guide to recovery from schizophrenia.* New York: Guilford.

Mueser, K. T., & Glynn, S. M. (1999). *Behavioral family therapy for psychiatric disorders* (2nd ed.). Oakland, CA: New Harbinger.

Mueser, K. T., Noordsy, D. L., Drake, R. E., & Fox, L. (2003). *Integrated treatment for dual disorders: A guide to effective practice.* New York: Guilford.

Mueser, K. T., Sengupta, A., Schooler, N. R., Bellack, A. S., Xie, H., Glick, et al. (2001). Family treatment and medication dosage reduction in schizophrenia: Effects on patient social functioning, family attitudes, and burden. *Journal of Consulting and Clinical Psychology, 69,* 3–12.

Murray-Swank, A., & Dixon, L. (2005). Evidence-based practices for families of individuals with severe mental illness. In R. Drake, M. Merrens, & D. Lynde (Eds.), *Evidence-based mental health practice: A textbook* (pp. 425–452). New York: W. W. Norton.

Pilling, S., Bebbington, P., Kuipers, E., Garety, P., Geddes, J. R., Orbach, G., et al. (2002). Psychological treatments in schizophrenia: I. Meta-analysis of family intervention and cognitive behavior therapy. *Psychological Medicine, 32,* 763–782.

Pitschel-Walz, G., Leucht, S., Bäuml, J., Kissling, W., & Engel, R. R. (2001). The effect of family interventions on relapse and rehospitalization in schizophrenia: A meta-analysis. *Schizophrenia Bulletin, 27,* 73–92.

Rapp, C. A. (1997). *Strengths model: Case management for people suffering from severe and persistent mental illness.* New York: Oxford University Press.

Schooler, N. R., Keith, S. J., Severe, J. B., Matthews, S. M., Bellack, A. S., Glick, I. D., et al. (1997). Relapse and rehospitalization during maintenance treatment of schizophrenia: The effects of dose reduction and family treatment. *Archives of General Psychiatry, 54,* 453–463.

Social workers outnumber other mental health professionals. (1999). *NAMI Advocate* 21(2), p. 1.

Solomon, P., Draine, J., Mannion, E., & Meisel, M. (1996). Impact of brief family psychoeducation on self-efficacy. *Schizophrenia Bulletin, 22,* 41–50.

Solomon, P., Marshall, T. B., Mannion, E., & Farmer, J. (2002). Social workers as consumer and family consultants. In K. J. Bentley (Ed.), *Social work practice in mental health: Contemporary roles, tasks, and techniques* (pp. 230–253). Pacific Grove, CA: Brooks/Cole.

Substance Abuse and Mental Health Services Administration. "Evidence-based mental health system transformation." Downloadable at www.samhsa.gov.

Substance Abuse and Mental Health Services Administration. *Family psychoeducation implementation resource kit.* Downloadable at www.samhsa.gov.

Sullivan, H. S. (1972). The onset of schizophrenia. *American Journal of Psychiatry, 7,* 105–134.

Tarrier, N., Lowson, K., & Barrowclough, C. (1991). Some aspects of family interventions in schizophrenia: II. Financial considerations. *British Journal of Psychiatry, 167,* 473–479.

Tracy, E. M. (2002). Working with and strengthening social networks. In A. R. Roberts and G. J. Greene (Eds.), *Social workers' desk reference.* New York: Oxford University Press.

CHAPTER 16

Mature Adults

Working With the Depressed Aging Patient

Marjorie R. Zahn
Bruce S. Zahn

INTRODUCTION

The clinical social worker typically interfaces with older adult clients and their families in a variety of settings, providing diverse services ranging from assessment to clinical treatment to referral. The social worker has the unique perspective of being able to view the elderly client as a "whole" person and to carefully evaluate a broad range of aspects of that person's life and their impact on health and mental health. Social workers in very different roles can be instrumental in helping the depressed elderly to make significant changes in mood, behavior, and relationships with others. Due to the wide range of services the clinical social worker may provide across diverse settings, opportunities exist for the social worker to introduce a variety of cognitive-behavior interventions that can be vital to improving quality of life of these often challenging clients.

This chapter discusses the ways in which cognitive behavior therapy (CBT) techniques can be used by social workers across different milieu to assist elderly clients who may be suffering from depression. These settings include the client's home, an inpatient or outpatient mental health facility, a hospital or medical setting, a long-term care facility, or a hospice setting.

Because the role of the social worker can be so varied, we discuss how the use of cognitive-behavior techniques can be beneficial in all areas of intervention with depressed elderly clients, expanding beyond the concept of the "treatment" paradigms of 15 to 20 sessions of formal individual therapy. This chapter gives an overview of how cognitive behavior techniques can be integrated throughout the range of services social workers may provide to elderly clients. Clinical examples demonstrate the use of CBT in a variety of settings.

LITERATURE REVIEW

Much of the literature in the field of aging over the past 20 years has discussed a continued growth in the aging population as the generation of baby boomers moves into old age. At the same time, advances in medical technology and health care have occurred, allowing for a larger aging population to also be living much longer than older adults of previous generations. In 2003, the older population (persons 65 years or older) numbered 35.9 million. They represented 12.3% of the U.S. population, or about one in every eight Americans. It has been estimated that by 2030, there will be about 71.5 million older persons, more than twice their number in 2000. People aged 65 and older represented 12.4% of the population in the year 2000, but are expected to grow to be 20% of the population by 2030 (Administration on Aging, 2005). While medical advances have allowed some people to enter their older years with fewer health problems, the diversity of our elderly population with regard to age span, racial and ethnic background, socioeconomic status, and physical and emotional health requires a mechanism to provide numerous vitally needed services to a large and changing group of older adults.

Little is known about the treatment of depression in the elderly, including prevalence, assessment, and treatment (Thompson, 1996; Walker & Clarke, 2001). According to one survey of physicians, only 8% reported working with the elderly (Levendusky & Hufford, 1997). The reasons for avoiding this segment of the population are unclear but may include stigma and stereotypes (Leszcz, 1997). Complicating the picture is the observation that the elderly are not always forthright about their emotional symptoms. They may believe that psychological disorders are a sign of weakness, and among this population there is considerable stigma associated with mental health care (Casey & Grant, 1993; Leszcz, 1997). The elderly may underreport their symptoms or misattribute their symptoms to some other disorder. Patient reluctance, combined with undertrained practitioners, leads to under diagnosis and mistreatment of depression in the elderly.

The comprehensive picture of individual needs, which is central to the social work tradition, suggests that the clinical social worker may be the professional who is most likely to come into contact with depressed elderly clients in medical and clinical settings (Kirst-Ashman, 2003). The social worker is often the primary contact person encountered by the older adult or a family member in a hospital, long-term care facility, or a hospice setting. In mental health settings, the social worker may provide both clinical and case management services to clients and families.

The diversity of services provided by social workers to older adult clients in various settings, coupled with a growing elderly population, suggests that the numbers of competently trained social workers will need to increase in order to adequately serve the older adult population. While the National Institute of Aging (1987) found that fewer than 30,000 U.S. social workers were either working full-time or part-time with the elderly, projections suggest that, by 2010, 60,000 to 70,000 social workers will be needed (Council on Social Work Education/SAGE-SW, 2001, p. 1). In an effort to increase the study of gerontological issues in social work education programs, the Council for Social Work Education (CSWE) has undertaken a major initiative to provide training to social work faculty and incentives to students who specialize in the field of aging. The $5.2 million Transforming Geriatric Social Work Education Program, managed by CSWE, "supports the incorporation of gerontology in curricula at 67 schools of social work, in both BSW and MSW programs" (O'Neill, 2003, p. 3).

Cognitive and behavioral interventions in social work practice have many advantages over other interventions with the elderly. The didactic approach of CBT "may be acceptable to elderly patients who may be biased against traditional psychodynamic psychotherapy" (Casey et al., 1993, p. 300). In addition, excessive dependency and potential regression are minimized by the collaborative nature of the relationship (Leszcz, 1997). Finally, CBT is focused on the "here and now," is focused and practical, goal oriented, and educative, typically challenging maladaptive beliefs such as "you can't teach an old dog new tricks" (Morris & Morris, 1991).

CBT is both a skills-based intervention designed to increase efficacy of coping ability and a depth therapeutic approach that can quickly clarify long-held beliefs (schemata) and assumptions about self, world, and future that are at the core of many depressed individuals' thinking. One of the assumptions about the conduct of CBT relates to the structure of therapy.

Many of the methods in CBT are directly focused on challenging irrational or distorted assumptions. These thoughts may initially seem quite true, not only to the depressed elderly client but also to family members and other caregivers who identify with the distorted assumption that depression and loss are *necessary* and logical outcomes of aging. For example, a significant challenge to social workers intervening with the depressed elderly client is to resist "buying in" to the sometimes overwhelming "evidence" from multiple sources regarding the elderly client's loss of function and meaning in life. Striking a balance between acceptance of *some* losses, while still maintaining a realistic perspective on what the elderly client *can* still do, is fundamental to the cognitive behavior method.

In terms of technique, much of the literature on CBT is scarce when it comes to applications to the depressed elderly. The prevailing assumption is that the same methods and techniques that have been demonstrated to be efficacious and effective with adult populations can be extrapolated to older adults. One of these assumptions relates to the structure of therapy.

The formal structure of therapy is typically divided into three phases: (1) socialization to cognitive behavior treatment, (2) formal treatment phase, and (3) relapse prevention (Laidlaw, Thompson, Dick-Siskin, & Gallagher-Thompson, 2003). Yet, it is relatively uncommon for social workers to conduct formal psychotherapeutic services with elderly clients in an ongoing basis in medical and long-term care facilities, as these psychotherapeutic services are often contracted with other mental health providers, such as psychologists and psychiatrists. Therefore, the social worker who works with the depressed elderly client needs to be especially skilled at rapid case conceptualization and the ability to target cognitive and behavior methods in strategically focused interventions. These interventions may be as brief as a single session, or might extend over a long period of time in informal therapeutic contacts, such as during family meetings or discharge planning conferences.

ISSUES/APPLICATIONS ACROSS VARIOUS SETTINGS

In-Home Services

Because of the desirability of maintaining elderly clients in their own homes whenever possible, the scope and range of in-home services for older adults has grown considerably over the past two decades. Social workers may see elderly clients in their homes in conjunction with other health care providers through a home-health agency or may provide individual in-home services through an array of community-based programs. Services the social worker may provide in a home setting are diverse, ranging from assessment to planning and referral and from supportive services to individual and family counseling.

Despite the wide range of services that may be provided, there are some common issues experienced by older adult clients in their own homes. A social work assessment of an elderly client must encompass not only a diagnostic assessment of one's emotional functioning, but also a practical assessment of one's continued ability to perform a variety of activities of daily living required to live independently. For many older adult clients, issues related to the need for increasing dependence on family, friends, and paid caretakers may become the central focus of counseling. While many older adults living independently may experience a variety of emotional changes including an increase in depression and anxiety, the need to maintain a sense of one's self-sufficiency seems to be a major factor in causing emotional distress.

One possible explanation for this focus may be that the concept of dependence versus independence is related to a belief system that values one's ability to function on one's own and devalues the process of asking for help. While individual belief systems may emerge based on a variety of personal experiences, the emphasis on independence as being desirable is also strong culturally supported. Therefore, the use of a cognitive-behavior approach that challenges long-held beliefs about dependence and independence may be an important component of working with older adult clients in their own homes.

CASE STUDY

Paul was 79 years old and had been living alone in his home since his wife died 6 years ago. After his wife's death, Paul had to take over some of the tasks that were primarily accomplished by his wife. To his surprise, Paul found that he really enjoyed and became quite proficient at grocery shopping and preparing meals. Paul had been able to maintain his household and his personal care fairly well. He received occasional assistance from his daughter and son-in-law, who lived 10 miles away. He also visited them at their home once or twice a month.

Although Paul and his wife had many friends as a couple, Paul was able to maintain an active social life after her death. He met three longtime friends for breakfast at the neighborhood diner every Thursday and enjoyed a game of poker with his buddies one or two nights a week. Most of Paul's friends lived within 5 miles from his home, although one lived almost 15 miles away.

At a recent doctor's appointment though, Paul received news that really hit him hard. He was diagnosed with macular

(continues)

degeneration, a visual condition that results in serious visual impairment and sometimes blindness. The physician told Paul that because the course of the illness can vary greatly, he would recommend that Paul stop driving as soon as possible. Paul's daughter, who was with him at the doctor's office, told him she wanted to discuss a plan for getting him more help when he could no longer drive. Paul refused to discuss this with her, went to his bedroom, and wouldn't come out for two days. He refused to eat and wouldn't talk to anyone. His daughter, who was worried and stayed at his house with him, finally called a home health agency for an assessment.

When the home health social worker came out the first time, Paul refused to speak to her, but the second time he came downstairs and sat in the room with her. From speaking with the daughter, the social worker began to suspect the giving up his car represented a major loss to Paul. Therefore, she talked with Paul about his beliefs about independence and dependence, and how the concept of driving came to symbolize these constructs. Paul remembered lessons he learned as a child, which taught him "to be strong and not to ask for help." The social worker also asked him about his first car. Paul said he remembered feeling "like I had wings. I could go anywhere and do anything." He remembered thinking "I'm really a man now."

Paul's social worker spent several sessions talking with him about these beliefs and acknowledged his feelings of loss related to driving. She also actively encouraged him to evaluate some of the ways in which he could still accomplish the activities and enjoy his friendships, even if he was not able to drive. By challenging his assumptions with data that he hadn't previously considered, Paul became willing to consider other ideas about independence and dependence that were not quite so black or white.

The social worker was able to introduce the idea that people who are not able to drive can still be highly functioning, productive citizens, and worked with Paul to evaluate the advantages of modifying his beliefs against the disadvantages. She also worked with him use the techniques of examining the evidence and the experimental method to "road test" some new ideas about independence and "manliness." Paul soon began to conclude that he could make plans to ask his friends to drive for social occasions or to use public transit when necessary, and that this did not mean that he was any "less of a man." He came to accept his visual disability and to adjust his lifestyle so that he could still function at the highest possible level. His symptoms of depression soon abated, and he was able to continue with many of the activities he had previously enjoyed.

Services in a Hospital or Medical Setting

For many older adults who do not experience major emotional or psychological problems as they age, the opportunity to interact with a social work professional occurs in a hospital or medical setting and is focused primarily on health-related changes. One risk factor for depression among the elderly that may be encountered is related to vascular processes. The "vascular hypothesis of geriatric depression" holds that elderly patients with vascular risk factors appear to be more susceptible to geriatric depression (Delano-Wood & Abeles, 2005). Other medical risk factors known to be associated with late-life depression include hypertension, coronary artery disease, and diabetes (Delano-Wood et al., 2005).

The relationship between depression and medical issues in the elderly is often manifested in excess disability. Excess disability is impairment in functioning beyond what would be typical for a particular disorder. For instance, a depressive episode can exacerbate a preexisting medical condition or lengthen the recovery process, resulting in increased morbidity and health care utilization. Additionally, depressed participants undergoing rehabilitation for physical impairments (a fractured hip, for example) tend to have poorer outcomes, as they experience decreased motivation, become easily fatigued, and feel discouraged about their recovery (Cohen, 1997).

Elderly clients may enter the hospital for an infinite number of medical reasons that are complicated by family and living considerations. A thorough biopsychosocial and family assessment can provide a wealth of information to the social worker and other members of the treatment team. Despite the different reasons for admission among hospital patients, however, there are some issues that seem to be somewhat universal among older adult patients. Changes in medical status generally result in loss in level of functioning. While the effects of that loss may vary somewhat, depending on whether the situation is temporary or more permanent, the psychological issues present during the hospital stay may vary little.

Issues related to loss in level of functioning frequently trigger concerns about one's continued ability to live and function independently. When other family members are involved in the older person's life, these concerns may elicit a variety of cognitions and emotions and sometimes may lead to disagreements about the best course of action for the older adult. Occasionally, decisions must be made during a hospital stay about whether the older person can return home or will require a higher level of care. Because of her role as a liaison between the medical staff and the patient and family, the social worker is in the unique position to assist the family in making these decisions and helping both the patient and his or her family process the implications and emotional issues related to such decisions.

Other issues that are relevant to older adults in a medical setting are concerns about increased dependence on others, changes in significant relationships, and fears about illness and death. Indeed, many depressed elders express their depression through somatic symptoms, a condition that is often referred to as *somatization*. Others may complain of confusion and memory impairments, claiming that there must be something medically wrong with them. This is referred to as *pseudodementia*, and is often symptomatic of depression once dementia has been ruled out.

Dysfunctional beliefs about illness may serve to deflate resolve and decrease motivation to combat depression. The depressed elder in an inpatient hospital setting may adopt the sick role and exhibit severe lethargy and anhedonia, complaining that he has no energy or desire to engage in activities such as participating in physical therapy sessions, going to religious services, or taking care of simple activities of daily living, which have the potential to enhance recovery and quality of life. The depressed elder in this situation begins to narrow his sphere of activities to include only those activities associated with the illness, such as doctor's appointments and medication administration. Family and friends may notice conversations revolving solely around illness-related topics to the exclusion of other hobbies, interests, or activities.

The meaning of illness can be traced to core beliefs about sickness and health that are developed early in life. Interpreted through a negative filter of pessimism, illness becomes an albatross around one's neck, signaling gloom and doom. The rule in such self-handicapping thinking is that "As long as you've got your health, you've got everything." A corollary of this belief is "As long as I'm sick (and in need of medical care), I cannot be happy."

CASE STUDY

Anthony was a 73-year-old Italian immigrant who had been in America since he was a young man in his twenties. He had lost his wife 2 years ago, and was looked after by his only daughter who lived a few towns away. A proud and strong-willed man, Anthony continued to live in his cozy rowhouse since his wife's death, where he tended a small garden and enjoyed talking with neighbors about the community and the local sports teams. He had closed his tailor shop several years ago in order to take care of his wife, Amelia, who had developed Parkinson's disease. A diabetic, Anthony continued to self-administer his medication, although he never exercised and still ate foods that were not on his "safe" list prepared by his daughter.

One day, Anthony suffered a serious fall in his home and had to be taken to the hospital. He was stabilized there while the medical staff kept him for observation and more tests. When he woke up the next day in the hospital, he became agitated and morbid, refusing to eat meals or take care of himself.

Later in the morning, the unit social worker made a visit to Anthony and interviewed him. He explained in a thick accent that he did understand why he was being held in the hospital "against my will." "I am going to die here, aren't I?" he stated. "Why else wouldn't they let me go home? " he said despondently.

The social worker understood that Anthony was most likely suffering from temporary relocation stress, and educated him about the procedures in the hospital. In addition, she called his daughter and asked her to attend a conference as soon as possible regarding the disposition of his discharge. She used a brief problem-solving model, asking Anthony to consider the range of all possible explanations for his continued hospital stay, not just the one that he had arbitrarily concluded. When they evaluated the list of possible explanations for continued hospital stay and the probability of each, they mutually agreed that the most reasonable explanation was that the medical staff wanted to make certain that he was "medically mended" before allowing him to go home. When Anthony's daughter arrived at the hospital later that day, he had calmed down considerably and was prepared to discuss discharge options.

Services in a Mental Health Setting

For some older persons, chronic behavioral health issues ranging from mood disorders to psychosis to substance abuse problems have resulted in lifelong contact with mental health professionals. These interactions and experiences have led to a number of assumptions and beliefs on the part of the older adult about the providers of mental health services. For other older persons, however, an initial contact with providers of these services may not occur until one is elderly and may be related to a variety of medical or adjustment problems. Dementia, stroke, Parkinson's disease and other neurological changes may lead the older adult client to seek or be referred for mental health services. Such later life incidents of emotional distress may also have a profound effect on the older person's perceptions about providers of mental health services.

For the clinical social worker in an inpatient, outpatient, or partial psychiatric hospital setting, the assessment phase of treatment with an older adult client is critical. An assessment must include a complete bio-psychosocial history, as well as a thorough survey of current functioning. A pertinent medical history is also an essential component of such an assessment and should contribute to the case conceptualization. While the role and function of the social worker may vary depending on the particular setting and population, once the assessment case conceptualization is completed, a treatment plan must be devised that reflects the clients' individual needs and level of functioning. Treatment in an inpatient or outpatient setting might include individual or group therapy as well as adjunctive therapies provided by the social worker or other mental health professional. A cognitive behavior focus would be beneficial in helping the older adult client to overcome some of the misperceptions and distorted beliefs about medical changes, personal and functional losses, later life changes, and decreased functioning.

The final responsibility of the social worker in an inpatient or outpatient mental health setting is usually referral. While this can appear to be a straightforward effort to ensure continuity of care, it can also involve a more complex process in which the social worker can help the older adult to understand and "invest" in his or her continued movement toward maximal emotional health and behavioral functioning. Because the therapeutic benefits of this referral process can be diverse, this may be an area in which the social worker can have a great impact on elderly clients.

Whether the social worker is interacting with the client in order to complete the assessment and case conceptualization, to provide direct treatment, or to facilitate follow-up care, some common issues may be encountered when working with the older adult client in a mental health setting. While the client's diagnosis, previous mental health treatment, and current medical and emotional status will have an effect on the issues being presented, the social worker will find it useful to identify specific difficulties found among this older adult population.

For example, a common theme associated with an older adult population is loss. While later life losses may be related to death of family and friends or to loss of functioning due to health issues, older adults with chronic mental health or substance abuse problems may also experience a sense of loss in older age related to missed opportunities and successes. When providing group therapy for this population, the theme of loss can be useful in "joining" a group of older adult clients who may have very different backgrounds.

CASE STUDY

Fred was a despondent, frail man on dialysis whose withered appearance belied his 64 years of age. He had led a rough and tumble life, having had a history of alcohol and substance abuse, as well as some brushes with the law for assault. He had several jobs over the years, mostly as a short-order cook or food prep man at a couple of the classier restaurants in town when he was sober. He had been married and divorced three times, and had five grown children who lived in the area but who rarely visited him.

In the partial hospital program, Fred stayed in a corner of the therapy room, appearing more of a bystander than an active participant. When he was asked by his social worker about his interest in engaging in potentially interesting and satisfying activities, Fred disavowed any such interest and looked squarely in his eyes. "Hey, man," he said in a dry and raspy voice. "You commit the crime, you do the time! I've been nothing but trouble for everybody all my life. I just want to be left alone now, so I don't mess up anyone else's life. I have nothing good to contribute to the others here."

Fred's social worker acknowledged his feelings, but asked him if he was interested in testing out his ideas about payment for his "crimes." He was encouraged to make a list of all of the "bad" things that he had done over his lifetime, and weigh them against the "good things" to see if the "good scale" balanced in his favor. His social worker also challenged him to consider sharing his idea about having nothing positive to contribute with the other members of the group, and test out his belief that one must be *necessarily condemned* to *always* suffer for human errors. When he bravely did so one day, he found to his surprise that the others in the group were willing to "commute his sentence," based on "good behavior" with his peers during the partial hospital program. Finally, Fred was asked to explore his beliefs about his faith and its relation to the concept of forgiveness, just as he would forgive a good friend for errors made in the course of living and learning. He was encouraged to use a modified Thought Record, using a double-column technique (see the following chart) to identify negative and distorted depressogenic thoughts, and talk back to them using a voice of loving kindness and forgiveness.

(*continues*)

Condemning Thoughts	Forgiving Thoughts
"You do the crime, you pay the time."	"I've paid enough. Now it's time to get on with things and help others as well as myself. That's surely going to put me in the plus column."
"I've been nothing but trouble for everybody all my life."	"I've had my share of trouble, but I've also done some good things, too. And my life isn't over yet! Now's the time to start changing things for the positive!"
"I have nothing good to contribute to the others here."	"That remains to be seen. I'll try to get real *now* and give it my all. That's the best I can do, and I'm willing to try. I'll let the chips fall where they may."

Services in a Long-Term Care Setting

The social worker employed in a long-term care facility may have the most challenging responsibilities when providing services to older adult clients and their families. A nursing home or long-term care placement of an older person may elicit a myriad of emotions and concerns on the part of family members and may involve a difficult physical and emotional adjustment for the older adult. The role of the social worker in this setting is multifaceted and may include intake, assessment, liaison with other health professionals, insurance and financial verifications, case management, and a great deal of contact with families. Although it is less likely in this setting, an appropriately trained social worker can also provide individual or group counseling. In many long-term care facilities, however, counseling or psychotherapy is a contracted service provided by private practitioners or practitioner groups. For this reason, the social worker in this setting must be able to use the opportunities available to provide a "therapeutic" experience to residents and families each time a contact is made.

Often the social worker is the first person to greet the older adult and his or her family upon admission and this initial contact may help to establish a more positive focus and easier adjustment. Cognitive behavior techniques can be used even in this initial contact to gain a better understanding of the older adult's beliefs about nursing home placement and to provide an alternative perspective that might help ease the transition period. For example, the social worker might learn in an intake interview with an older person that his belief about nursing homes is that "you go to a nursing home to be lonely and to die." In this case, the social worker might try to use this initial contact to gently introduce the idea that social interaction and companionship is possible in the long-term care setting. The social worker can also use her role as a case manager to help monitor the adjusting resident's view of nursing home life and to provide an alternative perspective whenever possible. In this way, she can help to ensure a continued therapeutic experience that decreases irrational thinking and focuses on coping with each day's challenges.

In interactions with family members, the social worker also has the opportunity to provide a realistic portrait of the common adjustment difficulties of long-term care placement. The family should understand that some older people may experience a period of depression with sleep or appetite disturbance and social isolation and that, while for some residents the depression will get better on its own, for others some kind of treatment or psychological intervention might be required. Because families of new residents may be experiencing many different emotions, including sadness, guilt and even anger, the social worker can provide support and reassurance by helping the family to have realistic expectations about the adjustment period and an understanding of what services the facility can offer during that time.

While the issues that are critical to nursing home residents are similar to those seen among older adults in the other settings already mentioned, the nursing home resident often seems to experience an intense kind of loneliness and isolation that can be devastating to one's sense of self-worth. Therefore, it may be beneficial to address this issue early in the resident's stay and to attempt to gain an understanding of what beliefs and ideas are helping the older adult to maintain this isolation. A cognitive behavior approach does not assume that the resident needs to interact more with peers or would benefit from more social activity. However, the social worker may use her developing relationship with the client to help her reach an empathic understanding about what is happening in the client's world and this may provide some clues about how to help the resident move past this phase.

CASE STUDY

Ethel was a 73-year-old homemaker who lost her husband of 46 years several years ago. She had two caring children who lived in neighboring communities, both of whom dutifully looked after her despite their busy family lives and careers.

About 4 months ago, Ethel had a mild stroke that left her partially paralyzed on her right side. As a resident in an assisted

(continues)

living facility, she continued her recuperation following a brief stay in a nursing rehabilitation center. She had limited use of her left hand, and she ambulated with a tripod cane due to weakness in her left leg. She had considerable difficulty performing routine activities of daily living such as dressing herself and bathing. It seemed that everywhere she turned, Ethel felt defeated by her disabilities. There were mild residual cognitive deficits from the stroke, including some impairment in memory. Her thinking was generally concrete.

The physical therapy exercises designed to strengthen her grip and ability to walk independently resulted in marginal progress, and Ethel became more and more angry and frustrated. Feeling betrayed by her body, she finally came to the conclusion that her life would never be the same, and that there was nothing that she could do about this tragedy. She was not actively suicidal, but she maintained a passive death wish. "I can't use my arm and leg anymore. This is going to be the death of me." Ethel's negative and distorted thoughts sounded like this: "There's nothing that I can do anymore." "I'll never be happy again." "I'm totally dependent on other people now." "Nobody cares about me."

In a small, structured group led by an a social worker trained in cognitive behavioral therapy, Ethel was first taught to assess her symptoms of depression. She was instructed in the basics of CBT by learning about the connection between her perceptions and evaluations ("I am totally disabled"), her moods (dysphoria), and her behaviors (lethargy). In a group exercise, she and her peers practiced responding with spontaneous thoughts and associated feelings to pictures of various landscapes from travel magazines, noticing that the same picture (event) could evoke different thoughts (positive, neutral, or negative) and moods (happy, neutral, sad).

For example, when looking at a picture of the seashore and boardwalk, one peer related fond memories and a happy mood, while Ethel shared her feelings of sadness and loss associated with her automatic thought ("I'll never be able to walk the boards again or enjoy the Jersey shore."). She also participated in small-group exercises with several peers, reading and discussing various scenarios from her workbook that described situations not unlike those she had experienced, noticing that the same situation could be viewed with various degrees of optimism or pessimism. In a group discussion led by the social worker, Ethel began to see that her view of her current physical condition was influencing her mood, although she did not yet understand how to perceive her reality differently.

In ensuing group sessions, Ethel was encouraged to define what she meant by the term *disabled,* and group members worked to point out to her how her definitions encompassed the categorical distortion of black-or-white thinking. She began to examine the evidence that she was "totally disabled" by using her peers to help her to collect and record small successes in participating in pleasurable "blues busting" activities. She was also encouraged to gather evidence of ways in which she was not disabled, using a three-column form, What I Can Do, designed to record three levels of achievement: (1) What I Can Still Do, (2) What I Can Still Do, with Some Difficulty, and (3) What I Can No Longer Do (Zahn & Davis, 2001).

Ethel was then taught to begin to challenge her self-evaluations and predictions by using the Life Event Enjoyment Index (Zahn et al., 2001). First she planned an activity with some potential for personal enjoyment with the help of the nursing staff, such as slowly taking a walk to the garden. Then she rated her prediction of how much enjoyment she would get out of it on a scale of 0 (none) to 100 (maximal). She then engaged in this activity and performed a post-rating of her enjoyment (Figure 16.1). Through repeated experimentation and encouragement from the nursing home staff, Ethel began to see that her initial evaluations were negatively biased, and often just plain wrong. By suspending judgment, she was apt to be much more motivated to try activities that she had previously shunned because she was convinced that they would be unpleasant.

Finally, Ethel learned how to identify "fuzzy" thoughts (cognitive distortions) that were blurring her view of herself, her abilities, and her surroundings, resulting in negatively biased associations and perceptions and dysphoric mood states. Through practice on structured examples in her workbook, Ethel began to increase her skill at catching these "mental tricks" that were blurring her view of life and interfering with her progress in recovery. In the following weeks, Ethel learned and practiced a variety of coping skills designed to improve her mood and enthusiasm for engaging in daily activities in the assisted living facility. She practiced writing down and role playing how to talk back to her negative and "fuzzy" thoughts using a simplified two-column thought record (My Best Friend Technique), just as she would encourage a good friend who was feeling discouraged about her residual deficits by using compassionate suggestions based on sound reasoning. She also used a similar method to examine the evidence for her thoughts more objectively by using the image of a neutral observer.

(continues)

Prerating: *Before* engaging in any planned activity, circle the number in the box that best describes how much *enjoyment* you *predict* you will get out of that activity.

Postrating: *After* engaging in the activity, circle the number in the box that best describes how much *enjoyment* you *actually* got out of that activity.

Event: The event I plan to do is _____

Before	After
100	100
90	90
80	80
70	70
60	60
50	50
40	40
30	30
20	20
10	10
0	0

What I learned about my prediction: _____

FIGURE 16.1   Life Events Enjoyment Index

With the encouragement of the social worker, the nursing home staff was able to also engage Ethel in a number of CBT-related activities by using props to reinforce learning. One such prop was called "The Perspective Box" (Zahn et al, 2001). The technique is explained as follows: "In the middle of a Pennsylvania cornfield every fall, one farmer uses his tractor to create a large maze. People come from miles away to try to make it through the twisting, turning passages of the maze. At certain places in the labyrinth are areas where people can climb up a ladder to look out over the field to get a better perspective on

their situation, and help them make it through the maze."
Sometimes our thoughts are like that maze. We can get so
locked into our negative/inaccurate thoughts that it seems as if
there's just no way out. Have you ever had a problem like this?
How did you go about solving it? Did you turn the problem
around in your mind until you saw it from a different angle?
Looking at problems from different angles or perspectives can
often be quite helpful when you feel stuck on a particular problem. That's why we will use The Perspective Box to help put
problems in a new light."

The Perspective Box is a cardboard box decorated with
bright yellow construction paper on five sides, and dark construction paper on the sixth side (see Figure 16.2). Ethel's negative

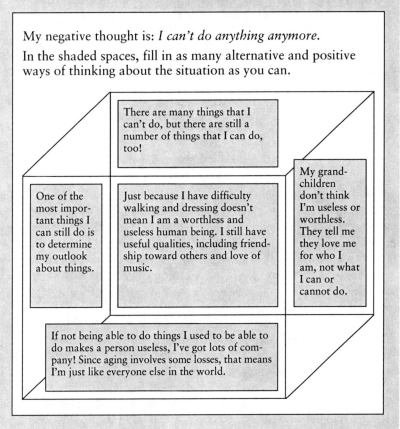

My negative thought is: *I can't do anything anymore.*

In the shaded spaces, fill in as many alternative and positive
ways of thinking about the situation as you can.

There are many things that I can't do, but there are still a number of things that I can do, too!

One of the most important things I can still do is to determine my outlook about things.

Just because I have difficulty walking and dressing doesn't mean I am a worthless and useless human being. I still have useful qualities, including friendship toward others and love of music.

My grandchildren don't think I'm useless or worthless. They tell me they love me for who I am, not what I can or cannot do.

If not being able to do things I used to be able to do makes a person useless, I've got lots of company! Since aging involves some losses, that means I'm just like everyone else in the world.

FIGURE 16.2   The Perspective Box

(continues)

thought, "I can't do anything anymore" was written on a self-adhesive note and attached to the dark side of the box. The box was passed around the group, while various participants volunteered their positive, accurate, and encouraging thoughts. These ideas were written on self-adhesive notes as well and affixed to the bright yellow sides of the box. When the box was finally returned to Ethel, she was instructed to examine all sides of the box, reading the positive messages aloud. When she found a thought that she found to be unmistakably true and believable for her, she peeled off the positive note, as well as the negative note, and attached them back-to-back. She now had a coping card that helped her to gain a new perspective on her situation.

In ensuing sessions, Ethel began to become more adept at using a variety of cognitive and behavior techniques to help her to adjust to her new level of functioning. She became more determined to learn new activities with a potential for pleasure that did not require her to ambulate a great deal, such as playing cards, and she began to reevaluate her definition of herself as disabled. She now referred to herself as *re-abled*, a term that made her smile with a sense of accomplishment, as she sought to make each day one of challenge and self-discovery.

FUTURE DIRECTIONS

As the older adult segment of the population continues to grow due to the aging of the baby boom generation and the medical advances that allow individuals to live longer, there will be a need to provide a range of services to an increasingly diverse elderly cohort. Whether these services are provided in hospitals, mental health settings, long-term care settings, or in the older adult's own home, the social worker is likely to be the first point of contact via social services, as well as a vital provider of clinical services.

While the demand for clinical services for this cohort increases, the expectations and opportunities for the social work professional will also expand. Social workers will not only be required to be expertly knowledgeable in the field of gerontology but they will also be required to provide treatments that are innovative, efficacious, and effective. Incentives have already begun to be offered to social workers who seek additional training in geriatrics. Social workers who are able to provide a range of interventions to help clients turn depressive thinking, moods, and behaviors into more adaptive and productive functioning will find themselves at the cutting edge in the field of gerontology.

Cognitive behavior therapy is the most researched clinical intervention with older adults, and a number of evidence-based treatment packages have been developed (Scogin, Welsh, Hanson, Stump, & Coates, 2005) and shown to be effective. While much research on the use of cognitive behavior therapy with the elderly still needs to be conducted, studies to date have demonstrated that CBT is highly beneficial with the elderly.

As the social work profession begins to support training in both gerontology and in CBT, social workers are expected to expand the opportunities for CBT practice using both traditional applications in clinical practice, and developing creative and timely interventions with the older adult, his or her family, and extended caregivers. One of the potential applications of CBT relates to the use of single-session interventions, or brief informal applications to the patient, the family, and the milieu. In this way, the social worker has the ability to cast the widest net possible in service of assisting older adults to maximize positive health-promoting behaviors and attitudes.

REFERENCES

Administration on Aging. (2005). *Statistics on the aging population*. Retrieved from www.aoa.gov/prof/Statistics/statistics.asp.

Casey, D. A., & Grant, R. W. (1993). Cognitive therapy with depressed elderly inpatients. In J. H. Wright, M. E. Thase, A. T. Beck, & J. W. Ludgate (Eds.), *Cognitive therapy with inpatients* (pp. 295–314). New York: Guilford.

Cohen, G. D. (1997). Gaps and failures in attending to mental health and aging in long term care. In R. L. Rubinstein & M. P. Lawton (Eds.), *Depression in long term and residential care: Advances in research and treatment* (pp. 211–222). New York: Springer.

Council on Social Work Education/SAGE-SW (2001). *A blueprint for the new millenium*. Retrieved from www.cswe.org.sage-sw.

Delano-Wood, L., & Abeles, N. (2005). Late-life depression: Detection, risk-reduction, and somatic intervention. *Clinical Psychology: Science and Practice, 12*, 207–218.

Kirst-Ashman, K. (2003). *Introduction to social work and social welfare: Critical thinking perspectives*. Pacific Grove, CA: Brooks/Cole.

Laidlaw, K., Thompson, L. W., Dick-Siskin, L., & Gallagher-Thompson, D. (2003). *Cognitive behavioral therapy with older people*. West Sussex, UK: John Wiley & Sons.

Leszcz, M. (1997). Integrated group psychotherapy for the treatment of depression in the elderly. *Group, 21*, 89–113.

Levendusky, P. G., & Hufford, M. R. (1997). The application of cognitive-behavior therapy to the treatment of depression and related disorders in the elderly. *Journal of Geriatric Psychiatry, 30*, 227–238.

Morris, R. G., & Morris, L. W. (1991). Cognitive and behavioral approaches with the depressed elderly. *International Journal of Geriatric Psychiatry, 150,* 124–129.

National Institute of Aging. (1987).

O'Neill, J. V. (2003). *Educators focus on aging: Social work education in aging moves out of the shadows. NASW News.* Retrieved from http://caster. ssw.upenn.edu/gswi/overview/nasw_article.html.

Scogin, F., Welsh, D., Hanson, A., Stump, J., & Coates, A. (2005). Evidence-based psychotherapies for depression in older adults. *Clinical Psychology: Science and Practice, 12,* 222–237.

Thompson, L. W. (1996). Cognitive-behavioral therapy and treatment for late-life depression. *Journal of Clinical Psychiatry, 57*(suppl. 5), 29–37.

Walker, D. A., & Clarke, M. (2001). Cognitive behavioral psychotherapy: A comparison between younger and older adults in two inner city mental health teams. *Aging and Mental Health, 5,* 197–199.

Zahn, B. S., & Davis, B. (2001). *When the golden years turn blue.* Unpublished manuscript.

PART V

Focus on Adult and Problem Areas

CHAPTER 17

Cognitive Behavior Therapy for Anxiety Disorders

Joseph A. Himle

INTRODUCTION

Social workers provide the majority of psychosocial services to persons with mental disorders in the United States (Lin, 1995). Community-based epidemiological studies find that when grouped together, anxiety disorders are the most common mental health conditions in the United States apart from substance use disorders (Kessler et al., 1994). Anxiety disorders are also associated with substantial impairments in overall health and well-being, family functioning, social functioning, and vocational outcomes (Mogotsi, Kaminer, & Stein, 2000). Given the high prevalence, substantial functional impairment, and considerable help seeking of anxious clients in social work settings (Chess & Norlin, 1991), it is imperative that social workers become familiar with these conditions and with associated, evidence-based psychosocial interventions. The initial portion of this chapter includes a brief description of the anxiety disorders followed by a more detailed review of the cognitive behavior interventions indicated for these conditions.

The Diagnostic and Statistical Manual of Mental Disorders (American Psychiatric Association, 2000) describes five distinct anxiety disorders. Social phobia (social anxiety disorder) is the most common anxiety disorder in the United States. Social phobia is defined as fear of one or more social or performance situations in which the individual is exposed to the scrutiny of others. Individuals with social phobia are concerned that they will act in a way that will be humiliating or embarrassing. Over 13% of the U.S. population will meet criteria for social anxiety disorder at some point in their lifetime (Kessler et al., 1994). Social phobia subtypes include specific social phobia (e.g., public speaking, eating in public) and generalized social phobia (e.g., fear of most social situations).

Specific (simple) phobia is also a very common anxiety disorder with over 11% of the population meeting criteria for this condition over their lifetime (Kessler et al., 1994). Specific phobia is defined as a marked and persistent fear of a specific object or situation (e.g., flying, heights, animals) that is associated with avoidance or else is endured with dread.

Approximately 5% of the U.S. population meets criteria for generalized anxiety disorder (GAD) (Kessler et al., 1994). GAD is characterized by repetitive, difficult-to-control worries about a number of events or activities. These worries must persist for at least 6 months and must be accompanied by at least three of a list of six symptoms which include restlessness, fatigue, difficulty concentrating, irritability, muscle tension, and sleep problems.

Panic disorder and agoraphobia are common (3.5% and 5.3%, respectively) and related conditions (Kessler et al., 1994). Panic disorder is comprised of a pattern of recurrent unexpected panic attacks. Panic attacks are sudden surges of intense anxiety that reach their peak with 10 minutes and involve at least 4 of a list of 13 symptoms. These symptoms include but are not limited to shortness of breath, rapid heart rate, dizziness, feelings of unreality, and concerns about going crazy, dying, or losing control during an attack. Many individuals with panic disorder feel a strong need to leave the situation once a panic attack occurs in order to get to a place of safety. Because of this need, persons with panic disorder often begin to avoid situations in which escape would be difficult or help not available because of concern about having a panic attack. This pattern of avoidance is known as agoraphobia. Agoraphobia often occurs along with panic disorder but agoraphobia without panic attacks can also be diagnosed. In most of these situations, another problem such as a seizure disorder or irritable bowel syndrome functions somewhat like a panic attack in that these conditions become associated with concerns that an episode will occur in a place far from home, where help may not be available.

Another somewhat less common anxiety disorder is obsessive-compulsive disorder (OCD). OCD involves two main symptoms, obsessions and compulsions. Obsessions are recurrent, intrusive, thoughts, ideas or impulses that are outside of a person's voluntary control. Common obsessions include thoughts about contamination, making a terrible mistake, harming others, religious blasphemy, and symmetry. Typical compulsions include checking, straightening, washing, touching, hoarding, and repeating. Most individuals with OCD have both obsessions and compulsions whereas some experience obsessions or compulsions alone. The lifetime prevalence of OCD is 2.5% in the U.S. population (Karno, Sorenson, & Burnam, 1988).

The final anxiety disorder discussed in this chapter is posttraumatic stress disorder (PTSD). PTSD involves several symptom types that occur in response to a traumatic event that involved death, threatened death, or serious injury to one's self or others. These symptom types include reexperiencing (e.g., repetitive flashbacks, nightmares), avoidance and numbing (e.g., avoiding PTSD-related stimuli, restricted affect), and increased arousal (e.g., easily startled, hypervigilance). The lifetime prevalence of PTSD in the United States is 7.8% (Kessler, Sonnega, Bromet, Hughes, & Nelson, 1995). In order to meet criteria for any of these aforementioned anxiety disorders, individuals must experience either significant impairment or marked distress resulting from the disorder.

COGNITIVE BEHAVIOR THERAPY FOR ANXIETY DISORDERS

Prolonged Real-Life (in vivo) Exposure

Real-life or in-vivo exposure to fearful stimuli, has been a mainstay of CBT for anxiety disorders for several decades (Rachman, Marks, & Hodgson, 1973; Watson, Gaind, & Marks, 1971). The main theoretical underpinning of this technique rests on the observation that when individuals are exposed to fearful stimuli under the proper conditions, reduction in fear occurs (Marks, 1987). Reduction in fear association with prolonged confrontation of fearful stimuli is known as habituation (Marks, 1987). The concept of habituation posits that the body cannot maintain an acute fear state for an indefinite amount of time. In a sense, the body is thought to "tire" of producing substantial amounts of sympathetic activity, resulting in a reduced state of arousal over time.

Much of the initial empirical support for prolonged exposure to fearful stimuli came from studies examining its effect on specific (formally known as simple) phobias. Recent meta-analytic studies support the value of prolonged exposure for specific phobias (Mendez, Rosa, & Orgiles, 2005). For many specific phobias, therapeutic exposure can be applied fairly simply. For example, an individual with a spider phobia could be assisted by a therapist as they gradually confront progressively more challenging stimuli associated with spiders, possibly beginning with a child-like drawing of a spider and finishing with a spider snake resting on their shoulders.

There are several general guidelines to conducting therapeutic in vivo exposure therapy. First, it is important for the person confronting the fear to do so for extended periods. Empirical studies support the value of extended confrontation of phobic stimuli compared to brief encounters. A usual rule of thumb is for exposure sessions to continue for approximately 90 minutes. A second important exposure guideline is for the phobic individual to end the session on a positive note, ending the session only after fear is substantially reduced. In order to accomplish this objective, it is usually essential for the phobic individual to learn a scoring system in order to characterize his or her level of fear. The most common strategy for rating fear is to use a 0 to 100 subjective rating of distress (SUDS; Wolpe, 1973) with 0 indicating calm and 100 noting terror. When exposure is conducted with the help of a therapist, the phobic individual is usually asked to provide a rating of anxiety every few minutes during an exposure session. This rating is useful in judging when it is advisable to conclude a therapeutic exposure session. With self-conducted exposure therapy, the phobic individual is directed to also use SUDS to rate fear during exposure sessions. Just how much reduction in subjective anxiety is required in order to safely terminate an exposure session is not known, but clinical impressions suggest that it is best to end a session when the client's subjective anxiety has declined by about half and has dropped below 50. Ideally, sessions would be ended when the fear declines to zero but this is often not possible within the confines of a 90-minute session.

The fourth guideline for therapeutic exposure, graded exposure, is somewhat controversial. The bulk of contemporary research in the area of specific phobia support the value of confronting phobic stimuli gradually in order to make the experience more acceptable for the phobic client and therapist. Graded exposure involves constructing a hierarchy of progressively more challenging confrontations with the phobic stimulus. The hierarchy often begins with an exercise of mild to moderate difficulty (e.g., looking from a second story window) and then progresses through a sequence of steps that ultimately culminate with an activity that would be challenging for most people (e.g., looking over a balcony rail 70 stories up). With graded exposure, SUDS scores are used to construct the hierarchy and to manage the pace of treatment. When building a hierarchy of progressively more challenging exposure exercises, the therapist and the client typically brainstorm a series of encounters with the phobic stimulus without regard to arranging them sequentially from easier to more difficult. Once the potential exposure tasks are identified, SUDS scores can be assigned to each potential encounter and then the tasks can be arranged hierarchically. Graded exposure sessions also involve the therapist using

SUDS scores to determine when it is time to move from one confrontation to the next. A generally good standard here is to move from one step
to the next (e.g., from viewing a snake at a distance of 5 feet to 2 feet)
when the SUDS score drops by at least half. Ideally, movement from
one item to the next would proceed when all anxiety is extinguished with
a given step, but clinical impressions suggest that this is difficult given
that the SUDS score usually involves a combined rating of current anxiety and anxiety related to the next anticipated encounter with the phobic stimulus.

The value of graded exposure notwithstanding, more rapid forms of
exposure have also shown promise in the treatment of phobic disorders.
Several studies have demonstrated the utility of more rapidly paced, single-
session exposure therapies (Gotestam, 2002; Koch, Spates, & Himle,
2004; Ost, 1997). This treatment involves encouraging clients to come in
close contact with the phobic stimulus as quickly as possible and to remain in place until their fear subsides. The empirical support for single-
session therapy suggests that the pacing of therapeutic exposure, at least
for fears of animals and insects, is likely best determined by the preferences of the client and the clinician.

A final general guideline to conducting therapeutic exposure therapy
involves the need to focus one's attention on the phobic stimulus. Studies
comparing the benefits of exposure therapy performed while distracted
versus while focusing attention on the phobic stimulus, consistently find
focused exposure to be superior (Sartory, Rachman, & Grey, 1982).
Focus on the phobic stimulus can often be enhanced by the therapist encouraging dialogue about the nature of the phobic stimulus throughout
the exposure session (i.e., describing the various parts of the spider).

Specific Application of Prolonged Exposure: Specific Phobia, Social Phobia, Agoraphobia

Many specific phobias are straightforwardly treated with prolonged exposure. Arranging for graded confrontation of animal or insect phobias
typically involves securing the appropriate target stimulus and simply
bringing the animal/insect and the client closer together. Many situational
fears can also be confronted with similar relative ease. For example, a
height phobic could gradually confront progressively higher floors in
a building. However, certain situational specific phobias can present lo-
gistical challenges when attempting to arrange for graded exposure exercises. Flying phobia presents a common example of this challenge.
Commercial airlines are not likely to accommodate graded exposure to
taxiing on the tarmac followed by repetitive high-speed trips down the
runway and so on. Flying fears and other situational phobias (e.g., fears

of high bridges in an area where there are no other available bridges) require creative approaches for successful exposure therapy. With flying phobias, a small aircraft with a flight instructor could be chartered in order to allow for progressively more challenging encounters with flying-related stimuli. Another option is to conduct exposure to difficult-to-arrange situational specific phobias in imagination. Although imaginal exposure has been found to be effective for specific phobias (Rentz, 2002), outcomes are often reduced compared to real-life methods (Dyckman & Cowan, 1978). Recent advances in virtual reality computer technology provide another alternative for difficult-to-arrange exposure to certain phobic disorders. Reports of successful exposure therapy delivered via virtual reality technology have been published for flying (Arbona, Osma, Garcia-Palacios, Quero, & Banos, 2004), height (Huang, Himle, & Alessi, 2000), and other situational specific phobias (Wald, 2004).

One final issue related to the exposure therapy of specific phobias relates to fears of blood and medical procedures. Persons with these phobias are likely to faint upon exposure to blood/medical stimuli whereas clients with other specific phobias almost never report fainting related to confronting their fears (Thyer, Himle, & Curtis, 1985). This problem can be addressed by directing clients to lie flat during initial exposure exercises and to apply vigorous tension to major muscle groups to elevate blood pressure and prevent fainting during exposure (Hellstrom, Fellenius, & Ost, 1996).

Social phobias can also present challenges for therapeutic exposure. Clients with generalized social fears of most social situations can often find several opportunities for exposure to social interactions in daily life. For these individuals, interacting with sales clerks, asking for directions, and stopping people to ask for the time can be a good beginning for exposure therapy. However, in certain situations, prolonged, graded exposure exercises for challenging social situations can be difficult to arrange. For example, a client with fears of presenting at a monthly executive board meeting cannot arrange for this group to assemble for repetitive exposure exercises until his or her fear subsides. In these situations, imaginal exposure to vivid descriptions of the feared situations can be helpful. Difficult-to-arrange exposure to social situations can be enhanced with group methods wherein social phobic clients can meet together to rehearse social encounters both within and outside of the group sessions (Andersson, 2003). Virtual reality programs for public speaking situations can also allow for prolonged repetitive exposure to this common, difficult to reproduce, social anxiety problem (Anderson, Rothbaum, & Hodges, 2003). Overall, recent meta-analytic studies support the value of exposure-based methods for social phobia (Federoff & Taylor, 2001; Feske & Chambless, 1995).

Prolonged exposure for agoraphobia typically involves graded exposure to locations and situations in which help is not available in case of a panic attack. Exposure hierarchies for agoraphobia often include visiting grocery stores, shopping malls, driving on expressways, or using public transportation. The usual exposure standards that apply to other phobic disorders fit well with agoraphobic fears. However, for some individuals the hierarchy begins with stepping outside of the home for the first time in years. In these difficult circumstances, the social worker may need to visit the client in his or her home in order to facilitate initial exposure exercises. Early exercises may involve spending time in the yard or walking in the neighborhood. It is important to note however, that successful exposure therapy for many persons with agoraphobia does not necessitate that a therapist direct the treatment. Substantial evidence exists that supports the value of computer or book (Ghosh & Marks, 1987) guided exposure therapy. Clients who are able to direct their own therapy can be at an advantage in that it is not necessary to fade out the therapist as therapy progresses. However, clinical experience suggests that severely agoraphobic clients may need to be accompanied by a therapist or family member at the early stages of exposure therapy.

Another important issue related to prolonged exposure for agoraphobia relates to *safety behaviors*. This term refers to several protective acts that are commonly performed by agoraphobics designed to prevent or reduce anxiety in phobic situations (Marom et al., 2003). Typical safety behaviors include carrying water bottles and outdated antianxiety medications, using distracting reading materials, eating specialized foods, and so on, all of which are designed to reduce the intensity of anxiety and to prevent full-scale panic attacks. Often clients believe that these behaviors have allowed them to narrowly escape catastrophic consequences related to panic attacks such as smothering, having a heart attack, going mad, or even dying. Although it may be difficult to withdraw established safety behaviors early in treatment, it is essential for the client to eventually discontinue these activities in order fully benefit from exposure therapy. Overall, meta-analytic studies support the efficacy of cognitive behavior therapy for agoraphobia, both with (Van Balkom et al., 1997) and without (Mehta, Mattick, Andrews, Hadzi-Pavlovic, & Christensen, 1990) panic disorder.

Specific Application of Prolonged Exposure: Panic Disorder

A somewhat more recent application of therapeutic exposure therapy, pioneered by Barlow and colleagues (Barlow, Craske, Cerney & Klosko, 1989) involves the application of direct exposure to the sensations associated with panic attacks. The theory driving this exposure innovation rests on the observation that persons experiencing panic disorder report that panic attacks can be triggered via exposure to internal sensations (e.g., dizziness, elevated heart rate, shortness of breath) that have been associated with previous panic attacks. These panic attacks are thought to occur as a result of conditioned associations between certain bodily sensations and full panic attacks, much like external cues such as grocery stores or highway driving might also trigger panic attacks. Much like exposure to external panic cues, internal bodily sensations can be repetitively reproduced using various exercises such that they no longer elicit substantial anxiety or panic attacks. Once clients have repetitively confronted these sensations over weeks of treatment, they often report that they no longer feel dominated by panic sensations but instead report mastery over them. This type of exposure is generally referred to as internal cue or interoceptive exposure therapy (Barlow et al., 1989).

Some internal cue exercises can be relatively straightforward to devise whereas others can require a good deal of clinician ingenuity. Sensations such as breathlessness can be reproduced by asking the client to hyperventilate or restrict their breathing by inhaling through a straw. Exposure to dizziness can be achieved via whirling about and rapid heart rate can be produced by running in place or up and down a stairway. Other sensations, such as feelings of unreality or depersonalization require more creativity and can be reproduced by directing clients to stare at their hand or a point on the wall for an extended time or to look at a bright light followed by attempting to read immediately afterward. The reader is directed to Barlow and Craske's treatment manual (Barlow et al., 1989) for further examples of interoceptive exposure exercises.

One issue of interest related to internal cue exposure relates to the length of exposure sessions. Although ideal from an exposure perspective, clients are generally unable to whirl about, hyperventilate, or run in place for hours without interruption. In practice, many interoceptive exposure exercises are conducted by asking clients to produce the symptoms for a brief time (usually 1 minute) followed by a brief rest (usually 1 minute), followed by further exposure, and so on. For certain sensations, voluntary hyperventilation for example, clients may not be able to continue the exposure for much longer than 20 minutes without undue discomfort. In these cases, multiple sessions can be scheduled over the course of the day ultimately reaching a total of 60 to 90 minutes of exposure. Other panic sensations, such as exposure to heat, can be delivered continuously for extended periods in a similar fashion to exposure to environmental stimuli associated with other phobic disorders. The research literature evaluating the efficacy of internal cue exposure is somewhat problematic in that internal cue exposure is usually tested as one of a group of specific interventions aimed at reducing panic attacks (Barlow et al., 1989). However, more recent studies isolating the effect of interoceptive anxiety support the value of this intervention (Margraf, Barlow, Clark, & Telch, 1993).

Specific Application of Prolonged Exposure: Obsessive-Compulsive Disorder

Prolonged exposure for obsessive-compulsive disorder (OCD) commonly involves exercises aimed at activating obsessional concerns and associated discomfort. For example, a person with obsessions related to dirt or germs would be directed to touch progressively more contaminated surfaces, starting with a rarely touched spot on a wall and ending with handling public restroom surfaces. Other examples of exposure therapy for OCD are quite logical extensions of the nature of the client's obsessional concerns. Persons with straightening obsessions exposure would be asked to put things out of order, persons with hoarding obsessions would be directed to throw items away, and checkers may be asked to use the stove or the door several times per day. However, none of these exposure efforts would be valuable without preventing, or at least delaying, the accompanying ritual. Shaking hands or handling contaminated surfaces would be of little use if the client immediately retreats to the restroom to wash his or her hands. Blocking the ritual, known as response prevention (Foa & Goldstein, 1978), allows the client to experience a gradual decline in distress associated with habituation to the anxiety-eliciting stimulus. For example, a client with hoarding obsessions would be asked to throw items in the trash (exposure) followed by resisting efforts to retrieve the item from the dumpster (response prevention).

An interesting issue concerning response prevention relates to the length of time the client is asked to delay ritualizing after confronting a challenging situation. It is quite clear that prolonged delays, or eliminating the ritual altogether is the best route given that brief delays in ritualistic behavior may not allow for habituation to occur (Foa et al., 1978). It may be tempting for the clinician to suggest a gradual pace of response prevention. For example, a client who washes his or her hands 100 times daily could be advised to reduce to 90 for the first week of treatment, 80 for the second, and so on. However, clinical impressions suggest that this gradual response prevention pace eventually leads to client frustration resulting from limited progress in achieving clinically meaningful change. For most clients, exposure intensity can be graded slowly but response prevention goals must be achieved more rapidly.

A second issue of interest relates to persons with primary obsessional OCD (Freeston et al., 1997). These clients often experience distressing thoughts (e.g., blasphemy, harm coming to loved ones, or actually physically or sexually assaulting others) without significant accompanying compulsive rituals. In these situations, exercises typically involve prolonged exposure to the content of the intrusive thoughts. Exposure to the thoughts is typically accomplished by listening to an audio loop tape containing detailed recordings of the client's most distressing obsessions (Himle & Thyer, 1989). Response prevention for primary obsessional OCD usually involves blocking attempts to reduce anxiety though reassurance from the self or others. Although a small amount of treatment research is available testing the value of imaginal exposure for primary obsessional OCD, existing studies support the value of this treatment (Himle et al., 1989; Freeston et al., 1997). Overall, meta-analytic studies confirm the efficacy of exposure and response prevention in the treatment of OCD with outcomes exceeding various control conditions and equaling the magnitude of response observed with medication treatment (Abramowitz, 1997).

Specific Application of Prolonged Exposure:
Post-Traumatic Stress Disorder

Exposure exercises for posttraumatic stress disorder (PTSD), like exposure for primary obsessions, involve repetitive exposure to distressing intrusive recollections. This task is also usually accomplished through the use of audiotaped recordings (Foa et al., 1999). Exposure therapy for PTSD usually begins with the client and the therapist collaborating to create a detailed narrative of the traumatic event associated with the onset of PTSD. For clients who have experienced multiple traumatic exposures, the usual method is to select the most challenging event for exposure (Zoellner, Foa, & Fitzgibbons, 2002). Well-constructed narratives usually include detailed discussion of the sights, sounds, smells, and other descriptive details of the event. Although exposure narratives of progressively more challenging detail can be introduced gradually, problems with brief, unplanned intrusions of more challenging recollections of the traumatic event(s) can interfere with the gradual pace of treatment.

Once the initial narrative is constructed and recorded, clients are asked to expose themselves to listening to the narrative daily as between session homework. These home sessions are usually 1 to 2 hours in duration. During the early portion of PTSD exposure, clinical impressions suggest that much of the exposure be conducted in the social worker's office given the substantial affect that is typically associated with exposure therapy for PTSD. The standard practice in the author's clinic is to conduct two to three in-office exposure sessions each week for the first 2 weeks of treatment. After this initial period, in-office sessions are scheduled 1 to

2 times weekly for about 12 weeks in total. As exposure therapy progresses, it is typical that clients will remember more details of the traumatic event, which makes it necessary to continuously update the exposure narrative with this new material. Standard practice is to add new details to the exposure tape as they are identified by the client.

Given the substantial affect elicited by exposure therapy for PTSD, it is important for social workers utilizing this treatment to provide support for clients and to educate clients that premature termination of treatment can be problematic. In the author's clinic, standard practice is to end each therapist assisted exposure session with a brief wind-down period in which the session is discussed and support is provided. During this period, the clinician also stresses the importance of regular adherence to exposure homework and future session attendance. In addition, telephone check-in calls are often scheduled to help ensure that the clients continue to conduct their homework exercises. Overall, meta-analytic studies confirm the efficacy of behavioral exposure therapy for PTSD (Bradley et al., 2005).

Anxiety Management Strategies

Two anxiety management procedures, breathing retraining and deep muscle relaxation, have been subject to some level of empirical investigation for certain anxiety disorders. Breathing retraining has been included among a group of CBT interventions used to treat panic disorder (Barlow & (Cerny, 1988). Breathing retraining typically involves directing the client to take in a normal capacity breath through the nose to the count of three followed a gradual exhalation through the mouth. The client is instructed to breathe deeply such that the diaphragm is expanded rather than shallow chest breathing typically associated with panic attacks (Meuret, Wilhelm & Roth, 2004). The value of breathing retraining in the treatment of panic attacks has been recently brought into question. Some clinicians believe that breathing retraining presents a contradiction to the more aggressive, confrontative approach characteristic of exposure therapy. With interoceptive exposure, clients are expected to welcome anxiety sensations as an opportunity to master them yet breathing retraining involves a palliative approach to managing panic. Research suggests that including breathing retraining in a package of other cognitive behavioral therapies (e.g., exposure to internal and external panic cues, cognitive restructuring) for panic disorder may actually reduce the effectiveness of the CBT procedure (Schmidt et al., 2000) although other studies support the utility of breathing retraining for panic disorder (Craske, Rowe, & Lewin, 1997). Further research is needed to determine the ultimate value of breathing retraining for panic disorder.

The utility of breathing retraining for generalized anxiety disorder is less controversial. Slow-paced diaphragmatic breathing is commonly included in multicomponent CBT treatments for generalized anxiety disorder (Kohli, Varma, & Nehru, 2000). Clients with generalized anxiety disorder can utilize controlled breathing when experiencing acute exacerbations of anxiety or for chronic tension. Controlled breathing has not been evaluated as a stand-alone treatment for generalized anxiety disorder but clinical impressions suggest that clients with generalized anxiety can benefit from this procedure.

The utility of controlled breathing for other anxiety disorders has not been empirically evaluated but it is important to note that available evidence suggests that anxiety management procedures may interfere with in-session fear reduction when paired with real-life exposure exercises compared to exposure alone (AuBuchon & Calhoun, 1990).

Various forms of progressive muscle relaxation (Jacobson, 1938) have been used to treat anxiety disorders. Among the most commonly studied muscle relaxation is a modified Jacobsonian method known as applied relaxation (Ost, 1987). The procedure involves a progressive technique wherein the client applies tension to a selected body part followed shortly by a release of tension. Typical sequencing begins with the hands and arms, progressing through the face, head, neck, shoulders, chest, abdomen, buttocks, legs, and feet. Each muscle group is tensed for approximately 5 seconds followed by a relaxation period of 15 seconds. Clients are encouraged to take special notice of the difference between the sensations associated with tension and the feelings accompanying muscle relaxation. With practice, this process allows anxious clients to detect signs of bodily tension and to respond with focused relaxation efforts. This basic procedure takes approximately 20 minutes to complete. The full procedure is usually followed by a series of exercises designed to eventually reduce the amount of time it takes for the client to achieve relaxation. The first of these exercises involves a release-only phase wherein clients are advised to relaxing muscles sequentially without applying tension beforehand. Cue controlled relaxation follows, which involves pairing the verbal cue, relax, with a pattern of breathing designed to bring about relaxation more quickly. Differential relaxation is introduced next in which clients are asked to conduct cue-controlled relaxation while some muscle groups are in use. Differential relaxation continues by advising clients to practice cue-controlled relaxation while sitting or walking in various locations. At this point, clients are typically able to achieve a relaxed state within 60 to 90 seconds. The next step, known as rapid relaxation, involves the clinician and the client mutually designating a series of cues such as sitting down in a chair or turning on the television as a prompt to practice a brief relaxation exercise. Rapid relaxation directs the client to take one to three deep breaths paired with the self-instruction "relax" before exhaling. The final step of applied relaxation, application training involves practicing newly acquired relaxation skills in a variety of stressful situations. Clients are directed to enter potentially anxiety-evoking situations and to apply rapid relaxation at the first sign of distress.

Specific Applications of Applied Relaxation: Panic Disorder and Generalized Anxiety Disorder

The efficacy of applied relaxation in the treatment of panic disorder has been investigated in several studies. The results of these investigations have been mixed. Applied relaxation has been found to be superior to various control groups, and equal to multicomponent CBT strategies (Ruhmland & Margraf, 2001). Applied relaxation has also been compared to "pure" cognitive therapy (i.e., cognitive therapy without additional procedures such as exposure) but the results of these studies have been mixed with some studies finding equal outcomes (Ost & Westling, 1994) and others reporting superior outcomes with cognitive therapy (Beck, Stanley, Baldwin, Deagle, & Averill, 1994). Research findings aside, clinical impressions suggest that palliative applied relaxation methods can be somewhat difficult to match with exposure efforts aimed at courageously tolerating panic symptoms in order to learn they are not dangerous.

Various relaxation strategies, including applied relaxation, have also been successfully used for generalized anxiety disorder (GAD) (Borkovec, Mathews, & Chambers, 1987). Like breathing retraining, muscle relaxation procedures do not suffer from compatibility problems with prolonged exposure for patients with GAD given that exposure is not a commonly used intervention for GAD.

Systematic Desensitization for Anxiety Disorders

Systematic desensitization for phobic disorders involves a combined approach that includes exposure in imagination along with relaxation therapy (Wolpe, 1958). This technique is based on the theory of reciprocal inhibition (Wolpe, 1958). This theory posits that fear cannot be present when an individual is relaxed. Systematic desensitization initially involves training the client to achieve a deep state of relaxation using progressive muscle relaxation procedures. Once the client is able to achieve a state of relaxation, the next step is for the clinician to present imaginal scenes involving the phobic object or situation. Clients are asked to signal to the clinician if they experience increasing tension resulting from the imaginal exposure exercise. If tension is signaled, the image is withdrawn and relaxation efforts are resumed until the tension is reduced. Once this occurs, the phobic image is again presented and the process continues until the image no longer elicits tension. The phobic images are typically presented hierarchically from mildly to highly distressing. Once all the imaginal scenes can be confronted without significant tension, the client is encouraged to confront the phobic stimuli in real life.

Scientific support for the value of systematic desensitization is well established. However, available evidence suggests that real-life exposure to phobic stimuli is likely more effective than imaginal methods (Dyckman et al., 1978).

Cognitive Therapy for Anxiety Disorders

Cognitive therapy focuses on the relationship between thoughts and emotions. The central theory of cognitive therapy posits that problematic emotional states result, at least in part, from faulty, inaccurate thinking (Beck, Rush, Shaw, & Emery, 1979). These inaccurate thoughts are referred to as cognitive distortions (Beck et al., 1979). Common cognitive distortions experienced by clients associated with anxiety disorders include: *catastrophizing*—clients view their phobic stimuli or anxious feelings as horrible, terrible, or dangerous; *mind-reading*—clients jump to conclusions that others are viewing them negatively without sufficient evidence to support this view; *predicting the future*—clients assume that they will not be able to tolerate upcoming confrontations with fearful stimuli, which often results in avoidance; and *selective abstraction*—clients attend to a single negative aspect of a given experience until the entire experience is viewed as a failure (adapted from Beck, 1995).

Cognitive therapy is a collaborative process wherein the social worker and the client work together to assess the accuracy of the client's thinking with the aim of helping the client to think more clearly about himself, his current circumstances, and his future. A Socratic dialogue is initiated by the social worker with the goal of discovering information counter to the distorted thought using the client's past experiences, current circumstances, and future possibilities to gather data counter to the belief in question. For example, the client who avoids social gatherings for fear that she will surely be rejected and humiliated, would be encouraged to examine past predictions of disaster associated with social gatherings and whether they were always associated with rejection and humiliation, whether previous rejections were really so terrible—especially compared to the hardships of social isolation, and whether it is possible that the gathering may actually lead to a positive social relationship. In support of in-office dialogue, clients are also advised to "test out" the validity of their thoughts by conducting behavioral experiments in the community. These experiments typically involve targeted prospective activities designed to gather more information counter to a firmly held distorted thought. For example, if a client with panic disorder believed that he or she might die if he or she went to the store, a series of prescribed visits to various shops in the community may serve as a compelling "test" of the validity of this catastrophic prediction.

The later stages of cognitive therapy often include attention to correcting faulty personal rules or core client beliefs. These beliefs are usually referred to as maladaptive schema (Beck, 1995). Maladaptive schema often associated with anxiety disorders include beliefs such as: "I must be perfect," "Everyone must like me," "Anxiety is a sign of weakness and is abnormal," "I must always be comfortable." Schema such as these are thought to produce cognitive distortions and associated distressing emotions. For example a person who holds the belief "I must be liked by everyone" may experience significant anxiety related to social interaction and may be especially likely think that it is "terrible" if someone ends a conversation prematurely or fails to give them a hearty greeting when passing in the hallway. These schema can be addressed using several strategies (Beck, 1995). One common strategy is the cost-benefit analysis that involves examining the pros and cons of rigidly holding a given belief (Beck, 1995). Another helpful strategy involves examining how the beliefs interfere with the accomplishment of major life goals.

Specific Applications of Cognitive Therapy: Panic Disorder

Many clients with panic disorder hold erroneous beliefs about the potential consequences that might arise from panic attacks. Common thoughts related to panic include concerns about dying, passing out, having a heart attack, going mad, vomiting, falling over, suffocating, and so on. Clients with panic disorder often experience a vicious cycle wherein they notice an anxiety symptom, worry about it worsening, which in turn leads to stronger and larger numbers of symptoms, followed my even greater concern, and so on. Ironically, these catastrophizing worries almost never come to pass.

When working with a client who experiences panic attacks, the cognitive therapist can use several sources of information to help the client counter his or her distorted thoughts. The first source of information is the client's own panic history. The therapist can question the client about how many panic attacks, large and small, he has experienced. Next, the client can be asked to estimate how many times these attacks have been associated with a particular thought (e.g., "I am going to fall over") and exactly how often the feared consequence has taken place. Almost always, the concern has never actually come to pass. If the concern has occurred, it is likely that the event has been very rare and chances are good that the consequences were not especially dire. A second useful source of information is other people who suffer from panic disorder. In this situation, the therapist can offer information about the number of clients with this disorder seen in the history of the clinic, the estimated grand total of panic attacks experienced by this client group, the number of catastrophic predictions that were associated with these panic attacks, followed by a review of the number of actual clinicwide disasters. A third source that can sometimes be helpful is to provide information about the nature of panic symptoms. For example, if a client has concern that she will faint during a panic attack, she can be informed that blood pressure and heart rate are generally elevated during a panic attack and that fainting usually requires low blood pressure and heart rate thus making it very unlikely that she will actually faint during an attack.

A final important source of information in the cognitive therapy of panic disorder involves the use of behavioral tests. Even after examining their own panic history, hearing of the experiences of other clients with panic disorder, and learning about the nature of their panic symptoms, most panic disordered clients continue to worry that their panic attacks may be more dangerous than others and that terrible consequences will actually occur in their case. This issue makes it important for the client to conduct behavioral tests to build more data counter to his catastrophic beliefs. Most individuals with panic disorder are aware that catastrophic consequences have not yet occurred but most individuals believe that these events have been narrowly averted with various behaviors, often "just in time." These "safety behaviors" (Marom & Hermesh, 2003) include leaving the situation, taking a drink of water, distracting one's self, taking a tranquilizer, and so on. Each of these safety behaviors interfere with the client's ability learn that disastrous consequences are actually not about to occur. Behavioral tests for panic disorder involve allowing attacks to occur without intervention in order to see that terrible consequences do not actually take place. Later, as an advanced test, panic symptoms can be aggravated and still found not to produce catastrophic outcomes. In sum, all four sources of information can be brought together to build a compelling rational response to erroneous thoughts about the potential consequences of panic attacks. Overall, meta-analyses confirm the value of cognitive therapy in the treatment of panic disorder (Van Balkom et al., 1997). It is important to note that much of the research related to the efficacy of cognitive therapy involves testing the efficacy of multicomponent interventions that include cognitive therapy among a group of CBT interventions, thus making the specific contribution of cognitive restructuring impossible to determine. However, studies using methods that isolate the effects of cognitive therapy confirm the value of this intervention for panic disorder (Gould, Otto, & Pollack, 1995).

Specific Applications of Cognitive Therapy: Social Anxiety

The application of cognitive therapy for social anxiety disorder is relatively straightforward. Excessive concern about the consequences of social rejection, mind-reading that people are reacting negatively without clear evidence, and negative predictions that participating in a given social event will lead to disastrous outcomes, all provide an opportunity for the client and therapist to collaborate together to counter these anxiety-provoking thoughts. One central theme usually involves helping the client to recognize that social rejection is often difficult to confirm, is a necessary risk if one is to become more comfortable in social situations, and that the consequences of social avoidance and resultant isolation are worse than the actual consequences of a social rebuff. The client's past experiences with challenging social situations often provide ready examples of predicted social catastrophes that turned out to be false, friendships that occurred even after displaying discomfort and other social imperfections, and social rejections that were not really so horrible. One interesting method helps to further test whether social mistakes are really so terrible. This strategy involves encouraging the client to produce social blunders on purpose in order to gather contemporary data about the true consequences of social imperfections. These blunders could include dressing out of fashion, calling someone the wrong name, applying a stain to one's clothing or face, or even deliberately behaving somewhat inappropriately. This method allows the client to see that the outcomes of these behavioral tests support the belief that social mistakes are somewhat uncomfortable, but not tragic. Overall, empirical evidence supports the value of cognitive therapy for social anxiety (Feske et al., 1995). Again, many studies involve multicomponent interventions that can make the specific effect of cognitive therapy difficult to detect, however, studies that allow for the specific effect of cognitive therapy to be detected have confirmed the value of cognitive therapy for social phobia (Fedoroff et al., 2001).

Specific Applications of Cognitive Therapy:
Generalized Anxiety Disorder

The core diagnostic feature of GAD is excessive worry that is difficult to control. Worries often represent exaggerated concern about future hardships. It is as if the person can tell the future, and the future looks bleak.

These concerns typically involve worries about finances, the well-being of children and other loved ones, health, faltering interpersonal relationships, and career concerns. Cognitive therapists help clients address these excessive worries using several strategies. One central method involves comparing the number of terrible hardships the client has predicted versus the number of actual awful outcomes that have occurred. For example, a client with excessive worries about his or her teenage child getting into a car accident may be helped by reviewing that over the past year the child may have been out on the road over 250 times, that each trip was accompanied by at least 20 worries about the child getting into an accident, that the total number of accident predictions in the past year exceeds 5,000, yet still no terrible accident. If some hardships have occurred, the therapist can at least build a case that the client does not predict catastrophe well. In addition to assessing the client's ability to predict horrible events, the cognitive therapist may also discuss the ability of the loved one or the client to cope with hardships. Often worried clients stop when they imagine that a feared outcome has occurred. The cognitive therapist can help the client to remember whether his or her loved ones eventually coped with the hardship and recovered. If recovery was difficult or incomplete, the client and the therapist can work together to build new coping and problem solving skills for these challenging situations.

Another interesting issue related to the cognitive therapy of generalized anxiety disorder relates to excessive worry about worrying, or what is often referred to as "meta-worry" (Wells, 2005). Many clients with GAD become very concerned that excessive worry will result in significant physical or emotional harm. The cognitive therapist can address this concern by using the client's own history of worry, the worries of others, and the lack of scientific data to support the notion that worry is dangerous to help the client counter the thought that worry will cause catastrophic harm.

Maladaptive personal standards, or schema, also play a large role in GAD. Beliefs such as "I must achieve excellence in everything I do" or that "My job is to see to it that no one in my family experiences hardship" or "I must have emotional control at all times" can be addressed and replaced with a more balanced views such as "It would be nice to do well but that is not always possible" or "Hardships are difficult but some problems make children stronger and more resilient." The cost-benefit analyses and other strategies can fit well as methods to moderate overly rigid personal standards that contribute to excessive worry.

The specific contribution of cognitive restructuring in the CBT of GAD has not been extensively studied, however limited research (Gould, Otto, Pollack, & Yap, 1997) and clinical impressions suggest that it is an important component of multicomponent CBT interventions for GAD.

Specific Applications of Cognitive Therapy: Obsessive-Compulsive Disorder

Clients with OCD experience several cognitive misinterpretations that can be addressed via cognitive therapy. These misinterpretations include the belief that thoughts must be controlled, that the likelihood of the occurrence of severe harm is great, that the individual has great responsibility to avoid any activities that could be harmful to others in any way, and that one must be certain and perfect (Obsessive Compulsive Cognitions Working Group [OCCWG], 1997). Clients may experience all or just one of these general misinterpretations. The performance of rituals often allows clients to maintain firmly held distorted beliefs. For example, if a client experiences the obsession that the stove is likely to malfunction resulting in the house burning down, checking the stove repetitively may interfere with the client learning that the stove is very unlikely to malfunction. In addition to questioning the client about previous predictions of stove fires versus the actual number of stove fires, blocking compulsive checking also provides contemporary data regarding how likely stove fires are. Excessive feelings of responsibility for harm can be addressed by carefully examining a client's actual level of responsibility for harm versus the amount of responsibility held by others. This can be illustrated using a pie chart that depicts the relative amount of responsibility for harm held by the client versus the amount of responsibility shouldered by others.

Many clients with OCD misjudge the impact of mistakes (e.g., losing one's home because of making a mistake in writing the monthly check). This distortion can often be addressed by examining the number of actual events that would have to occur before the actual catastrophe occurred (e.g., multiple notices would be sent, telephone calls from the mortgage company, formal legal papers, etc.). These data can be utilized by the client in response to the concern that a dreaded event will occur if he or she is not extremely careful.

A growing amount of research suggests that cognitive therapy results in similar levels of improvement compared to exposure and response prevention. Cognitive therapy and exposure and response prevention can be also be used together with cognitive therapy often preceding exposure therapy. There is essentially no research available to help social workers decide between cognitive therapy, exposure and response prevention, or both combined for an individual client. However, clinical impressions suggest that client preference is important and that cognitive therapy can be especially helpful when clients are initially reluctant to begin exposure therapy.

CONSIDERATIONS AND CONCLUSION

Although most of the empirical support for CBT for anxiety disorders discussed here comes mainly from studies of individual therapy, the efficacy of group CBT for many anxiety conditions is also well established. Studies of group CBT for panic disorder/agoraphobia (Mitchell, 1999), social phobia, obsessive-compulsive disorder (Himle et al., 2001), and PTSD (Foy, Ruzek, & Glynn, 2002) have all yielded positive outcomes compared to various control and comparison conditions. In addition to symptom improvement, group therapies provide several additional benefits including group support, group encouragement for treatment adherence, and efficient use of trained CBT practitioner resources. However, most of the group treatments that have been subjected to empirical testing involved groups comprised of members experiencing one specific primary anxiety disorder. Many practitioners are simply unable to assemble groups of persons with a single anxiety disorder without undue wait times. This problem makes it likely that most group therapy will be done in specialty anxiety disorders treatment centers or in major cities where patient flow is sufficient to form groups efficiently. However, there is some evidence that positive outcomes can result from participation in CBT groups that include individuals with various anxiety disorders (Barrett, 1998). This is especially true when grouping together persons with various phobias, panic attacks, and generalized anxiety disorder in the same group. Clients with OCD and PTSD may not fit as well in mixed groups (Himle, Van Etten, & Fischer, 2003).

Involving family members in the CBT of anxiety disorders is also an important consideration. Family members and clients benefit when clinicians provide education to family and friends about the nature of anxiety disorders and the principles of CBT. Family members can accompany fearful clients on community-based exposure outings (e.g., trips to the mall, theater), discourage compulsive rituals, provide social reinforcement for adherence to CBT homework, and give encouragement during setbacks. Clinical impressions and a limited research literature suggest that CBT outcomes can be greater when families are involved in treatment (Mehta et al., 1990). Social workers can be especially helpful with family treatment given that many social workers have specialized training in family treatment.

Overall, social workers play an important role in the treatment of persons with anxiety disorders. For many clients, especially those with limited resources, the social worker is the main source of clinical service they receive. Social work's historical focus on the person-in-the-environment fits well with the CBT approach for anxiety disorders given its emphasis on exposure to anxiety-evoking stimuli in the environment. Unfortunately, many social workers do not have appropriate training in CBT for anxiety disorders. Many schools of social work simply do not provide the classroom training, field experiences, and direct supervision that are required to learn CBT (Barlow, Levitt, & Bufka, 1999). Given the number of anxiety disordered clients that social workers are likely to encounter in practice, there is a clear need for more training in CBT for social work students and practitioners.

REFERENCES

Abramowitz, J. S. (1997). Effectiveness of psychological and pharmacological treatments for obsessive-compulsive disorder: A quantitative review. *Journal of Counseling and Clinical Psychology, 65,* 44–52.

American Psychiatric Association. (2000). *Diagnostic and statistical manual of mental disorders* (4th ed.). Washington, DC: Author.

Anderson, P., Rothbaum, B. O., & Hodges, L. F. (2003). Virtual reality exposure in the treatment of social anxiety. *Cognitive & Behavioral Practice, 10,* 240–247.

Andersson, G. (2003). Cognitive-behavioral group therapy for social phobia. Basic mechanisms and clinical strategies. *Cognitive Behaviour Therapy, 32,* 216.

Arbona, C. B., Osma, J., Garcia-Palacios, A., Quero, S., & Banos, R. M. (2004). Treatment of flying phobia using virtual reality: Data from a 1-year follow-up using a multiple baseline design. *Clinical Psychology & Psychotherapy, 11,* 311–323.

AuBuchon, P. G., & Calhoun, K. S. (1990). The effects of therapist presence and relaxation training on the efficacy and generalizability of in vivo exposure. *Behavioural Psychotherapy, 18,* 169–185.

Barlow, D. H., & Cerny, J. A. (1988). *Psychological treatment of panic.* New York: Guilford.

Barlow, D. H., Craske, M. G., Cerny, J. A., & Klosko, J. S. (1989). Behavioral treatment of panic disorder. *Behavior Therapy, 20,* 261–282.

Barlow, D. H., Levitt, J. T., & Bufka, L. F. (1999). The dissemination of empirically supported treatments: A view to the future. *Behavior Research and Therapy, 37,* S147–S162.

Barrett, P. M. (1998). Evaluation of cognitive-behavioral group treatments for childhood anxiety disorders. *Journal of Clinical Child Psychology, 27,* 459–468.

Beck, A. T., Rush, A. J., Shaw, B. F., & Emery, G. (1979). *Cognitive therapy of depression.* New York: Guilford.

Beck, J. S. (1995). Cognitive therapy: Basics and beyond. New York: Guilford.

Beck, J. G., Stanley, M. A., Baldwin, L. E., Deagle, E. A., & Averill, P. M. (1994). A comparison of cognitive therapy and relaxation training for panic disorder. *Journal of Consulting and Clinical Psychology, 62,* 818–826.

Borkovec, T. D., Mathews, A. M., & Chambers, A. (1987). The effects of relaxation training with cognitive or nondirective therapy and the role of relaxation-induced anxiety in the treatment of generalized anxiety. *Journal of Consulting & Clinical Psychology, 55,* 883–888.

Bradley, R., Greene, J., Russ, E., Dutra, L., Westen, D., & Russ, E. (2005). A multidimensional meta-analysis of psychotherapy for PTSD. *American Journal of Psychiatry, 162,* 214–227.

Chess, W. A., & Norlin, J. M. (1991). *Human behavior in the social environment: A social systems method* (2nd ed.). Boston: Allyn & Bacon.

Craske, M. G., Rowe, M., & Lewin, M. (1997). Interoceptive exposure versus breathing retraining within cognitive-behavioural therapy for panic disorder with agoraphobia. *British Journal of Clinical Psychology, 36,* 85–99.

Dyckman, J. M., & Cowan, P. A. (1978). Imagining vividness and the outcome of in vivo and imagined scene desensitization. *Journal of Consulting and Clinical Psychology, 48,* 1155–1156; *36,* 85–99.

Fedoroff, I. C., & Taylor, S. (2001). Psychological and pharmacological treatments of social phobia: A meta-analysis. *Journal of Clinical Psychopharmacology, 21,* 311–324.

Feske, U., & Chambless, D. L. (1995). Cognitive behavioral versus exposure only treatment for social phobia: A meta-analysis. *Behavior Therapy, 26,* 695–720.

Foa, E. B., & Goldstein, A. J. (1978). Continuous exposure and complete response prevention in the treatment of obsessive-compulsive neurosis. *Behavior Therapy, 9,* 821–829.

Foa, E. B., Dancu, C. V., Hembree, E. A. Jaycox, L. H., Meadows, E. A., & Street, G. P. (1999). A comparison of exposure therapy, stress inoculation training, and their combination for reducing posttraumatic stress disorder in female assault victims. *Journal of Consulting & Clinical Psychology, 67,* 194–200.

Foy, D. W., Ruzek, J. I., & Glynn, S. M. (2002). Trauma focus group therapy for combat-related PTSD: An update. *Journal of Clinical Psychology, 58,* 907–918.

Freeston, M. H., Ladouceur, R., Gagnon, F., Thibodeau, N., Rheaume, J., Letarte, H., et al. (1997). Cognitive-behavioral treatment of obsessive thoughts: A controlled study. *Journal of Consulting & Clinical Psychology, 65,* 405–413.

Ghosh, A., & Marks, I. M. (1987). Self-directed exposure for agoraphobia: A controlled trial. *Behavior Therapy, 18,* 3–16.

Gotestam, K. G. (2002). One session treatment of spider phobia by direct or modeled exposure. *Cognitive Behavioral Therapy, 31,* 18–24.

Gould, R. A., Otto, M. W., & Pollack, M. H. (1995). A meta-analysis of treatment outcome for panic disorder. *Clinical Psychology Review, 15,* 819–844.

Gould, R. A., Otto, M. W., Pollack, M. H., & Yap, L. (1997). Cognitive behavioral and pharmacological treatment of generalized anxiety disorder: A preliminary meta-analysis. *Behavior Therapy, 28*, 285–305.

Heimberg, R. G., Dodge, C. S., Hope, D. A., Kennedy C. R., Zollo, L. J., & Becker, R. E. (1990). Cognitive behavioral group treatment of social phobia: Comparison with a credible placebo control. *Cognitive Therapy and Research, 14*, 1–23.

Hellstrom, K., Fellenius, J., & Ost, L. G. (1996). One versus five sessions of applied tension in the treatment of blood phobia. *Behaviour Research & Therapy, 34*, 101–112.

Himle, J., & Thyer, B. A. (1989). Clinical social work and obsessive-compulsive disorder. *Behavior Modification, 13*, 459–470.

Himle, J. A., Rassi, S., Haghighatgou, H., Krone, K. P., Nesse, R. M., & Abelson, J. (2001). Group behavioral therapy of obsessive-compulsive disorder: Seven versus twelve-week outcomes. *Depression and Anxiety, 13*, 161–165.

Himle, J. A., Van Etten, M., & Fischer, D. J. (2003). Cognitive-behavioral group therapy for obsessive-compulsive disorder: A review. *Brief Treatment and Crisis Intervention, 3*, 215–225.

Jacobson, E. (1938). *Progressive relaxation.* Chicago: University of Chicago Press.

Karno, M. G. J. M., Sorenson, S. B., & Burnam, A. (1988). The epidemiology of obsessive-compulsive disorder in five U.S. communities. *Archives of General Psychiatry, 45*, 1094–1099.

Kessler, R. C., McGonagle, K. A., Xhao, S., Nelson, C. B., Hughes, M., Eshleman, S., et al. (1994). Lifetime and 12-month prevalence of *DSM-III-R* psychiatric disorders in the United States. *Archives of General Psychiatry, 51*, 8–19.

Kessler, R. C., Sonnega, A., Bromet, E., Hughes, M., & Nelson, C. B. (1995). Posttraumatic stress disorder in the national comorbidity survey. *Archives of General Psychiatry, 52*, 1048–1060.

Koch, E. I., Spates, R., & Himle, J. A. (2004). Comparison of behavioral and cognitive-behavioral one-session exposure treatments for small animal phobias. *Behaviour Research and Therapy, 42*, 1483–1504.

Kohli, A., Varma, V. K., & Nehru, R. (2000). Comparison of efficacy of psychorelaxation and pharmacotherapy in generalized anxiety disorder. *Journal of Personality and Clinical Studies, 16*, 43–48.

Lin, A. M. P. (1995). Mental health overview. In R. L. Edwards (Ed.), *Encyclopedia of social work* (19th ed., Vol. 2, pp. 1705–1711). Washington, DC: NASW Press.

Margraf, J., Barlow, D. H., Clark, D. M., & Telch, M. J. (1993). Psychological treatment of panic: Work in progress on outcome, active ingredients, and follow-up. *Behavior Research and Therapy, 31*, 1–8.

Marks, I. M. (1987). *Fears, phobias, and rituals.* New York: Oxford.

Marom, S., & Hermesh, H. (2003). Cognitive behavior therapy in anxiety disorders. *Israel Journal of Psychiatry & Related Sciences, 40*, 135–144.

Mehta, M., Mattick, R. P., Andrews, G., Hadzi-Pavlovic, D., & Christensen, H. (1990). A comparative study of family-based and patient-based behavioural management in obsessive-compulsive disorder. *British Journal of Psychiatry*, *157*, 133–135.

Mendez, X., Rosa, A. I., & Orgiles, M. (2005). Differential efficacy of the psychological treatments for animal phobia: A meta-analytic study. *Psicothema*, *17*, 219–226.

Meuret, A. E., Wilhelm, F. H., & Roth, W. T. (2004). Respiratory feedback for treating panic disorder. *Journal of Clinical Psychology*, *60*, 197–207.

Mitchell, C. G. (1999). Treating anxiety in a managed care setting: A controlled comparison of medication alone versus medication plus cognitive-behavioral group therapy. *Research on Social Work Practice*, *9*, 188–200.

Mogotsi, M., Kaminer, D., & Stein, D. J. (2000). Quality of life in the anxiety disorders. *Harvard Review of Psychiatry*, *8*, 273–282.

Obsessive Compulsive Cognitions Working Group [OCCWG]. (1997). Cognitive assessment of obsessive-compulsive disorder. *Behaviour Research & Therapy*, *35*, 667–681.

Ost, L. (1997). One versus five sessions of exposure in the treatment of flying phobia. *Behaviour Research & Therapy*, *35*, 987–996.

Ost, L. G. (1987). Applied relaxation: Description of a coping technique and review of controlled studies. *Behaviour Research & Therapy*, *25*, 397–410.

Ost, L. G., & Westling, B. E. (1994). Applied relaxation versus cognitive behavior therapy in the treatment of panic disorder. *Behaviour Research & Therapy*, *33*, 145–158.

Rachman, S., Marks, I. M., & Hodgson, R. (1973). The treatment of obsessive-compulsive neurotics by modelling and flooding in vivo. *Behaviour Research & Therapy*, *11*, 463–471.

Rentz, T. O. (2002). Active-imaginal exposure: Examination of a new behavioral treatment of specific phobia. *Dissertation Abstracts International: Section B: The Sciences & Engineering*, *63*, 2071.

Ruhmland, M., & Margraf, J. (2001). Efficacy of psychological treatments for panic and agoraphobia. *Verhaltenstherapie*, *11*, 41–53.

Sartory, G., Rachman, S., & Grey, S. (1982). Return of fear: The role of rehearsal. *Behaviour Research and Therapy*, *20*, 123–133.

Schmidt, N. B., Woolaway-Bickel, K., Trakowski, J., Santiago, H., Storey, J., Koselka, M., et al. (2000). Dismantling cognitive-behavioral treatment for panic disorder: Questioning the utility of breathing retraining. *Journal of Consulting & Clinical Psychology*, *68*, 417–424.

Thyer, B. A., Himle, J., & Curtis, G. C. (1985). Blood-injury-illness phobia: A review. *Journal of Clinical Psychology*, *41*, 451–459.

Van Balkom, A. J. L. M., Bakker, A., Spinhoven, P., Blaauw, B. M. J. W., Smeenk, S., Ruesink, B. (1997). A meta-analysis of the treatment of panic disorder with or without agoraphobia: A comparison of psychopharmacological, cognitive-behavioral, and combination treatments. *Journal of Nervous & Mental Disease*, *185*, 510–516.

Wald, J. (2004). Efficacy of virtual reality exposure therapy for driving phobia: A multiple baseline across-subjects design. *Behavior Therapy*, *35*, 621–635.

Watson, J. P., Gaind, R., & Marks, I. M. (1971). Prolonged exposure: A rapid treatment for phobias. *British Medical Journal*, *1*, 13–15.

Wells, A. (2005). The metacognitive model of GAD: Assessment of meta-worry and relationship with DSM-IV generalized anxiety disorder. *Cognitive Therapy & Research, 29*, 107–121.

Wolpe, J. (1958). *Psychotherapy by reciprocal inhibition.* Stanford, CA: Stanford University Press.

Wolpe, J. (1973). *The practice of behavior therapy.* New York: Pergamon.

Zoellner, L. A., Foa, E. B., & Fitzgibbons, L. A. (2002). *Cognitive-behavioral treatment of PTSD.* In M. B. Williams, J. F. Sommer (Eds.), *Simple and* complex *post-traumatic stress disorder: Strategies for comprehensive treatment in clinical practice* (pp. 75–98). Binghamton, NY: Haworth.

CHAPTER 18

Depression and Suicidal Behavior

A Cognitive Behavior Therapy Approach for Social Workers

Lili Daoud

Raymond Chip Tafrate

INTRODUCTION

Because of its prevalence in our society, depression is often referred to as the "common cold" of mental illness. Social workers will certainly encounter clients with a variety of mood-related disorders, regardless of the setting in which they choose to work. As common as depression may be, as professionals we are challenged by the complexity of client presentations, whose vulnerability and resilience will be determined by medical issues, the schemas formed in childhood, current cognitive style, and coping skills, and available social support. The challenge lies not only in correctly assessing factors that contribute to dysfunction, but also in formulating a treatment plan that includes interventions that will result in positive outcomes for the client's disturbance.

Although the notion of external causation is a popular view regarding depression, a cognitive behavior therapy (CBT) conceptualization is less likely to create a state of helplessness and blame, and is more likely to support empowerment of the individual. Key elements of empowerment, as defined by Chamberlin (1997) include access to information, ability to make choices, assertiveness, and self-esteem. A CBT conceptualization leads the client away from a negative view of the future and external circumstances, and instead emphasizes an internal locus of control, in which internal resources of empowerment and strength are discovered, regardless of the existing external circumstances.

Of course a wide variety of external events or life circumstances that generate stress can be contributing factors in precipitating a depressive episode. Nonetheless, despite an association between stress and depression, many people who are subjected to high levels of stress do not develop depression, and ongoing stressful experiences, do not lead inevitably to vulnerability, failure to adapt, and psychopathology (Bernard, 1993). Cognitive behavior theory attempts to deconstruct individual differences in vulnerability, adaptation, and development of psychopathology, through systematic assessment of a client's thoughts and behaviors, and use of empirically validated interventions. This chapter presents an overview of depression, demonstrates empirical support for CBT, and clarifies its potential usefulness in social work settings. Assessment and managing suicide risk is also addressed as important components of a complete treatment package.

DEPRESSION: DESCRIPTION OF SYMPTOMS

In order to begin a thorough assessment, it is important to gain a clear understanding of the severity of symptoms, as well as formulating a hypothesis about the factors that might be maintaining and perpetuating the patient's problems. While affective, cognitive, and behavioral symptoms are widely recognized as main problem areas for depressed clients, Dozois and Dobson (2004) also emphasize somatic symptoms and social functioning as areas requiring assessment. In a study done by The World Health Organization, common elements of depressive experiences were identified in subjects across four different countries: Iran, Japan, Canada, and Switzerland. The symptoms included sad affect, loss of enjoyment or pleasure (anhedonia), anxiety, tension, lack of energy (lethargy), loss of interest, inability to concentrate, and ideas of insufficiency, inadequacy, and worthlessness. Depressive experiences around the world appear to share a common foundation. Some components of assessment that are useful to consider are provided in the following text and are adapted from Dozois and Dobson (2004).

Affective symptoms are those symptoms that inform the therapist about the patient's mood. These may include depressed mood, guilt or a sense of worthlessness, loss of interest, hopelessness, and suicidal ideation.

Severity of the depressive state can be measured with specific instruments such as the 21-item *Beck Depression Inventory*–Second Edition (BDI-II; Beck, Steer, & Brown, 1996), or through self-report using *subjective units of disturbance scale* (SUDS). A weekly SUDS measure of self-reported depression can be requested from the patient by asking how he or she feels on a scale of 0 to 10 in terms of depression, with 10 being the most depressed he or she has ever been and 0 as no depression. It can be helpful to ask the client, as a measure of expectation, where he would like to be most of the time when they near his goal in treatment. Most of the clients we work with report 2.5 to 4 as a reasonable goal. Explaining to the client that most people are not a 0 or 1 most of the time can affirm realistic treatment goals.

Cognitive symptoms consist primarily of negative or irrational thinking. Although depression is associated with a preponderance of negative thinking, the overwhelming lack of positive thinking appears to also be specific to depression (Dozois & Dobson, 2001). Themes of hopelessness about the future, guilt about past behaviors, blame, worthlessness, disinterest, and sometimes death can permeate the inner thinking lives of depressed clients. These cognitive symptoms are powerful factors in terms of perpetuating dysfunction, particularly from the perspective of a cognitive model. If a depressed individual can become increasingly competent at identifying and restructuring cognitive distortions, the dark cloud of depression will often lift. The key to interventions directed at distorted, dysfunctional, or irrational cognitions is to challenge the client to change the cognitions related to environmental stressors, life's daily struggles, self-evaluations, and predictions about the future.

Behavioral symptoms that might help the therapist in assessing improvement over the course of treatment include the appearance, movements, and mannerisms of the client, as research demonstrates that depressed individuals make less eye contact, speak slower than nondepressed individuals, and exhibit a decrease in overall body and hand movements (Schelde, 1998). Many clients become tearful or cry during the initial sessions. The time spent crying usually lessens once the therapy begins to take effect. Observing the intensity and time spent crying, in session, can be another behavioral symptom that can indicate progress in the early stages of treatment. Having clients monitor crying episodes outside of sessions will also serve as another behavioral indicator of improvement or lack thereof. Depressed individuals might also tend to stay in bed and not engage in activities that they found pleasurable before the onset of the depressive episode. Subsequently, the client will benefit from an assessment of daily activities that could include attention to personal appearance and other self-care issues. Leahy and Holland (2000) emphasize reward planning and activity scheduling as components of behavioral intervention. Reward planning can include buying something new or having a manicure. The client can be encouraged to complete a pleasurable activities inventory by listing things he used to do before he was depressed that were associated with a pleasant outcome. He can begin to reintegrate some of those activities into his schedule. Activity scheduling can be as simple as taking a short walk alone or with a friend. Because of the low energy and concentration impairment often associated with depression, tasks that were routine in the past, may feel overwhelming. Therefore, it is reasonable to break down tasks into smaller steps (e.g., if the laundry needs to be done, an acceptable step for the day might be to sort the laundry). Persons, Davidson, and Tompkins (2001) believe it is imperative to facilitate behavioral change and thus introduce behavioral interventions, before cognitive interventions. The rationale for this is that so long as the patient is not functioning, the lack of functioning serves as compelling evidence to support the depressed patient's negative cognitions ("I can't do anything").

Somatic symptoms are physical symptoms that include complaints such as headache, constipation, back pain, chest pain, dizziness, musculoskeletal complaints, and weakness (Simon, VonKorff, Piccinelli, Fullerton, & Ormel, 1999). These aches and pains can sometimes be emphasized by the client over affective symptoms. Therefore somatic symptoms are an important piece of the assessment for depression, as specific cultures demonstrate an elevation in somatic complaints as evidence of depression. Chinese immigrants, for example, may not report the emotional issues directly, but will express their distress by describing more physical symptoms (Mak & Zane, 2004). When working with individuals from unfamiliar cultural groups it may be important to ask specific questions concerning somatic complaints.

Social dysfunction or maladaptive interpersonal behaviors can be another area of concern. Coyne's (1989) interpersonal reward model postulates that depressed individuals begin to complain, which gains reassurance and attention. Initially these individuals receive positive reinforcement because of the complaining, but then the self-preoccupation eventually leads others to reject them, which further reinforces their negative self-image (Leahy & Holland, 2000). A lack of meaningful interpersonal interactions or pleasurable activities can certainly negatively impact the course of a depressive episode. Assessing the client's social skills deficits and implementing interventions to address these deficits can be part of a complete treatment plan for individuals with depression. Assertiveness training, boundary setting, and interpersonal problem solving may be useful in increasing social competency and success. Such skills may also decrease the chances for relapse.

ISSUES FOR THE BEGINNING PHASE OF TREATMENT

Because a client's self-talk contributes to a construction of reality and consequential behaviors and feelings, it is important for the clinician to distance herself from the pessimism and negative predictions about circumstances and outcomes. For beginning practitioners it can often be difficult not to buy into the client's negative view. In addition, the first few sessions are a time when the client needs to feel understood and accepted. Psychomotor retardation as a symptom of depression will cause the client to need more time to respond; therefore, patience is essential on the part of the clinician during this time. One productive way to begin the treatment process is to ask the client about any past treatment, and to discuss what aspects of that treatment were helpful or unhelpful.

Practitioners who adhere to a CBT framework work to socialize clients into the model. This often begins by informing the client of the structure of sessions, and the process of efficient information gathering in order to alleviate any anxiety or feelings of rejection, when the therapist interrupts or changes the course of the assessment session. The primary focus of the first few sessions will be assessment, so the clinician will be asking many questions in a short period of time, thus it is helpful to ensure that clients are made aware of this. Clients who have engaged in other types of therapy are often surprised at the directive style of the clinician and quick pace of CBT.

In order to create an effective treatment protocol, making a correct diagnosis during assessment is essential. Research demonstrates that depression has a high rate of comorbidity with other Axis I disorders. Although depression appears to be relatively simple to diagnose, clinicians can make two common mistakes when evaluating clients. The first mistake is that the therapist may focus on a client's anxiety, substance use or psychotic symptoms, and ignore underlying symptoms of depression. Thus, the practitioner may fail to recognize depression as an important issue due to the presence of other psychopathology. The second error is not adequately diagnosing other problems because of the presence of depressive symptoms. Complex comorbidity patterns, such as the presence of personality disorders, when overlooked, can interfere with treatment adherence and progress. Several case examples follow to highlight these assessment issues.

Another issue to consider at the beginning phase of treatment is *client suitability*. Cognitive behavior therapy may not be suitable for certain individuals. The client must be willing to be active in treatment and to understand that the process may at times be challenging. Those clients, who are simply exploring their past and have no specific behavioral issue to address, may do better with another treatment modality or a generally

CASE STUDY 1

Geri, a 14-year-old female, has been in treatment since an early age. She was in a variety of foster homes until age 5, and was subsequently adopted. She is described by her adoptive parents as a nice young lady who has difficulty focusing in class, and on occasion engages in impulsive behaviors. She has many friends who she enjoys spending time with, and does not present with irritability or obvious sadness. She has been treated with stimulants for ADHD, which was diagnosed at age 8. On initial screening with the *Beck Depression Inventory* (BDI), she had a score of 31, which indicates a depression of severe intensity. She was not able to articulate her feelings, nor her thoughts until she completed the BDI. No one had considered depression, because she didn't present in the typical way that most adolescents present with depression.

CASE STUDY 2

Victor is a 47-year-old male with a history of depression. He has been on a variety of medications including the tricyclics, SSRIs, and MAO inhibitors, and none has made any significant difference in his feelings of depression or his ability to function. Victor reports that every clinician he has seen has focused on his depression, and he presents as severely depressed with a score of 33 on the *Beck Depression Inventory* (BDI). Currently he has difficulty sleeping because he reports that he takes a long time to eat, then he lets the cat out, gets ready for bed, and can't figure out why the night goes by so quickly and suddenly it is 5:00 A.M. Victor begins to slowly and shamefully report that he does some weird things. Victor's primary diagnosis was obsessive compulsive disorder (OCD). He engages in rituals and compulsions that prevent him from functioning adequately. The OCD symptoms interfere with his life to such a significant degree that he subsequently feels depressed.

supportive therapist. Upon further exploration and careful listening, the therapist will find that even among clients with vague complaints, some degree of cognitive distortions and difficulties with emotional regulation will exist and may potentially be addressed with CBT interventions. Recent studies demonstrate that even psychotic patients can benefit when the focus of the therapy is on issues of daily living, rather than on the psychotic thinking. For obvious reasons, patients with organic brain disease or trauma to the brain may benefit depending on their level of impairment.

BASIC COGNITIVE AND BEHAVIORAL CONCEPTS AND ASSUMPTIONS

Behavior therapy is founded on the premise that when environmental consequences are linked to particular behaviors, the consequence either increases (reinforce) or decreases (extinguish) the likelihood of a person responding in the same manner when confronted with similar stimuli in the future. This theory of change is also based on the client's prior learning history, and the ability to integrate new learning experiences.

While Beck was developing his cognitive theory in the mid 1970s, Peter Lewinsohn was developing a behavioral theory of depression. According to Spett (2005), Lewinsohn argued that the essence of depression is a low rate of behavior, and this low rate of behavior causes all the other symptoms of depression. Lewinsohn hypothesized that the low rate of behavior was secondary to a lack of reward from the environment. If a clinician can teach the depressed patient how to elicit higher rates of reward, the depressed patient's rate of behavior will increase, and the depression will lift. If the patient increases activities that she enjoys, improves social skills so that she won't be rejected as often, and gets out of bed even when she doesn't feel like it, she will likely experience improvement in depressive symptoms. As noted earlier, behavioral activation is often an important first step in any CBT treatment program for depression and is recommended in several treatment manuals (Freeman & Gilson, 1999; Leahy et al., 2000).

Cognitive models of depression assume that individuals respond to life events behaviorally and emotionally based on their interpretation of those events. Therefore, the cognitive model of therapy does not attempt to change the trigger, but rather focuses on changing the individual's perception of the trigger or activating event in order to decrease disturbance. The thinking of the client must be revealed and be open to restructuring by the therapist, the client, or both. A major premise of cognitive theories is that dysfunctional cognitions can be accessed and restructured in order to effect behavioral and emotional change. Cognitive theory also acknowledges that aspects of depression are rooted in reciprocal causal relationships, and that change in one area such as emotions, will likely produce change elsewhere (Persons et al., 2001).

Although cognitive behavior therapists are sometimes viewed as unempathic and unemotional because of the focus on method, protocol, and active therapist involvement, in reality, the therapist–client relationship is highly valued (Beck, 1995; Ellis, 1987; Young, 2003). A genuine relationship that includes respect, caring, and acceptance forms the foundation for using CBT skills. Other important assumptions included in most CBT models is the value of empiricism, a focus on functioning better in the present, and the efficient use of time (Freeman, Pretzer, Fleming, & Simon, 2004; Young & Matilla, 2002).

Both behavioral and cognitive models have their foundation in learning theories. Learning occurs when an individual is able to do or think something new or different. The goal of getting better, as opposed to simply feeling better, is attained through techniques that assist the client in learning new ways of thinking and practicing behavioral assignments that increase overall competence. New skills become integrated into the client's daily life. Thus, CBT can be framed within a developmental learning model rather than a linear medical model.

For example, take a client who finds herself in a phase of life in which developmentally she is challenged to move forward and lacks the skills or knowledge to do so. The client lacks the skills, not necessarily because of deficient chemistry, but because this difficult situation has not been encountered before. When one meets such a challenge, by definition the individual is *unconsciously incompetent*. The client may be confused and shamed by the inability to be effective without help and may begin to have thoughts that she is stupid, worthless, and unable to function. The client becomes aware of the lack of knowledge, by virtue of feeling helpless, hopeless, and overwhelmed, and subsequently the client feels *consciously incompetent*, as she admits that she cannot get beyond the issues at hand without professional help. The social worker, or other mental health professional, will provide the client with the opportunity to find ways to start working on getting better, or becoming more competent, rather than just feeling better. As the client learns and practices the skills presented within the context of CBT, she becomes *consciously competent*. She must still concentrate on what she is doing in order to meet with some level of success. As her skills become more automatic with practice, she becomes *unconsciously competent*. The client no longer has to think about what she is doing. She is now thinking more consciously, managing her emotions more appropriately, problem solving more effectively, and seems to have a better handle on life. This process can be compared to learning to speak a new language. Practice will increase the chances for success. This is the primary reason why homework is such an important component of CBT.

In their text, *Direct Social Work Practice: Theory and Skills*, Hepworth and Larsen (1990) present a conceptualization of social work practice that is consistent with the assumptions of cognitive behavioral practice:

Though it is the primary source of information, verbal report is vulnerable to error because of possible faulty recall, distorted perceptions, biases and limited self-awareness on the part of clients. It is thus vital to avoid the tendency to accept client's views, descriptions, and reports as valid representations of reality. Similarly it is important to recognize that the feelings expressed by clients may emanate from faulty perceptions or may be altogether irrational.

The cognitive therapist attempts to facilitate the patient's awareness of distorted thinking patterns, or cognitive distortions, and provides interventions that help to change the distortions but also understands that when dealing with humans, the process of discovery must be supportive and affirming of the individual's emotional status.

Historically, there has been significant debate over whether interventions based on purely behavioral models or cognitive models are most effective for helping clients. The battle of behavior therapy versus cognitive therapy is similar to the nature versus nurture struggle for which we will also likely never have a satisfactory answer. The interrelatedness of behavior and cognition is so strong as to warrant a change of name for an organization previously known as *Association for Advancement of Behavior Therapy*, which was recently changed to *Association of Cognitive and Behavioral Therapy*. Regardless of which side we choose, Leahy and Holland (2000) report that the behavioral model is a useful part of cognitive therapy, as behavioral assignments are essential to examining and testing the patient's cognitive distortions. The patient's response to a behavioral assignment will provide insight into the distorted automatic thoughts. For example, suggesting that a client have a manicure might elicit a response that informs us of her self-view of worthlessness or undeservingness. From a practical standpoint the practitioner needs to consider both thinking patterns and behaviors and how they typically go together for a specific client.

EMPIRICAL SUPPORT FOR CBT AND DEPRESSION

Numerous studies support the efficacy of CBT for the treatment of depression (Beck, 1976; Blackburn & Bishop, 1979; Dobson, 1989; Rush, Beck, Kovacs, & Hollon, 1977). Cognitive therapy can be effective for treating severe forms of depression and in combination with antidepressant medications is sometimes more efficacious than either treatment alone (Reinecke & Didie, 2005). Many qualitative and quantitative reviews now conclude that cognitive therapy: (a) is effective for reducing depressive symptoms, (b) is at least comparable, if not, superior to medication treatment, and (c) is associated with lower rates of relapse in comparison to medication treatments (Dobson, 1989; Hollon & Beck, 1986. Confirming Dobson's results, Glaoguen, Cottraux, Cucherat, and Blackburn (1998) in their meta-analysis found that cognitive therapy (CT) was significantly better than no treatment, antidepressant medication, and a group of miscellaneous therapies. However, in contrast to Dobson's finding of a clear superiority of CT over behavior therapy (BT), Gloaguen and colleagues found that CT was comparable to behavior therapy alone. A more recent meta-reanalysis completed by Wampold, Minami, Baskin, and Tierney (2000) also supports the effectiveness of CT for depression. However, this study concluded that all bona fide psychological treatments for depression are equally efficacious. In order for a treatment to fit the criteria of bonafide it had to meet the following criteria: (a) the therapist had to be trained in the specific therapy at a graduate level; (b) the sessions were face to face and treatment was individualized for the patient; (c) treatment contained psychologically valid components (as evidenced by two of the following: a citation made to an established approach, a description was contained in an article, and the description contained a reference to an established psychological process, or a manual existed to guide delivery of treatment). Gloaguen and colleagues (1998) completed a meta-analysis that resulted in demonstrating that CT and BT are equally efficacious.

In the midst of what may be perceived as a cognitive revolution, a debate has arisen stemming from the highly visible results of the National Institute of Mental Health Treatment of Depression Collaborative Research Program study (NIMH TDCRP), which concluded that CBT was not effective in the treatment of severe depression (Elkin, Shea, Watkins, and National Institute of Mental Health Treatment of Depression Collaborative Research Program, 1989). The issues present on both sides of the debate are of a methodological nature. Criticisms of the studies include researcher allegiance, lack of stringent selection criteria, exclusion of some studies while including others, and use of the BDI as the only measure of depression. When taken together, CBT seems to have a relatively large base of support for treating clients with depression. However, it is certainly not the only approach that is empirically supported but nonetheless remains an important option.

ALBERT ELLIS'S RATIONAL EMOTIVE BEHAVIOR THERAPY (REBT) MODEL

Albert Ellis's rational emotive therapy was developed in the 1950s. Ellis was becoming disillusioned with the process of psychoanalysis, and proposed that people have a biological and social tendency to easily and naturally raise their healthy preferences and desires into unhealthy and self-defeating demands (Ellis, 2003). Ellis has demonstrated three ways in which people do this. If they do not perform well, or as they *should*, then they are worthless. If other people do not treat them fairly, then the other people are damnable. Third, if their lives are not stress free, then they simply cannot be happy at all (Ellis, 2003) .

Albert Ellis's REBT model uses cognitive restructuring to change irrational thoughts. He distinguishes between two types of evaluations. In his REBT model he states that clients can evaluate life's difficulties and challenges either rationally or irrationally. He also addresses the validity of the thought as well as the utility. Is the thought logical and grounded in reality and is it helpful? Ellis and other rational emotive behavior theorists, writers, and practitioners make up a major school of thought regarding the importance client's evaluations (McMullin, 2000). Ellis uses several quotes in the REBT resource book for practitioners to demonstrate his philosophy:

Epictetus: *People are disturbed not by things, but by the views they take of them*

Shakespeare: *There is nothing either good or bad, but thinking makes it so.*

Milton: *The mind is its own place, and in itself can make a Heav'n of Hell, and a Hell of Heav'n.*

The Bible (Proverbs 23:7): *As a man thinketh in his heart so is he.*

REBT focuses on four major types of irrational beliefs that create disturbances (Dryden, 2003):

1. *Demands (DEM):* Elevating personal desires to moral dictates or rules that are imposed on the self, others, or the world. This type of thinking is often verbalized in words like *must, ought,* and *should.*
2. *Awfulizing (AWF):* Exaggerating the consequences or level of hardship associated with aversive events. This type of thinking is often indicated by client statements like "It's awful, terrible, horrible."
3. *Low frustration tolerance (LFT):* Underestimating one's own ability to deal with discomfort or adversity. Often heard in statements such as "I can't stand it or tolerate it."
4. *Depreciation beliefs (DEP):* Blaming or condemning people "in total" for specific behavioral acts. For example if another doesn't conform to my desires, he or she is "bad or worthless."

The following are some sample distinctions between irrational (IR) and rational (RB) beliefs related to the four major categories:

Demands

(IR) *I must have my boyfriend's love* or *He should love me.*

(RB) I would like to have my boyfriend's love, but there is no law that exists that says he has to love me.

Awfulizing

(IR) *It would be awful not to be loved by him.*

(RB) I would be disappointed and sad if he didn't love me, but it certainly is not the end of the world.

Low Frustration Tolerance

(IR) *I can't stand the idea of ever being separated from my boyfriend.*

(RB) I don't like thinking about being apart, but I have certainly tolerated other breakups.

Depreciation Belief

(IR) *My boyfriend would be a rotten person if he breaks up with me.*

(RB) I may feel frustrated because I can't control his choices, but exercising his free will doesn't make him a globally bad person.

REBT theory states that when confronted with negative events, we have a choice of feeling bad, but not becoming depressed and disturbed (DiGiuseppe, Doyle, & Rose, 2002). REBT differentiates between healthy and unhealthy negative emotions. It is healthy to experience some level of negative emotion in response to a negative activating event, rather than feeling indifferent to the event. Irrational thinking is likely to intensify and prolong negative emotional experiences.

A basic part of the REBT model is the A-B-C assessment. Although real-life situations are far more complicated than such a theory may encompass, it is a simple way to have clients begin to focus on and structure their thinking in more rational ways. In this model the A represents *an activating event* that can be external or even a thought itself. The B is the *belief* about A. The C is the *consequence* that results from B about A. Most people with disturbances believe that the activating event causes the resulting C, feeling or behavior. According to A-B-C theory, it is the B about A that drives C. We often hear someone saying, "He insulted me (A) and that made me so angry (C)." The A or activating event is someone insulting. The illusion is that this event created angry feelings or C. The question is then, why do some people react negatively to being insulted, while others walk away? The answer is based in their belief about some aspect of A.

Clinical example:

CLIENT: All week I have been thinking about all the problems that I have, and I am getting more and more depressed. I don't know if I can ever change.

THERAPIST: What were you telling yourself when you were making yourself depressed?

CLIENT: I'm not sure.

THERAPIST: Well, do you see the musts and shoulds you are putting in there? I must feel better, I should not be feeling this way. I should change.

CLIENT: I have to get better right away. Yes, I am using *demandingness* a lot.

THERAPIST: That's correct. It also sounds like you are saying that you should not have so many problems. If you said, I would prefer not to have so many problems, but I do and I will work on them without putting so many demands on myself particularly in the area of immediate changes, then you wouldn't get so depressed about your problems. You would feel like you could stand it, not feel so bad about yourself and perhaps agree that you didn't like the situation but could certainly tolerate it.

Readers interested in a more detailed description of REBT theory and practice are referred to Walen, DiGiuseppe, and Dryden (1992).

BECK'S COGNITIVE THERAPY

As originally formulated in the 1960s, the emphasis in Beck's cognitive therapy was to help clients identify *distortions in thinking about the reality of life events*, and to replace those distortions with more *accurate and realistic perceptions and appraisals*. While this is still a major focus, the Beck model has evolved to include three levels of cognitions: automatic thoughts, assumptions, and core beliefs.

Automatic Thoughts

Human beings are constantly thinking and making evaluations about the world around them. Automatic thoughts are part of this ongoing inner dialogue that naturally occurs with everyone. They are *spontaneous and fleeting*, and are thought to exist *just below the level of conscious awareness*. They may also take the form of images or memories. With minimal effort, most people are able to tune into this inner dialogue and identify specific thoughts as they occur moment to moment. In terms of working with depressed clients, it is important to identify those automatic thoughts that are negative, distorted, and associated with periods of low mood. Initially, the focus is on helping clients notice the thinking that takes place when they feel most down. Again, it is important to assess the automatic thoughts exactly as they are experienced when sadness or a sudden change in mood occurs. Initially, it may seem as though clients report a wide variety of automatic thoughts related to their sadness and depression. However, in a short time they will likely notice recurring patterns. In addition, once the other underlying cognitions (assumptions and core beliefs) are identified, the content of automatic thoughts becomes more understandable and easier to predict.

Assumptions

Assumptions can be conceptualized as *rules* or *attitudes* that guide daily actions and also set expectations (Greenberger & Padesky, 1995). These assumptions are often not directly expressed verbally by clients, as they may themselves be unaware of them, and therefore they are not easily accessible to the practitioner. Since assumptions give rise to the automatic thoughts, one way to identify them is to make *inferences from recurring themes* found in automatic thoughts. Assumptions, when stated, typically take the form of "if-then" statements, or "should" or "must" statements. For example, "If I try to get close to others then they will reject me," or "Even if I try hard, (then) I probably won't succeed anyhow." Assumptions can be problematic to the extent that they are exaggerated, distorted, and are maladaptive when applied rigidly across situations. Assumptions are believed to develop in response to early childhood experiences and interactions with others. Persistently negative or even traumatic experiences can lead to negative assumptions about oneself and result in negative expectations or attitudes regarding others and the future. Maladaptive assumptions actually are a coping skill developed to deal with the negative schema.

Core Beliefs

Core beliefs are proposed as the "deepest" or most abstract level of cognition. Core beliefs contain the most centrally held ideas related to self, other people, and the world. These are rules that are held with great conviction. Negative core beliefs underlie maladaptive assumptions and distorted automatic thoughts. For example, one may believe at a fundamental level that he is worthless and does not measure up favorably when compared to others. Thus, core beliefs may determine the way an individual automatically interprets reality, especially in ambiguous or stressful situations. The advantage for practitioners in conceptualizing maladaptive assumptions and core beliefs lies in the larger roadmap that it provides to help direct interventions in the most effective manner. For example, using Judith Beck's (1995) cognitive conceptualization model, let's take a look at a specific *client. Carmine is a 27-year-old college graduate beginning work at a new job.*

A.   The Cognitive Model as Applied to Carmine
  1. Typical Current Problems
      Writing reports, volunteering for overtime, social withdrawal, lack of assertiveness.
  2. Typical Automatic Thoughts
      I can't do this, I am a failure, I will never make it here.→ sad
      I should be more involved and doing more.→guilty
      What if they don't like my work? What if they fire me?→ anxious
  3. Core Beliefs
      I am inadequate and incompetent.
  4. Assumptions or Conditional Beliefs
      If I fail at this job then I am a failure as a person.
      If I ask for help, then I am weak.
  5. Rules
      I must work harder than everyone else.
      I should excel.
  6. Therapist's Goals
      Decrease self-criticism, teach basic cognitive tools to dispute dysfunctional automatic thoughts and restructure negative thoughts; do problem solving around improving written reports; address social skills that will improve social withdrawal.

One can begin to see that Carmine's beliefs, which likely developed earlier in his life, predisposed him to interpreting events in a negative way. He did not question his beliefs, but rather accepted them as absolute and true. The thoughts and beliefs did not cause the depression, but once the depression took hold, these thoughts supported the maintenance of the depression.

SUICIDE RISK ASSESSMENT:
WHEN DEPRESSION BECOMES DANGEROUS

Despite extensive research into variables that might contribute to suicidal behaviors, evaluating suicide risk continues to be both clinically difficult and scientifically imperfect for mental health providers. Studies that have attempted to categorize individuals and construct a suicide profile have been, for the most part, inconclusive, as assessing suicide risk is not a static process. In spite of the best efforts of family and professionals, suicide took the lives of 30,622 people in 2001 (Centers for Disease Control and Prevention [CDC], 2004). One in seven patients hospitalized for major depression will die by suicide (Powell, Geddes, Deeks, Goldacre, & Hawton, 2000). Although depression is strongly associated with suicide, most depressed individuals do not commit suicide and many nondepressed individuals make suicide attempts. Depression is not a necessary nor a sufficient cause (Reinecke et al., 2002).

There are risk factors outside of the symptoms of the disorder that indicate a greater probability for potential fatal behavior. The most critical risk factors for suicide completion (in order of their seriousness) are: (a) the medical seriousness of previous suicide attempts, (b) history of suicide attempts, (c) acute suicidal ideation, (d) severe hopelessness, (e) attraction to death, (f) family history of suicide, (g) acute overuse of alcohol, and (h) loss/separations (Peruzzi & Bongar, 1999). A history of serious suicide attempts may be the single best predictor of completed suicide (Moscicki, 1997). From a purely cognitive perspective, hopelessness may be a helpful short-term and long-term predictor of suicidal risk among adults and thus feelings of pessimism may be an important target for therapy. A cognitive model considers maladaptive cognitions to be a central pathway to suicidal behavior (Rudd, Rajab, & Joiner, 2004). Most researchers agree that motivation toward suicidality comes from a belief that the problem the individual is facing is too large and overwhelming to ever be solved, and that suicide is the only solution or escape. The individual has essentially run out of options. At this point a formal risk assessment is in order.

Treatment of suicidal patients is systematic, strategic, and problem focused with an initial emphasis on challenging beliefs that support feelings of hopelessness (Reinecke et al., 2002). Marsha Linehan has published a suicide crisis protocol in pocket form, which can be obtained at www .behavioraltech.com. Her risk assessment format in basic form is as follows:

- Summarize the problem. What precipitated the crisis?
- Emphatically instruct not to commit suicide. Give advice and make direct suggestions.

- Generate hope.
- Validate and soothe while focusing on affect tolerance.
- Reduce high risk environmental factors by removing lethal means. Increase social support.
- Address function of current suicide ideation.
- Get a commitment to a plan of action.
- Troubleshoot the action plan.
- Anticipate recurrence of the crisis and reassess suicide risk.

Berk, Henriques, Warman, Brown, and Beck (2004) have developed a 10-session treatment protocol specifically for suicidal individuals. The key element in the early phase of treatment is teaching the patient skills in order to become their own therapist outside the session. Many clients who have not had CBT treatment have no idea that their behaviors are often driven by their thoughts. Teens who are hospitalized for a suicide attempt will often report that when they had thoughts of suicide, they didn't realize that they had a choice to not follow through on the attempt. The middle stage of treatment, sessions four through seven, focus on cognitive restructuring and behavioral change. What are the recurring themes in the individual's automatic thoughts? These themes can be addressed using Socratic questioning or dysfunctional thought records. The later sessions address relapse prevention. This relapse prevention piece explores any possible future crisis and solidifies the patient's coping skills. Beck and colleagues recommend that booster sessions be offered to the client whenever he or she might feel the need to reconnect.

Finally, Leahy and Holland (2000) provide a structured interview format for practitioners to use in evaluating suicidal risk. Their approach consists of 38 questions regarding current and past behaviors. We recommend this format for those who are unfamiliar with how to conduct a risk assessment interview.

SUMMARY

In an effort to demystify depression and empower clients, CBT offers a structured approach to dealing with the negative thought patterns and reduced behaviors present in most depressed clients. The beginning phase of treatment includes a thorough assessment of client symptom patterns, the development of a supportive and collaborative therapeutic relationship, and a process of socializing the client into the CBT model. Once treatment begins, clients are exposed to a variety of cognitive and behavioral techniques designed to increase skills that become integrated into the client's life. In addition, several models of CBT exist from which practitioners can choose, the most common being the theories of Beck and Ellis. Finally, consideration must be given to assessing and intervening with clients who may be at risk for suicide.

REFERENCES

Beck, A. T., & Weishaar, M. E. (1995). Cognitive therapy. In R. J. Corsini & D. Wedding (Eds.), *Current psychotherapies* (5th ed., pp. 229–261). Itasca, IL: Peacock.

Beck, J. (1995). *Cognitive therapy: Basics and beyond.* New York: Guilford.

Beck, A. T., Steer, R. A., & Brown, G. K. (1996). *Beck Depression Inventory— Second Edition.* San Antonio, TX: The Psychological Corporation.

Berk, M. S., Henriques, G. R., Warman, D. M., Brown, G. K., & Beck, A. T. (2004). A cognitive therapy intervention for suicide attempters: An overview of the treatment and case examples. *Cognitive and Behavioral Practice, 11,* 265–277.

Bernard, M. E. (1993). Are our emotions and behaviors helping you or hurting you? In M. E. Bernard & J. L. Wolfe (Eds.), *The RET resource book for practitioners.* New York: The Albert Ellis Institute for Rational Emotive Behavior Therapy.

Blackburn, I., & Bishop, S. (1979). *A comparison of cognitive therapy, pharmacotherapy, and their combination in depressed outpatients.* Paper presented at the annual meeting of the Society for Psychotherapy Research, Oxford, England.

Centers for Disease Control and Prevention, National Center for Injury Prevention and Control. (2004). Web-based Injury Statistics Query and Reporting System (WISQARS). Retrieved July 28, 2005, from www.cdc.gov/ncipc/wisqars/default.htm.

Chamberlin, J. (1997). A working definition of empowerment. *Psychiatric Rehabilitation Journal, 20,* 43–46.

Coyne, J. C. (1989). Thinking post-cognitively about depression. In A. Freeman, K. M. Simon, L. E. Butler, & H. Arkowitz (Eds.), *Comprehensive handbook for cognitive therapy* (pp. 227–244). New York: Plenum.

DiGiuseppe, R., Doyle, K., & Rose, R. D. (2002). Rational emotive behavior therapy for depression: Achieving unconditional self acceptance. In M. A. Reinecke & M. R. Davison (Eds.), *Comparative treatments of depression* (pp. 220–246). New York: Springer.

Dobson, K. S. (1989). A meta-analysis of the efficacy of cognitive therapy for depression. *Journal of Consulting and Clinical Psychology, 57,* 414–419.

Dozois, D. J. A., & Dobson, K. S. (2001). Information processing and cognitive organization in unipolar depression: Specificity and co-morbidity issues. *Journal of Abnormal Psychology, 110,* 236–246.

Dozois, D. J. A., & Dobson, K. S. (2004). Depression. In M. M. Anthony & D. H. Barlow (Eds.), *Handbook of assessment and treatment planning for psychological disorders* (pp. 259–299). New York: Guilford.

Dryden, W. (2003). *Rational emotive behavior therapy: Theoretical developments*. New York: Brunner-Routledge.

Elkin, I., Shea, T., Watkins, J., and National Institute of Mental Health Treatment of Depression Collaborative Research Program. (1989). *Archives of General Psychiatry 46*, 971–982.

Ellis, A. (2003). Differentiating preferential from exaggerated and musturbatory beliefs in rational emotive behavior therapy. In W. Dryden (Ed.), *Rational emotive behavior therapy: Theoretical developments* (pp. 22–34). New York: Brunner-Routledge.

Ellis, A., & Dryden, W. (1987). *The practice of rational emotive therapy*. New York, Springer.

Freeman, A., Pretzer, J., Fleming, B., & Simon, K. M. (2004). (2nd ed.). Clinical applications of cognitive therapy. New York: Kluwer.

Freeman, A., & Gilson, M. (1999). *Overcoming depression: Cognitive therapy approach for the taming of the depression beast*. New York: Graywind.

Gloaguen, V., Cottraux, J., Cucherat, M., & Blackburn, I. (1998). A meta-analysis of the effects of cognitive therapy in depressed patients. *Journal of Affective Disorders 49*, 59–72.

Greenberger, D., & Padesky, C. A. (1995) *Clinician's guide to mind over mood*. New York: Guilford.

Hepworth, D. H., & Larsen, J. (1990). *Direct social work practice: Theory and skills* (3rd ed.). Chicago: Dorsey.

Hollon, S., & Beck, A. T. (1985). Cognitive and cognitive-behavior therapies. In A. E. Bergin & S. A. Garfield (Eds.), *Handbook of psychotherapy and behavior change*, 3rd ed. (pp. 443–482). New York: Wiley.

Leahy, R. L., & Holland (2000). *Treatment plans and interventions for depression and anxiety disorders*. New York: Guilford.

Mak, W. S., & Zane, N. (2004). The phenomenon of somatization among community Chinese Americans. *Social Psychiatry and Psychiatric Epidemiology, 39*, 967–974.

McMullin, R. E. (2000). *The new handbook of cognitive therapy techniques*. New York: W. W. Norton.

Moscicki, E. K. (1997). Identification of suicide risk factors using epidemeiologic studies. *Psychiatric Clinics of North America, 20*, 499–517.

Persons, J. B., Davidson, J., & Tompkins, M. A. (2001). *Essential components of cognitive-behavior therapy for depression*. Washington, DC: American Psychological Association.

Peruzzi, N., & Bongar, B. (1999). Assessing risk for completed suicide in patients with major depression: Psychologists' view of critical factors. *Professional Psychology: Research and Practice, 30*, 576–580.

Powell, J., Geddes, J., Deeks, J., Goldacre, M., & Hawton, K. (2000). Suicide in psychiatric hospital in-patients. Risk factors and their predictive power. *British Journal of Psychiatry, 176*, 266–272.

Reinecke, M. A., & Didie, E. R. (2005). Cognitive behavioral therapy with suicidal patients. In Robert I. Yufit, & David Lester, (Eds.), *Assessment, treatment, and prevention of suicidal behavior*. (pp. 205–234). New York: Wiley.

Rudd, M. D., Joiner, T. E., & Rajab, M. H. (2004). *Treating suicidal behavior: An effective time limited approach.* New York: Guilford.

Rush, A. J., Beck, A. T., Kovacs, M., & Hollon, S. (1977). Comparative efficacy of cognitive therapy and imipramine in the treatment of depressed outpatients. *Cognitive Therapy and Research, 1,* 17–37.

Schelde, J. T. M. (1998). Major depression: Behavioral parameters of depression and recovery. *Journal of Nervous and Mental Disease, 186,* 141–149.

Simon, G. E., VonKorff, M., Piccinelli, M., Fullerton, C., & Ormel, J. (1999). An international study of the relation between somatic symptoms and depression. *New England Journal of Medicine, 341,* 1329–1335.

Spett, M. (2005). *Behavior therapy vs. cognitive therapy.* Retrieved from http://members.aol.com.njacbt/article13.htm.

Walen, S., DiGiuseppe, R., & Dryden, W. (1992). *A practitioner's guide to rational emotive therapy* (2nd ed.). New York: Oxford University Press.

Wampold, B. E., Minami, T., Baskin, T. W., & Tierney S. C. (2002). A meta-(re)analysis of the effects of cognitive therapy versus "other therapies" for depression. *Journal of Affective Disorders, 68,* 159–165.

Young, J. (2003). Schema Focused Workshop presented at Cornell Hospital, New York.

Young. J., & Matilla, . (2002). Schema-focused therapy for depression. In M. A. Reinecke & M. R. Davison, (Eds.). *Comparative treatments of depression.* New York: Springer.

SUGGESTED READINGS

Beck, J. (1995). *Cognitive therapy: Basics and beyond.* New York: Guilford.

Bernard, M. E., & Wolfe, J. *REBT resource book for practitioners.* www.rebt.org.

Burns, D. (1999). *The feeling good handbook.* New York: Penguin.

Burns, D. (2003). *The original therapist's toolkit.* www.feelinggood.com.

Freeman, A., & Gilson, M. (1999) *Overcoming depression: Cognitive therapy approach for the taming of the depression beast.* New York: Graywind.

Leahy, R. L., & Holland (2000). *Treatment plans and interventions for depression and anxiety disorders.* New York: Guilford.

Mullin, R. (2000). *The new handbook of cognitive therapy techniques.* New York: W. W. Norton & Company.

Persons, J. (1989). *Cognitive therapy in practice.* New York: W. W. Norton.

CHAPTER 19

Treatment of Suicidal Behavior

Arthur Freeman
Donna Martin
Tammie Ronen

Thou shalt not kill.

—Exodus 20

And Samson put his arms around the two middle pillars supporting the building, and threw all his weight against them, his right arm against one and his left arm against the other; and he cried out, "May I die with the Philistines."

—Judges 16:29–30

And flinging down the silver in the sanctuary he [Judas] made off and went and hanged himself.

—Matthew 27:5

INTRODUCTION

The treatment of the suicidal individual is perhaps the most weighty and difficult of any of the problems confronted by the clinical social worker. The idea of the client being inclined to end his or her life has consequences for the client, the clinician, the client's significant others, for the family, a school or work group, and ultimately, for the society as a whole. Suicide is multifaceted with significant religious, sociological, psychological, legal, and economic consequences. Suicidal risk increases with each new depressive episode and there is a 15% chance that clients suffering from recurrent depression, severe enough to require hospitalization, will eventually die by suicide (Segal, Williams, Mark, & Teasdale, 2002). However, although suicide has been the disorder most associated with depression, more so than with other disorders, it is not automatically a "required" part of depression. Some clients with depression may not be suicidal. They will continue to suffer with their depression, but the thought of taking their own life would be foreign to them. Clients with anxiety disorders may also have suicidal ideation as part of the clinical picture. Some frequent comorbid pathology with suicidal behavior includes alcoholism, panic attacks, drug abuse, chronic schizophrenia, conduct disorder in children and adolescents, impulse control deficits, schizophrenia, and problem-solving deficits.

Foa, Keane, & Friedman (2000) state that while suicidal and self-destructive behavior is not part of the core posttraumatic stress disorders (PTSD) it is recognized as a major associated feature of PTSD and should therefore be a major part of the therapeutic focus with this group.

A full understanding of the basic dynamics of suicide from a cognitive perspective is essential for treatment. The theoretical underpinnings of suicidal ideation and intent are essential for the clinician who will, inevitably, be confronted by the individual who thinks about, plans for, or attempts some form of self-injurious or suicidal behavior. When suicide is an issue, the clinician must work quickly to establish rapport with the client, use a more direct problem-solving approach, and assume a more active role in restructuring of the client's thoughts, behaviors, and affect than is typical in the treatment of many other emotional problems. A depressed client may have a history of episodes of depression over many years, but will return to therapy, albeit depressed, the next week. The suicidal client poses the risk that there may not be a next week.

Suicide is part of a spectrum of problems that we have termed *self-directed negative behavior*. This spectrum starts with rather mundane negative internal dialogue and becomes increasingly more dangerous as it moves toward suicidal behavior. It is the latter part of the spectrum that will be the focus of this chapter.

SELF-DIRECTED NEGATIVE BEHAVIOR

Behaviors such as cutting of oneself, verbal suicidal threats, suicidal "gestures," and other behaviors often labeled as "acting out" are all self-directed negative behavior (SDNB). In the most severe circumstance, the behavior may involve completed suicide. Whatever the DSM diagnosis, SDNB will cut across all diagnoses and all age levels. The specific behaviors include self-denigrating/debasing thoughts, that is, what have been labeled as negative cognitions. The self-directed negative behavior also includes self-inflicted violence (e.g., cutting, carving, burning, scratching, hair pulling, self-inflicted bruising, wrist banging, interfering with the healing of wounds, or excessive nail biting). In all their varying degrees these behaviors appear clinically in many disorders and may arise spontaneously or after exposure to some other person who self-harms. Self-directed negative behavior seems to be escalating and it is likely that the present estimate that 1% of the population has engaged in some form of this behavior is likely an underestimation.

Suicidal harmful behavior appears in all ages and characterizes clients in a large spectrum of life. Herbert (2002) proposes that the rates of suicidal behavior rise sharply during the teenage years so that it comes to rank among the half dozen most common causes of death among older adolescents while the peak is between the age of 15 to 19 years old.

There seems to be a connection between self-harm and suicide that remains unclear. There is clearly a range of behaviors, and we believe that the clinician must view each on a continuum of severity. Several questions are raised. Do patients move along this SDNB continuum in a stepwise fashion? Does the level of depression or nature of the disorder predict the type of negative self-directed behavior? Do these behaviors arise spontaneously or are they "contagious?" What part does the Internet and exposure to other self-injurers play in the development of this behavior?

Our premise is that the best way to view these behaviors is as overlapping behaviors that run from low severity to high severity. While we see these behaviors as a continuum, we do not see them as sequential, requiring the individual to move through each one in turn. Each of these behavioral "types" requires a different set of interventions. Thus, we are proposing a more conceptual and treatment-planning emphasis that targets specific SDNB. The following diagram illustrates the continuum.

Degree of Severity of Life Threat

LOW   MEDIUM   HIGH

Self-Denigration/Debasement

Self-Punishment

Self-Harm

Self-Abuse

Disregard for Personal Safety

Self-Injury

Self-Destruction (Suicide)

The number of individuals in each group decreases with the severity, so that the most frequent behaviors seen in clinical practice are the negative views of self. We would define each of the types in the following way.

Self-Denigration/Debasement

The individual tends to verbally and cognitively demean and debase himself both internally and externally. He is prone to negative expectations inasmuch as he has a negative perceptual bias. Both episodically and stylistically this individual is prone to depression. His view may be stated directly (e.g., "I'm so dumb," or "No one would want to be with me.").

Self-Punishment

The individual will deprive herself of enjoyable activities or experiences inasmuch as she believes that she should "pay a price" for thoughts, actions, transgressions, or feelings in the present or past. This is related to and is often a sequelae of guilt and/or shame (e.g., "I deserve the bad things that happen to me," or, "I cannot go to the movies with my friends because I did not study enough last night.").

Self-Harm

The individual engages in behaviors or activities that *may* have a negative impact on his life (Brown, Henriques, Sosdjan, & Beck, 2004). This would include smoking, avoidance of prescribed medication, potentially life-threatening activities such as unprotected sex with multiple partners, or the choice of occupation. There is no guarantee that the risk-related behavior will cause self-directed injury. The risk factor may, in fact, be antidepressive in nature (e.g., "I am invulnerable and the risk is worth it" or, "There's no sure way of predicting that these things *will* hurt me.").

Self-Abuse

The individual engages in activities that have, or will likely have a direct negative impact on her present life circumstance. This would include extensive and regular use of alcohol and addictive drugs (both illegal and prescription). Also included would be overeating, bulimia, and anorexia (e.g., "Sure they have a negative effect but I only do it on weekends and I can stop whenever I want," or, "These things reduce my anxiety and that makes it worth the risk.").

Disregard for Personal Safety

Individuals place themselves in situations, circumstances, and relationships that are, and will be, hurtful, dangerous, or potentially lethal. They may be in abusive relationships, involved as a victim of abusive family members, or place themselves into situations of high risk (e.g., going to an area of their city at night that is known to be dangerous. (They might think "I cannot get out of this family/relationship. I am helpless to fight back.")

Self-Injury

Individuals involve themselves in a pattern of bodily damage such as burning, cutting, or ingestion of poisons. They may refuse needed and necessary medication. They may describe the self-injurious behavior as distracting them from their psychic pain, and/or a way of attracting attention or calling for help. Included would be parasuicidal behavior (e.g., "Look what I have to do to get anyone to notice me," or, "I need this as a release.").

Self-Destruction

The individual takes clear and powerful action to end their life. The means are not important, and the destruction is sooner rather then later. If they survive they are often surprised (e.g., "There is no hope for things to get any better so that I will act to end my life," or, "Anything is better than living this awful life.").

We continue by examining the last three areas of this continuum.

ASSESSMENT OF SUICIDAL THINKING

A client may be identified as suicidal in the course of the clinician's discussion with the client, by a family member concerned about the client's safety, or by the client themselves. The clinician must complete a clinical assessment of suicidal ideation, evaluate the client's family history for suicidal behavior, examine the risks and client resources, and then quickly conceptualize the client's problem(s), and plan strategies for intervention. To achieve maximum impact and effectiveness, the techniques or combinations of techniques are specifically selected to suit the goal of working with the suicidal client, counseling based on the clinician's conceptualization of the problem(s), the availability of the client's strengths and repertoire of adaptive responses, and the clinician's skill and style.

The clinical interview and assessment of the suicidal client must include the following points:

1. What are the expressed reasons for contemplated or planned suicide?
2. Are there comorbid problems?
3. What is the individual's level of depression and/or anxiety?
4. What is the individual's level of hopelessness?
5. What is the individual's level or degree of suicidal intent?
6. Is there a suicide plan?
7. Is the suicide plan vague or specific?
8. What is the client's level of impulse control?
9. What is the likelihood of the client exercising impulse control?
10. What are the individual's situational stressors?
11. What are the individual's vulnerability factors?
12. Is there a family history of suicide?
13. What are the client's coping strategies?
14. Is there active and current substance use and abuse?
15. What is the individual's attitude toward death and suicide?
16. What are the deterrents to making a suicide attempt?
17. Are there facilitators of suicidal behavior?
    a. Does the individual have the means of killing him or herself?
    b. Are there cultural and/or religious factors that make death by suicide attractive or acceptable?
    c. Does the individual have a personal attraction to death?
    d. Has there been a suicide of a family member or of a friend?
    e. Is there a decreased value on safety?
    f. Is there an increased threshold for pain?
    g. Has there been recent media attention to suicide?
18. Will (can) the client list alternatives to suicide?
19. Can the client and therapist develop *one* alternative to suicide?
20. Does the client have plans for the proximal future?

The sources of data for the assessment can be the client's self-report, report of significant other(s), clinical interview, rating scales, and objective testing.

ASSESSMENT OF VULNERABILITY

The vulnerability factors serve to drive their threshold for responding even lower. The vulnerability factors have a summative effect causing the threshold of response to lower even further. These vulnerability factors include:

1. *Acute illness.* This may run the range from a severe and debilitating illness to more transient illnesses such as headaches, virus infections, and so on.
2. *Chronic illness.* In situations in which the health problem is chronic, there can be an acute exacerbation of the suicidal thinking.
3. *Deterioration of health.* In aging, there may a loss of activity due to the body's inability to perform up to the expectations once appropriate at other times in one's life.
4. *Hunger.* During times of food deprivation, the individual is often more vulnerable to a variety of stimuli. In literature, Jean Valjean was willing to break the conventions of society. We have all been warned that when we are hungry, we should not attempt to shop for food because of the probability of overpurchasing food.
5. *Anger.* When individuals are angry, there appears to be a loss of appropriate problem-solving ability. There may be a loss of impulse control or overresponding to stimuli that may more usually be ignored.
6. *Fatigue.* In a similar fashion, fatigue decreases both problem-solving strategies and impulse control.
7. *Loneliness.* When individuals see themselves as isolated and apart from others, leaving this unhappy world may seem to be a reasonable option.
8. *Major life loss.* With the death of a significant other through death or through loss of divorce or separation, individuals often see themselves as having reduced options, or lack a caring for what happens to them.
9. *Poor problem-solving ability.* Certain individuals may have impaired problem-solving ability. This deficit may not be obvious until the individual is placed in situations of great stress. Being able to deal with minor problems may never test the individual's ability.
10. *Substance abuse.* The abuse of many substances can increase suicidality. This may be of two types of, acute problems where the client's judgment is compromised during periods of intoxication, and more chronic problems in which judgment may be impaired on an ongoing basis.
11. *Chronic pain.* Chronic pain may have the effect of causing the individual to see suicide as one method for achieving surcease from the pain.
12. *Poor impulse control.* There are certain clients who have poor impulse control because of organic (hyperactivity) or functional problems. Clients with bipolar illness, borderline, antisocial, or histrionic personality disorders may all have impulse control deficits.
13. *New life circumstance.* Changing jobs, marital status, homes, or family status all are stressors that are vulnerability factors.

TYPES OF SUICIDAL BEHAVIOR

We would identify four types of suicidal behavior. None is mutually exclusive of the others. The first type we would term the *Rational Suicider*. This is the individual who sees his death by suicide as a reasonable and rationale act. Having made that statement we would hasten to point out that very few of the suicidal clients that we have seen fall into this category. These clients generally do not seek counseling, but are seen in the hospital (generally on a medical unit) when a planned suicide fails. They do not come into a therapist's office to discuss or debate the rationality of their suicidal intent. This type of suicide is being discussed by legislators, medical-legal ethicists, and by clergy. The therapist's role with the Rational Suicider is unclear. It is essential to not accept every suicidal client's position that his or her suicide is rational. It may be a function of hopelessness.

The second type of suicidal individual is what we term the *Psychotic Suicider*. This is the individual whose suicidal actions are directed by inner voices and often by command hallucinations. Hospitalization and medication would be the treatment of choice for this individual. Treatment on an outpatient basis is less workable because of the need to titrate the antipsychotic medication to the therapeutic levels as quickly as possible.

The third type of suicidal individual is what we term the *Hopeless Suicider*. This individual has, in *his* or *her* personal view, no options other than to die. The therapeutic goal becomes helping the person to either develop options other than suicide, or to utilize the options that are available though unseen. The hopeless individual is the most frequently seen client in therapy. The suicidal individual generally experiences hopelessness and views suicide as a reasonable, prime, or sole method for achieving relief. All individuals have an option list of alternative actions they might use in problematic situations to avoid reaching the stage of hopelessness. However, for the seriously depressed client, whose problem-solving abilities are compromised, these options appear unavailable or inaccessible, thereby increasing the sense of hopelessness.

The final type of suicidal individual is what we term the *Impulsive or Histrionic Suicider*. This individual acts in ways that appear to be self-destructive although the intent is not necessarily suicidal. These individuals take great personal risks, act in ways that make it appear that they have little or no concern for their safety, may make numerous "gestures" that are disfiguring or painful though not fatal (e.g., cutting or scoring body parts with sharp objects). Among groups that are already at high risk, this places them at even greater risk. Chief factors among these are alcohol and substance abuse. Although the use of alcohol or drugs may be seen as an attempt to manage one's distress by self-medicating, this is rarely successful. From a cognitive perspective, alcoholism and substance abuse potentiate the risk of suicidal behavior by reducing one's ability to inhibit impulsive behavior, reducing adaptive problem solving, exacerbating ongoing stressors, and leading potentially supportive persons to withdraw from the individual. It is not surprising, then, that alcohol and substance abuse are common among groups with the highest rates of self-destructive behavior—individuals who have made prior suicide attempts. The relationship between alcohol abuse, drug addiction, and suicide has been actively studied for more than 50 years. Karl Menninger, in his book *Man Against Himself,* argued that alcohol and drug abuse were conceptually similar to a range of other potentially dangerous behaviors in that they unnecessarily increased the risk of illness, accidents, or death. As such, they might be considered to be unconscious suicide attempts. Similarly, Farberow characterized alcohol and drug abuse as "indirect suicides," and Shneidman views them as contributing to "subintentional deaths." This may place substance use at the midway point on the SDNB continuum. In some respects, however, the relationship between alcohol or substance abuse and suicide is far more direct. Severe intoxication with alcohol is, in some cases, an intentional attempt to poison oneself. Moreover, alcohol is frequently ingested along with barbiturates or other drugs as a means of potentiating their lethality. Alcohol is consumed along with medications in more than 20% of attempted overdoses, and during the hours before overdose attempts in an even larger percentage of individuals. Some drug abusers fall into the group we have labeled "impulsive" or "histrionic." Repetitive SDNB may reflect, in part, attempts to reach the "perfect high." This may involve taking more of the drug than they usually take, experimenting with new and more powerful drugs, or combining drugs, all in the service of achieving the greatest high. For example, Stuart, age 29, described his use of heroin in the following way: "It's better than the best sex. It's better than the best meal. It's the warmest, most wonderful and very best feeling I've ever got. It's like being wrapped in cotton candy. Each part of me is feeling soft and nice. The higher I get, the better I feel. After a while nothin' means nothin'."

THERAPEUTIC INTERVENTIONS

Whether suicidal behavior is the reason for intervention or whether the client has been referred because of other problems (such as anxiety, depression, PTSD, or others) once risk factors for suicidal behavior present, this should become the main focus of the therapist. Therefore, a routine assessment of *all* clients should include careful evaluation of current suicidal ideation and past history of suicidal attempts. If there are risk factors for suicide, this must be addressed before any other treatment is initiated to make sure the client is safely managed (Foa, Keane, & Friedman, 2000).

The first important part of therapy is establishing the rapport and building trust and motivation of change. The clinical social worker should be active, empathetic, and facilitate change behavior (Congress, 2004). That might be difficult due to the fact that clients in crisis may express feelings of anger, anxiety, fear, or depression that might affect communication. Parad and Parad (1999) state that although clients in crisis are often less defensive, the emotional overlay communications may make establishing contact difficult.

While working with suicidal clients it is important for the clinical social worker to involve the family members both in assessment as well as in therapy (Congress, 2004). This is crucial both to identify all risk factors, but also for establishing support of the close family.

Segal et al., (2002) report several kinds of therapies that had been applied to depressed suicidal clients and found to be effective: behavioral approaches that emphasize the need to increase participation of clients and reinforce pleasure-giving activities; cognitive therapy that aims at changing the way the person thinks about images and interprets events; and interpersonal therapy that stresses that learning to resolve interpersonal disputes and changing roles will help client change.

During the initial phase of therapy which, for the suicidal client, may be one or two sessions, the clinician helps the client to recognize the behavioral style, specific thoughts (among his or her ongoing stream of thoughts) that are associated with negative thinking, the degree of depressed affect, and the suicidal thinking and drive. Once the client can be helped to identify the style and recognizes these thoughts, the therapist teaches the client to record the thoughts, quantify the emotions experienced, and begin to adaptively respond to or challenge these automatic thoughts. The emphasis on identification and monitoring of automatic thoughts and behaviors is an essential part of cognitive therapy (CT) treatment. Since negative, self-depreciating, or other problematic and dysfunctional thoughts become a habitual part of the depressed client's life without the client's cognizance of their presence or relationship to his or her distress, they are a central focus of the counseling. For some more chronically suicidal clients the suicidal ideation is part of their normal repertoire of response. When they are under stress, the suicidal thoughts become automatic and appear, to the client, to be just one more way of coping. Herbert (2002) warns therapists that they can face the two extremes while treating adolescents with suicidal behaviors. The client might present with a lack of energy, helplessness, and powerlessness of events being out of control on the one hand, but at the same time, might present with a sense of strength, power, and even release once the client has reached the decision to commit suicide and then feels happy about it.

One of the problems and pitfalls of therapeutic work with the suicidal client is for the therapist to end up in a debate about suicide with the client. The two sides of the debate are first, for the client:

Resolved: Killing myself is a reasonable, honorable, intelligent, thoughtful course of action and that any attempt to hinder or stop me is the result of the hindering individual's lack of recognition of my pain and need to escape.

For the therapist the assigned part of the debate is:

Resolved: I must do everything that I can do to keep my client from hurting or killing herself.

The issue in the course of the preceding debate is that the therapist is constantly on the defensive and the client's motivation to change is limited. The goal of the counseling is to help the client to identify an alternative to suicide through the Socratic dialogue. The lower the client's threshold for responding, the greater will be the likelihood of their responding.

It is essential to actively and directly explore the client's immediate suicidal thoughts. A common fear of therapists is that if they mention or question the client's suicidality they may, in fact, be "suggesting" it as an option.

Jim, a 42-year-old male, commented that, "When you raised the issue of suicide I was very upset. I had never used that word myself. I was thinking of 'ending it all.' When you raised it I felt better. After all, if you weren't scared of it, maybe you could help me." It is helpful to have the client monitor his thoughts of self-harm for review within the next counseling session. It is helpful and important for the therapist to encourage the client to continue recording his thoughts so that these specific thoughts can be addressed in the counseling. The therapist has to begin the questioning of the thoughts very early in the counseling and to help the client to challenge his idea that there are very limited numbers of responses that he can make and that suicide or self-harm is high on that list.

As therapist and client explore the client's thoughts and reactions in recent situations described by the client, the client may need help in identifying the attendant emotions and learning to quantify them. Clients are often unclear about distinguishing statements that reflect emotions from those that reflect thoughts. They may need assistance in recognizing that many statements containing the word *feel* (e.g., "I feel stupid," "I don't feel as though I'll succeed") reflect thoughts despite the presence of the word *feel*. Clients with extreme difficulty labeling emotions may need to be provided with a list of possible emotions (e.g., depressed, sad, nervous, lonely, angry, hopeless, etc.) so that they can start with a multiple-choice approach.

Once the client becomes aware of his automatic thoughts and their relationship to his or her depressed and/or angry feelings and self-damaging or injurious thoughts and actions, the therapist focuses back to the concept of the cognitive distortions or thinking errors that are stylistic of the person's thinking. Understanding the various types of distortions (e.g., all-or-nothing thinking, overgeneralization, mental filtering, etc.) enables the clients to understand and label the thinking errors that contribute to their emotional distress and suicidal thinking. The labeling of cognitive distortions is also helpful for clients to begin to speak the therapist's language, to "see" things in a CBT manner, and to recognize the style and format of their distorting.

Overcoming depression: Cognitive therapy approach for the taming of the depression beast. (Gilson & Freeman, 1999), *The Ten Dumbest Mistakes That Smart People Make and How to Avoid Them* (Freeman & DeWolfe, 1992) are excellent self-help books for the purpose of educating clients about cognitive distortions. We must recognize, however, that suicidal clients may not be willing to read *any* book because they are far more focused on their here-and-now experience.

The depressed and suicidal client may not think of him or herself as worthy of any defense. In her view, she deserves to die. The therapist must work to point out that anyone deserves a defense, and that her hopeless view is a product of the depression. Inasmuch as the client believes her negative thoughts to be true, irrefutable, and permanent, and any attempt to question, dispute, or challenge the negative thinking as unreal, contrived, or rationalization, she may protest any attempt to adaptively respond to her negative, hopeless thoughts. The therapist must keep in mind that the client needs to be taught these strategies through didactic work and modeling, with constant monitoring of the client's developing skill. We might use the following example to help the client understand the need and importance of adaptive responding (establishing a defense):

"Suppose that I have been jailed for allegedly committing a crime. I am brought to trial and the State's Attorney presents 95 witnesses in 9 days of testimony attesting to my guilt and complicity. At the conclusion of the prosecution's arguments, my attorney for the defense rises and says: 'Your honor, ladies and gentlemen of the jury. My client is a nice person and is, more than likely, innocent. Thank you. The defense rests.' "

The therapist then inquires of the client what he would judge is his chance of being acquitted. The client response is usually that the chances of an acquittal are poor to none. The therapist points out that the reason for his being found guilty on all charges did not come from the charges but rather from the lack of a defense. The therapist then offers the following scenario:

"I have been charged with a crime and the State's Attorney produces 95 witnesses in 9 days of testimony attesting to my guilt. My defense attorney then produces a single witness for the defense, Mother Teresa. She testifies that on the day in question, I was meeting and having lunch with her and the Pope. Now what are my chances for an acquittal?"

At this point the client usually agrees that there is a far better chance for an acquittal based on having such a powerful witness in my corner. A third scenario is then offered:

"Suppose the same situation exists, and my attorney cannot get Mother Teresa. She does, however, produce 52 witnesses in 5 days attesting to my innocence. What are my chances of acquittal now?"

In this way, the client can be helped to see that the innocence or guilt is not based solely on the charges leveled against one, but depends, in large part on the defense one offers.

COGNITIVE TECHNIQUES

The following are the primarily cognitive techniques for challenging suicidal automatic thoughts.

1. *Understanding idiosyncratic meaning.* It is essential for the therapist to question the client directly on what she means when using the words *depressed, suicidal, upset,* or *anxious.* While this may appear to be intrusive, it can be structured by the therapist so that additional information is obtained (e.g., "Let me be certain I understand what you mean by _____" or "Can you describe what you were feeling when you were upset?").
2. *Questioning the evidence.* Through the use of questions such as: "What evidence do we have that that is true?" or "How could we test that idea out?," the therapist assists the client in examining the validity of his thoughts.
3. *Reattribution.* "It's all my fault" is a common statement made by clients in situations of relationship difficulty, separation, or divorce.

While one cannot dismiss this possibility out of hand, it is unlikely that a single person is totally responsible for everything going wrong. If the therapist takes a position of total support (i.e., "It wasn't your fault" or "You're better off without her") the therapist runs the risk of sounding like friends and family that the client has already dismissed as being a cheering squad, not understanding his position.

4. *Examining options and alternatives.* The suicidal client is the prime example of an individual who sees him or herself as having lost all options or for whom the best choice, among his or her few choices, is suicide. Since depression significantly interferes with the client's problem-solving abilities, this cognitive strategy focuses on helping the client to generate additional options. Even adding one more option increases the client's options by 100%.

5. *De-catastrophizing.* Depressed and suicidal clients frequently catastrophize experiences. Questions that might be asked of the client include, "What is the worst thing that can happen?" or "If it does happen, how will your life be different three months from now?" This technique helps to challenge the "Chicken Little" style of thinking.

6. *Advantages and disadvantages.* Having the client list and discuss the advantages and disadvantages of maintaining a particular belief ("Dying will solve my problem"), feeling (sad), or behavior (staying in bed) as well as the advantages and disadvantages of changing the belief or behavior can help the client to gain balance and a broader perspective regarding an issue or event. This may be seen as one of the scaling techniques. This technique, when applied to the suicidal client, includes helping the client to look at beliefs that contributed to his or her suicidal ideation ("I must be perfect to be loved by others" or "I will never be able to get another job like this one"), but also to the beliefs regarding suicide, per se. The purpose of this activity is to enable the client to see more advantages for living than dying by listing (a) the advantages and disadvantages for living and (b) the advantages and disadvantages for dying. While there will, undoubtedly, be some overlap on the two lists, the differences will be important. Suicidal clients readily list advantages for dying (e.g., "It will solve my problem" or "I won't have the pain to suffer"), but will need the therapist's help in generating advantages for living (e.g., to give this CT a chance to work), and disadvantages for dying (e.g., not being here to benefit from counseling). When the client cannot identify any reasons for living, the therapist should encourage the client to recall his or her reasons for living prior to the onset of depression and to consider whether these hold true for the client presently. The client is encouraged to keep his copy of the lists and to review it when suicidal ideation occurs.

7. *Fantasized consequences.* In this technique, the client is asked to fantasize a situation and to describe the images and attendant concerns. Often, in verbalizing his or her concerns, the client recognizes the irrationality of his or her ideas, or, if the fantasized consequences are realistic, the therapist can work with the client to assess the potential danger and develop appropriate coping strategies.

8. *Turning adversity to advantage.* There are times when an apparent disaster can be used to advantage (e.g., losing one's job can be a disaster but may, in some cases, be the entry point to a new job or even a new career). The therapist, through questioning, hypothesizing, or even sharing experiences of other individuals, may help the client to recognize the potential for positive opportunities.

9. *Guided association/discovery.* This collaborative, therapist-guided technique involves the therapist working with the client to connect ideas, thoughts, and images. By providing the conjunctions to the client's verbalizations with statements such as: "And then what?", "What would that mean?", "What would happen then?" "So what if that was true?", the therapist guides the client along various therapeutic paths, depending on the conceptualization and therapeutic goals.

10. *Replacement imagery.* For a client in distress this may mean generating an alternative solution to a problem and imaging its success. On the other hand, if the image is one of a suicidal act, it may mean replacing the destructive behavior (e.g., overdosing on pills) with a life-enhancing one (e.g., discarding the pills).

11. *Externalization of voices.* By having the therapist role play part of the dysfunctional thoughts, the client can get practice in adaptive responding to them. Initially, the client can verbalize his or her dysfunctional thoughts and the therapist can model adaptive responding. When roles switch and the therapist role plays the dysfunctional thoughts, he or she can, in a gradual manner, become an increasingly difficulty dysfunctional voice for the client to respond to. Clients normally "hear" the dysfunctional voices only in their heads. When they externalize the voices, the client can, hopefully, recognize the dysfunctional nature of the thoughts, while at the same time the therapist can hear the tone, content, and general context of the thoughts and generate strategies for intervention.

12. *Cognitive rehearsal.* The client can imaginally practice particular behaviors. For example, the overly accommodating client in the process of developing assertiveness skills can envision a situation in which he or she will have to use the skills (e.g., confronting an employer for a raise). By first generating a reasonable scene and practicing it imaginally, the client can investigate several alternative approaches. This is akin to having a pilot practice on a simulator to gain skills.

13. *Self-instruction.* The client can start with direct verbalization by saying self-instructions out loud. With practice, the client can learn to say the instructions without actual verbalizations (subvocalize) and eventually the instructions can come automatically. The client can then be taught to offer direct self-instructions or in some cases counterinstructions to suicidal behaviors.

14. *Thought stopping.* Dysfunctional thoughts often have an avalanche effect for the individual and can be difficult to stop. Therefore, thought stopping is best used when the thoughts start, not in the middle of the process. In order to "stop" the thought, the client can be taught to picture a stop sign, "hear" a bell, or think the word "stop." Any of these can help to stop the progression and growth of the suicidal thoughts. Given the propensity for the downward spiraling of depressed clients, this technique can be helpful in stopping the negative thinking before it concludes with suicide as the only viable option.

15. *Focusing.* There is a limit to how many things a person can think about at once. By occupying the client's mind with neutral thoughts, he or she can block dysfunctional thoughts for a limited period of time. This might involve counting, focusing on calming and pleasant images, or focusing on external stimuli. While this technique is a short-term strategy, it is very useful to allow the client time to establish some degree of control over his or her thinking.

16. *Direct disputation.* While cognitive counseling does not advocate arguing with a client, there are times when direct disputation is necessary. The imminence of a suicide attempt is an example of when this technique is appropriate. When it seems clear to the clinician that the client is going to make an attempt, the therapist must directly and quickly work to challenge the hopelessness. Disputation coming from outside the client may, in fact, engender passive resistance and a passive-aggressive response that might include suicide. Disputation, argument, or debate are potentially dangerous tools and must, therefore, be used carefully, judiciously, and with skill. If the therapist becomes one more harping contact, the client may turn the therapist off completely, precluding any opportunity for the therapist to help the client.

17. *Cognitive dissonance.* When what one thinks and what one feels are in conflict, anxiety is the result. The client who is considering suicide is often dissonant for family, cultural, or religious reasons. Previous learning tells the client that suicide may be seen as bad, wrong, or sinful. As long as there is dissonance, suicide is less likely. However, when the dissonance is resolved, he or she feels less pressure and can

effect a suicide. The goal of utilizing dissonance with the suicidal client is to move the client away from a suicidal resolution to a more effective means of problem solving. The client may complain that his death will be meaningless or go unnoticed. Having him examine the effect of his death on children or family can be effective as a deterrent, but should be used cautiously, since it can also foster thoughts of infanticide to protect the children from suffering without a parent.

18. *Paradox or exaggeration.* By taking an idea to its extreme, the therapist can often help to move the client to a more central position vis-à-vis a particular belief. This technique, however, should be reserved for limited usage by experienced therapists, given the hypersensitivity to criticism and ridicule exhibited by some clients. Care must be taken to not insult, ridicule, or embarrass the client or to give the impression that the therapist is making light of the client's problems. The therapist who chooses to use the paradoxical or exaggeration techniques must have (1) a strong working relationship with the client, (2) good timing, and (3) the good sense to know when to back away from the technique.

The need for the client's active involvement and participation is essential when suicide is the issue. The self-help work includes any and all of the cognitive techniques just discussed, along with relevant behavioral techniques. The techniques are taught in the office and can be practiced and used as part of the client's homework. The particular homework, nature and number of interventions, and amount of work all need to be appropriate to the problem, within the skills of the client, and collaboratively arrived at and developed. The homework can begin in the very first session by having the client produce an initial list of both problems and goals for discussion at the second session, having the client maintain an activity schedule for the week, or have the client try a new behavior or manner of responding that was introduced within the session.

REPETITIVE ATTEMPTS

A history of prior suicide attempts is one of the strongest predictors of future suicidal behavior. Although repeat attempters constitute only a small proportion of suicidal individuals, they are among the most challenging and difficult of patients. Retrospective studies of completed suicides reveal that approximately one-third of persons who commit suicide have made a prior attempt. Moreover, as was once observed, "The probability of completing suicide is especially high in the first year or two after the initial nonfatal suicide attempt." This pattern of making repeated suicide attempts is particularly insidious in that it may reflect the establishment of a self-destructive "coping style," and may desensitize the individual to the dangerousness of their behavior such that they make increasingly more lethal attempts. Moreover, it may tend to "desensitize" or alienate those around the patient, contributing to a loss of support and social isolation.

If there is a truism in psychology, it is that the best predictor of future behavior is past behavior. The same applies in predicting suicide. A history of prior suicide attempts has been found to be associated with suicidal ideations, subsequent attempts, and completed suicides.

Recent research suggests that subtypes of suicide "repeaters" may exist and that differences in the prognosis for repeat attempters may exist depending on the "seriousness" of their prior attempts. Patients who have made "serious" suicide attempts appear to demonstrate an increased risk of further attempts and completed suicide. Our confidence in these findings is limited, however, as no association was found between the seriousness of the initial suicide attempt and the risk of repeated attempts. Moreover, there is inherent danger in underestimating the risk of subsequent suicide attempts by patients who have made "nonserious" prior attempts. As one researcher states, "the individual who has made a feeble suicide attempt, is resistant or antagonistic toward treatment and denies any difficulty or even effort at self-injury is apt to have little or no treatment. . . . The young woman who has taken a few aspirins, has little or no symptomatology, and admits that her act was impulsive, is apt to find a medical counterpart in terms of labeling the problem as an unimportant one. This denial should not be accepted since the individual who toys with suicide may eventually become the individual who becomes a fatal suicide" (p.).

Although the specific items may differ, their clinical utility remains in that they appear to reflect more general underlying characteristics that place persons at risk for suicide. Such characteristics include impulsivity, social isolation, relatively severe psychopathology, alcohol or substance abuse, poor occupational adjustment, and limited coping abilities. The risk of repeated suicide attempts appears to be heightened when the "goal" of the initial attempt is not realized, and the precipitating stress remains. As a consequence, these individuals tend to experience one crisis after another and may come to employ suicide attempts as a habitual style of coping with problematic situations.

We do not wish to overgeneralize, however, in describing chronically suicidal patients. It is important to recognize that, as individuals, their motives for attempting suicide may vary. The prediction of suicide remains a clinical, rather than a statistical, endeavor. As with other patients, then, it remains important to assess their individual beliefs and cognitions. Automatic thoughts provided by chronically suicidal patients include such beliefs as "I deserved to be punished" and "I always knew I couldn't live past 30." In treating chronically suicidal patients, it is important to maintain regular sessions and to provide them with a continuity of care, even during periods in which they are not overtly hopeless or suicidal. During these hiatuses, we have found it helpful to aggressively treat the underlying affective or personality disorders as well as alcohol or substance abuse. Given the severity of the dysphoria, anxiety, and anger experienced by these patients, psychotropic medications are often a useful component of a comprehensive treatment program. Similarly, occupational training and placement may be recommended as a means of stabilizing their work situation, and they might be encouraged to live with friends or family as a means of reducing their sense of isolation. Several authors have recommended outreach programs, such as weekly telephone contacts with their therapists or home visits as a means of maintaining therapeutic contact and alleviating their sense of alienation from others. Although these approaches have been found to reduce patients' feelings of depression, a consequent reduction in suicide rates has not been observed.

In addition to the time and energy often expended in treating chronically suicidal patients, they can be difficult in that their behavior frequently antagonizes both their therapist and the medical treatment staff. The apparent manipulativeness of their suicidal behaviors, their difficulty in actively engaging in psychotherapy and in completing homework assignments, and the generally slow rate of improvement readily contribute to feelings of helplessness, hopelessness, and resentment on the part of the staff. These feelings, however, can cloud one's clinical judgment and contribute to a loss of empathy for the patient. They lead to increasingly strenuous efforts on the part of the staff to "control" the patient's behavior. These attempts, however, ultimately are futile. They reinforce the patient's feelings of powerlessness, reduce their sense of responsibility for their own actions, and undermine their legitimate or adaptive attempts to influence their environment. Moreover, these feelings disrupt the development of the collaborative rapport that is central to cognitive therapy. The therapist and patient are no longer working together toward a common goal but are attempting to "protect themselves" from the narcissistic injuries inflicted by the other. When this occurs, it is often helpful for the therapist to "disengage" from the emotions of the moment and to reflect on his or her personal automatic thoughts. In what ways, for example, is the patient behaving in a manipulative manner? Might the patient's behavior, alternatively, be seen as highly maladaptive—the only way the patient sees for resolving his or her predicament? What are the consequences for you, the therapist?

Nonetheless, the prediction of suicidal acts by persons with a history of alcohol or substance abuse, or of prior self-destructive behavior, and the treatment of factors contributing to this style of adaptation, continue to be important problems. Despite the fact that we have a reasonably good understanding of factors associated with an increased risk of suicide, we have not been able to use these items, either individually or in combination, to predict the behavior of specific individuals at specific points in time. Moreover, they have not contributed to our understanding of the intrapsychic processes of chronically suicidal individuals.

The reasons for these difficulties are both statistical and conceptual in nature. Bayesian statistical theory precludes us from predicting low base-rate behaviors, such as completed suicides. Our attempts to increase the base rate by examining high-risk groups, such as persons with a history of prior suicide attempts, are ultimately unsatisfactory as they lead us to overlook increasing numbers of potentially suicidal individuals. The generalizability of our findings are reduced as we limit the nature of our samples. Moreover, there is a presumption that "suicidal risk" is a characteristic of the individual and that it is "there to be found" if only we had the right assessment techniques. We would suggest, however, that this assumption is incorrect. Suicidal risk or intent is not a static entity, but varies from moment to moment and setting to setting. It reflects the ongoing and variable contributions of a range of cognitive, interpersonal, physiological, and environmental factors. Cognitive assessment instruments, such as the Hopelessness Scale (HS), appear to be strong predictors of an individual's behavior because they are state-dependent measures of the individual's perceptions. Consistent with cognitive theory, it is these perceptions that mediate the individual's behavior on a moment-by-moment basis.

Recent reports suggest that individuals suffering from alcohol or substance abuse are at an increased risk both for attempting, and for successfully completing, a suicidal act. Studies completed in Britain, for example, suggest that between 36% and 48% of male suicide attempters have difficulties with alcohol abuse. Similarly, one researcher reviewed the literature to that date regarding factors associated with increased suicide risk and estimated that 15% of individuals suffering from alcohol abuse die by committing suicide. The significance of this finding is highlighted by the fact that less than 1% of persons in the general population die by suicide. Further evidence for a relationship between alcohol abuse and suicide is provided by retrospective studies of individuals who have committed suicide. The literature suggests that between 15% and 26% of suicide completers suffer from alcohol abuse. Given that approximately 5% of the general population suffers from alcohol abuse, these findings strongly, suggest that an association exists between alcohol abuse and suicide. The treatment of a suicidal individual who is acutely intoxicated or who has recently taken illicit drugs is quite difficult. An argument can be made that it is impossible to treat persons who, because of alcohol or drug use, are not capable of cogently discussing their concerns. As such, suicidal patients suffering from alcohol or substance abuse should be admitted to an inpatient unit for detoxification. An initial period of drying out, during which withdrawal symptoms are monitored, provides the therapist with the time necessary to conduct a more thorough evaluation of the patients' current situation, to interview family members, and to develop a comprehensive treatment program. Initial interventions are typically directed toward eliminating their drinking or drug use, and toward providing them with more appropriate problem-solving strategies. Patients with a history of alcohol or substance abuse typically have little motivation to participate in therapy. They tend, quite often, to minimize the severity of their difficulties and to overestimate their capacity to resolve their problems. Cognitive distortions, such as these, can be addressed in a direct manner with structured interventions. We have often found it useful, for example, to encourage a patient's spouse and children to express their feelings and concerns openly to the patient during family therapy sessions. Not uncommonly, there has been a conspiracy of silence among family members, in which they have refrained from honestly expressing their concerns because of a fear that this would exacerbate the problems at home. The legitimacy of this fear, however, is also open to exploration through rational responding and other techniques. The use of the drug of choice lowers whatever self-control the individual has, promoting more impulsive and self-destructive behavior. A central component of treating the chronically suicidal patient involves preparing him or her for future crises. A goal is to resolve problems before they become too severe and to provide the patient with a range of coping strategies. As these approaches can be quite pragmatic, they may seem more like counseling or guidance to the patient rather than psychotherapy per se. Nonetheless, we believe that they are highly valuable and should not be dismissed. Specifically, it is often helpful to identify situations that are likely to precipitate suicidal feelings and then identify the specific automatic thoughts, images, and emotions that are elicited. Gestalt techniques may be employed to heighten their sense of "realism" and allow clients to envision how they would typically respond. We then prepare them to meet these challenges by reviewing alternative techniques for gaining control over their affect and resolving the situation. Problem-solving approaches can be employed during sessions, then, to prevent difficult situations from developing into crises, and to assist the patient in developing more effective coping skills. Specifically, we endeavor to help the patient recognize that

- Suicide attempts are a coping strategy.
- There are more effective alternatives available.
- It is not adaptive to behave impulsively in problematic situations. Rather, the patient should attempt to identify the "cues" that more effective coping may be necessary.

    For example, a combat veteran with a history of four serious suicide attempts recognized that he "gets a warm feeling . . . a tension . . . like I have to jump out of my skin . . . then, I have to do something" prior to his self-destructive behaviors. He was then trained to use this "warm feeling" as a cue that something was upsetting him, that he should reflect on what it was, and that he should list several ways of dealing with it. If these were unsuccessful, he could call his therapist or the crisis line before acting on the impulse.
- Present the patient with possible crises-practice alternative approaches to coping. Have the patient imagine the most effective strategy, how he'd feel when it worked, and write it down for ready reference.

In sum, chronically suicidal patients appear to require more extended and intensive treatment. Medications and supportive, problem-oriented techniques are used in conjunction with cognitive interventions designed to clarify and resolve underlying beliefs and assumptions.

DEVELOPMENT OF THERAPEUTIC RELATIONSHIP

Several assumptions are made when doing short-term cognitive psychotherapy. Among these are assumptions that the patient will be able to develop a trusting, therapeutic collaboration quickly, and that he or she will be able to reflect on his or her emotional experiences. Many individuals, especially those with a history of having been abused (verbally, physically, sexually, emotionally) appear to experience difficulty in meeting these prerequisites of short-term psychotherapy. Their sense of distrust and social alienation inhibits the development of a therapeutic rapport, and the intensity of their mood swings frequently leaves them feeling overwhelmed. They tend, as a consequence, to avoid reflecting on automatic thoughts and images, as these engender tremendous amounts of anxiety, guilt, and rage.

With these difficulties in mind, modifications of standard cognitive therapy techniques are necessary when working with suicidal individuals. Given their feelings of social alienation and distrust, a supportive, non-confrontational approach is often helpful. Trust must be earned through their experiencing a supportive and accepting relationship with the therapist. We have often found it helpful to acknowledge these difficulties directly. Patients who feel alienated might also be encouraged to conceptualize understanding as a continuum, to reflect on the degree to which they felt understood by the therapist, and to discuss the specific instances in which they felt understood or misunderstood during the session. Similarly, it might be noted that no one can fully empathize with their personal experiences; however, others, including the therapist, may be able to empathize enough to be of assistance. With such patients, it is helpful to inquire regularly as to whether they believe they have expressed their concerns and feelings clearly, and whether they feel they have been adequately understood.

As rapport is established, it may be helpful to identify and reflect the patients' feelings of suspiciousness and anger to them as they occur during session, and have them note the range of situations in which they occur outside of therapy. Traditional cognitive techniques may then be introduced in assisting the patient to evaluate the underlying beliefs. For example, to ask:

- Are others actually malevolent?
- What are the benefits and costs to me of maintaining a vigilant and suspicious approach?
- In what ways am I vulnerable? Not vulnerable? What influence do I have over this specific situation? Do I actually need complete security or control? Is it necessary to behave aggressively toward self or others or are there alternatives?
- Am I really a potential "victim"?

As in cognitive therapy with other patients, our emphasis is on assisting the individual to identify specific beliefs that maintain his difficulties, and to develop his ability to evaluate these beliefs objectively. Catharsis, although important, is not our only objective. Although it is critical that the individual feel capable of openly discussing his concerns, and of acknowledging the depth and significance of his experiences, this is not sufficient for the alleviation of symptoms. Rather, we wish to encourage the individual to identify the beliefs, assumptions, and coping strategies that had developed as a consequence of his proximal and distal life experiences, and to assist him in developing more adaptive alternatives.

SUMMARY

The key to successful counseling with the depressed and suicidal client is to (1) establish rapport with the client, (2) understand the individual client's idiosyncratic assumptions and dysfunctional thinking patterns, (3) help the client to question or challenge his decision to die, (4) help the client develop more adaptive coping skills, and (5) help the client to maintain his or her therapeutic gains. Based on an understanding of the cognitive counseling model, the conceptualization of the client's problem(s), and an understanding of the client's thinking and schema, the cognitive therapist develops the strategies for intervention and specific techniques to be used with the suicidal client. The therapist must develop an armamentarium of cognitive techniques, and the skills to use these effectively in ways that are appropriate for each individual client. Although our clinical interventions are currently effective in reducing immediate suicide danger, an alternative approach may be useful in guiding the development of techniques to reduce the long-term risk for individuals with the greatest potential for dying at their own hand.

With these goals in mind, the therapist may wish to encourage patients to do the following:

1. Get more information about their illnesses. Be reality based, and do not catastrophize or minimize outcomes.
2. Share feelings with others including family, friends, support group, and therapist.
3. Develop problem-solving capacities.
4. Employ structured techniques such as relaxation, autohypnosis, and guided imagery as a means of reducing physical pain.
5. Identify new activities they can pursue that will be enjoyable, meaningful, and satisfying.
6. Adopt an attitude of attacking problems in contrast to experiencing passive resignation.
7. Identify, clarify, and develop coping capacities and personal strengths.
8. Identify new goals for life. That is, things they can look forward to and can work to accomplish.

As with other patients, it is important to identify and resolve therapist automatic thoughts and assumptions that hamper therapeutic progress. Such beliefs might include the stigma attached to illness, the belief that their situation is futile, or a perceived withdrawal by family and friends from the client because of a fear of ultimate death of the client.

However, it is also important to note that suicidal and other destructive behaviors are sometimes hard to address and if the therapist is not sure of his or her capabilities to protect the client, it might be recommended to hospitalize the client. At least until the client is ready for acquiring new skills and knowledge for helping him or herself change.

REFERENCES

Congress, E. P. (2004). Crisis intervention and diversity. In R. A. Drofman, P. Meyer, & M. L. Morgan (Eds.), *Paradigms of clinical social work, Vol. 3* (pp. 125–144). New York: Brunner-Routledge.

Foa, B., Keane, T. M., & Friedman, M. J. (2000). *Effective treatment for PTSD.* New York: Guilford.

Herbert, M. (2002). The human life cycle: Adolescence. In M. Daview (Ed.), *The Blackwell companion to social work* (2nd ed., pp. 355–369). Oxford: Blackwell.

Parad, H., & Parad, L. (1999). *Crisis intervention book 2: The practitioner source book for brief therapy.* Milwaukee, WI: Family Service Association.

Segal, Z. V., Williams, J., Mark, G., & Teasdale, J. D. (2002). *Mindfulness based cognitive therapy for depression.* New York: Guilford.

CHAPTER 20

Comorbidity of Chronic Depression and Personality Disorders

Application of Schema Mode Therapy

Steven K. Bordelon

INTRODUCTION

While the focus of some of the previous chapters was depression, in this chapter we will discuss the treatment of comorbid chronic depression and personality disorders. The treatment needs of this population differ significantly from the treatment of those with depression. Our task is to explore recent developments tailored for this comorbidity.

Social workers have long held that their obligations are to those most in need, those most vulnerable. Social workers in various settings encounter multiproblem families, clients in crisis, stress in relationships, jobs, or school. Among these clients the frequency of depression and personality disorders is quite high. Whether in social service agencies, medical social work, or private practice, skills are needed to work with those struggling with comorbid chronic depression and personality disorders. Estimates of the co-occurrence of these two diagnoses range widely. Of those diagnosed with major depressive disorder (MDD), 30% to 80% will have a comorbid personality disorder during their lifetimes; and as many as 50% of those with borderline personality disorder (BPD) will experience MDD at some point during their lifetime. Further, those with this comorbidity often do not respond well to common pharmacological treatments for MDD, or they suffer frequent relapses (Feske et al., 2004). This chapter discusses recent treatment advances in the cognitive behavior field relevant to this population. These treatment advances show promise in the efficacy of working with these clients, and enables social workers to approach these clients in a manner consistent with the social work values of respect and compassion that are foundational to the profession.

Social workers need a therapeutic approach that is effective in providing relief from symptoms in the context of a therapeutic stance of genuine respect for the client. This chapter is an attempt to present a treatment style that successfully engages these clients, and provides a sense of understanding, acceptance, and empathy. With such an alliance established, change becomes more possible in problematic internal factors that reinforce chronic depression.

LITERATURE REVIEW

In one study, 79% of those with major depressive disorder (MDD) suffered from one or more current comorbid mental disorders, including anxiety disorder (57%), alcohol use disorder (25%), and personality disorder (44%) (Melartin et al., 2002). And those with personality disorders tend to have more severe depression than those without personality disorders (Comtois, Cowley, Dunner, & Roy-Byrne, 1990; Skodol et al., 1999). Another study found that a mood disorder with an insidious onset that is chronic and progresses in severity is likely to lead to a personality disorder diagnosis in young adults (Comtois et al., 1990; Skodol et al., 1999).

In comparison with other *DSM-IV* personality disorders, avoidant, borderline and dependent personality disorders were most specifically associated with mood disorders, particularly depressive disorders (Rossi et al., 2001). In another study, obsessive-compulsive personality disorder was also found to be associated (Hirschfeld et al., 1999).

In regard to treatment for this population, successful treatment for depression is associated with improvement in personality disorders (Comtois et al., 1990). And there are indications for the need to integrate into the treatment of personality disorders, the treatment for depression and anxiety (Beck, Rush, Shaw, & Emery, 1979).

There are several effective cognitive behavior treatment models for depression (Beck, in Greenberger & Padesky, 1995b; Greenberger & Padesky,

1995a; Yapko, 1997; Seligman, 2002; ACT, in Hayes, Strosahl, & Wilson, 1999). More recently, there are models developed specifically for chronic depression (Segal, Williams, & Teasdale, 2002; Arnow, 2005). But for the comorbidity of chronic depression and personality disorders, treatment models such as dialectical behavior therapy (Linehan, 1993a) and/or Schema Therapy (Linehan, 1993b) are indicated.

SCHEMA MODE WORK

In this chapter, I'll emphasize the schema therapy model. It is an integrative treatment that is effective with the comorbidity chronic depression and personality disorders. Those interested in this model should read the latest book *Schema Therapy, A Practitioner's Guide* by Jeffrey Young and his associates (2003). While Young and associates speak definitively about their Schema therapy model, Dr. Young developed schema therapy because traditional cognitive behavior therapy (CBT) was ineffective for many patients with chronic depression and personality disorders. A *schema* is defined as a set of cognitions, emotions, somatizations that are traits an individual has, and which can become activated in response to certain environmental triggers. Some of the typical schemas for someone with comorbid depression and personality would be abandonment, defectiveness, failure, and mistrust/abuse. These schemas develop in an early aversive environmental context in which similar problematic events were repeatedly experienced. The schema is subsequently reinforced in the individual's experience through numerous life events.

For example, a client with an abandonment schema might perceive abandonment by the social worker if the social worker is late for a meeting or a session. A client in my practice was late with a payment from a previous session. While waiting for a session to begin, he was worried about being told I would not continue to see him because he was late with his payment. His abandonment schema became activated in that situation.

Depending on the severity of the dysfunction, an individual may do well with schema therapy as originally developed. However, when working with the comorbidity of chronic depression and personality disorders, it is likely the schema mode work, will be the indicated treatment. The more severe the dysfunction the less likely schema therapy, as originally developed, will be helpful. The reason for this is that those with severe dysfunction tend to have several schemas, and they tend to flip quickly from one schema to another, and it becomes extremely difficult to establish a coherent focus in treatment. From this difficulty, schema mode therapy was developed by Dr. Young and his associates.

Schema mode therapy entails identifying which modes the patient experiences most often. A mode is a schema, or set of schemas, that is currently active for an individual. The mode can be either adaptive or maladaptive in the current context. It is a mood state in which certain schemas are operative. The predominant modes then become the main focus of the treatment. Mode work is a recent development that is explained fully in Young's book. Recently, research has been done comparing schema therapy to Otto Kernberg's latest model.

INDICATIONS FOR MODE THERAPY

Among other indications for mode therapy, patients with comorbid chronic depression and personality disorders are appropriate for mode therapy. Patients with this comorbidity can often be stuck in therapy, are likely to have a rigid avoidant coping style, and tend to have intense emotional dysregulation. In the language of mode work, they flip from one mode to the other quickly, and tend to intensely experience a particular mode when they are in it. Also, they are likely to have persistent relationship difficulties. Because of severe emotional distress, they often experience suicidal and/or parasuicidal behaviors. This chapter explores the benefits of mode work with these particular difficulties while maintaining a therapeutic approach of connection and compassion; this alliance is crucial for the approach to be effective.

IDENTIFYING MODES

The first task in mode work is to label the predominant modes of a patient. This is done through observing affective states while interviewing the patient, through listening for various modes experienced in daily life outside therapy, and when possible, to hear the observations of those connected with the patient regarding behavior and feeling states. There is also the Young-Atkinson Mode Inventory, available at www.Schematherapy. com, that the client can fill out to help identify the modes most significant for the patient. There are numerous therapeutic benefits involved in this process of labeling modes; it lays the foundation for the development an Observing Self (Young, Klosko, & Weishaar, 2003), the central skill in mindfulness practice. Labeling modes helps in developing a nonjudgmental stance (Hayes et al., 1999), and it enables the patient to identify the cycling of the modes that keeps them trapped in chronic depression.

The categorization of various mood states gives the therapy a sense of structure, and helps in treating specific aspects of the patient. This helps keep the patient from seeing themselves in a globally negative way. It is much less threatening to an individual to discuss one part of him or herself, (e.g., the angry part), without feeling labeled as being an angry person. Putting the angry mode in the context of several others parts helps keep the client from feeling overwhelmed. In labeling modes, the therapist and patient together observe emotions and behaviors without negative judgment from the therapist, and this serves as a model for the patient so the patient can develop the skill of being nonjudgmental. In this context, identifying the cycle of chronic depression is more easily attainable. Through this process, a therapeutic bond is developed that helps with the limited reparenting role of the therapist. As mentioned, limited reparenting is the necessary foundation for effectiveness in mode work.

THE FIVE COMMON MODES

There are a total of 10 modes identified in schema mode therapy. I focus on the five most common modes for those with chronic depression and personality disorders. They are:

1. the abandoned/abused mode (or vulnerable mode)
2. the detached protector mode
3. the angry mode
4. the punitive mode
5. the healthy adult mode

1. The Abandoned/Abused Mode

Schema therapists refer to this mode as the vulnerable child mode. When in this mode, the individual is childlike in behavior and affect. This vulnerable child mode is of central importance in this model; it is the mode that is most targeted for exposure and healing. It is also the mode that is the most painful to experience because of the associated intense anxious and depressive affect. With the comorbidity of depression and personality disorder, many schemas are likely to exist with the vulnerable mode. However, when they are in this vulnerable mood state, the predominant schemas, or themes, are often abandonment and mistrust/abuse. The patient expects that when in relationships they will be abandoned and/or abused by others. These themes are generally common in the history of these patients. In the process of identifying modes, it is crucial to help patients see how they have built their lives around avoiding the emotional pain of the vulnerable mode, and how they protect themselves from it with other modes. They experience the vulnerable mode as intolerable and try to avoid it at all costs. It is important to demonstrate that at one point in their lives it was understandable to avoid this mode which seemed overwhelming.

The main task of therapy, however, is to actually help them embrace their vulnerable mode. And as well, to appreciate that some of the most significant aspects of who they are as a human being are found in this vulnerable part of themselves. Their desire for their core needs to be met (e.g., relationships in which they feel loved, respected, and acknowledged) exists in the vulnerable mode. The process of embracing this mode begins as the patient is able to see that avoidance of the vulnerability isn't working, it's just reinforcing the pain, and fueling the chronic depression. Through strengthening the healthy adult mode the patient is better able to manage and tolerate this vulnerable part of him or herself.

2. The Detached Protector Mode

This is often a primary mode for these patients. In this mode, one avoids painful thoughts, feelings, events, and interactions. This mode is often a central obstacle to accessing and healing the vulnerable mode in therapy. It originally develops as a defensive posture to protect against the overwhelmingly painful affect experienced in the vulnerable mode. An example might be the individual who is well practiced in numbing painful emotions through pushing them out of mind when they start to surface, and might use alcohol or drugs to assist in the numbing process.

3. The Angry Mode

This mode is activated when individuals perceive that their core needs are unmet. The key feature in identifying this mode is when one is childlike with their inappropriate expression of anger; often out-of-control rage in which they may become destructive or abusive. In their mind, they are reacting to feeling deprived of some core need (e.g., feeling abandoned, abused, misunderstood, etc.).

4. The Punitive and/or Demanding Mode

In schema mode work, the punitive mode is described as an internalization of the negative statements of others (e.g., voices of the parents that the child eventually took on for him or herself). One of my young adult male patients whose parents continually denigrated him told him that he was not worthy of getting the good things his higher-achieving cousins were getting. He learned to anticipate this reaction from them, and eventually started saying similar things to himself before his parents would say them. This led to the development of a punitive mode, so that now he often is very demeaning of himself, even to the point at times of replicating the physical abuse he received from his parents by hitting himself as hard as he can. His parents were also overly demanding, which fueled a failure schema (i.e., "I'll never be enough in their eyes, I'm a failure.").

5. The Healthy Adult Mode

This is the mode in which one is able to set boundaries for him or herself, and able to be respectful of the limits of him or herself and others. One is able to assert his or her needs appropriately. In this mode, one is willing to tolerate the distress of painful feelings without turning to maladaptive coping behaviors. It is this mode that needs to be enhanced and strengthened so that it replaces the automatic response of the maladaptive coping modes. To assess this mode, identify with the client areas where he or she manages from a healthy adult mode (e.g. handling an irritable coworker calmly), and he or she may be quite effective in that context. The therapy builds on the strengths already demonstrated in the healthy adult mode.

By labeling modes with a patient, we are attempting to establish a self-observing stance wherein he or she is able, with emotional neutrality, to see various parts of him or herself. Upon labeling the modes, the cyclical pattern of the modes that keeps the patient stuck in chronic depression is identified. While at times, this can create a sense of hope and optimism in the client because they probably have never viewed themselves from this angle, it also can create a sense of confusion, or disorientation. This is a positive development because it indicates that they have become disillusioned by their old automatic coping styles, and therefore see the need for new ways of coping.

Exploring the Origins and Adaptive Value of the Modes

Once the patient's modes are identified, the next step is to explore how the modes originally developed, and how the patient's coping styles were adaptive to the situation in which they first emerged. Chronically depressed individuals often benefit from seeing that there are valid origins to their emotional, behavioral, and cognitive styles. These patients often think of themselves as defective *because* they have been depressed for a number of years. Therefore, it can be quite validating to them to explore how their depressive style made sense in response to some earlier stressor in their life, and this style has become habituated. Also, exploring the valid origins of their depressive style with the clinician enhances their experience of feeling cared for and supported in the therapy relationship.

Let's consider a clinical example in which the modes were labeled and the origins were explored. An adult female client, age 35, reported a great relationship with her father until age 12 to 13 at which time he changed. Her father suddenly stopped showing her affection, and withdrew his affection from her. Her interpretation of his withdrawal was that he abandoned her, and that she was not good enough, defective. As we label the modes, it is best to have the patient name them in accord with how they experience the mode. She named her vulnerable mode, which involves the schemas of abandonment and defectiveness, the "hurt part." At times she would respond to her father from the angry child mode, "mean part," in which she would have "rage fits" toward her parents. At root to her rage was that she was not getting a core need met (i.e., emotional support): "They didn't accept me." She also engaged in rebellious behavior that helped her escape from the pain experienced in the context of a rejecting father. This was her protective detachment mode which she called "clear the mind part": "When running with my friends, I didn't have to think about the pain of being at home." Her punitive mode developed as she began to denigrate herself for having behaved in ways that were displeasing to her parents; for example, "I'm a bad person because I disappoint and embarrass my parents." This is the internalization of what she heard from her parents, especially her mother.

She developed another coping mode to protect her from the intolerable pain of the vulnerable mode. This was an overcompensation mode in which she became very attentive to the needs of others while discounting her own needs. The overcompensation mode, often seen in depressed individuals, is similar to the detached protector mode in that it is another type of maladaptive coping mode. She developed this coping response to try to keep others pleased with her so they would not leave or abandon her, nor would they see her in a negative way. She named this mode the "pleaser part." This was her default mode (i.e., the mode the individual spends most of their time in). We also identified many examples throughout her adult years of her healthy adult mode. One example is in her occupational life where she sets healthy boundaries, and often asserts herself appropriately.

We labeled her predominant modes using her language: hurt, clear the mind, pleaser, punitive, and healthy adult. We also explored their origins. In this process, she felt validated in seeing the development of her coping styles in the context of suddenly feeling abandoned by her father after years of closeness. We were able to see how she, at that age, would understandably react as she did. And that these reactions, coping styles, became automatic responses. And the source of her chronic depression can be understood in the cycling of these modes. It is important to clarify that validating the origins of her modes does not mean approval of her interpretation of the events, nor does it mean agreement with her response pattern. It is simply validating her experience and response as understandable. Labeling modes and exploring their origins only makes sense if a connection is made with the patient's reasons for seeking treatment.

Connecting Modes to Presenting Problem and Symptoms

The patient must be able to identify the modes at work in the problems they want to help with. Staying with this case of our 35-year-old adult female, her presenting problem was a periodic loss of control with gambling along with an ongoing sense of depression and anxiety. She described her husband as being very critical of her when the house was not perfectly straightened. She tried diligently to keep the house up to avoid his criticism. But at times, she became so enraged with him that she would curse at him, and become "verbally abusive" to him. She intensely regretted these out of control behaviors, and that became another source of depression for her. Feeling overwhelmed with stress and sadness, she turned to gambling at times to try to deal with the stress. However, she deeply regrets these gambling episodes because she spends too much money doing it, and this elicits more criticism from her husband when he finds out. At times, she has suicidal thoughts, in the context of trying to relieve the overwhelming pain.

We related her primary modes to her presenting problems and cycle of chronic depression. As mentioned, her default mode was the pleaser part (overcompensation mode) in which she is overly attentive to the needs of others to avoid her fear of abandonment. This is the mode she is in most of the time at home with her husband. As a result, she is always trying anxiously to focus on what he might think is messy in the house, and then clean it prior to him seeing it. Being in the pleaser mode, most of the time, while disregarding her own needs, leads to a build up of resentment because her needs are not addressed. This leads to periodic rage episodes, the angry mode, the "mean part." Following this, her punitive mode takes over and she denigrates herself because of her negative behavior toward her husband. Upon punishing herself, she flips back to her vulnerable mode in which she feels more depression and abandonment. Overwhelmed by this, she turns, at times, to gambling to clear her mind; the detached protector mode. While she's able to numb herself from intense emotional pain for a while, often on the way home from gambling, she denigrates herself intensely (punitive mode), and her depression just becomes more intense (vulnerable mode), and at this point, she often becomes suicidal seeking relief from the overwhelming pain. Seeing this cyclical flipping through her modes in her presenting problems enabled her to briefly step out of the storm, and become a nonemotional observer.

Interventions With the Modes

Upon labeling and exploring the origins of the primary modes, establishing interventions with each mode is the next step. Again, we will focus on modes that are usually predominant with this population. The interventions described in schema mode therapy have cognitive, experiential, and behavioral components. Another benefit of this model is that the interventions vary depending on the mode one is working with at a particular time. As mentioned, this enables a highly structured and targeted therapeutic approach.

Intervening With the Vulnerable Mode

A central feature in mode work is to heal the vulnerable mode so that patients do not continue to live their lives avoiding what appears to them to be intolerable. This healing occurs through exposure to their painful emotions with skills to learn tolerance versus avoidance. They need to be exposed to the distressing affect of the vulnerable mode, and realize that they are better able to manage it than they thought. At a younger age they developed coping and/or survival skills to manage as best they could, but now they have access, with the therapist's help as needed, to skills that will enable them to appropriately manage these difficult emotions and memories versus avoidance of them.

Traditional cognitive and behavior therapies are usually ineffective with these patients when in the vulnerable mode because of the intensity of the feelings. Efforts at being rational are engulfed in the flood of emotion. Plus, challenging the irrationality of this mode is often perceived by the patient as invalidating, and the therapeutic relationship is harmed. At any point that a patient is in the vulnerable mode with the therapist, the appropriate therapeutic approach is one of support. The therapist should be affirming the expression of vulnerability and encouraging the patient's right to assert her needs. Experiential work, rather than traditional CBT, is indicated with the vulnerable mode.

Experiential work occurs most effectively in the context of imagery exercises. The focus in imagery exercises at this point is to identify the mode(s) that are the most significant obstacles to accessing the vulnerable mode. For example, the detached protector may be the main obstacle to accessing the vulnerable mode. In this case, the imagery exercise should first focus on debating the detached protector mode to decrease its avoidant behavior and allow access to vulnerable mode.

Let's discuss one way to structure an imagery exercise with the goal of accessing the vulnerable mode. The patient is asked to remember the age she was when the detached protector was first developing. In most cases, the patient is able to do this easily. The patient would be instructed to close her eyes, and to allow a distressing event to come to mind, focusing around the time the detached protector was first developing (e.g., around age 12 to 13). Once an event is imaged, the patient is instructed to have three separate images of herself: one in the vulnerable mode, one in the detached protector, and one in the healthy adult. The detached protector is to remain to the side, and told not to interfere at this point as the patient's healthy adult mode enters into conversation with the vulnerable mode. Using the names of the modes established by the patient, the patient's healthy adult asks the vulnerable mode, often imaged as a sad or scared child, to express its feelings and thoughts about the event imaged. Upon doing so, the vulnerable mode is affirmed for expressing affect, and encouraged to assert what it needs in the current situation. The vulnerable mode is the part of the patient that usually remains hidden, does not express itself, and does not feel entitled to ask for its needs to be met. The patient's healthy adult mode is to be supportive of the vulnerable mode, and coach the vulnerable mode in expressing affect, and asserting the right to emotional support, stability, safety, and so on.

The therapist then instructs the healthy adult, in the imagery exercise, to support the vulnerable mode with what he or she needs to hear in regard to themes pertinent to that patient. For example, this might involve telling the vulnerable mode that the painful experience of rejection or abandonment was not its fault. This is aimed at counteracting a common internal attributional style (e.g., self-blame for their pain), seeing themselves as defective or as a failure are common schemas with chronic depression.

It can take time for some patients to get to the point of accessing the vulnerable mode in imagery, and once there, it may be that their healthy adult mode is not developed enough to work with the vulnerable mode as needed. If this is the case, the therapist needs to instruct patients to add the therapist into their imagery exercise. The therapist models appropriate communication and support of the vulnerable mode. Gradually, the patient's healthy adult takes over that role. This experiential exercise exposes the patient to the vulnerable aspects of him or herself that they have avoided. Through repeated exposures, the patient experiences what seemed intolerable as tolerable, and the avoidance that fuels chronic depression decreases.

Intervening With the Detached Protector
This mode is often the main obstacle to accessing the vulnerable mode. An effective intervention here is to explore and debate the advantages and disadvantages of the detached protector.

In one imagery exercise with a patient, he was unable to focus on any one distressing event, and we discussed how the detached protector was keeping him from engaging in the imagery exercise knowing it would be emotionally distressing. Instead of imagery with eyes closed, we did an empty chair exercise in which we imaged his healthy adult mode in one chair, and the detached protector mode in another. We were both surprised to hear him confronting his avoidant tendency so effectively and powerfully from his healthy adult mode. He confronted his detached protector by saying, "You cannot keep running from problems because I will never get better if I don't learn how to deal with my sadness. By running, you're just making things worse." It is not unusual for patients to say that it "feels strange" to make these statements, or that they "feel confused" afterward. He debated with the detached protector the advantages and disadvantages of it in his life. He was able to state that while it played a helpful role when he was a young child and felt overwhelmed, it is now interfering in his life, preventing him from growing, and it is now keeping him depressed. Had the patient's healthy adult mode been unable to confront the advantages and disadvantages adequately, the therapist should role model this until the patient's healthy adult is able to do it. Again, this type of work helps decrease the intensity of the automatic response of the detached protector coping behavior so that the vulnerable mode can be accessed.

A behavioral intervention aimed at decreasing the detached protector would be to establish a stimulus hierarchy with behaviors that are contributing to their depression (e.g., stepwise behaviors to decrease social withdrawal). Social isolation and anhedonia are common with chronic depression, and should be attended to early in treatment. Behavioral work is perhaps the strongest method to help patients generalize mode work to various life situations. In this context, patients deliberately place themselves in situations that would generate vulnerable affect while disallowing themselves to flip into an ineffective coping mode.

Intervening With the Angry Mode

Again, this mode is indicated by a childlike expression of anger, in which there may be a loss of control, or the anger is disproportionate to the situation. This mode is often rare, or only experienced periodically, for individuals with chronic depression and personality disorders. However, at any point the patient is in the angry mode, whether angry at the therapist or others, the therapist first allows venting, then, empathizes with the valid need that was unmet, and finally, does reality testing regarding the ineffectiveness of inappropriate anger. These three steps should be taken in that order. While the patient is venting, the therapist allows the venting, stays emotionally neutral, and repeats, "And what else are you angry at?" until the patient says "That's everything that's bothering me." This allows him or her to fully express his or her anger in the context of being listened to by the therapist. Often the angry mode is triggered by feeling that some need has not been met (e.g., not being listening to, or treated unfairly). When finished venting, the therapist empathically addresses the valid needs that were frustrated. There is usually some reasonable basis to the angry mode. The therapist acknowledges the validity of the patient's need, and the right of the patient for that need to be met. Upon feeling heard and understood by the therapist, the patient will likely be more receptive to reality testing from the therapist in regard to communicating one's needs. The patient needs help to focus on how his or her inappropriate expression of anger usually makes others withdraw or become critical, and the patient feels even more misunderstood. The therapist communicates that while the need is valid, the way it was communicated made the problem worse. A behavioral intervention is to practice appropriate expression of anger as well as to assert one's needs.

Intervening With the Punitive and/or Demanding Mode

The sooner this mode is diminished, if not extinguished, the better. This process is begun early in therapy as the therapist models a nonjudgmental stance with the client, and works with the client to do the same. But often in order to extinguish this mode, imagery work is needed. The origin of the punitive/demanding mode is the internalization of the parental voice. The indicated exercise is for the patient to do an imagery exercise in which the critical parent is confronted by the patient's own healthy adult mode if possible, or by the therapist until the patient's healthy adult mode is able to do it. The confrontation should result in the patient giving appropriate responsibility to the parent for their overly punitive and/or critical behavior; while the vulnerable child, also in the image, is freed from blaming himself or from the overwhelming fear of the critical/demanding parent. This imagery work often requires a strong confrontational approach of the therapist in regard to the punitive parent. This can lead to the patient being defensive of the critical parent. In these situations, the therapist explains that his parents, like all parents, are imperfect; this does not mean they were all bad, but they made mistakes and it had significant consequences for the patient. The patient now needs to give them responsibility for their mistakes, and stop blaming himself inappropriately. This pattern of self-blame has been with him throughout his life, and it contributes to being trapped in chronic depression. Decreasing the punitive mode decreases the intensity of the internal attributional style so common with these patients.

Strengthening the Healthy Adult Mode

This mode is strengthened behaviorally through identifying and building on the successes of the patient as early as possible in the treatment. The therapist needs to find how the patient successfully set boundaries with others, or where the patient has been respectful of others while demanding respect for himself. Help the patient apply this skill in other areas of his life. Explore strengths and talents, and help the patient build into his life behaviors that he finds gratifying (Linehan, 1993a). Engaging in activities that offer a sense of accomplishment and gratification diminishes depression, and enhances patients' ability to manage the vulnerable aspects of themselves.

Limited Reparenting

Foundational to mode work is that the therapist responds to the patient in a manner that is consistent with the needs of the vulnerable mode. Limited reparenting involves a balance of nurturance and limit setting. The patient needs to feel secure and connected in the relationship with the therapist. The therapist must be willing to provide this for the patient in mode work. Discomfort with intense emotion, or with an emotional bond, on the part of the therapist, poses problems with being effective in this model.

Also, comfort with limit setting is important in working with these clients. Clinicians need to be aware of and assert their limits in regard to how much they can provide for a patient without building resentment. When a therapist has intense anger or is resentful toward a patient with this comorbidity, it is likely that the patient will perceive abandonment and/or feel unsupported emotionally. To be effective with limited reparenting, therapists need to be aware of their own schemas, and to be able to adequately manage them. Limited reparenting is emphasized in this model as perhaps the most important aspect of working with these patients. The experience of being connected with the therapist helps resolve the sense of abandonment of the vulnerable mode.

Crisis Management

Patients with the comorbidity of depression and personality disorders often struggle with chronic suicidality and/or parasuicidality. As in the DBT session format, management of this behavior should be the first priority in the treatment with these patients (Seligman, 2002). In each session, the clinician reviews suicidal/parasuicidal behaviors since the last contact.

Crisis events in schema mode therapy are managed through awareness of the modes activated when in a crisis, and interventions involve attention to the needs of the vulnerable mode that led to the crisis. As always, the therapeutic stance is one of limited reparenting, balancing attention to connection and limit setting. Identification of the mode the patient is in when suicidal is essential when managing a crisis. This occurs while discussing his or her suicidal ideation. It is important to listen to the patient's tone of voice, and attend to his or her affective state. Ask the patient what mode he is in. As his familiarity with his modes increases, he often becomes astute at identifying which mode he is in. With those experiencing chronic depression and personality disorders, suicidal ideation occurs most often while in the vulnerable mode. When feeling overwhelmed with the pain of abandonment and being alone, suicidal thoughts may occur as a means for relief. Or parasuicidal behaviors will often occur as a way to distract him from the intensity of the emotional pain.

The indicated response from the therapist is to diminish his sense of abandonment using the therapeutic relationship or other trusting figures in his life. The therapist, in this model, will recommend increasing the number of contacts with the patient until the crisis has subsided in order to reduce the sense of abandonment. This can be done by brief daily telephone calls until the suicidality has decreased. The increased contact helps diminish the sense of abandonment as he feels attended to and cared for. This intervention may be all that is needed if there is an adequate bond or alliance with the therapist.

Involving others is another helpful step in managing chronic suicidality. Identify with the patient others who the patient can trust, and with whom the patient is willing to take a risk in regard to disclosing her suicidal thoughts. Practice in session with the patient how to disclose this to the other. Usually, those chosen by the patient for disclosure already know, or at least strongly suspect, that the patient has been suicidal. This disclosure with a trusting figure can benefit the patient in several ways. First, if the patient is in a crisis, this person can assist with safety planning (e.g., they can stay with the patient until the crisis subsides). Second, by disclosing to others, the patient may feel some relief in that the other person does not reject her, but is supportive. This lessens the intensity of feeling defective that decreases the pain of the vulnerable mode.

The therapist should consult with other therapists when managing difficult cases like these because of the intense emotions involved and because of decisions regarding the patient's safety. When managing a crisis with the patient, decisions about the need for hospitalization are complex. The basic question is whether the patient will be safe until the next contact, whether by telephone or in person. If uncertain about a patient's safety, take action to protect the patient. *Options:* increase the level of contacts with the therapist, have the patient stay with a supportive peer, or have the patient voluntarily admit herself to the hospital. Hospitalization should be the last resort, but it must be used if there are no other adequate options to maintain safety. If the patient refuses to admit herself, then the therapist must initiate involuntary hospitalization. A limit should be set as early as possible in treatment that the patient must agree to follow the instructions of the therapist when in a crisis.

When suicidal from the angry mode, the therapist works with patients in a similar manner described earlier; allow them to vent their anger, empathize with the unmet need, and reality test. Explore, as well, whether harming oneself to express anger or get revenge is worth the negative impact to the patient while the other is minimally impacted. Suicidality from the angry mode is not too common with this population.

Suicidality from the punitive mode emerges as a way to punish themselves for being defective, or failing at something. The appropriate response for the therapist would be to focus on the origin of the punitive mode. It is the internalization of the parental voice that created the punitive mode. Giving in to the punitive mode and harming oneself is allowing the voice of the punitive parent to have power over the patient. Again, the needed intervention involves exploring with the patient the costs/benefits of empowering the parental voice by harming herself.

Let's consider a clinical example of managing suicidality from the mode context. This case involves a male in his late 50s. He lives alone; his wife died several years ago; they were unable to have children; he is retired with a very secure pension. He has experienced chronic depression and chronic suicidality since childhood. He grew up in a home in which he was compared by his parents to an older sister. His parents denigrated him for not being as good as his sister. This led to the development of several schemas, among them being failure, defective, and abandonment. His vulnerable mode is his default mode. The pain of the vulnerable mode often leads to the consideration of suicide for relief. In discussing his suicidal ideation, the clinician has identified a pattern that occurs at times in regard to mode flipping. The client starts thinking of how successful his sister is in her life; she has a family, and she has a successful career. He compares himself to her, and he immediately experiences the vulnerable mode in which he sees himself as a failure: he's defective because he has no family, he is not working. He then flips into the punitive/demanding mode in which he says to himself, just like his father would have said: "You're worthless; you don't deserve happiness in your life. You need to be motivated like your sister. Get your act together." This leads him to flip back into the vulnerable mode in which he feels rejected, abandoned, and sad, like he felt when his father said similar things to him. At this point, under the weight of feeling like a failure, defective, as well as abandoned, alone, he "can't take it," and turns to suicidal thoughts for relief from the emotional pain of the vulnerable mode.

In working with this patient, an intervention in regard to managing his chronic suicidality has been to focus on increasing the number of telephone contacts when he's experiencing a suicidal crisis. It is crucial for him to experience in relation to the therapist a secure and trusting relationship in which he feels accepted as he is, and cared for. His experience of the therapist as "someone who is there for me" is discussed openly. He has committed to calling the therapist prior to harming himself. He cannot commit to no suicidal thoughts, nor even to no suicidal behavior, but he is able to commit to calling prior to taking action to harm himself. The telephone calls are usually very brief. Triggers for suicidal thoughts are discussed as well as the modes he was in at the time. The therapist and patient are able to refer to patterns of modes at this point. His experience of calling the therapist, and a few other trusting figures in his life, give him the experience of connection and decrease the intensity of the vulnerable mode. When in contact with someone who accepts him, who is nonjudgmental, and does not compare him to others, the pain of the vulnerable mode subsides, and the fuel for suicidal ideation is reduced.

Because of the rigidity in these patients of the cognitive-emotional-behavioral patterns, many repetitions of these interventions are needed. Patience is required on the part of both the therapist and the patient. It may take years with many of these patients to develop healthy coping skills to adequately manage their vulnerabilities.

CONCLUSION

Social workers in a variety of settings have contact with individuals in which an effective working alliance is needed. Social workers need tools and skills to quickly develop a connection while also focusing on ameliorating problematic behaviors. This poses a significant challenge for the field.

The skills developed by Young and his associates offer a unique opportunity for the social work profession. The incorporation of the therapeutic tools of schema mode therapy appear to be a good fit for the challenges social workers face in field practice when working with this comorbidity.

Social workers have historically valued a respectful stance toward clients. This model, as well as DBT, places such a supportive therapeutic stance as foundational to their work with patients. Beyond that, mode therapy enables an alliance to form very early in the contact with the patient, and it offers to the clients a manner of considering their problematic behaviors and/or mood states in the context of various aspects of themselves. This provides a realistic spectrum of the various parts of themselves, and this in turn decreases a sense of being overwhelmed. Identifying modes and the cycling of modes often helps clients feel understood and perceived in a nonjudgmental way. This facilitates motivation on the client's part to ally with the social worker in the task at hand.

REFERENCES

Arnow, B. (2005). Cognitive behavioral analysis system of psychotherapy for chronic depression. *Cognitive and Behavioral Practice, 12*, 6–16.

Beck, A., Rush, J., Shaw, B., & Emery, G. (1979). *Cognitive therapy of depression.* New York: Guilford.

Comtois, K. A., Cowley, D. S., Dunner, D. L., & Roy-Byrne, P. P. (1990). Relationship between borderline personality disorder and Axis I diagnosis in severity of depression and anxiety. *Journal of Clinical Psychiatry, 60*, 752–758.

Feske, U. et al. (2004). Clinical outcome of ECT in patients with major depression and comorbid borderline personality disorder. *American Journal of Psychiatry, 161*, 2073–2080.

Greenberger, D., & Padesky, C. (1995a). *Clinician's guide to mind over mood.* New York: Guilford.

Greenberger, D., & Padesky, C. (1995b). *Mind over mood: A cognitive therapy treatment manual for clients.* New York: Guilford.

Hayes, S. C., Strosahl, K. D., & Wilson, K. G. (1999). *Acceptance and commitment therapy: An experiential approach to behavior change.* New York: Guilford.

Hirschfeld, R. M., Iketani, T., Kiriike, N., Stein, M. B., Nagao, K., Nagata, T., et al. (1999). Personality disorders and depression: Comorbidity. *Depression and Anxiety, 10*, 142–146.

Linehan, M. M. (1993a). *Cognitive-behavioral treatment of borderline personality disorder.* New York: Guilford.

Linehan, M. M. (1993b). *Skills training manual for treating borderline personality disorder.* New York: Guilford.

Melartin, T. K., Rytsala, H. J., Leskela, U. S., Lestela-Mielonen, P. S., Sokero, T. P., & Isometsa, E. T. (2002). Current comorbidity of psychiatric disorders among *DSM-IV* major depressive disorder patients in psychiatric care in the Vantaa Depression Study. *Journal of Clinical Psychiatry, 63*, 126–134.

Rossi, A., Marinangeli, M. G., Butti, G., Scinto, A., Di Cicco, L., Kalyvoka, A., et al. (2001). Personality disorders in bipolar and depressive disorders. *Journal of Affective Disorders, 65*, 3–8.

Segal, Z. V., Williams, J. M. G., & Teasdale, J. D. (2002). *Mindfulness-based cognitive therapy for depression: A new approach to preventing relapse.* New York: Guilford.

Seligman, Martin E. P. (2002). *Authentic happiness: Using the new positive psychology to realize your potential for lasting fulfillment.* New York: Free Press.

Skodol, A. E., Stout, R. L., McGlashan, T. H., Grilo, C. M., Gunderson, J. G., Shea, M. T., et al. (1999). Co-occurrence of mood and personality disorders: A report from the Collaborative Longitudinal Personality Disorders Study (CLPS). *Depression and Anxiety, 10,* 175–182.

Yapko, Michael D. (1997). *Breaking the patterns of depression.* New York: Broadway Books.

Young, J., Klosko, J., & Weishaar, M. (2003). *Schema therapy: A practitioner's guide.* New York: Guilford.

CHAPTER 21

Working With Adult Survivors of Sexual and Physical Abuse

Beverly White

INTRODUCTION

For many reasons working with adult survivors of childhood sexual and physical abuse is broad and complex. Factors such as the age of the child when the abuse occurred, the severity and duration of the abuse, and the relational attachment to the abuser make generalizing victim responses to events of abuse a daunting task. Equally problematic are the aftereffects of the abuse on survivors. Yet, it seems safe to say that for many child survivors, the abuses were traumatic and induced life-altering thoughts regarding trust, safety, intimacy, and feelings of fear, guilt, confusion, shame, and self-blame. Victims of childhood sexual and physical abuse often have other familial and situational problems that are traumatizing as well (Palmer, Brown, Rae-Grant, & Loughlin, 2001). In fact, the overlap between the possible effects of sexual abuse and the effects of a matrix of disadvantaged and disrupted family factors from which the abuse so often emerged is often considerable. This raises the question of how often sexual and/or physical abuse operate as independent casual elements to adult psychopathology (Muellen, Martin, Anderson, Romans, & Herbison, 1993).

A national survey of 2,000 adults (Finkelhor, Hotaling, Lewis, & Smith, 1990), whose results show that 27% of the women and 16% of the men reported a history of childhood sexual abuse, suggests that the prevalence of adult survivors is formidable. The implication of this statistic for mental health and social service providers is that adult survivors probably appear in significant numbers among our clients and patients. As mental health providers, we often see the multiple and multifaceted sequelae of the posttraumatic responses as displayed by the adult survivors. Though posttraumatic stress disorder (PTSD) is one diagnostic feature of adult survivors, often an individual survivor will have multiple diagnoses such as recurrent major depression, bipolar affective disorder, generalized anxiety disorder (GAD), substance abuse and borderline personality disorder (BPD), making it a challenge to provide effective treatment interventions specifically linked to ameliorating childhood abuse-related issues. Research indicates that service providers often find it difficult and stressful to treat survivors because of the patients' resistance to change, their ways of relating to helpers, and the emotionally demanding nature of the work (Palmer et al., 2001). Survivors often have difficulty being responsible for their own lives and may have used self-destructive behaviors, such as substance abuse, to cope with their feelings (Beutler & Hill, 1992; Briere, 1992; Herman, 1992; Valentine & Feinauer, 1993). As a worker addresses one symptomatic issue, there may be an unfolding of more intrinsic and pervasive pathology. The aftereffects of childhood abuse often adversely affect interpersonal skills and relationships (Palmer et al., 2001), further complicating and impeding effective service delivery and treatment.

Social workers especially play important roles as service providers to many adult survivors who present as clients or patients in a variety of social systems: medical, legal, protective, and therapeutic (Anderson, Weston, Doueck, & Krause, 2002). In the traditional social work role of linking or referring individuals to needed resources, the social worker is key in helping adult survivors who have difficulty managing their lives to access resources. Key in this role is choosing the strategies that most empower the survivor and facilitate a successful outcome (Anderson et al., 2002). To this end, social workers assume the role of a trainer in helping survivors learn, for example, effective social problem-solving skills. Through the roles of advocate, supporter, champion of rights, and representative for clients "dealing with the court, the police, social agencies and other organizations" (Sosin & Caulum, 1989, p. 28), social workers develop a pragmatic connection with the adult survivor. This is especially important in avoiding the attrition that is characteristically high, given the difficulties many survivors have with maintaining interpersonal relationships. In fact, the inclusion of case management services in a study to test the benefits of CBT for depression in low-income medical outpatients, where the majority of study members were Hispanic and African American, (Chambless & Ollendick, 2001) significantly reduced the dropout rate.

Only a few decades ago, it would have been the exception to find social workers in the role as therapists in private practice or working in industry, now it is a frequent phenomena (LeCroy & Stinson, 2004). Clinical social workers are well trained to provide a variety of therapeutic services such as individual, group, and family therapy. In the past decade it has become particularly important for clinical social workers to demonstrate treatment effectiveness. This development is related to social work's increased emphasis on accountability to clients and third-party payers and a desire to further the knowledge base of the profession. The challenge for workers is to effectively implement evidence-based interventions that will enhance the success rate of treatment for these often complex and difficult clients and will reduce the negative effects of trauma work in order to avoid or lessen worker burnout.

LITERATURE REVIEW

Since the inclusion of PTSD in the *Diagnostic and Statistical Manual of Mental Disorders* in 1980 (*DSM-III;* American Psychiatric Association Press), a fair amount of literature has been generated on the general topics of trauma, PTSD, and sequelae disorders by leaders in the field such as B. A. van der Kolk, J. L. Herman, E. B. Foa, S. Epstein, P. Janet, J. Briere, and work championed by the Harvard Medical School Trauma Clinic. An operative definition for psychic trauma has been the injurious and disordered physiological, psychological, emotional, and behavioral state that results from mental or emotional stress or physical injury (Perry, Conroy, & Ravitz, 1991), especially in the presence of an actual or perceived life-threatening event. In other words, they are the terrifying experiences that rupture people's sense of safety, predictability, and invulnerability (van der Kolk, van der Hart, & Burbridge, 1995). It is suggested that what distinguishes people who develop PTSD from people who are merely temporarily overwhelmed is that people who develop PTSD become "stuck" on the trauma, in that they keep reliving it in thoughts, feelings, or images (van der Kolk et al., 1995). A community study of the long-term impact of the sexual, physical, and emotional abuse of children (Muellen, Martin, Anderson, Romans, & Herbison, 1996) concluded that a history of any form of abuse was associated with increased rates of psychopathology, sexual difficulties, decreased self-esteem, and interpersonal problems. The study also claimed that abuse of all types was more frequent in people from disturbed and disrupted family backgrounds.

Information regarding the biological aspects of trauma is also well represented in the literature. The capacity to store and recall information is one of the amazing and powerful features of the human brain (Perry et al., 1991). There is information suggesting that people who experience traumatic events develop a distinct set of physical signs and symptoms that include intrusive and recurring recollections of the traumatic event (dreams and flashbacks), numbing of general responsiveness and physiological hyperactivity, increased arousal and hypervigilance. From a biological perspective, there is information that the organic patterns unique to PTSD are associated with alternations in noradrenergic, the hypothalamic-pituitary-adrenocortical axis, the endogenous opioid system, the diurnal sleep cycle (Davidson, 1992; Friedmann, 1991). Recent studies found that women with a history of childhood abuse exhibited increased pituitary-adrenal and autonomic responses to stress compared with controls (Heim, Newport, Heit, Graham, Wilcox, Bonsall, et al., 2000). This study also suggests that early traumatic experiences play a preeminent role in the development of mood and anxiety disorders.

There is well-established and increasing empirical evidence that cognitive and cognitive behavior therapies are effective for the treatment of disorders that are typical among adult survivors of sexual and physical abuse. For more than 40 years, models of psychotherapy that have emphasized brief, solution-focused treatment have gained immense popularity and respect (Beck, 1996). Much of that gain in stature has to do with the vigor with which these approaches have been investigated empirically (Beck, 1996). There are several benefits for implementing evidence-based techniques such as cognitive behavior therapy (CBT). Among them is that they use empirical data in the professional literature to guide assessments and interventions that facilitate client change (Vandiver, 2002). In empirical research comparing cognitive and cognitive behavior therapies with other therapies, including medication therapy, CBT and related therapies have demonstrated positive results with long-term effectiveness for the treatment of the following disorders: depression (Blatt, Zuroff, Bondi, & Sanisolow, 2000; Organista, Munoz, & Gonzalez 1994; Persons, Bostrom, & Bertagnolli, 1999), anxiety disorders such as phobias (Halweg, Fiegenbaum, Frank, Schroeder, & von Witzleben, 2001), panic disorder (Borkovec & Costello, 1993; Craske, Meadows, & Barlow, 1994; Stuart, Treat, & Wade, 2000; Telch, Schmidt, Jaimez, Jacquin, & Harrington, 1995; Wade, Treat, & Stuart, 1998), and obsessive-compulsive disorder (Franklin, Abramowitz, Kozak, Levitt, & Foa, 2000); eating disorders (Tuschen-Caffier, Pook, & Frank, 2001), and substance abuse (Parks &

Marlatt, 1999). There are few controlled outcome studies assessing the efficacy of cognitive therapy with such clinical disorders as borderline personality disorder (BPD). However, one study completed by the National Institute of Mental Health (NIMH) found cognitive behavior therapy to be superior to interpersonal therapy over a 16-week period for treating difficult clients with borderline personality disorder (Dean, 2001).

DISCUSSION OF PROBLEM—WORKING WITH DIFFICULT CLIENTS USING CBT

Individuals develop cognitive schemas (fundamental or core beliefs that influence how we think, feel, and act) about self and others on the basis of psychological needs in five areas: safety, trust, esteem, control, and intimacy (Bowlby, 1969; Epstein, 1991). Beck's cognitive model suggests that these schema generate a variety of automatic thoughts that occur almost reflexively in response to problem-provoking situations. Distorted thinking leads to distorted feelings and actions. Changing beliefs leads to changes in emotions and behaviors (Beck, 1996).

Trauma disrupts the cognitive schemas of victims of abuse. Past trauma influences the shaping of schema. The schema that forms in response to early trauma provides a model for how to interpret future events and for determining affective and behavioral responses (Cunningham, 2003). These, in turn, emerge as patterns of responses that further influence the responses to future situations. In this way, traumatic memories help establish pathways for the perception, interpretation, and response to problematic situations (Beck, 1996). Their strength is determined by credibility of source, age at acquisition and *reinforcement.*

The key to undoing these problem areas is to effect a change or reformation of these core beliefs that are a part of the cognitive schemas. In doing so, cognitive behavior treatment techniques are designed to foster a change in the belief system, which, in turn, should lead to changes in the individual's emotional, cognitive and behavioral responses to schema-incited events. The theoretical strength of the cognitive model lies in the conceptualization of how problems are caused and maintained and can be reshaped (Beck, 1996).

Basic Treatment Strategies

The role of memory in the formation and maintenance of schemas is central and essential. The cognitive behavior approach to treatment emphasizes the contextual aspects of memory as essential to the therapeutic process. It is insufficient to know what a client remembers. It is also imperative that the social worker gains an understanding of how the client remembers a given situation or situations. The concept of emotional/behavioral memory goes a long way toward explaining how and why a critical event can be central to the experiencing of depressive or anxious feelings and thoughts, even when the event is in the remote past.

Emotional/behavioral memory functions, for the most part, unconsciously and automatically (Beck, 1996). By referring to previous experiences, people frequently resort to cognitive short cuts that permit value judgments and evaluations without having to actually test situations empirically. The following are some basic CBT strategies that social workers can use in whatever roles they play in working with the multidisordered adult survivor (Beck, 1996).

1. *Focus on developing trust in the relationship and a collaborative strategy.* A trusting relationship can most easily be established when the worker openly acknowledges how difficult it must be for clients to trust based on the number of painful experiences they have had in the past. Then the worker must carefully define the relationship and must be consistent, straightforward, and trustworthy, so that the client knows what to expect.

2. *Choose an initial focus of treatment or service with the client that will lead to some immediately felt progress.* Identify behavioral goals, especially, that can be broken down into their tiniest component parts, so they can be tackled one small step at a time. Developing these goals can often be useful at an early point in treatment and service delivery, because it takes the focus off of the difficulties involved in maintaining trust and intimacy, it helps to build an authentic relationship, and it actually addresses underlying and formative psychological issues.

3. *Reduce or eliminate dichotomous (black and white) thinking early in working with clients.* As the main contributor to extreme actions, mood swings and dilemmas faced by those that are difficult to treat, reducing dichotomous thinking should reduce symptom intensity, as well as help modify underlying assumptions and provide alternate resolutions to many dilemmas. To change dichotomous thinking, the therapist should point out examples to the client as they occur and then discuss whether thinking in terms of gray areas would lead to more realistic and adaptive responses.

4. *Deal with transference issues.* In cognitive terms *transference* can best be understood as clients responding to the worker based on generalized beliefs and expectations they have about relationships, rather than according to how the worker behaves as an individual.

When strong emotional reactions occur that appear to be related to transference reactions, the worker must deal with them promptly. Cognitive treatment practitioners suggest the following process:

a. Develop a clear understanding of what the client is thinking and feeling.

b. Resolve misunderstandings and misconceptions clearly and explicitly.

c. Convey that the client will not be rejected or attacked because of emotional reactions.

d. Teach the client to expect and accept "transference" reactions as part of the treatment/learning/changing process.

5. *Address the client's fear of change by directly examining the risks involved in trying things a new way.* Motivational interviewing (Miller & Rollnick, 1991)—the goal of which is to move a client from saying "No" to change to saying, "I'll think about it"—can be a particularly effective cognitive technique for addressing the survivor's resistance to changing behaviors. It involves validating the client's experience and acknowledging his or her control in making a decision. Psychoeducation and a cost-benefit analysis of their current behavior and the proposed changed behavior are often useful motivational techniques. One common fear among the difficult to treat is that therapy and support will end as soon as problems are overcome. If this is the case, the worker will need to clarify that termination of therapy and/or supportive services will, as much as it is within the control of the parties involved, be a collaborative decision (as are other decisions about treatment and services).

6. *Help clients increase control over their emotions by acknowledging their emotions and modeling appropriate ways to respond to them.* The worker can help clients look critically at their thoughts in a problem situation and develop alternative coping strategies. These strategies involve learning adaptive ways to express emotions. While developing these more adaptive responses, the worker should proceed slowly and should continue to talk about the client's concerns regarding the risks in changing behavior patterns. This is a prime time for rehearsal and "what if" scenarios to help clients with the performance of new behaviors and coping with rejecting reactions. These reactions may come from family members, friends, and other members of their social environment in an attempt to maintain the homeostasis of their relationships with the client.

7. *Improve impulse control by acknowledging and dealing with the client's initial response to changing behavior, "Why should I?"* Workers can convey to clients that they are not trying to enforce societal

norms, but rather are helping them to choose whether to act on an impulse. The process of developing impulse control involves:

a. Identification of impulses

b. Exploration of the pros and cons of controlling impulses

c. Development of alternatives to responding to impulses and rehearsing them

d. Examination of the expectations and fears that block promising alternatives

e. Providing skill training or coaching necessary for the client to utilize new alternatives

Additionally, the worker needs to discuss what the impulsive behavior means to the client as well as the motivation for performing that behavior. For example, self-mutilating behavior may come from a desire to punish others, punish oneself, obtain relief from guilt, or as a distraction from more aversive thoughts and feelings. Knowing the motivation behind the behavior can help in developing alternative coping strategies.

8. *Build on the client's resiliency: Strengthen the client's sense of identity.* Help clients identify their positive characteristics and accomplishments and provide them with positive feedback regarding their resourceful decisions and effective coping. In addition, have them evaluate their own actions realistically as a means of strengthening their own ability to provide positive self-reinforcement. The client–therapist relationship presents the single most important opportunity for providing positive feedback; the therapist can provide positive feedback to the client by recognizing difficult risks the client takes in the process of making changes in his or her life.

Stages of Change

As previously mentioned, a key role for social workers is assessing and choosing strategies that most empower the survivor and facilitate a successful outcome. One danger of treatment and service failure lies in applying intervention strategies that are inconsistent with the client's level of readiness. Prochaska, DiClemente & Norcross's (1992) transtheoretical model, first developed in the treatment of smokers to effect smoking cessation, helps to conceptualize and assess a client's readiness for change. The model consists of five distinct stages. In the *precontemplative stage*, the client denies problems. In the *contemplative stage*, the client acknowledges problems without acknowledging specific need to change. Again, motivational interviewing, psychoeducation and cost-benefit analyses are often useful techniques to help the client transition progressively between the stages. In the *readiness stage*, the client realizes that the cost of continued behaviors outweighs the perceived benefits and strategies for change are developed (e.g., "I'll get treatment for this"). Helpful techniques and tasks to employ here would be to help the client identify social supports, assist in assessing and problem-solving obstacles, and verifying self-efficacy for changing behaviors. Planning for relapse prevention and developing coping strategies for relapse, are also essential tasks at this stage. In the *action stage*, plans aimed at encouraging small initial steps, and developing strategies for follow-up support are emphasized. In the *maintenance stage*, change has been established for a length of time and is periodically reevaluated. It is important to reinforce internal rewards. The client may relapse and resume old behaviors. Here it is helpful to evaluate triggers for relapse in order to develop better coping strategies and supports. Adult survivors may be at different stages for different proposed changes, and they can oscillate between stages.

METHODS OF TREATMENT

From cognitive and cognitive behavior models of intervention many other methods of treatment have emerged. They include Marsha Linehan's dialectical behavior therapy (DBT), a popular cognitive behavior model currently in use for the treatment of clients with borderline personality disorder (Dean, 2001). It has received extensive empirical support. DBT identifies a wide range of potentially risky or dangerous behaviors associated with borderline personality functioning. The initial emphasis of the model aims to establish and maintain behavioral self-control. Patients are provided a highly structured treatment design that emphasizes effective self-monitoring. Journals are routinely kept and the model emphasizes group and individual treatment sessions. Once behavioral self-control is established, the model shifts to the identification of core belief systems that lead the individual to feel vulnerable, unworthy, and unable to tolerate frustrations (Dean, 2001).

Francine Shapiro's eye movement desensitization and reprocessing (EMDR) is an information-processing (cognitive) approach for clients with PTSD (Shapiro, 2001). During EMDR the client attends to past and present experiences for brief sequential measures of time while simultaneously focusing on an external, bilateral stimulus. Then the client is instructed to let new material become the focus of the next set of dual attention. This sequence of dual attention and personal association is repeated many times in the session. EMDR integrates behavioral techniques such as stress inoculation therapy, exposure therapy, and systematic desensitization. While EMDR is somewhat controversial, ongoing empirical studies indicate potential benefits for adult survivors and those diagnosed with PTSD.

Marlatt and Gordon's (1985) relapse prevention therapy (RPT), originally designed as a maintenance program for addictive behaviors, also combines behavioral and cognitive interventions. In the most general sense, RPT is a behavioral self-control program designed to teach individuals who are trying to maintain changes in their behavior how to anticipate and cope with the problem of relapse.

D'Zurilla and Goldfried's (D'Zurilla & Nezu, 1990) social problem-solving approach is cognitive-behaviorally based as well. Interventions for this approach follow four basic steps: (1) define the problem; (2) generate alternative solutions; (3) choose the best solution, make a plan and execute it; and (4) evaluate the outcome.

Schema-Focused Approach

Young (1990) presented a basic CBT conceptual framework for how schema work and how to effect schematic change that, again, can be used by social workers in whatever treatment or service interactions they may have with adult survivors. Young combined object relations principles with cognitive techniques. In so doing, he forged interventions aimed at modifying or correcting basic cognitive distortions. In turn these interventions are meant to heal and correct early problematic experiences and change long-term patterns, such as those that exist for adult survivors of childhood sexual and physical abuse. In understanding how schemas work and exert their influence on feeling, thought and behaviors, Young (1990) proposed three processes: schema maintenance, avoidance, and compensation.

Schema maintenance involves reinforcements used to keep the schema intact. Cognitive distortions, negative interpretations, and predictions of life events are part of the schema-maintenance process. Cognitive distortions can consist of overgeneralizations, catastrophic thinking, "should" statements, externalization of self-worth, personalization, disqualifying the positive, minimization, and dichotomous thinking. The schema will highlight or magnify confirming information and will minimize or deny information that contradicts it. Schema maintenance works behaviorally as well as cognitively. The schema will generate behaviors that tend to keep the schema intact. It is important to point out the secondary gains there are for the client in maintaining the cognitive distortions. Socratic questioning that leads the client to the inconsistencies of the negative and distorted beliefs is also helpful. For example: "When you say you're a failure at life, do you mean at some things some of the time or all things all of the time? If the patient says, "All things all of the time," the worker can point out that this isn't true of anyone (Young, 1990).

Schema avoidance involves ways in which people avoid activating schemas. When schemas are activated this causes extreme negative emotion. People develop ways to avoid triggering schemas in order not to feel this pain. There are three types of schema avoidance: cognitive (not to think about upsetting events), emotional (automatic or voluntary numbness or shutting down, sometimes accomplished by substance abuse), and behavioral (acting in such a way to avoid situations that trigger schemas, and thus psychological pain). Superstitious thinking and behaviors may fit in this category. Gradual exposure and systematic desensitization may be helpful coping techniques for avoidance behaviors (Young, 1990).

Schema compensation involves the ways an individual behaves that appear to be the opposite of what the schema suggests in order to avoid triggering the schema. People who are functionally dependent on others may structure aspects of their life so that they don't have to depend on anyone, even when a more balanced approach may be better. For instance, a man may refuse to go out with a woman because he is afraid of becoming dependent and will present himself as someone who doesn't need other people. He goes to the other extreme to avoid feeling dependent (Young, 1990).

Young (1990) defined 16 specific schemas for clinical purposes and conjectured that most clients have at least two or three of these schemas and often more. The following case presentation will contextually illustrate six of these defining schemas:

1. *Emotional deprivation.* Refers to the belief that one's primary emotional needs will never be met by others. These needs include nurturance, empathy, affection, protection, guidance and caring from others. Often, parents were emotionally depriving to the child.
2. *Abandonment/Instability.* Refers to the expectation that one will soon lose anyone with whom an emotional attachment is formed. The person believes that, one way or another, close relationships will end imminently. As children, these clients may have experienced the divorce or death of a parent. This schema can also arise when parents have been inconsistent in attending to the child's needs. For example, there may have been frequent occasions in which the child was left alone or unattended for extended periods.
3. *Mistrust/Abuse.* Refers to the expectation that others will intentionally take advantage in some way. People with this schema often expect others to hurt, cheat or put them down. They often think in terms of attacking first or getting revenge afterwards. In childhood,

these clients were often abused or treated unfairly by parents, siblings, or peers.

4. *Social isolation/Alienation.* Refers to the belief that one is isolated from the world, different from other people, and/or not part of any community. This belief is usually caused by early experiences in which children see that either they or their families are different from others.

5. *Defectiveness/Shame.* Refers to the belief that one is internally flawed, and that, if others get close, they will realize this and withdraw from the relationship. This feeling of being flawed and inadequate often leads to a strong sense of shame. Generally parents were very critical of their children and made them feel as if they were not worthy of being loved.

6. *Failure to achieve.* Refers to the belief that one is incapable of performing as well as one's peers in areas such as career, school, or sports. These clients may feel stupid, inept, untalented or ignorant. People with this schema often do not try to achieve because they believe that they will fail. This schema may develop if children are put down and treated as if they are failure in school and other spheres of accomplishment. Usually the parents did not give enough support, discipline, and encouragement for the child to persist and succeed in areas of achievement (Young, 1990).

CASE STUDY 1

Jacob is a 29-year-old, single White male, living alone and attending a master's level program in graphic design. Initially, Jacob presented concerns regarding his interpersonal relationships. He stated that he had difficulties establishing and maintaining relationships with both males and females. Additionally, he claimed that he was having difficulty concentrating, was performing poorly in school, was compulsively overeating, and was suffering from anergia. His mood fluctuated between feeling very anxious (pacing, easily distracted, racing thoughts) to very depressed (hypersomia, anhedonia, thoughts of hopelessness). Jacob also experienced social phobia, dependency issues, and low self-esteem.

Born to a middle-class family of four (he has an older sister), Jacob reported having an unstable family life for as long as he could remember. Diagnosed as having a learning disability at age 5, he was sent to a special education school, and subsequently, considered himself a misfit within his family and community. Jacob described his father, a successful engineer, as being cruel, often verbally and physically tortuous to his mother and himself (not his sister), and emotionally detached. Jacob described his mother, a housewife, as being emotionally absent from her family, primarily due to her alcohol dependency. She virtually never intervened when Jacob's father would use violent corporal punishment for the slightest perceived or actual misconduct. Jacob also witnessed brutal assaults by his father toward his mother. She left the family when he was 8, after being "caught" having an affair. His parents divorced when Jacob was 13.

Jacob's father permitted only brief and infrequent telephone contact with his mother after she left. She would send gifts and cards for major holidays. And he saw her periodically during a brief interval of family therapy, just prior to the divorce. Jacob remembered his father often saying that his mother was unstable and would never be allowed to set foot in his home again because, "She had left a good suburban home, husband and children to live with her drunkard boyfriend in the city." Jacob was 14 when he first ran from home, and traveled alone to the city to be with his mother. He had "trashed" his room out of anger, fear and frustration, when he thought he would again be severely beaten for having poor school grades. He believed that there was no way he could remain in his father's home after that act of defiance.

His mother had married the man she went to be with when she left her family. She was still consuming alcohol daily, though her husband had presumably stopped. Jacob found it difficult to interact honestly with or to trust either his mother or her husband, though he did like being in the city. He returned to live with his father after 3 weeks, when his father threatened to take his mother to court. After he returned, his father forbade him to visit his mother for any reason as long as his father was supporting him.

Despite his alleged "learning disability," Jacob said he was mainstreamed into regular classes in public middle school at the age of 10 and did fairly well until eighth grade. Due to his paternal family's community and political influence, Jacob was placed in regular high school classes. He graduated with fair grades and, under his father's insistence, took courses, mostly art related, at the local community college. He worked part-time as a store clerk as well, until he obtained a bachelor's degree in art design at age 23. After graduation, he worked at various low-skill, low-paying jobs, while continuing to live with his father. At age 26, while in therapy for depression following his break-up with his first girlfriend—she had "pushed

(continues)

for sexual intercourse and he terminated the relationship"—he decided that he had to move out of his father's house. He had no skills, however, to get a job that would support him. With his sister's help, he applied and was accepted into a master's program at a city college. Through the school, he found two roommates to share an apartment close to the school.

There was no significant medical history. In general, Jacob appeared to be in good health, was conscious about taking care of himself by exercising (especially bike riding), and was taking vitamins daily. He ate compulsively when depressed and anxious, yet appeared to be only slightly overweight. He was a nonsmoker, and drank at least one beer daily. He denied personal history of alcohol dependency or abuse and no illegal drug use.

As related by Jacob, he remembered being involved with therapists since he was assessed for his learning disability and shyness. He also recalled brief involvement with family therapy at age 13 just before his parents were divorced. Following the divorce, Jacob was in therapy as a teenager for severe panic attacks and generalized anxiety disorder for 5 years. He had a bad reaction to medication (Paxil) that had been prescribed and has since refused to take any psychotropic medicines. Jacob was in therapy again for depression, as previously mentioned, following the end of his relationship with his only girlfriend when he was 26 years old. He did not like his first therapist who was a male. He subsequently procured the services of a female therapist. He ended this therapy after 2 years because he and the therapist agreed there was no more she could do for him regarding his depression, which had not ameliorated and at times, for Jacob, had worsened. She suggested that he increase his social life at school. He did not think much of that suggestion.

The precipitant events that prompted Jacob to enter therapy at age 29 were (1) a devastating argument he had with his male roommate, when he discovered that the roommate was planning to move in with his girlfriend, whom he hoped to marry; (2) a tremendously humiliating tirade he delivered to a young lady, who showed interest in him and to whom he was attracted, when he discovered that she was a prostitute; (3) the realization that his poor school performance may preclude him from graduating and his father was refusing to continue to support him.

Origins of Key Core Beliefs

Mother failed to meet Jacob's needs. → *People, particularly White women are rejecting and unable to provide emotional support or connection.* Mother modeled depressive and unstable behavior. → *People, particularly White women are emotionally unstable and unpredictable.* Mother allowed father to physically and emotionally abuse Jacob and then she left him entirely. → *People, particularly White women are coldhearted, will not be there for you and will abandon you.*

Father was physically and emotionally abusive to my mother and me. → *Men will hurt, abuse and humiliate you; I always get more than my share of hardship in life.* Father berates mother's lifestyle and the fact that she left a safe and secure home to go in the world and be with a drunkard. → *The world is a dangerous place.* Jacob is labeled as having a learning disability, while father and family members are considered to be high achievers. → *I always get the short end of the stick; I don't quite measure up the way I should, despite what I do; I have always been a misfit.* Intimacy was not valued in the family. Mother was banished for "having an affair." → *There's something wrong with my needs for intimacy and my sexuality.*

Maintaining Factors

1. An environmental reinforcement for many of Jacob's schematic beliefs—*"People, men particularly, will hurt, abuse and humiliate you; the world is unfair, unaccepting and dangerous; I will always be a misfit; and I get more than my share of hardship"*—occurred when he was significantly beaten by a gang of African American male youths, who also stole his expensive mountain bike. This took place when, while in present therapy, Jacob chose to ride his bike in a predominately low-income, African American and Hispanic neighborhood on the night before Halloween (traditionally known as "Mischief Night").

2. An avoidance reinforcement for the schematic beliefs that, *"People, White women particularly, are rejecting, coldhearted, unpredictable and unstable and emotionally unsupportive,"* occurred whenever Jacob refused to interact with female classmates or church members, even when they initiate interactions with him by inviting him to participate in social activities. "They're not giving me enough signals."

3. An avoidance reinforcement for the schematic belief that, *"I don't quite measure up the way I should, despite what I do,"* occurred when Jacob's school performance suffered largely due to his mood disorders.

4. A compensatory reinforcement for his schematic belief that, *"There is something wrong for my need for intimacy and my sexuality,"* occurred when Jacob viciously berated the alleged prostitute.

(continues)

It is noteworthy that Jacob did not appear to generalize his beliefs about the rejecting, coldhearted, and unstable nature of women to females of color.

Treatment Goals

The initial goals for treatment were to help Jacob identify and prioritize three treatment objectives and ways we could measure progress with these objectives. Through this process, the worker attempted to forge a positive working alliance with careful attention to transference and countertransference issues. *Impediment:* Jacob's difficulties with interpersonal relationships, particularly his distrust of women. Another goal of treatment was to build on the desire to take better care of self, and to seek ways that would allow him to take good care of himself even when he felt depressed and anxious. This, in turn, helped to improve affective moods. *Impediment:* This may be a long process and it was not clear that Jacob would tolerate treatment for the time required. Medication may be helpful and more immediately effective if Jacob were willing to consider this as an option.

Treatment Outcome

Jacob decided that his first objective was to finish his portfolio so that he could graduate and start in earnest to look for a professional job. This objective was subdivided into smaller objectives. Three objectives that seemed to promise the most immediate guarantees for success were (1) scheduling appointments with professors to work out a realistic schedule for getting past-due work completed; (2) identifying and establishing a good support team to keep Jacob on track for his schoolwork; and (3) structuring his daily activities. Jacob also began taking fitness classes at the school gym, and paying close attention to his food intake by writing down what he ate and when. Particular techniques employed to accomplish these objectives included identifying cognitive distortions through Socratic questioning, assessment of change readiness for each objective identified, motivational interviewing, social problem solving, systematic desensitization, cognitive reframing and a lot of rehearsal, especially to build his support team and to keep in contact with them.

Gradually Jacob acquired the focus and discipline needed to complete his portfolio. His self-esteem increased and he developed better interpersonal skills. He did not graduate with his class, because he had to drop some of his courses in order to focus on others. He found a job, however, that enabled him to take summer courses. With his completed portfolio, he began job hunting. Jacob's interpersonal relationships improved slightly through the use of desensitization techniques and rehearsals. With greater and improved social skills, Jacob began to socialize with a female classmate.

CASE STUDY 2

Rosa, a 32-year-old Hispanic female, is awaiting conviction and sentencing for prostitution, drug trafficking, drug possession, and vehicular assault while driving under the influence of alcohol and crack cocaine. She was self-referred and probably sought help in order to present herself in a positive light in the eyes of the court. She is HIV+ and ruminates about opportunistic infections and stress levels related to health status.

Up to the age of 9, Rosa lived with her parents, and an older half-brother. Rosa described her parents' relationship as tumultuous. Her parents' verbal and physical altercations led to her mother storming out with her older sibling when Rosa was 9 years old. Rosa held onto the car bumper pleading with her mother not to leave. She was dragged over two long blocks. She received multiple lacerations and bruises, but no permanent physical injuries.

Rosa remained with her father, who often drank heavily. She had no contact with her mother. Her father began to sexually abuse Rosa shortly after her mother left. The events of sexual abuse were intermittent, occurring when her father was particularly mournful about her mother. Within a year and a half after her mother left, child protective services were called when Rosa's teacher found a journal entry where Rosa talked about wanting to kill herself. Rosa was sent to talk with the school counselor who she told about the sexual abuse. As a result, Rosa was placed in a foster home and her father was arrested. It was at this time that she began displaying verbally defiant behaviors. She was truant from school and often stole from her foster homes. She had no contact with her father or her mother. Shortly thereafter, Rosa was remanded back to her mother's custody. Rosa reported that her older brother would sexually and physically assault her until she left her mother's home at age 16 to live with older male friends.

At age 14, Rosa began to display suicidal and self-injurious behaviors. She was psychiatrically hospitalized four times, and

(continues)

in several partial hospital programs over a 7-year period. Rosa reported that she attempted to continue going to school once she left her mother's home, but it was difficult and she began to prostitute. She said she used alcohol heavily to drown out the pain from thinking about parents, brother, and what was becoming of her life. Rosa then tried illegal drugs to numb the pain. Rosa was first incarcerated at age 19 for drug trafficking. She received a physical examination upon admission to the prison system and discovered that she was HIV+.

Between the ages of 19 and 32, Rosa was incarcerated twelve times on drug-related charges. She reported eight acute psychiatric hospitalizations and three 30-day admissions to the state hospital for major depression, several suicide attempts, and self-mutilating behaviors (superficially cutting her thighs and arms). She would attempt suicide by overdosing on street drugs, psychotropic medications, or drinking alcohol to the point of blacking out. Rosa had also been in several drug detoxification and rehabilitation programs. She had lived with several men and women, and in shelters. She had one relationship that she considered "serious," with a woman, but it had ended badly when Rosa resumed using drugs after finding out that her father had died when she was 29. She had no significant work history.

Rosa presented with depression, anxiety, flashbacks of early childhood traumatic events, hypervigilance to external stress and disappointment, inability to modulate affect, insecurity, impulsivity and poor social skills.

Origins of Key Core Beliefs

Mother abandoned Rosa at age 9. Father began to sexually abuse her. Parents fail to meet Rosa's need for protection, trust, and security. → "I'm no good. The world is an unsafe place; people will hurt you, so try to either hurt them first or avoid them. People will not be there to meet my needs."

Family rejection; childhood behavioral problems; did not receive a formal education. → "People will reject me. I have nothing to offer anyone except my body. Life sucks for me, but not for everyone else. The world owes me."

Vicious Cycle/Maintaining Factors

1. A maintenance reinforcement of schematic beliefs that, I'm no good; the world is unfair; I'll always be a miserable and hopeless failure; what's the use in trying new behaviors and planning for the future, existed because of Rosa's unstable living arrangements that fostered moment-to-moment decisions with no ability to make plans and follow through.

2. A maintenance reinforcement of schematic beliefs that *people will be cruel, critical, and rejecting; I have nothing to offer the world except my body; the world is unsafe* occurred when Rose would prostitute or sell illegal drugs.
3. Avoidance reinforcement for all her schematic beliefs occurred through her long history of alcohol and substance abuse. There was no cognitive, emotional, or behavioral information to alter her beliefs.

Treatment Goals

The initial goals for treatment with Rosa were to rehearse appropriate behaviors for the upcoming court case and improve social relationships by learning prosocial skills through relationship with therapist. This goal was subdivided into several smaller goals that included getting to appointments on time, dressing appropriately for official business occasions, and interacting productively with service providers. Barrier to treatment included her antisocial personality style making a therapeutic alliance difficult to establish and maintain, her tendency to externalize blame and responsibility for current plight and pain, her real-life stressors (e.g., HIV+ health status and possible incarceration), which has kept her on a high level of emotional reactivity.

Treatment Outcome

Due to prior arrests, and through the use of motivational interviewing, Rosa agreed to go for drug and alcohol detoxification and rehabilitation and to give daily urine samples for drug screening. Weekly treatment sessions were scheduled provided Rosa's urine screens were clean. The first three sessions were spent working on treatment objectives, expectations, and evaluation. Rosa rehearsed being on time for our sessions. We worked on her monitoring and charting automatic thoughts and cognitive restructuring. We did several desensitization exercises that were presented as coping techniques to be practiced at least three times daily as homework assignments. After the fourth session, we began scripting for her court appearance with the help of her lawyer and doing the homework assignments that centered around rehearsing and testing alternative behaviors in social interactions. She learned to better identify and negotiate resources.

Equipped with better social skills, and improved self-confidence, Rosa connected with a neighborhood activist group that rehabilitated low-income neighborhoods and some abandoned homes. She volunteered to do apprentice work to learn skills that she could later market. Rosa's court hearing is still pending.

SUMMARY

The mechanisms by which psycho-physiological "memories" of fear and arousal that result from childhood traumatic stress disrupt and encode psychic schema make an individual vulnerable to the development of various psychiatric disorders. Research suggests that adult survivors of childhood sexual and physical abuse may develop multiaxial disorders, especially if the severity or duration of the early trauma(s) was extensive and the child did not receive therapeutic interventions at or near the time of the traumatic event(s). Adult survivors may present as chronically depressed (perhaps with suicidal ideations and behaviors) and anxious, socially inept, substance abusing, and personality disordered.

Social work professionals work with trauma survivors in a variety of settings. They are in key roles for providing effective education, treatment, training, and services for adult survivors. Working with this population of adult survivors can be at best challenging and at worst overwhelming. This chapter attempted to equip social workers with an evidence-based treatment framework to effectively enhance their work with this population (i.e., a cognitive behavior model).

CBT-oriented models have at their foundation the identification and challenging of core beliefs related to the self and others. Key techniques used for assessment of readiness for change, motivation, cognitive restructuring, and behavioral coping and performance techniques have been presented. An overall goal treatment is guiding the client in identifying and increasing behavioral alternatives to usually exaggerated behavioral expressions, as well as promoting a stronger capacity to cope with perceived threat or challenges. Cognitive behavior activities can be equally affective for treatment and services with individuals or in a group setting depending on the capacity of the individual to tolerate the dynamics of group work. Social workers should feel free to explore CBT approaches from this point of view.

Given the scope of this topic, much could not be included in a single chapter. Of particular interest would be the impact of treating trauma survivors on social work clinicians and strategies that can be employed to buffer the negative effects, such as identifying special training and supports.

REFERENCES

Anderson, L. E., Weston, E. A., Doueck, H. J., & Krause, D. J. (2002). The child-centered social worker and the sexually abused child: Pathway to healing. *Social Work: Journal of the National Association of Social Workers, 47,* 368–378.

Beck, A. T. (1996). Beyond belief: A theory of modes, personality, and psychopathology. In P. M. Salkovskis (Ed.), *Frontiers of cognitive therapy*. New York: Guilford.

Beutler, L. E., & Hill, C. E. (1992). Process and outcome research in the treatment of adult victims of childhood sexual abuse: Methodological issues. *Journal of Consulting and Clinical Psychology, 60*, 204–212.

Blatt, S. J., Zuroff, D. C., Bondi, C. M., & Sanisolow, C. A. III. (2000). Short- and long-term effects of medication and psychotherapy in the brief treatment of depression: Further analyses of data from NIMH TDCRP. *Psychotherapy Research, 10*, 215–234.

Briere, J. N. (1992). *Child abuse trauma: Theory and treatment of the lasting effects*. Newbury Park, CA: Sage.

Borkovec, T. D., & Costello, E. (1993). Efficacy of applied relaxation and cognitive behavioral therapy in the treatment of generalized anxiety disorder. *Journal of Consulting and Clinical Psychology, 61*, 611–619.

Bowlby, J. (1969). *Attachment and loss: Attachment* (Vol. I). London: Hogarth.

Chambless, D. L., & Ollendick, T. H. (2001). Empirically supported psychological interventions: controversies and evidence. *Annual Reviews of Psychology, 52*, 685–716.

Craske, M. G., Meadows, E., & Barlow, D. H. (1994). *Therapist's guide for the mastery of your anxiety and panic II & agoraphobia supplement*. Albany, NY: Graywind.

Cunningham, M. (2003). Impact of trauma work on social work clinicians: Empirical findings. *Social Work: Journal of the National Association of Social Workers, 48*, 451–459.

Davidson, J. (1992). Drug therapy of posttraumatic stress disorder. *The British Journal of Psychiatry, 4*, 309–314.

Dean, M. A. (2001). *Borderline personality disorder: The latest assessment and treatment strategies*. Kansas City: Compact Clinicals.

Diagnostic and Statistical Manual of Mental Disorders (3rd ed.) (1980). Washington, D.C.: American Psychiatric Press.

D'Zurilla, T. J., & Nezu, A. M. R. (1990). Development and preliminary evaluation of the Social Problem-Solving Inventory. *Psychological Assessment, 2*, 156–163.

Epstein, S. (1991). The self-concept, the traumatic neurosis, and the structure of personality. In R. Hogan (Ed.), *Perspectives in personality* (Vol. 3A, pp. 63–98). London: Jessica Kingsley.

Finkelhor, D., Hotaling, G., Lewis, I. A., & Smith, C. (1990). Sexual abuse in a national survey of adult men and women: Prevalence, characteristics, and risk factors. *Child Abuse and Neglect, 14*, 19–28.

Franklin, M. E., Abramowitz, J. S., Kozak, M. J., Levitt, J. T., & Foa, E. B. (2000). Effectiveness of exposure and ritual prevention for obsessive-compulsive disorder: Randomized compared with nonrandomized samples. *Journal of Consulting and Clinical Psychology, 68*, 594–602.

Friedmann, M. J. (1991). Biological approaches to the diagnosis and treatment of posttraumatic stress disorder. *The Journal of Trauma and Stress, 4*, 67–91.

Hahlweg, K., Fiegenbaum, W., Frank, M., Schroeder, B., & von Witzleben, I. (2001). Short- and long-term effectiveness of an empirically supported treatment for agoraphobia. *Journal of Consulting and Clinical Psychology, 69,* 375–382.

Heim, C., Newport, D. J., Heit, S., Graham, Y. P., Wilcox, M., Bonsall, R., et al. (2000). Pituitary-adrenal and autonomic responses to stress in women after sexual and physical abuse in childhood. *The Journal of the American Medical Association, 284,* 592–599.

Herman, J. L. (1992). *Trauma and recovery.* New York: Basic Books.

LeCroy, C. W., & Stinson, E. L. (2004). The public's perception of social work: Is it what we think it is? *Social Work: Journal of the National Association of Social Workers, 49,* 164–174.

Marlatt, G. A., & Gordon, J. R. (Eds.). (1985). *Relapse prevention: Maintenance strategies in the treatment of addictive behaviors.* New York: Guilford.

Miller, W. R., & Rollnick, S. (1991). Enhancing motivation for change in substance abuse treatment. In W. R. Miller & S. Rollnick (Eds.), *Motivational interviewing; Preparing people to change addictive behavior* (pp. 214–234). New York: Guilford.

Muellen, P. E., Martin, J. L., Anderson, J. C., Romans, S. E., & Herbison, G. P. (1993). Childhood sexual abuse and mental health in adult life. *The British Journal of Psychiatry, 163,* 721–732.

Muellen, P. E., Martin, J. L., Anderson, J. C., Romans, S. E., & Herbison, G. P. (1996). The long-term impact of the physical, emotional, and sexual abuse of children: A community study. *Child Abuse and Neglect, 20,* 7–21.

Organista, K. C., Munoz, R. F., & Gonzalez, G. (1994). Cognitive-behavioral therapy for depression in low income and minority medical outpatients: Description of a program and exploratory analyses. *Cognitive Therapy & Research, 18,* 241–259.

Palmer, S. E., Brown, R. A., Rae-Grant, N. I., & Loughlin M. J. (2001). Survivors of childhood abuse: Their reported experiences with professional help. *Social Work: Journal of the National Association of Social Workers, 46,* 136–145.

Parks, G. A., & Marlatt, G. A. (1999). Relapse prevention therapy for substance-abusing offenders: A cognitive-behavioral approach. In E. Latessa (Ed.), *What works: Strategic solutions: The International Community Corrections Association examines substance abuse.* (pp. 161–233). Lanham, MD: American Correctional Association.

Perry, B. D., Conroy, L., & Ravitz, A. (1991). Persisting psychophysiological effects of traumatic stress: The memory of "states." *Violence Update 1,* 1–11.

Persons, J. B., Bostrom, A., & Bertagnolli, A. (1999). Results of randomized controlled trials of cognitive therapy for depression generalized to private practice. *Cognitive Therapy & Research, 23,* 535–548.

Prochaska, J. O., DiClemente, C. C., & Norcross, J. C. (1992). In search of how people change: Applications to addictive behaviors. *American Psychologist, 47,* 1102–1114.

Shapario, F. (2001). *Eye movement desensitization and reprocessing: Basic, protocols, and procedures* (2nd ed.). New York: Guilford.

Sosin, M., & Caulum, S. (1989). Advocacy: A conceptualization for social work practice. In B. R. Compton & B. Galaway (Eds.), *Social work process*. Belmont, CA: Wadsworth.

Stuart, G. L., Treat, T. A., & Wade, W. A. (2000). Effectiveness of an empirically based treatment for panic disorder delivered in a service clinic setting: 1-year follow-up. *Journal of Consulting and Clinical Psychology, 68*, 506–512.

Telch, M. J., Schmidt, N. B., Jaimez, L., Jacquin, K. M., & Harrington, P. J. (1995). Impact of cognitive-behavioral treatment on quality of life in panic disorder patients. *Journal of Consulting and Clinical Psychology, 63*, 823–830.

Tuschen-Caffier, B., Pook, M., & Frank, M. (2001). Evaluation of manual-based cognitive-behavioral therapy for bulimia nervosa in a service setting. *Behavioral Research and Therapy, 39*, 299–308.

Valentine, L., & Feinauer, L. L. (1993). Resilience factors associated with female survivors of childhood sexual abuse. *American Journal of Family Therapy, 21*, 216–224.

van der Kolk, B., van der Hart, O., & Burbridge, J. (1995). Approaches to the treatment of PTSD. In S. Hobfoll & M. de Vries (Eds.), *Extreme stress and communities: Impact and intervention*. Norwell, MA: Kluwer Academic.

Vandiver, V. L. (2002). Step-by-step practice guidelines for using evidence-based practice and expert consensus in mental health settings. In A. R. Roberts & G. J. Greene (Eds.), *Social workers desk reference* (pp. 731–738). New York: Oxford University Press.

Wade, W. A., Treat, T. A., & Stuart, G. L. (1998). Transporting an empirically supported treatment for panic disorder to a service clinic setting: A benchmarking strategy. *Journal of Consulting and Clinical Psychology, 66*, 231–239.

Young, J. E. (1990). *Cognitive therapy for personality disorders: A schema-focused approach*. Sarasota, FL: Professional Resource Press.

CHAPTER 22

Substance Misuse

An Issue of Degree, Assessment, and Empathy

Sharon Morgillo Freeman
Donald Osborn

INTRODUCTION

Substance misuse, across many different patient populations, has become a prevalent treatment issue in contemporary social work practice. For some individuals, misuse can permeate all aspects of the individual's life, to the point of substance dependency. For others, the substance misuse may bring death or near-death experiences through excessive use, toxicity, or a drug overdose. Despite these dangers, individuals continue to misuse substances. Others readily admit substance misuse is a problem in and of itself, or that it contributes significantly to other problems in their lives. Yet still others come to therapy as a referral (or demand) from a family member or the court system. For all of these patients, the issue of substance misuse has manifested itself in difficult and possibly painful life problems. These patients may be tired of the repeating cycle and come to the realization that their substance use can no longer continue because of the pervasive and negative consequences to themselves and their significant others. They come to the social worker's office under pressure, seeking help, desperate for relief, peace, and direction on how to manage their lives in a more adaptive manner.

Other types of patients may seek therapy for issues other than their primary substance misuse or abuse. They choose to not disclose their substance misuse history, or view their misuse as a minor concern and/or downplay the impact of substance misuse in their lives. In fact some may see substance misuse in a positive light, in that the effect of the substance, in their view, helps them to cope with life. With this patient, social workers may find they may be something of a detective. The social worker knows that "something" is not right in the patient's "story" and begins to search for clues and to test out various explanatory hypotheses. For example, the clinician may find that the presenting problem for a couple, such as difficulty communicating in their marriage, is a direct result of substance on the part of either or both of the partners. As therapy progresses, it becomes clear that the secret of substance use is like the secret of an extra marital affair. Use of the substance becomes a priority in the user's life. As a result, the spouse experiences issues of abandonment, betrayal, deceit resulting in a relationship that is suffering from a lack of honesty, stability, and fidelity.

Another type of client common to many treatment settings is the adolescent with substance problems and a coexisting self-esteem disorder. After some investigation, it is not uncommon for the social worker to discover that the adolescent's behavior changes dramatically over a short period of time, such as a weekend. Use of a substance, such as alcohol, disinhibits the shy adolescent and allows the adolescent to behave in a more outgoing manner in order to feel accepted by peers. Soon the adolescent realizes this combination (alcohol and social interactions) helps him feel more self-assured and outgoing. The seduction to continue substance use becomes complete when the adolescent perceives that he is acceptable only when with friends and alcohol to the neglect of family, healthy activities, and schoolwork.

Finally, the difficulties commonly encountered confusing substance misuse and personality disorders will be discussed in detail highlighting differentiation, recognition of common patterns, and an overview of behavioral manifestations and treatment.

This chapter begins with a general overview of substance-related disorders and the diagnostic criteria. This is followed with a discussion of CBT techniques for treating this population as well as a review of the neurophysiologic basis of addiction and reward pathways. We examine the impact of substance use and misuse on the patient, the family, and social worker in the therapeutic process. Assessment of substance misuse and differentiation of co-occurring disorders will be targeted as they relate to social work practice, including comparisons of behavioral manifestations of substance dependence versus personality disorder or brain impairment. Finally, recommendations are made regarding future directions in therapy and research.

SUBSTANCE MISUSE DISORDERS

Social workers see firsthand the impact substance misuse has on the lives of their patients, as well as others in the patient's life. Some consequences are more obvious, such as a change in physical appearance. Other consequences are related to family members when substance misuse impacts the individual's relationship and emotional responses within the family, peer relationships, school and work, or relationship to institutions such as churches, clubs, and other social groups. Substance use can complicate the therapeutic process and ultimately test the skill, training, and professional competency of the social worker. Ultimately, the use of substances to the point of misuse, abuse, and dependence negatively impacts the overall quality of that person's life.

Substance misuse does not automatically equate with pathology, crisis, or damage to the family system or person. It does however represent a powerful signal that indicates potential underlying problems, actual severe problems, or the root-cause of a person's presenting pathology. Accurate identification, management, and referral of these patients are critical to provide appropriate care, avoid unnecessary delays, avoid the cost of loss of work time, and social or psychiatric sequelae. Despite the stigma and discrimination often applied to persons who misuse substances, the disease of addiction boasts higher rates of remission than other behavior-related medical disorders such as diabetes, heart disease, and obesity (Kahan, Wilson, & Becker, 1995; SAMHSA, 2003). The use of substances to alter one's mood is as old as human existence. In some cases substance use remains in the realm of the mysterious, the stigmatized, and taboo akin to other disorders treated historically by shunning and secluding the afflicted (e.g., leprosy). It is puzzling and sad that society has failed to progress any further in sophistication for treating behavior-related medical problems such as this, but the reality is that as an international society we remain aloof when it comes to substance misuse and its treatment.

Comorbid psychiatric and medical conditions can make identification of substance misuse disorders or addiction difficult. Once substance misuse, addiction, or dependency has been identified, the clinician must decide whether to confront and treat the individual or to refer the individual to a substance abuse specialist. The choice of treatment options should be based on clinical criteria, patient motivation for change, ability to change, and environmental variables. The social worker should be familiar with general assessment guidelines for substance misuse spectrum disorders with and without confounding comorbid conditions such as medical and psychiatric problems.

These patients often present with multiple family, social, and occupational problems in addition to a possible substance misuse problem (National Institutes on Alcohol Abuse and Alcoholism, 1993). Often the signs and symptoms of alcohol or benzodiazepine withdrawal have often been mistaken for anxiety disorders or stimulant misuse. Other causes of anxiety can include agitated depression, caffeinism, or sleep disturbances, which the clinician needs to rule out before diagnosing or treating a person as a substance misuser (Ahmed & Koob, 1998; Freeman, 2004; Koob & Le Moal, 1997; Wells, 1997). Many patients with personality disorders, brain injury, and possibly mental retardation in addition to the use of substances often appear to manifest drug-seeking behaviors; however, the manifested behaviors are expected adaptations as opposed to unhealthy substance misuse driven behaviors (Freeman, 2004a).

Mood-altering substances are generally chosen based on three criteria: ease of access, rapid onset of action, and activation of the brain reward system (Koob & Bloom, 1988; Koob et al., 1997; O'Brien, 2001). We perceive this release of dopamine as a "rush" and of a sense of well-being that is highly rewarding, and therefore reinforcing (Portenoy & Payne, 1992). The therapist must remember that the process of chasing the rush of a drug alone does not in and of itself warrant the diagnosis of a substance abuse, only the misuse of the substance. The following sections discuss the biological-psychological-social components that must be in place for a substance disorder to be diagnosed.

SCREENING INSTRUMENTS

There are a number of brief screening instruments for chemical addictions with little evidence that any one is better than another. The most frequently used instruments include the following five:

1. The Alcohol Use Disorders Identification Test (AUDIT) (Babor, de la Fuente, Saunders, & Grant, 1992) takes about 2 minutes and provides the patient with immediate feedback on their drinking behaviors.
2. The four question CAGE questionnaire is the easiest and often used in emergency care settings because it is simple to remember. The four questions begin with the letters in the word CAGE: (1) have you tried to CUT down on your use?, (2) have you been ANNOYED by

someone telling you that you drink/use too much?, (3) Have you felt
GUILTY regarding your use?, and (4) have you needed an EYE-
OPENER to get rid of withdrawal symptoms in the morning? (This
last question is rarely voiced exactly stated this way. The idea is to
find out if the individual uses the substance to allay the discomfort of
withdrawal symptoms.)

3. The Michigan Alcoholism Screening Test (MAST) (Selzer, 1971) is a
   24-question test that requires a yes or no response to each question.
   The individual amassing five or more points would be placed in the
   alcoholic category. There is also a short version, the SMAST, comprised of 13 questions, and a geriatric version, the MAST-G.
4. The Drug Abuse Screening Test (DAST) is an adaptation of the
   MAST for drug use as opposed to alcohol use.
5. Finally there is the TWEAK questionnaire which includes the assessment questions for Tolerance, Worried about use, Eyeopener, Amnesia and K (for C) cutting down on use.

SUBSTANCE WITHDRAWAL

Withdrawal is a neuroadaptative, not pathological, process that is the result of the adaptation of the body's nervous system to repeated stimulation by a chemical (O'Brien, 2001). Withdrawal therefore is only one
of many symptoms that signals the social worker that a person's body
has adapted to long-term ingestion of certain categories of chemicals.
(See Figure 22.1) Taking a stimulant for a long period of time causes the
user to become used to the effects. Once the person stops using the stimulant his or her body will react with symptoms that are uncomfortable
such as tiredness, headache, and irritability. This response is diagnosed as
substance withdrawal. The greater the quantity and frequency of the sub-
stance(s) used determines the severity of tolerance, and therefore intensity
of withdrawal. Medical complications of withdrawal may include feeling
severely ill, and at worst, seizures, stroke, and even death. The practitioner can gauge the onset of withdrawal symptoms if the time of last use
is known. In addition, obtaining the person's experience and history of
previous withdrawal experiences can assist the therapist to prepare for
medical complications and possibly transport to emergency services.

Medical Considerations

Not all patients who misuse substances who wish to discontinue the drug
use will require 24-hour medically monitored detoxification procedures.

Opiates: Withdrawal from the use of heroin and other opiates is of gradual onset, and while not life-threatening, can cause the patient significant
discomfort and distress. Opiate withdrawal typically begins within 4 to 8
hours after last use, peaks at 35 to 72 hours, and subsides in 7 to 10 days,
depending on the class of substance and patient health status (Jaffe, 1997)

Alcohol: The first sign of alcohol withdrawal, tremors, generally begins
within a few hours after the last drink. Hallucinations, if they occur,
indicate severe withdrawal syndrome and are referred to as Delirium
Tremens or DTs. Delirium tremens are relatively rare and usually begin
between 24 and 48 hours after last drink. The most serious complication
of alcohol withdrawal, grand mal seizures, may occur as long as 3 days
after the last drink (Goodwin, 1997).

Benzodiazepines/Barbiturates: Sedative hypnotic withdrawal signs are
parallel to alcohol withdrawal; however, time of onset is highly variable
due to the half-lives of the various drugs. For example, the short-acting
barbiturates including pentobarbital, secobarbital, meprobromate and
methaqualone symptoms begin approximately 12 to 24 hours after last
dose. The longer acting drugs such as phenobarbital, diazepam and chlor-
diazepoxide may not peak until the fifth or seventh day, which is one of
the characteristics that make these longer acting substances attractive for
medical detoxification protocols (Wession, Smith, & Seymour, 1997).

Hallucinogens: There is no known physiologic withdrawal pattern from
any of the classes of hallucinogens, however, there are reports of persistent
personality changes as a result of chronic use (Ungerleider & Pechnick,
1997). Hallucinogens such as lysergic acid diethylamide (LSD) have an
adverse reaction pattern that includes hallucinogenic "flashbacks" occurring weeks or months after ingestion. The flashbacks are unpredictable
and sometimes include paranoia and depression placing the person at risk
for self-harm (Ungerleider & Pechnick, 1997).

Amphetamine and Methamphetamine: Withdrawal from stimulants begins
with extreme fatigue, depression, and anhedonia. This phase is often
referred to as the "crash" phase and the intensity depends on the drug
used and the chronicity of use. The symptoms increase in intensity for 12

FIGURE 22.1   Withdrawal Symptoms

to 96 hours post last ingestion followed by extremely intense drug craving that makes the person vulnerable to relapse (King & Ellinwood, 1997). Substances such as cocaine, for example, are highly associated with suicidal behaviors in the crash phase requiring close monitoring to prevent completion. Most insurance companies do not cover inpatient hospitalization for cocaine and other amphetamine withdrawal due to the lack of physiologic measures of the withdrawal syndrome. This author recommends evaluation for preventative psychiatric admissions for suicidal ideation if the patient is determined to have a plan and intent with substance rehabilitation therapy following the worst of the craving cycle.

Inhalants: Inhalants include a variety of substances. This includes a number of substances that (a) vaporize, and (b) create a "lightheaded" effect. The most commonly used substances are glue, paint, hair spray, deodorant, thinners, solvents, correction fluid, cleaning fluid, refrigerant gases, whipped cream propellants (whippets), lighter fluid, and gasoline. The resultant behavior appears similar to alcohol intoxication and occurs rapidly after use, without the odor of beverage alcohol, making it more difficult to detect in an individual. Very few chronic inhalant abusers benefit from drug treatment programs due to the severity of brain injury as a result of their use (Sharp & Rosenberg, 1997). There is no known withdrawal syndrome; however, permanent neurological disorders are not uncommon (Sharp & Rosenberg, 1997).

Marijuana: Marijuana is another substance with no known withdrawal syndrome and no apparent tolerance development. Users report obsession with obtaining the next dose and difficulty discontinuing the drug for any period of time suggesting a dependency syndrome. The major long-term effect of chronic marijuana use is known as "amotivational syndrome," which manifests as a disinterest in performing any of the major life tasks such as work or family development. This syndrome has been argued to develop from the social aspects of being preoccupied with the substance as opposed to the substance itself, but neither hypothesis has been proven to any great degree.

Source: Reprinted with permission from Freeman, S. M. (2005).

FIGURE 22.1   Withdrawal Symptoms (Continued)

For patients who have serious or even fatal withdrawal potential, it is important to evaluate the patient and/or refer to the most appropriate setting in which to conduct the detoxification process. Detoxification alone is only the initiation of readiness for treatment, not the actual treatment for the disease (Freeman, 2005).

Detoxification eliminates the active chemical from the brain, however, the brain has sustained long-term changes and is now hypersensitive to cues (triggers) or reminders of the substances as well as stimuli in general. In order to account for the long-term brain and behavior changes, the clinician must plan a well-designed, highly structured, and proactively scheduled follow-up treatment protocol following detoxification. General guidelines dictate that the social worker begins by educating the patient on current treatment procedures that are well established as safe and effective. The social worker, as a primary care provider, may need to be the central person in the treatment protocol: organizing, coordinating, information collecting, and information sharing.

SUBSTANCE MISUSE AND CHRONIC PAIN

Long-term unremitting pain conditions, or chronic pain, affect huge numbers of persons worldwide. In the United States approximately 86 million people are affected with chronic pain conditions that impact their basic levels of functioning. In addition these conditions result in lost time from work, decreased productivity, inability to enjoy recreational activities, increased utilization of medical services and financial effects in the amount of an estimated $90 billion annual losses (American Chronic Pain Association [ACPA], 2003). One factor regarding motivation for misuse lies in the effect of a drug on the brain's reward system. Opioid receptors are involved in the pathways responsible for pain relief, pain processing, and euphoria. This confusing system makes it difficult to differentiate between someone who has developed the expected responses of tolerance and withdrawal phenomena to opiate pain relievers and requires higher doses for relief.

SUBSTANCE MISUSE AND PERSONALITY DISORDERS

People who misuse substances can be challenging, frustrating, sabotaging and even annoying to others due to their behaviors and thinking patterns. Substance misusing behaviors are often mistaken for severe personality disorders given the parallels in presentation. Both disorders usually begin in early to mid-teenage years and include the defense mechanism commonly referred to as "other-blaming." Substance misusing persons tend to develop strongly held, minimally adaptive and highly inflexible coping mechanisms in order to protect their self-esteem, avoid addressing harmful behaviors, and to protect their substance use to avoid experiencing the pain and discomfort of withdrawal (Freeman, 2005). It is usually these mechanisms that are activated when the topic of their substance misuse is brought up by the social worker, family member, or employer. Therefore, the diagnosis of an Axis II disorder risks the strong possibility that attributing an enduring pattern of behaviors is being made on temporary behaviors that will probably extinguish upon discontinuation of substance use and with therapy. It is important to remember that behavioral changes due to long-term substance misuse take at least 1 year to begin significant reversal. It is therefore generally considered inappropriate to diagnose a person with an Axis II disorder either within the first year of nonsubstance use, or during active use.

The following list outlines those parallel presentations that often confuse the diagnostic picture with persons abusing substances and persons with personality disorders (Freeman, 2005):

1. There is often support system exhaustion (family, employment, financial, social).
2. Among the primary reactions and defenses are "other-blaming."
3. The changes in behavior can usually be traced to early to mid-teens.
4. Both disorders tend to progress over time as behaviors and drug use escalates.
5. There is often exacerbation and remissions with frequent crises.
6. There are often many apparently manipulative interactions.
7. Both disorders are at risk for affective disorders and exhausted support systems.
8. There is inadequate/limited/poor problem-solving skills.
9. There are multiple failure experiences in all aspects of life, and with substance use there is the additional neurobiological changes precipitated by the drug itself (Freeman, 2005).

Once these behaviors have been identified, a careful assessment of each area is important to determine the psychodynamic and biological basis of the presentation for accurate diagnosis. In many cases only one of the two disorders is present; however, there are many cases as well where the disorders co-occur. In order to differentiate, it is important to conduct an evaluation that is significantly different from the evaluation for other DSM-IV/ICD-10 disorders such as affective disorders, or psychotic disorders.

Some basic recommendations regarding substance misusing persons include:

1. Do not rely on the patient to self-report for information. This information is likely skewed, protected, and limited despite a presentation of cooperation.
2. Obtain collateral information from all sources connected with the patient. This author recommends not only family, friends, medical practitioners, and previous social workers, but the patient's pharmacy as well.
3. Undertake time line follow back (Sobell & Sobell, 1998). This technique allows the patient to identify her own use progression of substance use as well as behavioral escalation in a nonthreatening collaborative manner.
4. Refer the person for a thorough history and physical evaluation to rule out physical causes of his symptoms.
5. Many persons who misuse substances have suffered head trauma, may have mild mental retardation problem, or a history of learning disabilities that was never diagnosed. These problems may offer a neurological explanation for the maladaptive presentation (Freeman, 2005).

COGNITIVE AND BEHAVIOR TREATMENT OPTIONS

Modified Stages of Change Model

For almost two decades one model of change has stood as the standard bearer in conceptualizing the stages of change in therapy. Prochaska and DiClemente (1986) developed a simple and useful model for understanding the stages of change (SOC) that patients progress through in the therapeutic process. According to Freeman and Dolan (2002) the five-step SOC model widely accepted in substance misuse treatment settings lacks the specificity that is an essential part of the cognitive behavior treatment model. The basic model includes the stages of *precontemplation, contemplation, preparation, action,* and *maintenance* stages. The basic model was revised by Freeman et al. (2002) and expands upon the original by addressing five additional components of *noncontemplation, anticontemplation,* precontemplation, contemplation, *action planning* (as opposed to Preparation), *action, lapse activation and redirection, relapse and redirection, termination,* and maintenance. This expansion and specification from a five-stage model to a ten-stage model allows for the treatment planning specificity that is the hallmark of CBT (Freeman et al.,

2002). The revised model of change (see Table 22.1) allows for increased precision in assessing a patient's level of motivation. The additional stages reflect the experiences of patients and the clinician both in and out of the therapeutic process.

MOTIVATION FOR CHANGE IN AN INPATIENT TREATMENT SETTING

Given the importance of identifying motivation for change in a population that consists of persons who are in treatment settings reluctantly, involuntarily (under coercive pressure) or may change their mind on an hour by hour basis, Freeman (2005) determined it necessary to create an objective list of behaviors that would be easily understood by both patient and health care worker. Behaviors were categorized in a manner that roughly corresponded to the SOC model as described by Prochaska and DiClemente (1998). The list of behaviors was then grouped and categorized in five sets of 20-point scales in a fashion resembling the Global Assessment of Function (GAF) in the *DSM-IV-TR* (American Psychiatric Association [APA], 2000). Most staff on inpatient treatment units are familiar with the use of 10-point scale systems to identify levels of severity. For example, the most commonly used 10-point severity scale is the patient pain scale used by many hospitals to ask a patient to rate his or her level of pain on a scale from 0 to 10 with 10 being the worst pain imaginable. The Motivation Scale is used by the clinician to rate a patient's motivation for change on a scale from 0 to 100, with 100 being the highest level (Freeman, 2005). The use of "loss of control" as a frame of reference was suggested and added to the scale descriptions in order to provide additional weight to the choice of level. For example, scores ranging from 0 to 20 include those patients who demonstrate and verbalize a desire to retain 100 percent of control over all issues, decisions, and treatment planning. This person has entered treatment voluntarily, however, once he is on the unit, refuses to participate or even attend meetings or lectures, is defensive or even verbally violent when asked questions, discusses cravings overtly and with great pleasure, and often refuses to discuss or participate in aftercare planning with his team (Freeman, 2005). This patient would most likely meet the criteria for noncontemplation, or even anticontemplation despite the fact he is currently a patient on an inpatient treatment unit.

The remaining groupings correlate with the stage of change and the level of control the person is demonstrating. Table 22.2 shows the Freeman Inpatient Motivation Scale (Freeman, 2005).

TABLE 22.1 Substance Use Intoxication and Withdrawal Symptoms

Symptom	Alcohol	Amphetamine	Cocaine	Cannabis	Hallucinogen	Opiates	Sedative/Anxiolytic	Inhalants	MDMA/Ecstasy
Hypertension	WD	I	I	–	I		WD		I
Tachycardia	WD	I	I	I	I	WD	WD		I
Bradycardia						I		I	
Rapid respirations	WD	I	I		I	WD	WD		
Hallucinations	WD	I	I	I	I		WD	–	I
Delusions	WD	I	I	I	I		WD	–	I
Hyperphagia			I	I					I
Nystagmus	WD				WD (PCP)		WD		
Piloerection					I		WD		
Ataxia	WD			I		I			
Chills/diaphoresis	WD					WD			
Papillary dialation		I	I			WD			
Rhinnorhea and lacrimation						WD			
Severe cravings	WD		WD			WD	WD		
Panic/anxiety	WD	I	I	I		WD	WD		
Coarse tremors	WD		I		I	WD	WD	WD	

Symptom							
Seizures	WD	I				WD	
Body aches	I	WD				WD	WD
Abdominal cramps						WD	WD
Confusion/agitation	WD	I	I	I		WD	WD
Dysphoria	WD	WD	I		WD	WD	WD
Paranoia	I	I	I			WD	
Somnolence	WD	WD				WD	WD
Hyperreflexia	WD	I		I		WD	WD
Hyperpyrexia	WD	I	I			WD	WD
Intense dreams/nightmares	WD	WD				WD	WD
Insomnia	WD	WD	WD		WD	WD	WD
Memory disturbance	WD	I	I			WD	
Diarrhea	WD		I			WD	
Parasthesias	WD				WD	WD	
Yawning						WD	
Death	WD	I	I		I	WD	I

Note: WD = withdrawal; I = Intoxication/overdose

Source: Adapted with permission from Freeman, S. M. (2005). Substance misuse disorders in A. Freeman & S. M. Freeman (Eds.), *Cognitive Behavior Therapy in Nursing Practice.* (pp. 113–144). New York: Springer.

TABLE 22.2   Freeman Inpatient Motivation Scale

Motivation: "A state of being that produces a tendency toward action." Step one states "We admitted we were powerless" and "that our lives have become unmanageable." It is with these concepts in mind that motivation for treatment should be evaluated.

This classification system is intended for use in inpatient substance use treatment settings. It has not been evaluated for applicability to other settings.

Directions for Coding: The process for coding is similar to the GAF scale in *DSM-IV*. Individuals should meet at least three items in the category to qualify for that range.

Score 0–20
Voices disinterest in treatment or is in treatment by "forced choice."
Does not participate in group, recovery support meetings.
Exhibits defensive responses to inquiries or questions.
Voices overt references to cravings with intent to use and/or continue use.
Refuses to develop aftercare/continuing care plans.

Score 21–40
Participates minimally in groups and therapy, and/or arrives chronically late.
Is vague or argumentative in response to questions/suggestions.
Makes references to substance use that is euphoric in content.
Voices doubt and/or reluctance about abstinence.
Verbalizes the correct/expected responses but the content is superficial
    (e.g., Talking the talk but not walking the walk).

Score 41–60
Participates in group discussions but talks about peers as opposed to self.
Is adamant about doing things their own way.
Verbalizes statements that imply uniqueness rather than similarities with others.
Cannot verbalize specific plans for abstinence.
Has not developed a "one day at a time" mind-set or philosophy.
Minimizes seriousness of recovery/relapse planning.

Score 61–80
Participates actively in treatment, but avoids "pain-laden" topics.
Expresses a "one day at a time" mind-set.
Is reluctant in compliance to treatment and aftercare plan.
Does not have a specific plan to integrate self-help support groups
    (AA/NA/SMART, etc.).
Voices understanding and acceptance of seriousness of recovery plan and
    abstinence.
Participates actively in treatment, discusses embarrassing or shame-based issues.

TABLE 22.2   Freeman Inpatient Motivation Scale (Continued)

Score 81–100

Confronts peers' denial and rationalizations appropriately.

Has a specific, appropriate aftercare plan that has been developed with treatment team members.

Readily agrees to suggestions made by treatment team and a willingness "to do whatever it takes" attitude.

Has begun to explore potential sponsor candidates or has contacted previous, current sponsor.

Impediments to Change

Noncompliance, denial, and manipulative behaviors are almost watchwords in substance misuse literature. These and other equally derogatory attributions are used by health care professionals to explain lack of progress in treatment, early termination from treatment or disagreements with the social worker, or treatment recommendations. Placing responsibility for lack of progress in treatment on the shoulders of the patient is not only overly simplistic; it may in fact be blatantly incorrect. Instead of throwing failure to progress in treatment into the noncompliance bucket, it may be much more useful to evaluate impediments to change that are deterring the patient from forward movement in his or her desire to attain and maintain sobriety. That means evaluating the social worker, the environment, and the system as well as the patient.

The Freeman Impediments to Change Scale—Substance Use (FICS-SU) details various factors that contribute to problems encountered in therapy (Freeman & McCloskey, 2004; Freeman, 2005) (see Figure 22.2). The scale is divided into four main factors with 10 to 11 subfactors related to each item listed. The four main areas of impediments are (1) Patient factors, (2) Practitioner/Therapist factors, (3), Environmental factors and (4) Pathology factors (Freeman, 2005). Lack of patient skill to control substance use or comply with therapeutic regimen and expectations is listed as one of the patient factors. The scale allows for evaluation of impediments in an objective, nonjudgmental and targeted fashion (Freeman et al., 2004; Freeman, 2005). Once the impediment(s) have been objectively identified it is then a matter of developing a treatment plan incorporating or targeting these processes in the treatment. If an environmental factor is an inefficient or limited support network, this factor will continue to exert negative pressure on the progress until the clinician and patient evaluate this problem, develop goals, and reduce the impact (Freeman, 2005).

Instructions: For each of the following impediments, identify the contribution of that issue to the problems being encountered in therapy. It will be essential for the therapist to review all the areas with the patient.

0 = no importance; 1 = some importance; 2 = moderate importance; 3 = great importance; 4 = major importance

Patient Factors	
1. Skill deficit regarding techniques to control substance use and/or comply with therapeutic regimen/expectations	0 1 2 3 4
2. Negative cognitions regarding previous treatment experience or abstinence failure(s)	0 1 2 3 4
3. Negative cognitions regarding the consequences to others about altering substance use	0 1 2 3 4
4. Experiences secondary gain from disease symptoms	0 1 2 3 4
5. Experiences significant primary gain from substance use	0 1 2 3 4
6. Fear of changing one's actions, thoughts, feelings	0 1 2 3 4
7. Motivation to discontinue substance use has not reached contemplative stage	0 1 2 3 4
8. General negative mind set regarding ability to control use or stop use	0 1 2 3 4
9. Limited or restricted self-monitoring/monitoring of others	0 1 2 3 4
10. Frustrated with lack of treatment progress over time/or perceived stigma of being in therapy	0 1 2 3 4
11. Insufficient personal resources (physical, cognitive, or intellectual) to control substance use	0 1 2 3 4
Practitioner/Therapist Factors	
1. Insufficient therapist skill/experience with substance use	0 1 2 3 4
2. Patient and practitioner distortions are congruent	0 1 2 3 4
3. Limited or insufficient socialization of patient to treatment generally and to specific treatment model	0 1 2 3 4
4. Incomplete or absent collaboration and working alliance	0 1 2 3 4

FIGURE 22.2   Freeman Impediments to Change Scale—Substance Use

Practitioner/Therapist Factors (Continued)					
5. Insufficient or inadequate data regarding patient's history	0	1	2	3	4
6. Therapeutic narcissism	0	1	2	3	4
7. Timing of intervention was not aligned with patient and/or did not match motivation level	0	1	2	3	4
8. Therapy goals are unstated, unrealistic, or vague: There is misalignment of patient goals with therapy goals	0	1	2	3	4
9. Evaluation of developmental process does not take temporal factor of substance abuse into account or is overestimated	0	1	2	3	4
10. Generalized negative beliefs (discriminatory) about substance use or unrealistic expectations of patient	0	1	2	3	4
11. Insufficient flexibility and creativity in treatment planning	0	1	2	3	4
Environmental Factors					
1. Environmental stressors preclude changing	0	1	2	3	4
2. Significant others actively or passively sabotage therapy	0	1	2	3	4
3. Agency reinforcement of pathology and illness via compensation or benefits	0	1	2	3	4
4. Cultural or family issues regarding seeking help	0	1	2	3	4
5. Significant family pathology and/or active substance use in the home	0	1	2	3	4
6. Demands made by family members or significant others directly conflict with the therapeutic plans or activities	0	1	2	3	4
7. Unrealistic or conflicting demands on patient by institutions or other external source	0	1	2	3	4
8. Financial factors limit change (inability to access care)	0	1	2	3	4
9. System homeostasis	0	1	2	3	4
10. Inadequate or limited support network	0	1	2	3	4
					(continues)

FIGURE 22.2   Freeman Impediments to Change Scale—Substance Use (Continued)

Pathology Factors					
1. Patient flexibility severely restricted resulting in movement constraints in treatment compliance	0	1	2	3	4
2. Significant medical/physiological problems	0	1	2	3	4
3. Difficulty in establishing trust	0	1	2	3	4
4. Autonomy press	0	1	2	3	4
5. Severe impulsive response pattern independent of substance use	0	1	2	3	4
6. Confusion, dementia, or limited cognitive ability	0	1	2	3	4
7. Symptom profusion	0	1	2	3	4
8. Dependence upon external controls	0	1	2	3	4
9. Severe self-devaluation	0	1	2	3	4
10. Severely compromised energy	0	1	2	3	4

FIGURE 22.2   Freeman Impediments to Change Scale—Substance Use (Continued)

CBT AND SUBSTANCE-RELATED DISORDERS

Once therapy has begun and it is clear that the primary disorder is substance related, additional techniques may be employed that are similar to those used with personality disorders. The clinician must remember that due to disruption of normal brain chemistry, these patients may be unable to grasp abstract concepts early in recovery and respond much better to concrete, clear, and concise direction (Freeman, 2005). Goals, including homework assignments, must be concrete, easy to measure and remember and execute. In therapy sessions the clinician must set firm, kind, and clear boundaries that are strictly adhered to in order to avoid circular discussions and debates with the patient. Some of the techniques recommended by Freeman (2005) are:

1. *Avoid history reviews after initial assessment is completed.* Storytelling is not only nonproductive; it is a waste of time. The stories will only reconfirm what is already known and therefore the clinician must redirect back to the agenda of the session.
2. *Avoid focusing on the crisis of the day.* Many patients will often start the session with the most recent argument with a spouse or

employer, financial crisis, and so on. It is again imperative to redirect the patient to the current agenda and discourage the use of the session for general problem "dumping." This guideline does not apply of course to those stories that indicate immediate or impending harm to the patient or others.

3. *Evaluate individual motivation for change.* Do so using the revised SOC model (Freeman et al., 2002).

4. *Focus on behavioral demonstration of motivation as opposed to the patient verbalizing motivation.* If the patient is saying "I really want to beat this thing, I am really going to work hard," the patient needs to be evaluated for what he or she is actually doing to demonstrate this motivation. For example, attendance at 12-step meetings or homework, follow through, and clean drug screens.

5. *Set firm limits, boundaries.* Even small "revisions" of limits by clinician of patient can send the message that "slips" are OK.

6. *Coordinate care planning with other professionals throughout therapeutic relationship.* It is imperative that all professionals treating the patient stay in contact on a regular basis. It is usually up to the social worker to be the initiator of communication and the coordinator of information.

In addition to these above recommended interventions, Freeman (2005) recommends the following interventions for working with substance misusing patient in general:

1. There must be a high degree of structure for both homework, and each session.

2. Limit expectations for patient-generated problem solving until it has been assessed that problem-solving techniques are in place and active.

3. Use a concrete approach with avoidance of any abstract conceptual expectations

4. Remember that the choice of primary substance will likely point to the schematic structure underlying the substance misusing personality developments.

5. Integrate the information provided by the schema uncovered in therapy when planning outcomes related to use of substances as the schema will likely activate craving to use the drug.

6. Identify external sources that may reinforce the person's use of substances.

7. Set goals to disempower the above sources.

8. Identify those areas of support that increase likelihood of abstinence.

9. Refuse to participate in storytelling by the patient, especially story content that includes euphoric recall of substance ingestion.
10. Keep therapeutic goals proximal, realistic, directive, and patient driven.
11. Include an education component to therapy without sermonizing or preaching.
12. Assist the patient in identifying those automatic thoughts (ATs) that trigger, activate, or fuel craving responses.
13. Overemphasize the use of self-instruction techniques (especially the 12-step slogans such as "one day at a time").
14. Identify areas of vulnerability and develop specific plans of deflection (people, places, things).
15. Remain cognizant of both positive and negative transference.

CASE STUDY

Identifying Information

"Raul" is a 48-year-old Hispanic male. He is currently in the sixth year of an eight-year sentence for operating a motor vehicle while intoxicated by alcohol, resulting in death and bodily injury to a pedestrian. He states that his drinking went "out of control" when his daughter died of a gunshot at age 11, almost 24 years ago. Client also presents with use of marijuana and cocaine.

Background

Raul began to drink at age 12. His first intoxication was at age 13. Marijuana use started at age 16, and cocaine use started at age 22. Due to death of his daughter, he reports that he has had serious periods of depression. During these depressive episodes he will use alcohol as first drug of choice. He is now nearing the end of his incarceration and has voluntarily come to treatment. He is due to be released in approximately 24 months.

Current Situation

This interview took place 3 days after formal admission to the treatment program in a federal prison system in the United States. His stated goal for treatment was to help him lead a drug-free lifestyle after his release from prison and develop emotional stability.

Substance Use History

Raul reported that his daughter died at age 11 due to being struck in the head by a bullet. She was waiting for the school bus when gang-related violence broke out. Raul stated that his daughter died in his arms. He has blamed himself for her death as he was going to drive her to school. Subsequently, he increased his alcohol intake during depressive episodes, holidays, his daughter's birthday, and the anniversary of her death.

His alcohol intake was one case of beer a day. During this time he would also smoke marijuana and snort cocaine. He was not able to recall the amount, frequency, or duration of his substance misuse history. He does acknowledge periods of blackouts (loss of memory) and being "buzzed out" for 1 or 2 days at a time. It was during this time that he committed crimes due, he said, to depression on the third anniversary of his daughter's death. Raul states he never had any previous treatment for substance-related problems or depression.

Psychiatric History

By self-report and a review of the facility record, he has never been referred to or sought treatment. He stated, "While here in prison I try to keep myself wrapped up (private). I especially don't want any shrinks crawling in my head or taking any of their psycho drugs." When asked why he is seeking treatment he states, "While here I've done a lot of thinking. I have even started to get religious. I need help so I don't do anything stupid to come back." Raul admits he wants to be drug-free but still thinks about his daughter and the pain he has caused to another family. After some discussion, Raul agreed to a mental health consult as well.

Support System

Raul has a wife who remains faithful and supportive in her visits. Raul's parents are alive and supportive but have health problems. He also has an older brother and a younger sister who are supportive, along with their spouses who visit on a frequent basis. He is the only one in his family who has a substance abuse problem. Upon release he plans to go back to his community where he has two job prospects.

Prescribed Medications

He is not presently taking any medications.

Diagnostic Impression:

Axis I   a. Dysthymic Disorder
          b. Alcohol Dependence Sustained
            Partial Remission
          c. Polysubstance Abuse (marijuana, cocaine)
Axis II None
Axis III None
Axis IV Incarceration
Axis V Current: 60
         Past Year: 50

Case Discussion

Raul presented in the office in the sixth year of an eight-year sentence. He stated that while incarcerated he has not had any alcohol, though it was available illegally. However, as he was preparing for his release within the next 24 months, he was concerned about returning to drinking. He continued to be impacted in thinking, feeling, and behavior by his daughter's death, the emotional cost of his drinking, and the resultant driving death. Thus, he was at high risk for relapse given the ease of access to alcohol upon release and continued unresolved grief issues. He stated that even if alcohol were not available, he would turn to marijuana and/or cocaine.

His family support remained strong, as well as an employment possibility with job experience and skill. Raul has recently increased his motivation to seek help and be open. Part of this can be attributed to a self-exploration on faith issues. Treatment will also evaluate underlying mental health issues and support faith development.

His prognosis remains guarded, as treatment will begin in a secured environment. He will be given a baseline drug screen before the start of treatment and then during treatment. Upon release, treatment in a less restrictive environment will begin. Treatment applications will be in a supportive environment. Treatment will focus on thoughts, feelings, and behavior associated with presenting issues.

Treatment Conceptualization

Raul has a complicated presentation with four major hypothesized themes: (1) posttraumatic stress related to the death of his daughter and the accompanying blame that he contributed to or caused her death, (2) chronic alcohol dependence abuse of substances that keep him involved in illegal activity (in order to obtain his drugs), (3) severe legal consequences including prison sentence of eight years, and (4) guilt concerning the vehicular homicide.

Although the problems are all related, the therapist would need to prioritize this patient's issues into a series of several short goals to which Raul must agree, be capable of meeting, and remain obtainable and measurable within a controlled setting. In addition, the therapist would have to evaluate the multiple cultural issues inherent in a Hispanic family living in the United States in a high-crime, low-income neighborhood. This evaluation would prevent therapeutic error regarding recommendations, understanding, and communication with this patient.

An important part of the therapy would include Raul's willingness and skill in doing homework. Unless Raul learns the therapy through the out-of-session work, he will be at increased risk for relapse. A second feature of the therapy will be Raul's maintaining and building a solid support system. Third, he will also need to listen to and respond to his substance-seeking internal dialogue. Once the dialogue is explicated, Raul will need to learn how to respond to it using the Automatic Thought Record (ATR). Fourth, Raul will need help to grieve and deal with his daughter's loss. Again, his role would need to be explicated and addressed.

The patient's relapse prevention plan would have to be tied to his choices of illegal activities providing the logical connection between the two in a way that brings in Raul's motivation for change as opposed to the therapist's demands for change. The patient has sustained a huge personal loss in the death of his daughter, which heightens the perception of a loss of control in his life. It would therefore be important for Raul to feel a sense of control and ownership for his relapse plan in order to increase the potential for follow through.

Finally, given Raul's community problems it would be important to preplan for healthy activities, counseling, and family support postrelease. A multimodal approach that encompasses pharmacotherapy, psychotherapy, family sessions, and building an external support network must all be in place.

Treatment Recommendations
1. Attend structured support groups during and after incarceration (locate groups before discharge).
2. Attend psychoeducation group to receive education on the biopsychosocial impact of alcohol and polysubstance drugs.
3. Attend individual and group psychotherapy to examine issues of unresolved grief, bereavement, and anger.

4. Monitor automatic thoughts in subject, frequency, and duration that relate to feelings of negative mood and unproductive or relapse behavior.
5. Assist client in replacing negative self-defeating thinking with positive accurate self-enhancing talk and behavior.
6. Establish motivation for sustained recovery free from mood-altering substances.
7. Continue drug testing during and after incarceration. (this often gives the patient a sense of relief as they don't have to think about using).
8. Explore the possibility of obtaining Acamprosate pharmacotherapy for alcohol cravings if this continues to be a problem for this patient.
9. Focus on specific issues related to self-forgiveness of guilt regarding daughter's death.

OTHER TREATMENT CHALLENGES

1. The clinician must remember that the patient will not be "cured." Patient will need external support and supporters, possibly for the rest of his life. Clinicians must be very active in helping the patient to establish supports and then work at maintaining external supports.
2. Inasmuch as these patients often "other-blame," care must be taken to walk the fine line between confrontation of denial, and taking responsibility for their actions.
3. The patient often associates with others who substance-misuse. The substance abuse culture may, in fact, have become a central part of his social and family life. Leaving or minimizing contact with this social system may be experienced as a great loss to the individual.
4. Limited or ineffective problem-solving ability has, in many ways, contributed to the present problems. Problem-solving training and/or the use of concrete, focused "rules" (e.g., 12 steps) is very useful. This obviates the need for poorly prepared problem solvers to engage in that complex activity.
5. The discomfort anxiety involved in the idea that one may, in the future, be uncomfortable is a major contributor to the maintenance of abuse. The substance becomes a source and technique for lowering arousal that is perceived by the individual as uncomfortable.
6. The idea that "None are so blind as those that will not see," is nowhere more true than in the treatment of individuals who misuse substances. The denial and minimizing of the pain, negative impact,

loss of job, family, and function that are the sequelae of substance abuse can be a hindrance to treatment. Carefully, concretely, and convincingly, the clinician must address the patient's avoidance or even protection of their use.

7. The clinician working with these patients will often hear, "I can stop and/or control my use whenever I want to." This unrealistic view of the difficulty and problems of curtailing use is not unusual and is, in fact quite typical. The unrealistic view of one's personal ability to affect control must be addressed through many personal experiments.

8. Similarly, there is often an unrealistic view of one's ability to change or even affect one's life circumstance. Often there has been so much interpersonal damage that jobs are no longer secure, and relationships are no longer viable.

9. Treatment is a process. This process can be long, difficult, and energy consuming. Ideally, it would benefit all if there was a simple and easily effected cure. The "magic bullet" is still being sought by patients and researchers alike. Until that magical cure is discovered, therapy must be multifaceted and require hard work for clinician and patient.

10. Some patients expend vast amounts of time and energy in seeking to maintain their addiction without getting into legal or health-related difficulties. Therapy, detoxification, or treatment may be sought as a quick way out of discomfort. The withdrawal process may become intolerable because of the symptoms.

11. The comorbidity of other health-related problems makes the treatment more complicated. Several professionals may be involved, requiring a coordinator for all of the medications, time, therapies, and support.

12. The patient may be a poor historian. His view is often limited by the fact that he may have been under the influence of a substance at the time an event occurred, or may have developed cognitive dysfunction (e.g., memory impairment) related to long-term use.

13. Prescribed medication may complicate the treatment. Some medications may exaggerate the "high" from the substance of choice. Further, there is the potential for self-harm in the mixing of prescription, nonprescription (over the counter) or "street" drugs.

14. The very chronicity of the problem complicates treatment. The patient may state that this is who he is and this is what he is. The way that the patient presents for treatment is, in many cases, how he or she is known and identified by family and his or her social milieu.

15. The substance of choice is self-reinforcing by either eliminating anxiety, triggering the brain reward system, or by avoiding unpleasant situations.

16. The possible use of various substances as an attempt to adaptively cope with problems must be noted. Moving the patient away from self-medication to a more organized and controlled regimen is often problematic, frightening, complicated, and difficult.
17. Patients with a long treatment history may be confused by the various treatment models to which they have been subjected. Is it their family? Is it their biology? Is it their thinking? Is it their brain chemistry? It is important for the treating clinician to attempt to integrate and synthesize the previous treatment(s) to assist patients in moving on in the present treatment setting and CBT model.
18. The complications of diagnoses on Axes I, II, and III, with severe psychosocial stressors on Axis IV must be addressed in a comprehensive treatment protocol.
19. Patients may seem challenging, adversarial, or even threatening. More experienced clinicians have learned when to push and when to back off.
20. Given that through experience, the patient has learned the language, techniques, and courses of detoxification, recovery, and relapse, he or she may appear to know more than the therapist. Here the collaborative approach works best. By inviting the knowledgeable patient to use his or her knowledge in support of change rather than using the knowledge as a defense can make use of previous learning.
21. Using a concrete approach rather than a more abstract approach will be more successful in that long-term substance misuse may be related to present cognitive impairment.
22. When stressed, the patient may come to the treatment session "high" resulting in poor focus and state-dependent learning. When the patient is high, the session should be cancelled until a time when the time can be used effectively.
23. The style, verbalizations, actions, or ideas of patients may engender negative countertransference. The clinician needs to be aware of any negative personal responses and be able to deal with them appropriately within supervision, or peer support.
24. When the patient is involved with the criminal justice system, the clinician must be very clear as to the lines of control and report. Who is privy to the patient's notes? What can and cannot be reported? To whom are reports made? These lines must be clarified and discussed with the patient at the onset of treatment.
25. Finally, the clinician must be educated, trained, and certified in substance misuse work. It is not for all clinicians, and many can do more harm than good by virtue of their lack of understanding of the disease. (Based on Freeman, 2005)

SUMMARY AND FUTURE DIRECTIONS

Substance use and misuse is not unusual in any community setting, and is much more prevalent in populations experiencing psychological distress, symptomatology and/or longstanding psychopathology. Practitioners specializing in the psychiatric health care services networks must be adept at identifying not only the possibility of substance misuse, but the possibility of presentations that mimic substance misuse in order to provide treatment that is appropriate, helpful, and accurate (Marlatt & Kilmer, 1988; Miller & Rollnick, 1991). A patient treated for an anxiety disorder with benzodiazepines and guided imagery who is actually misusing or dependent upon stimulants is not only wasting time and money, but the practitioner is treating a nonexistent condition. On the other hand, treating a patient with a chronic pain condition for misuse of opiates when in fact the symptoms and behaviors are either expected responses to opiates, or expected responses to undertreatment of pain is equally misguided (Freeman, 2004b, 2005). This places the patient at risk for long-term neurological damage as well as embarrassment and anxiety about his or her identified dependence upon opiates.

Another area of assessment that is an emerging science is the area of motivation for change. One model for understanding the change process was developed by Prochaska et al. (1986). The simple and useful five-step SOC model is widely accepted in substance misuse treatment settings, however, it lacks the specificity that is an essential part of CBT. The basic model that includes the stages of precontemplation, contemplation, preparation, action, and maintenance discussed by Freeman and Dolan (2001) is an exciting addition to understanding change in health recovery.

Assessment and treatment of persons must be done carefully and with all available information about substance misusing disorders because presentation of symptoms and behaviors can often mimic other disorders such as head trauma, undertreated pain conditions, and personality disorders. As science continues to move forward evaluating not only the neuroadaptive and biological components of the substance misuse disorders, but the human behavioral factors that project from the disease process, we will move toward a greater understanding of a very serious disease process.

REFERENCES

Ahmed, S. H., & Koob, G. F. (1998). Transition from moderate to excessive drug intake: Change in hedonic set point. *Science, 282*(5387), 298–300.

American Chronic Pain Association (ACPA). (2003). *American Chronic Pain Association: Medications and chronic pain.* Retrieved April 11, 2003, from www.theacpa.org.

Babor, T. F., de la Fuente, J. R., Saunders, J., & Grant, M. (1992). The Alcohol Use Disorders Identification Test. Guidelines for use in primary health care. Geneva, Switzerland: World Health Organization.

Chan, A. W. K., Pristach, E. A., Welte, J. W., & Russell, M. (1993). Use of the TWEAK test in screening for alcoholism/heavy drinking in three populations. *Alcoholism: Clinical and Experimental Research* 17: 1188–1192.

Diagnostic and Statistical Manual of Mental Disorders, 4th ed. (DSM-IV), Text Revision (2000). Mood disorders, American Psychiatric Association, pp. 297–343.

DiClemente, C. & Prochaska, J. (1998). Toward a comprehensive transtheoretical model of change. In W. Miller & N. Heather (Eds.), *Treating addictive behaviors*, 2nd ed. pp. 3–24. New York: Plenum Press.

Freeman, A., & Dolan, M. (2002). Revisiting Prochaska and DiClemente's stages of change: An expansion and specification to aid in treatment planning and outcome evaluation. *Cognitive & Behavioral Practice, Association for Advancement of Behavior Therapy, 8,* 224–234.

Freeman, A., & McClosky, R. D. (2003). Impediments to effective psychotherapy. In R. L. Leahy (Ed.) *Roadblocks in cognitive-behavior therapy: Transforming challenges into opportunities for change.* New York: Guilford.

Freeman, S. M. (2005). Substance abuse. In S. M. Freeman, & A. Freemen (Eds.), *Cognitive behavior therapy in nursing practice* (pp. 113–144). New York: Springer.

Freeman, S. M. (2004a). CBT with substance misusing patient. In S. M. Freeman & A. Freeman (Eds.), *Cognitive behavior therapy in nursing practice.* New York: Springer.

Freeman, S. M. (2004b). The relationship of opioid treatment in chronic pain conditions: Implications on brain reward response. *Journal of Addictions Nursing, 15,* 1–8.

Gavin, D. R., Ross, H. E., & Skinner, H. A. (1989). Diagnostic validity of the Drug Abuse Screening Test in the assessment of DSM-III drug disorders. *British Journal of Addiction* 84: 301–307.

Goodwin, D. W. (1997). Alcohol: Clinical aspects. In J. H. Lowinson, P. Ruiz, R. B. Millman & J. G. Langrod (Eds.), *Substance abuse: A comprehensive textbook* (3rd ed., pp. 144–185). Philadelphia: Williams & Wilkins.

Jaffe, J. H. (1997). Opiates: Clinical aspects. In J. H. Lowinson, P. Ruiz, R. B. Millman, & J. G. Langrod (Eds.), *Substance abuse: A comprehensive textbook* (3rd ed., pp. 195–204). Philadelphia: Williams & Wilkins.

Kahan, M., Wilson, L., & Becker, L. (1995). Effectiveness of a physician-based intervention with problem drinkers. *Canadian Medical Association Journal, 152*(6), 851–859.

King, G. R., & Ellinwood, E. H. (1997). Amphetamines and other stimulants. In J. H. Lowinson, P. Ruiz, R. B. Millman, & J. G. Langrod (Eds.), *Substance abuse: A comprehensive textbook* (3rd ed., pp. 247–270). Philadelphia: Williams & Wilkins.

Koob, G. F., & Bloom, F. E. (1988). Cellular and molecular mechanisms of drug dependence. *Science, 242*(4879), 715–723.

Koob, G. F., & Le Moal, M. (1997). Drug abuse: Hedonic homeostatic dysregulation. *Science, 278*(5335), 52–58.

Marlatt, G. A., & Kilmer, J. R. (1998). Consumer choice: Implications of behavioral economics for drug use and treatment, *Behavior Therapy, 29,* 567–576.

Miller, W. R. & Rollnick, S. (1991). *Motivational interviewing: Preparing people to change addictive behavior.* New York: Guilford.

National Institute on Alcohol Abuse and Alcoholism (NIAAA). (1993). *Eighth Special Report to the U. S. Congress on Alcohol and Health.* ADM-281-91-0003. Rockville, MD: NIAAA, 203–232.

O'Brien, C. (2001). Drug addiction and drug abuse. In J. G. Hardman, L. E. Limbird, & A. G. Gilman (Eds.), *Goodman & Gilman's The Pharmacological Basis of Therapeutics* (pp. 621–643). New York: McGraw-Hill.

Portenoy, R. K., & Payne, R. (1992). Acute and chronic pain. In J. H. Lowinson, P. Ruiz, R. B. Millman, & J. G. Langrod (Eds.), *Substance abuse: A comprehensive textbook* (2nd ed., pp. 691–721). Philadelphia: Williams & Wilkins.

Prochaska, J. O., & DiClemente, C. C. (1986). Toward a comprehensive model of change. In W. R. Miller & N. Heather (Eds.), *Treating addictive behaviors: Processes of change.* New York: Plenum Press.

SAMHSA. (2003). *Results from the 2002 National Survey on Drug Use and Health: National findings.* NHSDA Series H-22. DHHS Publication No. SMA 03-3836. Rockville, MD: Office of Applied Studies.

Selzer, M. L. (1971). The Michigan Alcoholism Screening Test: The quest for a new diagnostic instrument, *American Journal of Psychiatry 127,* 1653–1658.

Selzer, M. L., Allen, J. P., & Columbus, M. (1985). Assessing alcohol problems: A guide for clinicians and researchers. [NIAAA Treatment Handbook Series 4] [HE 20.8308/2:4] Bethesda, MD: NIAA, 386–392.

Sharp, C. W., & Rosenberg, N. L. (1997). Volatile substances. In J. H. Lowinson, P. Ruiz, R. B. Millman, & J. G. Langrod (Eds.), *Substance abuse: A comprehensive textbook* (3rd ed., pp. 303–327). Philadelphia: Williams & Wilkins.

Sobell, M. B. and Sobell, L. C. (1998). Guiding self-change. In W. R. Miller & N. Heather (Eds.), *Treating addictive behaviors,* (2nd Ed.). pp. 189–202. Plenum: New York.

Ungerleider, J. T., & Pechnick, R. N. (1997). Hallucinogens. In J. H. Lowinson, P. Ruiz, R. B. Millman, & J. G. Langrod (Eds.), *Substance abuse: A comprehensive textbook* (3rd ed., pp. 280–289). Philadelphia: Williams & Wilkins.

Wells, A. (1997). Cognitive therapy of anxiety disorders. New York: John Wiley & Sons.

Wession, D. R., Smith, D. E., & Seymour, R. B. (1997). Sedative-hypnotics and tricyclics. In J. H. Lowinson, P. Ruiz, R. B. Millman, & J. G. Langrod (Eds.), *Substance abuse: A comprehensive textbook* (3rd ed., pp. 271–279). Philadelphia: Williams & Wilkins.

CHAPTER 23

Grief and Bereavement

Ruth Malkinson

INTRODUCTION

The commitment to helping individuals, families, groups, and communities has long been part of social work's practice. It is therefore obvious that adversities along the life cycle such as death and dying, and the treatment of typical grief and bereavement that follow will be part of the social worker's repertoire. Many of social work's interventions have been aimed at assisting clients to adapt to changing life situations by using their inner strengths. The changes involved in death, dying, and bereavement are sometimes so shattering and beyond the individual's comprehension and outside of the normal parameters for coping that social work interventions are required to provide unconditional availability and unconventional assistance. Such interventions may at times challenge the social worker for any of a number of reasons. The social work therapist must ask, "What do I do to help this individual or family?" "How do I help these individuals, families, and often, whole communities?" These systems may have experienced devastation as a result of natural or manmade disasters. They may be unable to cope with a loss of a person, a home, or a way of life. For example: An event such as 9/11 in 2001 was just such a disaster. The aftermath required the involvement of social workers in providing help to individuals, families, and communities who suffered the trauma of terror. This was remarkable in that while the social

521

work professionals were making heroic efforts to assist victims, they were, at the same time, themselves experiencing the effect of the trauma (Boss, 2002).

Although helping families with a dying relative, and families or individuals who have experienced a loss through death is among a social worker's routine concerns, it is nevertheless recognized as a "loaded" subject that challenges the professionals. Unlike many other social problems, death is one issue that professionals are likely to encounter in their own lives and in fact will have to deal with eventually as mortal human beings. In other words, death is an inevitable event that professionals have to deal with in relation to themselves as well as their clients. The medical revolution has placed death in the backyard and its avoidance has become common routine in contemporary society (Fieffel, 1987). However, its avoidance does not replace the inevitability of its occurrence. Moreover, not only did death not disappear, the number of losses and casualties resulting from wars, terror attacks, traffic accidents, suicide, homicide, and natural disasters is ever increasing, bringing the issue to the forefront and necessitating intervention programs at all levels.

The terms *bereavement*, *mourning*, and *grief* that are used in this chapter are now applied interchangeably. More specifically, *mourning* refers to the set of practices and acts as defined culturally, socially, and religiously, and it provides a framework of guidelines for the bereaved and the community to which the bereaved belonged. *Bereavement* is referred to as the objective situation of an individual who has recently experienced the loss of someone significant through death thus emphasizing the social external component of the process while *grief* represents the internal emotional response to the loss (Stroebe & Stroebe, 1987, p. 7).

The position taken in this chapter is one that views loss through death as an external and uncontrolled (most of the times) event followed by a process of accommodation to its consequences known as bereavement, and applying a cognitive perspective as an effective mode of intervention for the use of social workers. A characteristic of cognitive therapy (CT) is its focus on the individual's cognitions and its meaning construction in response to various events. Similarly, cognitive grief therapy approaches loss through death and dying as adverse events affecting one's way of thinking about oneself, others, and the world depending on the extremity of the circumstances.

Also, we elaborate on the cognitive approach to loss through death and the ensuing grief reactions, processes, and outcomes applying cognitive assessment and interventions with case illustrations. Importantly, a distinction between functional and dysfunctional bereavement processes is made, as related to different belief systems (rational and irrational). The importance of cognitive assessment in planning an intervention will be

stressed with case illustrations of specific interventions that can assist social workers when working with bereaved individuals.

LITERATURE REVIEW

In our lifetime we will experience the loss through death of a significant
other. Grief is a human, normal, and universal reaction to a loss.

How do we adapt to the loss? What is an adaptive response? When
is grief considered too complicated? When is it appropriate to intervene?

The answers to some of these questions underwent remarkable
changes within the last few decades. One such change took place in the
field of grief and bereavement in how it views the grief process, its aims
and its outcomes (Malkinson, 2001, 2005). An important shift has been
from Freud's (1917/1957) conceptualization of grief as a normal process
leading to breaking the bond with the deceased (i.e., *decathexis*)—a conceptualization that was the foundation of both research and clinical
work—to viewing bereavement as a process of reorganizing one's life and
worldview without the deceased, where bonds will remain intact and un-
broken (Klass, Silverman, & Nickman, 1996). From the perspective of relinquishing bonds, normal grief reaction following loss through death, its
course and identified symptoms that frequently are experienced by the bereaved, are ascribed to within a time frame. The reactions immediately
following the loss are intensified and expected to decrease over time. The
duration of normal grief process leading to relinquishing the bonds with
the deceased was considered to be 2 to 3 years (Rando, 1988, 1993;
Sanders, 1993). A wealth of literature has described in detail the course
of grief as stages (Bowlby, 1980), phases (Ramsay, 1979; Sanders, 1989),
components (Bugen, 1977), tasks (Worden, 2000/1991), or tracks (Rubin,
1981, 1993) including biopsychological reactions (i.e., changes in appetite,
sleeping habits, physiological and social functioning) as part of the normal grieving process.

From the continuing bonds perspective there is no final point to
grieving; rather it views grief as a process of accommodating to the loss
as dynamic that continues to preoccupy the bereaved in his or her search
for the meaning to life without the deceased (Neimeyer, 1999). It is a
process in which the relationships with the inner representations of the
deceased continue long after loss has occurred (Malkinson & Bar-Tur,
2005; Rubin & Malkinson, 2001).

In recent years, more studies have focused on the long-term outcome
of the grief process, suggesting that throughout the years it becomes less
intense but never really ends. With these conceptual changes in mind,
"young" (acute) grief, the *mature phase* and the *aging of grief* are terms

recently introduced to signify the enduring nature of grief (Malkinson et al., 2000, 2005; Malkinson, Rubin, & Witztum, 2000; Rubin et al. 2001). The implications of these conceptual changes on defining adaptive and maladaptive course and outcome of grief and on therapeutic intervention will be examined.

Different forms and circumstances surrounding the death event seem to affect the process, its duration, intensity, and outcome. Factors identified to affect the normal course include the circumstances of the death: sudden and unexpected death events such as suicide, homicide, and terror attacks (Malkinson et al., 2005) man-made or natural disasters—also termed as *violent death* (Rynearson, 2001) or "powerful situations" (Janoff-Bulman, 1992) that are outside the range of usual human experience and hence more likely to have a markedly distressing, traumatic, or overwhelming effect (American Psychiatric Association, 1994); types of lost relationships, for example, loss of a child, are known to impose additional stress on survivors and are associated with higher risks (Rubin, 1993; Sanders, 1993), social-cultural context within which grief is experienced (Stroebe, Gergen, Geregen, & Stroebe, 1992; Malkinson, Rubin & Witztum, 2000); gender, age at time of the loss, previous experiences with loss, and personality variables such as resilience and availability of adequate support networks (Bonanno et al., 2002).

HOW IS NORMAL GRIEF DEFINED?

What constitutes normal grief varies greatly from culture to culture. Different cultures have different views and customs on the mourning process that follow a death event, but all view it as one necessitating some kind of adjustment that takes place over time. In many cases the society or culture provides a set of mourning guidelines specifying what is expected of the bereaved and the community (Witztum et al., 2000).

As mentioned previously, recent approaches to bereavement are reexamining the necessity of finality as a component of successful bereavement resolution. Bereavement and its outcome following death are more widely regarded as a response to a stressful event that necessitates both reorganization and the acceptance of a new reality that excludes the dead person (Parkes & Weiss, 1983). Klass et al., (1996) argued that instead of emphasizing breaking bonds ("letting go") in the bereavement process, the negotiation and renegotiation of the meaning of the loss over time should be emphasized. While death is permanent and unchanging, the process of bereavement does change, affecting the mourner differently at different times over the rest of his or her life. These authors therefore regard the bereavement process not as recovery, closure, or resolution, but rather as an accommodation, in which one continually adapts one's preexisting knowledge, emotions, and experiences to the new reality.

Prigerson and colleagues (1999) conceptualized complicated grief distinct from a normal uncomplicated one. Normal grief or uncomplicated grief reactions, as it is referred to, are those that, though painful, move the survivor toward an acceptance of the loss and the ability to carry on with his or her life and investing in new relationships and maintaining a sense of self-efficacy. Uncomplicated grief is characterized by feeling saddened by the death of an intimate, but nevertheless, believing that life still holds meaning and the potential for fulfillment. In uncomplicated grief one's ability to trust others, maintain one's positive attitudes is alien to those with complicated grief. An important aspect of uncomplicated grief is the will to reinvest in interpersonal relationships and activities, and a willingness to explore new relationships and roles despite the pain of the loss. In contrast, in complicated grief, bereaved persons view their lives as having stopped, with no future. They don't believe that life holds anything worth investing in. According to Prigerson et al. (1999), in complicated grief, bereaved persons feel acute separation distress and a sense of emptiness that do not decrease over time.

In the following illustration we can see how the traumatic loss of a son, 23 years earlier, has been experienced by a mother who throughout the years has been oscillating between her questioning "why" he did it, and accepting the son's wish to see his death as triumph and not as something to mourn.

> My son committed suicide 23 years ago. Since then he has been with me every day. There isn't a day that I am not thinking of him, talking to him and in a way being with him. I still ask myself why he did it despite the fact that in the letter he left he asked us, his parents, to see his death as a triumph not as bereavement. (A quote from an interview with a 87-year-old artist talking about her son's death, May, 2003).

Is this continuous oscillation normal? Is it an indication of pathological grief? The answer lies with the choice of the model one applies to understand the bereaved mother.

To summarize, concurrently, the bereavement process is no longer viewed as solely comprising a stage or task model, as suggested by Bowlby (1980) or Worden (2000/1991), but rather as a process that includes coping with the stress evoked by the death event on the one hand, and ongoing relationships with the deceased on the other (Rubin, 1993; Stroebe & Schut, 1999). The latter approaches have shifted from expecting a predetermined course and outcome of bereavement to emphasizing that there is no one predictable pathway through grief and regarding it as an idiosyncratic process (Neimeyer, 1999, 2000).

Literature Review on Behavior and Cognitive Behavior Therapy in Grief

There is an agreement among theoreticians and clinicians that regardless of the theoretical adherence of different models of grief therapy, caring, support, availability, and empathy are central ingredients that go above and beyond a specific mode of intervention (Raphael, Middelton, Martinek, & Misso, 1993). Also, all forms of intervention, regardless of their theoretical adherence, focus on the loss and are typically structured and time-limited (e.g., the more traditional psychodynamic treatments, Raphael, 1983; Raphael et al., 1993; or treatments based on coping and stress responses, Horowitz, Bonano, & Holen, 1993; or treatment based on cognitive constructionist perspective, Malkinson, 2001; Neimeyer, 2005).

For quite a while research studies on the effectiveness of intervention programs with bereaved clients have been scarce and only recently have been applied more routinely. Among those carried out are a comparison of different treatment modalities and interventions at different points in time following the death event (Mawson, Marks, Ramm, & Stern, 1981; Schut, de Keijser, van den Bout, & Stroebe, 1997). The findings in these studies suggested that timely interventions were more effective in alleviating the symptomatology of grief and reducing the risk of subsequent pathology among high-risk bereaved persons, as compared to a delayed treatment control group (Raphael et al., 1993). The study by Kleber, Brom, and Defares (1992) compared different therapeutic modalities (trauma desensitization, hypnosis therapy, and psychodynamic therapy) and found them to be very effective in reducing stress response symptoms but substantially less effective on psychosomatic ones. No indication was provided on the degree of grief resolution achieved as a result of intervention.

Behavioral therapies for complicated grief were among the first to be reported in the bereavement literature including Gauthier and Marshall's (1977) technique for behavioral desensitization to the loss. Their assumption was that pathological grief is maintained largely through social reinforcement to the bereaved's repeated pattern of behavior using flooding procedures. Their treatment strategy to reduce the emotional distress included a rescheduling of social reinforcement. Although it originated from the psychodynamic framework, Ramsay's (1979) pathological grief model was one of the first reported behavioral models to be applied effectively in cases of complicated grief. In the context of individual therapy he employed flooding techniques to enable expression of feelings, followed by reintegration. In line with Ramsay's flooding technique, a technique of behavioral "guided mourning" was developed by Mawson and his group (1981), who carried on an outcome study to examine its effectiveness. The behavioral "guided mourning" approach involved reliving avoided painful memories and feelings related to bereavement along with the use of homework. The reported results showed improvement among the guided mourning patients (N = 6) after three, 60- to 90-minute sessions given over a period of 2 weeks, which they maintained through a follow-up 28 weeks later. The control group was instructed to avoid grief and painful memories of bereavement.

The study of stressful life events has expanded to include man-made and natural disasters and violence. This has been followed by developing intervention programs for victims to assist them in restoring their shattered worldview by way of searching for alternative interpretations. Cognitive therapies (CT) and cognitive behavior therapies (CBTs) were found suitable and effective (Kleber et al., 1992) particularly with individuals suffering from posttraumatic stress disorder (PTSD), depression, anxiety, and chronic or traumatic grief (Black, Newman, Harris-Hendriks, & Mezey, 1997; Clark, 1986; Kavanagh, 1990; Kubany & Manke, 1995; Resick & Schnicke, 1995; Richards & Lovell, 1997).

A central tenet of CT and CBT is that emotional disturbance and behavioral symptomology are maintained as a result of distorted thinking that can be modified with the use of a variety of cognitive, emotional, and behavioral techniques both during and between sessions in the form of homework assignments. CT and CBT are being applied increasingly in cases of acute and prolonged grief following death—combining guided imagery, exposure techniques, thought-stopping, cognitive restructuring, breathing exercises, and skill acquisition—all aimed at assisting clients to adapt to a new reality that excludes the deceased (Beck, Wright, Newman & Liese, 1993; Ellis, 1995; Foa & Rothbaum, 1998; Mahony, 1991; Neimeyer, 1999; Resick et al., 1995). Among general principles of CT that relate to the phase of acute or prolonged grief are interventions that focus on the here and now and can be empirically validated and specifically define target strategies (Gauthier et al., 1977; Hackman, 1993; Kavanagh, 1990; Mawson et al., 1981; Sireling, Cohen, & Marks, 1988). More recent CT interventions focus on assisting the bereaved person to reconstruct new meanings (Neimeyer Keese, & Fortner, 2000). From that perspective the idiosyncrasy of cognitive processes among the bereaved is emphasized although grief reaction following loss is regarded as universal.

THE COGNITIVE MODEL OF BEREAVEMENT

From the cognitive perspective, a loss through death is an adverse external event over which one has no control but nevertheless that changes one's belief system and its related emotions and behaviors. Grief is not only an emotional process but also one of cognitive and behavioral adaptation to the consequences of the loss. Yet, the role of cognitions has typically been viewed as less central than that of emotions, perhaps due to the latter's overt as opposed to cognitions' more covert nature. It may also be that emotions often have a flooding effect during the acute crisis following a death. Particularly when the cause of death is more sudden and traumatic (i.e., homicide, suicide, accidents, and natural or man-made disasters), emotions seem to dominate over cognitions, especially during the acute phase.

In traditional therapies, the emotional dimension of the process of grief is the focus of intervention. The presence or absence of anger, depression, shame, and guilt reactions have customarily been regarded as crucial indicators for understanding and evaluating short- and long-term bereavement outcomes, and also normal and complicated forms of bereavement (Rando, 1993). Traditional models maintain that exaggerated emotional responses, the absence of these emotions, or avoiding their expression are indications of complicated grief. This approach explains why most traditional interventions apply cathartic techniques in order to help the bereaved person alleviate the intensity of these emotions (Worden, 2000/1991); cognitions are seen only as the byproducts of emotional disturbance. Therapists' tendency to emphasize emotions as central to the process of grieving has led them to neglect its cognitive aspects (Rando, 1988).

In contrast, the cognitive perspective emphasizes the relationship between one's emotions and behaviors and one's cognitive evaluations about oneself, the world, and the future (Beck, 1976; Gauthier et al., 1977; Gluhosky, 1995; Malkinson, 2001, 2005). The death event is assumed to have a profound impact on the person's most fundamental assumptions (Janoff-Bulman, 1992) or assumptive world (Parkes, 1975, 1993), the fundamental cognitive structures or schemata about the self and the world (Beck, 1976; Horowitz, 1986; Janoff-Bulman, 1992), and the belief system about the self, others, and the world (Ellis, 1962, 1989, 1993; 1994a; 1994c). A death event deconstructs the existing views that a person holds about life and relationships, requiring a painful internal process of cognitively reorganizing what has been shattered following the external event, of modifying one's knowledge, thoughts, and feelings, of giving up old meanings to life, and of forming new ones (Gluhosky, 1995; Horowitz et al., 1993; Kavanagh, 1990; Kelly, 1955; Neimeyer, 1999,

2005). The loss event is new information that has to be processed and then assimilated (revising and processing new information into preexisting cognitive structures) or accommodated (adapting preexisting knowledge to the new reality) (Epstein, 1993; Horowitz, 2001; Piaget, 1950; Warren & Zgourides, 1991). Whether primarily cognitively processed or emotionally experienced, the cognitive perspective asserts that the more traumatic the event is, the greater its impact on one's belief system and other cognitions. Thus, the cognitive approach upholds that, for the grieving process to take an adequate course toward functional and satisfying outcomes, grief-related cognitions should be identified, included, and treated as an equal part of intrapsychic processes (Gluhosky, 1995; Kavanagh, 1990; Malkinson, 2001; Malkinson & Ellis, 2000; Rando, 1988).

According to the cognitive approach, maladaptive grief takes the form of distorted thinking related to the deceased rather than negative evaluations of oneself that is dominant in depression.

One of the first studies to observe complicated grief as a distinct grief syndrome was by Prigerson and colleagues in 1995 on 82 widows. A distinction between aspects devoted to the deceased and those of the self was found. The authors' conclusion was that it is possible to distinguish between depression and complicated grief following loss. The salient feature in complicated grief is preoccupation and emotions directed toward the deceased (Malkinson et al., 2000). Feelings of intense grief among bereaved persons is often related to their viewing the loss as an intended rejection while the distorted thinking is interpreted as "how could he/she have done this to me?" (Beck, 1976) or as a confirmation for being worthless ("I am guilty and a worthless person for not saving my dear son's life") (Malkinson et al., 2000). In depression, preoccupation and emotions are directed toward the self and the distorted thinking is typically "I am a worthless person and my life will never change."

During stressful life events, people often use maladaptive cognitive processes—referred to by Beck (1976, 1989, Beck et al., 1993) as *cognitive distortions*, and by Ellis (1962) as *irrational beliefs*. From a cognitive-constructivist approach focusing on changing distorted cognitions (correcting cognitions) undermines and limits the richness of the human tendency to organize the knowledge and life experiences in the form of stories (creating a story). When a disruption occurs according to cognitive-constructivists, it forces the individual to reconstruct and retell the story and replace the shattered one (Mahoney, 2003; Neimeyer, 1999; Neimeyer et al., 2000).

In this chapter, a combined creative-corrective approach to working with the bereaved is presented with emphasis on cognitive assessment as a tool for social workers. The ultimate goal is to determine how best to facilitate an adaptive grief process with individuals who experience traumatic loss or complicated grief.

THE ABC MODEL OF REBT APPLIED TO GRIEF AND BEREAVEMENT

The ABC model (Adversity—Beliefs—Consequences) presented here is based on a cognitive theoretical model originated by Ellis (1976, 1986, 1989, 1991, 1994) as a suitable model to be applied in treatment of bereaved individuals. Like other cognitive models, REBT emphasizes the centrality of cognitive processes in understanding emotional disturbance following an adverse event, distinguishing between two sets of cognitions that people construct, rational and irrational ones and their related emotional and behavioral consequences that differ qualitatively. These two sets of cognitions mark the difference between adaptive and maladaptive outcomes following undesirable events (Ellis, 1994b). In applying this model to bereaved persons the aim is to assist individuals to experience a more adaptive course of grief while distinguishing between functional reactions to loss and prolonged dysfunctional ones. This distinction provides guidelines for the assessment of bereaved individuals' interpretation to their experience of loss, and offers cognitive, emotional, and behavioral strategies for facilitating an adaptive course of bereavement in cases of loss. Clinical illustrations follow the description of an outline of the REBT model.

Several tenets underlie the ABC model of REBT (Ellis, 1991).

- The origins of emotional disturbance are cognitive, emotive, and behavioral.
- Cognition is a mediator between an event and its emotional consequences.
- Dysfunctional emotions largely follow from irrational thinking (demandingness).
- Humans are born with a biological predisposition to think irrationally. Some are born with a greater tendency and will therefore exhibit more irrational thinking.

The biological tendency to think irrationally coexists with the healthy human tendency to actualize oneself (Ellis & Bernard, 1985). According to the REBT model, people's emotional consequences (C) are not solely determined by the activating event (A) but largely by the beliefs (B) they have about the event. Death (especially traumatic sudden and unexpected death) may be regarded as an adverse external event (A) that affects one's belief system (B) and, consequently, one's emotions and behaviors (C). "People's cognitions, emotions and behaviors are not pure but part of an organismic or holistic interaction" (Ellis, 1994a, p. 217). A cyclical interaction occurs among the event (A), the beliefs about the event (B), and the emotional and behavioral consequences (C) (Ellis 1994/1962).

Irrational or dysfunctional beliefs are absolutist evaluations or demandingness that past, present, or future life events should, ought, or must be different from the way they are, largely resulting in emotional upsetness at point C (consequence). "Awfulizing," low frustration tolerance and self-damnation are forms of irrational demandingness that are often followed at point C by emotional upsetness such as depression, anxiety, extreme shame, and guilt. The human tendency to think irrationally often reaches a peak following a death event, because bereaved individuals tend to think that death should not have happened to them or that it is too painful for them to withstand (Ellis, 1976, 1986). On the other hand, rational, functional beliefs (B) are realistic evaluations of adverse events (e.g., "how sad and unfortunate that this happened to me"; "my life will never be the same, it's sad and painful"), and their related emotional consequences (C) are negative but not as upsetting: sorrow, sadness, regret, frustration, and concern (Ellis, 1995).

The REBT perspective distinguishes between functional adaptive and dysfunctional maladaptive consequences in reaction to loss. Grief is a process of experiencing the pain of the loss and searching and re-searching for a new meaning to life without the dead person, and it is also a process of reconstructing and restructuring one's "irrational" (dysfunctional) thinking to a more rational (functional), realistic mode. It is oscillation between grieving the loss and having to make choices regarding the reality of the loss (Stroebe et al., 1999; Neimeyer, 1999).

In REBT, distorted or irrational thinking (e.g., dogmatic demandingness about oneself, others, and the world) is considered a major factor in emotional disturbance (Ellis, 1994/1962, 1993b; Ellis & Dryden, 1997; Walen, DiGiuseppe, & Dryden, 1992). However, overreaction or its lack to the death of a loved one is not "right" or "wrong," not preferred or undesirable, but rather it is related to a specific set of beliefs (cognitions) that are functional or dysfunctional (adaptive or maladaptive). In the case of loss through death, negative emotional reactions (e.g., sorrow, sadness) are regarded as relating to adaptive cognitions (e.g., "life has changed forever, and it's sad and painful"; "the doctors did all they could do to save my child, I don't blame them." "I know we did everything to keep him alive but that didn't help and he died"). Maladaptive grief on the other hand, is seen as a negative emotion related to a continuous reconstruction and persistently upholding maladaptive cognitions (e.g., "life is not worth living without my loves one"; "I can't stand my life without my loved one"). A common dysfunctional interpretation among bereaved individuals relates to the experience of pain; when the experience of grief is perceived as too painful and unbearable ("grieving is too painful") or when the reality of the loss is too difficult to comprehend ("I don't even want to think about him or her as dead") avoidance of experience is the emotional consequence. In other words it is having a secondary reaction over the primary referred to as a secondary disturbance or secondary symptom (Walen et al., 1992). Thus, from the cognitive perspective, complicated grief is defined as persistence over time of distorted, irrational beliefs as the dominant set of cognitions affecting the emotional consequences (Malkinson, 2001, 2005; Malkinson et al., 2000).

Within the REBT conceptual framework, the grief process is an adaptive form of thinking and emoting that helps the bereaved persons to construct their disrupted and at times shattered belief system into a more meaningful one. Thoughts about death are not avoided nor constantly remembered, but are rearranged into a system of sadly deploring but successfully living with the bereaved person's great loss. Grief that has a healing effect and that adapts to the sad reality, which no longer includes the deceased, involves pronounced negative emotions such as sadness, frustration, and pain. Yet it minimizes unhealthy, self-defeating feelings of depression, despair, horror, and self-deprecation.

In addition, while those individuals who have functional beliefs are still traumatized and feel very badly about their loss, those with dysfunctional beliefs tend to feel continuously devastated and also create secondary symptoms about their primary bad feelings. As Moore (1991, p. 10) pointed out: "Not only does cognition significantly influence emotion but emotion appears to significantly influence cognitions." Particularly following a traumatic death event, people tend to have not only some self-defeating (irrational) evaluations of the event, but also self-defeating evaluations about their disturbed emotions (secondary symptoms or disturbances). For example, a father who lost his teenage son in a road accident (adverse event) feels angry with his son (emotional consequence), he is telling himself that he was careless and he should have taken better care of himself (belief); he then tells himself that he shouldn't think this way about his son and gets more angry at himself for even considering such a terrible thought. The father's anger directed toward himself over feeling anger at his son is a secondary symptom or secondary disturbance (Walen et al., 1992). In such cases, an irrational pattern of response is often more dominant than a rational one.

The REBT model stresses that irrational beliefs are dysfunctional because they are exaggerated evaluations of events over which the person has less control as compared to the choice of interpretation of the event that the person can exert. The belief-consequence connection, according to this model, will most probably result in a case of overreliance on irrational beliefs in dysfunctional emotional and behavioral consequences that in turn will increase stress and reduce the individual's coping resources. Like other CBT and CT models, REBT uses a variety of cognitive (disputation, thought restructuring and reframing), emotional (guided imagery) and behavioral (practicing skills as homework assignments) interventions to improve the person's coping, reduce emotional disturbance and increase the self-control especially when circumstances are uncontrollable. As a psychoeducational model it relies on the individual's active involvement both during and between sessions (homework assignments) in changing and adopting a more rational evaluation of the event resulting in more functional, emotional, and behavioral consequences. The application of the REBT model using these guidelines to reduce stress and burnout, as a syndrome comprising cognitive, emotional, and behavioral components, was reported in a study of a stress management training program to female blue-collar workers (Malkinson, Kushnir, & Weisberg, 1997).

COGNITIVE ASSESSMENT

The purpose of the grief process is to make sense of the loss and to construct a meaning to life without a loved one, and then integrate this sense into one's beliefs that were shattered. It involves a painful search of what was lost never to be regained and what could be remembered in spite of the pain these memories elicit. In this sense the grief process is similar to weaving in which each thread is important. This emphasizes the importance of a detailed cognitive assessment.

In addition to a general demographic assessment (details about the loss, the circumstances of its occurrence, relationship to the deceased, etc.) in cases of grief CT it is important to conduct an accurate and comprehensive assessment of the bereaved person's perception of the loss. Cognitive assessment includes two parts; (1) assessing the "story," the narrative with focus on the way the event is described, and (2) an assessment of the functionality of the cognitions that includes details about the activating event and the individual's beliefs, emotions, and behaviors (DiGiuseppe, 1991; Malkinson, 2005).

To formulate a hypothesis regarding the client's thinking and its interaction with emotions and behaviors (Beck, 1976; DiGiuseppe, 1991; Kavanagh, 1990), and meaning construction, the social worker should first seek to explore details concerning the activating event (A).

Exploring the death event in detail in addition to assessing the cognitions and emotional consequences may have a cathartic effect, because telling the "story" includes one's interpretation of how one feels about it, and at the same time offers an opportunity to express both rational and irrational thoughts the client may have about the event itself or thoughts about the self, others, or the circumstances surrounding the loss (Malkinson, 1996, 2001, 2005). It is essential to explore with the client the personal meaning of the loss event. This includes how the loss is verbalized and what specific words (e.g., "Life has lost its meaning") do or do not mean to the client.

The client's detailed perception of the death event should be elicited during the intake sessions, in conjunction with the collection of general demographic information and the person's underlying schema or assumptions about the self, others, and the world so as to elicit the individual's irrational beliefs (DiGiuseppe, 1991). A detailed assessment of the client's perceptions of the activating event (A) will assist in identifying the client's loss-related irrational beliefs (B) that underlie specific emotional consequences (C) (Malkinson, 2001) and it will also enable the social worker to make a distinction between functional and dysfunctional responses (B, C) to the death. This distinction is especially pertinent to sudden, traumatic events that are characteristically negative and overwhelming, but as Ellis (1994a) emphasized, dysfunctional thoughts about the adverse event coexist with functional, healthy thoughts ("It's so painful but I did all I could to help her").

Additionally, assessing avoidance-related cognitions is of special importance as they shed light on the variety of thoughts the bereaved holds that maintain the avoidance. "I avoid going to the graveside because if I go it means that she is dead and I don't want to think of her as a dead person." These thoughts will be assessed as rational or irrational according to the emotional consequences they elicit and vice versa. It is the thought behind the behavioral or physical consequence that will determine the course of the intervention.

Encouraging the client to tell a detailed "story" entails three important elements: (1) catharsis, (2) assessment of the client's dysfunctional cognitions and the related emotional consequences to be corrected as well as identifying functional ones and strengthening them, and (3) attentive listening provides an important opportunity for the therapist to hypothesize about possible alternatives for the client to retell the story, paying special attention to the person's linguistic style.

The following is an example of how the death event as an activating event is perceived and told by a bereaved mother during the first intake session. She relates that the decision to come to therapy occurred when she realized that her initial decision to be strong and to carry on with life "as if nothing happened" turned out to be too difficult, painful, and, in fact, impossible. Assessment will typically involve questions about the circumstances of the loss as well as additional demographic details, but most important is the mother's interpretation of the event:

SOCIAL WORKER: Tell me, what brought you here?

CLIENT: It is hard for me to tell you. I don't understand what is happening to me. It feels like I am losing control over my life. I was always strong and in control but since the death of my son I am no longer in control and it frightens me. My oldest son was killed few months ago in a road accident while a friend was driving the car. We lost not only our beloved son but a very talented musician. We were devastated but decided that for the sake of the other two sons we must continue with life and carry on as we did before. I am a school teacher and I returned back to work after the "shiva" (the first seven days of mourning). I try to do the work. I must do it. I don't want the others to think that I am not functioning. I fear their pity.

This bereaved mother's account of the loss of her son demonstrates how a detailed account of A (activating event) does not necessarily have to focus on the event itself (i.e., the traffic accident), but may instead comprise personal factors exacerbating the client's loss, such as the sudden and painful loss of a talented son's personality. In presenting what had happened, the mother believes that life should go on. The feeling of failure in keeping their efforts to be strong and "carry on with life" is creating an additional stress (a secondary symptom) of anxiety for her: "I must be strong and continue to live in spite of the terrible loss." Her and the family's efforts to do so are unproductive. This excerpt also reveals diagnostic information concerning the client's belief system (B) and its emotional and behavioral consequences (C).

It is possible to hypothesize from this assessment that the bereaved mother holds irrational beliefs about herself and her grief: "Life must go on and I must be strong otherwise people will pity me and that means I'm a weak person," and "I must not loose control." In this case illustration, the mother's grief (C) which is regarded as a normal, healthy response to a sudden loss is being interpreted as weakness and she fears that experiencing it might result in losing control over her life and worse that all people will pity her. The themes of "carrying on with life" and not losing control for fear of being pitied and the meaning attributed to weakness and failure will be further explored.

In view of this mother's assessment, a treatment plan was developed to include information and explanation about the healthy adaptive aspects of grief, normalization and legitimating of feelings of pain and grief, and pointing out the inappropriateness (correcting) of the client's thought about others' pitying her as a weak person. A distinction between adaptive feelings of grief and maladaptive feelings of anxiety was made and discussed throughout therapy. The mother was helped to accept her grief and pain as a part of a normal process of coming to terms with her beloved son's loss. Discussing her grief with her colleagues rather than viewing herself as a failure for not being able to "carry on with life" after the trauma of the loss was not important. In this specific case, the issue of carrying on with life, the fear of losing control and being pitied was related to the client's background of the Holocaust. The meaning attached to it as part of the story was understandable as well as why sensitivity was so pronounced. Experiencing such a traumatic loss necessitated finding both similarities and differences between past experiences and the present grief (re-creating meaning). Ways to avoid its intensification were explored in the light of past history; and the difference between losing control over one's feelings following such a tragic loss as part of grief in contrast to not having control over the loss itself was investigated as an alternative meaning construction.

INTERVENTION THROUGH REBT FOR GRIEF

Grief as a process of reorganizing one's life and searching for a meaning following a loss through death is a painful experience. Pain in grief is undesirable but at the same time is unavoidable. The thought of experiencing pain is oftentimes too stressful so that many bereaved are involved in finding ways to avoid or bypass it only to realize that this is impossible. Helping clients therapeutically to not fear pain but rather accept it is a normal part of grieving as well as teaching them ways to handle or manage the pain that will facilitate a more adaptive process (Malkinson, 1996, 2005; Malkinson et al., 2000; Sanders, 1993).

This element of pain is similar to the catastrophic misinterpretation observed in panic disorders and PTSD (Clark, 1986; Moore, 1991; Warren et al., 1991). The REBT approach legitimizes pain and sadness as functional (healthy) negative emotions that are a normal part of coming to terms with traumatic and tragic loss. Pain is the emotional expression of the understanding and recognition of the fact of death. Moreover, the process of giving up old beliefs regarding the dead person and adopting new ones based on the new reality cannot be experienced without pain and sadness.

It is assumed that in dysfunctional acute as well as in complicated, especially prolonged grief, a secondary symptom (e.g., stress, anxiety) regarding pain may stem from irrational beliefs (demandingness) such as

"This death is so sad in itself that it shouldn't also be painful," or "I must be able to control the pain or else I will go crazy." In some cases, people even demand from themselves that they must have great pain, especially when they blame themselves for possibly forgetting the deceased. In all, the human quest to avoid pain and increase pleasure is seriously disturbed when experiencing a traumatic event like that of death (Ellis, 1962, 1986; Epstein, 1993).

REBT-based interventions for the acute phase and complicated grief have five aims toward facilitating an adaptive process:

1. Identifying irrational beliefs (demandingness directed to self, others, and the world: "I must not cry, if I do, I am a weak person," "I must be strong and in control") and their emotional (e.g., anxiety), behavioral (e.g., avoidance), and physiological consequences (e.g., breathing difficulties, heart palpitations).
2. Explaining and teaching the connections between beliefs (B) and consequences (C) whether emotional (e.g., feeling anxious when crying), behavioral (e.g., avoiding situations that might elicit pain) or physiological (e.g., feeling as though there is a bone in my throat, choking, and sleep disturbances).
3. Identifying and assessing individual specific consequences (i.e., specific language to describe emotions, behaviors and specific physiological reactions such as, "I must not give up, strong is my motto").
4. Teaching and practicing appropriate adaptive (rational) cognitive, emotional, behavioral, and physiological grief responses. (Ellis, 1993, 1994a; Ellis et al., 1997; Malkinson, 1996).
5. Assisting the bereaved persons in retelling and reconstructing their story within which the deceased is included ("this part of my life seems like a new chapter in my life story which excludes my husband; and I realize that all my life I was a compliant person but since his death I rebel against the world's injustice!").

There are a number of interventions that are applied beyond a specific phase or form of grief and they include the following:

- Provision of *information* about grief; its components, process, and outcome with particular attention being paid to gender and cultural-sensitive issues.
- *Normalizing* the process and its emotional and behavioral consequences. The overwhelming effect of the event creates an additional stressor to the bereaved, especially when the circumstances of the loss were horrendous. The feeling of loss of control over one's reactions is a frightening although a real one. For example, it is common

among the bereaved to react as follows: "I feel like I am going crazy," "something must be wrong with me if I can't stop crying." A possible response focusing on normalizing this experience is "it is human and normal to feel like that when one has experienced such a loss" or "how can one not cry or feel 'crazy' when one's world has shattered?"

- *Legitimizing* the temporary feeling of helplessness and loss of confidence that one get over the pain and sadness. When a client says: "I don't believe I will ever get over it," or "with the loss of my dear one my life has ended and I see no point in carrying on," along with assessing the possibility of thoughts of committing suicide, the therapist can reply: "you have full right as of now to think that way."

INTERVENTION IN THE ACUTE PHASE

Acute grief is, as the term implies, the initial reactions to the loss event. Often these reactions include intense emotional reactions combined with a sense of being overwhelmed. Therefore, interventions during this phase are aimed to facilitate a more adaptive, healthier course of grief and to help and support the bereaved individual gain a greater sense of control over his or her life. In addition to the three general interventions previously mentioned, suitable strategies for this phase include thought stopping, cognitive rehearsal, reframing (Ellis et al., 1997; Meichenbaum, 1986) without actually challenging or attempting to change the irrationality of the individual's beliefs (Malkinson, 1996, 2001). Teaching deep breathing that can be exercised at any moment of experiencing stress or flooding increases the client's sense of control and reduces the stress (Foa et al., 1998; Meichenbaum, 1986). Breathing, in contrast to relaxation, is not perceived by the bereaved as inappropriate and when applied and practiced helps the bereaved to identify moments of stress and attend to them. Breathing is also a physical way to thought stopping.

A Dialogue With Repetitive Thought

A dialogue with the repetitive thought "Why?" or "how could this have happened to me?" are questions with a flooding effect frequently encountered during the acute phase. Creating a dialogue with a "why?" question is another way of increasing cognitive control over an inner sense of not having one. Following the normalizing of the sense of flooding of the question "why?," the social worker distinguishes between the loss as an external uncontrollable event and its cognitive processing as a way to increase the feeling of control. This is followed by an introduction of the dialogue idea wherein answering the why question minimizes its flooding effect and increases the sense of control.

The following is an excerpt of applying this intervention with Sheila, a woman client age 60 who a few months earlier lost her husband from chronic heart disease. He had been ill and cared for by her for a number of years and died at age 75.

SHEILA: I can't stop thinking why, why did he die? How could he have left me? I know that his condition deteriorated and he always said his greatest fear would be to sit in a wheelchair and be incapacitated but why, why did he die?

SOCIAL WORKER: This is a justified question and what is the answer?

SHEILA: That's the problem that the question keeps popping over and over again.

SOCIAL WORKER: Let's think of an answer because without an answer the question as you described it will keep popping up.

SHEILA: I have no answer to that question.

SOCIAL WORKER: In a way this is an answer, can you tell yourself when the "why" question pops again "I have no answer to that question?"

SHEILA (LOUDLY): Why, why? And she answers: "I have no answer to that question."

SHEILA: Rationally, I know that it is irrational. I realize that I need not insist on finding an answer.

SOCIAL WORKER: You are right in realizing that as of now there is no point in insisting on finding an answer. How do you feel now with the answer of "I don't have an answer and I need not insist on finding one"? Do you feel more, less or the same level of flooding?

SHEILA: Less.

SOCIAL WORKER: Good, that helps you take a better care of yourself in moments of great pain and sadness. Paradoxically, not answering the question increases your sense of helplessness. So, I suggest you practice and apply it when you feel distressed as well as in between these feelings so you master its use.

In the next session the following was told by Sheila:

I cried and couldn't stop thinking that he left me never to return. My life is worthless and I couldn't stop thinking why? And then I remembered what you told me and said to myself that I don't have to insist on finding an answer. It helped because then I could think that actually he didn't want to see himself deteriorating and being depended. He loved life and dreaded the thought of being incapacitated. I also told myself that I wouldn't want to see him in such a terrible state of not functioning. It helps me and eases the pain but gives way to the yearning which is so intense and at times unbearable.

By having the dialogue with the "why" question and giving up the insistence of finding an answer, an answer was found and allowed the client to touch upon the yearning to her beloved husband, and focused the following sessions on ways to handle the pain involved in thinking about him.

The intervention in this case focused on the distinction between grief as painful process involving functional negative emotions, as opposed to a disturbed painful process that is maintained by adopting distorted interpretations resulting in dysfunctional emotions. An important element in an adaptive process is coming to terms both with the loss and the pain that it elicits. As therapy progressed Sheila became less anxious and less depressed but was sad, grieving, and significantly less avoidant of her pain. She resumed previously avoided activities, such as returning to a holiday resort they used to go to when her husband was alive and not condemning herself for yearning for him and feeling sadness whenever she thought how her life changed. The therapy was a process of regaining partial control, and of reestablishing an acceptable equilibrium between mind, feeling, and behavior.

COGNITIVE THERAPY FOR COMPLICATED GRIEF

Recent literature reviews (Wortman & Silver, 1989) have questioned some well-established notions regarding the "grief work" assumption that the failure to follow a predetermined course of grief will almost certainly result in some form of complicated, dysfunctional grief. Interventions deriving from the more recent stress and coping (Lazarus & Folkman, 1984) and meaning construction (Neimeyer, 1996) models regard grief as more adaptive when the bereaved individuals go through a cognitive (and emotional) experience by way of confronting the loss and of constructing a meaningful narrative, without necessarily having to detach themselves from the deceased (Neimeyer, 1996; Silverman, Klass, & Nickman, 1996). The implications of these reconsiderations put forth cognitive therapies as an efficient mode for grief intervention, viewing cognitions as significant in understanding human disturbance (Beck et al., 1993; Ellis, 1993).

Dysfunctional grief is defined by REBT therapists as one persisting over time with no diminishing effect of dominant irrational (distorted) beliefs regarding the loss event, the deceased and the self (Malkinson, 1996, 2001, 2005).

According to the REBT approach, during the acute phase of grief, the bereaved require help in accepting their grief and pain through general cognitive behavior strategies (e.g., using coping statements, thought stopping, cognitive rehearsal, and cognitive reframing, dialogue with the persistent question), combined with information giving, normalizing the process and legitimizing idiosyncratic responses. As was discussed elsewhere (Malkinson, 1996, 2001, 2005; Malkinson et al., 2000) in cases of complicated dysfunctional grief, challenging and correcting distorted beliefs is more timely, and the employment of rigorous "disputation" interventions combined with behavioral strategies (Ellis, 1994a) and diverse cognitive behavior methods (Kubany et al., 1995), may be more effective to change the client's more rigid beliefs to a more rational, desirable set of beliefs (Malkinson, 1996). In complicate grief, REBT interventions will most likely include rigorous logical empirical pragmatic disputation combined with the employment of other forms of empirical disputation (i.e., thought stopping, reframing, practicing rational statements and alternative behaviors). The wide range of strategies in CT has been described at length by Ellis et al. (1997), Beck (1976), and Freeman and White (1989).

Complicated Grief: Balancing Negative Emotional Response Through Letter-Writing

A major tenet of REBT is the notion that when death of a loved one occurs, negative feelings are part of the normal process of grief. As was noted earlier, it stresses the distinction between adaptive (functional) negative emotions and maladaptive (dysfunctional) ones. Among adaptive negative emotions are sadness ("life has changed forever"), pain ("it is painful to realize that I will never see my loved one again"), anger about behavior not at the person ("he didn't think about the outcomes"), and concern ("I couldn't help it"; "I will miss my loved one"). In contrast, maladaptive negative emotions are more extreme, intense, and prolonged: depression ("my life is worthless"), anxiety ("I can't stand the pain, it's not fair. It shouldn't be so painful"), rage ("how could he/she do this to me?"), guilt ("it's my fault, I wish I were dead") (Malkinson et al., 2000).

The aims of REBT-based interventions for complicated grief are similar to those in acute phase grief: identifying distorted cognitions and their emotional, behavioral, and physiological consequences; explaining teaching the belief consequence (B-C) connection and correcting dysfunctional beliefs with the aim to facilitate an adaptive process. Assessing idiosyncratic consequences and in particular identifying secondary symptoms (a distorted belief about a dysfunctional cognition or emotion) and assisting in a search for alternative ways of retelling one's shattered story.

In line with the REBT tenet of normalizing grief responses, the application of strategies such as "as if" dialogue or Rational Emotion Imagery (REI) (Maultsby, 1971; Ellis, 1993; Malkinson, 2005) provide a means to legitimately allow the bereaved to express and experience in imagery otherwise unexpressed or feared thoughts or secrets that he or she may hold or experience.

The use of letter-writing as an intervention to facilitate in cases of pathological grief was developed by Van der Hart (1987) and applied successfully in numerous cases (for details see Malkinson & Witztum 2005). In its first formulation it was applied as a leave-taking ritual toward breaking the bonds with the deceased. Nowadays, with the growing empirical support for the "continuing bond" concept, the main purpose of its use is to facilitate an adaptive process of meaning making (Neimeyer, et al 2000, 2005). Presently, one of the main purposes of this approach is to help the bereaved express their thoughts and feelings through writing as a way of searching and constructing alternative cognitive and emotional processing in creating a new meaning so that life after the loss may take its adaptable course. Letter-writing is a planned intervention aimed at helping the client in organizing life following the death of a loved one, and continue the construction of the disrupted life's narrative.

The healing potential of writing is well established (Pennebaker, 1997; Smyth, Stone, Hureitz, & Kael, 1999). Writing is putting into words thoughts and feelings about the writer's past, present, and future life. Dreams, hopes, traumas, and losses are materials that can be expressed through writing. Writing involves cognitions and emotions and has psychological as well as physical health benefits (Smyth et al., 1999). The incorporation of writing in grief has become widespread and is applied in a number of ways over a limited time or carried out daily for a period of time (Miller, 2002; Pennebaker & Beall, 1986). Whatever the chosen structure or setting, writing is believed to help the individual express the pain in a "private" way with the "writer" choosing the words, the pace and emotions, and a reconstruction of the narrative in a more organized way (Malkinson & Witztum, 2005).

A female client in her late twenties was referred to grief therapy 11 months after her brother was killed in military action. She said she felt depressed, cried a lot, gave up her work and had lost interest in life. A detailed assessment was conducted on the circumstances that had led to her feelings of depression and her related cognitions. There were four siblings, her brother and three sisters. The client's brother was the oldest, and she and her brother were very close. Bursting into tears, she said she felt depressed as life no longer seemed worth living ("it will never be the same; what is the purpose of it all?"); anger was also expressed at her brother for not taking better care of himself ("he always thought of others before himself, he should have been more considerate of himself"); and she feared she would never be able to forgive him.

The client also revealed that she was condemning herself for her inability to overcome her intrusive thoughts (secondary symptom), especially during a time when she thought she ought to support her parents whose lives were shattered. Complicated grief was assessed as related to the cyclical interaction between irrational beliefs (demandingness) and disturbed emotions (depression), apparently preventing an adaptive course of grief. Depression and anger toward the deceased brother were the emotional consequences of the distorted interpretation. In the intervention with this client, alongside logical disputation (mostly questions to evaluate the event empirically and how sad it was, logically arguing with the client's distorted thinking and challenging it), the letter-writing technique (Malkinson et al., 2005; Van der Hart, 1986) was the main strategy employed.

REI was applied in which she imagined a dialogue between her and her brother in the "as if" manner (Malkinson, 2001) to explore her cognitions related to circumstances of the past, to focus on the "here and now," and as an appraisal of the future. Identifying distorted cognitions and making a distinction between facts ("My brother died") and her "if only" thoughts or interpretations about these facts ("If only he had taken a better care of himself," or "If only I had another chance to see him") as well as teaching the beliefs-consequence connection. The imagined dialogue was rehearsed and practiced with a focus on functional, adaptive emotions (sadness, pain, and frustration). As she practiced the difference between rational and irrational thoughts, she was able to emotionally experience sadness as distinct from depression. As sad as the death event was and obviously had remained, it was the client's evaluation that had to be changed into an adaptive one.

A one time letter-writing "as if" to her brother was suggested as the first anniversary of his death was approaching. After explaining and preparing the client, a homework assignment (toward the end of the third session) was given to her. She was requested to write an "as if" letter to her brother. It was suggested that, as the anniversary of his death was approaching, she would go to the cemetery with someone of her choice and read the letter aloud "as if" to her brother. The homework was prescribed as a way of practicing rational (functional) thinking and also as a leave-taking ritual (Van der Hart, 1987; Witztum & Roman, 1993).

Preparation for her visit to the cemetery included going through the details she feared would be too painful and thus might be avoided. Pain was to be part of the experience. In order to overcome a secondary symptom (pain is the primary reaction and her irrational thought that "it must not be painful" lead to a secondary symptom of avoidance of the pain: "It shouldn't be too painful") it was crucial to attend to the client's pain tolerance and show her that, though painful, she could stand the anticipated pain of the letter-reading visit.

In the following session, the client described writing the letter "as if" to her brother and how painful it was to tell him how much she misses him, how angry she felt toward him for not taking care of himself and how life without him lost its meaning. She cried as she wrote the letter but felt she had to do it. She described her visit with her sister to the cemetery. She related how, in spite of her being tense, she had told her brother all the thoughts and feelings she experienced following his death, her concern and love for him. She cried in the session as she was telling it and felt very sad, though less angry toward him and less condemning of herself for not being able to control her depression. She said she felt relieved. After two more sessions, when it was apparent that the client's grieving was more adaptive, therapy was terminated.

Three months later, in a follow-up session, the client reported being less depressed, saying that, though she felt the sadness and the pain of her brother's death, she also thought that, "If he could have talked to her he probably would have wanted her to continue with her life and remember him." She looked sad but more at peace.

CONCLUSION

The quote from Ecclesiastes (3:1-9) best captures the idea that we as social workers and human creatures have to face death and grieve upon experiencing a loss: "For everything there is a season, and time for every matter under heaven: . . . a time to be born, and a time to die; . . . a time to mourn and a time to dance." In this chapter the view taken was the one that adapting to loss is dynamic and a continuous process of searching for meaning of what has changed forever. The way we were before the loss, our individual identity, the nature of our interpersonal fabric and the quality of our relationships are but few. Some of what we were will be transformed into elements of our personal history and memory shaped by our unique experiences with the deceased including language, intimacy, visions, hopes, and despair. At a time when a traumatic life experience such as the sudden death of a loved one has created total chaos, cognitive therapies, with their focus on one's beliefs make it possible for the bereaved to create a sense of coherence between what was lost and the new meaning that has yet to be found.

From that stance as social workers, our interventions focus on assisting the bereaved in experiencing grief as a combined cognitive, emotional behavioral, and physical process with a focus on telling and retelling the disrupted life story by employing a variety of interventions to enhance an adaptive outcome to the loss.

REFERENCES

American Psychiatric Association. (1994). *Diagnostic and statistical manual of mental disorders* (4th ed.). Washington, DC: Author.

Beck, A. T. (1976). *Cognitive therapy and the emotional disorders.* New York: International University Press.

Beck, A. T. (1989). Cognitive therapy. In A. Freeman, K. M. Simon, L. E. Beutler, & H. Arkowitz (Eds.), *Comprehensive handbook of cognitive therapy* (pp. 21–36). New York: Plenum Press.

Beck, A. T., Wright, F. W., Newman, C. F., & Liese, B. (1993). *Cognitive therapy in substance abuse.* New York: Guilford.

Black, D., Newman, M., Harris-Hendriks, J., & Mezey, G. (Eds.) (1997). *Psychological trauma.* London: Gaskel.

Bonanno, G. A., Wortman, C. B., Lehaman, D. R., Tweed, R. G., Haring, M., Sonnega, J., et al. (2002). Resilience to loss and chronic grief: A prospective study from preloss to 18 months postloss. *Journal of Personality and Social Psychology, 83,* 1150–1164.

Boss, P. (2002). Ambiguous loss: Working with families of the missing. *Family Process, 41,* 14–17.

Bowlby, J. (1980). *Loss: Sadness and depression.* London: Hogarth Press.

Bugan, L. A. (1977). Human grief: A model for prediction and intervention. *American Journal of Orthopsychiatry, 47,* 196–206.

Clark, D. (1986). A cognitive approach to panic. *Journal of Behavior Research & Therapy, 24,* 461–470.

DiGiuseppe, R. (1991). Rational-emotive model of assessment. In M. Bernard (Ed.), *Using rational emotive therapy effectively: A practitioner's guide* (pp. 151–170). New York: Plenum Press.

Ellis, A. (1962). Reason and emotion in psychotherapy. Secaucus, NJ: Lyle Stuart.

Ellis, A. (1976). The biological basic of human irrationality. *Journal of Individual Psychology, 32,* 145–168.

Ellis, A. (1986). Discomfort anxiety: A new cognitive behavioral construct. In A. Ellis & R. Griager (Eds.), *RET handbook of rational emotive therapy* (Vol. 2, pp. 105–120). New York: Springer.

Ellis, A. (1989). The history of cognition in psychotherapy. In A. Freeman, K. M. Simon, L. E. Beutler, & H. Arkowitz (Eds.), *Comprehensive handbook of cognitive therapy* (pp. 5–20). New York: Plenum Press.

Ellis, A. (1991). The revised ABC's of rational-emotive therapy (RET). *Journal of Rational Emotive and Cognitive Behavior Therapy, 9*, 139–172.

Ellis, A. (1993a). The history of cognition in psychotherapy. In A. Freeman, K. M. Simon, L. E. Beutker, & H. Arkowitz (Eds.), *Comprehensive handbook of cognitive therapy* (pp. 5–21). New York: Plenum Press.

Ellis, A. (1993b). Rational-emotive imagery: RET version. In M. E. Bernard & J. L. Wolfe (Eds.), *The RET resource book for practitioners.* New York: Institute for Rational-Emotive Therapy.

Ellis, A. (1994a). General semantic and rational emotive behavioral therapy. In P. P. Johnson, D. D. Burland, & U. Klien (Eds.), *More e-prime* (pp. 213–240). Concord, CA: International Society for General Semantic.

Ellis, A. (1994b). Post-traumatic stress disorder (PTSD): A rational emotive behavioral theory. *Journal of Rational Emotive and Cognitive Therapy, 12*(1), 3–26.

Ellis, A. (1994c). *Reason and emotion in psychotherapy. A comprehensive method of treating human disturbances, revised and updated.* New York: A Birch Lane Press Book.

Ellis, A. (1995). Rational emotive behavior therapy. In R. J. Corsini & D. Wedding (Eds.), *Current psychotherapies* (5th ed., pp. 162–196). Ithaca, IL: Peacock.

Ellis, A., & Bernard, M. E. (Eds.). (1985). *Clinical application of rational-emotive therapy.* New York: Plenum Press.

Ellis, A., & Dryden, W. (1997). *The practice of rational emotive behavior therapy.* New York: Springer.

Epstein, S. (1993). Bereavement from the perspective of cognitive-experiential self-theory. In M. S. Stroebe, W. Stroebe, & R. O. Hansson (Eds.), *Handbook of bereavement: Theory, research and intervention* (pp. 112–125). Cambridge: Cambridge University Press.

Fieffel, H. (1987). Grief and bereavement: An overview and perspective. *Society and Welfare, 7*, 203–209. (in Hebrew)

Foa, E. B., & Rothbaum, B. O. (1998). *Treating the trauma of rape.* New York: Guilford.

Freeman, A., & White, D. M. (1989). The treatment of suicidal behavior. In A. Freeman, K. M. Simon, L. E. Beutker, & H. Arkowitz (Eds.), *Comprehensive handbook of cognitive therapy* (pp. 231–346). New York: Plenum Press.

Freud, S. (1917/1957). *Mourning and melancholia. Standard edition of the complete psychological works of Sigmund Freud.* London: Hogarth Press.

Gauthier, Y., & Marshall, W. L. (1977). Grief: A cognitive-behavioral analysis. *Cognitive Therapy Research, 1*, 39–44.

Gluhosky, V. L. (1995). A cognitive perspective on bereavement: Mechanisms and treatment. *Journal of Cognitive Psychotherapy: An International Quarterly, 9*, 75–80.

Hackman, A. (1993). Behavioral and cognitive psychotherapies: Past history, current application and future registration issues. *Behavioral and Cognitive Psychotherapy, 21*(Suppl. 1), 1–75.

Horowitz, M. J. (1986). *Stress response syndrome.* Northvale, NJ: Aronson.

Horowitz, M. J. (2001). *Stress response syndromes: Personality styles and interventions* (4th ed.). Northvale, NJ: Aronson.

Horowitz, M. J., Bonano, G. A., & Holen, A. (1993). Pathological grief: Diagnosis and explanation. *Psychosomatic Medicine, 55,* 260–273.

Janoff-Bulman, R. (1992). *Shattered assumption: Towards a new psychology of trauma.* New York: Free Press.

Kavanagh, D. J. (1990). Towards a cognitive-behavioral intervention for adult grief reactions. *British Journal of Psychology, 157,* 373–383.

Kelly, G. A. (1955). *The psychology of personal constructs.* New York: Norton.

Klass, D., Silverman, P. S., & Nickman, L. (Eds.) *Continuing bonds.* Washington, D. C.: Taylor & Francis.

Kleber, R. J., Brom, D., & Defares, P. B. (1992). *Coping with trauma: Theory, prevention and treatment.* Amsterdam: Alphen a/d Rijn Swets Zeitlinger.

Kubany, S. E., & Manke, F. P. (1995). Cognitive therapy for trauma-related guilt: Conceptual bases and treatment outlines. *Cognitive and Behavioral Practice, 2,* 27–61.

Lazarus, R. S., & Folkman, S. (1984). *Stress, appraisal and coping.* New York: Springer.

Mahony, M. J. (1991). *Human change processes.* New York: Basic Books.

Mahony, M. J. (2003). *Constructive psychotherapy: Practices, processes, and personal revolutions.* New York: Guilford.

Malkinson, R. (1996). Cognitive behavioral grief therapy. *Journal of Rational-Emotive & Cognitive-Behavioral Therapy, 14,* 156–165.

Malkinson, R. (2001). Cognitive behavioral therapy of grief: A review and application. *Research on Social Work Practice, 11,* 671–698.

Malkinson, R. (2005). *Cognitive grief therapy: Constructing a rational meaning to life following loss.* New York: Norton.

Malkinson, R., & Bar-Tur, L. (2005). Long term bereavement processes of older parents: The three phases of grief. *Omega, 50,* 103–129.

Malkinson, R., & Ellis, A. (2000). The application of rational-emotive behavior therapy (REBT) in traumatic and non-traumatic grief. In R. Malkinson, S. Rubin, & E. Witztum (Eds.), *Traumatic and non-traumatic loss and bereavement: Clinical theory and practice* (pp. 173–196). Madison, CT: Psychosocial Press.

Malkinson, R., Kushnir, T., & Weisberg, E. (1997). Stress management and burnout prevention in female blue-collar workers: Theoretical and practical implications. *International Journal of Stress Management, 4,* 183–195.

Malkinson, R., Rubin, S., & Witztum, E. (Eds.). (2000). *Traumatic and non-traumatic loss and bereavement: Clinical theory and practice.* Madison, CT: Psychosocial Press.

Malkinson, R., Rubin, S., & Witztum, E. (2005). Terror, trauma and bereavement: Implications for theory and therapy. In Y. Danieli, D. Brom, & J. Sills (Eds.), *The trauma of terrorism: Sharing knowledge and shared care, an international handbook* (pp. 467–477). New York: Haworth Press.

Malkinson, R., & Witztum, E. (2005). Cognitive intervention with complicated grief: Letter-writing as a leave-taking ritual in a search for meaning. In

R. Malkinson (Ed.), *Cognitive grief therapy: Constructing a rational meaning to life following loss.* New York: Norton.

Maultsby, M. J., Jr. (1971). Rational emotive imagery. *Rational Living, 6,* 24–27.

Mawson, D., Marks, I. M., Ramm, L., & Stern, R. S. (1981). Guided mourning for morbid grief: A controlled study. *British Journal of Psychiatry, 138,* 185–193.

Meichenbaum, D. (1986). Cognitive-behavior modification. In F. H. Kanfer & A. P. Goldstien (Eds.), *Helping people change* (pp. 60–72). New York: Pergamon Press.

Miller, L. (2002). Psychological interventions for terroristic trauma: Symptoms, syndromes and treatment strategies. *Psychotherapy: Theory/Research/Practice/ Training, 39,* 283–296.

Moore, R. H. (1991). *Traumatic incident reduction: A cognitive emotive resolution of post-traumatic stress disorder (PTSD).* Clearwater, FL: Moore.

Neimeyer, R. A. (1996). Process interventions for the constructivist psychotherapist. In H. Rosen & K. Kuehlwein (Eds.), *Constructing realities* (pp. 371–411) San Francisco: Jossey Bass.

Neimeyer, R. A. (1999). *Lessons of loss: A guide to coping.* New York: McGraw-Hill.

Neimeyer, R. A. (2000). *Lessons of loss: A guide to coping.* Keystone Heights, FL: Psychoeducational Resources, Inc.

Neimeyer, R. A. (2005). Re-storying loss: Fostering growth in posttraumtic narrative. In L. Calhoun & R. T. Tedeschi (Eds.), *Handbook of Postraumatic Growth: Research and practice.* Mahwah, NJ: Lawrence Earlbaum.

Neimeyer, R. A. (in press). *Complicated grief and the quest for meaning: A constructivist contribution.* Omega: Journal of death and Dying.

Neimeyer, R. A. Keese, N. J., & Fortner, B. V. (2000). Loss and meaning reconstruction: Proposition and procedures. In R. Malkinson, S. Rubin, & E. Witztum (Eds.), *Traumatic and non-traumatic loss and bereavement* (pp. 197–230). Madison, CT: Psychosocial Press.

Parkes, C. M. (1993). Bereavement as a psychosocial transition: Processes of adaptation to change. In M. S. Stroebe, W. Stroebe, & R. O. Hansson (Eds.), *Handbook of bereavement: Theory, research and intervention* (pp. 91–102). Cambridge: Cambridge University Press.

Parkes, M. (1975). Determinants of outcomes following bereavement. *Omega, 6,* 303–323.

Parkes, C. M., & Weiss, R. S. (1983). *Recovery from bereavement.* New York: Basic Books.

Pennbaker, J. (1993). Putting stress into words. *Behavior Research and Therapy, 131,* 539–548.

Pennebaker, J. W., & Beall, S. K. (1986). Confronting a traumatic event: Toward an understanding of inhibition and disease. *Journal of Abnormal Psychology, 95,* 247–281.

Piaget, J. (1950). *The psychology of intelligence.* New York: Harcourt Brace.

Prigerson, H. G., Frank, E., Kasl, S. V., Reynolds III, C. F., Anderson, B., Zubenko et al. (1995). Complicated grief and bereavement-related depression as distinct disorders: Preliminary empirical validation in elderly bereaved spouses. *American Journal of Psychiatry, 152,* 22–30.

Prigerson, H. G., Maciejewski, P. K., & Rosenheck, R. A. (1999). The effects of marital distress and marital quality on health and health service among women. *Medical Care, 37,* 858–873.

Ramsay, R. W. (1979). Bereavement: A behavioral treatment of pathological grief. In P. O. Sjodeh, S. Bates, & W. S. Dochens (Eds.), *Trends in behavior therapy* (pp. 217–247). New York: Academic Press.

Rando, T. A. (1988). *Grieving: How to go on living when someone you love dies.* Lexington, MA: Lexington Books.

Rando, T. A. (1993). *Treatment of complicated mourning.* Champaign, IL: Research Press.

Raphael, B. (1983). *Anatomy of bereavement.* New York: Basic Books.

Raphael, B., Middelton, W., Martinek, N., & Misso, V. (1993). Counseling and therapy for the bereaved. In M. S. Stroebe, W. Stroebe, & R. O. Hansson (Eds.), *Handbook of bereavement: Theory, research and intervention* (pp. 427–456). Cambridge: Cambridge University Press.

Resick, P. A., & Schnicke, M. K. (1995). *Cognitive processing therapy for rape victims: A treatment manual.* New York: Sage.

Richards, D., & Lovell, K. (1997). Behavioral and cognitive approaches. In D. Black, M. Newman, J. Harris-Hendriks, & G. Mezey (Eds.), *Psychological trauma* (pp. 264–274). London: Gaskel.

Rubin, S. (1981). A two-track model of bereavement: Theory and application in research. *American Journal of Orthopsychiatry, 51,* 101–109.

Rubin, S. (1993). The death of a child is forever: The life course impact of child loss. In M. S. Stroebe, W. Stroebe, & R. O. Hansson (Eds.), *Handbook of bereavement* (pp. 285–299). Cambridge: Cambridge University Press.

Rubin, S. S., & Malkinson, R. (2001). Parental response of child loss across the life cycle: Clinical and research perspective. In M. S. Stroebe, W. Stroebe, & R. O. Hansson (Eds.), *Handbook of bereavement* (pp. 219–240). Cambridge: Cambridge University Press.

Sanders, C. M. (1989). *Grief: The mourning after.* New York: John Wiley.

Sanders, C. M. (1993). Risk factors in bereavement outcome. In M. S. Stroebe, S. Stroebe, & R. O. Hansson (Eds.), *Handbook of bereavement: Theory, research and intervention* (pp. 255–270). Cambridge: Cambridge University Press.

Schut, H. A. W., de Keijser, J., van den Bout, J., & Stroebe, M. S. (1997). Cross-modality grief therapy: Description and assessment of a new program. *Journal of Clinical Psychology, 52*(3), 357–365.

Sireling, L., Cohen, D., & Marks, I. (1988). Guided mourning for morbid grief: A replication. *Behavior Therapy, 29,* 121–132.

Silverman, P., Klass, D., & Nickman, S. L. (1996). Introduction: What's the problem? In D. Klass, P. Silverman, & S. L. Nickman (Eds.), *Continuing bonds* (pp. 3–27). Washington, DC: Taylor & Francis.

Stroebe, W., & Stroebe, M. (1987). *Bereavement and health: The psychological and physical consequences of partner loss.* Cambridge: Cambridge University Press.

Stroebe, M. S., Gergen, M. M., Geregen, K. J., & Stroebe, W. (1992). Broken hearts or broken bonds: Love and death in historical perspective. *American Psychologist, 10,* 1025–1212.

Stroebe, M. S., & Schut, H. (1999). The dual process model of coping with loss. *Death Studies, 23,* 1–28.

Smyth, J. M., Stone, A. A., Hureaitz, A., & Kael, A. (1999). Effects of writing about stressful experiences on symptom reduction in patients with asthma or rheumatoid arthritis. *Journal of American Medical Association, 281*(14), 1304–1309.

Van der Hart, O. (1986). (Ed.) *Coping with loss.* New York: Irvington.

Van der Hart, O. (1987). Leave taking rituals in mourning therapy. *Society & Welfare. Special Issue: Bereavement and Mourning, 7*(3), 266–279.

Walen, S., DiGiuseppe, R., & Dryden, W. (1992). *A practitioner's guide to rational-emotive therapy.* New York: Oxford University Press.

Warren, R., & Zgourides G. D. (1991). *Anxiety disorders: A rational emotive perspective.* New York: Pergamon Press.

Witztum, E., & Roman, I. (1993). Psychotherapeutic intervention with unresolved and pathological grief following loss of an adult parent. In R. Malkinson, S. Rubin, & E. Witztum (Eds.), *Loss and bereavement in Jewish society in Israel* (pp. 117–138). Jerusalem: Cana—Ministry of Defense.

Worden, J. W. (2000/1991). *Grief counseling and grief therapy: A handbook for the mental health practitioner.* New York: Springer.

Wortman, C. M., & Silver, R. (1989). The myth of coping with loss. *Journal of Consulting & Clinical Psychology, 57,* 349–359.

CHAPTER 24

Eating Disorders

Laura L. Myers

INTRODUCTION

> Eating disorders are of great interest to the public, of perplexity to researchers, and a challenge to clinicians. They feature prominently in the media, often attracting sensational coverage. Their cause is elusive, with social, psychological, and biological processes all seeming to play a major part, and they are difficult to treat, with some patients actively resisting attempts to help them. Nevertheless, there is progress to report both in terms of their understanding and treatment. (Fairburn & Harrison, 2003, p. 407)

In this chapter, the definitions, prevalence, prognosis, warning signs, and treatment will be presented for (a) anorexia nervosa (AN), (b) bulimia nervosa (BN), (c) eating disorder not otherwise specified or atypical eating disorder (AED), and (d) binge-eating disorder (BED). An emphasis is placed on the recent research evaluating the use of cognitive behavior therapy (CBT) to treat each of these disorders.

ANOREXIA NERVOSA

The distinctive core psychopathology for both anorexia nervosa (AN) and bulimia nervosa (BN) is a person's constant concern and evaluation of his or her shape and weight. While most people assess themselves on a variety of domains (i.e., academics, sports, relationships, work, parenting skills), people with eating disorders judge their own self-worth almost exclusively on their shape and weight. One could argue that the main difference between clients with AN and clients with BN is how successful the client has been in his or her goal of weight loss, as part of the criteria for diagnosing AN requires a weight loss of 15 percent of total body weight. Others might perceive the difference as a matter of severity, with clients with AN having a more severe body image disturbance, therefore continuing to feel overweight even at extremely low weights (Fairburn et al., 2003).

The operational definitions of AN and BN are still in a state of flux, changing significantly with each new edition of the American Psychiatric Association's (APA) diagnostic manual. The current criteria for AN, as defined by the APA in the fourth edition of the *Diagnostic and Statistical Manual of Mental Disorders* (*DSM-IV;* 1994), include: (a) Refusal to maintain body weight at or above a minimally normal weight for age and height (weight loss leading to maintenance of body weight less than 85% of that expected, or failure to make expected weight gain during a period of growth, leading to body weight less than 85% of that expected); (b) Intense fear of gaining weight or becoming fat, even though underweight; (c) Disturbance in the way in which one's body weight or shape is experienced, undue influence of body weight or shape on self-evaluation, or denial of the seriousness of the current low body weight; (d) In postmenarcheal females, absence of at least three consecutive menstrual cycles.

There are two subtypes of AN. A person with the restricting type of AN attempts to lose weight by reducing his or her intake of calories, exercising excessively following food intake, and frequent fasting. A person with the second type of AN also restricts food intake, but usually as a result of the starvation, participates in periods of binge-eating and purging. The purging may involve self-induced vomiting, or the abuse of laxatives, diuretics, or enemas. Sometimes purging is used after only small amounts of food are eaten (Herrin & Matsumoto, 2002).

Prevalence

The prevalence of eating disorders is difficult to ascertain, as people who suffer from these disorders are usually secretive until the physical and medical consequences make it impossible for them to hide their problem. Indeed, clients with eating disorders who lose a great deal of weight are often envied by friends and family members for their great self-control. Therefore, unless the psychological or physical symptoms become extreme, many eating disorders remain undiagnosed. Research has estimated the prevalence of AN in adolescent women at 0.7%, with 19 females and 2 males per 100,000 people (Fairburn et al., 2003).

Prognosis

The onset of AN most often occurs during the mid-teen years, and usually begins with dieting, which then develops into extreme and unhealthy food restriction. Some people with AN grow out of the disorder naturally as they mature through adolescence. Others get entrenched in their compulsions toward weight loss, and require intensive treatment to overcome the disorder. In 10 to 20%t of clients with AN, the disorder proves to be intractable (Steinhausen, 2002). The mortality rate among people with AN is 12 times the normal rate, usually resulting from starvation, suicide, or extremely low potassium levels (Herrin et al., 2002). Hall and Ostroff (1998) estimate that 10% of people who suffer with AN die as a result of complications of the disorder.

Warning Signs and Symptoms

The main warning sign that a person is developing AN is very rapid weight loss and/or extreme weight loss. Clients with AN practice a severe and extreme restriction of food intake. They generally avoid all foods that are considered fattening. In an effort to compensate for even small amounts of food eaten, clients with AN might participate in a compulsive exercise regime, use self-induced vomiting, or misuse laxatives or diuretics to rid their bodies of extra pounds (Fairburn et al., 2003). They may turn to vegetarianism in an effort to avoid extra fat. Most clients with AN eat only a limited number of foods, and they may develop other rituals around food intake to help reduce their calorie intake, such as cutting their food into tiny bites, chewing each bite of food a certain number of times, or constantly drinking water or diet soda (Herrin et al., 2002). These types of behaviors can sometimes be observed by social workers in a variety of settings, including schools, counseling centers, medical clinics, foster care and adoption agencies, and anywhere adolescents and young adults are served food.

Psychological symptoms of AN include depression, anxiety disorder, irritability, mood swings, impaired concentration, loss of sexual desire, and obsessive thoughts. Clients with AN often withdraw from friends and family and become very isolated as obsession with their weight and body shape increases. As part of their obsession with food, some people with AN will spend a great deal of time shopping for and preparing food for family and friends, but will eat only small amounts or none at all (Herrin et al., 2002).

Physical symptoms may include heightened sensitivity to cold, constipation, fullness or bloatedness after eating, dizziness, fainting, absence of menstruation, dry skin, hair loss, crying without tears caused by dehydration, fine downy hair, called lanugo, on the back, forearms, and side of the face, cold hands and feet, cardiac arrhythmias, and muscle weakness (Fairburn et al., 2003). More serious signs that AN might be affecting a person's heart include fatigue, light-headedness, bluish, splotchy hands and feet, slowed or irregular heartbeat, shortness of breath, chest pain, leg pain, rapid breathing, and low blood pressure. Another serious complication of AN is osteoporosis, caused by the reduction of estrogen, which leads to bone loss. During adolescence, when bones are still developing, this bone loss can be particularly devastating (Herrin et al., 2002).

Cognitive Behavior Treatment

Compared to BN, the treatment of AN has been the subject of surprisingly little research. Of course, one of the problems with all eating disorders is that as long as the clients are successful in controlling their shape and weight, they often do not consider the behavior a problem and will not seek help. Unlike BN, however, because of the severe weight loss, parents, teachers, and others close to the client suffering with AN can often recognize the problem regardless of whether the client is seeking help.

There has been very little research on CBT for clients with AN (Wilson, 1999; Wilson, Vitousek, & Loeb, 2000), and outcomes are inconsistent. Ball and Mitchell (2004) recently compared CBT to behavioral family therapy, probably the most widely used treatment for clients with AN (Robin, Gilroy, & Baker, 1998). Treatment involved 25 1-hour sessions over a 12-month period, and was based on the treatment manual developed by Garner and Bemis (1982). Of the total sample, 60% had good outcomes, defined as weight within 10% of average body weight and regular menstrual cycles. There were no significant differences between the outcomes for CBT and those for behavioral family therapy. These findings are modest, however, in that a majority of the clients did not fully recover from eating disorder symptoms, and the more severely disordered patients required hospitalization during the treatment (Ball et al., 2004).

Because treatment outcomes are still inconsistent with this population, Lappalainen and Tuomisto (1999) emphasize, "The importance of an individual analysis should not be underestimated. Understanding the functions of 'anorectic behaviour' is a challenge, because it is a result of a multi-faceted interaction between inherited and learned behaviours affected by a cultural context" (p. 174). Although their research on CBT has been inconclusive, Fairburn et al. (2003) do offer four components of the treatment of AN that summarize the opinions of many professionals working with this disorder. The first is to motivate the client to accept that they need help. Second, the client's weight needs to be restored. Behavior therapy is the treatment generally used during this early phase of treatment. Reversing the effects of malnutrition usually results in a significant improvement of the client's overall state. This step may have to be completed in a hospital, especially if there are indications of suicide risk, severe and rapid weight loss, or medical complications, such as edema, severe electrolyte imbalance, hypoglycemia, or infection.

The third component of the treatment of AN involves clients' distorted thinking regarding their weight and shape, their disordered eating habits, and their overall psychosocial functioning. A behavioral family-based treatment has shown to be helpful with younger adolescent clients with AN (Lock, le Grange, Agras, & Dare, 2001; Russell, Szmukler, Dare, & Eisler, 1987). The final issue in the treatment of AN is the question of compulsory treatment. Many clients with AN do not feel weight loss is a problem, and therefore do not seek or want treatment. These clients are sometimes admitted to a hospital against their wishes and fed intravenously to ward off the extreme effects of starvation, including death. The decision to treat a client with AN against his or her wishes should never be taken lightly (Fairburn et al., 2003; Russell, 2001).

CASE STUDY

The anorexic child refuses to maintain even a minimally normal body weight. She is intensely afraid of gaining weight, a fear that is fueled by a distorted perception of her body's shape and size. No matter how thin she gets, she sees herself as fat and unattractive, and this distortion in perception usually becomes more severe the more weight she loses. (Herrin et al., 2002, p. 4)

One young woman, named Allie, was attending college with her husband. She was extremely thin, and had always attracted positive attention for her weight. Allie was always dieting, and ate virtually nothing at most meals. At age 19, she was brought in to the emergency room by her husband due to light-headedness and repeated fainting spells. For the year prior, she reported having gone from 101 pounds down to 94 pounds. At 5'6", she was clearly more than 15% below her ideal body weight. She reported that she had not had her menstrual period for over 2 years, but as it had always been sporadic since she started menstruating at age 14, she had not been concerned. Allie was

(continues)

diagnosed as having AN, nonpurging type. Over the next 14 months, with individual cognitive behavior therapy on a weekly basis, as well as intensive nutrition education, Allie was able to increase her weight back to 105 pounds and her menstrual cycles became fairly regular, ranging from 34 to 45 days. She still dieted, however, and reported periodic episodes of binge-eating and purging through vomiting. Her husband reported that when attending dinner at her parents' home, Allie would sometimes eat the entire main course intended for six people before the meal was served. She would follow this with vomiting, and a period of depression. During this time, her therapist diagnosed her with atypical eating disorder (discussed later), as she no longer met the criteria for AN, and the binge-eating and purging was too infrequent to meet the criteria for BN. The therapist felt, nevertheless, that the eating disorder was still serious enough to warrant a diagnosis, and believed that any negative event in Allie's life could easily trigger another more serious episode of AN.

Approximately 2 years after her emergency room visit, Allie got pregnant. During her entire pregnancy, she reported having had only two episodes of binge-eating and purging. She gained 24 pounds during her pregnancy, and the baby was born healthy. She continued to see her therapist, and felt the eating disorder was behind her. Unfortunately, complications caused by an estimated 6 years of AN (age 13 to 19) created serious health issues throughout her adult life.

BULIMIA NERVOSA

While clients with AN generally restrict their calorie intake in order to lose a significant amount of weight, clients with BN may be attempting the same goal, but experience frequent episodes of binge-eating, or uncontrolled overeating. These are usually followed by some type of purging behavior to help get rid of the unwanted calories. These clients sometimes describe themselves as failed anorexics (Fairburn et al., 2003). As with AN, there are two subtypes of BN, the purging type and the nonpurging type. The purging type uses self-induced vomiting or the abuse of laxatives or diuretics to control weight gain, and the nonpurging type uses fasting and excessive exercise to compensate for binge-eating (Herrin et al., 2002).

The current criteria for BN, as defined in the *DSM-IV* (APA, 1994), include: (a) recurrent episodes of binge-eating; (b) recurrent inappropriate compensatory behavior to prevent weight gain, such as self-induced vomiting, misuse of laxatives, diuretics, enemas, or other medications, fasting, or excessive exercise; (c) these behaviors have occurred, on average, at least twice a week for 3 months; (d) self-evaluation is unduly influenced by body shape and weight; and (e) the disturbance does not occur exclusively during episodes of anorexia nervosa (p. 549). If the client meets the criteria for both BN and AN, only the diagnosis for AN is made. The distinguishing factors between BN and AN are the presence of significant weight loss and the absence of menstrual cycles in the criteria for AN.

Defining the terms used in the criteria for BN has prompted numerous debates, including the presence and frequency of binging, the size of the binge, the presence and frequency of purging activity, and the presence of distorted body image. Binging is defined in the criteria for BN as being characterized by both of the following: (1) eating, within any 2-hour period, an amount of food that is definitely larger than most people would eat during a similar period of time and under similar circumstances; and (2) a sense of lack of control over eating during the episode, such as feeling that one cannot stop eating or control what or how much one is eating (APA, 1994).

Schlundt and Johnson (1990), believing that the classification of food intake as a binge is subjective and differs from client to client, define a binge as "the ingestion of any food substance or quantity that violates the individual's idea of dieting and thereby increases anxiety regarding weight gain" (p. 4). They argue that for different clients, a binge may involve the consumption of thousands of calories, a normal-sized meal, or even a single doughnut. In response to this argument, two types of binges have now been classified. The objective binge meets the DSM definition previously given. A subjective binge is a binge during which the client eats a normal or even a small amount of food, but feels the loss of control characteristic of a binge (Fairburn, 1995).

Prevalence

The prevalence rates of BN are difficult to ascertain as many people suffering from this disorder do not seek help. In addition, because there is not the significant weight loss found in AN, there are usually not obvious physical signs of BN. Prevalence rates of BN offered by researchers vary significantly from study to study, depending on the age and race of the sample and the criteria used. Fairburn et al. (2003) estimate that 1 to 2% of 16- to 35-year-old females have BN, with 29 females and 1 male per 100,000 population. They further assert that eating disorders are found predominantly among white women living in Western societies.

Prognosis

The average age of onset for BN is slightly later than AN. BN usually starts with dieting, much like AN. In about 25% of the cases of BN, the criteria for AN are met for a period of time before developing into BN. Extreme food restriction and the resulting weight loss are interrupted by repeated binge-eating episodes (Sullivan, Bulik, Carter, Gendall, & Joyce, 1996). On average, people who seek help for BN have suffered with the disorder for 5 years. Approximately 30 to 50% of those diagnosed with BN still have a serious eating disorder 5 to 10 years later, although in many cases it evolves into an atypical eating disorder (Fairburn, Cooper, Doll, Norman, & O'Connor, 2000).

Warning Signs and Symptoms

Clients with BN attempt to restrict their food intake, and while they are sometimes successful at keeping a low body weight, they generally maintain a fairly average weight. The most obvious warning sign for BN that a social worker might observe is a fluctuating pattern of extreme food intake restriction and large food intake amounts. Some people who suffer with BN complain of stomach flu symptoms or complain that certain foods do not digest well. Many show signs of depression, anxiety disorders, and compulsive behaviors, and a smaller group abuse substances (including appetite suppressants), and possibly injure themselves. People who vomit regularly might suffer from heartburn, chronic sore throat, hoarseness, difficulty swallowing, swollen cheeks, redness or calluses on the back of their hands from using their fingers to induce vomiting, redness around the mouth due to exposure to stomach acid, red blood spots around the eyes from the pressure of vomiting, and large numbers of cavities (Fairburn et al., 2003; Herrin et al., 2002).

Cognitive Behavior Treatment

Research has found that cognitive behavior therapy focusing on the specific eating behaviors and the distorted thinking is the most effective treatment for clients with BN. Current CBT therapies are based on a treatment manual originally developed by Fairburn, Marcus, and Wilson (1993). Components include self-monitoring, reducing environmental cues to binge, meal planning, introducing forbidden foods, problem-solving skills, relaxation training, nutrition education, and cognitive restructuring (Fairburn, 1988). Treatment usually involves 20 individual sessions stretching over 5 to 6 months, with 30 to 50% of the clients making a complete and lasting recovery (Fairburn et al., 2003). Research suggests that these programs "produce substantial improvements in both eating behavior (including, in episodes of overeating, a reduction in the use of other methods of weight control and in the level of dietary restraint), as well as an improvement in attitude about body shape and weight" (Kennedy & Garfinkel, 1992, p. 311).

The three main goals of CBT include (a) establishing a regular eating pattern; (b) evaluating and changing beliefs about shape and weight, and (c) relapse prevention. These goals are what define the three phases of CBT for BN. In Phase 1, the therapist helps the client establish an eating pattern that includes three meals and two snacks per day. This phase usually lasts 6 weeks and 8 sessions (2 sessions the first 2 weeks, weekly thereafter). Clients monitor their eating patterns by recording what is eaten throughout each day, when, where, whether the episode constitutes a binge, and when purging occurs. Eating on a regular schedule helps counteract binging, and thus reduces purging behaviors.

Phase 2 begins after the client has established a fairly regular eating pattern, and binging and purging is usually significantly reduced. Increasing the types of food that are eaten is a goal of this phase. The client then creates four lists of food, ranging from least threatening to most threatening. Another goal of this phase is to help the client change his or her beliefs that have contributed to body dissatisfaction, dieting, and eating disorder behaviors. A third goal of this phase is increase problem-solving skills. Some clients use binging and purging to cope with difficult and unpleasant situations. Problem-solving techniques are used to help clients learn alternative ways of coping with stressful situations. The final phase of CBT, Phase 3, is focused on relapse prevention. Clients learn to identify warning signs and develop strategies to use in case of relapse (Spangler, 1999).

More advanced research has shown CBT to be as or more effective in treating BN than supportive psychotherapy, focal psychotherapy, exposure with response prevention, behavior therapy, and treatment with antidepressants (Fairburn et al., 1993). While antidepressant drugs result in a quick decline in the frequency of binging-and-purging behavior, the effect is not generally sustained and the improvement is not as great as that obtained with CBT. Combining antidepressant drugs with CBT provided few consistent benefits over CBT alone (Fairburn et al., 2003).

Despite this clear finding in the research that CBT can help many clients with BN, Mussell et al. (2000) found that few psychologists are actually providing this therapy for their patients with BN. Based on this finding, several areas of research have surfaced. A recent study (Chen et al., 2003) compared group and individual CBT. The group CBT was adapted from the manual for individual CBT written by Fairburn et al. (1993). Group sessions lasted 90 minutes, were closed, and began with only six patients per group. Both individual and group CBT were effective in reducing the BN symptoms, and the improvements were maintained at 6 month follow-ups. This suggests that group CBT may be a cost-effective alternative to individual CBT for clients with BN (Chen et al., 2003).

Self-help manuals have also been developed by the leading professionals in the eating disorders field (Cooper, 1995; Fairburn, 1995; Schmidt & Treasure, 1993), and have been offered as a treatment to be completed unassisted or "guided" by a therapist. Outcome research has been very promising, and self-help manuals may prove to be another cost-effective and readily available alternative to the standard individual CBT (Bailer et al., 2004; Birchall & Palmer, 2002). Another group of researchers (Bara-Carril et al., 2004) is investigating the use of CD-ROM-based self-help CBT for clients with BN. The outcome showed significant reduction in binging and purging behaviors at posttreatment and follow-up. Yet another group (Bakke, Mitchell, Wonderlich, & Erickson, 2001) has considered the use of telemedicine to treat clients with BN in a rural setting. They used a telecommunication link to treat two women with BN using individual CBT, and both were abstaining from binging and purging behaviors at their 1-month follow-up.

CASE STUDY

Instead of the self-starvation that is characteristic of anorexics, bulimics engage in periodic bouts of binge eating. These are always followed by a period of contrition during which the bulimic tries to undo the effects of the binge, either by purging, abusing diuretics or laxatives, or fasting and/or exercising to the extreme. (Herrin et al., 2002, p. 9)

Sara left home to attend college at age 18. She came from a happy home, with parents who were slender, attractive, and always watching their food intake. Sara was a straight-A student throughout high school, had lots of friends, and was generally a very happy adolescent. When her body started changing during her late teens, she gained approximately 10 pounds (from 115 to 125 pounds). On her 5'8" frame, she was still very slender, but as her hips and bottom started to fill out, her mother started commenting on her looks in certain clothing. Soon after she moved away to attend college, Sara gained another 5 pounds. She started having trouble keeping food down after large meals.

She didn't feel nauseous, but reported that the food would involuntarily come back up into her mouth after eating. After reporting this phenomenon to her mother and even one doctor, and having several tests run to make sure there was nothing physically wrong with her, Sara started to realize that she could now vomit at will.

She started vomiting every time she felt she had either overeaten or had eaten something particularly fattening. Periodically, she would even binge on forbidden foods, such as ice cream, cake, and bread, knowing she could get rid of the unwanted calories. The binge-eating and purging became routine, occurring up to five times a day. Her weight dropped to 115 pounds by the time she left school and started working. In the stressful work environment, the symptoms increased. She would purge after every meal eaten in a restaurant, which was usually one or even two a day. When she returned home at night after a long day, she would often binge and purge throughout the evening to return to a sense of control. Sara also ran two to three miles a day and attended several exercise classes each week. Her weight was 105 pounds during this time, low enough for a diagnosis of AN. She was on birth control pills throughout this time so her menstruation continued on a regular 28-day cycle.

In her late twenties, after 11 years suffering from BN, Sara went to a counseling center where she was diagnosed with BN and received 20 weeks of CBT to help her get her eating under control. Partly due to the therapy, and possibly partly due to a normal maturation process, she was able to develop a healthy eating pattern, completely stop binge-eating and purging, increase her weight to 120 pounds, and maintain it throughout a 2-year follow-up period. At long-term follow-up (5 years after therapy ended), Sara weighs 130 pounds, exercises intermittently, and is generally happy with her shape and weight.

ATYPICAL EATING DISORDER

A third eating disorder is defined in the *DSM-IV*, called eating disorders not otherwise specified, also referred to as atypical eating disorder (AED). This is a category for eating disorders that are considered severe enough to warrant a diagnosis, but do not meet the specific criteria for either AN or BN. For example, the client may not quite meet the weight loss requirement of AN or may still be menstruating. Or they may meet all the criteria for BN, except the binging and purging behaviors have not occurred with the required frequency or duration. These eating disorders can be as severe and as long lasting as BN and AN, and should not be over-looked by clinicians and counselors simply because the criteria for BN and AN are not met.

There are no clear prevalence estimates for AED, however, there has been research regarding the distribution of eating disorders. Fairburn et al. (2003) report that the occurrence of AED is the most common diagnostic category among the three DSM-defined eating disorders, with AED comprising approximately one-half of the cases of diagnosed eating disorders. The estimates are made more difficult as research suggests that clients with AN, BN, and AED tend to migrate between the three disorders.

As symptoms of AED vary from client to client, research on treatment tends never to look exclusively at a sample with AED. Instead, research on clients with BN will sometimes distinguish between clients who meet the full criteria for BN from those who fail to meet some symptom and are thus categorized as AED. Likewise, research on AN will sometimes include a portion of the sample who is diagnosed with AED as they fail to meet all criteria of AN. Therefore, to gain even an elementary understanding of treatment of this possibly large group of clients, one must look at the outcome research that has been completed on the other eating disorders, including AN, BN, and BED.

BINGE-EATING DISORDER

Binge-eating disorder (BED) is an eating disorder in which binge-eating is the central feature. Cooper and Fairburn (2003) explain that the diagnosis of BED is still somewhat controversial and the criteria for making a diagnosis of BED has still not been agreed upon by professionals. The criteria for BED was introduced into the *DSM-IV* (APA, 1994) in two ways. First, BED was offered as an example of "eating disorder not otherwise specified," described as "Recurrent episodes of binge-eating in the absence of the regular use of inappropriate compensatory behaviors characteristic of BN" (p. 550). BED was also included in the *DSM-IV* appendix in which proposed diagnostic categories are defined. BED is defined as: (a) recurrent episodes of binge-eating (defined in previous discussion of BN); (b) episodes are associated with three (or more) of the following: (1) eating much more rapidly than normal, (2) eating until feeling uncomfortably full, (3) eating large amounts of food when not feeling physically hungry, (4) eating alone because of being embarrassed by how much one is eating, or (5) feeling disgusted with oneself, depressed, or very guilty after overeating; (c) Marked distress regarding binge-eating is present; (d) The binge-eating occurs, on average, at least 2 days a week for 6 months; (e) The binge-eating is not associated with the regular use of inappropriate compensatory behavior (e.g., purging, fasting, obsessive exercise) and does not occur exclusively during the course of AN or BN (p. 731).

The distinguishing factor between BN and BED is the absence of compensatory purging in BED. However, there is some controversy in trying to distinguish between BED and the nonpurging BN. Drawing the line to determine which clients with nonpurging BN should be diagnosed with BN and which should be diagnosed with BED has become a research question for many professionals working with eating disorders. The question has led to a change in the criteria for nonpurging BN that some researchers feel has resulted in almost eliminating the diagnosis of nonpurging BN. Cooper et al. (2003) argue that this is a disservice to the field, and offer revised diagnostic criteria for BED and nonpurging BN so that clients can be more accurately diagnosed.

Prevalence

One study (Smith, Marcus, Lewis, Fitzgibbon, & Schreiner, 1998) evaluated almost 4,000 men and women and found an overall prevalence rate of 1.5%, finding BED more prevalent than BN. Yanovski (1999) estimated a prevalence of 2% in community samples. Fairburn (1995) suggests that the distribution of BED may be significantly different than BN. Men and women are more evenly affected by BED, and African American women seem to have increased risk of BED. The age group affected by BED is also broader, with people aged 20 to 50 being at increased risk.

Other research considers the association between BED and obesity. Fairburn (1995) points out that "It is a common misconception that *all* people with BED are overweight. Community studies indicate that only about half are overweight (defined as having a body mass index of 27 or more)" (p. 25). Yanovski (1999) found 25 percent of severely obese individuals to have BED. Smith et al. (1998) found the prevalence rates of BED among overweight individuals (2.9%) to be almost double that of the overall sample (1.5%).

Prognosis

Findings regarding the prognosis of BED are mixed. Fairburn et al. (2000) suggest that the disorder tends to remit spontaneously with only 18% of the individuals studied having any form of eating disorder at the end of a 5-year study. Other studies (Agras, 1999; Crow, 2002) found that 38% of BED patients still met the criteria for the disorder at 1-year follow-up and an additional 55% of the sample met the criteria for other eating disorders. Thus only a small portion of the sample had fully recovered, suggesting that BED does not simply remit over time. One study (Spurrell, Wilfley, Tanofsky, & Brownell, 1997) found that the average age that individuals with BED sought treatment was 45 years old and many had experienced the onset of symptoms 20 years earlier.

Warning Signs and Symptoms

BED shares the core eating disorder psychopathology, including preoccupation with shape and weight, the degree to which self-worth is influenced by weight, low self-esteem, poor social adjustment, and high rates of comorbid psychiatric disorders. BED is also associated with poor social functioning, high levels of disability, and more health problems. In addition, of course, BED is linked with obesity and overweight, along with the accompanying adverse physical and mental health consequences (Wilfley, Wilson, & Agras, 2003).

Cognitive Behavior Treatment

Wilson and Fairburn (2000) point out that "research on the treatment of BED is at an early stage" (p. 351). Some of the shortcomings of this early research include weak assessment measures, insufficient controls, short follow-up periods, and samples made up almost exclusively of clients who also meet the criteria for obesity. Yanovski (2003) states that "Our challenge in the future is to understand better the ways in which BED and obesity co-exist, and to find treatment strategies that will relieve the distress and dysfunction due to this disordered eating while enhancing appropriate weight loss or preventing future weight gain" (p. S119).

CBT for BED has been adapted from the much studied treatment protocol used with BN, although a group format is generally used with BED (Wilson et al., 2000). Studies show that CBT as well as interpersonal psychotherapy lead to a decrease in binge-eating behaviors, but do not cause weight loss (de Zwaan, 2001). Another study (Agras, Telch, Arnow, Eldredge, & Marnell, 1997) combined CBT and weight loss treatment and found that abstinence from binge-eating was associated with sustained weight loss at 1-year follow-up. A study by Wilfley (1999) found that 59% of clients with BED participating in a group format CBT were still free of binge-eating behaviors at 1-year follow-up. Self-help forms of CBT for clients with BED also show promising results (Carter & Fairburn, 1998). Two of the well-established self-help books (Cooper, 1995; Fairburn, 1995) are aimed at helping all people who suffer from binge-eating, including those with BN and BED.

It should be pointed out that CBT with clients with BED is not intended to produce weight loss, although in some cases weight loss does occur. The more traditional behavioral weight loss treatment (BWLT) uses increased dietary restriction to reach its primary goal of weight loss. Studies have shown that BWLT has resulted in both a reduction in binge-eating as well as loss of weight. One strength of BWLT is that it is more widely available than CBT (Wilson & Fairburn, 2000). A limitation is that interventions involving BWLT have consistently resulted in weight regain at follow-up (Jeffery et al., 2000). While BWLT has been effective in reducing binge-eating in obese patients, Nauta, Hospers, and Jansen (2001) found that at 6- and 12-month follow-ups, CBT was superior to BWLT in terms of the continued remittance of binge-eating behaviors. CBT was also more effective in reducing concerns about shape, weight, and eating. However, because BWLT produces greater weight loss and is more available as it does not require the same professional training and expertise, additional research should consider the long-term effects of this treatment method.

CASE STUDY

A 32-year-old man, Samuel, came into a treatment center for a lifelong struggle against obesity. He had been dieting on and off his entire life and currently weighed 380 pounds. Samuel reported eating fairly normal-sized meals, but admitted to drinking approximately 128 ounces of sugar-sweetened soft drinks each day, as well as binging on snacks while he traveled to and from his workplace 28 miles from his home. He also admitted sometimes binging on large quantities of food after returning home in the evening to find his wife and son out for the evening. These binges happened approximately three times a week, and an example binge might include four sandwiches, a box of macaroni and cheese, two to four soft drinks, and two bowls of ice cream. Samuel clearly suffered from low self-esteem and some depressive symptoms. He was diagnosed with BED, and participated in 18 weeks of CBT. He was able to reduce his binge-eating episodes to no more than one per month. While weight loss was not a goal of the therapy, his weight did go down from 380 to 320 over the 6 months he was involved with the therapist. At a 12-month follow-up, Samuel still reported no more than one binge-eating episode a month, he now weighed 312 pounds, and was feeling much better about himself and his family.

CONCLUSION

Eating disorders are a vast problem in our society. Many people live with disordered eating patterns throughout their lives. Social workers are in a position to help many individuals with eating disorders who may present for treatment for their eating problems. Once social workers are trained to identify the warning signs of eating disorders, they will likely recognize people with eating problems in many environments, including middle and high schools, college campuses and counseling centers, community counseling centers, hospitals and clinics, and prisons. It is imperative that social workers be familiar with the most effective ways to treat eating disorders. In some situations (i.e., self-help manuals), the social worker can help guide clients through treatment that can help reduce or even eliminate their eating problems. Where more specialized treatments are needed, including hospitalization in extreme cases, social workers should be familiar with the resources that are available in their local area. Clearly, the goal in the field of eating disorders is to develop effective treatments that are cost-effective and are available to the people who need them. Overall, CBT offers the most promising treatment for these disorders. As in many fields, however, more research is needed before professionals can be satisfied with the outcomes of the available treatment.

REFERENCES

Agras, W. S. (1999). *Diagnostic significance of Binge Eating Disorder.* Paper presented at the annual meeting of the Eating Disorders Research Society, San Diego, CA.

Agras, W. S., Telch, C. F., Arnow, B., Eldredge, K., & Marnell, M. (1997). One-year follow-up of cognitive-behavioral therapy for obese individuals with Binge Eating Disorder. *Journal of Consulting and Clinical Psychology, 65,* 343–347.

American Psychiatric Association. (1994). *Diagnostic and statistical manual of mental disorders* (4th ed.). Washington DC: Author.

Bailer, U., de Zwaan, M., Leisch, F., Strnad, A., Lennkh-Wolfsberg, C., El-Giamal, N. et al. (2004). Guided self-help versus cognitive-behavioral group therapy in the treatment of Bulimia Nervosa. *International Journal of Eating Disorders, 35,* 522–537.

Bakke, B., Mitchell, J., Wonderlich, S., & Erickson, R. (2001). Administering cognitive-behavioral therapy for Bulimia Nervosa via telemedicine in rural settings. *International Journal of Eating Disorders, 30,* 454–457.

Ball, J., & Mitchell, P. (2004). A randomized controlled study of cognitive behavior therapy and behavioral family therapy for Anorexia Nervosa patients. *Eating Disorders, 12,* 303–314.

Bara-Carril, N., Williams, C. J., Pombo-Carril, M. G., Reid, Y., Murray, K., Aubin, S., et al. (2004). *International Journal of Eating Disorders, 35,* 538–548.

Birchall, H., & Palmer, R. L. (2002). Doing it by the book: What place for guided self-help for bulimic disorders? *European Eating Disorders Review, 10,* 379–385.

Carter, J. C., & Fairburn, C. G. (1998). Cognitive-behavioral self-help for binge eating disorder: A controlled effectiveness study. *Journal of Consulting and Clinical Psychology, 66,* 616–623.

Chen, E., Touyz, S. W., Beumont, P. J. V., Fairburn, C. G., Griffiths, R., Butow, P., et al. (2003). Comparison of group and individual cognitive-behavioral therapy for patients with Bulimia Nervosa. *International Journal of Eating Disorders, 33,* 241–254.

Cooper, P. J. (1995). *Bulimia Nervosa and binge eating: A guide to recovery.* London: Robinson.

Cooper, Z., & Fairburn, C. G. (2003). Refining the definition of Binge Eating Disorder and nonpurging Bulimia Nervosa. *International Journal of Eating Disorders, 34,* S89–S95.

Crow, S. J. (2002, November). *Does Binge Eating Disorder exist?* Paper presented at the annual meeting of the Eating Disorder Research Society, Charleston, SC.

de Zwaan, M. (2001). Binge Eating Disorder and obesity. *International Journal of Obesity and Related Metabolic Disorder, 25*(Suppl.), S51–S55.

Fairburn, C. G. (1988). The current status of the psychological treatments for bulimia nervosa. *Journal of Psychosomatic Medicine, 32,* 635–645.

Fairburn, C. G. (1995). *Overcoming binge eating.* New York: Guilford.

Fairburn, C. G., Cooper, Z., Doll, H. A., Norman, P., & O'Connor, M. (2000). The natural course of bulimia nervosa and binge eating disorder in young women. *Archives of General Psychiatry, 57,* 659–665.

Fairburn, C. G., & Harrison, P. J. (2003). Eating disorders. *Lancet, 361,* 407–416.

Fairburn, C. G., Marcus, M. D., & Wilson, G. T. (1993). Cognitive-behavioral therapy for binge eating and bulimia nervosa: A comprehensive treatment manual. In C. G. Fairburn & G. T. Wilson (Eds.), *Binge eating: Nature, assessment, and treatment* (pp. 361–404). New York: Guilford.

Garner, D. M., & Bemis, K. M. (1982). Cognitive behavior therapy for anorexia nervosa. In D. M. Garner & P. Garfinkel (Eds.), *Handbook of psychotherapy for anorexia nervosa and bulimia.* New York: Guilford.

Hall, L., & Ostroff, M. (1998). *Anorexia nervosa: A guide to recovery.* Carlsbad, CA: Gurze Books.

Herrin, M., & Matsumoto, N. (2002). *The parent's guide to childhood eating disorders.* New York: Henry Holt & Company.

Jeffery, R. W., Drewnowski, A., Epstein, L. H., Stunkard, A., Wilson, G. T., Wing, R., et al. (2000). Long-term maintenance of weight loss: Current status. *Health Psychology, 19*(Suppl.), 5–16.

Kennedy, S. H., & Garfinkel, P. E. (1992). Advances in diagnosis and treatment of anorexia nervosa and bulimia nervosa. *Canadian Journal of Psychiatry, 37,* 309–315.

Lappalainen, R., & Tuomisto, M. T. (1999). Functional analysis of Anorexia Nervosa: Some applications to clinical practice. *Scandinavian Journal of Behaviour Therapy, 28,* 167–175.

Lock, J., le Grange, D., Agras, W. S., & Dare, C. (2001). *Treatment manual for anorexia nervosa: A family-based approach.* New York: Guilford.

Mussell, M. P., Crosby, R. D., Crow, S. J., Knopke, A. J., Peterson, C. B., Wonderlich, S. A., et al. (2000). Utilization of empirically supported psychotherapy treatment for individuals with eating disorders: A survey of psychologists. *International Journal of Eating Disorders, 27,* 230–237.

Nauta, H., Hospers, H., & Jansen, A. (2001). One-year follow-up effects of two obesity treatments on psychological well-being and weight. *British Journal of Health Psychology, 6,* 271–284.

Robin, A. L., Gilroy, A., & Baker, A. (1998). Treatment of eating disorders in children and adolescents. *Clinical Psychology Review, 18,* 421–446.

Russell, G. F. M., Szmukler, G. I., Dare, C., & Eisler, I. (1987). An evaluation of family therapy in anorexia nervosa and bulimia nervosa. *Archives of General Psychiatry, 44,* 1047–1056.

Schlundt, D. G., & Johnson, W. G. (1990). *Eating disorders: Assessment and treatment.* Boston: Allyn & Bacon.

Schmidt, U., & Treasure, J. (1993). *Getting better bit(e) by bit(e).* London: Lawrence Erlbaum Associates.

Smith, D. E., Marcus, M. D., Lewis, C. E., Fitzgibbon, M., & Schreiner, P. (1998). Prevalence of Binge Eating Disorder, obesity, and depression in a biracial cohort of young adults. *Annals of Behavioral Medicine, 20,* 227–232.

Spangler, D. L. (1999). Cognitive-behavioral therapy for Bulimia Nervosa: An illustration. *Psychotherapy in Practice, 55,* 699–713.

Spurrell, E. B., Wilfley, D. E., Tanofsky, M. B., & Brownell, K. D. (1997). Age of onset for binge eating: Are there different pathways to binge eating? *International Journal of Eating Disorders, 21,* 55–65.

Steinhausen, H-C. (2002). The outcome of anorexia nervosa in the 20th century. *American Journal of Psychiatry, 159,* 1284–1293.

Sullivan, P. F., Bulik, C. M., Carter, F. A., Gendall, K. A., & Joyce, P. R. (1996). The significance of a prior history of anorexia in bulimia nervosa. *International Journal of Eating Disorders, 20,* 253–261.

Wilfley, D. E. (1999). *Group cognitive-behavioral treatment and group interpersonal psychotherapy in the treatment of Binge-Eating Disorder: A controlled comparison.* Paper presented at the Eating Disorders Research Society, San Diego, CA.

Wilfley, D. E., Wilson, G. T., & Agras, W. S. (2003). The clinical significance of Binge Eating Disorder. *International Journal of Eating Disorders, 34,* S96–S106.

Wilson, G. T. (1999). Cognitive behavior therapy for eating disorders: Progress and problems. *Behavior Research & Therapy, 37*(Suppl. 1), S79–S95.

Wilson, G. T., & Fairburn, C. G. (2000). The treatment of Binge Eating Disorder. *European Eating Disorders Review, 8,* 351–354.

Wilson, G. T., Vitousek, K. M., & Loeb, K. L. (2000). Stepped-care treatment for eating disorders. *Journal of Consulting & Clinical Psychology, 68,* 564–572.

Yanovski, S. Z. (1999). Diagnosis and prevalence of eating disorders in obesity. In B. Guy-Grand & G. Ailhaud (Eds.), *Progress in obesity research* (pp. 229–236). London: Libby.

Yanovski, S. Z. (2003). Binge Eating Disorder and obesity in 2003: Could treating an eating disorder have a positive effect on the obesity epidemic? *International Journal of Eating Disorders, 34,* S117–S120.

CHAPTER 25

Cognitive Behavior Therapy in Medical Settings

Vaughn Roche

INTRODUCTION

Clinical social workers have an opportunity to position themselves at the forefront of historic, philosophical change in 21st-century medicine. As is so often true for social work, the opportunity is associated with need. The need in this case is for the treatment of neglected mental illness among medically ill patients. Psychological disorders, especially depression and anxiety, are common among patients seen in hospitals, clinics, and other medical settings (World Health Organization [WHO], 2001). Yet these disorders go largely undiagnosed and untreated, or undertreated when recognized (President's New Freedom Commission on Mental Health, 2003). Often, emotional suffering is viewed as simply an unavoidable burden to be borne along with physical illness. Around 20 percent of patients seen by primary health care providers suffer from one or more mental disorders (WHO, 2001). Major unipolar depression alone is widespread among medical patients, yet it goes undiagnosed or inadequately treated in nearly 60% of patients seen by primary care physicians (Andrews, Sanderson, Slade, & Issakidis, 2000). Patients with serious and chronic illness have especially high rates of depression: 42% of hospitalized cancer patients; 45% of patients with recent heart attacks; 33% of patients with diabetes (Rifkin, 1992). Unnecessary emotional suffering is not the only consequence of untreated mental illness. Studies, including those using the most advanced tools of medical science, demonstrate the power of emotional suffering to cause physiological and behavioral changes that aggravate physical illness. As a prime example, depression can lead to noncompliance with medical care (DiMatteo, Lepper, & Croghan, 2000) and has been shown to increase mortality rates (Barefoot & Schroll, 1996; Cavanaugh, Furlanetto, Creech, & Powell, 2001; Wulsin, Vaillant, & Wells, 1999). The failure to diagnose and treat mental illness in the primary care setting is also associated with suicide. About half of suicide victims had seen a primary care provider within a month of their suicide (Luoma, Martin, & Pearson, 2002).

For social workers, in their role as advocates and clinicians, this unmet need would seem to create an obligation. This chapter argues that, if choosing to accept the obligation, social workers can become catalysts for vitally needed change within the medical field. In working toward that change, social work would also have an opportunity to elevate its clinical role in a setting where that role is frequently marginalized. While the mental and emotional suffering of patients goes undetected or neglected, social workers with clinical skills that could help are often preoccupied by such nonclinical tasks as planning patient discharges, reviewing patients' medical-insurance utilization, and counseling patients about financial matters. Their number in hospital settings, in particular, makes social workers the most likely mental health clinicians to come in contact with patients needing mental health intervention. Though they occupy such a frontline position, social workers might not have the support, the assigned clinical role, or the time to effectively assess and intervene psychotherapeutically with patients.

Cognitive behavior therapy (CBT) can be a persuasive tool in remedying the situation. While studies using the most advanced medical technology show the impact of emotional suffering on physical disease, other studies using the same technology are demonstrating CBT's effectiveness in relieving not just emotional suffering but physical suffering among medically ill patients. One significant study showing the power of CBT to change physiology, and relieve depression as a result, was performed at the University of Toronto. Using positron emission tomography, or PET scans, to chart activity in the brain, Goldapple and colleagues (2004) found that CBT changed brain metabolism much like the antidepressant drug paroxetine did, though CBT appeared to change brain activity from the cortex down and the paroxetine from the limbic area up. The most important finding was that CBT visibly changed physiology in producing the desired result of relieving depression. In doing this, the University of Toronto study offered the sort of "seeing is believing" proof that those trained in the biomedical model prefer in persuading themselves of the effectiveness of an intervention. Social workers can use such visible scientific evidence to promote the use of CBT among biomedical professionals. They can also demonstrate the effectiveness of CBT with the use of self-report tools proven to measure disorders like depression and anxiety. The Beck Depression Inventory (BDI) is one of the better-known tools, but many more are available. The Brief Symptom Inventory 18, developed through work with cancer patients, is an example of tools that measure not only depression and anxiety but somatization, which is particularly useful in treating medical patients. The proven validity and test-retest reliability of such tools make them ideal for measuring patient progress and the effectiveness of interventions provided them. In that way, they also provide solid data to be used in research to identify and support the most effective psychosocial interventions. Tools of the kind are in keeping with today's evidence-based health care practice. Given the time constraints of the medical setting, the efficiency of CBT also makes an argument for its use. It offers the advantage of its brief, directive approach, and it can be manualized for use by inexperienced therapists. CBT provided in group therapy form can reach many patients in a short amount of time. Its teaching of self-help techniques is also an advantage in helping patients whose poor physical health might keep them from regularly scheduled psychotherapy sessions.

While this chapter discusses the clinical benefits and techniques of CBT, it also acknowledges the likelihood that social work will have to campaign for its implementation in many medical settings. Doing so will require the field to utilize the skills of its two, sometimes warring schools of philosophy—community organization and direct clinical care—to accomplish the goal of integrating mental health care into medical care to improve overall patient care. The challenge is considerable, because the explanations for the neglect of mental illness among the physically ill are many and complex. However, one major obstacle to improved mental health care is posed by the traditional mind-body split of Western medicine. Western medicine's bias toward the physical as the origin of all illness, mental and bodily, carries the accompanying bias that all illness can be treated by physical means. This approach toward medicine has been labeled the biomedical model. Its dominance has marginalized attempts to broaden Western medicine's perspective to consider the patient's whole realm of experience—biological, psychological, behavioral, and social—in formulating and providing treatment. Even the field of psychiatry, once heavily focused on mental processes and psychodynamic or psychoanalytic psychotherapy, has gravitated to the biomedical model with the advancement and proliferating use of psychotropic medication. Gabbard and Kay (2001) argue that switching to a biopsychosocial model of medicine as proposed by Engel (1977) receives a great deal of talk but little action as managed care companies and major voices in the field of psychiatry favor drug therapy for mental disorders. Just as physicians treating physical diseases like cancer have been found to deflect from their patient's expression of emotional suffering (Greenburg, 2004), psychiatrists, limiting their encounters to brief medication management, may use the biomedical model, in part, as an emotional shield (Gabbard et al., 2001). The value of ever-improving psychoactive medication cannot be dismissed. Yet, its success and proliferating use may have further reinforced a biomedical model of patient care even among medical doctors devoted to mental health care (Gabbard et al., 2001).

The campaign at hand, then, must be to convert the biomedical model to a biopsychosocial model. It is a tall order. No less than the U.S. Surgeon General has called for the integration of mental health care into mainstream health care, particularly primary medical care (U.S. Department of Health and Human Services [DHHS], 1999). The Surgeon General's report found that the mind-body split was a major barrier to improving mental health care and a significant source of the stigma surrounding it. Overall, the Surgeon General's report was a call for an historic initiative in changing the perceptions and treatment of mental illness. But the reality of all initiatives, even those grounded in public policy, is that they succeed by the will of many individuals acting in common interest to accomplish the goal. Social work prides itself on being a field that looks unflinchingly at need and sees in it an opportunity. In the medical settings of the 21st century, social work has the opportunity to help meet a great need and bring about vital change in medical care.

LITERATURE REVIEW

The effectiveness of CBT in general has been well established and is documented elsewhere in this text. Its effectiveness in relieving depression and anxiety can be seen as especially critical in the context of treating medical patients. For example, research like that of Antonuccio, Danton, and DeNelsky (1995) showing CBT's effectiveness in comparison to medication in treating depression is especially encouraging when considering that medical patients may not always be able to tolerate antidepressant medication, either because of side effects or adverse interactions with the range of medications they may be taking for severe and chronic illness. In reviewing research on the more prominent mind-body treatments, including CBT, Astin and colleagues (2003) found that although research on psychosocial interventions has received much criticism, the quality of the research compared favorably with research done in other areas of medicine. Along with its general effectiveness, CBT has been found effective, with medication or alone, in relieving both the mental and physical suffering of chronic pain patients (Gallagher & Cariati, 2002; Loscalzo, 1996; Turk, 2003; Williams et al., 1993); diabetic patients (Jacobson & Weinger, 1998; Lustman, Griffith, Freedland, Kissel, & Clouse, 1998); chronic fatigue patients (Deale, Chalder, Marks, & Wessely, 1997; Sharpe et al., 1996); insomnia patients, fibromyalgia patients, irritable bowel patients (van Dulmen, Fennis, & Bleijenber, 1996).

The importance in treating psychosocial suffering is made apparent by studies finding that depression is a risk factor for increased mortality in breast cancer (Hjerl, Anderson, Keiding, Mouridsen, Mortensen, & Jorgensen, 2003); cancer in general (Lawrence, Holman, Jablensky, Threlfall, & Fuller, 2000); myocardial infarction (Barefoot et al., 1996). Depression was also found to impair the immune system (Schleifer, Keller, Bartlett, Eckholdt, & Delaney, 1996). The common combination of depression and anxiety not only worsens the patient's health and increases medical cost, but does so by interfering with compliance in medical treatment (Saravay & Lavin, 1994).

Depression and anxiety not only reduce quality of life, but increase the cost of health care among general medical inpatients (Creed et al., 2002). Depression has been shown to increase mortality rates (Barefoot et al., 1996; Cavanaugh et al., 2001; Wulsin et al., 1999).

That so much of the mental suffering among medically ill patients goes unrecognized, untreated, or undertreated would seem difficult to explain, given the large and accruing body of knowledge on the subject. Scientific articles detailing the neglect and its consequences appear in medical journals circulating among the very same physical care providers who fail to address their patients' psychosocial suffering. In their review of psychosocial, mind-body interventions, CBT included, Astin et al. (2003) found that psychosocial factors remain not only underaddressed in clinical settings but underemphasized in medical education as well. Social workers, in their roles as patient advocates and agents of change, can help through a third role as educators. The proven effectiveness of CBT— and demonstrating it—can be a powerful tool in education. But the educational process must be twofold. To build support for the use of CBT and to encourage referrals from physical care providers, social workers should first be prepared to discuss the scale and consequences of untreated mental illness among medically ill patients. Given the present state of affairs, social workers cannot assume that this knowledge is common. Social workers can spread their message through educational presentations to physician groups. They can work to secure a voice on hospital boards and committees. Hospital medical ethics committees are especially good vehicles for change; they played an instrumental role in addressing the controversial issue of undertreated physical pain at the turn of the century. The undertreatment of emotional suffering should receive no less attention. One organization that has already drawn a parallel between the problems of untreated physical pain and untreated psychic pain is the National Comprehensive Cancer Network (NCCN). The network of (18) cancer treatment and research centers has made psychosocial care a priority and has developed guidelines for its integration with medical care. The NCCN goal is to screen and treat every patient for psychosocial distress. Social workers can use initiatives like that of the NCCN to support their own.

Social workers have an abundance of evidence to support their case for a biopsychosocial model of medicine. The World Health Organization (2001) reports that unipolar depression is the greatest disabler on earth in terms of years lost to disease, and that mental and behavioral disorders are common among patients in primary care, the most common being depression, anxiety, and substance abuse. Andrews et al. (2000) say that 58% of depressed patients are neither diagnosed nor sufficiently treated in health care settings. The President's New Freedom Commission on Mental Health (2003) cited the separation of mental health and medical health systems as a major obstacle to mental health care. Among the commission's findings were (1) approximately half of all treatment for common mental health problems is provided in general medical settings, (2) primary care providers identify mental health problems at a low rate, (3) most adults with depression, anxiety, and other common mental disorders are not appropriately treated in primary care settings, (4) patients often do not follow through with referrals for specialty mental health treatment outside primary care settings, and (5) primary care providers could be pivotal in addressing mental illness but persistently do not identify, treat, or refer patients needing mental health care. The Commission recommended that primary care providers integrate mental health professionals, clinical social workers included, into their practice to provide patients with education, psychotherapy, case management and, if needed, referrals to specialty mental health care agencies. The presidential commission also recommended that treatment be evidence-based, a recommendation that CBT meets.

In championing a biopsychosocial treatment approach, social workers can offer doctors and other physical care providers the profound argument of the late George Engel, M.D. In 1977, Engel began appealing for the replacement of the biomedical model with a bio-psycho-social model (Engel, 1977). Engel championed the new model as one offering not only a more humanistic approach to medicine but a more scientific one that examined the patient's whole realm of experience—mind, body, behavior, and social environment—in diagnosing illness and formulating treatment. He argued that medicine, in holding fast to the biomedical model, was trapped in a 17th-century worldview that arbitrarily and superstitiously separated mind from body. He believed it a backward view to conceive illness narrowly to what can be physically and objectively verified at the body's cellular and molecular level (Borrell-Carrio, Suchman, & Epstein, 2004). Engel's reference to a 17th-century worldview stems from tacit Christian church restrictions of the time. These belief-based restrictions permitted scientific investigation of the body through such practices as dissection but precluded investigation of the mind and behavior, insisting they were matters of the soul and therefore matters of church and religion. Thus, Engel refers to this split of mind and body as a cultural construct, a "folk model" as opposed to a scientific model, yet one accepted as scientific because it inculcates generation after generation of doctors who seldom question the model's origins.

Engel acknowledged that the biomedical model's staying power was also due to its remarkable record of scientific breakthroughs, resulting in the marvel that is modern medicine. But he argued that its focus on body as machine and medicine as the means to fix that broken machine was incomplete and limiting. Engel formulated his argument after attending a conference where the psychiatry of the day, the 1970s, was being attacked as unscientific by some of its own practitioners. Some psychiatrists wanted to ground their profession in the same biological sphere as medicine and abandon the psychological sphere in order to reclaim what they believed was declining credibility. Engel responded that he believed all medicine was in crisis and that blame lay in "adherence to a model of disease no longer adequate for the scientific tasks and social responsibilities of either medicine or psychiatry" (1977, p. 129). Engel said that it would be ironic for psychiatry to retreat from being the one medical discipline that, as he saw it, concerned itself with the human condition and the patient as a person.

Nearly 30 years later, Engel's call for a biopsychosocial model of medicine appears to have gone largely unanswered. Although many doctors, researchers and others continue the plea, there are signs that efforts to institute Engel's model continue to be frustrated. Despite growing evidence that psychosocial conditions have a major impact on patients' physical health, and despite the medical field's pronouncements of support for the biopsychosocial model, patients continue to receive inadequate clinical attention for their psychosocial needs or none at all (Astin et al., 2003). The reason for the inconsistency in what is said and what is actually done may be due to what Astin and colleagues (2003, p. 131) cite as a "lack of exposure to the evidence base supporting the biopsychosocial model," including evidence showing the effectiveness of psychosocial interventions such as CBT. Pincus (2003) found that, in primary medical care, the failure to factor in psychological and social influences in a patient's care not only continued all these many years after Engel's call, but was getting worse. Pincus cited organizational structures that separate mental health care providers from physical care providers as well as lacking parity in insurance coverage for mental health care. Comparing articles published by medical researchers in *The Lancet* from 1978 to 1982, the years just after Engel's challenge to medicine, and articles published in *The Lancet* from 1996 to 2000, Alonso (2004) concluded that the biomedical model still dominated medicine's definition of health and illness. Alonso found that the biopsychosocial model had to some degree positively changed the public health sector's definition of health and illness and even improved doctor-patient relations, but that doctors and other medical practitioners had still not integrated psychosocial interventions into treatment plans.

From the abundance of studies, clinical trials, and public policy initiatives, social workers can draw strong evidence for their integration into multidisciplinary medical teams. Their training and sensibilities are critical to ensuring that psychosocial considerations are not overlooked, as they are for many reasons. In the case of diabetes, for example, two-thirds of patients suffering from depression go untreated because (1) physicians lack time with the individual patient, (2) lack training in diagnosing depression, (3) often view depressive symptoms as a secondary burden that the patient must simply endure (Lustman & Anderson, 2002). In the case of cancer patients, physicians with limited time have been found to avoid questions about emotions, sometimes through such observable strategies as ignoring the signs of depression, changing the subject or quickly reassuring the patient in what appeared to be strategies designed to insulate them from patients' emotions (Greenburg, 2004). On the part of the patients, such concerns as stigma and medicinal side effects have been known to inhibit discussion of emotional suffering. Clinical social work has a vital role to play, and this section of the chapter demonstrates the benefit of CBT in that role. The following case example illustrates how a social worker using CBT integrates psychosocial interventions into medical treatment.

CASE STUDY

Catherine, a 45-year-old woman whose esophageal cancer had been treated with surgery, radiation, and chemotherapy 5 years earlier, was referred to a pain medicine specialist. Catherine's cancer remained in remission, but chronic pain related to surgical scar tissue no longer responded to medication that had controlled the pain reasonably well in the years since her surgery. Most troubling, she reported, were spikes of incapacitating pain. She reported nearly daily episodes of chest pain that she feared would end in death. The pain medicine doctor planned to start Catherine on a course of narcotic medication. The doctor also wanted social work to assess Catherine because she had reported a history of major depression and work-related stress. The doctor also planned to increase the dosage of anxiety medication Catherine's family doctor had prescribed for anxiety and panic associated with the attacks of pain. Catherine said the anxiety medication helped but that it took 20 to 30 minutes to calm her. In that time, she would struggle to cope with rapid heart beat, hyperventilation, dizziness and the sense that she was caught in a death grip from which nothing could free her. She said her chest pain intensified as the panic progressed.

The social worker assessing Catherine conducted a step-by-step analysis of her pain and panic symptoms to determine the order of their onset. He guided her through a detailed reconstruction of her most recent episode. He sought detail on the social setting and circumstances in which the combined pain and panic attacks occurred. In keeping with cognitive behavior practice, the social worker sought especially fine detail on the thoughts that ran through Catherine's mind before, during, and after the attack. Together, Catherine and the social worker focused most intently on the thoughts immediately preceding the attacks. In this collaborative fashion, she and the social worker discovered that the attacks almost always occurred during a work or social situation in which Catherine felt pressured or feared embarrassment. For example, she was easily flustered by her boss's criticism of her work, however slight, and feared being humiliated in the eyes of coworkers. It became apparent that most of the attacks occurred at work. By analyzing several of the attacks in this detailed way, the social worker hypothesized that the excruciating spikes of pain nearly always followed the onset of panic symptoms. Less often, the patient would feel pain before the onset of panic, but it was clear that even in those instances, the rapid heart beat and hyperventilation of the panic would greatly exacerbate the chest pain by physically irritating the surgical scar tissue that was the source of the pain. The panic also tended to intensify the patient's perception of pain.

Using Socratic questioning and guided discovery (Beck, 1995; Burns, 1980; Taylor & Asmundson, 2004,) the social

(*continues*)

worker began to elicit and amplify the specific thoughts and beliefs that triggered Catherine's panic. It appeared that thoughts of physical and social catastrophe, and core beliefs that made Catherine vulnerable to these thoughts, triggered her panic attacks more often than not. This is the core of cognitive theory: that thoughts and underlying beliefs drive emotions and behavior. In this case, Catherine's catastrophic imaginings of social humiliation not only triggered her panic but the pain itself. Once the panic and pain began, she, in turn, imagined the ultimate catastrophe of death. As a first step in helping her control panic, the social worker educated and socialized Catherine in cognitive theory and the concept of catastrophic thinking. Just an understanding of how thoughts of catastrophe drive emotions and trigger the autonomic nervous system, escalating heart beat, hyperventilation, nausea, sweating, and so on, began to reduce her fear and thus the panic. Beck, Emery, with Greenberg (1985) offer one of the best understandings of the panic syndrome from a biopsychosocial perspective. The explanation demystified the experience for Catherine, presenting it as a process that can be contained and arrested through the logic of cognitive behavior techniques.

Taking the mystery out of her panic experience laid the base for teaching Catherine techniques to dispute the catastrophic thoughts driving her panic. First, the social worker taught her a simple validity-based, or evidence-based, technique to dispute her panic-triggering thoughts and weaken and defuse their effect. Catherine was asked to write down at the top of a page of paper the thought, "I will die from this." She was asked to draw a line down the middle of the page and write on one side "Evidence For" the thought and on the other side "Evidence Against" the thought. The social worker helped prompt her answers by asking such questions as: How many of her frequent attacks had ended in death? Given numerous attacks and recoveries, what was the likelihood that she would die from the panic experience? What was the worst that had ever happened during her panic? Recognizing the worst, had she survived it? The technique might seem overly simplistic and might even be viewed as "talking down" to the patient in the eyes of a clinician or person who has never suffered from panic. However, it is unexamined thoughts, speeding automatically and uncontrolled through the mind, that keep patients from engaging such basic logic when it is most needed. It is not that patients lack the intelligence or the ability to think logically; it's that their ability to think logically is overridden by these automatic thoughts and the resulting flood of emotion. The disturbing physiological effects that follow, such as rapid heart beat, hyperventilation and, in this woman's case, chest pain exacerbated by surgical scarring, tend to fuel a patient's catastrophic thinking. In Catherine's case, the disputation technique offered a structured exercise that enabled her to ground her thinking and engage logic. In the process she learned that what she had to fear most was the alarm that generated the attacks. At the same time, she learned that she could defuse the alarm by disputing and reconstructing her thinking to reflect reality, which was not catastrophic. The techniques also strengthened the patient's overall sense of control, the loss of which is a common and distressing experience for most patients.

Because Catherine's automatic thoughts of catastrophe had been strongly conditioned by so many panic attacks, the social worker assumed she might have difficulty turning directly to the evidence-based exercise when she felt panic coming on. To help her ground her thinking and engage her logical CBT stance, the social worker helped her write out a "coping card." On a 3 × 5 inch note card, he wrote a simple and pithy statement briefly summarizing what was actually occurring as the patient began to feel panic, reminding her that she had survived all previous attacks, and instructing her on what she could do to combat the attack, including who she might call to help calm her thoughts. She would keep the card with her at all times. Along with grounding her, it would serve as a touchstone to the collaborative and reassuring relationship she had formed with the social worker. The card proved effective at calming Catherine enough so that she could begin using the evidence-based exercise to dispute the thoughts that drove her panic.

The social worker also offered Catherine help in addressing anxiety outside of panic episodes. Using a script, the social worker recorded a guided imagery exercise designed to relax and distract Catherine when she felt her anxiety begin to rise. Such an exercise calls for a patient to sit or lie comfortably with eyes closed as they listen to the tape through headsets. The recorded script prompts the patient through some basic steps of body relaxation, and then describes vividly a comforting scene in which the patient imagines participating. Catherine chose a tropical beach scene that prompted her to imagine herself warmed by sun, soothed by gentle breezes and carried gently along the scene on a puffy white cloud. The recorded voice of the social worker, with whom she had developed a good therapeutic alliance, added reassurance to the relaxation. Rossman (2000) provides a comprehensive understanding of guided

(continues)

imagery and its benefit to the medically ill. Guided imagery scripts are generally available in handbooks on relaxation.

Once Catherine's panic attacks were controlled, she and the social worker began to use CBT to identify, dispute, and reconstruct automatic thoughts and underlying beliefs that made her especially vulnerable to criticism from others, especially her boss and coworkers. This social vulnerability is what had initiated most of her panic-pain attacks, which occurred mostly at work. In that setting, coping cards proved most helpful, because Catherine, a clerical worker, could not always leave her desk for a private place, as her boss had agreed she could. In time, using the thought-disputing and restructuring exercises away from work, she found it progressively easier to arrest and confront the automatic thoughts that had for so long driven her panic. Such thoughts and beliefs included, "I'm stupid," "They think I'm stupid," "I'm laughable," "I'll lose my job."

Catherine's case illustrates the impact and the crucial importance of addressing the full range of biological, psychological, and social factors in the treatment of medical patients. The social worker collaborated closely with doctors, nurses, and physician assistants on the multidisciplinary team. Each discipline's expert perspective was needed to understand how the patient's pain and panic were intertwined. It was critical for each discipline to share its understanding of the cause and treatment of the patient's suffering. It enabled the clinical team to differentiate between the role of biological, psychological, behavioral and social factors and to formulate an optimal treatment plan to address each. As a result of psychosocial interventions, Catherine eventually required less pain and anxiety medication, and the team doctor reduced her prescribed dosage accordingly. In providing intervention, it was critical for the social worker to have the doctor's full physical evaluation of the patient to be confident that the patient's pain and panic symptoms did not stem from a medical condition that might actually pose the risk of death. Catherine also benefited from that reassurance. That understanding was crucial to disputing her catastrophic conclusion that her pain and panic would cause death or never be controlled.

Time to intervene is often limited for social workers in a medical setting. Social workers may be assigned to several multidisciplinary teams and be subject to random call by doctors, nurses, and others working outside those teams. The resulting volume of patient referrals, often for on-the-spot needs, can severely limit time with each patient. If being treated for a chronic illness on an outpatient basis, the patient, if limited by physical mobility or transportation means, might find it possible to see their social worker only when scheduled to see their physician. Weeks and even months can pass in between. The ideal scenario of setting weekly therapy sessions with patients may not be possible in many cases. For all of those reasons, CBT's effectiveness, its time-limited design and its imparting of self-help to the patient make it ideal for treating patients within medical settings. That is not to say that social workers will not have the opportunity to see many patients in weekly sessions. They frequently do. They might even be assigned to a unit devoted solely to providing psychotherapy. Ideally, social workers should train extensively in CBT to meet any contingency. Formal training and supervision are available and some CBT interventions can be effectively learned and applied through manualized protocols. For reasons of limited space, this chapter limits itself to a look at some problems commonly encountered in medical settings and introduces some common techniques useful in helping almost any medical patient.

Since anxiety and depression are the most common disorders among the physically ill, it follows that social workers will want to familiarize themselves with some basic techniques to help relieve patients' symptoms and, in the collaborative nature of CBT, teach patients to use these techniques on their own. At the root of both anxiety and depression are distorted thoughts patients cannot cope with and may not be able to specifically identify. Patients are often ungrounded by these thoughts, especially patients newly diagnosed with chronic illness or suffering progressive setbacks from chronic illness. The social worker can help the patient begin to clearly identify these thoughts, weaken their impact on feelings and behaviors and replace them with more adaptive thoughts. In the process, the social worker and patient might begin to identify underlying beliefs that support these distorted, negative thoughts. They may be beliefs formed as a result of illness or long-held beliefs that have been activated and strongly pronounced by the stress of the illness. Working with the bulk of these underlying beliefs may take more time than the social worker and patient have to commit. But helping patients ground, or center, their most conscious thoughts can be a significant beginning in relieving their suffering.

Take, for example, Sam, a 38-year-old man diagnosed with a skin cancer that appeared as a small spot on his cheek. It was a form of cancer known only in rare cases to spread beyond skin surface. Doctors at two prestigious cancer treatment centers had confirmed the diagnosis. None could cite a case of serious physical illness or death associated with Sam's particular type of skin cancer. It was not known to spread. Treatment involved the simple surgical removal of the cancerous skin, performed on an outpatient basis by a dermatologist. Still, Sam slept very little at night. He was kept awake by thoughts of death and what would happen to his wife and two teenage children in his absence. He had begun to lose interest in ordinarily pleasurable activities. When he wasn't anxious, he felt depressed. He reported feeling guilty for obsessing about his health and being distracted from his family. He had also begun to avoid social settings because friends and acquaintances, not knowing the specifics of Sam's cancer, approached him with sympathy, believing that he might have terminal illness. They, like Sam, feared for his life. No amount of reassurance from doctors seemed to have any effect on Sam's outlook and thought-driven emotional symptoms.

The social worker taught Sam an evidenced-based, or validity-based, empirical technique to ground and examine the thoughts that drove his anxiety and depression. Sam's foremost thought was, "I am going to die." The doctor's reassurance that he would not die from his particular kind of cancer rang hollow because they were asking him simply to take their word for it. As in the case of Catherine, the social worker asked Sam to list the evidence for and against the thought that he would die. The exercise gave Sam more than the doctor's affirmative statements. It permitted him to compile evidence on paper so that he could begin to see, even literally see, that the evidence against his dying from his cancer far outweighed evidence that he would. In fact, Sam could list no concrete evidence to support his fearful thought. Not only did the exercise present a persuasive case against Sam's dying; it also diverted his mind from catastrophic thoughts and focused him on a productive exercise. In essence, the exercise was both cognitive and behavioral in nature. His "doing" the exercise helped distract him from anxious and depressing thoughts while at the same time it focused him cognitively on disputing those same thoughts. It grounded his mind, kept it from running free with anxious and depressive thoughts. He was instructed to repeat the exercise each time he was upset by his thinking, not just simply look at previously completed exercises. Over time, the exercise helped restructure Sam's thoughts so that his negative thoughts were fleeting and easier to dispute and replace with more adaptive thoughts.

Teaching use of such exercises for self-help purposes is standard in CBT and is all the more important for patients who may not be seen regularly by the social worker. To motivate Sam to use the evidence-based examination of his thoughts, the social worker taught him another basic technique that can be useful for any patient: the cost-benefit analysis. Sam was instructed to draw a line down the middle of a piece of paper, writing at the top "Doing the exercise" and listing the "cost" of doing the exercise on one side of the line and the "benefit" of doing it on the other. He was asked to repeat the exercise by evaluating the cost-benefit of not doing the exercise. Sam readily saw that the cost of not doing this homework would be suffering the very misery he sought help for. The same cost-benefit technique was extended to the usefulness of thinking anxious and depressing thoughts. That exercise reinforced Sam's understanding of how his thoughts drove emotions and behavior, and how his reaction interfered with his functioning. Eventually, Sam was able to compartmentalize his negative thinking and the use of these exercises to a regularly scheduled hour or two a day. His mood and functioning improved progressively.

Another especially anxious and depressing set of thoughts for Sam was driven by the underlying belief, "I'm selfish." It was especially difficult for Sam to identify that belief. It might very well have been a long-hidden core belief that was activated by the stress of his medical diagnosis. To help Sam put his finger on that belief, the social worker used the "downward arrow" technique (Burns, 1980). The technique repeatedly utilizes the question "If that is true, why is it so bad?" Each time Sam identified a conscious, troubling thought like "I'm spending too much time worrying about myself," the social worker would ask "If that is true, why is it so bad?" Sam would answer with another thought like "I'm not being a good father to my kids" and the social worker would again ask "If that is true, why is it so bad?" The questioning eventually led Sam to the basic core belief driving all these thoughts: "I'm selfish." The downward arrow technique is especially helpful in uncovering—getting to the bottom of—harsh self-beliefs hidden in the blizzard of troubling thoughts that medical patients frequently experience. Identifying and testing the validity of such basic distorted beliefs can help relieve a patient of an entire set of anxious and depressing thoughts.

These are just a few CBT techniques developed for general use and adapted for use with medical patients. Techniques learned in any CBT training program can be converted for application in the medical setting. Social workers in medical settings will discover that physical disease often activates or intensifies psychosocial problems that would bedevil patients even if they were not ill. A good understanding of how CBT can be applied specifically in medical settings is offered by Taylor et al. (2004); Moorey and Greer (2002); and White (2001). Turk, Meichenbaum and Genest (1983) offer classic instruction on helping patients cope with pain.

SUMMARY

The great need to treat mental illness among the medically ill presents clinical social work with an obligation and an opportunity. Accepting the challenge would befit a field that defines its professional mission broadly enough to encompass social advocacy and direct clinical treatment of individuals, couples, and families. CBT, with a growing base of scientific study to prove its effectiveness, offers clinical social work a tool that can help relieve the emotional and physical suffering of medical patients and improve health care as a whole. Its ability to demonstrate its effectiveness through scientific methods persuasive to doctors and other physical care providers can help redefine Western medicine. Combining its humanistic sensibilities with evidence-based CBT practice, clinical social work can bring a wholeness of perspective to medicine that emphasizes the full human experience and the unique worth of each patient. In turn, social work has an opportunity to elevate its clinical role in a setting where too frequently that role is marginalized.

REFERENCES

Alonso, Y. (2004). The biopsychosocial model in medical research: The evolution of the health concept over the last two decades [Electronic version]. *Patient Education and Counseling, 53*, 239–244. Retrieved March 21, 2005, from ScienceDirect database.

Andrews, G., Sanderson, K., Slade, T., & Issakidis, C. (2000). Why does the burden of disease persist? Relating the burden of anxiety and depression to effectiveness of treatment [Electronic version]. *Bulletin of the World Health Organization, 78*, 446–454.

Antonuccio, D. O., Danton, W. G., & DeNelsky, G. Y. (1995). Psychotherapy versus medication for depression: Challenging the conventional wisdom with data. *Professional Psychology: Research and Practice, 26*, 574–585.

Astin, J. A., Shapiro S. L., Eisenberg D. M., & Forys, K. L. (2003). Mind-body medicine: State of the science, implications for practice [Electronic version]. *Journal of the American Board of Family Practice, 16*, 131–147.

Barefoot, J. C., & Schroll, M. (1996). Symptoms of depression, acute myocardial infarction, and total mortality in a community sample [Electronic version]. *Circulation, 93*, 1976–1980.

Beck, J. S. (1995). *Cognitive therapy: Basics and beyond.* New York: Guilford.

Beck, A. T., & Emery, G., with Greenberg, R. L. (1985). *Anxiety disorders and phobias: A cognitive perspective.* New York: Basic Books.

Borrell-Carrio, F., Suchman, A. L., & Epstein, R. M. (2004). The biopsychosocial model 25 years later: Principles, practice, and scientific inquiry [Electronic version]. *Annals of Family Medicine, 2*, 576–582.

Burns, D. D. (1980). *Feeling good: The new mood therapy.* New York: New American Library.

Cavanaugh, S. V., A., Furlanetto, L. M., Creech, M. S., & Powell, L. H. (2001). Medical illness, past depression, and present depression: A predictive triad for in-hospital mortality [Electronic version]. *The American Journal of*

Psychiatry, 158, 43–48. Retrieved January 26, 2005, from Psychiatryonline database.

Creed, M. A., Morgan, R., Fiddler, M., Marshall, S., Guthrie, E., & House, A. (2002). Depression and anxiety impair health-related quality of life and are associated with increased costs in general medical patients [Electronic version]. *Psychosomatics, 43*, 302–309.

Deale, A., Chalder, T., Marks, I., & Wessely, S. (1997). Cognitive behavior therapy for chronic fatigue syndrome: A randomized controlled trial [Electronic version]. *American Journal of Psychiatry, 154*, 408–414. Abstract retrieved June 13, 2005, from Psychiatryonline database.

DiMatteo, M. R., Lepper, H. S., & Croghan, T. W. (2000). Depression is a risk factor for noncompliance with medical treatment [Electronic version]. *Archives of Internal Medicine, 160*, 2101–2107.

Engel, G. I. (1977). The need for a new medical model: A challenge for biomedicine [Electronic version]. *Science, 196*, 129–136.

Gabbard, G. O., & Kay, J. (2001). The fate of integrated treatment: Whatever happened to the biopsychosocial psychiatrist? [Electronic version]. *The American Journal of Psychiatry, 158*, 1956–1963.

Gallagher, R., & Cariati, S. (2002, October 2). *The pain-depression conundrum: Bridging the body and mind.* Content based on session presented at the 21st Annual Scientific Meeting of the American Pain Society. Retrieved January, 22, 2005, from www.medscape.com/viewprogram/2030_pnt.

Greenburg, D. (2004). Barriers to the treatment of depression in cancer patients [Electronic version]. *Monographs, Journal of the National Cancer Institute, 32*, 127–135. Retrieved January 27, 2005, from JNCICancerspectrum.

Hjerl, K., Andersen, E., Keiding, N., Mouridsen, H., Mortensen, P., & Jorgensen, T. (2003). Depression as a prognostic factor for breast cancer mortality [Electronic version]. *Psychosomatics, 44*, 24–30. Retrieved April 6, 2005, from Psychiatryonline database.

Jacobson, A. M., & Weinger, K. (1998). Treating depression in diabetic patients: Is there an alternative to medications? [Electronic version]. *Annals of Internal Medicine, 129*, 656–657.

Lawrence, D., Holman, C. D., Jablensky, A. V., Threlfall, T. J., & Fuller, S. A. (2000). Excess cancer mortality in Western Australian psychiatric patients due to higher case fatality rates. *ActaPsychiatrica Scandinavica, 101*(5), 382–388. Abstract retrieved April 6, 2005, from PubMed database.

Loscalzo, M. (1996). Psychological approaches to the management of pain in patients with advanced cancer [Electronic version]. *Hematology Oncology Clinics of North America.* Abstract retrieved June 13, 2005, from PubMed database.

Luoma, J. B., Martin, C. E., & Pearson, J. L. (2002). Contact with mental health and primary care providers before suicide: A review of the evidence [Electronic version]. *The American Journal of Psychiatry, 159*, 909–916.

Lustman, P. J., & Anderson, R. (2002, January). Depression in adults with diabetes. *Psychiatric Times, 19*, 1. Retrieved June 19, 2005, from www.psychiatrictimes.com/p020145.html.

Lustman, P. J., Griffith, L. S., Freedland, K. E., Kissel, S. S., & Clouse, R. E. (1998). Cognitive behavior therapy for depression in type 2 diabetes mellitus: A randomized, controlled trial [Electronic version]. *Annals of Internal Medicine, 129,* 613–621. Retrieved June 13, 2005, from PubMed database.

Moorey, S., & Greer, S. (2002). *Cognitive behaviour therapy for people with cancer.* New York: Oxford University Press.

Pincus, H. A. (2003). The future of behavioral health and primary care: Drowning in the mainstream or left on the bank? [Electronic version]. *Psychosomatics, 44,* 1–11.

President's New Freedom Commission on Mental Health. (2003). *Achieving the promise: Transforming mental health care in America.*

Rifkin, A. (1992). Depression in physically ill patients. *Post Graduate Medicine,* 9–92, 147–154.

Rossman, M. (2000). *Guided imagery for self-healing.* Tiburon, CA: H. J. Kramer & Novato, CA: New World Library.

Saravay, S. M., & Lavin, M. (1994). Psychiatric comorbidity and length of stay in the general hospital: A critical review of outcome studies [Electronic version]. *Psychosomatics, 35,* 233–252.

Schleifer, S. J., Keller, S. E., Bartlett, J. A., Eckholdt, H. M., & Delaney, B. R. (1996). Immunity in young adults with major depressive disorder [Electronic version]. *The American Journal of Psychiatry, 153,* 477–482. Abstract retrieved April 6, 2005, from Psychiatryonline database.

Sharpe, M., Hawton, K., Simkin, S., Suraway, C., Hackmann, A., Klimes, I. et al. (1996). Chronic behaviour therapy for the chronic fatigue syndrome: a randomized controlled trial [Electronic version]. *British Medical Journal, 312,* 22–26.

Taylor, S., & Asmundson, G. J. G. (2004). *Treating health anxiety: A cognitive-behavioral approach.* New York: Guilford.

Turk, D. C. (2003). Cognitive-behavioral approach to the treatment of chronic pain patients [Electronic version]. *Regional Anesthesia and Pain Medicine, 28,* 573–579. Abstract retrieved June 13, 2005, from ScienceDirect database.

Turk, D. C., Meichenbaum, D., & Genest, M. (1983). *Pain and behavioral medicine.* New York. Guilford.

U.S. Department of Health and Human Services. (1999). *Mental health: A report of the Surgeon General.*

van Dulmen, A. M., Fennis, J. F., & Bleijenberg, G. (1996). Cognitive-behavioral group therapy for irritable bowel syndrome: Effects and long-term follow-up [Electronic version]. *Psychosomatic Medicine, 58,* 508–514.

White, C. A. (2001). *Cognitive behaviour therapy for chronic medical problems: A guide to assessment and treatment in practice.* Chichester, UK: John Wiley & Sons.

Williams, A. C., Nicholas, M. K., Richardson, P. H., Pither, C. E., Justins, D. M., Chamberlain, J. H. et al. (1993). Evaluation of a cognitive behavioural programme for rehabilitating patients with chronic pain [Electronic version].

British Journal of General Practice, 43, 513–518. Abstract retrieved June 13, 2005, from PubMed database.

World Health Organization. (2001). *World Health Report.*

Wulsin, L. R., Vaillant, G. E., & Wells, V. E. (1999). A systematic review of the mortality of depression [Electronic version]. *Psychosomatic Medicine, 61,* 6–17.

PART VI

Directions for the Future

CHAPTER 26

Synthesis and Prospects for the Future

Arthur Freeman
Tammie Ronen

In its first days, social work as a profession strived to stay alive—to prove its importance, to sharpen its uniqueness in comparison with other professions, and to become advocators for those in need. As the profession matured and gained its high status among the helping professions, social workers became an integral part of every social, medical, and educational setting. Therefore, social workers can allow themselves to continue working toward their traditional goals but, at the same time, to collaborate with professionals from other disciplines and to emphasize integration rather than differentiation.

WHAT CHANGES WILL THE PROFESSION EXPERIENCE IN THE FUTURE?

The contents of social work interventions in the future will likely be highly determined by technological and medical advances. Modern society has discovered remarkable ways to extend people's lives, helping them live longer, live with illnesses that caused death in the past, and cope with traumatic threats to their lives. As an outcome, social work as a profession has begun developing new areas of intervention regarding health behavior. This area will probably become a chief focus of attention among social workers in the future—helping those who live longer to also improve their subjective well-being and their quality of life and find meaning in their lives (Huebner & Dew, 1996).

WHICH CLIENTS WILL SOCIAL WORKERS SERVE?

In its early days, social workers were involved mainly with the low socioeconomic classes, the poor and needy population. Changes in modern Western society, increases in crises and traumatic life events, economic changes, and life-prolonging medical interventions have all resulted in bringing social work interventions to a very broad population. Although the profession will always feel responsible for the low social class, social workers in the future will be involved much more with all social classes, and will especially focus on socio-ethno-cultural diversity (Anderson & Wiggins-Carter, 2004).

Among the various populations, we can pinpoint two in particular: senior citizens and children. As just mentioned, a longer lifespan necessitates different kinds of intervention enabling the older population to live better, to maintain independence, and to find meaning in their lives, as well as to learn to live with the impact of that longer life: accepting life's changes; living with various ailments, medical interventions, and handicapping conditions; and coping with loss and changing family roles.

At the same time, treating children at risk and in danger has become another focus for social work intervention. Increased recognition of children's rights, greater exposure of children to dangerous circumstances, and awareness of the importance of early development and emotional support for healthy human functioning will all continue in the future to raise the interest of social work as a profession to take responsibility for children's well-being, welfare, and life quality.

WHAT PROBLEMS WILL BE AT THE CENTER OF ATTENTION?

Modern life has enabled a shift from a human preoccupation with basic survival needs to questions about the quality of life. Consequently, the role of emotions have taken center stage in the development, maintenance, and resolution of human disorders in general (Mahoney, 1991, 2003; Wells, 2000). Power and Dalgleish (1997) emphasized that emotional disorders relate to the interaction between life events and cognitive features such as self-esteem (Baumeister, 1998, 1999). Recognition of the role of emotions in behavioral change and in human functioning has opened a whole new world to social workers, legitimizing a focus on internal events, affects, and awareness rather than a concern with mainly environmental causes for human disorders. Hence, loneliness, anxiety, depression, self-acceptance, and self-evaluation, like other components of emotions and emotional disorders, will become the crux of intervention.

WHAT SETTINGS WILL TYPIFY SOCIAL WORK INTERVENTIONS?

In contrast with individual intervention, which comprised the focus of attention in the past, future treatments will emphasize community-based, group, and family interventions. Research outcomes have highlighted the importance of social support for the human ability to cope and change; this professional understanding will increase the probability of involving the client's close environment (parents, teachers, peers) in the change process (Cohen & Willis, 1985).

WHAT THEORIES AND INTERVENTION METHODS WILL BE APPLIED?

Growing consensus in the profession about the need to address subjective well-being and emotional disorders will necessitate new modes of intervention. One cannot expect changes in emotions by merely talking about emotions.

New models of intervention will be applied, integrating traditional cognitive behavior therapy with modern developments of the theory—self-organization, self-representation, connectionism, and constructivism. All of these will incorporate techniques taken from constructivism, mindfulness, and positive psychology, with empowerment at the core of intervention (Mahoney, 2003).

WHAT WILL BE THE MOST IMPORTANT CHARACTERISTIC OF SOCIAL WORK PRACTICE?

Kazdin (1993) stated that any clinical practice that targets diverse populations should make sure of the evidence showing this intervention's success and should include special diverse assessment methods and intervention modes to meet clients' needs. Thus, we believe that the tendency for evidence-based practice, described both by Bruce Thyer and by Eileen Gambrill in this book, will become central to social work intervention. At the same time, the need to treat emotional processes will necessitate new intervention modes that are not necessarily based on verbal therapy.

WHERE ARE WE GOING?

With slashed budgets, the demand for short-term treatments, the need to supply evidence-based therapy, and the call for a focus on emotional disorders, we believe that CBT, with its modern developments, will become the treatment of choice for social work as a profession.

SUMMARY

Social work is a profession that relies predominantly on a "strengths perspective" and strives to move away from a medical model. As such, when social workers approach clients, rather than focusing on "what's wrong" with the client, they assess the individual in terms of "what's right" with the client. Social workers build upon client strengths in order to assist clients in identifying and meeting the broad range of life challenges. Many challenges can otherwise be defined as problems; some are just "challenges." Refugee resettlement, for example, is an area where there is little "wrong" with the client, rather external forces have created challenges beyond the "typical" problems that most people have. How clients adapt to change and a new environment, in the face of all that has transpired in their lives, is the challenge. In terms of cultural adaptation, here is where a cognitive and behavior approach can be useful.

We believed that it was important to frame the book in a way that it can help to interest and move social workers into the idea of the applications of CBT in a wide variety of settings. We tried to do this in a way that would be consistent with the current philosophies within the profession and to bring CBT into the mainstream of social work practice. By developing a comprehensive collection of theory, research, and treatment, the goal of the editors is to offer the social worker, no matter what her or his level, a basic text in CBT as it applies to clinical social work practice. Attempts were made in every area to utilize social workers as authors or coauthors. Our hope is that this book will have value as a text in social work programs, as a professional reference for the practicing clinical social worker, and as a resource book that will hopefully fuel further expansion of CBT in social work practice. This book presented the reader with many of the commonalities of CBT as a mode of intervention and social work as a helping profession. The main role of social work—helping people change—can be realized only by combining new theoretical knowledge with empirically tested intervention approaches that account for the cultural, social, economic, and political transformations typifying modern life.

As we tried to present in this book, CBT is not simply a series of techniques, or a mode of intervention. Rather, it constitutes a way of thinking about human functioning and needs, and a way of operating within the environment in order to achieve the most effective means for accomplishing one's aims. Being a cognitive behaviour therapist necessitates dynamic thinking, considering that no one correct approach or intervention exists for treating the variety of clients encountered in clinical social work.

The social worker as a therapist always needs to make decisions adapting available techniques to specific client-related factors—the individual client and problem—and to therapist-related factors—the service setting and the therapist's abilities, knowledge, and skills. The book is now out of our hands and into yours. Social change is at the heart of current social work practice and we believe that CBT will enhance that capability.

REFERENCES

Anderson, J., & Wiggins-Carter, R. (2004). Diversity perspectives for social work practice. In R. A. Dorfman, P. Meyer, & M. L. Morgan (Eds.), *Paradigms of clinical social work: Vol. 3. Emphasis on diversity* (pp. 19–33). New York: Brunner-Routledge.

Baumeister, R. F. (1998). The self. In D. T. Gilbert, S. T. Fiske, & G. Lindzey (Eds.), *Handbook of social psychology* (4th ed., pp. 680–740). New York: McGraw-Hill.

Baumeister, R. F. (Ed.). (1999). *The self in social psychology*. Philadelphia, PA: Taylor & Francis.

Cohen, S., & Willis, T. A. (1985). Stress, social support and the buffering hypothesis. *Psychological Bulletin, 98,* 310–357.

Huebner, E. S., & Dew, T. (1996). The interrelationship of positive affect, negative affect, and life satisfaction in an adolescent sample. *Social Indicators Research, 38,* 129–137.

Kazdin, A. E. (1993). Psychotherapy for children and adolescents: Current progress and future directions. *American Psychologist, 48,* 644–656.

Mahoney, M. J. (1991). *Human change processes*. New York: Basic Books.

Mahoney, M. J. (2003). *Constructive psychotherapy*. New York: Guilford.

Power, M., & Dalgleish, T. (1997). *Cognition and emotion: From order to disorder*. Laurence Erlbaum.

Wells, A. (2000). *Emotional disorders and metacognition: Innovative cognitive therapy*. Chichester, UK: John Wiley & Sons.

Index